LANGUAGE, READING AND LEARNING DISABILITIES

(Third Printing)

LANGUAGE, READING AND LEARNING DISABILITIES

psychology, neuropsychology, diagnosis and remediation

By

ALEXANDER BANNATYNE

Director, Bannatyne Children's Learning Center
Miami, Florida

Formerly

Member, Center for Advanced Practice
Adler Zone Center, Illinois

Associate Professor of Special Education
Institute for Research on Exceptional Children

Director, Learning Disabilities Research Project
Children's Research Center
University of Illinois
Urbana, Illinois

CHARLES C THOMAS • PUBLISHER
Springfield • Illinois • U.S.A.

Published and Distributed Throughout the World by
CHARLES C THOMAS • PUBLISHER
BANNERSTONE HOUSE
301-327 East Lawrence Avenue, Springfield, Illinois, U.S.A.

© *1971, by* CHARLES C THOMAS • PUBLISHER
ISBN 0-398-02182-1
Library of Congress Catalog Card Number: 70-143727

First Printing, 1971
Second Printing, 1973
Third Printing, 1976

With THOMAS BOOKS *careful attention is given to all details of manufacturing and design. It is the Publisher's desire to present books that are satisfactory as to their physical qualities and artistic possibilities and appropriate for their particular use.* THOMAS BOOKS *will be true to those laws of quality that assure a good name and good will.*

Printed in the United States of America
00-2

INTRODUCTION

The theme and focus of this book is language learning disabilities, even though a considerable portion of the book is devoted to the normal development and operation of language functions and reading during infancy and childhood. Learning disabilities as an area of study is a relatively new development which has attracted the interest of many people who work with children. To date, there have been few publications available to match this interest, and in particular, there has been a great need for a comprehensive reference book. It is hoped that this present volume will help fulfill that need by presenting a detailed description and analysis of a broad range of the causes and deviations of language learning processes in the first and second decades of life.

In order to make the rather extensive and complex subject of language and learning disabilities both useful and conceptually clear, I have chosen to break away from the traditional publishing format of separating the normal from the abnormal, and the theoretical from the clinical. To understand the abnormal, one must be knowledgeable about what is normal. Only through presentation of the abnormal in conjunction with a knowledge of the normal can we work out what has gone "wrong"; only then do we have standards against which to measure degrees and types of abnormality, and only then do we have an accurate knowledge of the *mechanisms* of both healthy and comparatively disturbed functioning. This makes the book useful for an understanding of normal children as well as of those with learning disabilities. In fact, although most of the contents of the book revolve around children with learning disabilities, much of what is said applies equally well not only to normal children but to other children requiring special education. In particular, the contents are often applicable to all grades of mentally defective

v

children, to those who suffer from primary organ disorders of communication, such as the deaf, and to noncommunicating children.

The chapters are arranged in such a way as to present accounts of normal behavior in a particular facet of language or human functioning before presenting the abnormal counterparts to this behavior. Thus, the nature of language, orthography, linguistic conventions and normal language development sets the stage for a discussion of primary emotional communicative dyslexia, which is a disorder directly related to those topics. Similarly, the chapters on neuropsychology, memory and the reading, spelling and writing processes naturally lead to a consideration of genetic dyslexia, minimal neurological dysfunction dyslexia and aphasia. Social deprivation and the emotional factors associated with language functioning are then treated separately as distinct sets of problems. Next, diagnosis and remediation are examined from the "tests and techniques" aspect, as closely related chapters which point to the needs of the future, which are discussed in the final chapter.

THEORY AND PRACTICE

The integration of theory with practice as a deliberate policy has, I believe, many advantages. The practical and clinical aspects of our work will then be the outcome of a sound, research-based system of knowledge—a union which permits a much sounder judgment in practical situations. Also, when theory and clinical practices are incorporated into one book, all who work in the field can obtain a clearer understanding of how the difficult transition is made from one to the other. It is strange that in the social sciences the integration of theory and practice, which is so crucial in terms of human lives, is rare. Note that I do not use the words *theory* or *theoretical* synonymously with *hypothetical* or *speculation*. A theory is a relational *system* or model and it may be supported in varying degrees of confirmation with irrefutable research evidence.

In this book, then, the integration of theory and practice takes two forms. The first is the insertion of practical information in the text when appropriate, as in the chapter on memory (Chapter VII). The second form of integration involves the whole plan of the book, in that chapters devoted to particular types of learning disabilities are interspersed with the more theoretical chapters which lead into them.

LANGUAGE AND READING AS MULTIDISCIPLINARY SUBJECTS

The traditional viewpoint of educators on language or reading has been restricted to the academic aspects of the subjects; they are studied only on the manifest level. I feel, however, that there is a need to get below these everyday aspects into a large variety of areas that were unexplained until recently (in this context), ones which involve the brain, genetics, sociology and personality relationships. Lenneberg (1967), with his *Biological Foundations of Language,* has given impetus to this fresh approach, one which is here further extended into language, reading and learning disabilities. I have attempted to set down concisely the neurological, psychological, emotional, motivational, cognitive, psycholinguistic, genetic and subcultural aspects of language and reading, both normal and abnormal but excluding sensory or motor *organ* defects. In other words, I have, I hope, collected together most of the large pieces of this immense jigsaw puzzle in order to present a first-attempt integrated picture of the whole subject. The attempt at presenting an integrated and comprehensive picture makes this a reference book which should probably be read in small doses, ones which may require rereading for full digestion. Unfortunately, knowledge in these various subjects is not linear and it is almost impossible to follow the traditional format of single-subject books. Even so, the layout of the book has been carefully designed, but since it was not possible for me to cross-reference within the text as much as I would have liked, the reader may have to "move around" from time to time for the purpose of refreshing his memory on specific points. This is a problem inherent in multidisciplinary subject matter.

As this is, in part, a reference book, it includes a review of the most significant theories in each of the fields discussed. This is particularly true in Chapter IV, where I have presented the particular viewpoints of some eight or nine authorities in the field of language development in infancy. These summaries provide a basis for understanding the synthesis which follows them, and, coupled with my own research findings, help illuminate the sources and evidence for the viewpoints expressed throughout the book.

One of my hopes in writing so comprehensively was that the contents would reach a very mixed and varied group of highly qualified professionals including psychologists, neurologists, senior educators, qualified learning disability remediators, speech therapists, senior social workers, psycholinguists, experts in language, educators of the deaf, qualified reading teachers and pediatricians. In the field of learning disabilities, people have written on psycholinguistics, motor functioning, visuo-spatial factors, etc., each as isolated topics. For some time, I have felt that there has been a great need in the area of language and learning disabilities to attempt to pool this and other relevant information into a synthesized whole. Because language and learning disabilities are, and must always be, multidisciplinary in nature, the variety of professional people involved can no longer meaningfully work in their separate compartments of knowledge. Each member of a research or diagnostic and remediation team must come to understand the basic theory of language underlying each of the various disciplines. By analogy, while the physiologist who designs pilots' aircraft seats does not design the airplanes, it does help him in his own aspect of the work to have a real knowledge of aerodynamics. Likewise, in learning disabilities, each of us must understand the work of those in other disciplines in order to avoid diagnostic errors. This book results from a long-term goal to provide a basis for cross-disciplinary understanding.

COMMUNICATION, MEANING AND READING

Reading as a subject of study, until recently, has received very little research attention from disciplines outside education. Almost all books on reading have been written by educators whose primary interest has been one of encouraging academic achievement. Traditionally, reading has been considered a visual process which is largely involved with *understanding*, a viewpoint which until recently has maintained its vogue for want of a cogent challenge. My own viewpoint permeating this book is that reading is the outcome of *language;* therefore, most of the content of the text is about what goes on *underneath* reading as a *total* process. Reading the printed word is decoding or code breaking and one only understands the passage read through the "inner language" auditory/spoken word in the mind *after* the passage has been decoded from print. Understanding is a quality of all language (not just reading) as a communication system and it is in the auditory/vocal system just mentioned that meaning resides. Recently, Bateman (1967a) stated this thesis rather well as the result of a research project:

> The rationale for the view of reading presented in part 1 [of her paper] developed slowly over many years. The research project presented in part 2 was one of four or five main lines of evidence which led the author eventually to reject the popular view of reading as a "meaningful, visual process" and formulated it rather as a, "non-meaningful, auditory process."

This is the identical conclusion to which I have come over a similar number of years (Bannatyne, 1966c, 1966g, 1967b). Because meaning is an attribute of all language, it has been discussed in those chapters which are concerned with conceptualizing and thinking. How concepts are associated with both auditory and written verbal *labels* is also treated at length in the relevant chapters. Reading as a *decoding skill* which functions automatically, once learned, is dealt with as a separate, though related topic in other passages.

I hope that this treatment of conceptualizing, language, reading and learning disabilities will tie together many loose ends for the wide variety of people who must necessarily come into contact with learning disability children.

ACKNOWLEDGMENTS

It is not possible to thank individually all those who have helped in a variety of ways with the contents of this volume. My interest in language and learning disabilities is a longstanding once from the time I became a teacher after World War II. This led me into psychology, and for many years I worked with emotionally disturbed children in school and clinic settings. Many of these children had learning disabilities.

The first major opportunity I had to pursue my studies of reading disability cases came when I was appointed as Psychologist to the Word Blind Center for Dyslexic Children in London, a Center I helped organize from its beginning. The parent body is the Invalid Children's Aid Association of which Princess Margaret is the very active President. Her interest in and visits to the Center, which she officially opened, and the encouragement I had from Dr. Alfred White-Franklin, the Honorary Medical Director, contributed greatly to the setting from which this book developed. The staff at the Center, Gillian Cotterell, Esther Hirsch, Betty Warburton, Eleanor Harrison, Tilde Stern and David Moseley, were very loyal and their work contributed many ideas and some of the content. The ICAA paid for a study tour I made of the United States, enabling me to visit many centers for learning disability and emotionally disturbed children from coast to coast. Dale Bryant, Ben Mirling, Gil Schiffman, John Money, Alice Garside, Richard Gregory (then at New York University from Cambridge), Ralph Rabinovitch, Sally Childs and Joseph Wepman were very kind and informative. Special mention must be made of Marianne Frostig, Marion Stuart and Samuel Kirk, to whom I owe a great deal.

Samuel Kirk invited me to join the Institute for Research on Exceptional Children at the University of Illinois and he, more than anyone, provided me with the opportunity to teach, do research and write. More recently, William Hurder, the new Director of the IREC, continued to encourage me in every way. The research project quoted in the text under my name was supported by the National Institute of Mental Health and the U.S. Public Health Service (Grant No. NB07346). Penny Wichiarajote did much of the testing and analysis of results.

My daughter, Katharine, has helped my study of language through her own speech development from birth to five years. Marianne Frostig, Phyllis Maslow, John Reddington and R.E. Orpet of the Frostig School read, edited and commented on many of the chapters. So also did my colleagues John Salvia, Elaine Jacobson and Marcia Solomon at the Children's Research Center, University of Illinois and Adler Zone Center. Joe Ann Jansen has carried through much of the routine work and typed the manuscript, giving up much of her free time to do so.

Many, many others have played a part in bringing this volume to completion and I thank them all.

I am grateful to the following publishers and/or authors from whose work I have quoted at length:

Adams, J.A.: *Human Memory.* New York, McGraw-Hill, 1967.

Anderson, J.O.: Aphasia from the viewpoint of a speech pathologist. *Journal of Speech Disorders, 9* (3), Sept. 1944.

Ayres, A.J.: Patterns of perceptual-motor dysfunction in children: A factor analytic study. *Perceptual and Motor Skills, 20*:335-368, M1-V20, 1965.

Ayres, A.J.: Reading—A Product of Sensory Integrative Processes. International Reading Association 12th Annual Convention, Seattle, 1967. Reprinted with permission of the International Reading Association and the author.

Bereiter, Carl, and Engelmann, S.: *Teaching Disadvantaged Children in the Preschool.* Englewood Cliffs, N.J., Prentice-Hall, Inc., © 1966.

Bernstein, B.: Aspects of language and learning in the genesis of the social process. *Journal of Child Psychology and Psychiatry,* Pergamon Press Ltd., 1961.

Birch, H.G.: *Brain Damage in Children: The Biological and Social Aspects.* Baltimore, Md., Williams & Wilkins Co., © 1964.

Birch, H.G., Belmont, L., and Karp, I.: Excitation-inhibition balance in brain-damaged patients. *Journal of Nervous and Mental Diseases*, 39 (No. 6), Baltimore, Md., Williams & Wilkins Co., © 1964.

Broadbent, D.E.: *Attention and the perception of speech.* © 1962 by Scientific American, Inc. All rights reserved.

Brown, R., and Fraser, C.: The acquisition of syntax. A paper in *Acquisition of Language*, Child Devel. Mono. No. 92, Vol. 29, No. 1, Ed. by Bellugi and Brown. © 1964 by the Society for Research in Child Development, Inc.

Calvert, J.J., and Cromes, G.F.: Oculomotor spasms in handicapped readers. *Reading Teacher*, Dec. 1966. Reprinted with permission of the International Reading Association and the author.

Chomsky, N.: *Syntactic Structures.* The Hague, Mouton & Co., Publishers, 1957.

Cohen, A., and Glass, G.G.: *Lateral dominance and reading ability. Reading Teacher*, 21 (No. 4), Jan. Reprinted with permission of the International Reading Association and the author.

Connolly, K.: The genetics of behavior. In *New Horizons in Psychology*, Ed. by B.M. Foss. Harmondsworth, England, Penguin Books, 1966.

Coopersmith, S.: Studies in self-esteem. © 1968 by Scientific American, Inc. All rights reserved.

Delacato, C.H.: *The Treatment and Prevention of Reading Problems*, 1954, and *The Diagnosis and Treatment of Speech and Reading Problems*, 1964. Courtesy of Charles C Thomas, Publisher, Springfield, Illinois.

Dykstra, R.: Auditory discrimination abilities and beginning reading achievement. *Reading Research Quarterly*, 1966. Reprinted with permission of the author and the International Reading Association.

Fry, D.B.: The development of the phonological system in the normal and the deaf child. In *The Genesis of Language*, Ed. by Smith and Miller. Cambridge, MIT Press, 1966.

Hebb, D.O.: *The Organization of Behavior: A Neuropsychological*

Lewis, M.M.: *Language Thought and Personality in Infancy and Childhood.* London, George G. Harrap & Co., Limited Publishers, 1963.

Lilly, J.C.: In *Handbook of Physiology Environment,* Chapter 46. American Physiological Society, 1964.

Luria, A.R.: *Higher Cortical Functions in Man,* Translated by Basil Haigh. © 1966 Consultants Bureau Enterprises, Inc., and Basic Books Inc., Publishers, New York.

Maccoby, E.: *The Development of Sex Differences.* Stanford, Stanford University Press, 1961, p. 26.

McGinnis, M.A., Kleffner, F.R., and Goldstein, R.: *Teaching Aphasic Children.* The Volta Review, June 1956.

Miller, G.A., Galanter, E., and Pribram, K.H.: *Plans and the Structure of Behavior.* New York, Holt, Rinehart and Winston, Inc., 1960.

Miller, W., and Erwin, S.: In *Acquisition of Language,* Child Develop. Mono. No. 92, Vol. 29, No. 1, Ed. by Bellugi and Brown. © 1964 by the Society for Research in Child Development, Inc.

Milner, P., and Glickman, S. (Eds.): *Cognitive Processes of the Brain.* © 1965 by Litton Educational Publishing, Inc., by permission of D. Van Nostrand Co.

Osgood, C.E., and Sebeck, T.A. (Eds.): *Psycholinguistics: A Survey of Theory and Research Problems,* with a Survey of Psycholinguistic Research, 1954-1964, by A. Richard Diebold, Jr. © 1965 by the Trustees of Indiana University. Reprinted by permission of the Indiana University Press.

Osgood, C.E.: A behavioristic analysis of perception and language as cognitive phenomena. In *Contemporary Approaches to Cognition.* Cambridge, Harvard University Press Pub.

Penfield, W., and Roberts, L.: Selections from Wilder Penfield and Lamar Roberts. *Speech and Brain Mechanisms.* © 1959 by Princeton University Press. Reprinted by permission of Princeton University Press.

Rosenthal, R., and Jacobsen, L.F.: Teacher expectations for the disadvantaged. © 1968 by Scientific American, Inc., All rights reserved.

Smith, I.M.: Spatial ability. In *Spatial Ability: Its Educational and Social Significance*. San Diego, R.R. Knapp, 1964.

Sperry, R.W.: The great cerebral commissure. © 1964 by Scientific American, Inc. All rights reserved.

Teuber, H.L.: In *Acquisition of Language*, Child Develop. Mono. No. 92, Vol. 29. No. 1, Ed. by Bellugi and Brown. © 1964 by the Society for Research in Child Development, Inc.

Thoday, J.M.: Quoted by Connolly, K., from The genetics of behavior, in *New Horizons in Psychology*, Ed. by B.M. Foss. Penguin Books, Ltd., 1965.

Wepman, J.: Auditory discrimination, speech and reading. *Elementary School Journal*, 60:325-333, 1960, The University of Chicago Press.

CONTENTS

LANGUAGE, READING AND LEARNING DISABILITIES

Chapter I

THE DIVERSITY AND INTEGRATION OF RESEARCH INFORMATION

R esearch studies of the psychology of language have tended to be somewhat unrelated to each other in the past, mainly because the subject is so vast. With two or three notable exceptions (Lenneberg, 1967; Osgood and Sebeck, 1965; Luria, 1966), few have attempted to draw together the various threads of knowledge which have been discovered nor have they tried to weave those threads together to see how they can be integrated. The study of language as a psychological phenomenon has often been approached via other sets of subject matter. For example, those psychologists who have been involved in a study of intelligence have investigated verbal ability as one factor of something called "g" (Spearman's general intelligence). Psychotherapy-oriented people have stressed the motivational and emotional aspects of language, while the neurologists, of course, have investigated the problem of language by identifying the functional areas of the brain which are involved. Developmental psychologists, such as Piaget, have traced the various stages through which language develops from infancy. The speech therapists, needless to say, until recently have been primarily concerned with articulation and hearing disorders and to some extent with the symptomatology of aphasia, while those dealing with ear deafness have been preoccupied with devising means of transmitting sounds directly or indirectly to the brain, e.g., hearing aids or Braille. The linguists have analyzed language in a variety of ways to make the principles on which it works more explicit.

Over the last few years, some educators, psychologists and neurologists have separately become interested in studying children suffering from reading disabilities, both from the practical

3

"what-to-do-with-them" point of view and from a desire to discover the nature of such linguistic disturbances. An interest in the educational aspects of reading disabilities has been shown by teachers for a very long time but, almost always, their approach has been less concerned with the workings of the mind or brain of the child than with devising *ad hoc* methods which will help the disabled reader or motivate him to pay attention to his work. Now that other professional people have turned their attention to examining the reasons why dyslexic children find it peculiarly difficult to learn to read and spell, more and more information has been forthcoming which links together or integrates the various disciplinary approaches to language. It is a truism to say that if one wants to know a great deal about *normal* functioning in any aspect of life, it is extremely rewarding to examine the *abnormal*, preferably in parallel. By analyzing what is wrong, one obtains a deeper insight into what the situation should have been had events proceeded normally. This applies to medicine and to studies of perception (R.L. Gregory, 1966), emotional development and cognition, as well as to the complex developmental states which underlie language. Recently, the widespread interest in dyslexia has resulted in an increasing stream of valuable hypotheses and research studies. Some of this work has been done by a variety of authorities in special centers in various countries around the world and many of the results will be presented in the text of this book. However, much of what I have written stems from my own work on the underlying nature of language and language disabilities which I have attempted to integrate with information gleaned from the books and journal papers on library shelves, some of it just waiting to be reanalyzed and integrated, often in ways the authors never intended.

Although some of this book is devoted to examining the nature of disabilities in language and reading, much of it is not. *Some chapters are devoted to the development and structure of normal language and reading while others discuss memory, neuropsychology and psycholinguistics.*

Unfortunately, much research into reading disabilities has

been carried out on small, clinically biased populations and this has led to very confusing results, not only from the research point of view but also from a theoretical standpoint. All kinds of children have been indiscriminately grouped together into a heterogeneous collection which has taken no account of the great diversity of symptoms manifested by individual children. In other words, *dyslexia* has become a label which means what it says, namely, the inability to cope with words. Into this category have been placed children who are clumsy or spatially disoriented, who cannot spell, who cannot remember sounds, who have a poor self-concept, who are too emotionally disturbed to concentrate on any schoolwork, and so on. I had the opportunity in London to investigate the nature of dyslexia idiographically and I made it one of my main objectives to try to classify, on a clinical judgment, discrete groups of various kinds of reading disability children who seemed within any one group to present similar symptoms. Of course, the homogeneity of each group was a relative matter and the definition of that group depended on the majority of the children near the center of the group *cluster* rather than on those who seemed to have two or three types of disability superimposed. The actual classification of these clusters is discussed later in the chapter. It is hoped that over the next few years, large-scale learning disability research projects will be carried out, based on representative samples of the entire school population covering an IQ range from 60 right to the top of the intelligence scale. Only then will the actual numerical incidence of the various categories or clusters of dyslexic children become known. Quite apart from the value of counting heads and identifying overlapping symptoms, there is much work to be done within each category to understand the actual processes involved in reading, processes which are not fully functioning in dyslexic children. Although some psycholinguists such as Osgood (1964) have drawn up excellent theoretical models of linguistic communication (see Chapter II) which show the numerous psychological stages through which language behavior must pass, much work remains to be done on the details of that behavior, its neuropsychological concomitants, its development and the motivations necessary to its successful use.

PANACEAS FOR READING PROBLEMS

In the United States, there has been a great interest in the teaching of reading to normal children and several admirable books have been written on the subject. It is interesting to note that books devoted to the subject of reading in schools often discuss at great length the reasons why so many children read poorly. Successful linguistic communication has such tremendous survival value for the human race that any failure immediately generates an anxious search for panaceas, but if we are to discover the best types of remediation, we must first understand the underlying nature of the disability. Peripheral organ defects such as abnormalities of the eyes, ears and vocal apparatus are not dealt with in this book even though some children do not learn to read because of such handicaps.

Many methods have been developed to teach children to read, whether those children are normal or not. A great deal of wasted time, money and energy has been spent on proving whether one method is better than another, on the philosophy that reading is a unitary function which can be developed by frequent doses of one particular stimulant or "verbal vitamin tonic." Reading is a very complex psychological process, the varied ingredients of which may differ in amounts from one individual to the next. One child may have slight central nervous system (CNS) visual defects whereas another may have equally slight auditory defects; one child may find decoding to be a particular problem while another may have difficulty in remembering sound-symbol associations. Still others may lack the necessary motivation to speak or to read their native language. The moral is that no *one* method can ever be generalized to cover the education of all, or even most, children. It is apparent that different children require different methods and that *the main educational and research problem is to find which methods of tuition work best with particular groups of children.* It is to be hoped that in years to come, considerable amounts of research will be devoted to discovering which individual children will benefit most from any given teaching technique. This applies to both potentially competent and potentially incompetent readers.

In its turn, this raises the question of differential diagnosis within an extensive cluster-classification system for both linguistically normal and linguistically abnormal children. One would hope that in the not too distant future, every child would be screened on school entry to discover which approach to reading and language training would be the most fruitful and, at the same time, to bring to light those children who have specific disabilities. With respect to these disability cases, clinical and school psychologists will need to be trained to carry out differential diagnoses, much research work having already gone into establishing which educational and psychological tests best achieve this. As a result of the findings of these diagnostic examinations, programs of instruction have been and are being devised which will enable such children to receive the specialized help they need. For example, children diagnosed as having certain visuo-spatial deficits can already be provided with training programs designed to improve their perception or knowledge of spatial relationships.

TYPES OF TERMINOLOGY AND DEFINITIONS

One of the urgent needs in the area of language and language disabilities is that of clarifying terminology and definitions. As with any discipline in its infancy, one entity acquires several different names or, conversely, several separate entities are given the same name. It is to be hoped that these diverse terminologies will quickly disappear and it is particularly appropriate that they should do so when one is communicating about communication. Throughout this book, the word *dyslexia* is used as a generic term to cover the whole category of reading and spelling disabilities which appear to have a primary cause in their own right and which cannot be said to be caused by retardation, emotional disturbances, aphasia, autism, etc., as these latter terms are usually defined. If we wish to indicate, then, a particular type of dyslexia, the appropriate adjective or phase should qualify the generic term. One authority in learning disabilities has said that he automatically uses the word *dyslexia* to mean that the cause of the reading problem lies in some abnormality of the brain. My personal view is that not only does this beg a research question, but it deprives us of a valuable generic word which is necessary to describe a particular disorder of functioning.

Many educators and psychologists have not been trained in the biological sciences and so are unaware of the value in hierarchical classification systems of generic terms, categories and definitions. Words like *food, mammals* and *organic* are easy to define in their central meaning but they become vague around their edges. Is calcium a food? Is the platypus a mammal? Nevertheless, such generic terms are essential for classifying knowledge and *dyslexia* is such a term. The way in which more precise subcategories can be subsumed under a given category can be seen in Table II on page 18.

There are many people in education, neurology and psychology who repeatedly say that we know little about the nature of dyslexia or, for that matter, about any of the processes underlying language functions. However, I have found that there is a wealth of literature on each one of the many different aspects of the educational, neurological and psychological processes involved in verbal communication. There is an even greater fund of knowledge in the peripheral areas impinging upon linguistic functioning and it is this material which I feel has been largely neglected. There is no doubt that to cover the field, one must be fairly conversant with current work in several different disciplines and perhaps only a broadly based research unit devoted to communication problems in childhood can hope to achieve this. There are still some educators who, at the mention of classification, will acclaim the importance of looking at and studying the "whole child." Quite often, such people will overstress the point that when we separate out groups of children or even analyze individual children into symptom categories, we begin to lose sight of "real children in a problem situation." These practitioners never stop to consider where education, medicine, the life sciences or, for that matter, any body of knowledge would be today if it were not for the people who set up "theoretical" models and then set out to investigate their validity. Usually, such models are the result of pondering on a great deal of practical everyday experience with "whole" children in schools, centers, clinics and hospitals. Applied science nearly always follows theoretical science, and education is, or at least should be, as much an applied science as an art. The most gifted, sympathetic and inspired teacher can become just that much more effective if she is supplied with carefully thought out systems of knowledge and specific teaching techniques based on them.

TAXONOMY

The essential elements of taxonomic classification systems dealing with living organisms are as follows:

1. The systems almost invariably have a hierarchical structure ranging down from a single all-inclusive category at the top to minute subdivisions and even, perhaps, to individual instances at the lowest level.

2. The grouping of cases in any one category on any given level works on a statistical frequency technique, those at the center of the distribution in any one group being the most characteristic of that group. Such clustering taxonomic procedures are common to most of the biological and social sciences (Sokal, 1966).

3. The underlying single principle or topic on which the clustering works must be consistent throughout the classification. In the case of learning disability children, one must classify according to *attributes* and their causes. Until recently, the taxonomic system in biology was largely based on morphology; however, this is now tending to give way to a more purposive functional classification. Much classificatory work in medicine and the social sciences has been founded on symptomatology groupings, but quite different causes can bring about very similar symptoms or vice versa, leading to a great deal of confusion. Therefore, this approach is rejected. Even a classification of individual cases in the social sciences or medicine can lead the

investigator into rather illogical tangles, particularly when one case after another presents *several* diverse symptoms or even several disorders. Therefore, classifying cases is out. This is certainly one of the major difficulties besetting the investigator of language and learning disabilities. As a result, attributes, characteristics and their causes or agents are classified, rather than cases.

4. The lower subdivided categories must all fall within their respective larger category on the level above.

5. The causal conditions (in terms of Aristotle's "four causes" outlined below) in any one branch of the classification should be compatible and consistent. Embodying two or more types of causality within one grouping can only lead to confusion. For example, genetic causes should be presented separately from disease-originated defects.

If any classification system is to have a constant validity, then each cell at each particular level will be a relatively homogeneous unit in terms of the attributes and causal agents classified, and the only way in which homogeneity can be achieved is to base the classification on either functional or etiological factors. In medicine and the social sciences, it is probably the latter which give the clearest, neatest and most useful system. Causality as a basis of classification enables one to define any particular symptom or case by referring to the other cells and (separately through measurement) to the degree to which the disability or talent is possessed by an individual. Therefore, a child who has several etiologically separate disabilities would appear in all the appropriate cells and, as with any profile system, one would obtain a much clearer picture as to the best course of treatment to adopt. In other words, a kind of hierarchical chart is drawn up which can be used as a set of integrated criteria against which any child could be matched across the board, so to speak (see Table II, page 18).

THE FOUR CAUSES

The only difficulty with an etiological classification is that, as Aristotle pointed out, there are at least four separate types of cause. Therefore, if one is not very careful to take into account the different types of causation within any one classification, the result is even more confusing than classifications based on symptoms only. In terms of human behavior. I would say that the four basic causes are as follows:

1. *The efficient cause:* This is the situation, instrument or agency which was responsible for initiating the "movement" or change in the first place. For example, in the case of brain damage, the original cause might be the total birth situation, including the mother's state or situation which gave rise to the damage. In the case of emotional disturbance, the original efficient cause might be the familial relationship setup or a traumatic situation which affected the child.

2. *The material cause:* The second type of cause of behavioral phenomena is the actual physical, neurological or psychological "material" of which the individual is composed and which has been modified in some way. For example, in neurological dysfunction cases, the material cause will be the actual lesion or malformation of the brain cells, while in other types of disorder it might be a defect in one of the sensory organs. In cases of emotional disturbance, the material cause would be the actual instincts, emotions and drives and their derivatives because within a psychological framework, the "content" of the mind becomes its material.

3. *The formal cause:* This cause is the design, plan, program or blueprint in accord with which the object or individual in question is shaped or built through time. In psychology and education, the formal cause would be the sum total of the innate and environmental programs "modifying" the individual and, as such, they can be divided into two major (interactive) subtypes of cause: those which are innate developing potentials (almost entirely genetic) and those which are environmental. There are a vast number of genetic and environmental plans or programs influencing the development of the individual child, plans which may be innate, environmentally determined or accidental but which all interact.

4. *The final cause:* This type of cause consists mainly of the *motivational goals* of the individual, some of which can be partially defined in terms of outside agencies. For example, if a child has to pass a school examination in the future and if his parents are exerting pressure on him to do so, the examination situation is, itself, the final cause of any stress which appears in the child. Prestige, status, money, fame, etc., are all examples of final causes; inasmuch as they may be somebody else's plan for a child, they may also be formal causes. In a different way, the situations or objects sought after as a result of human motivations are also final causes.

For an etiological classification, one must insure that the type of causation selected for any given category is relevant to the types of attributes being discussed. Emotional problems tend to require an explanation mainly in terms of efficient causes. Neurological impairment calls for material cause explanations on a neurosensorimotor basis. *Even so, a complete causal description of any state or event (of its type) would almost always involve all four types of causal explanation in major and minor roles.* Aristotle's concept of four causes has great value for the clarification of the variety of viewpoints and theories put forward by various people in the area of learning disabilities. Some exclusively emphasize material causes (e.g., "brain damage"), others efficient causes (e.g., parental or, separately, genetic factors), others formal causes (e.g., maturational lags) and yet others final causes (e.g., academic pressures). A well-rounded theory will take into account all four types of cause.

THE RELATIONSHIP OF TIME AND CAUSATION

I have already stressed the fact that a child may be afflicted with several etiologically separate disabilities which require cross-classification by level and type. However, a third consideration is extremely important in etiological diagnosis, namely, *time.* This makes the diagnostic problem very complex as, for example, when a child reaches the stage of being able to learn to read several years after the educational provision for the teaching of beginning reading to children has ceased. Therefore, when we talk about multiple causation, it can take two forms: the first is the contiguous interaction of several causes, and the second is a successive buildup through time of a series of consecutive causes. A child who is suffering from both genetic dyslexia and neurological dysfunction could be classed under the first type of multiple causation, whereas a boy with a maturational lag (whatever the original efficient cause) who gets out of step with the school system would be in the second category of multiple causation. As has been said above, a complete description of the characteristics of any child will always involve all four causes in major and minor roles. Table I summarizes many of these concepts of classification and causation. It is largely self-explanatory.

Sometimes, research will identify a "cause" of reading disabilities (using statistical and test techniques) because the "deficit" found in the children is significantly *correlated* with reading and spelling abilities. Often this cause is partway up the serial chain-of-causes ladder mentioned above; that is, the "discovered" cause may be in the middle of a series of causes (e.g., toxemia—brain cell malformation—maturational lag—poor motivation—reading disability). It is even possible that there may be several chained series of causes contributing to a reading disability. These separate chains may or may not coalesce—that is, they may act as an "integrated" resultant deficit (e.g., poor eye-hand coordination) or they may each separately contribute to a cumulative deficit, thus operating side by side (e.g., cultural deprivation and auditory neurological dysfunction).

THE INCIDENCE OF DYSLEXIA

Many educators have estimated the incidence of dyslexic children in the total school population and one or two have carried out research surveys. Depending on one's cutoff points, criteria and definitions, the figures range from ½ to 15 percent. If one limits the dyslexia group to children of average intelligence or above who, being otherwise emotionally, cognitively and physically normal, have abnormal difficulty learning to read, write or spell when compared with their intellectual peers, then the incidence will be *at least* 2 percent of the school population and

TABLE I

SCHEMATIC RELATIONSHIP OF CHARACTERISTICS TO ETIOLOGY IN LANGUAGE DISABILITIES*

Final Causes	Moral standards	Self-respect	Ambition	Identification	Conformity	
	(Any of these causes can have an influence on the characteristics listed below)					
Language Disability Characteristics	Emotional factors: Reaction, anxiety, nonmotivation, distractibility, etc. Visuo-spatial: Form constancy, scrambling, memory, mirroring, etc. Auditory: Memory, noise levels, closure, discrimination, etc. Motor: Balance, speech, fingers and hands, eyes, hyperactive, slow, etc. Integrational/conceptual: Generalizing, induction, deduction, relativity, etc.					
Formal Causes (Patterns) (Programs)	All maturational patterns: Inherited or acquired	Physiological factors: Health, food, sleep, exercise	Physical environment: Slum/city/rural opportunities	Home: Family relationships, organizations	School: Education, teachers' quality	Friends: Clubs, interests
	(Any of these causes can have an influence on the characteristics listed above)					
Material Causes (Body-Mind Total Situation)	Hormones, growth determinants	Physiological and neurological dysfunctioning	Motivational and emotional disturbances (May reflect in final causes)	Poverty of language and knowledge		
	(Any of these causes can have an influence on any of those on the lines above)					
Efficient or Original Causes	Genes from parents	Perinatal events	Disease	Accidental brain injury	**Culturally** deprived parents, grandparents, etc.	
	(Any of these causes can have an influence on any of those on the lines above)					

*This model can be adapted in a variety of ways to cope with most areas of human functioning. Note also that the inter-influence between causes can sometimes operate "downward" as well as upward on the above schema. The doctrine of the four causes comes from Aristotle's *Metaphysics*.

will be mainly boys. Gorton (1964) conducted a survey based on such criteria as these, together with a screening for secondary emotional disturbance, a history of speech defect or slow speech development, right-left disorientation, weak or incomplete orientation, hyperactivity or clumsiness, and a positive family history of more than one of these facets. This very restricted sample was screened from all the children aged nine to ten years attending several randomly selected schools in a local education authority district in England. The proportion of children exhibiting five out of the six symptoms was 2.01 percent of the total school population initially tested; it was 14 percent of the total sample of poor readers. Gorton found that 14.9 percent of the regular school population (excluding the mentally retarded) were reading more than one standard deviation below the norm for their age.

This is the only study which accurately assesses the incidence of severe reading disability and specific dyslexia in children while excluding the mentally retarded and emotionally disturbed.

Critchley (1964), in a survey of studies reporting the incidence of sex differences, averaged out the proportion of boys to girls as 4:1. In a center devoted exclusively to severe cases of dyslexia, I found that the proportion was over ten boys to every girl. The implications of these sex differences will be discussed later in the book.

Such a large proportion of disability in our schools goes largely unnoticed because there are, on the average, only one or two true dyslexic children to each classroom. Furthermore, they exhibit no external characteristics as do the partially sighted or the hard-of-hearing, nor are they mentally retarded. Therefore, it is easy for the teacher, principal or psychologist to assume that the problem is solely one of motivation or deviant behavior. For these and other reasons—some financial—the whole problem of dyslexia has been largely avoided by the public schools, thus leaving the field to a few pioneering language clinics, private centers and special schools whose policies have been deliberately aimed at the investigation and remediation of the problems of dyslexic children. It is to be hoped that this state of affairs will rapidly change so the dyslexic child will receive the specialized help he desperately needs.

AN OVERVIEW OF ABNORMAL LANGUAGE AND READING PROCESSES: DYSLEXIA

If such a heterogeneous group of children is to be understood, it becomes necessary to cluster-analyze the attributes of reading disability cases into a hierarchical classification system which will take the form of a hypothetical model. This does not mean that there is no factual basis for the model in real life. To the contrary, I have personally examined hundreds of reading disability cases in recent years. A thorough examination of the literature also yields evidence for identifying various categories of disorder. If we take all *reading* disabilities as our area of study, then within this, there will be several separate genera or major groups, one of which will be a grouping of those disabilities which, by definition, can be subsumed under the genus *dyslexia. Dyslexia, then, is one type of reading, spelling or writing disability which is not caused by low intelligence per se.* Thus, although dyslexia (and other learning disabilities) can occur in children of low intelligence, it is not *caused* by low intelligence. Dyslexia always refers to reading, spelling and writing disabilities *not primarily caused* by low intelligence, emotional disturbance, organ deficits, etc., although it may *also occur* in such children.

Taking the above points into account, the following brief definition of *learning disabilities* (the widest term) is a useful starting point: "A child with learning disabilities is one who has a number of specific deficits in perceptual, integrative, relational or expressive processes not attributable to sense-organ defects which impair learning efficiency. This includes children who have central nervous system dysfunction which is expressed primarily in impaired learning efficiency." If one substitutes *dyslexia* for the term *learning disabilities,* and limits the frame of reference to reading, spelling and writing, the modified definition becomes a reasonably accurate one for dyslexia. It would be possible to record and analyze dozens of definitions of learning disabilities, dyslexia and the numerous other concepts used in the literature, but perhaps an empirical classification chart, combined with the detailed descriptions in the text, can provide the best definition of all. If readers prefer operational descriptions to etiological causes as a method of defining attributes and their profiles, they will find them in subsequent chapters. Genetic dyslexia is described operationally in Table II.

The four groups or clusters of attributes in the table are more precisely delineated than their "parent" term *dyslexia*. None of the categories in the table are mutually exclusive and, therefore, many children fall into more than one category; that is, they combine in themselves the attributes of more than one type of dyslexia or possibly other disabilities. Thus a child can be both neurologically impaired and emotionally disturbed. Likewise, he may be a genetic dyslexic and a culturally deprived child. This overlapping multiple causation is a major source of confusion in many published research studies, the authors invariably analyzing their sample as a homogeneous "single-cause" group. Only by using statistical techniques which cluster-analyze symptoms or attributes will some sense of order develop in our knowledge of learning disabilities. Furthermore, it is only after such a clear clustering of homogeneous groups and subgroups that we can correctly experiment to discover which specific teaching techniques actually *do* remediate various deficits. The following overview of specific categories of dyslexia is deliberately brief, the immediate aim being to orient the reader in a general way prior to a reading of the content of later chapters when the same material will be examined in great detail.

Primary Emotional Communicative Dyslexia

This, the first group subsumed under dyslexia, has as its primary efficient cause a poor communicative (language) relationship between mother and child during the critical period of language development in infancy.

This is the most difficult kind of dyslexia to diagnose because the original efficient causes have invariably ceased to exist in any tangible form. They cannot be directly measured in any way and the only proof that they exist in the way described would be to

TABLE II

A HIERARCHIAL CLASSIFICATION OF THE CAUSES AND TYPES OF DYSLEXIA°

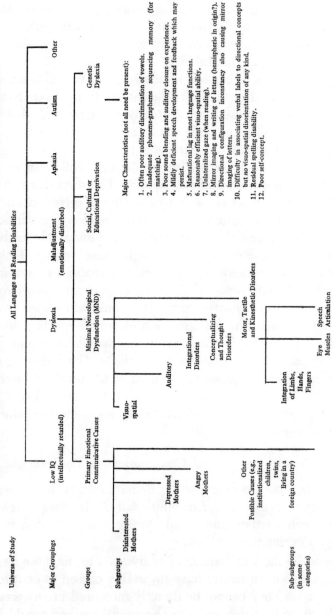

All Language and Reading Disabilities

Universe of Study

Major Groupings

Low IQ (intellectually retarded) · Dyslexia · Maladjustment (emotionally disturbed) · Aphasia · Autism · Other

Groups

Primary Emotional Communicative Causes · Minimal Neurological Dysfunction (MND) · Social, Cultural or Educational Deprivation · Genetic Dyslexia

Subgroups

Disinterested Mothers · Depressed Mothers · Angry Mothers · Other Possible Causes (e.g., institutionalized children, twins, living in a foreign country)

Visuo-spatial · Auditory · Integrational Disorders · Conceptualizing and Thought Disorders · Motor, Tactile and Kinesthetic Disorders

Sub-subgroups (in some categories)

Integration of Limbs, Hands, Fingers · Eye Muscles · Speech Articulation

Major Characteristics (not all need be present):

1. Often poor auditory discrimination of vowels.
2. Inadequate phoneme-grapheme sequencing memory (for matching).
3. Poor sound blending and auditory closure on experience.
4. Mildly deficient speech development and feedback which may persist.
5. Maturational lag in most language functions.
6. Reasonably efficient visuo-spatial ability.
7. Unlateralized gaze (when reading).
8. Mirror imaging and writing of letters (hemispheric in origin?).
9. Directional configuration inconstancy also causing mirror imaging of letters.
10. Difficulty in associating verbal labels to directional concepts but *no* visuo-spatial disorientation of any kind.
11. Residual spelling disability.
12. Poor self-concept.

°These categories are not mutually exclusive. Characteristics are classified, not children.

carry out an extensive longitudinal study. The best source of information is the mother herself, both directly and by observing her attitudes toward her children.

The subgroups shown under this category have one factor in common. During the critical phase of language development and differentiation, from birth to four years of age, the mother or mother-surrogate has not given her child sufficient verbal stimuli for the child to develop an accurately differentiated appreciation of the spoken language and/or clarity of speech. Language is composed of dominant sounds, sequences of sounds and even exclusion of sounds. The child must learn by imitation which sounds occur in which sequential contexts, and which other sounds he need not use at all; for example, in English, he usually strings together the phonemes for the word *mommy* in the right sequence fairly quickly; these, along with many other sounds, are reinforced by his day-to-day communication with his mother. If the mother does not speak very much during the child's formative years, he simply does not learn this basic information or the linguistic *conventions* that go with it. His vocabulary will be limited, speech development will be slow and speech defects common. The child will not listen properly and will be disinterested in auditory stimuli. If nothing is done to alter this pattern during the early school years, it may very well "congeal" in the course of normal neurological maturation and subsequently may be very difficult to modify.

The various subgroups are most easily categorized in terms of the type of mother and her emotional attitudes to the child. The nature of these mothers and other factors connected with primary emotional communicative dyslexia will be considered at length in Chapter V. The various uses of the word *emotional* in this book are elaborated in Chapter XIII.

Minimal Neurological Dysfunction Dyslexia

Under the heading of minimal neurological dysfunction (MND) dyslexia are included only those children whose brains are abnormal in the sense that they are qualitatively dissimilar by reason of malformed cells or areas that are not found in the normal population, which includes other types of dyslexic children. Also included in this category are those children whose brains are abnormally malformed or damaged for genetic reasons. They are not categorized as having genetic dyslexia, but as this is rather a subtle point and as it is difficult to make the distinction clear in one paragraph, the topic will be further examined when genetic dyslexia is described in Chapter IX.

Many different kinds of lesions can cause similar symptoms, and widely differing symptoms sometimes seem strangely to originate in apparently similar lesions. This may be caused by the possibility that some brain areas are "established" and programmed by environment and training in infancy and early childhood. Thus, different individuals will have the same areas differently programmed. The subgroups outlined below are, for the sake of clarity, relatively homogeneous, but the great variety and extent of possible cell impairment or malformation makes a categorization of MND attributes extremely difficult and much more like guidelines. Therefore, the following classification, while reasonably accurate, is rarely found to be so neat and precise in actuality. This does not deny the usefulness of a stylized map; such a cluster map must take into account the main neurological areas of the brain in terms of sensory, motor, conceptual and integrative functioning.

Briefly, the subgroups can be classified into visuo-spatial, auditory, motor-kinesthetic, conceptualizing and integrative disorders. Any permutation or combination of these areas may be impaired and deficiencies may range from a tiny lesion in one particular area to a generalized impairment over the whole cortex. In my own experience, it is rare to find an MND dyslexic child with only one narrow deficiency. Although in some cases the actual dysfunctioning of the child may be minimal, the impairment itself may sometimes be widespread in the brain; at least, that is the tentative conclusion one sometimes draws from neuropsychological testing procedures.

Genetic Dyslexia

Children suffering from genetic dyslexia have not inherited in the natural course of events the specific ability to acquire language functions easily. They form the lower end of a normal continuum which is found throughout the whole population, the continuum being linguistic or verbal ability. While environmental training can play a great part in the development or fulfillment of any particular talent, the talent itself with its maximum of potential is inherited. For example, almost everybody seems to accept that musical ability, the ability to draw, mathematical ability and even verbal ability, when found to excess in a talented person, are inherited. Some people agree that a lack of those abilities is in many cases inherited. More specifically, one would say that the tone-deaf person, the incompetent artist and the poor mathematician have just not inherited the given talent even though the subsequent cultural environment may have been favorable. The tone-deaf person may happily practice music for many years and not make a success of it. I suggest, then, that the genetic dyslexic child has not inherited those specific psychological abilities (or, of course, their broad neurological bases) which are necessary for the development of language functioning at a particular level. The concept of "level of functioning" is an important one. Sophisticated adult reading and writing is the equivalent of being able to understand and write simple music. In the last hundred years, universal literacy has caused us to discover that a small proportion of otherwise intelligent children are unable to learn to read or spell easily at a high level. If everyone, by law, had to be able to draw a face accurately, there would be many artistic "dyslexics" in the community; because we demand fluency in reading of everybody, there is a small proportion of children who suffer from dyslexia.

Intelligence, which is largely inherited in potential (Carter, 1962), is made up of several special composite abilities (P.E. Vernon, 1961), among which are verbal ability, spatial ability, musical ability and mathematical ability. There is also a motor-kinesthetic "ability," which may be one aspect of spatial ability. The following discussion will be primarily concerned with the inheritance and functioning of verbal and spatial abilities.

One of the most important characteristics of dyslexia is its incidence in terms of sex differences. There is a greater or lesser ratio of boys to girls, depending on the cutoff point in terms of severity. If the cutoff point is in the mild dyslexic area, the ratio of boys to girls may be 3:1 or 4:1; in the very severe cases, the ratio may rise to 10:1. There seems to be little doubt that genetic dyslexia is, in some way, a sex-linked characteristic, though not exclusively a male one. The inheritance pattern, in terms of genes, is probably a polygenic one as is height, for example.

Genetic dyslexic children do quite well in all those spatial tests which do not demand sequencing, and their visual perception in terms of relationships in two- and three-dimensional space is usually good. Their ability to conceptualize logically in terms of meanings is also usually quite competent. Their major problem is in handling linguistic or other types of automatic coding fluency. In fact, arbitrary (that is, nonlogical) sequencing tests are especially difficult and, in essence, learning to read and learning to spell as skills *are* nothing more than arbitrary, irregular sequencing processes mostly auditory in nature—processes which in most children rapidly become automatic with training.

Genetic dyslexic children tend to mirror-image letters and to have a poor lateralization of eye movements in one dimension, problems which are probably caused by a competent spatial ability which, itself, results from a relatively superior inherited development of the visual and motor cortices. Good visuo-spatial ability requires an equality of hemispheric dominance, even though there may be some kind of control center in the spatially dominant right hemisphere (see Chapter IX). Verbal-auditory abilities, by contrast, seem to require a strong dominance of one hemisphere, usually the left, for their successful and rapid processing. Using the right visual field for reading and the right hand for writing means that almost all linguistic material will be processed in the left hemisphere of the brain, and within that hemisphere, there will be an economy of neurological communication. The right hemisphere in people with good verbal ability can thus be suppressed in terms of most interference, be it visual, motor or auditory.

The cortical and psychological intersensory and motor associations of writing and reading processes in terms of symbols are usually represented as a triangle with the stimulus object at the apex, the sound-phoneme symbol for that object in one lower corner and the secondary visual symbol for the sound in the other corner (see Fig. 1). However, this may be an incorrect way of looking at linguistic processes. The stimulus object (e.g., a table) in early childhood (and because of early childhood, throughout life) is always first associated with an *aural sequence of phonemes* (e.g., the sounds *t-a-b-le*); later, when learning to read, these sequences of phonemes in their turn are always associated with a series of visual symbols (e.g., the letters *t-a-b-l-e*) which represent them. The visual symbol does not normally *directly* represent the stimulus object. It always works through

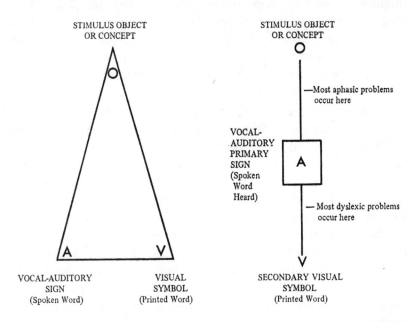

TRADITIONAL VIEW OF ASSOCIATIONS INVOLVED IN THE READING PROCESS. O-A IS LEARNED FIRST, THEN A-V (IN SCHOOL), WHICH GRADUALLY GIVES WAY TO O-V IN FAST READERS. THIS IS PROBABLY AN INCORRECT VIEWPOINT.

THE MOST LIKELY ASSOCIATION SYSTEM IS THE ONE WHICH HOLDS THAT ALL LANGUAGE SYSTEMS INCLUDING READING ARE CONTINUOUSLY PROCESSED AUDITORIALLY.

FIGURE 1. Intersensory and motor association systems of writing and reading processes.

the medium of auditory processes, no matter how much they may be compressed. (This may not be true in the case of pictograph languages or with the congenitally deaf, but this does not invalidate the argument, which is confined for the moment to phonetically symbolized languages.)

Genetic dyslexic children are probably better than others at appreciating visual stimuli and their interrelationships and they certainly know the shapes of all letters. Their major problem, I suggest, lies in the auditory area which must mediate in all linguistic functions. There is evidence to show that genetic dyslexic boys are less able to discriminate between arbitrary sequence of sound (Wolf, 1967) and that, by definition poor spellers, they find it difficult to associate to or remember sequences of sounds, even though they usually comprehend the meaning (associating a concept to a given word-gestalt of sound). Even so, their speech development is sometimes delayed and their fine auditory discrimination for some vowels may be poor. It should be emphasized that there is no question of deafness or ear defect of any kind.

Because the traditional orthography of the English language is extremely irregular (that is, the particular association of each auditory symbol to each visual symbol is only accurately identifiable in one single sequential word context), the task of reading and spelling largely becomes one of rote memory associations, each cued by several conventional contexts—the sequence of sounds, the sequence of letters in a word, the number of letters in the word, the sequence of words in the sentence and the conceptual content of the passage. The difficulty is increased when one realizes that the visual symbols must also be sequenced *separately* from the phonemes in a word context. In short, the sequences of sounds and their multiple arbitrary associations with sequences of visual symbols must always be learned by rote because there is no logical system to them. Spatial concepts, by contrast, are amenable to conceptual logic as, for example, in geometry, and the spatially capable person prefers a logical structure of principles from which he can work in any pure or applied field, such as physics, architecture or engineering. Spatially capable children, being part of this group, also prefer the logic of applied principles. On the other hand, the verbally able (auditory-type) person can more easily memorize arbitrarily associated or unsystematically linked material, such as objects and their linguistic signs and symbols. Languages are partially founded on a variety of arbitrary conventions, most of which are unsystematic in their coding systems. There are anecdotal reports that languages which are phonetically "logical" are less of a problem to dyslexic people. With this in mind, the additional burden of the eyes wanting to scan in all directions and of mirror images sometimes cropping up, makes the tasks of reading and spelling well-nigh impossible.

However, the major problems for the genetic dyslexic are (a) auditory fluency and sequencing, (b) auditory vowel discrimination and closure, (c) associating auditory symbols to sequences of visual symbols and (d) sound blending or vocal-motor sequencing. Therefore, the central emphasis in any training program must be on auditory and visual phoneme sequencing and training in careful listening and articulation, the whole approach to reading and spelling being phonic in nature. Techniques are available to help children in all these auditory, vocal and memory skills to which can be added directional training in one-dimensional scanning to establish eye muscle habits.

My own experience with genetic dyslexic children suggests that fathers in highly spatial occupations, such as surgeons, mechanics, dentists, architects, engineers and farmers, tend to have more genetically dyslexic children than do fathers in other occupations. Although the mothers and daughters in these families may be linguistically superior to the males, their verbal talents tend to be lower than they might be (Walker and Cole, 1965). In other words, the women in genetic dyslexic families, although nowhere near as handicapped as the men, will exhibit minimal symptoms; for example, their ability to learn foreign languages may be limited. Incidentally, highly intelligent dyslexics may teach themselves to read well by the age of ten, although afterward there is the residual problem of a severe spelling disability, recall of words being far more difficult than recognition. Thus, it will be seen that genetic dyslexia is a complex end result of a particular pattern of neurological inheritance, such a brain functioning reasonably well in most visual aspects and rather poorly in certain neurological auditory characteristics. Quite a large number of *normal* genes must be involved in the inheritance of a pattern of this sort.

Recently I have been noticing a syndrome of characteristics which might be a second type of genetic dyslexia. The main deficit areas are to be found in coding tasks and block design problems. However, the number of cases and families involved is too few to make any clear-cut statements about the nature of this genetic disorder, if it exists at all.

Genetic dyslexia will be further discussed in considerable detail in subsequent chapters, especially in Chapter IX.

Social, Cultural or Educational Deprivation Dyslexia

This type of dyslexia also warrants a chapter to itself (Chapter XII); therefore, this section will be devoted to distinguishing between cultural deprivation dyslexia and primary emotional communicative dyslexia, as well as to outlining briefly the nature of the disability.

Primary emotional communicative dyslexia is peculiar to the *particular* family in which it occurs. The main deprivation the child suffers is that of poor linguistic communication which is a facet of his relationship with his mother. Cultural or social deprivation dyslexia is more of a group or subculture problem and does not revolve around the personality of the mother in an idiosyncratic way. Sizable groups of people are failing to benefit from a thorough elementary education because, for complex reasons, they are unable to cope with what the schools have to offer.

Certainly there is no reason to believe that the children who have characteristics in this category have any neurological or psychological deficits in the usual sense. The published evidence indicates that several superimposed causes may be operating, namely, a language barrier between child and teacher, a subcultural value system which undervalues education and a lack of personal motivation in the father in the form of job ambition.

Therefore, the remedial antidote is equally complex. Reading centers and remediation classes sometimes have culturally deprived children referred for diagnosis and treatment and not infrequently these cases have still other aggravating causes of their dyslexia. A comprehensive and accurate differential diagnosis, though difficult to achieve, is essential if these children are to make satisfactory progress in language, reading and spelling.

In this type of dyslexia the main deprivation may be in the homes of the children, in the schools or in the neighborhood environment. Obviously, this is more a matter of emphasis than of sharp divisions. Quite often, the child has been hampered by a poor milieu across the board, so to speak, but it is of some value to be reminded that the home, school and a lack of neighborhood cultural facilities can each contribute separately.

Emotional Causes

There is sometimes confusion about whether emotional causes are primary, secondary or concomitant with dyslexia. Primary emotional dyslexia has been briefly described and needs no further elaboration here. The child who is dyslexic for any of the four main reasons (primary emotional communicative problems, neurological dysfunction, genetics or social deprivation) may suffer from *secondary* emotional problems such as poor work attitudes. Obviously, one has to deal with any negative attitudes during the first phase of remediating the child. It is also possible for a child to be backward through emotional disturbance for other reasons. The child with a severe reactive conduct problem will probably not learn to read well, but he also will not learn anything else; I would not describe such children as dyslexic, no matter how far behind their peer group they are in reading. Such children should be referred to schools for the emotionally disturbed, where they may improve once they receive individual remediation.

The classificatory grouping of causes in Table II accounts for almost all the points of view expressed by workers in the field of dyslexia, as well as for the reported symptomatology, however complex. In this "overview" chapter, it has not been my purpose to do more than hint at the various types of training required for the different groups and subgroups of dyslexic children described. Both diagnosis and treatment are quite complex because the groups are *not* mutually exclusive. It is common to find children who combine two categories or, much more rarely, even three. Perhaps one of the underlying reasons for the number of conflicting or confused results in much earlier research into reading disabilities has been the mixing together into one experimental group children with various etiologically different types of dyslexic symptoms. Emotionally disturbed children are sometimes included in such examples.

A large number of diagnostic tests is required on every physiological, neurological and psychological level for accurate differential diagnosis; there is a great need for rapid development of such tests.

Criticisms of the Classification System

Table II and its accompanying text have been criticized on several counts, mostly because the critics read more into the classification than was ever intended. Therefore, it is pertinent to emphasize the purpose and limitations of this taxonomic grouping and to answer some of the comments that have been made.

Table II is a collective *hypothesis* in diagram form about the possible origins of the observable symptoms presented by children to the teacher and research worker. Although there is a great deal of evidence in the literature which will be subsequently presented, as in all scientific investigation, no hypothesis is ever finally and conclusively proved—there is only more or less evidence to support it. The history of science is littered with supposed watertight cases of proof which have been shattered either by ingenious experiment, shrewd reasoning or recalculation. Proof is a continuum of the degree, quality and range of evidence; it is not something which either is, or is not, present.

Another point about the table is that it is limited to language and reading disabilities. Only too often conversationalists talk at cross-purposes because each has a quiet different universe of discourse without realizing it. One of the most common out-of-phase situations is where one person is discussing a state of affairs as it actually *is* where another is pointing out how it *should be,* ideally speaking. Table II is merely a first tentative, potentially evolving grouping of language and reading disability variables. Thus, mental retardation is only on the table to the extent that it is connected with language and reading problems. Other facets of mental retardation are irrelevant to the table. This is equally true of all the other cells shown. Any of the other major groups (e.g., emotionally disturbed and autistic children) could also be broken down into symptom groupings and, indeed, aphasia will be considered separately in Chapter XI. Other such chart elaborations of these major groups would be valuable contributions to our knowledge but each would then have its own universe of study. However, it is not my purpose to explore any of these other areas except insofar as they concern language and reading disabilities.

Some people have asked what is to be gained from the additional information derived from this type of classification system. The answer is that it makes people aware that *all* these diagnostic possibilities exist. Many educators and psychologists may not know that there is the possibility of, say, primary emotional communicative dyslexia or defective eye movements. The classification organizes knowledge systematically and because some of that knowledge may be new to some investigators, children are less likely to be misdiagnosed or inappropriately remediated. If we know what deficits a child has in this respect, the table can serve as a kind of reference checklist, and we can seek a remedial *solution* that much more accurately. Otherwise, we would have to rely on trial-and-error procedures for remediation and it may be months before we find the correct key from the hundreds available. Thus, there is a conservation of time and effort.

Other people have asked why the universe of study should not be extended to cover all learning disabilities rather than limiting it to only reading and language disorders. The reason is that one's universe of study in any classification must be a relatively homogeneous group *on that level;* otherwise, it would logically require an even higher category to link the disparities. Each discrete school subject in which learning disabilities can occur should have its own etiological classification table, even though the various tables may in part be identical.

Yet another criticism, this one from learning theorists, is that remediation should focus on the individual and his behavior rather than on etiology. The "medical model" is contrasted with behavior problems and their modification through shaping techniques. Krasner and Ullmann (1966) say,

> For example, if the psychologist decides that his goal is to reduce delusional speech he will respond with attention and pleasure to rational nondelusional verbal behavior and ignore or respond coldly to bizarre verbalizations. There are many issues touched on by this example. The psychologist after assessment formulates a program of treatment and assumes the responsibility for selecting behaviors whose emission by the patient are to be increased or decreased.

If, in the last sentence, one substitutes *doctor* for *psychologist* and *diagnosis* for *assessment,* and introduces the word *physiological* to qualify the word *behaviors,* then I suggest we *do* have the medical model. It may be a slightly unusual way of thinking about medicine, but the physician or surgeon fundamentally encourages or *increases* desirable (i.e., healthy, or acceptable) physiological behaviors and discourages or decreases undesirable ones (e.g., very high temperatures). The work of the learning theorists and behavior modifiers is a tremendous contribution to psychological knowledge, but their logic in terms of etiology and the four causes is, I think, dubious to some extent, being in many ways one of substitute terminology. A surgeon who corrects the shape of a congenitally malformed foot can do nothing about the efficient, formal or original material causes. But, like the operant conditioner, he can materially modify that foot "efficiently" in the here and now.

There is no fundamental difference between the medical model (be it surgical, psychological or physical) and behavior modification. Until medicine discovered drugs and other resources which directly reduced or eliminated the immediate material causes (e.g., bacteria or viruses), their medical practice was one of short-term behavior modification. Much of clinical and special educational psychological practice is still in the symptom analysis stage, during which symptomatic behavior modification is particularly appropriate. However, before too long many of these "abnormal or unacceptable behaviors" will be susceptible to *direct* neurophysiological treatment with drugs, surgery, electroneurology, genetic manipulation, *in utero* operations, hormone treatment and probably other methods not yet discovered. Using an analogy, first we must isolate the neuropsychological "viruses"— that is, the material causes of neuropsychological deficits—and to that end, we must identify and classify the facets of the disorders within our field of study. Once these syndromes are identified, we can work back, not only to modification, but ultimately through research to an eradication of the various material, efficient and formal causes. Some of them are already "assessed" by the behavior modifier; in other words, he makes a tentative diagnosis, usually of the immediate efficient and final (motivational) causes, and then prescribes a course of treatment, e.g., giving desirable tokens for healthy behavior. One day in the future, the "bizarre verbalizations" of the schizophrenic will probably be cured with injections or a surgical operation, or even prevented *in utero*.

Behavior modification will always have a valuable contribution to make in the wider scheme of remediation even after future research has isolated and controlled some learning disability "viruses." Inasmuch as some types of psychological and educational symptamatology such as a lack of motivation or poor work attitudes have entirely environmental causes (e.g., ineffectual teaching, a maladaptive emotional home life or negative social pressures, as in some subcultures), then behavior modification will be an essential tool.

Someone once suggested that there should be a group of genetic dyslexic children who are the visual counterparts of the ones I have described in more detail in Chapter IX as having particular auditory deficits. While it is no doubt true that many normal people do have poor visuo-spatial skills, this is not (if they are relatively *normal* though far below average) a handicap to reading. As the Johns Hopkins ophthalmologist, Dr. Herman Goldberg (1964), has pointed out, "The eyes play little part in producing a disabled reader." Obviously, all one has to be able to do visually is discriminate the shapes of the various letters, a relatively simple optical task for all people with normal vision and even for many with abnormal vision. People with abnormal visuo-spatial *neurological* deficits are a very different group who may have serious reading problems. In addition, to date there is no evidence for a cluster of dyslexic children whose reading problems of a visual nature are both homogeneous and attributable to a familial genetic factor.

Yet another criticism is that to be useful the classification system has to be continually extended into subgroups until the total population is splintered into a bewildering array of categories. This criticism, if it were applied to any other pure or applied science, would be ludicrous. Biology, education and nuclear physics, for example, all have extensive classification systems and gain by them. Any scientific knowledge is, to a large extent, simply an organizational classification of the known data, both relational and descriptive. It should be stressed once again that the units classified are symptoms, variables, attributes and their causes, and *not* the children who possess them. Furthermore, the categories of variables are not mutually exclusive. In a physical analogy, children can have measles, toothache and hiccups at the same time, all of which deter them from eating.

AN OVERVIEW OF ABNORMAL LANGUAGE DISABILITIES: APHASIA

Aphasia has interested many kinds of professional workers since the middle of the last century, and it is surprising how much of the early work has never been contradicted. Of course, it has been modified and amplified, and many new details have been written between the lines, so to speak. Many of these points are discussed at length in Chapter XI.

The symptoms and disabilities exhibited by the aphasic child are many and varied. They may have problems of auditory discrimination, a poor recognition of speech sounds; they also may have auditory figure-ground problems, an inadequate processing of auditory perceptions, an inability to relate information to its context, poor articulation or other speech problems and all manner of complex behavioral manifestations of cerebral impairment. The way in which these symptoms tend to cluster into various types of aphasia will be dealt with later in the book.

A Definition of Aphasia

As is so often the case with neuropsychological disorders, it is easier to say what aphasia is not rather than what it is. Thus, most definitions run roughly as follows: Aphasia is an impairment in language function probably caused by some form of neurological dysfunction which does not come under the categories of mental deficiency, deafness, dyslexia, peripheral speech deficits, emotional disturbance or social, cultural or educational deprivation. Aphasia has been traditionally divided into two categories, receptive (sensory) and expressive (motor), and as will be seen, much of the literature is devoted to a discussion of this oversimplified point of view. Another way of looking at aphasia is to consider the original causes of the disorder and here again there are two schools of thought which are not mutually exclusive. Some people have laid the blame on a developmental or maturational lag in language (for example, Bender, 1963) and have even suggested links with childhood schizophrenia. The second group holds that lesions in the brain are the most important cause of childhood aphasia. (Of course, there is little doubt that lesions are the most frequent cause of aphasia in adult patients.) There is every possibility that many aphasic children can be classified in each category and not a few probably in both. There are not very many younger children who have lesions after the onset of language development; nearly all the children coming into clinics and centers have suffered from language impairment from the earliest weeks of their life.

Psychoneurology and Psycholinguistics

The work of two men in the field of aphasia is of paramount importance; one is the Russian psychologist Luria, and the other is the American psycholinguist Osgood. Luria (1966) has made an extensive study of the higher cortical functions in man and has identified the neurological areas which, when damaged, seem to impair central language functioning. In all, he defines some seven categories of aphasia, his sample being mostly children and adults with specific brain lesions. Unfortunately, Luria does not title his categories with precision, sometimes using traditional terminology and sometimes his own. Therefore, I have taken the liberty of setting out a classification of the types of aphasia using terminology which stems from the process involved, the sensorimotor modality and the cortical area in which the lesions were found. Table XVI (page 509) sets out this classification. The first two lists of terms in the table are adequate to define any particular type of aphasia and, therefore, using this short form, the following terms are suggested for Luria's categories: *phonemic auditory aphasia, lexical auditory aphasia, semantic auditory-optic aphasia, oral-apraxic kinesthetic speech aphasia, deautomatized motor speech aphasia, articulemic motor speech aphasia and dynamic integrational aphasia.*

Osgood's work in psycholinguistics has contributed to our knowledge of aphasia because his multistage-process model of behavior (Osgood and Miron, 1963; Osgood, 1964b) delineates the various cognitive levels of psychological operation and the processes of decoding, association and encoding through which all behavior, including language, must pass in one form or another (see Chapter II). Osgood claims to be able to place aphasic patients fairly accurately into his psycholinguistic chart. Furthermore, it is possible to classify roughly the types of aphesia described by Luria in terms of this psycholinguistic model, particularly if the sensorimotor modality channels are added to the system.

Training and Remediation

Myklebust (1957) and McGinnis (1956) have both suggested techniques for training developmental aphasic children. The method propounded by Myklebust follows the normal development of language, the emphasis being on developing the child's "inner language" before teaching articulation, speech and conversation. McGinnis adopts the opposite procedure, finding that success comes more quickly if a child is first taught to articulate individual phonemes and only later is taught to build these into words and eventually sentences. It would seem that whereas Myklebust considers aphasia almost a cognitive problem, Mc-Ginnis regards it as a language *skill* deficit. As far as receptive aphasia is concerned, the work of Luria would suggest that the McGinnis method with its phoneme articulation is probably the better of the two techniques, but many of the excellent points made by Myklebust should certainly be used as powerful adjuncts to any training program for aphasic children.

Aphasia and Dyslexia

There is no doubt that many aphasic children and quite a number of dyslexic children have symptoms in common, although these may be more severe in aphasic cases. In fact, the *automatic* processing, in memory, of various sound units, both in hearing and in speech, is the one major symptom which most (but not all) aphasic and dyslexic children have as a central problem. All these points will be further elaborated in Chapters X and XI.

Chapter II

THE NATURE OF LANGUAGE

INTRODUCTION

That communication between the individual members of a species has immense survival value for that species is very obvious. What may not be so obvious is that while language is a form of communication which transmits denotative and connotative information from one human being to another (or even to animals), the language itself, except in special cases, is not the *information* being transmitted. Language may also, in most circumstances, facilitate individual thought processes internally by giving a verbal structure or organization to the "informational" systems we possess. In any complete linguistic communication system involving two individuals or groups of individuals, there are many separate elements, each of which not only must be defined but also must have its place in the system clearly indicated. Although it is impossible to do this in adequate detail in one chapter, some idea of the complexity of the problem can be derived from the following sections, which are mainly intended as background information for much of what follows later in the book.

SIGNS, SIGNALS AND SYMBOLS

There seems to be some confusion in the literature as to the exact meanings of these three words, even to the extent where one author will call all word-labels *signs,* whereas another will call them *symbols.* However, most authorities use the following definitions. *Signals* are sounds that serve an informational purpose and that may or may not be linguistic. *Signs* are those vocal utterances which have a discrete semantic meaning. Under this definition can be included all root-words, prefixes and suffixes—

in fact, all those "morphs" which can be considered as members of a "morph substitution class" (see page 43) as defined by Osgood and Sebeck (1965). *Symbols* are the visual written or printed shapes or geometric form outlines which, collected in clusters, represent meaningful vocal/auditory signs. Thus, the printed word symbolizes the vocal/auditory word. There is no inherent logic in these definitions because the words *sign* and *symbol* are used indiscriminately by many writers; the non-linguistic meanings of these two words are of no help because both signs and symbols can be nonlinguistic objects in their own right. To prevent ambiguity, it is convenient to restrict the use of the word *sign* to the vocal/auditory linguistic label and to use the term *symbol* to denote the printed or written equivalent for that label. As will be seen, a visual label is therefore a *symbol* for a sound label which, in its turn, is a *sign* representing the object or concept in question.

THE COMPONENTS OF LANGUAGE

Phonemes

All vocal signs (words) are composed of various sensorially recognizable discrete collections of sounds which are separately called *phonemes*. The operative word in this definition is *recognizable,* because different languages may utilize different sets of phonemes. These recognizable segments of sound are strung together sequentially to form spoken words, words which the competent listener decodes more or less automatically. One language may use many phonemes which are not found in another language; French, for example, makes use of phonemes which are not found in English. It should be realized that phonemes are really "categories of sound," each of which may contain much variation. The variations, if they can be separated (photographically), are single units of sound called *phones;* if two phones or phonemes are very similar they are called *allophones*. One or more phones may make up a phoneme. Consonants tend to be perceived as clear-cut phones or as a discrete collection of blended phones, whereas vowels do not appear to stop and start so clearly (Lindgren, 1965). It seems that the activity of the auditory speech perceptual system (perhaps the "auditory analyzers" of Luria, 1966) continuously sharpens, heightens and clarifies the incoming phonemic signals of a *known* language, once they are learned—usually in early infancy. Probably inhibitory neurosynaptic biochemical devices accomplish this (Eccles, 1965; John, 1967). That vowels seem to be less precisely delineated in speech has significance for the study of learning disabilities. As will be seen later, there is some evidence that certain types of dyslexic and aphasic children find it difficult to discriminate vowel phonemes auditorially and may even have a parallel articulatory problem. This has the further implication that auditory discrimination tests should concentrate more on vowel phoneme differentiation than they do at present.

Distinctive Features

Phonemes can be graded on whether or not they are formulated by several possible *distinctive features* which occur in articulatory and acoustic functioning. Lindgren (1965) has set out these distinctive feature patterns for English phonemes. He reports that Jakobson *et al.* (1952) originated this work and quotes them as follows:

> Any minimal distinction carried by the message confronts the listener with a two-choice situation. Within a given language each of these oppositions has a specific characteristic which differentiates it from all the others. The listener is obliged to choose either between two polar qualities of the same category, such as grave vs. acute, compact vs. diffuse, or between the presence and absence of a certain quality, such as voice vs. unvoiced, nasalized vs. non-nasalized, sharpened vs. non-sharpened (plain). The choice between the two opposites may be termed *distinctive feature*. The distinctive features are the ultimate distinctive entities of language since no one of them can be broken down into smaller linguistic units. The distinctive features combined into one simultaneous bundle form a *phoneme*.
>
> Any one language code has a finite set of distinctive features and a finite set of rules for grouping them into phonemes and also for grouping the latter into sequences; this multiple set is termed *phonemic pattern*. [However, the] distinctive features and the phonemes possess no meaning of their own. Their only semantic load is to signalize that a morpheme (the smallest meaningful unit in

language—e.g., a root, a prefix, and a suffix are morphemes) which, all other things being equal exhibits an opposite feature is a different morpheme.

Jakobson and Halle (1956) describe their view of how language units are constructed from distinctive features:

> The distinctive features are aligned into simultaneous bundles called phonemes: phonemes concatenated into sequences; the elementary pattern underlying any grouping of phonemes is a syllable. The phonemic structure of the syllable is determined by a set of rules and any sequence is based on a regular recurrence of this constructed model . . . The pivotal principal of syllable structure is the contrast of successive features within the syllable. One part of the syllable stands out from the others. It is mainly the contrast vowel vs. consonant which is used to render one part of the syllable more prominent.

Of course, languages differ considerably in the extent to which they make use of the various distinctive features as contrasts.

Jakobson *et al.* describe several more important types of coded information-bearing features of speech. Lindgren lists these as

> . . . *configurative features* which signal the division of an utterance into grammatical units of different degrees of complexity, particularly into sentences and words, either by singling out these units and indicating their hierarchy (*culminative features*) or by delimiting and integrating them (*demarcative features*). *Expressive features* (or emphatics) put the relative emphasis on different parts of the utterance or on different utterances and suggest the emotional attitudes of the utterer. There are also *redundant features* that serve an important role in different situations. For instance, in some cases of shouting or whispering, the normal distinctive features no longer serve, and the redundant feature takes over the distinctive function.

Lindgren then makes the following important statement:

> The suggestion throughout, although not explicitly stated has been to the effect that humans make decisions about what they are hearing at the lowest levels first (at the phonemic level), and then progressively make the decisions at higher levels (e.g., at the levels of syntax and semantics), or possibly on many levels simultaneously.

This statement parallels both the various speech and speech perception neuropsychological findings of Luria (1966) as described in Chapters VI and XI and the psycholinguistic sentence production model as proposed by Osgood (1963). In other words, in the progressive, sequential and hierarchial formation of an uttered sentence from the first stage of distinctive features to the final stage of transmitted information, there is a reasonable agreement on different "planes" of sound sequencing, neuro-psychological functions and psycholinguistic processes. The same holds true for the perception processes involved in decoding a heard sentence.

Tables III and IV were adapted by Lindgren from the work of Jakobson and Halle (1956) and Jakobson *et al.* (1952). It can be seen from Table III that the common vowel phonemes do not make use of the nasal-oral, tense-lax, continuant-interrupted and

TABLE III
SOME CHARACTERISTICS OF THE DISTINCTIVE FEATURES ON
THE ACOUSTIC LEVEL*

1. *Vocalic/nonvocalic*
   Presence vs. absence of a sharply defined formant structure.
2. *Consonantal/nonconsonantal*
   Low vs. high total energy.
3. *Compact/diffuse*
   Higher vs. lower concentration of energy (intensity) in a relatively narrow central region of the spectrum, accompanied by an increase (vs. decrease) of the total energy.
4. *Tense/lax*
   Higher vs. lower total energy in conjunction with a greater vs. smaller spread of the energy in the spectrum and in time.
5. *Voiced/voiceless*
   Presence vs. absence of periodic low-frequency excitation.
6. *Nasal/oral*
   Spreading the available energy over wider (vs. narrower) frequency regions by a reduction in the intensity of certain (primarily· the first) formants and introduction of additional (nasal) formants.
7. *Discontinuous/continuous*
   Silence followed and/or preceded by spread of energy over a wide frequency region (either as a burst or a rapid transition of vowel formants) vs. absence of abrupt transition between sound and such a silence.
8. *Strident/mellow*
   Higher-intensity noise vs. lower-intensity noise.
9. *Checked/unchecked*
   Higher rate of discharge of energy within a reduced interval of time vs. lower rate of discharge within a longer interval.
10. *Grave/acute*
    Concentration of energy in the lower (vs. upper) frequencies of the spectrum.
11. *Flat/plain*
    Flat phonemes in contradistinction to the corresponding plain ones are characterized by an upward shift of some of their upper-frequency components.
12. *Sharp/plain*
    Sharp phonemes in contradistinction to the corresponding plain ones are characterized by an upward shift of some of their upper-frequency components.

*From Lindgren (1965) and Jakobson *et al.* (1952).

TABLE IV
DISTINCTIVE-FEATURES PATTERN OF ENGLISH PHONEMES*

	o	a	e	u	ə	i	l	ŋ	ʃ	ʃ̂	k	ʒ	ʒ̂	g	m	f	p	v	b	n	s	θ	t	z	ð	d	h	#
1. Vocalic/nonvocalic	+	+	+	+	+	+	+	-	-	-	-	-	-	-	-	-	-	-	-	-	-	-	-	-	-	-	-	-
2. Consonantal/nonconsonantal	-	-	-	-	-	-	+	+	+	+	+	+	+	+	+	+	+	+	+	+	+	+	+	+	+	+	-	-
3. Compact/diffuse	+	+	+	-	-	-		+	+	+	+	+	+	+	-	-	-	-	-	-	-	-	-	-	-	-		
4. Grave/acute	+	+	-	+	-	-			-	-	+	-	-	+	+	+	+	+	+	-	-	-	-	-	-	-		
5. Flat/plain	+	-	-	+	-	-																						
6. Nasal/oral								+							+					+								
7. Tense/lax									+	+	+	-	-	-		+	+	-	-		+	+	+	-	-	-	+	
8. Continuant/interrupted							+		+	-	-	+	-	-		+	-	+	-		+	+	-	+	+	-	+	
9. Strident/mellow									+	+	-	+	+	-		+	-	+	-		+	-	-	+	-	-		

Key to phonemic transcription: /o/ - pot, /a/ - pat, /e/ - pet, /u/ - put, /ə/ - putt, /i/ - pit, /l/ - lull, /ŋ/ - lung, /ʃ/ - ship /ʃ̂/ - chip, /k/ - kip, /ʒ/ - azure, /ʒ̂/ - juice, /g/ - goose, /m/ - mill, /f/ - fill, /p/ - pill, /v/ - vim, /b/ - bill, /n/ - nil, /s/ - sill, /θ/ - thill, /t/ - till, /z/ - zip, /ð/ - this, /d/ - dill, /h/ - hill, /#/ - ill.

*From Lindgren (1965) and Jakobson et al. (1952).

strident-mellow distinctive features, whereas most of the consonants have a much wider range of characteristics. This work also has implications for those who, like Luria (1966), Sommers *et al.* (1961a) and Liberman *et al.* (1962), claim that feedback from the motor articulation processes is important in the development of the auditory discrimination of phonemes. Sommers *et al.* (1961b) have produced evidence that speech training in the articulation of phonemes significantly improved the reading comprehension of a large experimental group. Of course, the feedback would be both neurological and external. This articulatory acoustic-phonemic approach to language learning disabilities opens up many possibilities for future research.

Graphemes

The *grapheme* is the printed symbol equivalent of the phoneme. For example, *igh* in the word *light* is one grapheme representation of the phoneme that is also used in the personal pronoun *I*. In the word *white*, the phoneme is represented by a lower case *i*. In the word *by*, the phoneme is represented by the letter *y*, and in the word *buy*, it is represented by the phoneme *uy*; thus, it can be seen that a single phoneme can be represented by many graphemes. Conversely, a single grapheme, such as the printed letter *e*, can have several pronunciations as in the words *bet, he, the* (as commonly used in speech before a word beginning with a consonant), *canapé* (and other similar introduced French words), *little* (where the *e* is silent) and *shovel* (where the *e* is neutral). It will be apparent if this analysis is carried farther that phoneme-grapheme matching in the English language is highly irregular, since most phonemes are represented by more than one grapheme and vice versa.

The matching of phoneme to grapheme in a sequential fashion in writing is called the *orthography* of the language and the regularity or irregularity of the match varies considerably from language to language. Spanish has a fairly regular orthography whereas English and Danish are highly irregular or unsystematic in the matching process. Irregular orthography can present certain types of learning disability children with immense problems of memorization simply because each single phoneme-grapheme match in each word in the language must be independently learned in an arbitrary fashion by rote memory. This problem will be discussed in great detail in subsequent chapters.

Phones, phonemes, distinctive features and graphemes in their isolated states carry no semantic meaning; that is, they do not, in themselves, carry an intelligible communicative message from one individual to another (except, of course, in those cases where a phoneme or grapheme is also a word or exclamation in its own right). Phones and phonemes are the smallest units of the sound wave (compressed air) medium and it is only when they are strung together in a series that they have sufficient versatility to *code* a message. In the interests of flexibility (that is, to encode auditorially tens of thousands of meaningful words), it is more efficient for communication purposes to have an open-ended multiphoneme permutation/combination coding system as a medium. Although there are some rules, limitations and restrictions on the emission of meaningful strings of phonemes, an almost infinite variety of possible sequencing arrangements enables us to encode an almost infinite variety of meanings. An analogy is found in musical notation, where notes are sequenced in an infinite variety of melodies.

Morphemes

If the phoneme is the basic sound unit of speech, the *morpheme* is the smallest unit of meaning. Morphemes cannot be further divided into smaller elements conveying meanings and they usually occur in various contexts with relatively stable meanings (*Webster's New World Dictionary*, 1966). Osgood and Sebeck (1965), after discarding the use of words as linguistic units, utilize the term *morph* (instead of *morpheme*) as the minimal unit of language which conveys a meaning. In searching for a relatively independent consistent definition of a morph, Osgood and Sebeck suggest,

> The first unit to be considered is the *morph substitution class* (MSC) in terms of which it will be possible to define the key nucleus unit. . . . A morph substitution class is a set of single morphs (minimal

units with a meaning) which in a given context may substitute for each other. For example, in the sentence, "The singer broke the contract" the morph "sing-" in "singer" belongs to a morph substitution class which contains "sing-," "play-," "min-" and other members, since "The player broke the contract" and "the miner broke the contract" are possible utterances; "reform-" does not belong to the class since "re-form" consists of two morphs.

In their search for a minimal meaningful *nucleus*, Osgood and Sebeck next introduce the notion of a *thematic sequence*, which is defined as follows:

> In the example of "sing-er" above we saw that "re-form," although a sequence of two morphs and representing two morph substitution classes, behaved in the construction "reform-er" like a *single* morph substitution class, that containing "sing-," "play-," etc. A sequence of two or more morph substitutions classes will be said to constitute a thematic sequence, (1) if there is a single morph substitution class for which it may always substitute and yield a grammatical utterance and (2) if none of the morph substitution classes of the sequence is equivalent to, that is, has exactly the same membership as this single morph substitution class for which the sequence may substitute. The thematic sequence may be said to form a theme and to be an expansion of the single morph substitution class for which it may substitute.

Osgood and Sebeck then go on to define the term *nucleus*:

> A nucleus is either (1) a single morph substitution class which is not part of a thematic sequence or (2) a thematic sequence of morph substitution classes. Among single morph substitution classes are some which are expandable into thematic sequences but are not expanded in the particular construction analyzed and some which are not. In the sentence "the farmer killed the ugly duckling" there are nine morphs: (1) the (2) farm- (3) -er (4) kill- (5) -ed (6) the (7) ugly (8) duck- (9) -ling. There are seven nuclei: (1) the (a non-expandable morph substitution class) (2) farm-er (a thematic expansion containing two morph substitution classes) (3) kill- (a single morph substitution class expandable, e.g., into "un-hook-") (4) -ed (a non-expandable morph substitution class) (5) the (as above) (6) ugly (a single morph substitution class expandable into "un-god-ly") (7) duck-ling (a thematic expansion consisting of two morph substitution classes). There remains finally the distinction between nucleus boundaries which are also word boundaries and those which are not. There are a number of ways of stating the distinction which give practically the same results. The one adopted here is as follows: a nucleus boundary is an infraword boundary if and only if a fixed

number of nuclei may be inserted including those with zero members. Often nothing may be inserted. It is a word boundary in the excluded instance, that is, when insertions are possible and they are not fixed in number, e.g., if both three and five are possible. Usually an indefinitely increasing number of insertions is possible, that is, there is "infinite" insertion at word boundaries. In the above sentence no nucleus can be inserted between (3) kill- and (4) -ed and therefore it is not a word boundary. Between all the others, sequences of nuclei may be inserted of varying length and, in fact without limit. Thus between (1) "the" and (2) "farm-er" we can insert "very, headstrong, cruel, unlovable," etc., between (2) "farm-er" and (3) "kill-" can be inserted, "who lives in the house which is on the road that leads into the highway," etc. . . . The concept of nucleus as defined here is essentially a unit of which there is always a single fixed number in the class of words which are mutually substitutable in the same construction. . . . For example, it might well be investigated psychologically as a possible fundamental encoding or decoding unit.

In the same section, Osgood and Sebeck go on to indicate that the meaningful *nucleus* may be useful in the study of child development. They use it to resolve the question of whether a child develops morphology before syntactic construction, coming to the conclusion that *morphology does come first*, morphology being delineated as in the above quotations. It may also be true that future research in learning disabilities will profitably match up phonemes, graphemes and morphemic nuclei in various combinations which will facilitate the whole remediation process. It is quite easy to envisage systematic reading and writing programs firmly founded in a developmentally based tripartite matching procedure like the one just described.

In summary, we can say that spoken language in its smallest units is composed of distinctive features which in combination give rise to the phoneme. Morphemes or morphemic nuclei (on the morphological level) are built from groups of phonemes; these smallest units of meaning are grouped together to form words first, and then phrases. This leads us to a consideration of syntax, which is primarily concerned with the organization of sentences and the principles and processes on which they are constructed. From a study of syntax grammar develops, and grammar, obviously enough, differs from language to language. Languages differ in many respects on each of the component and organizational areas which have been identified above, but it is worth noting that groups of languages are thought to have many elements in common. It is the search for the invariance of language in tongues ancient and modern which is the concern of many of those who study linguistics.

LINGUISTICS

The above sections have been concerned with linguistics in the widest sense but, more and more, the term has become associated with *structural linguistics* and, particularly, with the objective investigation of the rules of syntax bereft of their semantic denotations (dictionary meanings) and their connotations (the affective or emotional and attitudinal associations to the meaning). Chomsky (1964) notes:

A generative grammar consists of a syntactic component which generates strings of formatives and specifies their structural features and interrelations; a phonological component, which converts a string of formatives with a specified (surface) syntactic structure into a phonetic representation; and a semantic component, which assigns a semantic interpretation to a string of formatives with a specified (deep) syntactic structure.

In this section, we will be mainly concerned with the syntactic component.

In his book *Syntactic Structures*, Chomsky (1957) put forward a comprehensive linguistic theory of syntax, which he defines as the study of the principles and processes by which sentences are constructed in particular languages. A sentence can be analyzed into its constituent parts by progressively breaking it down into noun phrases and verb phrases, then into nouns, verbs and other noun phrases, and then eventually into the component formatives (usually individual words). This is a hierarchical system of analyzing sentence structure and it can be presented in two ways. The first way is to progressively break down the sentence into more detailed elements in successive lines of analyses, and the second way is to make an outline of the elements (Table V).

The first method of breaking down the structure of a sentence gives more information than does the second, but both have par-

TABLE V
TWO WAYS TO ANALYZE A SENTENCE INTO ITS
CONSTITUENT PARTS*

Sentence

$NP + VP$	(i)
$T + N + VP$	(ii)
$T + N + Verb + NP$	(iii)
the $+ N + Verb + NP$	(iv)
the $+$ *man* $+ Verb + NP$	(v)
the $+$ *man* $+$ *hit* $+ NP$	(vi)
the $+$ *man* $+$ *hit* $+ T + N$	(ii)
the $+$ *man* $+$ *hit* $+$ *the* $+ N$	(iv)
the $+$ *man* $+$ *hit* $+$ *the* $+$ *ball*	(v)

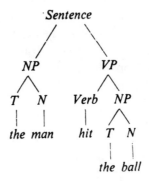

*From Chomsky (1957).

ticular uses. The former is useful in developing what are called the *transformational structures* of sentences (described below), and the second is rather useful for analyzing the spoken word into its constituents, particularly in analyzing the development of language in infancy. Chomsky and other structural linguists have developed a complex written symbolic notational system for labeling the various types of constituent parts that make up strings of formatives in sentences.

A sentence or phrase structure is subjected to a process of transformation when the original "kernel" sentence is altered into another overall form. For example, if the sentence, "The man hit the ball," is transformed into the passive form, "The ball was hit by the man," or into the form of a question (for example, "Was the ball hit by the man?"), transformation has occurred. Negation is yet another form of transforming the structure of the sentence. Transformational rules can operate on classes of utterances irrespective of their individual meanings. For example, the sentences, "They have arrived," "They can arrive" and "They did arrive" can all be generated by one transformation rule which, is this case, exchanges the first two segments (words) so that these statements become the questions, "Have they arrived?" "Can they arrive?" and "Did they arrive?" By this time, it will be apparent that structural linguistics have a lot in common with pure mathematics, intellectually speaking. A given number of "bits" are manipulated in more and more complex fashion and with an ever-increasing symbolic notation. For units, we have the parts from the more usual prediction-type sentences with their transitive and intransitive verbs (usually kernel sentences). We have passives, negatives, interrogatives, transpositions, exclamations, imperatives and deletions. From this, it will be seen that the non-semantic transcription of any language is an extremely complex and formidable task.

Fortunately, most children who have language learning disabilities are in the early stages of the language learning process and, therefore, the linguistic analyses which are most appropriate to them are more often of a simple kind. Two authors, Fries (1963) and Lefevre (1964), have contributed to a linguistic treatment of learning to read. While Fries adopts a traditional approach, the technique of Lefevre is to present, in a relatively simple way, the elements of syntactic structure and transformational techniques so that children will acquire a knowledge of the fundamental rules of generative grammar. Lefevre's book, after considering language development and intonation, proceeds to discuss sentence patterns, functional word groups, structure words, word form changes (the four word classes) and then spelling, word analysis and phonics. One quotation from Lefevre will summarize his approach:

> So far we have discussed several imporant patterns of the statement, a number of structural variants of those patterns and the intonation patterns that provide unifying configurations for entire meaning-bearing sentence structures. We have also mentioned noun markers,

verb markers, and question markers as they occurred in the sentences we examined. Now it is time to look at some of the word groups, expanded from single nouns and verbs, that may function as nouns and verbs in the common patterns we have previously discussed. *Understanding the systematic structuring of noun groups is more significant for reading and writing instruction than almost any amount of study of individual words that may fill these positions.*

There may be two ways in which this study of simple linguistic structure may be of value to some children with language learning disabilities. First, they may actually be taught simple linguistics so that they will acquire a more fundamental and direct knowledge of how language works. Second, by arranging the contents of workbooks in a pattern which corresponds to the developmental sequence of language acquisition, linguistically speaking, the learning disability child will be aided, because a more natural ordering of material usually facilitates learning. However, it should be mentioned here that there are many exceptions to this generalized developmental rule of remediation. These and other possible implications of linguistics for remediation will be discussed in Chapter XV. Yet another use of structural linguistics is to be found in the study of language development in infancy and early childhood; this will be discussed in more detail in Chapter IV.

PSYCHOLINGUISTICS

Osgood and Miron (1963) say, "Psycholinguistics is concerned with those (decoding) processes whereby messages are received and interpreted and with those (encoding) processes whereby messages are conceived and articulated." In practice, however, though they are primarily concerned with decoding and encoding processes in language, psycholinguists are by implication interested in the total psychology of language. Some of these facets are dealt with more appropriately in other chapters; therefore, this section will be mainly concerned with describing various psycholinguistic models of language behavior in preparation for a wider discussion of language development and language learning disabilities. Osgood and Miron have described some psycholinguistic models in *Approaches to the Study of Aphasia* (1963).

The learning position of single-stage language learning as put forward by Skinner in his book *Verbal Behavior* (1957) has been criticized and found wanting both by Osgood and Miron (1963) and separately by Chomsky (1959) in his classic paper entitled, "A Review of B.F. Skinner's Verbal Behavior." Interested readers are referred directly to these two works.

During an interdisciplinary conference on aphasia (Osgood and Miron, 1963), Weinreich suggested the functional model of language behavior illustrated in Figure 2. In this model, it can be seen that at the input stage, the listener (phoneme) or the reader (grapheme) registers these primary stimuli and, by decoding them in terms of grammatical structure, understands the meaning of the passage; this may set the person thinking. Alternatively, the stimulus to encode may come from outside the listening or reading situation; e.g., the person may see a sunset and may comment on its beauty to a companion. The person is, on the basis of grammatical rules, stringing together phonemes or graphemes and, through this output, communicating meaning-fully.

Wepman *et al.* (1960) have a slightly more elaborate model

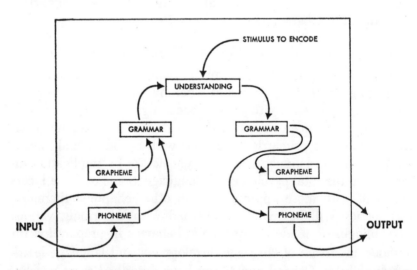

FIGURE 2. Weinreich's psycholinguistic model. *(From Osgood and Miron, 1963, p. 102.)*

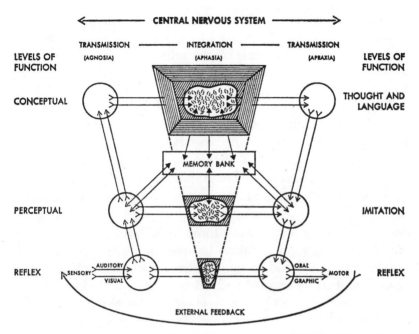

FIGURE 3. Psycholinguistic model of Wepman *et al.* (1960). *(From Osgood and Miron, 1963, p. 107.)*

(Fig. 3) which tends to emphasize more the conceptual and thinking aspects of language behavior. Since they are also concerned with abnormalities of language processing, Wepman *et al.* indicate where such disabilities as agnosia, aphasia and apraxia fit into their schema. On the input side, the term *reflex* refers to the automatic analyzing of the input material, which can be either auditory or visual. As will be seen, this tends to coincide with Luria's sensory analyzer stages, neurologically speaking, and with Osgood's psycholinguistic projection level. The simple sensory image is then perceived in the light of previous sensory experience, a process which takes place on the perceptual level. On the conceptual level, the subject completely understands the full nature and implications of the present experience, presumably mostly in the light of past experience; if this is not the case, the subject is suffering from agnosia, which is an inability to know or understand what is adequately perceived. The information is then further dealt with in a full integration process during which it will be related to previous experience, and decisions will have to be made by the subject on that information as to what is an appropriate active or communicative behavior as a next step. These decisions having been made centrally, the encoding process begins. The final thoughts, so to speak, are arranged sequentially, and through various automatic sequential habits which have been formed in infancy and childhood through imitation, the subject will structure the material linguistically and present it through either oral or graphic motor reflex systems.

Osgood (1964b) has elaborated a multistage-process model of behavior which is set out in Figure 4. Osgood divides the model into nine sections by defining three main levels—the projection, integration and representation levels—and three processes—decoding, association and encoding. These levels and processes have been described by Osgood and Miron (1963) as follows:

[The model] describes three levels of organization on both input and output sides; a *projection level* (assumed to be essentially isomorphic

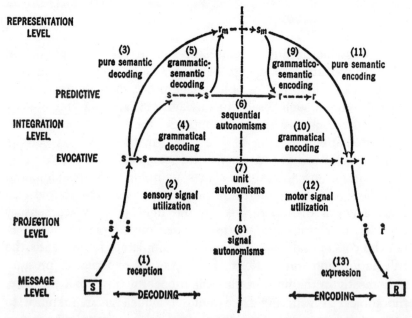

FIGURE 4. Osgood's psycholinguistic model. *(From Osgood, 1964, p. 106.)*

with external stimuli and unmodifiable through experience), an *integration level* (including both evocative unit integrations and predictive sequencing mechanisms), and a *representation level* (the decoded significances of signs as stimuli and the encoding intentions of signs as responses). It assumes three processes in the handling of information: *decoding processes* (reception, projection, integration and decoding the significance of input signals), *encoding processes* (intentional selection of meaningful units, their grammatical integration, and expression via motor pathways), and *associative processes* (associations among representational mediators, associations between sensory and motor integrations as wholes—here called sequential and unit automatisms, and wired in associations between input and output signals, i.e., reflexes). Although they are not shown in the diagram (for obvious reasons), it must be assumed that there are hierarchies of alternatives at every level, these alternatives varying in the probabilities of occurrence, for example alternative SS integrations given any particular subset of input from the projective system, alternative r_m's given any particular sensory integration and so forth.

In an appendix, they list several possible channels through which behavioral information may pass. These are the auditory, visual, tactile, motor and vocal (oral) channels. These channels not only apply to the projection level but also to the integrational and representational levels. Changes of channel may occur in any of the sections of Figure 4 but, of course, decoding is mostly (though according to Luria by no means completely) sensory, whereas encoding is primarily motor in function. Obviously, most input will be auditory or visual and the output will be motor (writing) or oral motor (speech).

Kirk and McCarthy (1961) have taken Wepman *et al.*'s and Osgood's models and used them as a basis for constructing a test of language functions, the Illinois Test of Psycholinguistic Abilities. A schematic diagram of Kirk's adapted clinical model of the communication process (Kirk, 1966) is presented in Figure 5.

As can be seen, this figure incorporates the channels (or in Wepman's language, the modalities) through which human beings operate linguistically. Note that the term *haptic* is a generic word which covers touch, some kinesthetic feedback and other proprioceptive sensory information. Thus at the input level we hear, see

Clinical Model of The Communication Process

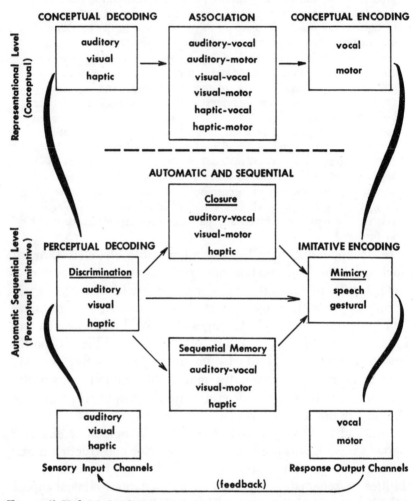

FIGURE 5. Kirk-McCarthy-Osgood clinical model of the communication process. *(From Kirk, 1966, p. 52.)*

or feel the stimuli, which are then discriminated at the perceptual decoding level. In the case of language, the *automatic and sequential association processes of closure and sequential memory are important* and I personally think that the arrows here should have a pointer on each end, indicating a two-way process. At the representational level, the processes are identical to those described by Osgood. However, at the encoding integrational level, Kirk makes use of Wepman's idea of imitation and mimicry in the acquisition of speech and gesture. It should be noted that the above models allow for external feedback only; that is, one either hears one's own voice or sees what one is writing and thus is able to monitor one's output to insure accuracy. It has also been suggested that this feedback helps to sharpen or heighten discrimination of sensory input at the perceptual level. As has been said, the model presented in Kirk (1966) and Kirk and McCarthy (1961) has been the basis for the Illinois Test of Psycholinguistic Abilities; this test is described in Chapter XIV. It is used primarily for the diagnosis of children with learning disabilities.

Yet another model of a different kind (Fig. 6) has been produced by Stevens and Halle (1967). These authors suggest that when someone is listening to language, the subject's brain works on a matching principle (akin to that which has been postulated for vision). The subject will make synthesized hypoth-

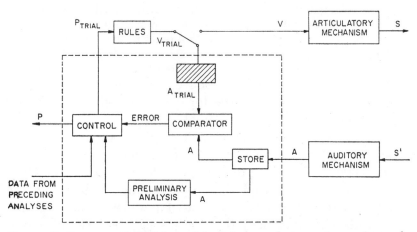

FIGURE 6. Stevens and Halle's model of the speech-generating and speech-perception process. The dashed line encloses components of a hypothetical analysis-by-synthesis scheme for speech perception; the shaded component indicates the capability of the model for effecting transformations between articulatory instructions and auditory patterns. (*From Stevens and Halle, 1967, p. 100.*)

eses about the pattern of the incoming stimuli by continuously matching the perceived patterns against existing internalized patterns which have developed according to various linguistic rules. The internal rules are possibly similar to those used in speech (Osgood adopts a similar theoretical position). Stevens and Halle go so far as to suggest that internally generated patterns are basic to both speech perception and speech production. Each speaker stores in his memory an "abstract" representation of the words in his language; these consist of segments which, in their turn, are "complexes of features." The order of the different segments in the sentence is determined by the syntactic rule components of the language, but while the final output is obviously linear in time, the vocal tract production itself is a complex arrangement of discrete segments and features. However, the authors go on to say,

There is no implication that the acoustic output must be necessarily decomposable into sequences of discrete segments or that instructions or features are directly recoverable from the signal. We *are* asserting that the acoustical output is a joint function of the abstract representation of the rules of the language, and the dynamics of the vocal tract, but we do not mean to imply that this is a linear function of the segments in the abstract representation; nor is there any reason to suppose that it must be served. As a result it cannot be expected that the underlying representation should in all cases be recoverable from the signal by simple techniques of signal analysis.

When a person listens to conversation, he uses the same phonological rules that he used for generating speech to decode the incoming signal. The essential point is that behind both speech and listening is some kind of matrix of abstract representation of segments and features, all of which are formulated into linear language according to fixed phonological rules. This whole conception of Stevens and Halle is very much in line with the work of Luria (1966), inasmuch as it postulates neurologically (and with some evidence) that the primary sensory and motor systems have "analyzers" which actively select from previous learning, *on a predetermined basis,* which signals are to be selected as significant or meaningful. Stevens and Halle suggest that their particular "abstract representation," which generates speech production (motor) and which analyzes incoming auditory signals, has a firm neurological basis in man.

Unfortunately, more recent studies have tended to indicate that speech and hearing (speech perception) *are not interdependent* with a common set of phonological rules. Lenneberg (1964) quotes the case of a boy who, although completely mute from birth, was able to acquire the ability to understand language. MacNeilage *et al.* (1967) have published a paper undermining the essential interdependence of speech production and speech perception. They say,

> The present study has shown that in spite of severely limited speech production capacities, the patient's phoneme perception is qualitatively similar to that of normal subjects in these various aspects of vowel and consonant identification and discrimination. This does not of course demonstrate that normal subjects do not use motor information for some of these types of perceptual performance. But it does suggest that motor information is not necessary to such performance.

Of course, although it can be taken as proven that speech and speech perception are *essentially* independent, this does not mean that there is no mutual feedback facilitation between the two. In fact, although the congenitally deaf can learn to speak to some extent and although the congenitally mute can learn to understand language, it is highly likely that feedback from speech to hearing and vice versa in normal people is extremely reinforcing linguistically. From the evidence already quoted (Sommers *et al.*, 1961b), there would seem to be little doubt that an improvement in articulating the language results in an improvement in perceiving the language.

Although there must be considerable feedback each way between speech production and speech perception and although there must be numerous neurological linkages between the two areas, I also personally tend to the opinion that they do not have a common generative "abstract representation of speech events." While one can listen to or read meaningfully (decode) a very large number of lexical items (words) on an almost infinite variety of syntactical "themes" in one's own language, unless particularly gifted, one usually speaks with a restricted vocabulary and a single syntactical style. Because of the immense internal and external feedback of vocabulary and syntactical style, a parallel commonality of speech production and speech perception may be built up in the motor articulatory and speech planning areas and in the appropriate auditory areas, thus enabling the individual to perceive incoming information more accurately. He will then encode and decode according to his own experience-built lexical and syntactical habits. This can be carried over to reading, inasmuch as he may better understand those authors who write in accordance with the rules of his own idiosyncratic syntax and vocabulary.

There are many implications in what has been said for helping children or adults with language learning disabilities. Within reason, it might become necessary to recast much of their course work, their remedial material and corrective exercises in a linguistic-style pattern which they can appreciate because it meshes with their own. Although such techniques would most obviously apply to those who already possess a reasonable degree of language ability, the technique might be found useful with some severe cases of adult aphasia, particularly if samples of their previous intact speech and writing were available. The usefulness of this approach with dyslexic children will be discussed later.

Note that learning disability children can have specific deficits in any of the nine sections of Table VI and often those deficits are multiple. Table VI is very important and should be studied in detail.

SPECIFIC ABILITIES AND INTELLIGENCE

There is a long tradition in psychology that intelligence can be analyzed into various factors or specific abilities, each of which enables the individual to perform more or less competently in equally specific areas of cognitive functioning. The number of psychologists and educators who have made contributions in this field is only matched by the array of factor patterns that they have produced. Spearman (1946) suggested a two-factor theory: first, a general factor of intelligence g, then a number of specific factors such as musical ability or numerical ability. P.E. Vernon (1961) has extensively reviewed most of the work on cognitive abilities, including his own research. It would seem that in the

TABLE VI
PSYCHOLINGUISTIC SCHEMA—SUMMARY DIAGRAM

3. CONCEPTUALIZATION REPRESENTATION	4. THINKING/RELATIONSHIP PROCESSING	5. OUTPUT CONCEPT/IMAGERY PLANNING
Complex sensorimotor imagery Associations with other concepts and images (Parietal areas of brain?)	Active, logical (?) *processing of relationships* between concepts and images (Midbrain? Penfield and Roberts, 1959)	Marshaling one's *own* thoughts systematically prior to encoding for communication (internal or external) (Frontal and midbrain?)

	9. MEMORY	
	Visual, auditory, motor, kinesthetic/haptic	
2. IDENTIFICATION, RECOGNITION AND RECALL OF DATA Sensorikinesthetic integration (Secondary sensory areas of brain?)	Memory for units Memory for sequences Memory for chunks Short-term memory Long-term memory Recall memory Recognition memory Memory for content (items) Memory for systems (relationships) (Midbrain and secondary areas)	6. PROGRAMMING OUTPUT Motor/kinesthetic sequencing of words Motor/kinesthetic sequencing of actions (Frontal and superior parietal?)

1. ACTIVE SENSORY RECEPTION	8. PRIMARY SENSORI-MOTOR COORDINATION	7. MOTOR OUTPUT
Data input: Visual Auditory Kinesthetic/haptic (Primary areas of brain)	Motor and sensory feedback between 1 and 7 (e.g., eye movements, voice movements)	Voice/vocal Handwriting, Communication typing Doing, constructing Action (Frontal and cerebellum?)

NOTES:
1. The memory processes in 9 are essential to all the other sections.
2. Most cognitive activities move in the order 1 through 7 with boxes 8 and 9 supplying association and feedback "information."
3. Semiautomatic functions tend to occur in the order 1, 2, 9, 6, 7 (e.g., typing).
4. Some motor functioning occurs on the input side (1, 2, 3).
5. Learning disability children can have specific deficits in any of the above sections and often those deficits are multiple.

majority of studies, the first factor to be extracted is nearly always a "Spearman-type" general factor of intelligence. The next two factors are frequently group factors, one being verbal, numerical ability and the second spatial/mechanical ability. If the hierarchical breakdown is continued, the verbal/numerical factor divides into separate verbal and numerical factors, each composed of various fluency factors (mostly of a skill nature). The spatial/mechanical group will break down into a pure spatial factor, a mechanical information factor and a manual dexterity factor. It is possible for these minor group factors to be further split into more specific factors, but in most factor analyses, these tend to be very unreliable statistically.

The *v*-factor (verbal ability) is broken down by Vernon into four main areas: verbal reasoning, verbal fluency, vocabulary and clerical ability. He analyzes the *k*-factor (spatial ability) into spatial ability, drawing ability, mechanical ability and practical ability. *These two factors, which are further described below, are extremely important and will be referred to frequently throughout this book.*

A descriptive definition of visuo-spatial ability would seem pertinent here: Visuo-spatial ability is the ability to manipulate objects and their interrelationships intelligently (psychologically) both directly (e.g., engineering, surgery) and symbolically or abstractly (e.g., geometry) in two-, three- or multidimensional space.

With respect to spatial ability, I. M. Smith (1964) has written an excellent book in which he devotes a chapter to the spatial factor and its subdivisions. He cites el Koussy (1955), who makes the following points:

> From the point of view of content, spatial aptitude may be subdivided into two-dimensional and three-dimensional, and static and dynamic aspects. From the functional point of view, it may be subdivided into visualization and manipulation sub-factors. Research has shown that there are differences in spatial aptitude from the kindergarten onwards and that boys show a superiority over girls. This superiority is not due to the effect of apprenticeship since it exists even when the same education is given to both sexes. It is more marked in three-dimensional tasks than in two-dimensional tasks. . . .

Smith himself has more to say about the nature of spatial ability.

> Analyses for aptitude for mathematics has shown that it consists of a heterogeneous group of capacities involving the general, numerical, verbal, memory and spatial factors. The numerical and spatial factors have a tendency to be weaker in pupils who are backward in mathematics, though normal in other subjects. . . . It seems that the factors

underlying the mental processes necessary for success with spatial material—considered as a global aptitude to obtain, manipulate and utilize spatial/visual imagery—may be differentiated into a visualization factor and a manipulation factor.

After an extensive analysis of mathematical and spatial ability, Smith puts forward the suggestion that *the spatial factor appears to have a greater claim for consideration as an essential basis for aptitude for mathematics than does either numerical or verbal ability.* Other points made by Smith are as follows:

> Mathematics can be regarded as a language only in a highly specialized sense. *It is certainly not a spoken language.* We communicate mathematical ideas in writing, either on paper or on a blackboard or by means of models or diagrams. Formulae and equations have to be read; only the most elementary expressions can be communicated orally. In order to follow an exposition in algebra, we must be able to compare one expression with another, or to relate one part of a formula to another. . . . It is sometimes said that the most able mathematician can think entirely in abstractions and have no need of diagrammatic props. But, this may be because these gifted individuals have their own internal "blackboards" and can *visualize complicated structures* without being aware that they are doing so. Certainly many mental calculators, such as Buxton, Colburn and the Bidders, reported that their calculations always proceeded in a visible form in their minds. . . . Much of the difficulty in teaching mathematics may arise from the need to communicate abstractions relating to configuration to many pupils (particularly girls), who do not think readily in terms of mental or visual imagery. Even in quite elementary mathematics, many such spatial concepts have to be assimilated, e.g., length, squareness, area, angle, direction, congruence, parallelism, volume, similarity, gradient, vector, symmetry, dimensions; and many other abstract concepts may be conveyed most conveniently by means of geometrical illustrations, e.g., continuity, maximum and minimum, limit, functionality, variation. [Italics added.]

In yet another chapter devoted to a consideration of spatial ability and conceptual or abstract thinking, Smith argues, on the basis of available evidence, that Spearman's tests of spatial perception, which had fairly high g-loadings, are good indicators of abstract reasoning ability. He goes on to say,

> If this is indeed the explanation of what Spearman calls the "anomaly of spatial perception" the unexpected fact that some spatial tests, such as the N.F.E.R. Spatial Test I, have very high g-loadings in

addition to very substantial k-loadings, takes on a new significance. If there are psychological grounds for regarding g and k as a single factor (and the analyses of Sultan's data suggests that this might be satisfactory statistically), then spatial tests have a strong claim to be regarded as true abstractions tests, if not super-g-tests. There would be good grounds for preferring them, because of their superior reliability, to concept-formation or sorting tests such as those of Goldstein and Scheere, Weigl, Vigotsky, Berg and others. As Vernon (1953) has pointed out, no one has yet proved that these are anything more than a rather unreliable test of g. Certainly the long-standing view of psychologists such as McFarlane (1925), Alexander (1935) and Spearman and Jones (1950), that there is a dichotomy between concrete and abstract intelligence, has been misleading. The corollary that spatial tests measure an ability to think concretely while verbal tests measure an ability to think abstractly seems to be based on the fallacy.

Smith goes on to suggest that the theory that there is an intimate association between form perception and the process of abstraction which has been put forward by Lorenz (1951) is a correct one. Lorenz suggests,

> Gestalt perception is nothing else than . . . the function of another constancy computer, which enables us to perceive the shape of an object as one of its permanent properties. . . . The original survival value of Gestalt perception indubitably lies in perceiving constant shape as the supremely important property of individual objects. . . . All effects of constancy, including that of Gestalt, are based on the single function of extracting the essential constant factor by abstracting from the inessential variable sensory data. The differentiation of this function contains an amazing development in the service of shape constancy, and it needs only to be driven one little step further to make possible an absolutely new operation miraculously analogous to the formation of abstract, generic concepts. . . . Very probably this function of generic recognition achieved by Gestalt perception is not the only phylological precursor of conscious abstraction. We know by much observational and experimental evidence that the human capacity of Gestalt perception far exceeds that of all animals. In my opinion, the great change of function just described is one of those indispensable conditions which had to be fulfilled in order to make possible conceptual thought and speech.

Almost all the above detailed points have great relevance to the study of language and learning disabilities, inasmuch as they also involve cognition, and they will be referred to and elaborated on frequently in later sections. *Of particular importance is the rationale and evidence for the statement that much (if not all) abstract thought and reasoning is not only visuo-spatial and non-verbal but also far more primary and perceptually direct than is verbal functioning. Thought is thought and words are labels.* Note, however, that spatial ability can be *used* in a very concrete way (involving abstract spatial principles), as when an engineer designs a bridge or a child plays with an erector set.

LEARNING, LANGUAGE AND THE BRAIN

The components of language, linguistics, psycholinguistics and general and specific cognitive abilities all have as their basis the human brain and its neurons. Over the last two decades, many neuropsychologists from their various disciplinary approaches have contributed much to our knowledge of the specific functioning of the various areas of the cerebrum. Some of these, such as Hebb (1949), have postulated theories of interneuron functioning in terms of neurological networks, etc., which could account for many psychological phenomena including memory. However, Hyden (1961) has postulated memory as a cellular RNA functioning and others such as John (1967) have put forward more complex wave theories (see Chapter VII). Penfield and Roberts, in their classic book *Speech and Brain Mechanisms* (1959), have done much through neurosurgery to identify the specific functions of various cortical areas. The Russian psychologist Luria (1966) has extensively mapped the functioning of the cortex by psychologically testing patients with lesions of the brain. There is little doubt that an extensive synthesis of our psychological and neuropsychological knowledge is imminent.

Those who study learning disabilities are rapidly forced into an extensive study of neuropsychology because a fair proportion of learning disability cases appear to have some kind of neurological dysfunction as the material cause of their immediate learning problems. There is extensive literature (in which Luria's work stands out as a high point) on the neuropsychology of language and learning disabilities, and while this will be thoroughly examined in Chapter VI, I think it appropriate at this point to set down my own broad conclusions and hypotheses as a frame of reference for what will come later.

The first point to be made is that the human being is a whole organism and that that whole organism is in a continuous state of developmental change. That would seem to be a rather trite statement but it is surprising how many people who work with children disregard its implications. About the only aspects of the child which would *not* seem to change are his innate potentials for development, the limits of potential being determined in almost every area by genetic inheritance. Even our ideas on potential limits are not static and many myths are being exploded by the great variety of work devoted to investigating the effects of the early stimulation of young children which is going on all around the world today. The early stimulation of babies and infants can occur in every aspect of the child's being, including motor functioning, verbal capacities, spatial manipulation of the relationships of objects, social skills, cognitive abilities, musical appreciation, mathematical abilities and, above all motivation to enjoy all these functions in a dynamic life-fulfilling way. However, the point to be made is that although we are not yet sure of the potential limits of children within the genetic framework, those limits must obviously exist. For example, it is inconceivable that all children could be trained to be Einsteins or Shakespeares, although many children with seemingly average intellectual capacities are trained up to university level as a result of early stimulation in infancy. It should be noted that even this has yet to be demonstrated. The conclusion is that environmental training is extremely important and it is in this area that learning theorists, using classical and operant conditioning techniques, have a great deal to contribute, and will do so even more fruitfully once the technology matches the infinite complexity of human learning. On the academic side of education, the learning theorists have constructed extensive curriculum programs, some in the form of textbooks and some for use in teaching machines. If many of these programs are dry and uninteresting to young children, this is only because this branch of education is, itself, in its infancy and the effort thus far has been concentrated on a logical step-by-step analysis of the subject tasks to be taught, rather than on the

intrinsic motivation of the presented material. It is to be hoped
that high-interest elements will be wedded to these curriculum
programs so that even dull children will obtain satisfaction from
them (Bannatyne, 1966b). In the area of personality disorders,
the learning theorists have also contributed much to our knowledge of behavior modification, particularly to that of severely
emotionally disturbed children. The techniques being developed
by Ferster (1967) with autistic children and by Hewett (1967a)
with emotionally disturbed children are excellent (see Chapter
XIII).

The genetic aspects of human development and behavior have
been seriously neglected in American psychology and education
for many decades; even today, there is only a slowly growing
appreciation of the role which genetics may play in the formation
of cognitive and personality variables. In this, I would include
language functioning, an area in which genetic factors have been,
until very recently, considered nonexistent. There is no incompatibility between genetic inheritance and learning theory unless
one subjectively and unscientifically decides to eliminate one or
the other for all practical purposes. The true scientific approach
is to try to discover the exact nature of the interplay between
genetic inheritance and those functions and activities which are
learned through conditioning or incidental training. Some authorities use the word *genic* to indicate that area of genetics which is
concerned with the inheritance of innate characteristics from the
parents. For me the word *genetics* includes this definition of *genic*
but carries with it the more desirable wider meaning of cognitive
and personality development within inherited potential limits—
limits which may be aspects of a continuous developmental program, e.g., the appreciation of spatial relationships from birth to
maturity, or, on the more conative-affective side, sexual development. Genetic limits in this sense mean the maximum potential
(in any area of behavior) that can possibly be developed by that
individual, e.g., physical height or the ability to memorize nonsense syllables at speed.

There would seem to be a vast area of unmapped genetic
developmental patterns in humans, an area of which biologists,

psychologists, educators and other social scientists are only slowly becoming aware. Ethologists such as Lorenz (1963, 1965), Harlow (1961, 1963) and Bowlby (1957) are already suggesting that human beings have a lot in common with their animal ancestors, namely, specific innate patterns of behavior which, in human beings, are probably slightly "blurred" in the interests of survival and training malleability. These are discussed in Chapter XIII. Likewise, specialists in language have been turning to an examination of possible innate factors which may be contributing to language learning processes. Recently, Lenneberg (1967) published the book *Biological Foundations of Language,* which will be discussed below. Research workers interested in problems related to deafness, such as McNeill (1965), have also suggested that innate factors probably operate in the realm of language acquisition. McNeill says, "The process of acquiring syntax is fairly well understood, and evidence is accumulating that children have a general capacity to acquire syntax, an inborn set of predispositions if you like, to develop a grammar of immense complexity and richness on the basis of very small amounts of evidence." It is worth noting that most children do this by the tender age of three years, whereas for an equally difficult subject, such as advanced algebra, they must wait for high school. Nobody, after reading the work of Lenneberg (1967), of Penfield and Roberts (1959), of Luria (1966), of the contributors to Mountcastle (1962) or of a dozen other neuropsychologists can doubt the fact that the brain is constructed to handle and process language in accordance with a neurology which has specific developmental and structural characteristics. Of course, aspects of the *content* of a particular langauge have to be learned, but while languages seemingly vary a great deal, as will be seen, they do in fact have many attributes in common.

The human brain has obviously evolved for other purposes as well as for the handling of language. Neuropsychologists, such as those mentioned above, generally accept the fact that the human cortex with its special functions has evolved from the less highly developed levels of the brain in a "vertical" fashion. The brain can be looked at in two ways: (a) in terms of levels from the so-called levels of the lower pons medulla functions up to the so-called higher levels of cortical functioning, or (b) in terms of its "vertical" structure, inasmuch as the sensory systems are actually continua from the lowest levels of CNS and brain functioning to the so-called associative cortical areas.

The human brain has evolved in a certain milieu which includes not only the physical attributes of land and air, but also social and individual survival needs. These have determined the actual structural functioning of the brain through the process of adaptation, and it is pertinent to explore the implications of this at this point. Recently, I had the opportunity to visit the Communications Research Institute in Miami, where the brain and communication system of the bottlenosed dolphin is being investigated. Lilly has written extensively on his findings (Lilly, 1964, 1965, 1967, 1968). The adult bottlenosed dolphin (*Tursiops truncatus*) has a brain roughly the size of the human being's, but has about 10 to 20 percent more cerebral cortex than humans. Some 96 percent of human brain surface is cortical, whereas the bottlenosed dolphin has 98 percent. The density of cells and the number and kind of major connections between cortical areas are very similar for the two species. However, the visual inputs of the bottlenosed dolphin are about one-tenth those of the human being; he has 120,000 fibers per eye to 1,200,000 for human beings. With respect to the ears, the bottlenosed dolphin has about 2¼ times the number of fibers humans have, and his hearing-frequency spectrum is five times that of Homo sapiens. Dolphins of this type have a communication-frequency band of 1,500 to 17,500 cycles. While the temporal lobes of the dolphin have approximately 2½ times the area of those of human beings, their occipital areas are very much smaller. Man and the dolphin have the same number of layers of cells in the brain. The entire vocalization equipment of the dolphin, apart from the larynx, is innervated by the seventh cranial nerve, and there is an intranarial pair of vocalization apparatuses, one on each side, each being served by about 30,000 fibers. Man, too, has about this number, so that although both species are much the same on the output side (except, of course, in terms of frequency), on the auditory input side the dolphin is considerably better equipped, neurologically speaking.

Bottlenosed dolphins can "mimic" simple tunes and most of the variations in the human voice. Dolphins can remember and reproduce a quite lengthy series of nonsense syllables very rapidly on the first trial. It should be mentioned that a "working relationship" has to be built with a particular animal before these humanoid noises can be evoked. Lilly (1964) says,

> If in contact close enough and long enough with persons who are speaking, these animals gradually modify the noises they emit and gradually acquire new noises which begin to resemble the noises of human speech. Slowly, but surely, some of these emissions begin to correspond to distinct human sounds; recognizable words are separated out. Modifications and variations of these words are produced in great profusion. Such flexibility and plasticity of the use of the phonation apparatus of these animals demonstrates an adaptive capability heretofore completely unsuspected. In a sense, these animals who are producing humanoid sounds have adapted to a totally new set of circumstances.

However, I am more concerned with the evolutionary reasons for the development of the specific characteristics of the dolphin brain, in terms of its adaptation to the requirements of living in the ocean, than with its similarities to the human brain. It will be seen that the environmental milieu has determined the phylogenetic development of the bottlenosed dolphin's brain. Lilly (1964) has written on this aspect of the neurological developments of the bottlenosed dolphin. Reviewing many findings from investigations of whales (including the bottlenosed dolphin), Lilly suggests that to live in the sea breathing air, with a mammalian physiology and a mammalian skin, requires a large brain for a successful adaptation. After discussing respiration, ingestion and nutrition, Lilly turns to the topic of sleep. He says,

> An apparently unique feature of their sleep pattern is that they sleep with one eye closed at a time. In a series of ten 24-hour experiments in our laboratory, it was found that closure of both eyes is an extremely rare event. The period of sleep for each eye totals 2 to 3 hours a day. This pattern may assure that the animal is always scanning his environment with at least half of his afferent inputs.

This has obvious survival value for catching food and avoiding danger, mostly sharks. With respect to communications, Lilly goes on to discuss sonic and ultrasonic emissions. He says,

Of course vision may be of little use in very murky water, at night without light, or in the depths of the sea. To compensate for this deficiency of vision, these animals have developed a sonic-ultrasonic echo ranging and recognition system. This active "sonar" system allows them to scan their environment and recognize objects at fairly sizeable distances in spite of the absence of light. . . . This sonar ability may allow each animal to detect the presence of friend or foe or food under any and all conditions. However, these animals apparently have additional means of receiving information from others of their own species by vocalizations and thus cooperating in food hunting, in their rescue operations, and in their attack and offense against sharks. . . . In our experience we discovered a particular whistle which they emit when they are in distress and which elicits the full cooperation of any animals within earshot. This whistle rises in frequency and then falls in frequency in a particular attention-getting and demanding fashion. We have also found that the first part of the distress signal, i.e., the part which rises in frequency, is used alone as an attention call when one animal is trying to attract the attention of others in the neighborhood. Vocal exchanges [occur] between pairs of dolphins which bear a resemblance to human conversation in that each animal transmits only during the silences of the other animal and that vocal exchanges in the proper sense of that term take place. Such exchanges are found for clicks and for whistles. These findings have given rise to a postulated dolphin language called Dolphinese. . . . The existence of such a language, if proved, will give these animals a means of cooperative adaptation to the marine environment par excellence which could not be obtained by individuals isolated from one another.

Most of the survival needs of the bottlenosed dolphin (and probably of other whales) involve the transmission and perception of sound under water. Vision and visual processes are relegated to a secondary or backup sensory role. Sonar and language communication are two quite different adaptive systems, the former being for the judgment of distance and the identification of objects, while the latter is for intercommunication between members of the species. Both would be functions of the temporal lobe, and it seems highly likely that this accounts for its being approximately 2½ times the size of the temporal lobe in human beings.

It is apparent that the structure of the brain in any species is largely determined by the environmental milieu in which the species lives, and by its adaptation for survival in that milieu. Obviously, sonar and Dolphinese, working as they do in the auditory area at very high speeds, require a comparatively enormous amount of temporal lobe neurological equipment for their satisfactory functioning under water.

Too often, I feel, we human beings become so immersed in our own species-specific milieu and communcations systems that we tend to think of them not only as the *only* possible ones but even as universal. However, it is by no means certain (in fact it is highly unlikely) that human language is the only intelligent language or that the human brain alone can process language. The lesson to be learned from the dolphins is that in all probability human language also evolved through adaptation for survival in a particular milieu and, even more important, in the communicative services of other survival needs. Like the dolphins, we probably required language to facilitate the hunting of food and the communal avoidance of danger. However, the dolphin did not require excellent eyesight (his environment being murky, he adopted sonar as a more efficient instrument for spatial sensing), whereas the human being evolved an excellent eyesight for spatial sensing in a clear air atmosphere. Therefore, the dolphin can fully integrate his sonar-spatial sensing systems with his auditory language functions entirely in the temporal area of the brain, whereas man requires far more elaborate connections between his visuo-spatial occipital lobe sensing system and his auditory language temporal lobe functioning. If one adds to the latter the very recent development of written language, with its visual symbols, the neurological connections required become extremely elaborate. If the hypothesis is true that our human appreciation of scientific and symbolic logic (as represented in mathematics and symbolic logic) is an abstract outgrowth of our visuo-spatial system, then the bottlenosed dolphin, having sonar (auditory temporal lobe) sensing as his basic system, may possess qualitatively a very different type of logic and cognitive appreciation of his environment from that of humans. It is a reasonable conjecture that the dolphin does not have to any degree the visuo-spatially generated logical reasoning abilities of the human species.

While much of what has been said is still neurologically speaking only at the exploratory stage of scientific investigation, there is far more "hard" material evidence for it than for much of the psychological theorizing which is current today. While I am all for speculation in science, it is wise to strive to insure that our speculations are compatible with the broad evolutionary trends of all life. Language learning systems are not necessarily unique to man. *The systems of dolphin and man have evolved genetically in quite different patterns for different milieus.*

LANGUAGE AND GENETICS

As is the case with most areas of human behavior, language has long been a battleground for those who believe it to be almost entirely environmentally determined and those who regard it as having an extensive biological basis. The latter point of view has been cogently argued by Lenneberg (1967) in his book, *Biological Foundations of Language,* wherein he describes in considerable detail the complex physiological and neurological equipment we inherit, a great deal of it for the sole purpose of processing linguistic material. Lenneberg makes a point which is being considered more and more by those who are concerned with a full integration of the nature and nuture elements in their explanations of human behavior. He says,

> It seems unlikely that genes actually transmit behavior as we observe it in the living animal because the course that an individual takes in its peregrinations through life must necessarily depend on environmental contingencies which could not have been "programmed and prepared for" in advance. Inheritance must confine itself to propensities, to dormant potentialities that await actualization by extra-organic stimuli, but it is possible that innate facilitatory or inhibitory factors are genetically transmitted which heighten the likelihood of one course of events over another. When put into these terms, it becomes quite clear that nature-nurture cannot be a *dichotomy* of factors but only an *interaction* of factors. To think of these terms as incompatible opposites only obscures the interesting aspects of the origin of behavior.

Connolly (1966) quotes Thoday (1965) on the same topic as follows: "Genotypy determines the potentialities of an organism. Environment determines which or how much of these potentialities shall be realized during development."

But neither of these authors stresses the existence or importance of genetically determined built-in developmental growth patterns. It is pertinent here to remember Aristotle's doctrine of the four causes. In any general discussion of human behavior, the usual efficient or original cause would be the genetic inheritance from the parents. This genetic cause is closely allied with the formal causes which are maturational and physiological patterns, many of which are laid down by genic inheritance—for example, sexual development. Thus, it would seem important in any study of language as one form of human behavior to search out the genetic foundations of language together with their genetically determined patterns of progressive development and, equally important, to discover exactly how environmentally determined training interacts with the language genotype. Several research projects are under way which should throw light on this interaction in the development of language in early childhood. Some of these projects are reported by Lenneberg (1967) and some by Bellugi and Brown (1964).

Following is a summary of the various factual and circumstantial sets of evidence which support the hypothesis that language in the human species is a behavior which, to a considerable extent, is genetically determined. These sets of evidence are (a) morphological characteristics, (b) intelligence, (c) language development in infancy, (d) sex differences, (e) the universal and spontaneous nature of language acquisition, (f) the common elements of human languages and (g) twin and family pedigree studies.

Morphological Characteristics

In human beings, there is an extremely complex species-specific internal and external structure of brain and body which operates biologically in the service of language communication. Vast numbers of books devoted to neurology or speech have described these biological structures in great detail and Lenneberg (1967) has set this material within an evolutionary and genetic framework.

Intelligence

There has long been considerable evidence that intelligence as a manifested cognitive process is inherited as a familial characteristic (Penrose, 1949; Carter, 1962). *Verbal ability is an inherent and major part of intelligence* (P.E. Vernon, 1961), and as such it, too, must have an inherited basis. It is the potential for language acquisition, the genotype *pattern* of maturational development and perhaps the cognitive style, which is inherited, rather than the data content of information on which intelligence operates. Additional evidence that verbal ability is to a considerable degree inherited is to be found in the incidence of genius and low intelligence. It is worth repeating that there are few educators or psychologists who believe that through any type of intensive optimum training any child can become a Shakespeare or a Milton. *These statements in no way contradict the fact that academic and experiential stimulation in early infancy and childhood can raise the intelligence of children to a considerable degree.*

Hunt (1961) has amassed considerable evidence and argued very cogently that we have insufficiently investigated the beneficial effects of an enriching environment during early physiological and psychological development. Educators have tended to underestimate considerably the limits of cognitive expansion within the genetic potential. It is as if education were only just entering the vitamin era which in the past raised health, height and weight limits considerably, expanding horizons of genetically determined physiological potentialities. We are currently discovering novel educational "vitamins" which likewise may raise intellectual potentials in many ways. I do not accept the validity of the steel wall many psychologists seem to erect between the principles of neurophysiology (genetic) and those of psychology, particularly learning theory.

Language Development in Infancy

McNeill (1965) says, "The process of acquiring syntax is fairly well understood. Evidence is accumulating that children have a general capacity to acquire syntax and an inborn set of predispositions to acquire grammar of immense complexity and richness on the basis of very small amounts of evidence." One should add the obvious fact that this almost invariably occurs before the age of five years. McNeill adds, "The capacity to acquire language may be transitory; it may reach a peak around ages 2 to 4 and decline thereafter; it may even disappear altogether as a special capacity with the beginning of adolescence." Here he refers to Lenneberg (1967). There is no need to labor the point that whereas young children can acquire an extremely complex communication system almost automatically, they are unable to parallel this ability with almost any other cognitive activity. In mathematics, for example, even with deliberate training, the very bright child of four who has a sophisticated knowledge of language cannot do more than simple addition and subtraction. Of course, the particular variety of language which the child learns is environmentally determined, but these are conventions of habitat rather like clothes on the body.

Sex Differences

One of the most neglected variables in psychological and educational research is that of sex differences. I have read many volumes where it is not even listed in the index as a topic, boys and girls being equated. The term *the child* and the pronoun *he* will refer to both girls and boys, a convention of writing which sometimes leads to inaccurate statements. Many papers have been written about psychological sex differences in children, but I can do no better than quote Maccoby's (1966) book, *The Development of Sex Differences*. In referring to verbal ability, she says,

> Through the preschool years and in the early years girls exceed boys in most aspects of verbal performance. They say their first word sooner, articulate more clearly and at an earlier age, use longer sentences, and are more fluent. By the beginning of school, however, there are no longer any consistent differences in vocabulary. Girls learn to read sooner and there are more boys than girls who require special training in remedial reading programs; but by approximately the age of ten a number of studies show that boys have caught up with their reading skills. Throughout the school years, girls do better on tests in grammar, spelling and word fluency.

With respect to number ability, Maccoby summarizes the evidence by saying that although girls learn to count at an earlier age, "Fairly consistently, however, boys excel at arithmetical reasoning in high school and these differences are substantially in favor of men among college students and adults." While other authors, notably P.E. Vernon (1961) and I.M. Smith (1964), have noted the superiority of males in spatial ability, Maccoby summarizes the evidence by saying, "While very young boys and girls do not differ on spatial tasks such as form boards and block designs by the early school years boys consistently do better on spatial tasks and this difference continues through the high school and college years."

Now, it is very obvious that many sex differences are at least partially caused by nurturance, social and other environmental influences, even though to date, research attempts to support this point of view are by no means clear-cut. However, looking at the whole of nature, it is extremely difficult to believe that the genetically determined biological differences between the sexes do not have their counterpart in the neurology and psychology of the human being. Phylogenetically the sexual characteristic of organisms is so basic that it is even exhibited by bacteria (Wollman and Jacob, 1956). Maccoby has a chapter in her book which summarizes research in sex differences. In the section devoted to "Cognitive Ability—Verbal," there are twenty-two research studies reported involving children three years of age and under, *and in eighteen of these, girls show superiority.* In the other four studies there was no sex difference; that is, the boys were not superior there either. The areas of study were the age of first speech, articulation, verbosity and verbal fluency, lengths of statement, vocabulary, grammar, reasoning (verbal) and general verbal skills. It is difficult to believe that environmental influences in the first three years of life could have such an overwhelming bias in favor of the female of the species, particularly as in some of these areas, boys attain a superiority later on (which I suspect is more in reasoning/thinking ability than verbal skills).

Two interesting reports of sex differences which would seem to be biologically based have been reported in the literature.

Bachrach (1964) reports that whereas males tend to stutter under conditions of delayed auditory feedback, females do not. These sex differences will be discussed in some detail in Chapter VI.

A more direct neurological sex difference is reported by J.P. Lansdell (1964). He found sex differences in hemispheric asymmetries of the human brain and described them as follows:

> Of interest in this respect is a recent investigation by Conel of a series of eight brains from four-year-old children; no consistent feature was apparent in the differences between the hemispheres. However, if the sex of the children is taken into consideration, two noteworthy differences emerge. Conel's Table IX shows that in four out of five female brains the amount of myelination is greater in the left FA-hand area than in the corresponding area on the right, while in the three male brains this difference is reversed. In Table X the number of exogenous fibers in layer I of areas FA and PB is greater on the right in the four female brains for which data are provided, but greater on the left in two of the three male brains. Neither of these comparisons reaches acceptable levels of statistical significance, but the importance of and the difficulty in obtaining these limited data may warrant a conjecture. Could these anatomical differences be related to the finding that side differences in the tactual thresholds on the thumbs of young children are not the same for the two sexes? Some earlier research may also be used in speculating about sex differences in cerebral asymmetry. An investigation of variations in cerebral venous drainage suggests that the right vein of Trolard is larger than the left in girls, and not in boys. Since this is often the major vein in the hemisphere opposite to that used in speech, is it possible that the differences in venous drainage are related to the superiority of girls over boys in certain verbal skills?

The Universal and Spontaneous Nature of Language Acquisition

Not only is language learned at an early age as indicated above, but it is a universal phenomenon which seems to occur regardless of culture. Most educators and even psychologists become so used to thinking of language in terms of the visual patterns involved in reading that they tend to underestimate the similarities of *the spoken word* across all languages. Alphabets and ideographs may vary greatly but vocal languages are, by comparison, relatively much closer together. Even more important is the fact that the spoken language is learned by tiny children quite spontaneously, that is, without the need for *formal* instruction. Most human characteristics which are "learned" spontaneously are universally and innately characteristic of the species. An analogous situation in motor functioning would be walking. By contrast, reading and driving a car can only be learned through the medium of formal instruction. It should be noted that while it is true that for some species simple universal characteristics do occur which have been learned through imitation (for example, the pecking of milk bottle tops by a species of bird in Southern England in order to drink the cream), language acquisition is a very complex human learning task which would be difficult to attribute entirely to imitative modeling. Lenneberg (1967) points out that infant language is *not* a carbon copy of the adult model but is a telegrammatically structured language in its own right. However, there is little doubt that imitation plays a definite part not only in the learning of language, but also in the acquisition of most other human activities whether or not they are innately based. Imitation of behavior is not a contradiction of the thesis that much human behavior has a genetic basis. Imitation is, as it were, at right angles to genetic factors. Indeed, imitation itself may be a species-specific developmental behavior pattern subserving the environmental "interests" of the learning processes involved in the development of yet other innate species-specific developmental patterns.

The Common Elements of Human Languages

All human languages have several elements in common which tend to remain constant, despite the modifying influences of other learned characteristics within a particular language. There are certain broad areas within which these common elements occur; they all possess distinctive features, phonemes, morphemes, syntactic features and the communication of semantic meaning. This last has been investigated by Osgood (1964a).

Twin and Family Pedigree Studies

The evidence for the inheritance of language potential coming from twin studies and family pedigrees was summarized by Lenneberg (1967). His results all indicated that "fraternal twins are much more prone to differences in language development than identical twins and that language disabilities tend to run in families." Also recently, Vandenberg (1967) has reported as a result of his own research work with identical twins that many language functions have a considerable genetic foundation and he even goes so far as to say that the ability to spell is mostly inherited.

Conclusions

If they are considered separately, each of the above seven sets of evidence can be partially undermined by arguing that environmental influences can account for the data equally well. However, the arguments become rather tortuous and they, themselves, very frequently have far less research proof than do the genetic ones. Incidentally, proof in science is never complete, even in the physical sciences. However, the seven points taken together and in detail are difficult to explain away. I am always puzzled as to why many environmentalists and particularly learning theorists wish to explain away all genetic and biological influences in the learning process at any cost. They will admit that the body is largely genetically determined but somehow, halfway through the brain, there seems to be that steel plate which cuts off the body from the mind. Everything below the plate may be genetically determined but everything above the plate must be environmentally accounted for. It is much more in keeping with our knowledge of psychology and biology to make no presuppositions about the nature of human behavior in terms of environmental versus genetic influences.

Most psychologists and geneticists would agree that environmental learning plays a *major part* in the formation of the human personality and cognitive abilities, but to ignore or to deny the probability and influence of genetic factors in human psychological behavior is rather irrational and foolhardy, in terms of both pure scientific theory and the applied sciences of clinical psychology and education. The viewpoint that genetically determined factors in human development or behavior are unmodifiable or unalterable is a complete misunderstanding of the nature of growth. Genetically determined patterns cannot develop in the absence of an environment any more than the body can develop without air or food. Each human body is open to a great deal of modification through environmental influences as the history of evolution and medicine demonstrates; so much more, then, can the environment influence those *psychological* developmental patterns which may be innately determined. Moreover, one can utilize the very same techniques used by the advocates (of which I am one) of enriching stimulation in early childhood. It is only rarely in education that the full potential of an individual is realized, even though the extent of that potential is, to a degree, genetically delineated. It is worth emphasizing that to the best of my knowledge, all genetically oriented psychologists and educators would say that the inherited bases of behavior have *programmed* into them large areas of potential functioning which *must* be learned if the individual and the species are to survive. One of these learned areas is to be found in the conventional aspects of language.

Chapter III

ORTHOGRAPHY, PERCEPTION AND THOUGHT

ORTHOGRAPHIC AND LINGUISTIC CONVENTIONS

The last section of the previous chapter listed some of the evidence supporting the thesis that human language has a considerable genetic and biological foundation; while it will be necessary to refer to, or elaborate on, the nature of that foundation from time to time, it is not a contradiction to say that human language contains a considerable number of conventional or environmentally determined elements.

A convention is any law, rule or regulation which has been, or is, solely determined by human beings (or animals) for the arbitrary regulation of any behavior. Examples are found in language, social relationships, physical activity (sports) and the law of the land.

Many linguists and other students of language structure are more concerned with a study of the attributes which all languages or groups of languages have in common than they are with investigating their idiomatic differences. However, for anyone who is primarily interested in how languages are *learned* in both their spoken and written forms, it becomes equally important to delineate accurately the characteristic conventions of any particular language. For example, it is thought that the incidence of specific reading disability in intelligent children (dyslexia) seems to be higher in those countries which have an irregular orthography (i.e., an irregular phoneme-to-grapheme correspondence). Such is the case with the English and Scandinavian languages. Makita (1968) comments that the rarity of reading disability in Japanese children is probably caused by the regular orthography of the language. Irregular morphology (combinations of morphemes) can make the learning of a language difficult from both the spoken and written aspects.

In English a tree is a /t-r-ee/, in French it is an /ar-bre/ and in German it is a /b-au-m/. This is but one instance of one type of linguistic convention; the list below sets out many others. It should be understood that this list is not necessarily complete, nor is it implied that these "conventions" are completely environmentally determined. Most of the items contain implicit universal elements which are most likely not inherited in terms of their specific content but rather in terms of their underlying structural processes. For example, phonemes and words appear to be neurologically processed in separate cortical areas (Luria, 1966) (see Chapter VI), and while all languages structure phonemes into words, the phoneme sequence within each word may be quite different in various languages. Another point worth noting is that all auditory/vocal activities occur *through time as a sequence of "pieces"* (unlike spatially static pictures or objects) with the consequence that many of the conventions of language are related to the *order* in which similar sequential units occur, be they phonemes, morphemes, words or sentences. Obviously, the unfolding meaning of a sentence will also partly determine the sequential arrangement of the words in it in a nonconventional syntactical way (see page 106). Syntax is only partly conventionally determined, as can be seen from scrambling sentences into *meaningless* arrangements.

Auditory/Vocal Conventions

The major auditory/vocal conventions are as follows:
1. The complete set of phonemes used in a language.
2. The particular phonemes used in each word.
3. The number of phonemes used in each word.
4. The sequence of phonemes used in each word.
5. The level or alteration of the pitch on which the word must be vocalized for a given meaning; this includes syllable accent, intonation, emphasis, question, exclamation, etc., and Chinese, in which changes of word pitch level convey separate meanings.
6. The clustering of vowels or consonants within words.
7. Vowel-dominated languages.

8. Consonant-dominated languages.

9. Click-dominated languages.

10. Simple or complex vowel and/or consonant preponderance.

11. Elisions, contractions and liaisons, as for example in French.

12. Auditory and speech spacing conventions, pauses, etc., sounds (features) which denote irony, sarcasm, humor, laughter, etc.

13. Morphology—inflection.

14. Syntax.

Visual Conventions

The major visual conventions are as follows:

1. Pictograph (i.e., primary) symbols representing the object; also called hieroglyphics.

2. Ideographic or logographic symbols which, in a sense, may have evolved from original pictographs.

3. Syllable-symbol representation of words.

4. Phonetic alphabets in which letters represent sounds.

   a. Number of visual letters in the alphabet.

   b. Shape of the individual letters in the alphabet, including simplicity or complexity of any given letter; style of the type script or writing (italics, cursive, etc.); number of symbolic explanatory aids (capitals, commas, periods, punctuation generally), and omissions and additions, as in Hebrew.

   c. The number of letters in a given word.

   d. The sequences (including grouping) of letters in a given word.

   e. The grouping together of sequences of words or morphemes without gaps (e.g., German).

Orthography (Phoneme-to-Grapheme Correspondence) as a Linguistic Convention

Conventions by definition are man-made and because conventions of the linguistic kind have evolved on a basis of immediate necessity through time, they often tend to be unpredictable. This is particularly true of the written version of the English language, because the spoken and written conventions of the many languages from which and through which it has evolved have been separately absorbed. Because these contributing languages (French, Greek, Latin, Anglo-Saxon, etc.) each had their own sets of conventions, some of which English absorbed along with the foreign words and expressions, the result was, and is, an extremely flexible but highly irregular coding system. In particular, the orthography of English is probably more variable than in any other phonetic language. From the point of view of anyone learning to read and write it, English orthography is very unpredictable. Of the twenty-six vowel phonemes, at least twelve can each be spelled in eight or more different ways. All the other phonemes have more than one grapheme equivalent. As if that were not confusing enough, most of the vowel graphemes are interchangeable. Thus the symbol *a* can represent a minimum of seven separate phonemes. The letter *e* also stands for seven phonemes, some of them held in common with *a*. The possible permutations and combinations of all phoneme/grapheme matchings run into several hundred. Added to this arbitrary complexity is the selection and sequence of the letters in each separate word, an area in which there are few rules to use as guides. This makes our language almost as infinitely variable as musical notation. The analogy is apt, since both are auditory sequencing processes of discrete or blended sounds. As will be seen, many children who find it difficult to learn to spell or read find it equally difficult to discriminate similar melodies.

Despite this orthographic tangle, more than two-thirds of our children rapidly absorb the linguistic conventions of their mother tongue, both receptively and expressively, always provided that suitable stimuli and instruction are present and the child is eager to learn. Later, such children are able to make phoneme/visual symbol associations relatively easily and rapidly, so much so that once a given word-set of associations has been made a few times, it tends to be remembered permanently in terms of both recognition (reading) and recall (spelling). Even if the orthography of the language is very regular, as it is in Spanish, it is still quite an *arbitrary* custom and there are no absolute first principles to which the child can refer to work it out, should he forget. If a particular serial association of phoneme/grapheme matchings is forgotten, the only course open to the child is to look it up in the dictionary or find out from those who know in school, his family or the community. To show the difference between a linguistic situation in which a child cannot remember that the sound /ē/ is represented by the symbol *ei* in a given context, and the mathematical situation in which he cannot remember that 2 + 3 = 5, one only has to conduct a little experiment on a suitable child. No amount of placing of letters in front of the child will help him to identify the sound /ē/, but if his counters are placed in front of him, he can work out for himself the answer to 2 + 3. An English child, A Greek child and a Chinese child, once they have been taught, can each add together 2 + 3 and get the answer 5, but if they were asked to write the visual symbol for the sound /ē/, very different answers would be obtained, provided, of course, that each had previously learned his own orthographic conventions.

As has been mentioned already, Makita (1968) reports that reading disabilities are rare in Japanese children, the incidence being under 1 percent. He attributes this to the unambiguity of Japanese scripts, particularly in terms of mirror imaging and alikeness of symbols. This ties in with Osgood's principle of interference in memorizing "pairs," which is discussed in detail in Chapter VII. The orthography of the Kana script is very regular and the graphemes are quite distinctive and specific. Kanji script, which is ideographic, is easier to learn initially but as the number and complexity of the characters increase, mastery of them becomes correspondingly more difficult. Presumably this is a memory capacity problem related to design configurations.

Once it is appreciated that phoneme/grapheme associations and their sequencing are qualitatively different from logic and natural law, one can begin to understand how it is possible that some intelligent children find it difficult to learn to read. Thus a child may not have the ability to remember by rote the conventional phoneme/grapheme associations of language and their sequential ordering in words and yet may be able intellectually to process conceptual material of a nonverbal nature which is based on natural law. At this point, it becomes necessary to mention again the notion of special cognitive abilities, particularly verbal ability and spatial ability. While there is no need at this point to enter into the full psychological implications of verbal and spatial ability, it is worth noting that whereas the former partially depends on an ability to make arbitrary rote associations between conventionally determined phonemes and graphemes, spatial ability very much depends on references to the first principles of natural law.

The Symbols of the Scientist and the Novelist

It is not an accident that while the auditory and visual symbols of most languages in the world occur arbitrarily and vary greatly, symbols as used in science, though conventional in a very restricted sense, tend to have universal recognition, visually speaking. The mathematician, chemist or physicist uses symbols to represent objects *directly* because he must be able to manipulate them in a situation which directly expresses or *is modeled by thought processes without any essential auditory medium.* This is not to say that auditory factors are not included in these processes. Inasmuch as the scientist must communicate thoughts in conversation, their visual symbols require auditory symbols as well, but the latter play an almost superficial secondary role to the need of the scientist to manipulate his thought symbols in a primary way. When the chemist writes a formula, he is able to manipulate the elements on paper as a direct substitute for manipulating them in the laboratory situation; when the mathematician abstracts numbers and manipulates them during various mathematical thought processes, he is substituting symbolic numbers on paper for actual objects in space; when the geometrician uses lines, dots and symbols on paper, he is substituting directly for distances and positions in external multi-dimensional space. The fact that in some of these and other scientific processes, auditory labels are used, is, empirically speaking, almost incidental, the purpose of the latter being the facilitation of communication. Theoretically, language could be used in a scientific way, but it is an elementary fact of social evolution that language neither developed as an adjunct to science nor has it as its main reason for being. While logicians may develop symbolic signs for human reasoning and linguists may endeavor to reduce language to a contentless abstraction organized by fixed rules, the *social* necessities of linguistic communication in everyday life continue uninterrupted and that is the situation within which the language learner finds himself.

Because scientific thinking *is* a matter of intellectually manipulating first principles, that is, the interrelationships of objects in terms of logical thought processes, the symbols themselves must be conventionally regularized to be subservient to those first principles; otherwise, the whole structure of scientific knowledge would be uncertain. Scientific symbols must be logically *necessary* in a conventional way if they are to model successfully the processes of nature they represent. For example, the symbol π in geometry must always have the same value. In terms of verbal ability, the novelist is hardly concerned with first principles in the usual sense of the words. The scientist may strive for a relatively permanent, unemotive, objective description of natural law and may wish to communicate this description to other people, but the novelist is usually concerned with a subjective interpretation of immediate personality states in a highly individualized series of situations, and he strives to communicate those states vividly. The scientist and novelist are very characteristic examples of two ways of experiencing life. The scientist organizes empirical data objectively in order to abstract the intrinsic principles of relevant interrelationships and communicates them as accurately and as unemotionally as he can. The novelist is concerned with handling and communicating the arbitrary, sometimes historical conventions of everyday life and their interrelationships, particularly in terms of feeling states. He is a typical representative of all those people who communicate "conventional" information in the highly verbal way described. One could replace the novelist with the journalist, the orator, the playwright, the politician or people in a hundred other occupations. The poet is the perfect paradigm of those who work in the arbitrary area of convention, no matter how unconventional his poetry may be, since unconventionality is logically an aspect of convention as a categorical concept.

By the very nature of language, verbally gifted people seem naturally to prefer to work in the areas of life which deal with other conventions. People involved in politics, religion, journalism, family life, ethical philosophy, some aspects of education, entertainment, social work and selling each work in their own respective sphere of convention and require a highly developed linguistic ability in order to communicate the essence of those conventions and the arbitrary feeling of the attitudes involved. The word *convention* is being used here in a more generic sense than its colloquial denotation of conformity to custom. This wider meaning implies that one is free to disagree with the convention, to analyze it subjectively, to modify it or to rebel against it—the essential element being an interest in convention, whatever form that convention or interest takes. On the other hand, most scientists, particularly those in the physical and biological sciences, are not at all concerned with convention as a dominant interest in their working life. Social scientists, however, do tend to have a foot in both camps, to use a conventional English metaphor. To be effective, the type of person who is occupied with the anthropological material and customs of which conventions are made should have an *innate neuropsychological capacity to absorb rapidly the arbitrary associations which characterize those conventions, be they customs, dogma, social laws, mores, political attitudes or the elements of spoken and written language.*

The Learning of Linguistic Conventions and the Importance of Memory

People who are talented at learning several foreign languages have (to use an analogy) a tape-recorder ability to *remember* completely arbitrary object-names, action-labels and other verbal associations, and to *recall* them immediately and automatically whenever they wish. They also have the ability to *memorize* all the other arbitrary conventions of sequences, of syntax, etc., in each of these languages; of course, this does not mean that they must make a formal study of the grammar of each language. Usually the grammar and syntax are acquired equally automatically. To the extent that one deliberately studies the rules and principles of one language or a set of languages and generalizes from them to others, he is no longer making completely arbitrary associations. It is very possible that people who can very easily and rapidly *associate* objects with phoneme and grapheme sequences (words) without the necessity of any logical connection are also people who will, in all probability, rapidly *learn* those other arbitrary conventions which are embodied in law, politics and mores, for example. Furthermore, it is in the nature of conventional social systems to depend on the linguistic communication between the participant members of the system for their existence. Conventional traditions, customs and languages themselves are used, passed on and modified by each generation in turn. This social *survival* of the species is one of the most fundamental reasons for language and, for that matter, the reason for any communication system between the individual members of any species. Memory is one of the fundamental keys to language processing (see Chapter VII).

According to Piaget, it would seem most unlikely that a child under four years of age could abstract the arbitrary principles of language. Therefore, the infant who can imitate easily object/phoneme associations and subsequently imitate (copy) and *memorize* phoneme/grapheme associations has a tremendous linguistic advantage over the child who cannot.

If it is accepted that the ability to cope with language is innate as a potential, and that some children and adults are gifted in this area, it should be equally true that in the other half of the verbal-population continuum there will be many with varying degrees of linguistic disability. It also follows that these particular linguistic disabilities must be the result of an innate inability to associate rapidly arbitrarily determined object/phoneme and phoneme/grapheme links. Such children simply cannot *remember* the arbitrary conventions (mostly associations) of verbal functioning; they also may not be able to remember (or learn) *social* conventions, which may cause them to become misfits (see Chapter IX). Some readers may contest the statement that individuals on the lower half of a normal curve are *normal* (in the sense that psychologically they have less talent), preferring to hypothesize that such individuals are "impaired" in some way. Sometimes embedded in this argument is the feeling that the implication of less talent leaves remediators no possibility of improving or training the children in question. This is not so, as almost *all* children from trainable defectives through normals to children in the genius class can definitely profit from special tutoring programs. Everyone in education and psychology should know that in every branch of teaching, our methods, our school systems and our curriculum content are woefully inadequate. Therefore, any type of enrichment program will rapidly improve the achievement and IQ level of the children in its care. However, a normal curve is just that, and any broad-scale enrichment tuition will slide the *whole* scale many points along the base line toward the positive end. It is also true that at the lowest end of the normal curve, there will be an increasing number of *abnormal* children, some being neurologically impaired, some mentally retarded, some emotionally disturbed, some autistic and so on; these may even form a separate hump on the end of the normal curve, just as midgets of many kinds form a small, discrete group on the lower end of the normal curve of height. But it is not these abnormal individuals who are under discussion here. The below-average children referred to above are quite normal in the usual educational and neuropsychological sense of the term.

If these children are linguistically less well endowed and if language is primarily a function of the auditory area, then it follows that the main difficulty with which these children have to cope in learning languages is to be found, neurologically speaking, in the auditory area. It should be understood that the brains of these children are *not* abnormal in any way; it is simply that the children have not inherited the neurological basis of auditory functioning to the same rich degree as some other children. Looking at the problem of the inheritance of special abilities in a wider context, most people readily admit that if a person is tone-deaf to music or is a specially gifted musician, the ability or the lack of it is mostly inherited. We do not think that there is anything abnormal about the brain of a tone-deaf individual. Similarly, if an artist can accurately reproduce a photographic likeness of a human face, he is regarded as having an innate talent, although it may be improved by training, and the inability to represent objects visually is not usually regarded as being caused only by environmental factors. However, no one is too concerned if a child is unable to draw faces or appreciate a tune, but human society now demands that *everyone* must learn to converse effectively and even more, must learn to read and write. The ability to read and write has been demanded of the population as a whole only very recently. Literate people have become so dominated by their visual-verbal accomplishments that they forget that to be able to read and write 180 years ago was a rare accomplishment. Therefore, reading and writing are not the result of mutations originally evolved for the specific purpose of communicative survival. Rather, they are a happy accident—an integration of many skills evolved for other reasons. In fact, all written communication is a very recent occurrence in the history of man, being no more than ten thousand years old. Therefore, although almost all children innately associate spoken words with objects and concepts, there is no specific *built-in* evolutionary reason why they should associate spoken words with their visual symbols. The implications of this for scholastic literacy will be investigated in later chapters.

The Possible Origins of Written Language

It would appear that the expression of language in written form is, in a sense, an evolutionary accident; the ability to associate phonemes with visual symbols is surely a by-product of other cortical functions which have survival value for their own sake. The ability to associate sounds with bodily needs is common to almost all animals; certainly all young animals make noises which the mother will interpret in a particular way, usually as an indication of danger or hunger. The ability to associate visual stimuli with bodily needs is also common to most animals: the young chick reacts to the color of its mother's bill and the mother bird to the shape of a hawk in the sky above (Hinde, 1966). Most animals in the higher species can be trained to react to symbols that substitute for some other object, whether the symbol is auditory or visual. No doubt the forest and the plain naturally provided animals with plenty of "signs" which warned them of approaching dangers. Presumably, the roar of a lion or the cry of a wolf would be associated in a very simple, primitive way with a memory image of the predator, though, of course, it is possible that in many cases the traditional fear was handed down without the predator being sighted. Still, the tradition could not have arisen if the predator had not been seen at some time by ancestors. Such vocal symbolism almost certainly had survival value in the most positive aspects of life. From the visual side, surely thirst conjured up a primitive image of a water hole and hunger for berries. Such could have been the beginnings of imagery and imagery is the forerunner of symbolism.

It is very apparent that if animals in the wild can associate a sound with a visual image and vice versa, human beings can, and this ability obviously had tremendous survival value. By imitating animal noises and other natural sounds, early man could communicate information or warnings about the animals concerned. Those hearing the imitated sound of an animal would conjure up by association the image of the animal concerned, and so an auditory/visual-image pathway would be established. Whether or not the cave artists of Lascaux may have drawn animals as symbolic representations in response to the animal noises made by other tribesmen, there can be little doubt that these early men were quite able to associate the real animal with both the sound it made and the pictorial representation of the animal. Probably the imitation of animal noises in rituals concerned with potential food and a fear of death had a great deal to do with the origins of language and its pictorial representation. During magical ceremonies, tribal members no doubt made the noises of animals killed for food and pictorially represented them on trees, earth, rocks or the walls of the caves. By spearing such representations, they would receive the power to be successful in the hunt. Similar tribal dances still exist in many countries today.

However, it is not the power to represent pictorially a visual image which is so remarkable, as this could easily result from the dexterity developed to fashion tools, an ability which could easily be converted to use as a graphic art. All people almost from the beginning of the Homo sapiens era seem to have developed decoration of a representational kind, even if only as a body paint or tattoo. It is the visual or other sensory image evocation in response to a *spoken* auditory cue with a specific reference in the absence of the original object which is particularly human, though perhaps dolphins, whales and some apes may also achieve it in a limited way.

It is suspected by some linguists that pictures which were drawn in response to an auditory symbol (e.g., the lowing of the bull) as a representation for the original animal or object were, with the early growth of the Phoenician and European languages, *gradually modified into letters* to represent the sounds rather than the original visual object. Some books, commenting on the origins of the alphabet, have series of diagrams that show how the original pictographs or hieroglyphics changed into visually represented phonetic symbols. No doubt a written phonetic alphabet tended to refine the auditory aspects of communication by giving phonemes an added emphasis.

Memory and spoken language both have great survival value. While this seems obvious, a point that is not often appreciated in educational circles during these days of a universal emphasis on reading and writing is that linguistic functions are essentially *auditory*. It also follows from what has been said above that a phonetic script perpetuates the efficiency of auditory linguistic processes. Compared with ideographic writing systems, a phonetic script incorporates the efficient qualities of simplicity and speed. Yet another concomitant advantage is the flexibility of a phonetic script, inasmuch as once new words have been auditorially established, they can immediately be represented by their equivalent written phonetic symbols using established linguistic conventions.

As has been previously pointed out, the phoneme/grapheme association is no longer systematic in most alphabet languages, the traditional orthography of the English language being extremely irregular. This is most unfortunate for those people whose auditory processes, though within the normal curve, are less able to cope (a) with very fine discriminations of sound, (b) with remembering the sequences in which they occur and, even more, (c) with remembering the sounds which are attached to the various graphemes in the context of particular letter-spelling sequences, which themselves are quite arbitrary in nature.

LANGUAGE, READING, PERCEPTION AND THOUGHT

There appears to be a considerable amount of confusion among many educators and psychologists as to exactly what the meanings are of such terms as *sensory, perceptual, conceptual, thinking, listening, reading, writing,* etc., and how they are interrelated and associated. It is difficult to present a comprehensive statement in prose of such a broad set of interrelationships; therefore, I have constructed a table (see Table VII, page 98) for the purpose. This text is intended only to lead into the table as a preliminary orientation.

The human brain seems to function on several levels and the work of neuropsychologists such as Luria (1966) and Penfield and Roberts (1959) tends to support my psychological viewpoint. Some of the following content has appeared in standard psychological textbooks over the past hundred years and some of it I believe to be original, while certainly the table and associational structuring are my own. An excellent paper by Osgood (1963) inspired these efforts to integrate both "pure" thought processes and printed symbols into the auditory/vocal language system as described by psycholinguists (Osgood, 1957; Wepman, 1960).

The Sensory Level

The first level is sensory, which includes hearing, seeing, movement sensing, touch, etc., as well as the activity of the primary areas of the cortex where the sensory signals are first received and—*from the sensation aspect only*—identified as having primary physical attributes, e.g., shapes, noises, colors, bulk. However, there is no recognition and no understanding on this level. Neurologically, it is very likely that this nonverbal sensory input is analytically decoded in this simple way in both the sense organs themselves and their respective primary cortical areas (Luria, 1966).

These functions, which operate well even in babies, must obviously be intact if a child is later going to learn to read in the usual way, yet unfortunately, many learning disability cases with primary neurosensory deficits remain undiagnosed, and I do not refer merely to the hard-of-hearing or partially sighted. By the time a child comes to learn to read, he has usually acquired a fully working auditory/vocal language; therefore, all he has to do is associate a visual code with this auditory/vocal code. Many learning disability cases do not have a competent auditory/vocal language and so, before examining the audiovisual linkage, it will be necessary to discuss the way in which auditory/vocal codes become associated with meaning. To do this, it is inadvisable to use the ambiguous term *word;* instead, we will substitute *sound-label* (and later on, *visual-label*). These terms are shorthand for, respectively, the spoken or heard word and the read or printed word, the latter representing the succession of phonemes which comprise the former.

The Perceptual Level

Much of the experience most people have throughout their lives is nonverbal, even when verbal activity is being processed coincidentally. We drive the car, watch television, listen to music, play sports and work in factories or on farms. This direct experiential material is built up selectively from birth, coming in through the body and its senses to a main memory store which seems to cooperate with other cognitive processes to cross-index, superimpose and freely associate the received images into categorical concepts or meanings. Thus, when we see a particular chair, we classify it nonverbally as one of those single-seated pieces of furniture in which one adopts a specific relaxed posture. A nonverbal infant conceivably could be unacquainted with the sound-label *chair*, yet might know its *function*. All of us utilize objects in our daily lives, the sound-labels of which we are ignorant— the names of the bones in our hands, for example. Thus, perception combines "identified" sensory input data with nonverbal meanings or concepts, the latter being a function of utilitarian attention or other survival-value experience. Neurologically, it is possible that this perceived meaningful material may, in terms of memory, be stored in what Penfield and Roberts (1959) call the "interpretive cortex." They say, "Psychical responses may be called experiential or interpretive. They have been obtained . . . only from certain portions of the temporal lobe cortex in either hemisphere." Much of this experiential or perceptual memory bank is nonverbal in the strict linguistic sense. The unit of perception then involves an *immediate* sensing of the environment. One perceives a single particular chair or a specific musical note at a given moment in time, recognizing it for what it is by comparing it with past cumulative experience.

The Conceptual Level

A concept can be defined as an enduring (and almost invariably progressing) coalescence of related images, usually in the form of a class (e.g., symphonies, governments, tables, furniture). Whereas a percept almost always involves an immediate meaningful interpretation of the environment, a concept may be manipulated *internally* without reference to the immediate nonverbal physical environment. However, if we ponder on a mental arithmetic problem or next year's vacation, we are *thinking*, that is, manipulating concepts internally.

The Thinking Level (Relational Operations)

Thought processes may take place through time, with or without continuous or intermittent nonverbal percepts. A watchmaker repairing a watch resolves his problem (on the basis of previous experience-built concepts) under circumstances of acute visual perception, with much of the problem-solving thinking being nonverbal. Thinking usually includes some form of reasoning, a process which involves the manipulation of the relationships between separate image-type concepts (e.g., "If I put the chair on the table, I will be able to replace the broken electric light fitting"). Thinking through *time* is more than a simple succession of concepts, because it involves a new ingredient, the *relationship,* which in the final analysis is itself an internalized model of either a coincidental happening or teleological event, depending on one's philosophical outlook. Many relationship models are in the form of abstractions; that is, they are statements of laws or principles which, though free of any particular content, can be applied to a content as necessary, e.g., an algebraic equation. Thus, thinking can manipulate symbols relationally in place of objects.

Signs and Symbols

A symbol can be defined as an object or thing which, being indelibly associated in the mind with another object or thing, serves as a recall agent for the latter. A flag can symbolize national identity, and spoken words can symbolize almost anything. An important point is that the symbolic object is, in its own right, *also* a primary object which is sensed, perceived and conceptualized. When these symbolic objects are verbal labels, we call the resulting percepts, concepts and relationship systems a spoken language. Obviously, the purpose of symbol systems such as spoken language is to enable us to communicate with each other, or to reason without always having to manipulate real objects directly. Instead of showing people how to put the chair on the table to get to the broken light, we can *tell* them by using sound-label substitutes. Thus, the spoken word may facilitate conceptualizing but it is *not* itself conceptualizing. Still less can verbal activity be equated with abstraction, which is a higher-order conceptualizing process frequently visuo-spatial in modality, as, for example, in abstract art or advanced geometry.

In the *written* form of languages, we have a system of secondary (visual) symbols which represent the primary (auditory/vocal) symbols—or, to prevent ambiguity, *signs*—which, in their turn, represent the perceived objects or coalesced concepts. These secondary printed symbols are also *objects in their own right* which are directly sensed, perceived and conceptualized just as are both the primary auditory signs and the original objects. Therefore, an auditory/vocal and written phonetic language itself expresses a sensory, perceptual and conceptual system, the latter two aspects being capable of symbolic expression through two symbolic systems, one auditory/vocal and the other visual. Thus words can be signs for other words, especially in the study of language, e.g., *noun, sentence,* etc.

The way in which the psychological imagery processes are cross-related with the two symbol systems is presented in some detail in Table VII (Bannatyne, 1967c).

Symbol Systems

If Table VII is examined carefully, it will be found to be largely self-explanatory. As one moves down the imagery or symbol-system columns, their content, the vertical developmental processes and the horizontal association processes become increasingly complex; this is not surprising, since the transition from the top left-hand sense-data corner to the lower right-hand reading/reasoning corner parallels the likely psychological ontogenesis of the human organism, in terms of cognitive language functions.

The developmental progression, although it may sometimes appear to operate on a continuum from sensing to thought, probably does not do so. It is highly likely (and at the sensory level fairly certain) that specific areas of the brain may take care of each of the psychological functions: sensing, memorizing (as an aspect of perceiving and simple conceptualizing) and thinking (Penfield and Roberts, 1959; Mountcastle, 1962). It is also probable that the two symbol systems, being of sensory origin, also each have their specific neurological territory, although they must have an extensive interface as well. And it is not a contradiction of the foregoing statements to say that all these neurological facets of the brain overlap and interlock in an unbelievably intricate intercommunication system. Psychologically, these are the association, control and feedback processes through which the functioning of the parts is integrated. The higher functions

TABLE VII
THE CLASSIFICATION OF IMAGES AND THEIR SYMBOL SYSTEMS BY TYPE OF PSYCHOLOGICAL PROCESS DURING DECODING OPERATIONS, AND BY IMPLICATION SOME ENCODING OPERATIONS*

Psychological Process	Images of Objects, Actions, etc. Non-verbal "Meaning" (Internalized)	Association Process	Primary Auditory Symbol System (Auditory-Verbal Signs)	Association Process	Secondary Visual Symbol System (Visual-to-Sound-Verbal)
Sense Data Awareness	Unidentified image, e.g., an object with a rectangular flat top, four legs, etc. (1)	No association (8)	The sensing of a series of sounds which have no concept associations although they may be perceived as unknown words, e.g., listening to an unknown language (12)	No association (19)	The visual sensing of a series of line configurations in patterned sequences, e.g., looking at a page of Chinese print as a nonreader (23)
Developmental Process (Down)	Familiarization through repeated sensing, usage, teaching, etc. (2)		Auditory-sound decoding into images through learned contingencies (13)		Visual decoding of the printed word through learned associations with sound-labels (words) (24)
Percepts	Recognition of an immediately present object, action, etc. (or its pictorial equivalent) as something repeatedly experienced in different situations, e.g., something one works on, eats from, puts	Learned-by-memory image-to-sound-label (word) pairing. Image and symbol have been repeatedly associated in experience (9)	Hearing a particular sound-label (word) or a simple string of such labels, and being able externally or internally to identify any image associated with that label, e.g., "See that table." Identification (14)	Learn-by-memory gestalt printed word sequence patterns associated with relevant gestalt sound-labels. Or for beginner readers or new words	The child beginning to read will learn to recognize (a) some whole visual word patterns as symbolizing a gestalt of sound (a word) and (b) some sequences of visually coded phonemes which he must blend. The ratio of (a) to (b) will depend on the "look-

	objects on (3)		grapheme-to-phoneme matching trials (20)		"say"-to-phonics teaching methods ratio, e.g., t-a-ble (25)
Developmental Process (Down)	Internal development through perception and memory of permanent integrated networks of image concepts, all interassociated (4)		Internal development of grammatical coding systems linking sound-labels—partly innate and partly mimicry in genesis (15)		The learning of visual grammatical sequences which more or less correspond with auditory sound-label grammatical systems (26)
Concepts	An internalized grouping of coalesced similar (or closely related) images within and across all sense modality experience. Concepts are usually generalized and form spatial and temporal hierarchical classes; e.g., these objects as a class have a flat working surface, legs being mostly empty space beneath, i.e., a meaning without a symbolic label or representational concepts (5)	(a) Automatic selection of context-appropriate image-label associates; that is, sound-labels pull out percept images or concept images. (b) Inasmuch as encoding takes place as an aid to decoding, we can say that the sound-labels are more or less automat-	Here there is a corresponding hierarchical classification of sound-labels, possibly into Osgood's "word form pools." Auditory closure operates in this system facilitated by familiarity of both concept and label and by the semiautomatic retrieval of habitual sequences of sound-label strings (phrases or sentences) *within* a particular concept class of images (e.g., the table is made of wood and has four legs). Thus some probabilistic pre-	Arbitrary printed word-sound-label associations or arbitrary grapheme/phoneme associations of irregular orthography (in English). Also learned are matched grammatical sequences of both sound and visual word-labels, i.e., automatic grammar cor-	Good readers must be able to recognize (i.e., perceive and conceptualize) the gestalt of sound in a printed word-label, or else be able to "sound it out" if the word is unfamiliar. Visually coded labels (words and morphemes) in visual word form pools will correspond (be associated with) their equivalent sound-label word form pool contents. Visual closure is facilitated both by familiarity and by the semiautomatic habitual letter and word sequences within their

Psychological Process	Images of Objects, Actions, etc. Nonverbal "Meaning" (Internalized)	Association Process	Primary Auditory Symbol System (Auditory-Verbal Signs)	Association Process	Secondary Visual Symbol System (Visual-to-Sound-Verbal)
		ically grammatically sequenced. Processes (a) and (b) are both probabilistic and take place within a generalized concept, i.e., they are (to adapt Osgood's terms) "homeostatic and qualifying" (Osgood, 1963) (10)	diction of sound-label and sequence is possible (16)	respondence associations (21)	associated concept-idea-class-area (27)
Developmental Process (Down)	Development of intellectual cognitive processes as studied and elaborated in the works of Piaget (6)		Development and understanding of sound-labels (words) for various *relations* possible *between* concepts (17)		Development of visual-label equivalent forms of relational sound-labels (28)
Thinking as a Dynamic	Nonverbal, nonsymbolic concepts and their in-	Probabilistic selection of	To the above (16) sound-label selection	Same as above in (21) but	The ability to decode conceptual meaning from

Process of Manipulating Interrelated Concepts	terrelationships (which incidentally are higher-order concepts) can be processed in accordance with the "thought-computer-*programs*" available. In other words, concepts can be sequentially reasoned with through time in accordance with the innate laws and acquired rules of thought, e.g., geometry. Note that lines, angles, planes, etc., and their interrelationships are *not symbolic*—they are true visuo-spatial abstractions. Symbolism and abstractions are far from synonymous. Also note that images, percepts, concepts and even their interrelational "modifiers" can be visuo-spatial, auditory, kinesthetic-motor, tactile, taste, olfactory, visceral, proprioceptive, temporal or any combination or permutation of these (7)	sequential concept (image) sound-label association, i.e., syntactical stringing or decoding or such. This process would be (to adapt Osgood's terminology) "multiplicative and quantifying." The selection of sound-labels in encoding or the thought process in decoding is also partly determined by the thinking program in use, i.e., the relationship associations *between* concepts (11)	processes can be added further *relational* sound-labels plus those semihabitual string sequences (sentences and phrases) which *match the laws and rules of "rational"* thought; e.g., legal terminology abounds with these sound-label sequences of a relational and interrelational type. On the other hand, original or unfamiliar thought-speech or sentencing, or reading, as in (29), is less habitual, less fluent, more hesitant (Goldman-Eisler, 1964) (18)	the sound- and visual-label associations and their grammatical sequences are more complex in accordance with the relational concept system they symbolize (22)	the printed word using many complex associations on several levels (all described in other sections of this table), e.g., reading a report of a scientific research project. This requires the reader to decode first in sound-label grammatical strings as described in (18). I am of the opinion that all *verbally* facilitated thinking, conceptualizing or perceiving on any level, whether decoding or encoding, always utilizes *auditory* symbols. Even so, much thought is nonverbal, e.g., in art, science and music (7). But when we read we first decode to the auditory stage and then use sound-label language as the medium for thought (29)

*Table may be read both across and down.

of abstract conceptualizing and thinking, together with the complex symbolic labeling and sequencing they involve, probably incorporate the lower neurological levels in their operation. Even so, one can obviously think in the absence of immediate sensory stimuli; therefore, the latter need not be present.

The childhood development of conceptual imagery and thinking has been investigated by many people, notably Piaget. The work of the "symbolic" logicians is also relevant to the laws, rules and principles of human thought. However, although Osgood, Wepman, Kirk and others have constructed excellent models for the hierarchical classification of language and conceptualizing processes, until recently no clear theoretical distinctions had been made between imagery concepts and the two symbol systems. Osgood (1963) has analyzed the relationship between meaning and sentences, particularly from the syntactical psycholinguistic point of view. This approach, with its "meaningless word form pools," "semantic key sorts," "cognitive mixers," etc., seems to me most fruitful if only because meaning or conceptualizing is theoretically distinguished from (and related to) words, syntax, etc. But though Osgood explores cognition, semantics and linguistics, he is not concerned with distinguishing between auditory and visual symbol systems (except to say very briefly once or twice that we do not speak the way we write, a factor which I consider may be an artifact of repeated polishing).

The essence of Osgood's thesis, as I interpret it, is that during the encoding of an assertion, nonword meanings selectively determine, on a probabilistic basis, one's choice of words and parts of words and their positional sequence. However, it is difficult to determine if Osgood considers abstract conceptual thought possible in the absence of internalized signs or symbols. Inhelder and Piaget (1958) now seem to lean toward the opinion that logical thought processes are not founded in verbal symbols or linguistic material.

Before going on to the part played by association, I would like to emphasize, in the interests of clarity and brevity, that I have somewhat oversimplified both my own conceptualizing of the whole topic and the neuropsychology involved. Like many other people, I consider that the sensory-neurological workings of the brain most likely operate on the basis of a stochastic selection of *bits* of stored information of any and all kinds and of matching, associating, integrating, decoding and encoding them meaningfully. Visual and auditory imagery may even be stored in operationally different memory systems (Bannatyne, 1966c), the former perhaps being a "spot" or bit-matching process, whereas the latter may be a more *gestalt-unit* sort of registration. This would explain some of the real problems a few dyslexic children have in matching a well-learned auditory/vocal language to (or from) its visual/written version. It also is in accord with Osgood's contention that the *word* is the base unit of language. By implication, I would suggest that the *concept* is the base unit of thought and that it is not only obviously a prior development to language phylogenetically and ontogenetically, but also the reason for the existence, content and structure of language. This seems obvious, but linguists often endeavor to abstract the structure of language in the absence of meaning. Meaning is the main determinant of the structure of language.

Thinking, Reasoning and Language

Although language is not thinking, it is a symbolic medium for facilitating, expressing or communicating thought, and it does so with varying degrees of accuracy. Sometimes, for example, when speaking at speed, one chooses a word to express a concept even though one knows it is not an exact match. Nevertheless, since language, or more precisely words, phrases and sentences, *roughly mirror* thought processes, it is possible (as the symbolic logicians have done) to use them or their abstracted equivalents to study the nature of thinking. As thinking (i.e., conceptualizing and reasoning) cannot occur in a vacuum—we have to think about something—the total process involves one or more of the following: (a) actual sensory external objects (watch repairing), (b) the internal images of those objects (the artist who paints from memory, the composer whose memory imagery is auditory or the choreographer whose memory imagery is partially kinesthetic), (c) primary auditory sign-symbols (speaking and listening) or (d) secondary visual symbols (reading and writing). All these, usually in various continuously shifting permutations and combinations, participate in thinking and reasoning, but only (a) and (b) can be the subject matter which is the *content* of the thinking. The thinking and reasoning aspect is a process of internally *manipulating* this content; the term *manipulating* is used because when actual objects, as in (a), are represented in cognition as an immediate concept/content, they *are* often being manipulated concurrently by the hands, usually using extensional tools (hammers, trucks, radar, computers, etc.) at the bidding of thought/reason.

Apart from the image/concept content, what extra quality does thought/reason have which *internally* manipulates objects? The answer is that *thinking models relationships in space-time* which involve *active changes* wrought by some physical or biological agent or agents in the widest sense of those words. Note that the active change may be zero because "staticity" is one extreme end of the change continuum. These internalized models of changing the space-time relationships of external objects (or rather their internal equivalents, namely, images, percepts and concepts), when processed by the human brain, *are* thinking and reasoning. Even the assertion, "I am happy," denotes a certain endocrinological ego-environment homeostasis, an interactional, continuing space-time relationship.

These internalized relational elements between image-type concepts are actively utilized in the neural thought processes so that the human organism can simulate or postulate trial or modeling manipulative "runs" of the image/concept data without having to deal with or handle the objects themselves. It is not too much to suggest that thinking and reasoning evolved because there was (and is) an immense survival value in the organism being able neurologically to *simulate* (in images or symbols and sometimes abstractly) actual, possible or even hypothetical series of interrelated events without the actual events occurring, or without the objects themselves being present. A definition of *thought* in those terms would be the dynamic (neurological) manipulation of internalized models and their interrelationship structures, all of which attempt more or less to simulate reality (e.g., planning a road system or even an abstract painting). Language labels sometimes facilitate this process.

These thinking and reasoning relationship manipulations are the *key* to the nature and structure of all meaningful language as a symbol system. In fact, I am of the opinion that morphemes, words, phrases, sentences and, from another angle, syntax are no more or less than auditory or visual *labels* strung together as the communicative *matching equivalents* for pure sensory-originated (in the past) image concepts and their direct (thought) interrelationships. The communicative aspect may be internally facilitative, externally transmitting or both.

We can summarize the above discussion as follows:

1. Thought is the fundamental reason for the existence of language.
2. Thought is not language in the "word-sentence" sense of the term.
3. As well as concepts, an essential part of thinking is to be found in the manipulative relational elements between concepts (including objects).
4. These relational factors have reality in space-time changes.
5. The factors can exist as internalized dynamic (or passive-observational) models which can be manipulated hypothetically.

Most important of all, the relational elements themselves can be symbolized (or represented) on the verbal word level; moreover, these verbal equivalents of space-time relationships only become truly meaningful when they interconnect concepts. Thus, for example, I can actually *look* at a bush between two trees, I can pictorially *imagine* a bush between two trees and I can *say or write,* "A bush between two trees." If the movement-change relation is added to the mix, usually in the form of a verb, I can say, "A bush is standing between two trees." The complete relationship of bush and trees is (a) in the present *time,* (b) standing (paradoxically a static *motion*) and (c) *between,* i.e., spatially in the center. Similar analyses can be made for auditory, kinesthetic-motor, tactile or visceral images or any other kinds of imagery including mixtures of these. Even abstraction in this context is a psychological image/concept phenomenon, essentially *nonverbal* in nature, which may sometimes be represented verbally. Emotional relationships in this context are, in essence, no different, as I consider them to be neurophysiological (endocrinological) relationships existing in space-time.

Much of the above section has stressed the association of image concepts with language symbols, particularly the auditory sign system. There is a need to clarify further the *association processes* between image concepts, their auditory sign (symbol) system and their visual symbol system.

Meaning/Sound-Label Associations

One point needs to be made very clearly. Syntax or the *sequence* of auditory sign-labels is, to a considerable extent, determined by the nonverbal thought *interrelationship* determinants linking purely nonverbal image concepts. Image concepts as internalized "things" are action-manipulated in space-time, selectively qualified with intrinsic attributes and quantified by relative evaluations, and it is the sequence of these factors which largely determines syntax, along with certain conventional, sequential, alternative transformations. For example,

The heavy	man	ate	the brown	bread
quantity	thing	action	quality	thing

If one asks why the sequence subject-verb-object (or its linguistic equivalent) occurs, the only answers are: first, that this is the visual temporal sequence of the event in terms of its cause-and-effect importance to the speaker, e.g., "The heavy man caused to be consumed the brown bread." The continuing conversation is probably centered around the heavy man and his diet. The first "thing" mentioned is usually the most important from the stage setting point of view; e.g., in the sentence, "The brown bread was eaten by the heavy man," the speaker no doubt feels that the bread was most important and the continuing conversation is probably centered around the bread. It is worth noting that habitual thought sequences develop cliché-like habitual word sequences, e.g., "What is for dinner tonight, dear?" These can be automatically processed at speed. However, original or strange thoughts (or, when speaking, words) may be very hesitantly processed (Goldmen-Eisler, 1964). In some languages, for example Latin, the verb may come at the end of the sentence, but this is a less efficient system of sequencing in terms of events occurring through time. Apparently, the Romans felt the action to be less urgent information than the object acted upon.

Meaning, Language and Labeling

I am not convinced that language is as *essential* to sophisticated thought as Piaget in his earlier works, Luria and many other speech/language-oriented authorities have indicated. In the above discussion and in Table VII, the functions of perceiving, conceptualizing and thinking have been clearly separated from auditory/vocal and written language processes. There is other evidence which supports this point of view.

Piaget (1962) himself has modified his position in his statement "that the root of logical operation lies deeper than the linguistic connections, and that my early study of thinking was centered too much on its linguistic aspect" (quoted by Furth, 1964). Furth further notes that the deaf "were found to perform similarly to hearing persons on tasks where verbal knowledge could have been assumed a priori to benefit the hearing. Such evidence appears to weaken a theoretical position which attributes to language a direct, general or decisive influence on intellective development."

Much conceptualizing in pure and applied science, mathematics and art is essentially nonverbal. An architect does not design a house with words nor the engineer a bridge with labels. When I personally am conceptualizing statistically, I *see* vectors with three-dimensional deviation contours running through clusters of minute people. For me, a factor analysis is a multidimensional series of microgalaxies in space-time rather than a nonfiction essay in table form. Nonverbal intelligence tests deliberately strive to assess those aspects of conceptualizing which are independent of language. It can be seen that most forms of nonlinguistic thinking are visuo-spatial or motor in origin (motor-spatial conceptualizing occurs in all sports), but music would be an example of nonverbal conceptualizing in the auditory modality.

Osgood (1963) talks about his "assertion that word units in the [word] Form Pool are meaningless." Indeed, he postulates a "Semantic Key Sort" as a sentence formation process through which are selected the most likely (probabilistic) linguistic units of word parts, grammatical sequences and associational, affective and denotative characters. However, Osgood is concerned with sentence formation and hence *communication*, and it is not clear whether or not he considers that meaning can be entirely separated from language in thought processes. An electronics engineer once described how, during the day, he had wired a television set incorrectly but did not know where the fault was. That night he lay awake and "in his mind's eye" retraced every wire and connection until he found the fault. But the imagery was not communicated and remained nonverbal.

Yet another case of nonverbal thought occurs when meanings or concepts have no verbal labels. Many theoreticians and innovators have to invent new words for new concepts, which indicates that the concept existed independently first and was in search of a label. This is, I suggest, the reason for Goldman-Eisler's (1964) observations that original linguistic material causes more frequent hesitancies and pauses than does the familiar. Apparently, one is searching for the obscure labels or meanings, depending on whether one is speaking or reading. If thought *were* language, there could be no hesitancies of the kind caused by an internal search for the most appropriate word-label.

Reading is itself an excellent example of the converse situation, namely, the extent to which language can become separated from meaning or conceptualizing. Almost everyone must have had the experience of superficially reading long tracts in books while thinking other thoughts. Or again, an advanced textbook in an unknown subject can be read aloud so that an expert listener understands perfectly, while the reader is unaware of the meaning. Some intellectually defective subjects with IQ's below 50 have mastered the *skills* of reading, but they are often unable to comprehend the meaning of the passages they read (Houghton and Daniels, 1966). Another example of the separation of language skills from conceptualizing occurs when secretaries type documents routinely without bothering to understand the text itself.

Bernstein (1961a) quotes Luria and Yudovich (1959) thus: "Speech is not only a means of indicating corresponding objects or relationships in the internal world, but abstracts, isolates, generalizes perceived signals and relates them to certain categories. Language marks out what is relevant, affectively, cognitively and socially, and experience is transformed by that which is made relevant." This is true up to a point, but I consider that Yudovich and Luria are substituting the term *language* for *thought* or at least are tending to equate the two. It is *intelligence* which "abstracts, isolates," etc., and while language may sometimes, or even usually, facilitate the process, as many an intelligence scale demonstrates, these cognitive functions can be equally demonstrated in a nonverbal direct way. Actions can easily communicate "affectively, cognitively and socially" and be very relevant in a nonverbal embrace.

Language helps to crystallize thought, but is not thought. It brings to thought a communicative facilitation even when it is labeled "inner speech." In a sense, all speech is "outer" to conceptualizing and relationship-manipulating processes. The mosaic of verbal rules, units and sequences which is language subserves one form of thought communication inasmuch as it constantly shifts to fit the mosaic of concepts it signals or symbolizes. Our thoughts to a greater or lesser degree automatically *select* language components on a best-fit basis to communicate primary meaning, which is essentially nonverbal.

There is even neurological evidence that words are meaningless labels which are associated with meaningful concepts elsewhere in the brain. If word labels *were* meanings, or were absolutely essential to meanings and reasoning, they would be stored economically all over the brain together with the sensorimotor experiences (memories, etc.) involved. This is not the case, since words are usually stored in specific areas in the left hemisphere in most people (Hecaen and Ajuriaguerra, 1964; Mountcastle, 1962; Zangwill, 1960). Penfield and Roberts (1959) state quite clearly that there are three separate brain mechanisms which record or store (a) specific events in present and past experience, (b) the concepts derived from each series of these particular events, and (c) *"the ganglionic equivalent of a word."*

They say, *Word memory:* Returning, thus, to speech and the speech mechanism, it is obvious that words which are first related to particulars come to be related to concepts. As time passes, there is formed within the brain the *ganglionic equivalent of a word* and the *ganglionic equivalent of a concept.* Experience over the years continues to reinforce the back-and-forth neuronal interrelationship between the two.

Later, Penfield and Roberts say: "It was pointed out in Chapter X that memory of concepts, which does not depend on one hemisphere as speech does, is separate from the speech mechanism." It is only necessary to add to such a clear-cut statement that Penfield and Roberts also state that there is a neurological area they term the "Centrencephalic System," which is "that central system within the brain stem which has been, or may be in the future demonstrated as responsible for integration of the function of the hemispheres [and the] integration of varied specific functions from different parts of one hemisphere." The centrencephalic system is hypothesized to be "a conceptual storehouse," clearly separable from the speech mechanism. Furthermore, the "highest level of integration [is] located not in the frontal lobes but in the diencephalon and mesencephalon." I suggest that the centrencephalic system is the conceptual/thinking equivalent of categories 5 and 7 in Table VII; that is, it is the neurological counterpart of psychological nonverbal conceptualizing and relational thought processes. Penfield and Roberts' "recording of specific events" fits neatly into categories 1 and 3 in Table VII, whereas storage and processing can be identified with categories 14 and 16. Category 17 would exist only as an integrational process. These general topics will be further discussed in Chapter VI.

Auditory-Label/Visual-Label Associations

Thus far, the discussion has elaborated the relationship of syntactical sequences to meaning sequences, and the image/concept to sound-label association. There remains clarification of the association of the auditory symbol system to the visual symbol system.

Teaching children to read has led me to the conclusion that they learn to associate sound-labels with visual-labels (and vice versa) on *both* a gestalt whole-word basis and a phoneme/grapheme analytical/synthetic basis. Of course, there will be a bias toward keeping with one method to teach the child to read, but children taught to "look and say" will eventually develop a somewhat crude phoneme analysis and blending attack for use with new or difficult words. Although children taught through phonics analyze most words, there are some words with distinctive visual patterns which they seem to recognize immediately as a gestalt. Most research tends to indicate that a combined method with an emphasis on code-breaking phonics is the most efficient technique for teaching reading (Chall, 1967). Usually the three-quarters of school-entry children who are verbally competent will rapidly learn to read by any method and often in spite of the teacher. This does not mean that the process cannot be made more pleasant and efficient if interesting code-breaking phonics techniques are used.

However, the least competent quarter of beginning readers together with the severe reading disability cases are quite a different educational proposition. Slight differences in teaching techniques or sensory training may bring about startling differences in attainment. By studying the language problems of learning disability cases, one can learn a great deal about what is happening in normal language processing.

From the auditory/visual frame of reference, the associative processes involved in visual language decoding (reading) or encoding (spelling and writing) take the "meaning" for granted, since the child can easily comprehend the passage when it is read aloud to him. To read and spell, all the child has to do is turn the gestalt of letters into sounds, or the gestalt of sounds into letters; the association of meaning is a separate problem, as indicated above. Most of us as competent adult readers can read, write or spell words instantly, but the beginner or poor reader who cannot recognize or spell a particular word has to cope with it with an analytical attack of some kind. Content may provide some clues, but often there is insufficient evidence for even a reasonable guess.

As was pointed out earlier, the phoneme/grapheme matching (orthography) system in English is notoriously irregular in both decoding and encoding. Here, decoding refers to recoding the visual graphemes into auditory phonemes, and encoding to translating the auditory phonemes into visual graphemes, which in turn have to be decoded or encoded in terms of meaning. (The fact that there are *two stages* (or sets) of both decoding and encoding in reading and spelling is never mentioned or made clear by most writers.) Because phoneme/grapheme orthography is so irregular, each paired association, as it appears in sequence in each word, has to be learned by rote memory in association with the only permanent feature of that word, namely, its meaning in context. The dog is a *bow*-wow; the knights *bow* to the Queen; the archer aims his *bow;* the *bough* is on the tree. The girl ties her hair with a *bow* because her *beau* is coming to meet her.

The phoneme/grapheme rote memory association (within a word "content-meaning") is extremely difficult to establish in many reading disability cases. Even more difficult to ingrain in the memory is the rapid automatic sequencing of these associations, which, after all, is what reading or spelling is. The major problem for most of these children lies in their poor ability to identify rapidly auditory phonemes and in the fluent sequencing (blending) aspects of the phoneme/grapheme association. The concept which best summarizes the nature of these rapid memorizing functions in phoneme/grapheme association is *fluency,* and it will be remembered that verbal fluency is one of the major areas of cognitive sex differences. Fluency will be considered again in much greater detail in later chapters.

Auditory Discrimination of Phonemes

Usually, children do not need to hear the separate phonemes within a word when they hear or speak them in normal conversation. No doubt to some extent, the economies of the neurological computer do demand a "bit" storage of sounds, possibly in two separate places, one for listening and one for speaking. This process is largely automatic and the sequences of "bits" become, to all intents and purposes, gestalts of sound which are near enough to their most popularly used phonetic equivalent. Because reading disability boys often do not or cannot listen accurately, their registration and production of words may be somewhat distorted (slurred, phonetically inaccurate, etc.). In the course of normal conversation, the auditory closure of the people who are listening (closure copes with accent variations, etc.) makes appropriate allowances for these mispronunciations, so in everyday conversation they do not matter. However, in reading and spelling, they can be a distinct handicap because any distortion of phonemes creates even more chaos and irregularity with grapheme processing. When spelling unfamiliar words, we apparently internally sequence the phonemes and transpose them into graphemes. If (a) the phonemes are distorted, (b) phoneme/grapheme correspondence is inherently irregular and (c) the phonemes are auditorially unseparated in an "outburst" of sound, then the grapheme-sequencing (and hence letter-sequencing) output on paper will be equally chaotic. Likewise, in reading, even if the less able reader with these three handicaps can split up words into purely visual grapheme segments, his ability to decode them into their respective sequences of correct phonemes (which would then be blended into gestalts of sound) will also be distorted.

THE AUTOMATIZATION OF LANGUAGE

Although the term *automatization* is relatively new, the idea which it expresses, namely, an integrated pattern of automatic habits, is an old one. All language, whether spoken, perceived, written or read, is, in the literate person, a habitual skill or tool which conveys meaningful information. Once the deliberate period of learning, usually in infancy or childhood, is through, all the processes of decoding and encoding become fully automatic overlearned skills which, like all other tools, have no use until they are put to work. Habit formation in many areas of behavioral activity, including language, appears to be a built-in characteristic and capacity of the human mind. Task acquisition, no matter how simple or complex, seems initially to require considerable deliberate effort but, as many studies have shown, as practice proceeds, one moves through a sequence of learning progressions and plateaus which become successively less conscious and more automatic behavioral patterns.

That this is the case in language learning ability is neatly expressed by Whiting *et al.* (1966). They say,

> It is believed that a critical feature of the normal reading is the automatic performance of decoding, leaving the reader free to concentrate on the *meaning* of the written material or the flow of ideas. . . . In brief, normal readers appear to decode "automatically" while consciously attending only to comprehending. Normal handwriting and spelling, similarly, involve automatic coding, with conscious attention given to meaning. The rapid and efficient performance of simple over-learned tasks has been termed automatization (Broverman, 1960, 1964 and Broverman, *et al.*, 1964). The term derives from the observation that highly over-learned behaviors tend to be carried out by human beings without consciousness of them, that is, automatically. Automatizers are thus able to perform simple repetitive and characteristically over-learned tasks quite rapidly. Weak automatizers on the other hand tend to be less adept performing such automatic-type behavior.

Whiting *et al.* carried out a small research project to determine the extent of automatization in dyslexic and normal children. Unfortunately, most of the nonautomatization tests could be classified as highly spatial tests, while most of the automatization tests were various forms of verbal fluency. Thus, it is very possible that the results of the study have nothing to do with automatization but rather with the difference between the visual/spatial and auditory/vocal modalities.

From another point of view, automatization is a synonym for rote memory, a process which can take place in any of the sensory or motor modalities, in any combination of sensorimotor modalities or in the area of cognitive-intellectual relationship functions.

An example of the latter occurs when children learn their multiplication tables in arithmetic. They see the tables, they hear them and they memorize the relationships between numbers of objects.

The automatic memorization of language skills is even more complex than learning multiplication tables by rote memory; this is discussed at length in Chapter VII. In fact, the orthographic and linguistic conventions mentioned earlier in this chapter have to be overlearned until they operate quickly. Fortunately, if Luria, Lenneberg and others are correct, there is a considerable built-in neurological and neurosensory wiring system which so facilitates the automatization process that most speech production and speech perception language learning takes place in infancy. However, this is not so true of reading, which is a much more artificially acquired skill, and of course, the same is even less true for writing and spelling. Although mankind has been vocally communicative for tens of thousands of years, reading and writing are relatively recent developments which can usually only be acquired when they are deliberately taught in school or its equivalent. The problems encountered by some children because they are unable to automatize the associational elements involved in reading and spelling is considerable and their difficulties will be thoroughly investigated and discussed in later chapters.

Chapter IV

NORMAL AUDITORY/VOCAL LANGUAGE ACQUISITION AND DEVELOPMENT IN INFANCY AND CHILDHOOD

THE NEED FOR STANDARDIZED RESEARCH

I n a book on language and reading disabilities, it is obviously essential to establish the norms of development before embarking on detailed explanations of the abnormal, and this chapter is intended to survey our knowledge of infant language acquisition and development in the auditory/vocal modalities. One would expect that the single, most important function of the human race, communicative language, would have been exhaustively researched and documented, but such is not the case for children under three years of age. There are few studies and many opinions, although several interesting projects are now under way.

However, there is a great need for far more research, using large representative samples with discrete homogeneous subgroups, which will provide standardized data from which definite (though temporary) conclusions can be drawn. Several permanent institutes in various countries, devoted to pursuing large-scale developmental surveys, would be invaluable for testing the thousands of hypotheses which have recently emerged, usually from biased limited samples of children and infants. In particular, Piaget's excellent work calls for standardization on a worldwide basis. The cross-cultural comparisons would yield valuable developmental information. If "twin studies" were also carried out, the findings would help establish the degree to which genetic factors underlie Piaget's theoretical findings.

After studying children with severe reading disabilities for many years and having surveyed all the research and literature listed in the References section of this book, I have come to the firm conclusion that *at least 80 percent of reading disabilities are the result of auditory/vocal language problems* originating from a variety of etiologies. The importance of competent auditory/ vocal functioning to competent reading is illustrated by the fact that the blind learn to read relatively easily without vision, whereas the deaf almost invariably have a gross deficiency in reading achievement (Hargis, 1970).

EARLY STIMULATION

My own persuasion is that although heredity plays a considerable phylogenic part, many of our developmental *norms* for language are very much culturally established. The succession or order in which stages emerge is, of course, both pragmatically and genetically determined in the sense that most developmental processes are broadening maturational ones which continuously grow through discrete phases. The flower cannot exist before the bud, nor the bud before the germination of the seed. The great danger in standardized norms is that we come to regard them as both inevitable and absolute. We do not see them as somewhat flexible and relative—relative to our cultural and educational habits and customs. The point is not so much that we can alter the successive *order* of developmental stages or the *nature* of each separate stage; it is that our temporal standards are, to some extent, man-made, and that these imposed time sequences may have little to do with the natural innate time sequences *optimally possible.* For example, some intelligent children can begin to learn to read at three years of age in a most enjoyable way. Doman (1964) quotes several cases, and others are known to me personally. I suspect that most children could begin to read at four years of age.

Many teachers who still feel that education is an anxiety-creating process, involving negative pressures on the child (probably resulting from their own unfortunate experiences as pupils in school), raise their hands in horror, saying that one must not *force* anything on the child until he is ready. When challenged as to how one knows a child is ready and how that child acquires the skills and knowledge from life to reach such a stage of readiness, the answer is invariably vague. My next questions are always, "Do you never talk to a baby until he is ready to speak whole words, or until he can understand you?" and "Do you not allow a baby to walk until you decide he is ready?" In other words, I hold first that any educative process should always be enjoyable (and it is *naturally* so), and second, that the provision of reading situation materials in infancy is as beneficial as providing a floor on which a baby can learn to lie, flap around, crawl and eventually walk. The opportunity to profit from both materials and happy tuition should be provided for infants and children in almost *every* sphere of development at all ages and we should not prejudice the learning situation by depriving children of stimulating materials because of our preconceived developmental notions. Personally, in any developmental process, I believe in providing the child with material aids and preliminary "tuition" for one or two more advanced stages than the one where he presently is. There is a tremendous booster effect to learning which results from tackling upper-limit material as a part of the social and educational process. In this way, one breaks through learning plateaus far more rapidly. Of course, it is here assumed that the teaching process itself is essentially enlightened and interesting, and that the presentation of principles and processes is logically clear. Too many teachers are still unaware of the principles on which the subjects they are teaching are founded; this is particularly true of the skills involved in language and mathematics (Bereiter and Engelmann, 1966).

DEVELOPMENTAL AGE AND EDUCATIONAL SETS

The concept of "developmental age" is a useful one. Some children are really ready to begin to learn a new skill at, say, the age of three, while others may not be ready even at the age of eight. Our schools, unfortunately, all tend to work on a chronological age system of grading and promotion, a system which seems reasonable from physical and, to some extent, social standpoints. Hirst (1970), after reviewing the literature, quotes from her own research findings that while sex was a significant reading predictor variable at the first-grade level, age did not emerge as a significant predictor variable for first or second graders. Nor was age a significant predictor variable for success in the readiness test at the end of kindergarten. Hirst concludes quite flatly that age does not hold up as a significant predictor variable for academic success.

Emotionally, some children may be far more developmentally advanced than their chronological peers, while others may have a maturational lag. *Educational systems of the future will have to become far more flexible and ingenious if they are to cater to the developmental ages of individual children in a vast number of separate and not necessarily correlated aspects of mind and body.* A system of highly specialized "sets" in each subject in place of classes is most likely to solve the problem. Thus, a child who is good at mathematics would move rapidly up to the higher-mathematics "sets of children," while if the same child is poor at, say, French, he would move through the lower French groups. This is quite a different and more flexible system than streaming or age grouping. For many social and some sports activities, all the children could participate in a more scrambled fashion. A system of sets in a school solves many of the problems arising from the education of both gifted, average and below-average children—particularly since many talents and deficit areas are specific to one or two subjects.

THE ORIGINS OF SPEECH

This topic was long forbidden in learned societies because before the turn of the century, every second linguist speculated in endless papers about the origins of speech. Recently, Hockett (1960) has opened up the whole subject again but from a very original angle. He lists thirteen design features which may or may not be present in human or animal communication systems.

1. *Vocal/auditory channel:* Unlike physical systems of communication (e.g., the bee dance), use of the vocal/auditory channel leaves the body free for other activities that can be carried on at the same time.

2. *Broadcast transmission and directional reception:* The linguistic code signal can be heard by any auditory system

within earshot, and the source can be located by binaural direction finding.

3. *Rapid fading:* A signal does not linger for reception at the hearer's convenience, but writing down language overcomes this disadvantage.

4. *Interchangeability:* A speaker of a language can reproduce any linguistic message he can understand, but a stickleback can only communicate through fixed behavior patterns.

5. *Total feedback:* A speaker of a language hears everything of linguistic relevance in what he himself says. Hockett suggests that feedback internalizes language, a process which facilitates thought.

6. *Specialization:* Bodily efforts and speech sound waves serve no other function except as signals. (Note, however, that blind people can use speech sounds for sonar-type object location.)

7. *Semanticity:* A signal has the ability to trigger a particular meaningful result because there are fixed associations between elements in messages (words) and recurrent features of the world around us. When we say "Fire!" either there is a fire or we want rifles to fire.

8. *Arbitrariness:* In a semantic communicative system, the ties between meaningful message elements and their meanings can be arbitrary or nonarbitrary. In language, the ties are arbitrary. (This causes problems of memory storage in persons who are linguistically less competent.)

9. *Discreteness:* Each sound element in a word has a discrete meaning, so that a change in any of the elements may result in a different meaning. The opposite is seen in a continuous-change system such as pitch, which can connote a degree of anger.

10. *Displacement:* Through language, we can talk about things that are remote in space and time.

11. *Productivity* (of novel word combinations, etc.): Through language, we can say things that have never been said before and yet can be understood by the speakers of a

language. This feature is responsible for the changeability of language through time.

12. *Traditional transmission:* Detailed conventions of any language are transmitted extragenetically by learning and teaching. The human genes carry the capacity and motivation to acquire language.

13. *Duality of patterning:* The meaningful elements or morphemes in any language are represented by a small arrangement of a relatively small stock of distinguishable sounds (phones and phonemes) which in themselves are wholly meaningless. The combinations of these elements produce an infinite number of meaningful words.

Hockett goes on to say, "The problem of the origin of human speech, then, is that of trying to determine how such a system could have developed the four additional properties of displacement, productivity, duality and full-blown traditional transmission," which are not present in the protohominoids. He suggests that these human-language design features may have evolved through the ability to *blend sequences of sounds* in various permutations. Productivity through blending sounds probably preceded "any great proliferation of communicative displacement as well as any significant capacity for traditional transmission. A productive system requires the young to catch on to the ways in which whole signals are built out of smaller meaningful elements, some of which may never occur as whole signals in isolation." The system has survival value because "a child can be taught how to avoid dangers before he actually encounters them." This involves displacement and traditional transmission. According to Hockett, duality of patterning, that is, the infinite variety of the manipulative sequencing of phonemes, was the last property to be developed in human language. This evolutionary step was the major breakthrough because "without it language could not possibly have achieved the efficiency and flexibility it has."

It is interesting that Hockett should emphasize that the two most essential and uniquely human *skill* design features of language itself are productivity (of original words and sentences) and duality of patterning, the rearranging of phonemes into sequences called words, which can carry arbitrary but fixed meanings. Hockett automatically assumes that these developments must have evolved genetically. One would assume that the evolutionary changes in these respects would have been primarily neurological, inasmuch as the brain must have developed the ability to communicate meaning through an arbitrary, intrinsically nonmeaningful, phoneme-sequencing *coding* system.

Another important point stressed by Hockett is his suggestion that the ability to *blend* sounds vocally and discriminate them may have been a key factor in this evolution of a *coding* process. As will be seen from the work of neuropsychologists, psycholinguists and reading researchers, the characteristics of phoneme discrimination, blending, arbitrariness, duality of patterning and productivity (in the sense of *planning* sentences) are of key importance in linguistic competence and performance.

It is now necessary to examine further the development of language in the human child from the viewpoint of a series of different authors; I will then attempt to synthesize their ideas with my own.

JEAN PIAGET

Piaget's (1965) approach to language is quite empirical, being mainly conceived in terms of human communicative *relationships* (self and others) and the psychological purpose of linguistic behavior. The following categorizations result.

Egocentric Speech

The child does not bother to know whether or not anyone is listening and his speech is not directed to anyone. He talks for his own benefit and, in a sense, is his own listener. Egocentric speech can be divided into three categories:

1. *Repetition or echolalia:* This is the repeating or mimicking of sounds made by others. It is similar to babbling even when words are used and is devoid of social character.

2. *Monologue:* The child will talk to himself as if he is merely vocalizing internal psychological processes. This is a kind of thinking aloud.

3. *Dual or collective monologue:* In these situations, the speech produced is similar to that in the monologue situation, but the second person or group serves as a stimulus to vocalization.

Socialized Speech

This is true conversation which communicates thoughts and feelings even if they are, at first, primitive in nature. Socialized speech is divided into the following categories:

1. *Adapted information:* This is a true exchange of thoughts in which the child understands the listener's contribution and structures his own remarks accordingly.

2. *Criticism:* This category includes all comments on the behavior, conversation or work of others which assert the child's own superiority.

3. *Commands, threats, requests, etc:* These usually subserve the child's own immediate needs in the sense that the listener is the instrument through whom satisfaction will be gained.

4. *Direct questions:* These are questions which obviously require a direct answer from a specific person or group.

5. *Answers:* These are the child's own replies as a listener to the commands, questions, etc., of other people.

The "socialized speech" classification applies equally to adults, even though, on occasion, one presumes that adults also speak egocentrically. Piaget counted the number of egocentric and socialized speech forms of language, dividing the former by the latter. In this way, he was able to put a figure to the linguistic maturity (my own phrase) of various children. This is a valuable idea which could be considerably extended in a suitable test form.

In his book, *The Language and Thought of the Child,* Piaget (1965) also explored the verbal understanding of older children. True social intercommunication requires each participant to have a consciousness of himself as a subject, together with an ability to differentiate between self-subject and object without confusing the identities of each. Furthermore, one must cease to look on one's own viewpoint as the only possible one, even to the extent of synthesizing it with the view of others.

Because most of Piaget's findings are concerned with observed relationships between (a) self and self and (b) self and others, his categories are of limited use to those interested in the mechanisms of language and reading disabilities. Piaget does not analyze human communication linguistically, neurologically, psycholinguistically, biologically or physically—only socially. In other words, he does not interweave language with cognitive functions such as thought and spatial or numerical reasoning. Likewise, language is incidentally related to play and fantasy but in all these observational studies the inherent attributes, features and qualities of language itself are not systematically examined.

The same criticisms are partially true of the next author but it should be pointed out that a direct analysis of the development of the characteristics of language is not the purpose of either Piaget or Lewis. Rather, both are concerned with maturational patterns of observable language *behavior*.

M.M. LEWIS

The infant does not learn to speak or later to read in a social vacuum and, of course, many maturational factors within the child's own makeup contribute to his linguistic development. Until recently, very few investigators had explored the overt development of speech, language and thought in early infancy; by far the most thorough investigation was the one carried out by M.M. Lewis (1963) in his book, *Language, Thought and Personality in Infancy and Childhood*. Following is my own summary of his findings and conclusions, though I must take the responsibility for the wording and organization given here. This summary is intended to whet the appetite of the reader, who is encouraged to read the book in full.

Initial Development
Spontaneous Cries

There are two types of spontaneous cries:

1. *Discomfort cries* are an innate vocal response to urgent

bodily conditions, e.g., hunger, pain or discomfort. The sounds involved are mostly narrow vowels (*e, E, ae, a*), often nasalized, while the first consonants are *w, l, g, h.* these may later be followed by the often nasalized front consonants *m* and *n*. The former tend to result from straight vocalizing, while the origins of the latter may be the sucking motion of the mouth and lips.

2. *Comfort noises* occur a little after the discomfort cries begin and tend to be open vowels such as *a, o, u*. The early consonants stemming from relaxed gurgling noises are back ones, namely, *g, x, k, r*. Subsequently, the oral front consonants *p, b, m,* and *t, d, n* appear.

Babbling

This occurs sometime after the sixth week and is to be distinguished from comfort noises because babbling is a playing-with-sounds vocalization for its own sake as a source of pleasure. Repetitive vocalizations quickly follow which give the child even more pleasure. Babbling contains the rudiments of two developmental factors:

1. Manipulating a material medium for esthetic creation and enjoyment as an art.

2. Skill in making the sounds which will develop into complex speech. Lewis points out that comparatively few of these sounds will ultimately be used in the mother tongue, a point made by earlier authors.

Imitation

Along with Lewis and many others, I consider imitation one of the most important factors in a child's acquisition of language. He discusses three developmental stages of imitation:

1. *Responsive sounds,* which include any noises the child makes in response to visual or vocal stimulation by others. Reinforcement, smiling, holding, etc., is important at this stage.

2. *Action responses* by the baby, who obtains approval for physical responses to vocal stimulation and may even come to imitate the particular sounds himself.

3. *Actual imitation,* through which the child can utter sounds which are already associated with real meanings for him. This capacity, once present, means that the infant can participate in true rudimentary communication, but this does not occur with the first word a child utters. He may say *mama* for weeks before his cognition develops to the point where he learns that it is associated with one or more people or objects in his environment.

Development of Meaning

Meaning comes slowly to the infant, but there are *classes* of meaning and Lewis traces these developmentally.

Manipulative Effects

An infant's speech is manipulative when it results in someone performing a task he wants performed. A call to his mother directed at bringing her to his side is such a case.

Declarative Effects

This is a simple declaration of satisfaction, usually uttered when the child is contented. It is mainly an expression of an inner state and to a slight extent may be informational.

The Stabilization of Meanings

Only through a great variety of associated experiences can an infant slowly begin to realize that a particular word stands for a particular person or object. For example, it may take many, many months to establish that *mommy* stands for his mother and nothing else. This is a discriminative process which evolves out of his basic baby-language.

Basic Baby-Language

Lewis says that there are "six archetypal nursery words throughout the world: six sound patterns broadly of these kinds: mama, nana, papa, tata, dada. . . ." The nasalized forms come to be used for communications involving basic biological needs, whereas the relaxed nonnasal forms signify states of contentment or amusement in play. Imitation and babbling reinforce these sounds.

Secondary Baby-Language

The above baby-language is often augmented by words which reflect the patterns of adult language. They are usually onomatopoeia, e.g., *bow-wow* and *yum-yum*.

Expansion and Contraction of Meanings

These are well-known characteristics of the speech of one-, two- and three-year-old infants. Expansion of meaning is most common during the earlier stages of naming things and contraction tends to come slightly later as the vocabulary increases. *Ducky* is generalized to all flying things, until it is superseded by *airplane, bird, sparrow, kite,* etc. Besides form-similarity, the child may generalize on the basis of function, position, action and social need. Quite often a new word is an amalgam of the old generalized "baby" word and the child's rendering of the adult pronunciation of the new word.

Emotional Conative and Cognitive Development

Lewis stresses that words evoke emotional and conative responses both from the child and from the adult. Furthermore, these influences, through the medium of language, promote cognitive growth. The growth of meaning is a complex interaction of all three functions—affect, conation and cognition.

Perception

According to Lewis, a child learns to perceive the world around him in the course of his physical activity and his manipulation of his world. This growth of perception is related to the orexis (emotion plus cognition) aroused in him by his experience of this world: at the same time his growing perception is influenced by and influences his linguistic development.

Although perception may occur without language—for example, during Piaget's sensorimotor period of the first two years or so of life—once language enters "the process of symbolic mediation," it rapidly takes over to become the major means of symbolizing perceptions and communicating about them. Language intensifies perceptual experiences, reinforces attention and encourages remembering. Lewis quotes Bartlett's (1932) definition of a schema as "an active organization of past reactions and past experiences," which can be symbolized through images or language.

Conceptualizing

Here, Lewis quotes H.H. Price's (1953) definition: "A concept is a recognitional capacity which manifests itself also in absence." Language makes possible the ability to generalize in terms of universals; when a child "abstracts" *mama* from many sets of circumstances, we can see the rudimentary conceptualizing processes beginning to work. (I would also suggest that one can equally well generalize visuo-spatially in terms of universals, both realistically and abstractly.)

Ethical Behavior

Through language and the emotive undertones that accompany it, the child comes to understand patterns of approved and disapproved behavior. This is a conditioning process of reward and punishment which largely depends on linguistic communication. The process eventually leads to the introjection of the adult "ethical" situation as an internal control.

Discrimination of Attitudes

The child's developing attitudes modify and in turn are modified by his increasing verbal facility. The increasing need to communicate forces the child to adopt conventional words which express his feelings on a wider foundation than simply comfort-discomfort and satisfaction-dissatisfaction. Specific esthetic and ethical attitudes begin to emerge.

Discrimination of Situations

Pleasurable and unpleasurable feelings begin to be associated with recurring situations. This occurs as the infant learns the words (and their meanings) for various kinds of **approval** or disapproval, e.g. *clean, best, lovely, good, naughty*. Soon the child is able to generalize these qualitative judgment words as he recognizes a common perceptual pattern that can be labeled. All objects and situations which give pleasure are called *nice*. This is the beginning of abstraction, but it is not yet true abstraction. It is more related to a perceptual emotional state of mind. Similarly, *dirty* is such a state.

The Ethical Effects of Contrast

Opposites (e.g., *clean-dirty*) help the child to clarify meanings, particularly in terms of approval and disapproval. *Yes* and *no, nice* and *nasty, clean* and *dirty* all gradually become introjected as standards of judgment usually stemming, of course, from the established family attitudes to life—particularly the mother's.

Expressions of Self-Assertion and Self-Awareness

Lewis emphasizes the importance of four categories of directed speech which the child adopts as ethical expressive or declarative functions in his own right. The embryonic beginnings of ego development in the conscious sense of self-evaluation are discernable at this stage and age, and Lewis emphasizes the role of language in this process. He stresses speech directed at (a) the inhibition of others' actions, (b) the assertion of personal ability and prowess, (c) the expression of ownership and (d) the expression of self-awareness. The first three are self-explanatory and the fourth occurs when the child names himself, or says *I* or *mine*. This is a process of consciously relating objects or concepts to his own emergent identity and in the process he gradually differentiates himself from his environment and clarifies the interrelationships within it. Lewis stresses that deaf children are usually immature in personality development, because they are cut off from all these linguistic communications.

The Growth of Reference to What is Absent

This reference to things absent begins with the baby's first cry for absent milk, so to speak. His subsequent cries for his mother are of the same order but it is not until some months later that verbalized remarks about absent or hidden objects are under-stood and acted upon. When a child can appreciate that, say, a toy is not present by asking about it, then he has internalized not only an image of it, but also a vocal/auditory label for that image. This in turn leads to true linguistic intercourse in which he dis-cusses some topic or need with other people without it necessarily leading to action.

References to Time

Absence implies that, in the future, the object will be forth-coming or the person will return. Thus, the child gradually begins to understand references to future events and comes to use such terms as *later* or *yesterday*.

Questions

Questioning is one of the main promoters of the growth of speech in early childhood. The infant quickly comes to appreciate the inflection of the voice that indicates the asking of a question and becomes able to imitate it. Questions develop from the very simple query which almost any answer will satisfy, through nam-ing questions which help the child build a vocabulary, to true requests for information about events.

Internalized Silent Speech

In his book, Lewis emphasizes Vygotsky's (1962) ideas con-cerning "the directing functions of egocentric language when it becomes inner speech." Lewis claims that Piaget (1950), Luria (1961b) and Osgood (1953) also subscribe to this point of view, namely, that egocentric speech later becomes an internalized mediation process facilitating thought, particularly generalization and the analysis and synthesis involved in problem solving. The conclusion is that solitary play in infancy with its egocentric vocalization is one necessary forerunner of true adult thought. One has only to consider the restricted thought processes of the deaf-from-birth child to realize the part that inner language plays in the development of some cognitive processes.

Comments

I personally have reservations about the part that "ordinary" language plays in mediating thought processes. If one extends the definition of language to include all symbolic forms of communication (e.g., mathematics, music, art, gesture, physical contact), then I would agree. It is possible to make the mistake of *equating* language processes with thought processes, or even worse, of equating verbal thought with abstract thought, and nonverbal thought with concrete thought. Many great thinkers, after "discovering" new theories, have subsequently had to invent new words or mathematical symbols in order to communicate their thoughts. Some have practically invented a new vocabulary to explain their ideas and not the least of these is Piaget himself. Internalized words do facilitate abstract thought, but (to apply Piaget's principles of conservation and reversibility) *abstract thought is frequently made communicatively concrete by subsequently finding or inventing a suitable terminology.* Personally, I believe that much spatial thinking is both extremely abstract and nonverbal. However, these concepts will be further explored in later chapters. Suffice it to say here that I believe the terms *concrete, symbolic, thought, abstract, verbal, generalization*, etc., are so ambiguous that they require precise definition. To more or less equate intelligence and reasoning with verbal ability is not only inaccurate psychology, but an educational crime. Very recently several authorities including Piaget himself (1962) and particularly Furth (1964) have tended to draw back from the hypothesis that inner language must be present as a prerequisite for sophisticated reasoning, abstract thought processes or logical operations.

M.E. MORLEY

In her book, *The Development and Disorders of Speech in Childhood,* M.E. Morley (1965) and analyzes the development of speech and language by analyzing the various developmental levels on which the different speech processes occur.

Level I (see Fig. 7) is concerned with all the basic sensations and simple movements of the mouth and the vocal organs. The appropriate neurological and elementary feedback processes are

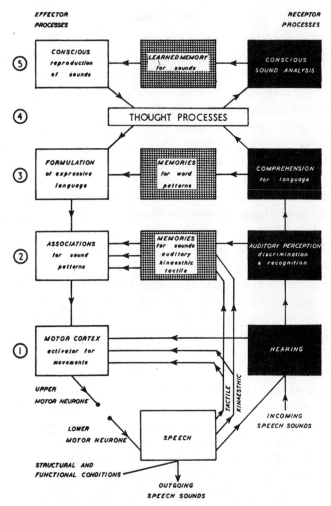

FIGURE 7. Some processes involved in speech.

Level I: Basic sensation and movements.

Level II: Receptor-effector processes for articulate sounds. Basic articulation.

Level III: Receptor-effector processes for integration of articulation with language.

Level IV: Mental processes associated with the reception and expression of thought through spoken language.

Level V: Involves conscious sound analysis and synthesis. *(From Morley, 1965, p. 6.)*

also operating. The infant can, to some extent, learn to interpret cries and noises other than its own, which it may imitate. A hearing loss would prevent or delay the normal development of speech on this level and presumably poor sight would limit associated visual experiences. Dysarthria could result on this level from defective muscular equipment in the speech organs.

Level II occurs as the child comes to discriminate sounds and to associate them with objects. Vowel and consonant sounds are being developed and the *patterns* of sounds required for subsequent verbal behavior are being laid down. The child babbles and imitates both others and himself. A partial hearing loss which results in poor auditory discrimination may cause a language delay on level II. Morley also tentatively suggests that a *limitation of auditory memory* may be the cause of poor comprehension and articulation. On the motor side, the main defect at level II is "the failure to reproduce accurately, in *the correct sequence,* the articulated sounds as used in speech." It seems to be the consonants which are mostly affected but vowel sounds may also be defective. This disorder of speech when it appears in older children or adults is known as *articulatory dyspraxia.*

Level III is the level on which "the developing thought processes influence the knowledge acquired through receptor activity and the ever increasing expression of ideas through executive language." Children with subnormal intelligence may, through imitation, develop through levels I and II and even make level III to a limited extent. However, for full development through this latter stage, a reasonable degree of intelligence is required. The disorders associated with sensory or motor failure on level III are mostly aphasic. Even though articulation may be normal (i.e., there is no failure of the auditory perception of level II), the child does not develop a normal understanding of spoken language. Such a disability is termed *developmental receptive aphasia.* The other type of aphasia, *developmental expressive aphasia,* occurs in children in whom the understanding of language appears to be adequate.

If such children are not using speech reasonably sensibly by four and a half years of age, some degree of expressive aphasia is apparent. Later, these children, if there is no spontaneous "recovery," may be able to learn in school, because they can comprehend normally even though their expressive language functions are limited.

Level IV occurs when language is directly linked with thought processes from both the comprehension (input-receptive) and formulation (output-expressive) aspects. Morley does not mention any disorders associated with this level, except that good intelligence is a necessary prerequisite. This is even more true on level V, which is concerned with the study of language as a subject, as in phonetics, linguistics, foreign languages, etc.

Many similarities are apparent when Morley's model of the levels of language functioning are compared with the psycholinguistic models of Wepman, Osgood and Kirk. Without actually using the terms *decoding, association* and *encoding,* she describes rather accurately the very same processes, levels and memory functions as the other authors.

L.S. VYGOTSKY

In his book, *Thought and Language,* Vygotsky (1962) puts forward his hypothesis that social interaction involving language between child and adult is the prime cause of attentional processes, voluntary movement and many other higher psychological functions. None of these evolve along pure lines, as language is inextricably mixed into their development.

However, Vygotsky holds that, at least for the first few months, thought and language develop from different origins and in different ways. "Intellectual" processes are evident in a child's activity in the form of purposeful actions well before speech occurs. Early vocal expressions are considered to be only emotional aspects of behavior, but within a month or two they become a means of social contact. At about two years of age, the developmental progressions of language and thought coalesce inasmuch as *thoughts* are verbally expressed. Prior to this, words are only associated with objects, people and emotional states. At this age, vocabulary expands rapidly and true relational meaningful speech occurs. For Vygotsky, speech cannot exist without prior thinking;

therefore, in a sense, he regards speech as a vehicle for thought, the two being separate entities in theory.

Comments

Kohlberg *et al.* (1968), in a four-part research comparison of several theories of "private speech" development in infancy, found that the "cognitive development" theory (of Vygotsky, Piaget and others), which has as its main determinants mental age and task difficulty, is the correct one. Their findings were more consistent with Vygotsky's specific theory that private (inner) speech represents a transitional stage to inner thought, into which it is transformed in time, than with Piaget's hypothesis that inner speech is an egocentric presocial manifestation which later disappears. I would suggest that finding a correlation between inner speech and a highly *verbal* intelligence test such as the Stanford-Binet Scale requires very circular reasoning, even though I agree that verbal ability and nonverbal IQ are also very likely to be highly correlated. However, a high correlation does not mean a causal relationship and I would suggest that further research should take into account the evidence quoted throughout this book that language codes thought, but is not thought; that a superior "thinking" ability requires a superior verbal coding ability for communication purposes (and verbal intelligence tests *communicate*), and that verbal and spatial abilities involve many nonreasoning *skills* such as fluency, perceptual speed, rote memory, etc. A much more subtle research might reveal that neither Piaget nor Vygotsky are right but that language coding abilities develop from "inner" egocentric speech into a full, mature, communicative *coding* system which facilitates both external, mature communication and "thinking" as a process of *nonverbal* manipulation of objects and their relationships. *In other words, language is an "inner" or "outer" communication-automatized skill process which subserves thought, but is not thought.* Images, percepts, concepts and thoughts are composed of cognitive equivalents for objects and their relationships (both of which can be concrete or abstract), which they *model.* One problem for research, then, is to develop more nonverbal techniques of communication for the measurement of relational thinking (e.g., block design) at an early age. At present, verbal communication as a skill contaminates nonverbal thought by processing it linguistically—because the infant *also* has to learn and develop nonverbal communication systems.

H.R. MYKLEBUST

Myklebust (1964), in his book *The Psychology of Deafness,* views language development from a phylogenetic point of view, stressing the fact that "the first verbal system acquired by man was auditory." Historically, auditory processing of language developed long before visual processing (reading); this pattern is also seen ontogenetically, inasmuch as the infant first learns to understand and use the spoken word long before he comes to read and write.

Myklebust holds that an infant first acquires meaningful experiences and only later comes to associate auditory symbols (spoken words) with those experiences. It takes up to nine months for the basis of "inner language" plus experience to develop to the point where the child can understand spoken words readily. During the second phase (up to the age of one year or so), this "receptive-language" stage rapidly grows and through a feedback process increases the inner-language development considerably. From twelve months to seven years, the normal child will develop his use of "expressive language," which initially will be confined to concrete concepts such as the names of objects and people or specific acts. Again, much feedback occurs as a child's speech reinforces his inner- and receptive-language functions. Once true expressive language is achieved, the infant is able to communicate meaningfully with others in an auditory/ vocal exchange of information. He can relate to others on a verbal level.

Myklebust goes on to say that "not until at least five years later does he have comparable facility with read-language." He does not take into account that many children are now taught to read meaningfully at four, three and even two years of age (Doman, 1964; Bereiter and Engelmann, 1966).

TABLE VIII
THE DEVELOPMENT HIERARCHY OF MAN'S LANGUAGE SYSTEM*

Verbal Symbolic Behavior
Visual expressive language—Writing
Visual receptive language—Reading
Auditory expressive language—Speaking
Auditory receptive language—Comprehending speech
Inner language—Auditory symbol and experience
Experience

*From Myklebust (1964). Table should be read upward.

Myklebust is on firmer ground when he emphasizes his overall approach to language as an auditory, speech and phonetic system:

In Western languages, reading is acquired by relating what the word looks like to what it sounds like. Only the *sophisticated reader* [my italics] can read without reference to how the words sound; even the sophisticated reader "regresses" and uses a "sounding out" process when he encounters a word which is difficult or with which he is unfamiliar.

A developmental hierarchy of man's language systems (Table VIII) is set out by Myklebust to illustrate this progressive growth through successive, functionally discrete phases beginning with primary sensory experiences in early infancy and ending with verbal symbolic behavior. It is worthwhile comparing these with Morley's levels as explained above.

This developmental hierarchy explains why an individual may be unable to write even though his other language functions are intact. However, if, for example, auditory receptive aphasia occurs on the second linguistic level, then the acquisition of all the later functions will be impeded in some way.

The following passage from Myklebust's book, although it stems from his interest in deafness, summarizes neatly the extreme importance of auditory processes in the acquisition of meaningful language. He says,

In actuality the child with deafness from infancy has a marked retardation in all aspects of language. Furthermore, no educational methodology known has been highly successful in overcoming this limitation. We must infer that when auditory language is lacking or seriously impeded reading and written language are restricted on a reciprocal basis. This concept of reciprocality or feed-back is useful in understanding the total hierarchy of language systems. . . . No child is born with language, but normally he is born with the capacity to acquire language, but because of the importance of auditory language in man's verbal symbol system, in doing so, he is confronted with one of the most difficult problems of learning known.

The "importance of auditory language in man's verbal symbol system" also confronts some types of dyslexic children with considerable problems, particularly on the two highest levels of the hierarchy of man's language system.

M. WOOLMAN

Woolman's (1965) standpoint is that of a learning theorist and his summary of language learning in infancy "rests heavily on the views of the learning process of Skinner [1938] and Keller and Schoenfeld [1950]. Differences in position and/or emphasis do occur and for these the writer [Woolman] bears sole responsibility."

Woolman suggests that the prime objectives of language learning are (a) language precision, descriptively and conceptually ranging from specificity to vagueness; (b) language extension, the ability to communicate through speech to a wide variety of people, and (c) language depth, the ability to understand language in terms of connotation, inference and implications.

The home, according to Woolman, may be placid, turbulent or verbally ambiguous in the sense that the parent anticipates the child's assumed wishes, or it may not use language as part of a reward system. Parents who do not themselves directly communicate may indicate intrafamilial love to the child through food, drinks or gifts of toys. The problem then becomes one of optimizing language growth potential; to this end, the child must have as a prerequisite "intensive experimental exposure as a foundation for the development of language." These children would fall into my category of primary emotional communicative dyslexia.

Levels of Language Organization

Woolman maintains that language disorders occur when the child is arrested at a particular level or develops only rudimentary language at higher stages. He suggests four levels of language organization, all of which are necessary to a full command of language:

The Discrimination Level

1. The infant learns to discriminate objects on the basis of multimodal sensations.
2. In this level, no language is required.

The Identification Level

1. After discrimination, the infant may learn that a specific sound is associated with a particular object.
2. The infant associates the production of certain sounds with quick reduction of certain needs; these functional sounds emerge as signals when the need recurs.
3. This stage is a sort of verbal labeling, and the infant must discriminate before he can label.

The Classification Level

1. Once a child gets a large body of "identifiers," he may need to place them in classes in order to be more efficient.
2. As an example, the word *pet* may be used to include dogs, cats, rabbits, ponies, etc.

The Conceptual Level

1. Class terms are directly reducible to perceptible objects or events, while conceptual terms, such as *ampere,* are not accessible to the senses.
2. Conceptual terms involve relating class terms with each other or with identifier terms.

Woolman lists the following preconditions for learning: (a) the existence of a state of need; (b) the goal-stimulus; (c) need as a behavioral catalyst, where the infant produces responses associated with reduction of the need and also can develop novel responses, and (d) contingency and the acquisition of new responses (generalization of the stimulus).

Woolman presents what he calls a *verbal contingency chain (VCC),* which indicates a general order of progression from discrimination to vocalization to true identification. The levels of the VCC are

1. The communicator.
2. Vocalization.
3. Modeling.
4. Selective emphasis.
5. General word term.
6. Identification.

It is clear that to begin language learning, there must be a communicator who is sensitive to the conditions required for language development, patient, knowledgeable, available over substantial periods of time and largely responsible for providing need-satisfactions (level 1). Level 2 has as its purpose an increase in the amount of infant vocalization at the prelanguage stage. Level 3 provides a simple and functional technique for "modeling" a word sound related to a need-satisfying object. In level 4, the communicator selectively emphasizes word-similar sounds from the stream of vocalizations produced by the infant. Level 5 is intended to set up the association between word-similar sound production and need-reduction. Finally, in level 6, the infant achieves the level of specificity necessary to assign an appropriate word term to the need-reducing object. He identifies the object by its relevant word.

The higher levels of language development come about because of increased efficiency in need-reduction by their usage.

Woolman's account of language learning is very detailed inasmuch as he is presenting a strictly environmental operant conditioning model of the process. For those not familiar with the terminology of learning theory, it is possible to translate many of the expressions into everyday equivalents; however, these will be less precise and will not be associated in the reader's mind with operant procedures.

There is no doubt that to the extent that the child does acquire language through formal or informal training, the process as described by Woolman is accurate and correct. However, in *most* children, this normal language learning process occurs almost automatically and spontaneously and when it does not, one has to search for deeper reasons. One of these reasons for the abnormal or incomplete acquisition of language may be (and sometimes is) a disruption of the learning-theory/operant-conditioning process described by Woolman. As for the other possibilities, Woolman tends to discount them as almost inconsequential. He does not mention that the genetic factors may themselves have built-in motivators (as is so often the case in species-survival innate developmental behavior patterns) which will provide their own rewards. It is very likely that the normal child naturally enjoys babbling even though he may never be rewarded for it. But the main point to be made is that if a built-in skill is either missing or defective for neurological or genetic reasons, the remediator may have to engineer "spare parts" educationally without necessarily bothering with motivation. Some learning disability children already have adequate motivation in the form of both built-in and socially acquired reinforcers.

Even though Woolman overstates the learning theory "case," all who work with children should realize that operant conditioning is a very important aspect of experience learning and, furthermore, that it can be an extremely valuable tool in the hands of an inventive educator such as Hewett (1967a) or Ferster (1967).

D.B. FRY

This author suggests that there are three aspects to the development of speech:
1. The learning of motor skills.
2. The mastery of the cues for recognition.
3. The building up of a store of linguistic knowledge that eventually forms the basis for both the production and reception of speech.

Fry (1966) emphasizes the importance of maternal reinforcement (as does Woolman) but he makes an important point when he stresses the crucial development of the capacity for *listening* in the early years.

The Babbling Stage

While babbling during the first year, the child tends to repeat the same syllables or sounds; in doing so, he is discovering "the possibilities inherent in the phonatory and articulatory muscle system. He is combining larynx action with articular action and using the out-going air stream. He also establishes the important auditory feedback loop linking his own kinesthetic impressions and auditory sensations. "Even in deaf children, "babbling usually develops at about the normal age and continues some time. But at a later stage, when, in the normal child, the auditory feedback would begin to assume some importance, babbling fades in the deaf child because he lacks the external auditory stimulus from an adult as well as the auditory stimulus from his own babbling."

The Development of Articulation

Imitation, says Fry, plays a very important role in articulation and the development of the phonological system. Family pronunciations and dialect attest to this imitative fact.

The child imitates specific sounds toward the end of the babbling stage but, of course, he relies on his earlier babbling experience. He learns intonation and precision of pronunciation and these efforts the mother and family reinforce with praise or action (need-reduction).

In acquiring a particular word, the baby first hears
. . . a group of sounds associated with a given situation; second, he learns to recognize the sounds; third, he makes his own attempt at reproducing the word, at first without associating it with the situation; fourth, he says the word in the situation in order to call forth a response; fifth, he changes his own utterance to make it match a pattern he has heard in order to obtain more certain and more satisfactory responses; sixth, he continues the modification process until the word gains the desired response from all the listeners in all appropriate situations.

Learning can be motor, too, and the muscle systems must have their memory traces which are linked with auditory (unit and sequencing) memory systems. After speech-learning is well established, auditory feedback is less important, as is demonstrated by adults who become deaf but retain a reasonably correct and fluent speech.

The Development of the Phonological System

The above acquisitions are really preparatory stages leading to the development of a full speech communication system.

The order in which phonemes are acquired varies but is determined by the fact that some sounds are "intrinsically more difficult to produce than others," and by a statistical frequency of presentation:

> In the second half of the first year the child begins with syllables containing only one vowel in the region /ae/ to /a/ and by the age of eighteen months he will probably have a vowel system containing perhaps eight to ten vowels including one or two diphthongs. The whole system of about twenty vowels is unlikely to be complete until about the age of three years.

The /m/ of *mamma* and /d/ of *dadda* are the first consonants, then come /p, b, t, n/. The velar sounds /k, g/ and the semivowel /w/ appear a little later. At the other end of the scale are the difficult sounds /r, θ, s, h, f/. The child also has to learn the distribution or sequencing of phonemes and the prohibitions on phonemes not used in English, for example, the sound /ng/ at the beginning of a word.

Acoustic Cues and the Phonemic System

The perception and recognition of specific incoming sounds is bound up with the use of acoustic cues to sort phomemes into various categories. This sorting appears to work on an exclusion principle of selection: e.g., this sound is /p/ not /t/, /p/ not /k/, /p/ not /b/, etc. The phonemic system evokes the cue system and not vice versa. The acoustic cues are apparently founded in the acquired distinctiveness of sounds—sounds which were previously indistinguishable to the child. Fry continues:

> There is not . . . a standard set of acoustic cues or a standard arrangement of cues for arriving at given phonemic solutions. For one thing sensitivity to change in a particular acoustic dimension is found to vary appreciably among individual listeners and this cannot fail to have an effect upon the way in which cues are combined in carrying out phonemic identification.

Fry does not elaborate further on the nature of acoustic cues nor does he give examples, but one gathers that they are identical to the "distinctive features" and other types of features described earlier in this chapter.

R. BROWN AND C. FRASER

Brown and Fraser (1964) have investigated experimentally the acquisition of syntax in very young children, and have adopted many of the techniques and terminology of those linguists such as Chomsky (1957), who have developed such constructs as generative grammar, syntactic structures, transformational structures and rules, all under the generic title of "structural linguistics."

Brown and Fraser review several studies to show that children "do indeed have rules of word construction [morphological rules] and of sentence construction [syntactical rules]." They then state that the rules of grammar are cultural norms and that it is necessary to abstract the generative grammar rules from the actual verbal behavior of children without superimposing preconceived notions of how they should be. Taking thirteen chidren around three years of age, the authors taped much of the children's speech in the natural setting of the home. They comment,

> Of course the child has not induced his grammar from his own sentences but rather from the somewhat more varied and complex sentences heard from adult speakers. A comparison of the recorded speech of mother-to-child with the speech of child-to-mother shows that the grammars induced by children from adult speech are not identical with the adult grammars that produced the sentences.

The investigators wished to discover the syntactic classes and the rules of sequential combinations of those class members.

The authors present many tables analyzing the one-, two- and three-word utterances of the children, of which the following (Table 6 in their article) is an example.

GRAMMARS SUGGESTED BY THREE-WORD UTTERANCES

(a) Eve's Grammar with the Articles Separated Out
Utterance— $(C_1) + (C_3) + C_2$
C_1— Daddy, Mommy, 's, See, That, There, Two
C_2— bear, bird, block, boat, etc.
C_3— a, the
(b) Eve's Grammar Allowing for Possessives
Utterance— $(C_1) + (C_3) + C_2$
C_1— 's, See, That, There, Two
C_2— bear, bird, block, boat, etc.
C_3— a, the, plus human terms

Note: ( ) means that selection of the enclosed is optional.

At this point they state, "The job of a grammar, however, is to predict sentences that are possible while *not predicting sentences that are impossible.*" The authors then note that the utterances of young children are "classifiable as grammatical sentences from which certain morphemes have been omitted." The sentences of Eve are intelligible "as abbreviated or telegraphic versions of familiar constructions. 'Mummy hair' and 'Daddy car' seem only to omit the possessive inflection." The researchers therefore analyzed all of the records in terms of adult simple sentences by assigning each utterance sentence to the sentence type it most closely approximated.

Having stated that an age-related increase in the length of utterance has been established (McCarthy, 1954), the investigators conclude that children all "reduce" English sentences in a similar fashion; they do not hit on different ways of achieving this telegraphic speech. "Omissions do not appear to be random or idiosyncratic. On the contrary, it looks as if across children and across sentences there is a consistent tendency to retain one kind of morpheme and drop another kind." Retained are final-position-in-sentence morphemes, reference-making forms and "[those] that belong to the large and expandable noun, verb, and adjective parts-of-speech."

Brown and Fraser state that it seems safe to say that children do not learn their telegraphic English from adults and they suggest that the basic cause is "an upper limit on some kind of immediate memory span for the situation in which the child is imitating and a similar limit of programming span for the situation in which the child is constructing sentences." The authors quote the digit-span scores of young children on the Stanford-Binet Intelligence Test (two digits at thirty months, three at thirty-six months and four at fifty-four months). However, memory span does not account for morpheme selection and the authors speculate on various possible reasons for that selection.

It is important not to lose sight of nonlinguistic behavior in connection with the development of linguistic patterns. Miller and Ervin (1964) suggest that some children choose "operator words" on the basis of their own action. One little girl used, *on* and *off* because she was always busy taking things off and putting them back on. Time is also important in that "sequential orders may arise either because one skill is dependent on the prior acquisition of another, because one is less often practiced, or because they differ in difficulty though are practiced equally."

Chomsky (1964) comments that small children may be able to understand quite complex sentences but may be unable to encode them except in a telegraphic style.

IMITATION

The child who is born with his sensory equipment intact is not in a *tabula rasa* state .neurologically, psychologically or sensorially. He has built into his brain a considerable number of automatic developmental programs inherited through the genetic code and, like any computer-organized extremely complex building operation, every aspect is phased so that it will become activated at its precise moment of necessity. The phased building of a great ocean liner by computer is a vastly simple operation alongside the "computerized" developmental processes within the human infant, child and adult.

It would appear from recent work on human vision (Pines, 1967; Bower, 1966) that contrary to most previous theories, human infants can see fairly accurately within a few days of their birth, and there seems every reason to believe that they can hear accurately over a wide range of frequencies. Motor/kinesthetic control may come much more slowly in some muscles, although shortly after birth the baby has a powerful clinging grip and touch, particularly in the area of the mouth and hands. Evidence for these points comes from the rooting and clinging reflexes observable in neonates.

The normal baby is soon able to hear a wide range of sound cycles per second and to make quite a wide variety of noises with its vocal apparatus. In the brain, the neurological areas of speech and hearing are lavishly interconnected internally (and of course environmentally), the feedback from one's own voice being extremely important to the development of speech. Perhaps the single most important factor in learning language is the repetitive imitation of sounds, first individually and later in sequence. The first noises the child makes are obviously of survival value because they are in the form of cries designed to attract the attention of the mother and impress on her the need for food or other ministrations to the child's comfort. Fairly rapidly, these cries are supplemented by the extremely primitive gurglings and babblings of the social situation which arises as the baby becomes aware of the mother as a source for food, warmth and attention. The importance of this relationship is discussed later in the chapter. Between the sixth and twelfth weeks, one begins to see the first signs of motor imitation; if one sticks out one's tongue, the baby will usually respond in a similar way without reinforcement. It is worth emphasizing that speech development involves motor imitation of the model as well as accurate hearing. The infant, by mimicking a sound, is intuitively discovering how to manipulate his own vocal equipment in the same way as the mother. Strictly speaking, auditory sensing is not imitation; it is the vocal motor output which is the imitation. (Note that the only possible way for any living thing to communicate with or manipulate its environment is through motor functioning. This is true even in the case of chemicial output, which must involve the use of muscles, however minute.)

If the imitation of sounds is primarily the function of the muscles involved with the voice, it can also be asserted that the sensing of speech, though mostly auditory, is in part visual. Most people understand better what another person is saying when looking at his face, because they not only tend to lip-read in a minor way but also to obtain context-supporting cues from the whole facial and gestural expression of the speaker. Of course, this interest in the face of the speaker is also a way of excluding other visual stimuli which might have tended to distract the attention of the listener. Therefore, through imitation the baby in its first few months (using its major senses and vocal-motor apparatus) gradually structures its cries and babblings into elementary forms of speech.

The extent and nature of the role played by imitation in the acquisition and production of speech and language is the subject of much discussion in the literature. Many writers consider imitation to be of key importance but usually leave it as an unexplained phenomenon (Wepman, 1960; Kirk, 1966; Penfield and Roberts, 1959; Brown and Fraser, 1964). Lenneberg (1964), while he concedes that imitation is essential, suggests that its role is less important than other genetic factors. Quite rightly, he regards the whole process of speech acquisition and production to be very complex. He notes that a mother's attempts to imitate the cooing sound of a three-month-old baby were a failure and, therefore, "We must conclude either that sound imitation is a mere fiction or if the infant should indeed strive for imitation, that he is innately equipped to hear similarities between his and his mother's vocalizations where, objectively, there are definite differences." Lenneberg himself emphasizes the importance of innate developmental patterns and I suspect that three months is a little young for a baby to imitate precise adult sounds; it is a great deal to expect the adult vocal apparatus to have the flabby, undifferentiated structure and quality of a baby's. Surely the imitative process itself is a developmental differentiating one rising to a peak between two and four years of age. Figure 8 illustrates the dynamics of the process.

This in no way denies that other developmental processes are not equally important or even more so. In fact, a table presented by Lenneberg (1964), "Relationship of the Capacity for Making Speech Sounds to Understanding Instructions as Illustrated by Children with Various Handicaps," suggests that "understanding is more significant for language development than the capacity for making speech sounds." With this evidence and conclusion I agree, even to the extent of saying that language subserves thought and thought structures language. This is quite compatible with the equally valid statements (a) that much language structuring and its development is innately determined; (b) that imitation or, if preferred, modeling behavior, is essential to speech production and, since imitation must include speech perception, expressive mutes can acquire receptive language, and (c) that language as a communicative skill, although it subserves thought, is not thought but a highly sophisticated, automatic, very flexible tool

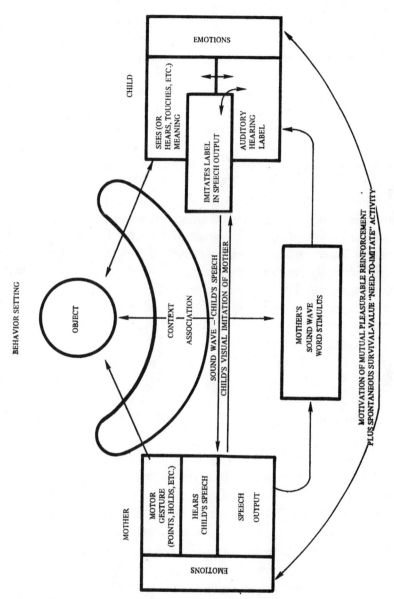

FIGURE 8. Interaction process during speech imitation.

of thought once the innate program is content-coded through imitation for local conventions. This complex developmental interaction of thought (understanding), specific innate patterning, imitation, automatic coding and decoding skills and convention demonstrates the need in the nonphysical sciences for fewer "either/or" discussions and more "How much of each and how are the components integrated?" studies. Imitation in some form is obviously essential to the acquisition of a *specific* language in all its conventional aspects. Each person in a community grows up to speak the language of the locality with its accents, idioms and inadequacies.

Some learning theorists such as Jenkins and Palermo (1964) conclude that language is all learned, claiming that psychologists have avoided explaining grammar and syntax in terms of conditioning. They outline three relevant learning paradigms which might facilitate language development, all of which involve mediation processes. The first paradigm is *stimulus-response chaining,* the second is *response equivalence* and the third is *acquired stimulus equivalence,* such as occurs in concept formation learning. Although there is not space here to present their case in detail, a few points can be made. It seems to me that all stimulus-response conditioning procedures, whether mediational or not, whether classical or operant, never take into account the power of the human mind to *think* and *in the process of thinking to manipulate the contents (concepts) of cognition internally prior to a possible manipulation of their objective equivalents in a similar way externally.* Jenkins and Palermo appear at first to have due regard for "the notion of reference" (to meaning). However they go on to say, "As the speaker becomes more and more practiced in the language, the precise semantic content may be supposed to recede in importance, and the (by this time) well-learned structural properties take over virtually unconscious control of the structure of utterances." Kagan (1964) commenting on their stimulus-response theoretical position, points out in detail that almost none of the factual evidence supports the theory. He goes on to say:

The child's early sentences are imitations of those parts of the adult utterances that are semantically meaningful and perceptually salient. Perceptual salience, I suggest, is based primarily on inflection and loudness and secondarily upon sequential position. The next step in this process may be the matching of utterances to the adult model through discrimination and differentiation and utilization of different sentence frames depending on the function of communication. The fact that the sentences of the five year old are relatively accurate may arise initially from an intimate interaction between similarities in meaning and inflection and only later from similarities in word sequence. This suggestion would agree with the data presented by Brown and Fraser.

The arguments against imitation in language development particularly in the area of syntax all assume that the child is being portrayed by those stressing direct imitation as, first, a parrot (language acquisition), and then as a mindless talking machine, the response depending on which stimulus button is pressed, and the strength of the response being proportional to operant (reward) reinforcement. But even a small child has inner survival-value needs and can utilize thought to manipulate the environment to attain those needs. The one-year-old child who says, "Mommy, drinkie" is reutilizing two imitated words in a logical, possibly original first-time request, with the emphasis, as Kagan and Brown and others suggest, on perceptually salient dimensions. Syntax, therefore, though it is imitated to a minor degree, is, I suspect, primarily and necessarily the result of associating word-labels to objects and their internally manipulated (thought) relationships, including one's own person. The word-labels themselves and their morphological inflections as familiar forms are mostly and primarily imitated. All the object-label or concept-label or inflection/morpheme/allomorph associations are learned extremely rapidly and soon become automatic in operation simply because the brain's memory system is innately *built* that way for survival through auditory/vocal communication.

During conversations with my daughter Kate from the age of one year to three years, I have many times noticed how more often than not she will learn (imitate and indelibly memorize) the pronunciation of a word or sentence she hears in *one trial*. Her auditory perception of language and vocal output in terms of key operation *words* (using telegraphic speech) has many qualities in common with a tape recorder. Moreover, once a key word is instantly memorized it is quite difficult to alter or modify it during normal conversation. It is as if the auditory/motor word memory system resists change, and it would seem that the older one gets the more resistance builds up. If the original mishearing and subsequent mispronunciation of a word (or sequence of words) is also the correct pronunciation of another word, it is difficult to eradicate. Kate said "another one" for "the other one" for many weeks because for her these phrases had (in semantic value) response and concept equivalence, even though the adult input stimuli were correctly presented throughout that period. Everyday single-word mispronunciations were more easily corrected by direct imitative teaching procedures using clear enunciation and visual cues. The latter procedure utilizes the word as a series of sounds which have an objectivity in their own right independently of their sign-meaning.

There are two aspects of this first early period of vocal imitation and it is necessary to separate them out rather artificially and examine each in turn. However, in life they are interlaced within one linguistic gestalt. The first aspect, which has been examined throughout this chapter, is the growth of language itself and the child's use of it as a cognitive function. The second is the emotional and feeling context which determines the child's attitudes to the language it is learning.

SELECTIVITY, REINFORCEMENT AND ENDOWMENT

By listening to the mother, by watching her facial movements, by repeatedly experimenting and by the natural growth of muscular control, the infant adds more and more sounds and even very simple meaningful words to his "vocabulary." Because language is to some extent a convention, each language and to a lesser extent each dialect has its own preferred sounds together with a preferred frequency of sound usage; in his first year or two, the child has these sounds emphasized and reinforced by constant vocal interchange with the mother. While these sounds are being encouraged to form a permanent foundation for future speech, other sounds are being screened out of the child's repertoire simply because the mother does not use them. Some African languages make considerable use of clicks, which are culturally reinforced in infancy. The English language makes almost no use of clicks and consequently English-speaking children who in babyhood quite frequently and spontaneously develop clicks soon forget them. Nevertheless English, being a blend of several quite diverse languages, has a wide diversity of phonetic elements, and indeed it is just this diversity of sound which when superimposed on a relatively inadequate phonetic Latin alphabet subsequently causes many children to have reading disabilities.

However, it is not only single sounds and simple blendings of sounds which are of fundamental importance to the learning of a language in infancy. The conventional sequencing of the phonemes is equally important and the child must learn this from the mother and family. Memorization and production of sequences of sounds are obviously necessary to the formation of words and sentences. For most children this is an almost automatic process which is innately predetermined and hence a speaking vocabulary is acquired with relative ease, although any natural or artificial flaw in the child's total language situation, be it innate or acquired, can hinder development and result in a language disability of some kind.

Probably some two-thirds of intact intelligent children will learn their native language adequately, even when there are minor environmental barriers to their doing so, because they are naturally well endowed with an accurate auditory discrimination, excellent neurological feedback, a strong desire and capacity to imitate, an efficient auditory memory and an even more efficient intersensory/motor integration system. In short, if they have a good neuropsychological verbal ability this will override minor linguistic inadequacies in terms of training and environment, while children who are less well endowed may have their problems aggravated by minor environmental shortcomings. Thus, a well-endowed child growing up in a rich linguistic environment will be highly successful verbally; a well-endowed child in a poor linguistic environment will usually make the grade. A poorly endowed child in a rich environment also often makes the grade and it is useful to realize this, particularly when the outcome may be in fine balance.

NATURAL REINFORCING RELATIONSHIPS

There is not much doubt that the first object to be "understood" by the baby is the mother's body, particularly her arms and breast and the sensation of swallowing warm milk. It is probably a very few weeks later that the sounds the child hears at various times becomes associated with the mother's body, namely her voice cooing, clucking and talking to the baby.

Ambrose (1960) and others have demonstrated the importance of the smiling reflex in the first months of the baby's life. It comes into play at about six to eight weeks and helps to reinforce the instinctual bond of attachment between mother and child which is common to all mammals. The smiling response causes pleasurable feelings (which *are* the attachment) and these in turn become associated with the sounds the mother directs toward her infant.

Thus the emotional side is extremely important inasmuch as it activates pleasant feelings in the child. If this pleasurable mutual relationship is firmly associated with the voice of the mother and the gurgles of the baby, the solid positive beginnings of a foundation for later linguistic communication will have been laid.

Over the first six months the baby will naturally tend to gurgle and make spontaneous noises which the smiles and clucking of the mother continually reinforce. Therefore, by six months the infant will have a fair range of noises well related to the mother on two counts—food and attachment. However, if the mother is negative in her relationship with the child, then language will be associated with those negative feelings (see Chapter V).

From four to six months onward, the child will begin vaguely to imitate sounds in general, but for some time, while the multiplicity of acquired sounds grows, few are extinguished. It should be noted that none of these sounds during the very early weeks is associated with a particular environmental object, visually speaking. The baby soon "realizes" that this making of noises is fully appreciated by the bountiful, smiling "object" in his environment, so he continues to produce even more. Probably dimly at first, at about six months, the infant becomes aware that this person may make one particular noise; the mother does this partly in imitation of the baby and the baby partly in imitation of the mother. In both cases the noise, which is usually the word *mama*, will be one of the simplest for the developing vocal organs to make. An *m* requires just a simple opening of the lips and the long *a* can be achieved by vocalizing through a relaxed open mouth.

Gradually, throughout the following year or two, the child *hears* more and more sounds and sound combinations, some of which, being continually reinforced and associated with everyday objects, become auditory symbols for those objects.

The imitative behavioral response, which is also separately reinforced, is essentially a vocal one. Therefore, it is in order to speak of an auditorially recognized vocabulary and an imitative speaking vocabulary, the latter developing at a much slower rate. In all cases the sounds, whether heard or said, can only have an associative meaning in terms of perceived objects or states, whether external or internal. Therefore, to speak meaningfully, a child must first perceive an object as an entity separate from the other objects in the environment; second, he must associate the sequences of heard sounds with that object, and third, he must learn to associate by imitative experimentation the vocal techniques for reproducing that sound. These steps are set out in more detail in the following list of the developmental cycling processes in language acquisition:

1. Object/concept recognition (nonverbal meaning).
2. Phoneme analysis and synthesis—receptive.
3. Speech perception of words as sequences of sounds.
4. Articulemic analysis and synthesis.
5. Speech production of words as sequences of sounds.
6. Appreciation of object relationships and self.

7. Sentence planning and syntax as a manipulative modeling (thought) process.

8. Meaningful conversational communication.

Note that speech perception, meaning and speech production cycle through the above steps continuously as language develops. The "conversations" may be single-word (*mama*) interchanges initially but they gradually move through telegraphic speech to become more mature linguistic forms. It should also be noted that an infant's thought is mainly concerned with objects and personal needs and not with the more subtle relationships represented in adult speech. These adult subtleties are usually expressed by all those words and phrases *not* used by infants in telegraphic speech. The thoughts are not there, so to speak; therefore, the words are not necessary.

LINGUISTIC PLANNING AND SENTENCE GENERATION

As a follow-up to the assertion that syntax is primarily dependent on thought and meaning processes (although some imitation and built-in sequencing attributes of the brain also contribute), some discussion is necessary on the possible ways in which the brain plans the syntax of utterances.

In their book, *Plans and the Structure of Behavior*, G.A. Miller *et al.* (1960) discuss plans for speaking. They consider the possibility that

> . . . the next word in our utterance will depend upon only the words that have led up to it, but not upon any plan for the words that may follow it. A nonanticipatory grammar would be exceedingly simple and since the mathematics of those systems has been carefully studied under the general topic of "Markov Processes," we would immediately know a great deal about the level of complexity of the sentence generator itself.

By demonstrating the astronomical amount of (operant) learning the child would need, to generate all those original sentences he speaks, the authors dispose of the Markavian model. As a further criticism (within left-to-right grammars) they note the process of embedding sentences within sentences. One could go further and note that almost every sentence uttered in normal conversation other than automatic questions or greetings is an original sentence, which in all likelihood the speaker has never uttered before. Most sentences in most books fall into that category. Nevertheless, it is fairly obvious that grammar exists and, furthermore, that although the actual words and concepts may vary infinitely, the vast majority of our utterances have syntactical structural characteristics in common. At this point the authors embark on a discussion of Chomsky's "structural linguistics." At the end of the discussion they say,

> The general picture of sentence generators that emerges from this analysis, therefore, is that we have a rather simple system for generating sentences like, "A boy hit a stick" (Chomsky calls these "kernel strings"). On top of that we have a system of transformations that operate upon the kernel strings to combine them or permute them, etc., into the endless variety of grammatical sentences. With such a theory it should be possible to do a fairly good job of speaking English grammatically with less than 100 rules of formation, less than 100 transformations, and perhaps 100,000 rules for vocabulary and pronunciation. Even a child should be able to master that much after 10 or 15 years of constant practice.

Miller *et al.* do not stop at this point, because they say that there is a great deal about sentence generation left unexplained by the structural linguistics theory of grammar.

There are several quotes of quotes which I would like to make from the above-mentioned book. The first is from William James and is quoted by Miller *et al.* on page 145: "One may admit that a good third of our psychic life consists in these rapid premonitory views of schemes of thought not yet articulate." The authors says, "James is describing a state of consciousness associated with an intention to execute a plan. The plan of the sentence, it seems, must be determined in a general way even before it is differentiated into the particular words that we are going to utter." Later the authors quote Karl Lashley; what follows is a part of Lashley's statement: "Analysis of the nervous mechanisms underlying order in the more primitive acts may contribute ultimately to the solution of even the physiology of logic." They then go on to discuss the "Whorfian hypothesis" advanced by Benjamin Whorf, who wrote, "The forms of a person's thoughts are controlled by inexorable laws of pattern of which he is unconscious. These patterns are the unperceived intricate systematizations of his own language—shown readily enough by a candid comparison and contrast with upper languages, especially those of a different linguistic family." Miller *et al.* comment on Whorf's theory in their statement: "But to say that the formal structure of the laws of grammar is similar to the structure of the laws of thought is very different from saying that the laws of grammar are the laws of thought, and that your thought must remain forever shackled to the conjugations and declensions of your native tongue." Once again relational thinking is regarded as separate from language, at least in some of its aspects.

It does not in any way deny the relative importance of structural linguistics, mediational learning theory, operant conditioning or biological, inherited, developmental and structural patterns to say that all of these subserve the processes of thought. It seems to me that language is merely a labeling system which subserves the communcation of thoughts internally or externally and that many of the complexities (particularly syntactical ones) that we attribute to something called *language* are in reality a reflection of the immense complexity of the cognitive *thinking* processes. Every "nonlabel" characteristic which can be attributed to language can equally well be attributed to thinking, and thinking, as has been said previously, is a dynamic internal modeling process for manipulating the images and concepts of objects and their interrelationships, and the suspected actual relationships of these objects in the external environment. In this context the word *object* includes everything external to the conscious mind of the thinker including his body, brain and unconscious mind. Thought integrates information in extremely complex ways and there is no reason why the integrational syntactical models for explaining utterances suggested by Osgood (1963), by Jenkins and Palermo (1964) and, in the area of structural linguistics, by Chomsky (1957) should not be applied equally well to the generation and formulation of thought processes. One only has to substitute the nonverbal images, concepts and relationship concepts, etc., for the word-labels used in facilitating the communication of those thoughts to turn the study of language, at least on the universal level, into a study of cognitive thinking processes. Some support for such a position is suggested by Goldman-Eisler (1964). Her research studies measured the fluency of speech in a variety of experimental situations in which the main variable was the originality or triteness of the concept/content of the speech. She presented the stimulus/content information in the form of nonverbal cartoons which the subject described, and found that the more unusual or original the stimulus material the more difficulty the subject had in formulating his descriptive speech, which was hesitant and slow. However, more commonplace material generated a much more fluent flow of speech. Goldman-Eisler concluded that one must add semantic and grammatical determinants to speech production along with the accepted sequential statistical probabilistic ones.

Goldman-Eisler's work, taken overall, tends to indicate that verbal activity is heavily dependent on thought construction. Why then have those who study language tended to relegate thought and meaning processes to a position of less importance in their studies? The answer is that *one* of the ways in which we communicate our thoughts is through language and it is easier to assume that the observable behavior, namely speech or its written equivalent, *is* the total phenomenon being investigated. It is interesting that Bertrand Russell studied formal thought processes in the form of symbolic logic, partly using language as a source of data. He assumed that language was a communicative vehicle for thought.

Original thought produces original sentences and any structure the sentences have is the communicative equivalent of the underlying structure of the thoughts which the word-labels in sequence represent. Thinking which is meaningful must be structured and organized in accordance with certain principles just as are all phenomena in science. What Chomsky (1957) and his followers have done is to set down the principles along which thought works *as it is represented in language.* And unfortunately we cannot communicate our thoughts about thoughts and language except through language. However, we can study other forms of communicated thinking as found in moving silent film, the solving of geometrical problems and so on. There is a rich field for comparative investigation and one result would probably be to discover how inadequate traditional linear language is for the communication of continuous integrated thinking.

Yet another psycholinguist and psychologist who has come to the conclusion that language is something which is qualitatively different from thought is Lenneberg (1967). He says,

> There is evidence that cognitive function is a more basic and primary process than language, and that the dependence-relationship of language upon cognition is incomparably stronger than vice verse. The cognitive function underlying language consists of an adaption of a ubiquitous process (among vertebrates) of categorization and extraction of similarities. . . . Words label categorization processes.

At this point I would refer the reader back to Table VII, which elaborates my own detailed view on how thought and language are associationally interrelated on various levels of cognition.

Chapter V

PRIMARY EMOTIONAL COMMUNICATIVE DYSLEXIA

INTRODUCTION

Throughout the previous chapters, two aspects of language development have been stressed. One is the inherited psychophysiological equipment and innate potential capacities, while the other is the environmentally (psychologically and culturally) determined conventional and arbitrary characteristics of speech and writing listed in Chapter III. Although it seems almost too obvious to state that hereditary developmental processes and environmental influences dynamically interact to produce continuously developing behavioral skills and abilities, it is surprising how many psychologists and other social scientists ignore or brush aside the biological genetic foundations of behavior. Therefore, before embarking on a clinical description of primary emotional communicative dyslexia, a brief summary of recent trends in the genetic bases of behavior is necessary.

THE ETHOLOGISTS AND BEHAVIOR

Over the last decade or two, men like Lorenz (1963, 1965), Thorpe (1963), Harlow (1963), Tinbergen (1951) and Bowlby (1957) (the first four working with animals) have observed, described and experimented with species-specific innate patterns of behavior which "mature" at various crucial periods during an animal's life to enable it (or them in a relationship situation) to adapt appropriately in the *relevant* and immediate ecology or environment, the final cause being survival of both individual and species. For example, immediately after birth, ducklings will attach to the first moving object in the environment and follow it around, presumably for safety, food and training, since the first moving object they see is *usually* their mother. However, if another moving object gets in the way first, the duckling will attach to it and follow it, be it a man or a football (Lorenz, 1952). The process of fixation on the relevant object in any of these patterns is termed *imprinting*. Since nature is only interested in the survival of the species, those individuals who, *because of unusual, inapposite, irrelevant or even bizarre environmental circumstances (ecological niches) not of their own deliberate making, are not imprinted in the usual survival-value way* would tend to act in an abnormal way or even die off; these events tend to increase the strength of the species-specific behavioral pattern, which in the above case is mother/infant attachment. Geese which imprint their attachment behavior on men later exhibit sexually to humans and thus do not reproduce. Many of these species-specific behavior patterns are difficult to eradicate by training or conditioning (Harlow and Kvenne, 1962; Breland and Breland, 1961) once imprinting is satisfactorily established in the appropriate environment, *viz.*, the environment the pattern evolved through adaptively for the purposes of survival in the first place. This template-like matching of an innate behavior pattern with its relevant environment in the interest of preservation also occurs in humans. And, as with animals, when the appropriately keyed environment is absent, distorted, actively hostile, blurred, bizarre or otherwise ill-fitting, *maladaptive* behavior results. Personally, I consider that many human emotional disturbances (especially conduct disorders) are caused by inappropriate environmental interference with species-specific developmental behavior patterns. Bowlby (1957), Foss (1961, 1963), Ambrose (1961) and others have published in this field of psychology.

An example of species-specific communication imprinting which may sometimes be partially modified by environmental isolation is recounted by Thorpe (1963). In a research into the acquisition of song melodies by chaffinches he found that if hand-reared chaffinches (isolated from older chaffinches) were (a) put in with other species of birds, (b) exposed to artificial sounds or (c) exposed to the sounds of other species of birds on the tape recorder, they would retain a largely innate appreciation of the tonal vocalizations of their own species and limit their imitativeness to chaffinch-like models. Even baby chaffinches isolated from all sound developed a basic song pattern in some respects like the usual one, and presumably this is innate. Two or three chaffinches raised together in isolation tend to produce an entirely individual but uniform song pattern; some of these patterns are quite unlike anything recorded in the wild. However, says Thorpe, once a song has been acquired and sung for a few days, it becomes fixed and subsequent changes are minimal, since there is a very generalized inborn basis to the songs.

The above account of chaffinch song has remarkable parallels with the effects of distorting environments or inapposite ecological niches on the characteristics of human language. As will be seen, isolated chaffinches are like children with disinterested mothers, and some twins may be akin to chaffinches reared together in isolation.

HUMAN LANGUAGE DEVELOPMENT AS A SPECIES-SPECIFIC BEHAVIOR PATTERN

Lenneberg (1967) has already gone on record as saying,

Generally, there is evidence that species-specific motor coordination patterns emerge according to a maturational schedule in every individual raised in an adequate environment. The emergence of such patterns is independent of training procedures and extrinsic response shaping. Once the animal has matured to the point at which these patterns are present, the actual occurrence of a specific pattern movement may depend upon external or internal stimuli (for instance, certain hormone levels in the blood) or a combination of the two.

Later Lenneberg adds, "There are certain indications for the existence of a peculiar language-specific maturational schedule," and "Language is a manifestation of species-specific cognitive propensities." It is not practical here to give further details of Lenneberg's theory, which he sets out more completely in Chapter IX of his book.

On the evidence Lenneberg presents for the inheritance of

language potentials, from our increasing knowledge of ethological principles (Lorenz, 1965) and our knowledge of how the brain is programmed for language (Luria, 1966), it is safe to assume that language development, acquisition and production are collectively (except for cultural content) a human species-specific innate (original efficient cause) behavior pattern (formal cause) and, furthermore, that if this development pattern finds itself, so to speak, within an incompatible environment or ecological niche (a second efficient cause), *the innate program will be distorted* (material cause), with the result that the individual concerned will be linguistically handicapped in some way. Thus, the individual will be maladapted for social communication and the survival value it holds for the species (final cause).

The fact that children have a fairly well-developed and rounded speech perception and production system in full operation by the age of three-and-a-half years (Brown and Fraser, 1964) suggests that the period of critical language development and its imitative imprinting is from birth to four years of age, with a peak somewhere between one and three years depending on the verbal ability inherited by the child. The term *peak* may be slightly misleading because in all probability the interactional language of both mother and child is best maximized throughout the period. However, it is the child's language development which may be at its most vulnerable during his second and third years of life. The developmental processes by which a child may acquire language in a normal way in his mother's (and others') presence have been fully discussed in the previous chapter. It is now necessary to consider some of the various abnormal environmental or ecological circumstances which may interfere with the normal acquisition of that species-specific function of humans called language.

COMMUNICATIVE DYSLEXIA: ENVIRONMENTALLY DISTORTED LINGUISTIC DEVELOPMENTAL PATTERNS

The environment within which the child learns his native language is obviously that of the home; in the very early months and years, the mother will be the main influence in terms of language. She, and possibly other members of the family, have the potential to supply all the environmental language stimulation necessary for the child to progress normally through the developmental patterns described in Chapter IV. The mother and family also are in the converse situation of being able to *deprive* the infant of the amount of linguistic stimulation necessary for normal language growth. They can spoil the ecological, verbal learning niche. In my work with dyslexic children, I have identified cases in which the etiology seemed to lie in the mother-child relationship and the mother's *distortion* of their mutual linguistic communication. Therefore, the grouping of this particular syndrome is most easily categorized in terms of the type of mother who originates the problem. Three types of mothers can be listed as follows: (a) the disinterested mother, (b) the depressed mother and (c) the angry mother. Each of these will be presented in turn, and then still other types of this form of dyslexia will be discussed.

DISINTERESTED MOTHERS

The disinterested mother tends to leave her infant alone to play by himself or possibly with other infant children because she is too preoccupied with her own personal activities. Usually, the child has to be in a situation where he cannot clearly hear adult conversation, because if he could, he would learn many phonemes and other language conventions in a relatively normal, if limited way. In some cases, the infant may be left in the care of a nanny or childminder who does not speak the child's native language. Children whose parents' work requires them to move frequently from one country to another are sometimes at risk in this way. A few career women may also neglect their children from the linguistic point of view. Even the suburban housewife who leaves her infant child alone in the playroom, in a playpen or in a baby carriage in the garden for hours on end may cause verbal damage, particularly if she also does not speak much at other times. Some schizoid mothers may fall into this category. When these children later go to school to learn to read, they may have great difficulty because they do not possess a sufficient foundation of basic language on which to build the more complex task of symbolic decoding and encoding, that is, reading, writing and spelling (see the section on H.R. Myklebust in Chapter IV). These children are not necessarily emotionally neglected in terms of affection, although quite often the two problems of emotional disturbance and communicative disorders occur *independently* in the same child (in the context of this chapter). Many of the characteristics exhibited by the children of disinterested mothers are also exhibited by the children of depressed mothers and vice versa. Therefore, what is said about one group of children (not mothers) sometimes applies to the other.

DEPRESSED MOTHERS

The problem with the depressed mother is rather self-explanatory. It should be made clear at the outset that the term *depressed* does not necessarily mean neurotic depression, although, of course, women with pathological depressive states may form a subgroup within this group. Many mothers may be depressed over a considerable period of time as a result of real situations such as the death of a parent or other children, or some other calamity such as financial failure or divorce. Simply because of the psychological nature of depression, they do not care to carry on long animated conversations with others, frequently not even with their own children. If a depressed mother has a baby or infant passing through the critical phase of language development and she does not talk to him very much, the child cannot learn to discriminate phonemes, their sequences, the contexts in which they are used or the emotional or objective situations to which they semantically refer. Note that for these children, the environmental learning process on which the acquisition of language depends in part is inadequate not only from the verbal content aspect but also from the reinforcement (reward) point of view. Normally, linguistic imitations are reinforced by repetitive stimuli, in conjunction with emotional rewards such as smiles, laughter, affection, praise and those other pleasurable and mutual feelings which encourage the child to *want* to remember and repeat the words he hears. These qualities are equally absent when the mother is depressed, disinterested or absent, even though the overall personality development of the children may eventually be quite dissimilar.

John was a ten-year-old boy whose mother had been very depressed throughout his first years of life because of a series of deaths in the family. A few days before John was born, the eldest son was killed in a street accident in front of the mother's eyes. When John was a year old, the mother's father, of whom she was very fond, suddenly died. After another eighteen months, when the boy was about two-and-a-half years old, an uncle of whom the mother was very fond also died. Her son John thus grew up to be a rather serious, very quiet child who, although quite emotionally stable (he received a reasonable amount of direct affection, kindness and sensible training) had never really learned to understand what language was all about apart from a rather rudimentary use of telegraphic communication. It was not that he could not speak or understand; he had a *poverty* of verbal communication which derived from his many years as an infant in a serious and semi-silent home. Although of average spatial intelligence, by the age of nine he was still unable to read. He preferred to do things for himself rather than to ask or converse about his needs. In his quiet, rather serious personal relationships with other children, his teachers and his family, he was relatively normal and personality testing revealed little of a neurotic nature. It is probable that to a slight degree, John also suffered from genetic dyslexia (described in Chapter IX). Despite this, it is likely that he would have been behind his peers in language skills even if he had been well endowed with verbal ability. His speech, though understandable, was imprecise and he found it rather difficult to decode quickly normal conversation; this was shown by his frequent demands for statements to be repeated.

Although there are few positive reinforcing attitudes to language in the children of disinterested or depressed mothers, there are also very few negative ones. The situation is neutral and therefore, in both cases, the outlook is quite hopeful, especially if an intensive speech training, listening and linguistics/phonics reading program is put into operation.

ANGRY MOTHERS

The children of angry mothers have much more to cope with. The difficulty is not so much a lack of communication between mother and child as the negative relationship feelings of fear and aggression which become contingently associated with verbal communication, although in some cases, poverty of communication may also be an aggravating factor. The mother who attacks her child with angry words and who may possibly accompany them with slaps causes the child to associate indelibly verbal communication with an internal sense of fear of, and perhaps reactive anger against, parental authority. Although there are many psychoanalytical undertones to this situation, it is quite possible to look on it as a simple conditioning process. Angry words from a powerful person arouse fear, and if these are part of a training program for any animal or human being, there is a tendency for the trainee to run away from the attacking behavior associated with it. If the child is able to react aggressively to the situation or actively to run away, not only will language development be affected but also conduct disorders may develop. However, if the child has a timid nature, the result in school will be an inability to face, accept and absorb verbal material. The more outwardly conforming the child appears, the more flight will take the form of a "blank wall" inability to concentrate, to pay attention or quite simply to understand what language, in its slightly more sophisticated forms, is all about. A fairly high standard of linguistic ability is demanded from quite young schoolchildren as is evidenced by the scholastic failure of many socially disadvantaged children (see Chapter XII).

Derek had had quite a stormy upbringing by a mother who was always angry with her children. He learned to speak quite satisfactorily although his vocabulary and quality of expression were rather limited and somewhat negative. Derek, even at the age of ten, was unable to bring himself to look at a printed page and it is quite possible that some of his teachers had reacted to his disability in a frustrated way which only served to reinforce his anxiety. During the six months it took Derek to *begin* to learn, I had to reassure him constantly, by word and action, that I was "safe" and would not attack him—a kind of informal desensitization. He also saw me helping other children learn to read in a friendly cooperative way. After months of refusals, he announced one day that he was going to learn to read and in the ensuing six weeks, did so, at least to a level at which he could read several books by himself. Obviously, some of the reading tuition he had received in four years of school had stuck. However, it took a few more months for him to value the printed word for the direct satisfaction it gave him rather than as a means of pleasing me.

This case history demonstrates the three "emotional" phases of language learning. The first, a spontaneous communicative interaction, is carried through in an atmosphere of affection and praise which, in Derek's case, had never really been fulfilled and hence had to be "built"—a phase whose first beginnings normally are observable a few weeks after birth. In the second phase, during skill-building learning in speaking or reading, there is now a built-in reinforced need to please the parent or teacher to obtain affection, praise and other rewards. This relationship must obviously be predominantly positive and constructive in nature. The third phase is when the child no longer requires direct affection and rewards from the adult; he can get an almost equally direct satisfaction from the *content* of the written word. The child learns to read for the sake of the entertainment or knowledge he gains directly from the book, which means, psychologically speaking, that the author has taken over some of the aura of a parent figure. This third phase takes place when some skill competence has been established, that is, automatization of speaking (in infancy) or reading (in school) has been effected.

TWINS

Another group of children who are somewhat at risk in their acquisition of language are twins who may be left by the mother to entertain each other both directly and conversationally. Occasionally, they may even develop their own private version of the language which later only slowly yields to standard English. As with other communicative dyslexic children, the condition need only be aggravated by a parallel dyslexic symptom of another type for the handicap to become scholastically serious.

Day (1932) has reviewed the early literature on the development of language in twins as well as conducting her own survey on eighty pairs of twins, five years of age and under. She presents detailed conclusions which need not be reported here, her general conclusion being that ". . . the evidence is clear that during the pre-school years, twins progress toward adult use of language at a relatively slow rate." This language retardation increases with age within the age period covered.

INSTITUTIONALIZED CHILDREN

Some children are still reared in those old-fashioned custodial institutions called orphanages which group together large numbers of infants in stimuli-less surroundings. Some of these children, by two or three years of age, have acquired a kind of "environmental autism" with its symptoms of withdrawal, inhibited language, rocking and other stereotyped behaviors. Even though these characteristics may be mild in many children, the overall level of language development can still be insufficient for later academic study. The more progressive countries no longer have these types of institutions, but isolated cases occur. Poor foster homes may contribute to a linguistic handicap if the child is insufficiently stimulated for any of the reasons described here. Kellmer Pringle (1965), in comparing the language and speech development of preschool children, found those living at home and in nursery schools in advance of the group in residential care nurseries.

TERMINOLOGY

The rather lengthy term *primary emotional communicative dyslexia* was chosen for this chapter for the following reasons. The word *primary* signifies that the causes (of whichever kind) etiologically act directly on the language development process itself without mediators. Therefore, *communicative dyslexia* (a convenient abbreviation) is not the secondary result of *some other state in the child* as, for example, occurs when a reading disability results from severe emotional disturbance (see Chapter XIII). The term *emotional* indicates that the efficient cause of the dyslexia is usually to be found in the mother's emotional state or, from a broader point of view, in the child's attitudinal environment. This does *not* imply that the child is emotionally disturbed. The third word in the title, *communicative,* describes the relationship area in which the disturbance or distortion occurs. These facets of the problem may not result in gross distortion of the child's ability to speak and hear in the early years, but the distortion may be sufficient to cause a critical failure when higher, more intricate language learning is demanded, e.g., reading.

REMEDIATION

Most of these communicative dyslexic children require a language development program. The teacher can formulate such a course from the information presented in previous chapters. Certainly, the lessons should encourage (a) spontaneous clear vocalization, (b) accurate listening, (c) training in all the conventions of language, (d) linguistic sequencing in conventional sentence transformations and grammar (Lefevre, 1964), (e) phoneme discrimination and articulation, (f) phoneme/grapheme matching and (g) copious amounts of conversation. Further details of these and other techniques will be found in Chapter XV.

CONCLUDING REMARKS

The classification of the types of dyslexia in Table II (page 18) should be referred to in order to position communicative dyslexia with respect to the other types. It should be remembered that none of the categories or subcategories of communicative dyslexia (or of any of the other types) are mutually exclusive. The classifications have to do with attributes, symptoms and the like, and not with "whole" children—even though colloquially, one may fall into the convenient habit of referring to one type of child or another. Almost all scientific classifications are, in a sense, hierarchical orderings of attributes into descendingly smaller categories. This has the advantage in the practice of education, psychology and medicine of allowing examination of the whole child as an individual made up of many attributes which separately have meaningful referential systems.

Communicative dyslexia of a "pure" uncompounded kind is, I suspect, fairly rare. In the few cases I have examined, most have been suspected of also having minimal neurological dysfunction, genetic dyslexia or cultural deprivation. Certainly, boys are much more vulnerable to communicative dyslexia than are girls, the reason being the slower linguistic development of boys in infancy (see Chapters II, VII and IX, and Maccoby, 1966). This maturational lag, by lengthening the critical period of language development, would add to the vulnerability of boys with respect to the possible environmental distortion of the innate species-specific acquisition pattern. Since the ability to acquire new language content seems to decrease with age (this has led to the excellent practice of teaching children foreign languages in kindergarten), communicative dyslexic children should be screened out and remediated as young as possible. This screening should take place at least during the first school years and, preferably, long before, a policy which calls for the urgent development of suitable batteries of infant language tests.

A further distinction is necessary; communicative dyslexia is peculiar to particular families and not to a subculture, and there is a clear difference between it and cultural deprivation, even though they may have much in common. Cultural deprivation may produce more of a "motivational" type of dyslexia and this possibility is investigated in Chapter XII.

Prevention of communicative dyslexia would be possible if mothers were made more aware of the need to stimulate their children linguistically during infancy. Newspaper, magazine, radio and television articles and programs could help to spread awareness.

Correction of preschoolers in nursery school programs is also an important development. Levenstein (1970) demonstrated significant improvements in general and verbal IQ's in a controlled study of low-income preschoolers who participated in a seven-month program of home sessions devoted to stimulating verbal interaction in mother-child dyads. In another study, B.B. Gray (1970) showed how programmed conditioning can accelerate the language training of young children. If such experiments come to be part of regular nursery school practice it is a reasonable estimate that reading disability problems of all kinds will decrease rapidly. Auditory/vocal language *is* what children learn to decode in the reading of a phonetic language. *Without that phonetic auditory/vocal language the written or printed code has no decipherable content.*

Wells (1970), in a study concerned with finding out the relationship between selected preschool play activities and achievement in reading, found no significant differences either in the kind of play or the amount of play. Some surprising findings came out of this research on twenty-eight middle-class children. The underachievers had spent significantly more time playing with their parents indoors and even in the case of outdoor play they played more often with their parents. The underachievers spent more time outdoors in winter and the data as a whole suggested that the activities of the underachievers were more adult-centered than were those of the achievers. The achievers averaged 2½ hours a day watching television while the *underachievers* watched for only 1 hour 50 minutes. (This last result confirms other studies in England which found that achievers watch television more than underachievers.)

Wells concluded that factors other than the preschool *play* activities investigated account for level of achievement in reading. It should be noted that the two groups were equated for intelligence and all had IQ's over 100. They were also equated on socioeconomic status, had no physical defects, lived with their natural parents in families of two or more children and came from families with no known severe emotional stress. Although it was not significant, there was a trend for the achievers to participate in artwork, to be read to and to play with puzzles and table games more than the underachievers. Certainly these activities, which *stimulate conversation,* plus television watching call for further research. Genetic differences in verbal functioning should also be investigated in future studies.

Chapter VI

A NEUROPSYCHOLOGICAL SYNTHESIS OF THE NATURE OF LANGUAGE

NEUROLOGICAL AND PSYCHOLOGICAL MODELS AND SCIENTIFIC INVESTIGATION

With the advent in recent years of the work of Penfield and Roberts (1959), Sperry (1964), Luria (1966), Hecaen and Ajuriaguerra (1964), Mountcastle (1962) and Eccles (1966), a newer, different approach to the problems of neuropsychological theory has developed. Most of the people writing in the above works have had direct access during operations to conscious living human and/or animal brains, enabling them experimentally to test subjects psychologically before, after and even during surgery. The result has been a realization that many of the previously accepted tenets of neurological theory are too simple or do not hold up to empirical investigation. Lashley's (1929) hypotheses, in particular, with their emphasis on a resultant behavioral output of the brain as a whole, have required considerable modification. Luria agrees with Pavlov, whom he quotes as follows: "These attempts to interpret the results of extirpation of isolated areas of the brain by using certain undifferentiated concepts of psychology are basically unsound." The "antilocalization doctrine" of Lashley has now been superseded by a new localization-of-function approach which has little to do with either the old one-to-one area-to-function correspondence, or the mass action neurology of Lashley. This up-to-date viewpoint regards the central nervous system as an integrated multiplicity of subsystems complexly cross-referenced to subserve specific behaviors (psychological and motor) in a survival-value way. Some of these functions are broad in behavioral scope but incredibly precise neurologically (e.g., the visual appreciation of movement), while others are narrow in scope and neurologically simple (e.g., spinal reflexes). Lansdell and Urbach (1965), reporting a research on neurological sex differences, state:

> Regardless of the specific cause, the data add to the mounting difficulties of the general "mass action" conception of complex brain function; the conception of extent of damage to separate systems in the brain seems more appropriate, particularly when considering the effects of lesions on non-cognitive factors and the associated hemispheric asymmetries and sex differences.

It is the tracing of these systems and subsystems and the unraveling of their intricate, integrative cross-connections in the areas of speech, language and thought which has been one of the major scientific preoccupations of the above authorities during the last two decades.

Although I will present in a crystallized form, so to speak, the more essential details of the psychoneurology of language, the latter is not the main intent of this chapter. For some time I have attempted to synthesize several sets of research information which have repeatedly, and usually separately, cropped up in the literature. The *first* is that mentioned above, namely, the neuropsychological information of Luria, Penfield and Roberts, and others. However, these authors do not mention sex differences as a major variable to be considered. The *second* collection of information to be incorporated is that presented by Lenneberg (1967), but he, too, does not refer to sex differences in language functioning. The *third* body of evidence is that concerned with verbal and spatial abilities as the major variables of cognition. Several authors are extremely interested in these topics, particularly P.E. Vernon (1961) and I.M. Smith (1964). These intellectual abilities are correlated with the *fourth* subject, namely, psychological sex differences, a much neglected variable in almost all neurological, psychological and, until very recently, educational research. The *fifth* and *sixth* topics are specific aspects of the relatively recent evolution of Homo sapiens and some additional genetic data concerning the inheritance of structured language potentials. Some evidence and speculation on slow maturation patterns and their implications for linguistic and social adjustment form the *seventh* and final element of the presented synthesis.

The research evidence for my "case" will be given in the text and any speculation will be at least implicitly indicated.

On this point, I would like to comment that all "proof" in scientific research is *circular* inasmuch as our criteria for proof are dependent on our previous proofs of more elementary systems and our often inaccurate and unsubtle understanding of the limits of our restricted knowledge. If the history of astrophysics, nuclear physics and molecular biology abound with examples of such "proofs" and "limits," how much more so is it the case in the higher life and social sciences. Let me give one example. Many psychologists include intelligence as a research variable in their projects (and some are concerned with extremely *behavioral* learning theory research) as if the IQ as manifested in test data had an external validity akin to that of the atom in physics. Intelligence is a prime example of the circular research argument in psychology and education.

IQ subtests are loosely constructed by individuals almost invariably with a completely *subjective* concept of what intelligence is, and very often the elements of the subjective compilation have been centrally drawn or abstracted from educational curricula which are even more subjectively established. Frequently, the sample is nonrepresentational on almost every classification variable known to psychosocial research: validity is established against other intelligence tests or, worse still, scholastic achievement; the inbreeding of items from traditional procedures is notorious, and all sex differences in performance are systematically eliminated. Yet often well-meaning scientifically oriented psychologists, while having a naïve faith in measured intelligence, will dismiss speculation as an idle waste of time, although it is probably two-thirds of the scientific process in terms of the advancement of integrated knowledge (the final cause of science). Some of Einstein's extremely elaborate scientific speculations (in the form of closely reasoned hypotheses) were not "conclusively" proved until the invention of space satellites decades later. Scientific proof is built slowly over time, section by section, sometimes awaiting the invention of more advanced techniques to allow the keystones of validity to be put into place. The hypotheses put forward in this and other chapters already have a reasonable degree of support but as with all scientific projects, conclusive proof is a never-ending effort. It is to be hoped that the acceleration of psychological and biological research will progressively provide more and more evidence for (or against) the data and ideas presented below.

SEX DIFFERENCES

Many authors writing about language skills have commented that in some linguistic skills, there are small, often significant differences between males and females. Example of such authors are P.E. Vernon (1961), M.D. Vernon (1957), Templin (1957), Morley (1965), Money (1962), Maccoby (1966) and I.M. Smith (1964). These sex differences are particularly observable in the field of reading disabilities, where boys predominate.

The neurological sex differences discussed by H. Lansdell (1962), J.P. Lansdell (1964) and H. Lansdell and N. Urbach (1965) strongly suggest that more research neurologists should follow up these promising leads (which were mentioned in more detail in Chapter II). Physiologically, Burke (1898) and Bayley and Jones (1955) suggest that there are definite sex differences in height, weight and bone age development in children. In the areas of emotional disturbance, school failure, delinquency, autism, social immaturity and defects of speech, hearing and vision, boys invariably outnumber girls (research cited by Bentzen, 1966). Even in areas of normal functioning there are numerous sex differences. Males tend to be more aggressive (Sears *et al.*, 1957) and boys' and girls' conceptual thinking is qualitatively different (Buddeke, 1960); J.J. Gallagher (1963) confirms Kagan's (1964) hypothesis that male aggressiveness may account for some superficial differences in cognitive thinking and expressiveness. Boys outnumber girls on color-blindness tests 7:1, according to Waddington (1965). That males exhibited far more artificial stuttering than did females under delayed auditory feedback was found in a research by Bachrach (1964). Boys and girls react differently in terms of anxiety feelings, according to Sarason *et al.* (1960).

Turning more to sex differences in language and related areas, one finds the literature so extensive that it is impossible to summarize it concisely. Therefore, it is necessary to select and quote from several key studies. P.E. Vernon (1960), in a survey of intelligence tests, comments that informational items show a considerable sex difference in favor of males whereas more purely linguistic ones tend to favor females; also, females are relatively superior in spelling (a sequential *fluency* process?) and are inferior in arithmetic. Verbal fluency as a female attribute will recur as a key variable again and again. Males are superior on spatial and mechanical tests; it is possible on the evidence that the range or spread of general intellectual ability is slightly more restricted in girls, but the evidence is not unanimous on this point.

Beard (1965), in a factorial study of the structure of perception, found girls superior in verbal *fluency* and Ballard (1920), in standardizing his reading tests, found girls superior in rate of reading (*fluency?*). Neale (1964), in her tests, also found that girls scored above boys in their rate of reading. Stephens *et al.* (1967) found no sex differences between boys and girls on an IQ test (California Test of Mental Maturity) or on the Metropolitan Reading Readiness Test which, in the light of what has been said earlier about the construction of such tests, is not surprising. Also, the samples they used were small and unrepresentative. Since eyedness has been shown to have little relation to reading ability (see below), their other negative findings on cross-laterality were to be expected. By contrast, a representative school sample study on reading readiness by Thackray (1965) states: "The girls showed a significant superiority over the boys in reading readiness skill tests involving auditory discrimination (1% level) using context and auditory cues (5% level); also in this study, on the Kelvin Measurement of Ability Test, the Vocabulary profile, and the two reading achievement tests, the girls showed a significant superiority over the boys." Other studies on auditory discrimination found similar differences. Dykstra, (1966) in an excellent study using a large, carefully structured representative sample, states: "Other findings included significant sex differences in performance on three of the auditory discrimination tests and on both reading tests. All such differences favored girls." Templin (1957) also found indications that girls are more proficient in discriminating speech sounds during the developmental period.

My own work with dyslexic children has led me to the conclusion that for mild cases, boys outnumber girls approximately 4:1, but in very severe cases, this ratio may increase to 10:1. Schiffman (1965) has summarized the sex ratio for remedial reading cases as reported by nine authors. The proportion of boys to girls runs from 2:1 up to 9:1. Burt (1937, 1950), in studying London children, found that boys outnumbered girls 2:1 in reading backwardness and defective auditory perception.

In her book, *The Development and Disorders of Speech in Childhood*, Morley (1965) makes the following statement:

> Contrary again to what we had expected we found little differences in the ages at which boys and girls first began to speak. Boys however experienced greater difficulty than girls in the use of oral symbols of speech with defective articulation or unintelligible speech occuring more frequently and persisting to a later age. Defects of articulation were found in twice as many boys as girls at five years of age, and in the proportion to 3:2 at 6½ years. Unintelligible speech at 5 years of age was three times as frequent in boys as in girls. Boys also experienced greater difficulty with the fluent use of speech and we found twice as many boys as girls who had a transient period of stammering.

Once again, it would seem as if a variation on the fluency theme was of key importance.

Reference has already been made in Chapter II to the research summary studies in the areas of verbal abilities made by Maccoby (1966). It will be remembered that in eighteen of the twenty-two Verbal Ability Research Studies involving children three years of age and under, girls were found to be verbally superior to boys while in the other four studies there was no difference. In none of the reported research projects were boys superior to girls in this early age range.

The net result of the above information about sex differences in verbal ability is an overwhelming support for the statement that girls are verbally superior to boys in general and that in some areas, this difference tends to hold right through into adult life.

Specific Areas of Female Verbal Superiority

Throughout the evidence presented above, there has been a tendency for *verbal fluency* to separate out as the particular variable in which females are most often superior to males. Rogers (1952) calculated the correlations of a large number of fluency tests with sex. An examination of the results suggests that the main areas in which females are superior to males are those of spelling and articulatory flow. The basis of these skills is, I suggest, the automatic recognition or recall of auditorially registered sequences of sounds as well as, perhaps, superior vocal-motor fluency. In other words, if the auditory input is excellent and the speech organs efficient, then output should be fast and fluent. This hypothesis is supported by the various studies reported above which indicate that females have auditory discrimination superior to that of boys. Presumably, the auditory analyzer (Luria, 1966) is even more efficient in females than in males. Even in terms of output, males stutter more than females, whether the stuttering is permanent or temporarily and artificially produced. Note that it is the automatic associative (linkage) aspects which seems to be superior, and not necessarily the quality of the concept, perceived objects or reasoning processes, which are being associated *to*.

For an analysis such as this, it is necessary to separate the *skills* of speaking, listening and reading from the conceptual content of the word or passage which is being spoken, heard or read. This separation is most obvious when a child or adult correctly articulates a lengthy passage read from an abstruse textbook, but does not have the slightest idea of what it all means. Such a person has acquired the ability *skills* to recognize and automatically associate sound to printed words using all the everyday conventions of the language, both phonetic and syntactical. It can be seen that in both theory and practice, these linguistic conventions and the skills associated with them can be clearly distinguished from the meaningful conceptual content which they may symbolize. Taken overall, the evidence presented thus far tends to confirm *that females are superior to males in various automatic language skills but that this sex difference is not true for the conceptualizing aspects of linguistic content.* A close examination of the research studies reported by Maccoby (1966) will confirm this conclusion. She says, ". . . girls maintain superiority throughout the school years in spelling and fluency, though not in vocabulary." One further point needs to be made here; automatic fluency skills in language are in psychological terms habitual or rote (unit or sequencing) memorizing abilities, which, in their turn, have been described psycholinguistically (Osgood, 1964b) as unit and sequential autonomisms. This naturally leads us to an investigation of the neuropsychological concomitants of efficient auditory and vocal sequencing memory systems. But before doing this, it will be profitable to ask if there are any psychological or sensory skills in which males appear to be superior to females.

Spatial Abilities

It is to be emphasized that the term *spatial ability* refers to an aspect of cognitive functioning which may or may not involve manual skills; certainly the latter are not essential to an operational definition. Spatial ability can be defined as the ability to manipulate objects and their interrelationships intelligently in multidimensional space, the latter including any number of dimensions from two to infinite. The intellectual manipulation may be theoretical, symbolic or abstract; it may utilize body-extensional tools (radar, telescopes, cranes, cars, etc.) or may be directly manual. Leaving aside physiological manual dexterity within which the sexes may be equal, *almost every research study into sex differences in the area of spatial abilities over the last half century has shown males to be superior to females.* Maccoby (1966) in her Classified Summary of Research in Sex Differences lists fifteen studies in the area of spatial ability, not including three studies using various Wechsler Intelligence Tests which have been standardized to eliminate sex differences. Of the fifteen, twelve are in favor of boys and for the other three tests, there is no difference; in none of the tests are girls superior to boys. It is worth contrasting this highly significant finding with the finding mentioned above in connection with verbal abilities. The superiority of boys in spatial tasks of an *intellectual* nature is not in evidence until approximately five years of age, but it is very likely that this is one aspect of the overall slower maturation of the male. Also, spatial ability is far more dependent on logical operations than are automatic verbal functions and we know from Piaget's work that true reasoning does not begin developing until the middle years of childhood. It should be noted that while in infancy there may not be any sex differences in spatial ability, the girls are not *superior*. I do not wish to reiterate at length evidence presented in Chapter II, but mention must be made of the reviews of spatial ability made by P.E. Vernon (1961) and I.M. Smith (1964). Both authors come to the unequivocal conclusion that spatial ability is a masculine trait.

I.M. Smith in his excellent book, *Spatial Ability: Its Educational and Social Significance* (1964), concludes that pure mathematical reasoning can be largely subsumed under the more general function of spatial ability. The equivalence of spatial ability with conceptual or abstract thinking is also stressed by Smith and several quotations of his on this point have been presented in Chapter II. Yet another point made by Smith is that verbal ability and spatial ability have been demonstrated by many factor analytical studies to be a bipolar factor. In other words, there is a generalized tendency within the population as a whole for a person having a preponderance of one type of ability to have less of the other. As there is a definite sex difference in these functions, this would mean that girls and women as a group would tend to be verbally superior, particularly in terms of automatic fluency, whereas the majority of boys and men would tend to be superior in spatial ability, mathematical ability and abstract conceptional reasoning, particularly of the visuo-spatial kind. To avoid confusion, it is necessary to reiterate that *verbal language skills of an automatic nature are cognitively quite separate from the conceptualizing and relational reasoning which are embedded within the strings of verbal labels.* Therefore, females do not necessarily reason more logically with words than do males. I will return to these points in the sections on the brain and laterality later in the chapter.

Evolutionary Explanations

The temptation to speculate on the evolutionary reasons for these verbal and spatial ability sex differences is too great, particularly as a "reasonable" evolutionary case, inasmuch as it can be found and stated, lends historical support to the other very extensive research evidence already discussed.

During the last half million years, human beings have spent most of their time evolving in a natural environment in which the men must be proficient at spatial activities, such as making tools, boats, houses, bridges, etc. Those men with poor spatial ability were liable to be killed, for example, because they could not make or throw a spear accurately, because they could not flight an arrow or because their canoe, being too unstable, turned over and caused them to be drowned. Thus, visuo-spatial ability has been built into many human males, and those having it to a superior degree have lived to produce sons who, in their turn, have inherited the ability. Visuo-spatial ability is a quality possessed to a high degree by engineers, architects, surgeons, dentists, sculptors, airline pilots, mechanics, craftsmen, etc.

Females, on the other hand (while of course they, too, require a considerable degree of visuo-spatial ability), have a much more primary interest in life, namely, that of rearing children in the complex, emotional, family situation of the home. Obviously, those women in the past who could successfully raise a family needed to be able to "manipulate" its members to some degree if harmony was to reign and their daughters were to grow up, reproduce and successfully rear their kind. The manipulation of emotions calls for *excellence of communication*, a fact well known to propagandists and writers the world over. A subtle molding and persuasion of family attitudes must have as its medium an equally subtle flow of language. Maccoby (1966) reports, ". . . boys catch up [to girls] in vocabulary and reading comprehension, but not in fluency, spelling and grammar." The differences between males and females in both spatial ability and verbal ability, though significant, are not great and the two characteristics are usually, by test construction, normally distributed. But at the extreme end of the normal verbal/spatial discrepancy curve for both sexes, individual cases occur who exhibit *marked* discrepancies. *Since the two aptitudes are a bipolar factor, males will be found who have good spatial ability and poor verbal ability, and females who have good verbal ability and poor spatial ability, relative to the particular individuals' overall ability* (I.M. Smith, 1964; P.E. Vernon, 1961). Many learning disability cases exhibit such discrepancies.

The Genetic Aspects of Language

A brief recapitulation of the evidence presented in Chapter II for a considerable degree of inheritance of language functions is necessary here because it is an important frame of reference biologically speaking for the subsequent discussion of the brain areas of speech and language and their functioning. Some of these reasons come from Lenneberg (1967).

It will be remembered that seven sets of evidence were presented: (a) the morphological characteristics of vocal organs and brain devoted to speech; (b) the evidence that intelligence, at least in its degree of maximum potential, is inherited; (c) the almost automatic occurrence of language development in early infancy, provided the environment is satisfactory; (d) the occurrence of definite sex differences which cannot be entirely attributed to training; (e) the evidence that language acquisition is a universal and spontaneous event common to all human beings; (f) the many elements that spoken human languages have in common across cultures and time scales, and, most important of all, (g) the hard evidence that twin and family pedigree studies have yielded for the inheritance of verbal traits as potentials.

Knowing the complex integrated nature of the neuropsychological and physiological bases of verbal and spatial abilities, there would seem to be little doubt that the inheritance pattern of both characteristics is a polygenic one. By anology, just as males are taller than females at least in adult life, and a large number of genes must contribute to this physiological end result, so it is highly likely that many genes must contribute to the extremely complex psychoneurophysiological structure which forms the permanent foundation for these basic psychological traits. It will be hypothesized later that a formal developmental cause (concomitant with this structure) is a marked physical and psychoneurological maturational lag in males, one which has been noted by many authorities.

Of course, the polygenic nature of the inheritance pattern will mean that in many individual cases, there will be females with excellent visuo-spatial ability and many males with excellent verbal fluency, just as there are tall women and short men. This fact does not negate the significant sex difference trend as a whole. Furthermore, because the sex differences are not great, environmental training, particularly in early infancy and childhood, can, in a sense, artificially reverse the innate tendency for a superior development of one particular ability over the other. In another sexual context, it is possible to bring up boys to be effeminate men or even homosexuals (and not all homosexuals have a feminine hormone system), even though physiologically they have mature male sex organs. I am stressing this point because there is a naïve view abroad that if some characteristic is innate, it is immutable in terms of training. Such a position is not tenable. It is extremely likely that if all our infant school systems were very efficient in the verbal training of boys and the spatial training of girls, the innate sex differences would largely be counteracted, though only while such training was in vogue in those specific schools. The points made here about nature versus nurture are relevant to many theoretical discussions in psychology and education. Biologists have never had any doubts about the influence of the environment in facilitating or inhibiting innate physiological development programs, and the brain with its psychological concomitants is no exception to the biological rule. It is the brain, then, which requires detailed investigation to determine the neurological bases for the various verbal fluency and spatial ability sex differences. Many of the points made in the above section will be referred to again in Chapter IX.

BRAIN AREAS OF SPEECH AND LANGUAGE AND THEIR FUNCTIONING

The brain consists of two hemispheres; by and large, the left hemisphere is responsible for the right half of the body and the right hemisphere "controls" the left half of the body, but of course, this is only a very generalized rule of thumb applying mostly to the "external" sensory and motor organs of the body. Some important areas of the brain are illustrated in Figures 9 and 10, which should help the reader locate areas of functioning mentioned in the text. Figure 9 illustrates the left hemisphere as looked at from the side of the head, and Figure 10 presents the same hemisphere in its medial aspect, that is, as if the brain had been cut straight through the center from front to back. Figure 9 shows those areas of the cortex (the thick outer layer of the brain) which are responsible for motor activity, semantic activity, auditory activity and visual activity. Each of the primary areas has impulses sent (projected) to it but it also retransmits impulses in various directions. Luria (1966) claims that the primary pro-

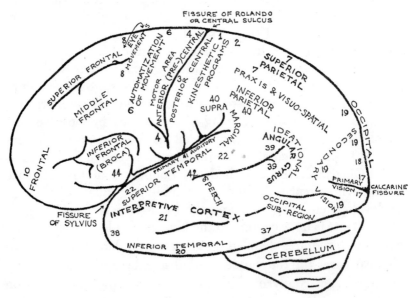

FIGURE 9. Left hemisphere (lateral aspect).

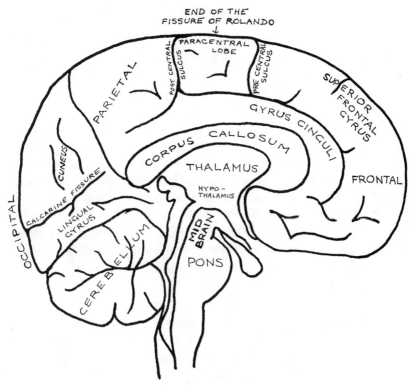

FIGURE 10. Left hemisphere (medial aspect).

jection and transmitting areas do not produce potentials that spread far over the brain, whereas stimulation of the secondary zones which surround these areas does give rise to such potentials. For example, the secondary auditory areas in the temporal region have well-developed associations with the inferior sections of the premotor and frontal portions of the cortex. Each major area of functioning will be dealt with separately. It should be noted that the sections below are not primarily concerned with giving information about lesions or the effects of lesions. Lesions are mentioned only because most of our knowledge of how the normal brain functions comes from the influence or effect of lesions. It is the normally functioning brain which I wish to describe and analyze in this chapter.

The Voluntary Motor and Kinesthetic Areas

Although the precentral gyrus of the fissure of Rolando is mainly concerned with motor activity and the postcentral gyrus with kinesthetic-sensory activity, the division of function is blurred. In fact, both the postcentral and precentral areas have afferent (incoming) and efferent (outgoing) groups of fibers showing the integrated functioning of this whole area (Penfield and Rasmussen, 1950). In the pre- and postcentral gyri, the sequence of responses to electrical stimulation on the surface of the cortex runs from the inside top of the hemisphere down to the lower end of the fissure of Rolando, an area which deals with the motor and kinesthetic functions of the body in the following order. At the top come the toes, then the legs, trunk, shoulders, elbows, the rest of the arms right through the fingers, the thumbs, the neck, the face, the brow, the eyelids, down to the lips and vocalization, the jaw, tongue and swallowing, and finally salivation down at the lower end of the two gyri.

The principal function of the secondary premotor area, that is, the area directly anterior to the precentral motor area, is the coordination and automatization of complex movements or series of movements. These coordinated sequences of programmed muscle activity involve the *cerebellum*. Luria (1966) says on this, "The channels of transmission of the impulses reaching the fields of the pre-central region are mainly tracts leading from the cerebellum through the red nucleus and the thalamus to the cortex. A large portion of this afferent system serves for the feedback of streams of impulses circulating in the extrapyramidal cortical-subcortical systems of the brain." Later Luria (1966) says,

> In man, the connections with the cerebellar system are particularly highly developed, owing to the assumption of erect posture and the importance of cerebellar coordination in the performance of goal-directed actions. Besides projection connections, the frontal fields possess extensive bilateral associative connections with the fields of the pre-central region and of cortical regions lying posterior to the central sulcus and on the medial and inferior surfaces of the hemisphere. As a result of these associative connections, as well as of those connections functionally uniting the various divisions of the cortex through the subcortical formations, the activity of all sections

of the cortex of the anterior and posterior parts of the cerebral hemispheres is integrated. Functional unity of all the higher mental processes is thereby achieved.

Elsewhere, Luria says that the performance of coordinated and goal-directed *acts* is represented in the whole frontal lobe.

The postcentral sections of the cerebral cortex to a large extent are concerned with kinesthetic sensing, although as has been stated above, some direct motor activity may also be initiated in this area. However, the postcentral area and the divisions immediately posterior to it are closely associated with precisely guided motor movements such as doing up buttons or writing. The secondary kinesthetic areas apparently store kinesthetic programs of movement which perhaps counterbalance the secondary-area precentral motor programs. Certainly lesions of this post-central area cause apraxic disturbances such as the inability to do up buttons or coordinate handwriting even though the visuo-spatial organization may remain intact. This is why it is essential when diagnosing learning disability cases for visual *or* apraxic problems to clearly separate the two. This may be difficult in the absence of "pure" sensory tests. Muscle systems and the coordination of muscular movements through kinesthetic feedback provide us with much of our appreciation of three-dimensional space, an appreciation which is quite separate from, but complements, our visual understanding of space. Therefore, when testing children for apraxia it is a good idea during some of the tests to have them close their eyes. Also, as the right hand is governed, so to speak, by the motor and kinesthetic areas in the left hemisphere, impairment in these regions will frequently cause writing defects. Other lesions in these areas can cause problems with eye movement or speech because the neurological control of the muscles concerned has in some way been impaired. Eye movements can also be incoordinated by lesions of the precentral motor areas (area 8).

From the work of Luria (1966) and Critchley (1953) there is evidence that the secondary parieto-occipital temporal junction may be responsible for associating written or printed symbols with their phoneme equivalents. Certainly lesions in this area in the left hemisphere cause Gerstmann's (1940) syndrome (see Chapter X), a complex disorder which causes a breakdown of the symbolic processes involved in reading and writing. However, phoneme/grapheme matching *may* be accomplished by long-range fiber connections integrating the auditory, visual and manual codes in their respective secondary areas.

Visual Processes and the Occipital Lobe

Throughout his book, Luria (1966) rejects the passive receptor theory of sensation and perception, instead insisting that cortical sensing of the stimuli is essentially an active process. At one point, he defines this theory as follows:

> Sensation is always an active reflex process associated with the selection of the essential (signal) components of stimuli and the inhibition of the non-essential, subsidiary components. It always incorporates effector mechanisms leading to the tuning of the peripheral receptor apparatus and is responsible for carrying out the selective reactions to determine the signal components of the stimulus. It envisages a continuous process of increased excitability in respect to some components of the stimulus and of decreased excitability in respect to others. In other words, sensation incorporates the process of analysis and synthesis of signals while they are still in the first stages of arrival.

A little later, Luria states that the sensory divisions of the cortex are the apparatuses responsible for this analytical procedure. Thus every act of visual perception incorporates both afferent and efferent mechanisms. This view of sensing as an *activity* which *selects* is to be contrasted with Broadbent's (1958) more passive "filter" theory presented in Chapter VII.

Some aspects of this active process of seeing have been described by R.L. Gregory (1966). Certainly the oculomotor movements involved in searching or scanning for visual stimuli contribute considerably to our visual perception of the environment. It is impossible here to give more than a brief outline of the highly complex series of biochemical and neurological events involved in the act of seeing. Therefore, it will be assumed that the reader knows much about the structure of the eye. To begin, I would like to quote Gregory as follows:

The retina has been described as an outgrowth of the brain. It is a specialized part of the surface of the brain which has budded out and becomes sensitive to light, while it retains typical brain cells lying behind the receptors and the optic nerve (but situated in the front layers of the retina) which greatly modify the electrical activity from the receptors themselves. Some of the data processing for perception takes place in the eye which is thus an integral part of the brain.

The fibers from the two retinas, called the optic fibers, cross over in the chiasma, eventually reaching the occipital region of the cortex after being relayed through the lateral geniculate body and nuclei of the thalamus. Almost all the fibers proceed directly to the areas surrounding the calcarine fissure (the primary visual areas), but a few afferent fibers go directly to the secondary visual regions surrounding the primary ones. All these visual areas have fibers running back to the retina and yet other associative fibers to the areas immediately surrounding them. There are point-to-point fiber connections from the surfaces of both retinas to the projection areas of the primary visual cortex, so much so that precise damage in this area of the brain will cause corresponding blank areas in the field of vision. Stimulation of the primary areas leads to a very precise excitation in the visual field but electrical stimulation of the secondary area immediately surrounding the primary one seems to be felt more widely throughout the occipital areas. However, when the next layer out is stimulated, it leads to a definite inhibitory effect (von Bonin *et al.*, 1942). The stimulation of *all* the primary and secondary visual areas results only in flashes, dots, rings and other undifferentiated sensations, according to Penfield and Roberts (1959).

R.L. Gregory (1966), like others, has come to the conclusion that visual perception is an active process of suggesting and testing hypothesis about the objects which come into our line of vision. He has demonstrated this by using ambiguous figures. When viewing ambiguous figures, we continually search for a solution to an impossible visual situation. Thus, the hypothesis continuously present themselves in rotation, each being entertained in turn as a possibility but none being acceptable, for none is better than the others. He says,

> The great advantage of an active system of this kind is that it can often function in the absence of reliable information—like a good officer in battle. . . . By building and testing hypotheses, action is directed not only to what is sensed, but to what is likely to happen and it is this that matters. The brain is in large part a probability computer, and our actions are based on the best bet in the given situations.

It is apparent that past knowledge of a visual nature is very important if rapid cross-referencing is essential to immediate recognition and the anticipation of future possibilities. Before the brain comes to any conclusion about the nature of the object it sees, in cases of complex stimuli, it may be necessary for the eye to perform a great deal of exploratory activity, all the while observing and *matching in terms of past experience.* This matching will make use of extensive neurological inhibition in the secondary visual areas. These points concerning matching are elaborated in Table IX (page 276).

Lesions in the primary visual area tend to lead to central blindness, but lesions in the wider secondary areas may result in a decreased ability to identify objects visually, presumably because their representation has been distorted and matching is difficult. Sometimes an individual with this problem is unable to integrate the parts of the objects he sees into a whole figure, although he can identify small parts separately. This type of disturbance, which is called opticagnosia, can be observed in the distorted and fragmented drawings of some children, particularly on such tests as the Bender Visuo-Motor Gestalt Test and the Memory-for-Designs Test (Graham and Kendall, 1960).

Tactile Sensing and the Appreciation of Space

Our appreciation of space is built up not only by motor activity and visual perception, but also by our tactile cutaneous senses. These primary senses also reside in the posterior central gyrus. Most people, when they are presented with an object they have to identify by touch (blindfolded, of course), can easily do so. In achieving this, they must make use of the secondary areas of the tactile sense which can be used for *matching with past experience*—just as was the case with our visual and auditory analyses of stimuli. Ayres (1965, 1967) considers tactile sense development crucial to maturation. Kinsbourne and Warrington (1963b) have developed a test to measure finger agnosia which, in short, means the inability to identify objects through touch. They suggest that finger agnosia is one aspect of Gerstmann's syndrome, a set of symptoms which some authorities suggest is not uncommon in children with learning disabilities (Critchley, 1964; Hermann, 1959).

As Luria points out, the perception of spatial relationships in man is more than just the combined activity of the three analyzers: the visual, the tactile and the kinesthetic. He stresses the importance of a sense of direction, which contributes to our general orientation in space. We also involve word-labels in this orientation process, words such as *left, right, up* and *down*. Consequently, " . . . these coordinates usually become defined by words and so become subject to the organizing influence of the language system." Visuo-spatial ideational factors may also be involved in our overall appreciation of space. Luria makes an interesting observation: ". . . a disturbance in the comprehension of the spatial relationships on a clock face and on a map, in which symmetrically opposite points are interchanged, is one of the most common symptoms of a lesion of the parieto-occipital divisions of the cortex."

I personally consider the contribution of the visuo-spatial areas of the brain to be of paramount importance in the development of thought processes, particularly in terms of logical reasoning ability. More will be said about this below and in subsequent chapters.

The Auditory Areas, Speech and Language

In the area of speech and language, Penfield and Roberts (1959) have delineated many of the major areas of the brain. Luria. (1966) has also made a great contribution, as have many others. Although questions of hemispheric laterality and brain dominance will be dealt with in detail below, it is necessary to state at this point that the vast majority of people use their left hemisphere for almost all speech and language purposes. In the following discussion, therefore, it will be assumed that the functions mentioned are taking place in the left hemisphere, unless otherwise indicated.

The Primary Projection Auditory Zone

This lies in the superior temporal area of the brain close to the fissure of Sylvius. It is possible that some analysis of sounds may take place in the organ of Corti in the ear itself before they are projected to the brain via the thalamus. The primary section of the auditory analyzer is arranged so that the various frequencies of hearing are organized systematically within it. The *secondary auditory* areas lie immediately around and below the primary fields covering much of the remaining superior and middle areas of the temporal lobe. In Luria's words, these "secondary fields of the nuclear zone of the auditory analyzer are responsible for the analysis and integration of sound signals and . . . these processes are carried out by the combined activity of the several cortical zones taking part in speech activity." As was indicated in Chapter II, speech is made up of many distinctive features and phones, some of which are combined into phonemes which, in their turn, are strung together to form particular words. Therefore, the hearing of speech involves the selective *differentiation* of these speech characteristics, a process which will also involve the inhibition of nonmeaningful sounds. In this respect, Luria mentions the problem a person has when listening to a foreign language of which he is ignorant. Such a person hears "a stream of unarticulated sounds, not only impossible to understand, but inaccessible for accurate auditory analysis." Of course Luria was not the first person to know of these speech perception centers; in 1874, Wernicke roughly identified this and other areas of speech perception and production. There seems little doubt that the primary auditory area, perhaps in conjunction with nearby secondary areas, actively analyzes (differentiates out) the incoming phonemes while the wider secondary areas contribute to a deciphering or *decoding* of the sequence of phonemes through time, resynthesizing them into individual and familiar gestalts of word sounds (not meanings). Lesions in the primary area cause impaired auditory discrimination and an acoustic agnosia.

Secondary Auditory Zones

It was established earlier in this book that motor speech functioning was not essential to semantic speech perception because people exist who can understand language auditorially quite well but who are otherwise mute. Recently, I saw an adolescent spastic boy who, apart from a few vague noises, had no vocalization but who was able to type a high school essay in history using his big toe on an electric typewriter; he certainly had never experienced his own speech feedback to the auditory areas, internally or externally. However, it is also highly likely that those of us who *do* have speech, use feedback from it to contribute to auditory discrimination and word-sound identification. This mutual interdependence of auditory speech perception, ideational meaning and speech production means that if one link in this language chain is dysfunctioning, disturbances in the other links are also likely to result. Therefore, lesions in the secondary auditory sensory areas are likely to result in aphasic disturbances of motor speech. This type of lexical aphasia and several others are discussed at length in Chapter XI.

The Matching Reformulation of Words in the Secondary Areas

As we turn our attention down to the *middle segment of the convex section of the left temporal lobe,* the importance of whole words increases. Patients with lesions in this area have difficulty in reproducing individual words or series of words in the correct order. It is even possible that some kind of *receptive* word form pool, a counterpart of Osgood's (1963) expressive word form pool, exists in these secondary auditory areas surrounding the primary area and lying near to it. This word form pool, formed initially through experience and coded in the memory system, would be instantly available for *part-word matching and syn-*

thesizing purposes. When we listen to another person speaking, we do not completely absorb into our total brain the actual sequence of phonemes *he* emits. Rather, the evidence suggests that we probably break down (analyze) the speaker's sound sequencing into a succession of phonemic units and *match these against our own equivalent succession,* experientially acquired and stored for the purpose in an acoustic memory system. From this point, the ramified associations (in other brain areas) to our *own* reformulated word-in-context take over; the phrase "other brain areas" includes those areas situated close by as well as more distant ones. If the heard word is incomplete, our word-matching process may enable us to "close" or complete the whole word. These remarks, although they are consistent with available evidence, must be regarded as a little speculative. However, discrimination, matching, sequencing and closure must all be involved in the auditory word-sound recognition process (see Chapter VII).

Word Meanings

Below and posterior to the above-mentioned immediate secondary auditory areas, we find that the situation becomes more complex. Patients with lesions in these areas will have difficulty associating objects with words and vice versa; it is as if the word has been severed or disassociated from its meaning. This amnesia or memory dysfunction is termed *anomia,* but it is clear that such patients suffer little loss of the sequential structuring of speech or hearing. When speaking spontaneously they are inclined to have to search for whole words. Therefore, it is highly likely that many (but not all) whole-word unit memories are retained in this wider secondary (or perhaps it should be called tertiary) area. Furthermore, it is not unreasonable to suggest that these particular word memories are associated with the meaningful experiential memories which, in turn, surround the "tertiary analyzer" areas.

Penfield and Roberts (1959), when stimulating below and anterior to the above secondary and tertiary areas, observed that patients hallucinated and produced memory images of various kinds. They have called this area the *interpretive cortex* and comment, "The 190 cases included all craniotomies under local anesthesia in which stimulation was carried out during a nine-year period. The location of stimulations might be anywhere on the accessible cortex. But psychical responses, consisting of *experiential hallucinations* or *interpretive illusions,* were produced only by stimulation of the temporal lobe."

Contrary to what Luria says, Penfield and Roberts were apparently unable to produce such psychical responses when stimulating the secondary visual areas in the occipital lobe. Judging from the examples given by Penfield and Roberts, many of these psychical states seem to be in the nature of waking dreams or reminiscences and they certainly involve a *time factor.* The "dreams" may involve both vision and speech perception, much in the nature, as Penfield and Roberts remark, of a moving film. It is interesting that the interpretive cortex covers the major portion of *each* temporal lobe including the inner or mesial surface, and there is no clear separation between the temporal speech cortex and the interpretive cortex in the dominant hemisphere. Penfield and Roberts then state categorically, "But there is no overlapping with the visual sensory cortex of the occipital lobe." They distinguish between the experiential responses which are in the form of memory flashbacks and the interpretive responses which appear to refer more to present experiences even though the interpretation may be based on actual experience from the past. In conclusion, Penfield and Roberts suggest that the interpretive cortex is concerned with ". . . a neuronal record of his own stream of consciousness which every individual forms." They continue:

> Consciousness, forever flowing past us, makes no record of itself, and yet the recording of its counterpart within the brain is astonishingly complete . . . the thread of time remains with us in the form of a succession of abiding facilitations. This thread travels through ganglion cells and synaptic junctions. It runs through the waking hours of each man, from childhood to the grave. On the thread of time are strung like pearls in unending succession, the "meaningful" patterns that can still recall the vanished content of a former awareness. No man can voluntarily reactivate the record. Perhaps, if he could, he might be hopelessly confused. Man's voluntary

recollection must be achieved through other mechanisms. And yet the recorded patterns are useful to him, even after the passage of many years. They can still be appropriately selected by some scanning process and activated with amazing promptness for the purposes of comparative interpretation. It is, it seems to me, in this mechanism of recall and comparison and interpretation that the interpretive cortex of the temporal lobes plays a specialized role.

The important sentence in the above statement is that the memory patterns can be *"appropriately selected by some scanning process and activated with amazing promptness for the purposes of comparative interpretation."* Surely an aspect of this scanning and activation must be by, or on behalf of, the spoken *word* perception process through which *meanings* (experiential nonverbal concepts as described in Chapter III) *are associated with the stimulus words.* Incidentally, to make matters more complicated, memories of previous speech could form part of the experiential and interpretive record; therefore, the term *nonverbal* must be modified to *nonverbal and experiential conversational* to distinguish such memories from the quite separate and different non-meaningful phonemic and lexical recognition matching systems discussed above.

Ideational Speech Area

Adjacent to the interpretive cortex is the posterior speech cortex which Penfield and Roberts have called the ideational speech area. It seems that the two areas overlap, judging from the results of stimulation. If one examines the stimulation diagrams in Penfield and Roberts' book,* one finds that this posterior ideational area, centered around the angular gyrus, is associated with the following symptoms: the inability to name objects, etc., with retained ability to speak; misnaming with perseveration, distortion and repetition, and confusion of numbers while counting. Many of these symptoms also occurred in Broca's inferior frontal area when it was stimulated. Indeed, most of the symptoms described occurred in different patients in the three speech areas: those in the temporal lobe, those in the motor areas and those in Broca's area. Penfield and Roberts go on to say, "There must be one single functional mechanism within the dominant

---
*Figure X-3, page 200, and Figure X-4, page 201.

hemisphere that employs all three cortical speech areas, and it seems likely that a subcortical center plays a most important role in the mechanism." Returning to the ideational speech area, it would seem that its essential function is one of labeling ideas, images and concepts. Usually, the whole intact word is involved— but if there are lesions in this area, it is more the *associational link* between the word and its image meaning which is absent rather than the image or the word separately. One might speculate that this is an auditory (word) to visuo-spatial-praxic meaning (concept) associational area. This description of the area is consistent with that of the areas immediately inferior to it, which are discussed in the next section. The use here of the word *concept* should not be confused with or assumed to imply *reasoning* or *thought processes*, which are *relational* in nature.

Temporal-Occipital Areas

Luria has found that patients who have lesions in the lower area of the brain, which connects the middle and inferior temporal areas with the inferior occipital lobe, exhibit a certain kind of symptom—they cannot remember the *meanings of words* although they may pronounce them faultlessly; there seems to be a severence of the connections between visual images (occipital) and their word names (temporal) very like that in the situation described above. Luria goes on to say,

> While they can readily copy drawings shown to them (even difficult ones), they cannot reproduce what they have drawn when the drawings are removed. Although words apparently retain their direct significance, they do not bring to mind the precise visual image that usually arises in a normal subject or in a patient with a lesion of the superior divisions of the temporal region. . . . the fact that the patient can copy drawings indicates that visual analysis and synthesis as such are preserved; the preservation of the phonemic aspect of speech indicates the normal working of the cortical divisions of the auditor analyzer.

Once again the problem seems an associational one. The point to be made here is that the temporal-occipital area is an associational interface in which visual objects and possibly concepts are linked with their word-labels.

Kinesthetic-Praxic-Visual Symbol Manipulation Areas

The functions in these areas have been described in some detail earlier in the chapter and, therefore, it is only necessary here to recapitulate in terms of language functions. The cumulative evidence indicates that this middle-to-superior parietal area, particularly in the dominant hemisphere, is very much concerned with the integration of the kinesthetic, tactile, visual and auditory information and skills which are seen to be functioning optimally during the process of writing. A person who is composing a story, for example, continuously generates thoughts which in terms of expressive language he first has to encode in the form of inner auditory/vocal language. The words involved then have to be broken down or further encoded into phoneme sequences which in their turn must be transposed into grapheme equivalents. The graphemes next have to be encoded in terms of individual letters, which is probably a visual process. These letters are next translated into kinesthetic-praxic preformed patterns of writing which then activate the efferent motor areas, causing the hand and fingers to write the words on paper. Certainly lesions in the main parietal areas interfere with many of the processes just described (Gerstmann, 1940; Nielsen, 1938; Critchley, 1953; Luria, 1966).

Kinesthetic Afferent Speech Regulation

From the evidence of lesions, it would seem that the primary kinesthetic postcentral region adjacent to the fissure of Rolando (in the vocal apparatus section) is mainly concerned with regulating speech patterns of the oral apparatus. The actual speech word patterns may be *kinesthetically* retained in the secondary areas immediately posterior to the primary kinesthetic region. However, according to Luria, patients with lesions in this area frequently incorrectly substitute for individual articulations within words. Usually, these sounds are similar in the articulation process as, for example, when /b/ is substituted for /p/. Very probably this area is closely synchronized with the premotor patterns of articulation discussed below.

The Premotor Areas and Motor Functioning

The primary motor area immediately anterior to the fissure of Rolando, which has already been described, is directly concerned with efferent output to the muscular systems of the body. Lesions in a particular area will disturb the functioning of the particular muscles involved. Obviously, if any muscles involving speech, writing or other linguistic activity are linked to damaged areas in the primary motor cortex, those functions will be impaired.

Directly in front of the primary motor areas is the premotor region, which accounts for over 80 percent of the whole precentral cortical region (Glezer, 1955). It should also be noted that the premotor area is closely connected with Broca's area which, in turn, is richly connected with the temporal lobes. Penfield and Roberts have found a superior speech cortex which is situated anterior to and at the top of the primary motor area, some of it carrying over or through to the medial side of the hemisphere. Penfield and Roberts note that when this area was removed in the patient, there was a disorder of rapid and complex movements for both speech and other movements. Certainly vocalization is disturbed in several ways by lesions in this area. Speaking more generally of the whole premotor area, Luria says, "Disturbances of complex motor actions are the most permanent signs associated with lesions of the premotor portion of the cortex." Later, he says, "This defect in kinesthetic synthesis arising from lesions of the premotor portion of the cortex leads to the disintegration of the kinetic structure of motor acts. . . ." Luria also refers to "kinetic schemes," the purpose of which is to organize series of movements. In short, the premotor area is concerned with the *integration of complex skilled movements.* Therefore, lesions in the superior speech area or any of the appropriate premotor zones will cause disturbances of articulation, writing or other automatically organized sequences of fine motor activity.

Eye movements which are extremely important in the reading process, are regulated by a complex neurological servomechanism in which retinal-image motion serves as feedback (Fender, 1964). Four feedback systems operate: the positioning of the image on the retina, depth perception, correct angle convergence and focusing (accommodation of the lens). The conjugate movement of the two eyes is regulated in area 8 of the superior frontal lobe (Woodburne, 1967), another example of highly specialized motor patterning of an automatic nature. Furthermore, it should be noted that it is very likely that along with the oculomotor areas (areas 8), the primary motor area in the left hemisphere "moves" the eyes from left to right, resulting in a synchronization of reading activities with oculomotor saccadic movement in the left hemisphere. The eyes evolved to track movement according to both Fender (1964) and R.L. Gregory (1966), the latter author suggesting that probability factors govern our perception of movement. Walsh (1964), reviewing the evidence, suggests that the frontal eye-motor areas are concerned with directing vision to a new point in the environment while the occipital regions regulate eye movements to keep the same objects in view. Presumably, this latter function is also served by the parietal-occipital interface area noted by Netter (1962). Lesions of the neurological areas regulating eye movements can cause severe reading disabilities (Lesevre, 1966).

The cerebellum also has numerous connections with many cortical areas, some of the richest two-way links being with the primary, motor, precentral analyzers. The reasons for this are obvious when it is realized that the cerebellum plays a large part in automatically regulating the individual's balance. Therefore, it plays an important role in fine motor coordination patterns involving eyes, proprioception (kinesthetic), vision and audition (Woodburne, 1967), all of which are involved in vestibular activity in the interests of body equilibrium. I suspect that lesions in the cerebellum may, through interference activity, cause problems in the reading process, especially in the area of fine oculomotor habituation and coordination. Quite often poor readers who are verbally competent in other ways display balancing disabilities. Earlier in the chapter, quotations from Luria were cited which stated that the cerebellum was closely involved with coordinated muscular goal-directed activity.

Mention has been made of Broca's area, which is directly in-

ferior to the premotor sections of the cortex. According to Mc-
Culloch (1943) Broca's area, when stimulated, tends to depress
the activity in the nearby sections of the brain and to inhibit
movements which have already begun. The major symptom of
patients with lesions in this area according to Luria is that they
have an inability to rapidly transfer from one articulation to
another. In other words, it is difficult for them to smoothly sequence articulemes in a complex synthesis, even though in many
cases they may be able to articulate isolated sounds. If Broca's
area is largely inhibitory in effect, then it would seem likely that
it counterbalances the more positive patterns of automatized
articulation present in the superior premotor areas.

The Frontal Cortical Areas

Lesions in the frontal regions of the brain can result in various
types of symptoms. There may be disturbances of posture or of
gait, ataxia of the trunk, perseveration of movement and, if epilepsy occurs, a general loss of consciousness. Penfield (1954)
suggests that this indicates neurological links between the frontal
areas and the reticular activating system. It has long been known
that frontal lobe lesions often cause patients to be emotionally
unstable, and this may be caused by neuron linkages with the
hypothalamic area. Netter (1962) says that some authorities have
indicated direct connections between the frontal lobes and the
hypothalamus (which seems to regulate temperature, blood pressure, appetite, sleep-waking mechanisms, aggression—at least in
the form of rage—and water balance), but these connections have
not yet been confirmed; however, indirect connections between
the prefrontal areas through the medial thalamic nuclei are well
established. Frontal lesions usually cause a decrease in the emotional activity of the patient but quite often excessive impulsive
behavior may occur. In this sense, there is a lack of organized
goal-directed behavior, as well as emotional instability which
may be largely passive but occasionally may be excessive.

Recently Valenstein *et al.* (1970) presented experimental evidence from samples of rats which suggests that there is much less
anatomical specificity within the hypothalamus than is commonly

supposed. The authors point out that species differences, prior experience and environmental conditions may also be essential and therefore a wider interpretation of drive states may be necessary for a full explanation. Few would quarrel with their point of view.

Luria suggests that the frontal regions of the brain are actually a part of the motor analyzer, but that the former does differ from the motor areas in a number of ways. He goes on to say,

> It is especially important to note that some fields (for example, the oculomotor Area 8) possess specific afferent-efferent connections with the optic areas whereas others (Areas 10, 45, and 46) are connected by a system of analogous afferent-efferent connections with Areas 22, 37, and 39 of the parieto-temporal region and with those sections of the superior temporal region (Areas 42 and 22) constituting part of the system of speech zones. These data indicate the structural complexity of the pre-frontal divisions of the cerebral cortex and the diversity of their connections with other divisions of the cerebral hemispheres. It may be concluded that not only do the pre-frontal divisions belong to the cortical system of the motor analyzer, but also, provisionally, that they play an important role in the afferent organization of movement. Since they receive afferent impulses from nearly all the more important parts of the cerebral cortex, they must be instrumental in the sorting of these impulses and in the transmission of them to the system of the motor analyzer.

Luria formulates his conclusions about the frontal lobes in the following way. He says that the frontal lobes "synthesize the information about the outside world received through the exteroceptors and the information about the internal states of the body and that they are the means whereby the behavior of the organism is regulated in conformity with the effect produced by its actions." It seems that patients with frontal lesions find it difficult to initiate desired actions and also to terminate them. They tend to perseverate and any actions which require a sequence of actions, such as those that occur in speech, are especially difficult for them. In other words, as Luria puts it, there is a gross disintegration of the preliminary synthesis of intended actions. Summarizing, he says, "It seems that what are most severely affected in patients with a lesion of the frontal lobes are the systems of preliminary synthesis, formed with the participation of speech connections and determinants of the subsequent course of nervous and mental processes." It is this operation of *planning speech activity* which is at least one concern of the frontal areas. The overall fragmentation of activity in the presence of lesions may also lead to intellectual deficits of analytical ability and to poor memory functioning. Therefore, it seems as if the frontal lobes are verbally responsible (at least in part) for generating syntactical structure in normal speech and even inner speech. All these findings are based on Luria's own observation and psychological testing of numerous patients (Luria, 1966).

The Centrencephalic System and Integration

Whereas Luria (1966) ascribes some intellectual functioning to the frontal lobes, which of course do interact in an integrated way with many other areas of the brain, Penfield (1938, 1952) and Penfield and Roberts (1959) consider that the evidence is greater for placing the highest level of integration in a group of areas collectively called the centrencephalic system. The frontal lobes, while they may plan or sequence (Luria, 1966) or possibly transform or store plans (Miller *et al.*, 1960), probably do not otherwise participate in logical or intellectual activity even though Luria suggests that they do. The negative evidence comes from Weinstein (1962), who found intellectual losses in cases of gunshot lesions only of the temporal and parietal lobes, not the frontal or occipital areas. Penfield and Roberts (1959) state that the neurophysiologist must disregard statements that the cerebral cortex acting as a whole can perform these integrated activities. They claim the evidence indicates that a definite central integration actually occurs and that specific areas of the brain facilitate such an integration. The centrencephalic system is defined as ". . . that central system within the brain stem which has been or may be in the future demonstrated as responsible for integration of the function of the hemispheres." The system lies within the diencephalon, the mesencephalon and probably the rhombencephalon, the latter having bilateral functional connections with the cerebral hemispheres.

Penfield and Roberts (1959) go on to say,

It has been suggested by our associate, Professor Herbert Jasper, that the definition should be enlarged to include "integration of varied specific functions from different parts of one hemisphere." We are forced to agree with him. The subcortical coordinating centers which will be described for speech in this monograph are integrating areas within one hemisphere. Thus, although the cen-trencephalic system would not include the cranial nerve nuclei of the brain stem, it would include all those area of subcortical gray matter (together with their connecting tracts) which serve the purposes of inter-hemispheral integration and intra-hemispheral in-tegration. It would seem that the corpus striatum, or basal mass of gray and white matter in each hemisphere, forms an extra-pyramidal motor mechanism and is probably not to be considered a part of the higher centrencephalic integrating system. The brain stem, as defined by Herrick, includes the thalamus on either side but not the cerebellum nor the cerebral cortex and their dependencies.

The neurological hypotheses implicit in the above statement have been tested in practical applications at the Montreal Neurological Institute on hundreds of patients. They go on to say, "This experience taken with evidence from many others on the reticular system with its "nonspecific" connections is a most important beginning of anatomical confirmation." The centrencephalic system is never divorced from the activity of other areas of the cortex, particularly the temporal lobes and the anterior portions of the frontal cortex. In normal waking life, consciousness accompanies this combined activity; however, it disappears with the interruption of activity in the centrencephalic system. The neurosurgeon can, at one time or another with one patient or another, remove each of the areas of the cortex without loss of consciousness, but any lesion or other agent interfering with the circulation of the higher brain stem is, say Penfield and Roberts (1959) accompanied by unconsciousness.

Penfield and Roberts (1959) then say,

Whenever a man speaks or writes, he must first select the concepts that best serve his purpose from a conceptual mechanism . . . the study of aphasics shows clearly that the speech mechanism is separable from it [the conceptual mechanism]. This necessitates the hypothesis that there is a conceptual store-house. One might easily consider that these concepts are preserved somehow in the *centrencephalic system*. But it would seem better to reserve the name centrencephalic for the system which is forever busy with the organization of the present.

They suggest that the centrencephalic system integrates word patterns from the speech mechanism and sends out integrating voluntary impulses through the cortical motor areas of voice control or hand control when speaking or writing. Concepts are selected by the centrencephalic system and each concept "rings up in turn" the appropriate words by acquired association, utilizing an automatic reflex action. Whether listening, talking or writing, each word complex, once learned, operates on an automatic reflex basis with its corresponding concept, so much so that at one point They also refer to the formation within the brain of the "ganglionic equivalent of a word," and the "ganglionic equivalent of a concept. Experience over the years continues to reinforce the back-and-forth neuronal inter-relationship between the two." *Therefore, it would seem that neurologically there is a firm research foundation for stating that language skills and storage systems together are structurally quite distinct and separate from the conceptualizing and thinking systems and that the first pair may not be identified with the second, either in theory or in practice.*

Weinstein (1962) in testing brain-injured soldiers has found the left parieto-temporal regions crucial to verbal intelligence test performance and I would suggest that this result occurs not so much because they could not "think" (manipulate concepts relationally) as because they could not conceptualize (generalize abstractly from like percepts). It is thus likely that concept storage and its associated word-labels were disorganized in these soldiers. Incidentally, the fact that "relatively few subjects sustained an intellectual loss (as defined by the Army G.C. Test) in spite of the brain injury" suggests that the cortex is not primarily involved in intellectual activity.

I would go even further than Penfield and Roberts and hypothesize that there might be three separate (but closely integrated) systems operating in the brain neurologically and psychologically. The first of these would be the automatic (with training) linguistic word skills and sequencing communicative system entirely devoted to language skills in the narrowest automatized nonsemantic sense. The second system would be the experiential precept and concept storage system or, in other words, our record of experience, both abstractive and continuously interpretive, which would be closely related to and organized by the sensory system, particularly the secondary cortical areas. It is even likely (Bannatyne, 1966c) that the storage and matching systems for the various sensory modalities or perhaps types of experience (abstractive or interpretive) may be neurologically speaking quite different in the way they operate. More will be said about this in the chapter on memory (Chapter VII). The third area or neurological system would be the *thinking system,* and I deliberately avoid the use of the word *conceptualizing* because in this context it is rather ambiguous. The thinking system is quite simply the area in which one *manipulates* concepts logically (and sometimes illogically), where one calculates or, more generally speaking, where one *reasons* about the *relationships* of concepts of all kinds and their organization.

This integration of a tripartite model of the brain and mind into (a) a communication system (decoding and encoding, or printout), (b) percept and concept memory storage systems in which abstraction is possible and (c) a reasoning or data processing system which may contain both innate and learned programs is itself a very reasonable hypothesis. Although in the above description I have used some computer-associated terms, I am not suggesting that the brain is hypothetically analogous to present-day computers. In fact, it is almost impossible to imagine any computer or organism which does not have these three separate functions (code, data and programs) at some level and any scientist discussing the workings of the human mind is almost forced into some such threefold framework. The psycholinguists have produced equivalent psychological systems for interpreting language behavior and Penfield and Roberts (1959) have come close to this, neurologically. Some of these points will be further amplified in the next section.

Summary of the Language Functions of the Brain

The following account of the language functions of the brain is really an overview of the material presented above and although some minor points may be speculative, on the whole there is considerable evidence (presented throughout this chapter) for the following summary.

It would seem that when we perceive speech, the sounds may possibly be analyzed a little in the organ of Corti but predominantly this takes place in the primary auditory area (area 41). Much of the preliminary analysis at this point would be in terms of distinctive features and phones. Next, the phonemes and groups of phonemes are probably structured into simple part-word units of sound in the area immediately surrounding the primary auditory center (area 42) and matched against existing previously experienced part-word or whole-word units in an automatic sequencing decoding process which is thus far nonsemantic. The "building" of a word from its phonemic elements no doubt requires considerable scanning and sorting in the wider secondary auditory zones. Whatever the details of the neurological mechanisms involved, sounds *are* assembled and matched against experience. The whole-word storage or word assembly system areas are probably sited in the posterior areas 22 and much of area 39 (the angular gyrus). The next stage is for the word to "pull out" the meaning or concept associated with it and the storage of the concept would depend on the sensorimotor modalities with which the concept is essentially concerned. Obviously, most concepts are multisensory in nature and will therefore be stored in a number of the secondary areas found in many parts of the cortex. However, more time-connected and communicative auditory concepts are likely to be stored in the interpretive cortex, whereas visual material of a percept-concept nature is likely to be stored in the secondary areas of the occipital lobes. Concepts of a visuo-spatial-praxic nature may be stored in the parietal areas, particularly in the right hemisphere, although the left hemisphere will also play its part. Note that there is no reason why stimulation in the interpretive cortex of the temporal lobes cannot pull together on a continuous scanning and matching basis sequences of visual or praxic imagery from the occipital and other areas (e.g., imagine riding a bicycle).

The communicated concepts will then be digested in the centrencephalic system and manipulated there in terms of the individual's existing thinking patterns or reasoning programs. Since thinking or reasoning must always involve perceptual and conceptual data or information there would be extremely rapid and constant interplay between the centrencephalic interrelational programs and the conceptual materials stored in the cortex in complex patterns. Once the individual decided to communicate a reply, the sequence of relational thoughts would contain the sequence of desired concepts and then both would pull out the appropriate words syntactically, a planning operation which probably takes place in the frontal lobes (Luria, 1966). It is important to realize that reasoning-thinking processes of a relational kind (e.g., add *this* to *that*) have a psychological objectivity of which we are consciously aware; therefore, they themselves can form the content of percepts and concepts which can be abstracted and labeled for communicative purposes. Storage of such relational concepts could be in the frontal lobes. Of course, this does not mean that the frontal lobes work in splendid isolation. Far from it; the frontal lobes almost certainly carry plans or organizational programs which synchronize the centrencephalic logic, the conceptual cortical images of all sensory kinds and the whole-word (essentially auditory) temporoparietal associations into a kind of sequential inner speech for the purposes of, and preparatory to, vocal-motor encoding. From this point on, the middle frontal area including areas 46 and 45, Broca's area (area 44) and the premotor area 6 all combine to structure the inner speech into articulation motor patterns. This is largely an automatic process which then fires the appropriate cells in area 4, thus innervating the muscles used in all the apparatus involved in voice production.

It is very likely that reading and writing involve other areas as well since both of these functions utilize visual symbols. There is little doubt that the parietal area in the left hemisphere is closely involved in these two processes (areas 7 and 40). Since reading in part depends on an elaborate system of integrated eye movements (area 8), the frontal lobes will be involved in an elaborate context-centered feedback operation founded on previously learned syntax patterns—the experienced reader seems to sense from the context how far the next saccadic eye movement "leap" must be (Morton, 1964). Thus, even the visual input during reading involves a sensory matching process for the purpose of identifying syntactical structure. This inner-outer syntax matching has implications for reading disability cases inasmuch as they may not be able to match their acquired idiosyncratic style of syntax with that of the author of the book being read.

Writing is an encoding process which very probably takes the same neurological route as speech production up to the point of "neurological" vocalization (see Table X, page 301). Instead of the final articulation, the frontal and premotor inner speech may be transposed into writing through the kinesthetic programs (areas 1 and 2) and the praxic and visuo-spatial informational (mostly alphabetic) feedback (area 7) of the postcentral and parietal areas. Spelling sequencing is determined primarily by articulatory vocal sequencing and *not* by visual sequencing (see Chapter XIII; see also Bannatyne and Wichiarajote, 1969a). Therefore, when writing it is highly likely that one uses almost every speech and language area of the brain.

If there is one important theme for language educators in the above discussion, it is that a broad and deep experience of all kinds of linguistic activity will greatly assist in the decoding and encoding of speech, reading and writing. One major key lies in the matching processes involved, whatever the sensory skill may be; if there is *a paucity of internal experiential data (as in communicative dyslexia) against which incoming signals have to be matched,* then the comprehension of the message will be that much less efficient. No doubt the same is true for conceptualizing and thinking. The implication is that during the critical period of language development in infancy up to five years of age children should receive as much stimulation as possible in all three areas so that they can build up experience in phoneme decoding, conceptualizing and purposeful thinking all in terms of linguistic communication.

LATERALITY AND HEMISPHERIC DOMINANCE

Laterality or lateralization of function simply means that a particular activity occurs more frequently on one side of the body than on the other or in one hemisphere of the brain rather than the other. Quite often the terms *laterality* and *dominance* are used synonymously by authors, but I prefer to keep the word *dominance* to describe what happens when a particular hemisphere or area of the brain dominates or suppresses the opposite hemisphere or other areas of the brain. Therefore, I will use *dominance* as a neurological term and not apply it to handedness or other sensorimotor activities except to indicate their neurological regulatory areas. Speaking of handedness and the tests used to determine laterality, I wholeheartedly agree with Benton (1962), who deplores much of the content and practice of present laterality tests. The vast majority of test items utilize activities such as hammering or writing for which a particular hand has been *deliberately trained*. Ideally, before testing for laterality, both hands should be given identical training or better still the test items should consist only of tasks which involve minimal or no training. Examples are clasping the hands and finding which thumb is placed on top, folding the arms, filing the fingernails and so on. After all, if manipulating a chisel with the left hand while it was being hammered, or shifting car gears with the left hand, were part of laterality testing, most Englishmen would appear to be left-handed. Tests of both unlearned and learned laterality have already been developed and used for research investigations (Bannatyne and Wichiarajote, 1969a, 1969b).

Sensorimotor Regulation and Hemispheric Dominance

In the lower animals and certainly in cats, the two hemispheres are symmetrical, each being able to learn tasks equally well and each being capable of operating almost as an independent brain. The two hemispheres are still somewhat symmetrical in operation in the monkey, although some small specialization may be present (Sperry, 1964). This left/right symmetry has probably evolved from "the same morphogenetic forces that cause left/right symmetry in our skeletal muscular system" (Nauta, 1962).

With the development of language in the human being, this hemispheric equivalence has given way in some respects to particular functions which tend to occur only in one hemisphere. Nevertheless, even in human beings, the muscular and primary visual systems appear to operate mostly on a simple cross-mirror pattern, although in exceptional cases, one hemisphere seems to be able to do the work for both sides of the body (Teuber, 1962). Lateralization of function is very complex, and some of the subtleties of the problem can be appreciated from Teuber's statement: "Apparently, central representation of sensory functions for the left hand is not a simple mirror image of the sensory representation for the right hand." Even so, the mirror imaging of written letters in children seems to originate in the *right* hemisphere (Bannatyne and Wichiarajote, 1969b).

There are several cerebral commissures which transfer information back and forth between the two hemispheres of the brain; these are the corpus callosum, the hippocampal commissure, the massa intermedia, the anterior commissure, the optic chiasm, the pons, the cerebellum, the quadrigeminal plate, the posterior commissure and the commissure of habenulae. Of these, the corpus callosum is the major communicating commissure and it, along with the others, has been studied extensively by Sperry (1964).

Before continuing with more detailed descriptions of the lateralization of function and cerebral dominance, it is necessary to describe the nature of the visual fields, their relation to lateralization and the fallacy of crossed-laterality problems in reading disability. As can be seen from Figure 11, the retina of each eye is split into two sections. The left half of each retina in each eye, marked *x*, registers the part of the visual field falling to the right of the mid-line of sight, whereas the right half of the two retinas, marked *y*, records what is happening in the visual field to the left of the midline of sight. The two left halves of each retina (viewing the right-of-midline field) travel back through the optic chiasm to the primary visual area in the left occipital lobe, whereas the left-of-midline field is ultimately registered in the right occipital lobe. Therefore, although one whole eye may be more efficient than the other, this has no meaning in terms of hemispheric lateral dominance in the brain because as has been explained, *the retina of any one eye is registered in both hemispheres.*

Cohen and Glass (1968) in a study of good and poor readers in the first grade and fourth grades, stated: "No significant rela-

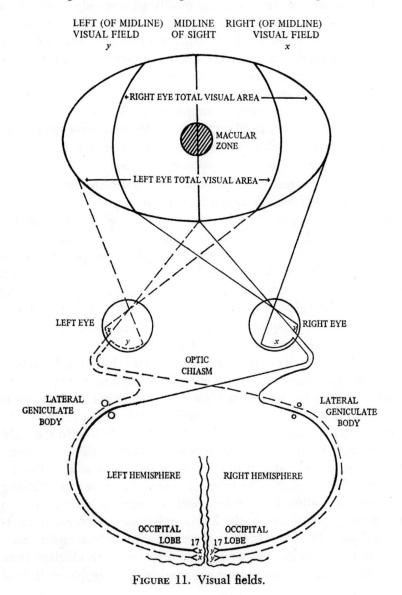

FIGURE 11. Visual fields.

tionship was found between crossed [eye-hand] dominance and reading ability in the total population studied." Stephens *et al.* (1967) found no correlation between crossed eye-hand preference and reading readiness scores of eighty-nine first-grade children. In yet another study, Belmont and Birch (1965) found no correlation between crossed eye-hand preference and reading ability, although Koos (1964) did find a significant difference in reading ability between the mixed eye-hand preference group and the unilateral group in the lower IQ ranges. Koos concluded that the influence of dominance categories varies with IQ level. It is also known to vary with the chronological age of the child, but in general, we can conclude that crossed eye-hand preference has little or no relationship to reading ability. The relationship of hand preference alone to reading ability will be discussed later.

Eyedness alone *may* have a slight causal relationship with poor reading. In a study of thirteen subjects with *neurological dysfunction,* Forness and Weil (1970) found that eight of the children were left-eyed although all but one were right-handed. Moreover, the subjects with the more severe reading disability tended to be left-eyed. Therefore, it may be that in some MND poor readers the "good" left eye is a little less efficient in registering stimuli in the right visual field. This hypothesis calls for further investigation.

The Organization of the Verbally Competent Brain

As has been said before, although some people seem to have their language functioning in the right hemisphere, the great majority of people process language in the left hemisphere and thus, during the rest of this chapter, any references to the left hemisphere mean that it is being regarded as the dominant hemisphere for verbal abilities unless the contrary is indicated in the text.

The vast majority of people are neurologically organized to process almost all language information and material in the left hemisphere. The implication of this is that they read in their right visual field (Sperry, 1964), write with their right hand, process words in the left temporal lobe (Luria, 1966) and process auditory/visual symbols in the left occipital lobe, at least on a visual interpretive level. (It is true that some visual and spatial aspects of the reading process may also occur in the right hemisphere.) However, as far as normal speech and hearing are concerned, it is possible by using the Waja (1949) technique to inject Amytal Sodium® into the intracarotid arteries of the right hemisphere and still have language functions proceed normally in most cases; however, if the opposite hemisphere is anesthetized, severe aphasic problems will usually occur. Therefore, as Sperry says, the right (or nondominant) hemisphere is usually suppressed during language functioning in persons whose left hemisphere is dominant for language purposes. In passing, he quotes the case of a boy born without a corpus callosum who developed language in both hemispheres.

Penfield and Roberts (1959) state that the muscles used in articulation are regulated from the appropriate areas in both hemispheres and that if either side is damaged or removed, the areas on the other side will soon take over the control of speech movement quite well. This is a logical finding as the speech organs are on the midline of the body. Eye movements are probably organized on both sides of the brain, but it is likely that the left hemisphere controls the key muscles which pull the eyes from left to right in saccadic movements while reading. Kimura (1964) has found that speech perception is more accurate in the right ear, which is directly connected with the left temporal areas. This finding is also reported by Milner (1962). That certain reading and writing deficiencies of a constructional spatial nature may occur in the right hemisphere is stated by Hecaen (1962). Hebb (1949) reports an experiment by Mishkin and Forgays who found that fluent readers of English, reading of course from left to right, recognized words to the right of the midline between two and three times better than words to the left of the fixation point, while readers of Hebrew recognized more words to the left of the midline. These results indicate which visual field is being used in the reading of English, and is a further confirmation that we use the left occipital lobe to see print while reading. In a research devoted to poster advertising, it was found that the public tended to locate items on the poster more or less randomly (except for the location of salient features) using the left-of-midline visual field, while they used the right visual field to read the printed copy. This fits in with the fact that during reading, we must almost always locate the beginning of the next line by using the left visual field.

It has been suggested by Denny-Brown (1962) that the left parietal area is mainly concerned with "propositional" activity which is verbal, visuo-spatial or constructive-praxic in nature, but Benton (1962) suggests that this area is concerned with symbolic processes, namely symbolic understanding, symbolic operation and symbolic expression. Sperry (1964) notes that the left hand and the right verbally nondominant hemisphere are superior in solving block arrangement tests, surely a visuo-spatial propositional task. Critchley (1953, 1964), along with earlier writers, has, also suggested such a symbol processing and symbol manipulation role for the left parietal areas. Further research evidence in this direction is given by Weinstein (1962) who reports that soldiers with gunshot wounds who have lesions in the parietal areas of their dominant hemisphere have significant deficits on army (verbal) intelligence retest scores and that these intellectual deficits are not shown by lesions in any other area, least of all the frontal and occipital regions. Therefore, on this evidence, verbal "intelligence" seems to mostly reside, so to speak, in the left parietal areas. However, I would suggest that as these areas are connected to a presumably undamaged centrencephalic system deeper in the brain (Penfield and Roberts, 1959), intelligent verbal concept *manipulation* or thought may only *appear* to be in the left parietal area even though the storage of verbal concepts may very well be located there.

The Organization of the Visuo-Spatial Brain

In this section I wish to put forward the hypothesis and present evidence for the existence in many people, mostly males, of a visuo-spatial brain which is differently organized in subtle ways from the highly lateralized, verbally competent brain. In a way, this visuo-spatial brain is the neurological equivalent of the person described by I. M. Smith (1964) who operates psychologically on his spatial ability rather than on his verbal ability. A preliminary description of this visuo-spatial brain is as follows: *While language functioning remains relatively dominant in (usually) the left hemisphere, and while both hemispheres actively participate in all behaviors involving spatial tasks, there is a spatial ability "executive control" center in the spatially oriented right hemisphere which dominates the whole brain including language functioning. The left hemisphere langauge functions subserve the more dominant right hemisphere spatial functions.* A psychological description of spatial ability, which can be defined as the ability to manipulate objects intelligently in multidimensional space, has been given earlier in the chapter and therefore the main concern here will be to present the neurological and behavioral evidence for the opening statements of this section.

First of all, it is self-evident that the manipulation of objects in three-dimensional space very frequently requires the subject to work in two or three visual dimensions which will involve both his visual fields and very often both hands. The architect at his drawing board, the engineer, mechanic, surgeon, dentist, airline pilot, car driver, factory worker, farmer, research scientist, sculptor, artist and designer usually utilize *both* visual fields and *both* hands in their daily work. This bilateral visuo-spatial activity must involve both hemispheres simultaneously at the very least in the motor, haptic, kinesthetic and visual areas. By "simultaneously" I do not necessarily mean that the two hemispheres function at identical levels continuously; it is possible that one hemisphere at a time may be actively suppressed in the interest of the momentarily attentive one. The alternation between the two may be rapid, or it may be dependent on the importance of the task being carried out in either visual field or by either hand; e.g., during which moment is the dentist manipulating the mirror with his left hand and the drill with his right? However, it is very likely that the two hemispheres act spatially in a fully integrated synthesis of simultaneous functioning in most visuo-spatial tasks.

I. M. Smith (1964) sums up his own information on handedness as follows:

The writer has not been able to find any experimental data relating to the possibility of an association between relatively high spatial ability and left-handedness. Lombroso [1891] has listed a number of artists, presumably men of high spatial ability, who were left-handed—Michelangelo, Leonardo Da Vinci, Raphael D'Montelupo, and Sebastian del Serle and Peter Scott. Burt [1950] has mentioned that many distinguished surgeons have been either left-handed or ambidextrous. There is an interesting and unexplained fact that left-handedness, like superior spatial ability, is more common among males than females. Burt found that just under six percent of boys and just under four percent of girls are left-handed. Clark [1957] found somewhat higher percentages, 8 percent and 5.9 percent respectively, the difference being statistically significant.

Wolf (1967) conducted research on thirty-two carefully selected dyslexic boys, "free of problems such as brain damage and severe personality-emotional disturbances." They were carefully matched with a control group of good readers on IQ, chronological age and other variables. The experimental group was found to be significantly less able on four Seashore Tests: rhythm, time, tonal memory and loudness. On the WISC (Wechsler Intelligence Scale, Children), there was *no difference* between the two groups on comprehension, picture arrangement, block design and coding, but the experimental group did perform better on the picture completion subtest. In addition, they were "left-foot-dominant, they evidenced a history of reading and spelling disability in their fathers, and a history of reading disability in their brothers but not their sisters, and their mothers had direction disorientation. A statistical tendency toward incomplete handedness was found ($p = .0575$)."

Unfortunately, most studies on reading disability cases do not control for intelligence or do not cluster the children into homogeneous groups, preferring to mix neurologically dysfunctioning children with communicative dyslexics and genetic dyslexic children. In other studies, the children are too old or the experiment has not included t-tests in its statistical analysis. Hecaen and Ajuriaguerra (1964) say,

> Our study (of laterality in poor readers) shows that the group of children with dyslexia is statistically different from the normal group when one considers the relative proportions of the lateral dominances, and that the children with dyslexia are not more often

left-handed than the controls but more often poorly lateralized. The high proportion of crossed dominance (ambidexterity) in the group of the youngest children with dyslexia is what appears to be most characteristic.

Tinker (1964), using only correlations in a rather unusual research design, found no correlation between handedness as a total figure and reading ability in either the disabled reader group or the normal reader group. However, the disabled reader group did have a low significant correlation between foot laterality and reading ability, and this ties in well with the above-mentioned study by Wolf. Perhaps foot laterality is more indicative of the innate lateralization of the limbs than is the somewhat *trained* laterality of handedness. On the findings of the above studies, we can conclude that there is some evidence of a link between poor reading skills and non-right lateralization of the limbs.

In a study involving tests of learned and unlearned handedness (Bannatyne and Wichiarajote, 1969b), left-handedness was tentatively found to be associated with several different "syndromes" (Varimax factors), one involving spatial competence, another involving immaturity and a third involving neurological dysfunction.

There is a need for a large definitive study using carefully selected laterality test items not involving training, the sample being clustered by (a) sex, (b) type of reading disability as defined in this book and (c) various types of verbal tasks, each involving various psychological functions, for example, memory (long-term, short-term, recall, recognition), fluency, spelling, etc.

In an investigation of touch pressure and point localization, Teuber (1962) found that although the various kinds of tactile deficits of the right hand were highly correlated, for the left hand there was no significant correlation between alterations in touch pressure and those in point localization. According to Teuber, "This finding is of particular importance to us because it shows a right-left difference quite independently of any assumptions about the exact site of the cerebral lesions." Teuber also lists several authorities who suggest that the left-handed may show a more diffuse representation of language mechanisms through both hemispheres than the right-handed. O'Leary (1962) reports that

Blau in his book *The Master Hand*, reviewed a large literature including twin studies and concluded that handedness is not inherited, but I suggest that it may be the acquired or learned tasks used in laterality tests which, so to speak, are not inherited rather than the fundamental tendency. I also suggest that the two hands should not be measured against each other; rather, each should be measured against the standardized test results of a large sample of left hands and, separately, right hands. Thus, though a surgeon or sculptor may be very skilled with the right hand and predominantly right-handed, his skill may be well above the national average when utilizing his left hand. In yet another study, Kolers and Boyer (1965) found that training a right-handed man's left hand on a complex task enables him to perform the task with his right hand, but training his right hand does not usually enable him to perform the task with his left. Is this because the left hand, when active, almost always involves the use of the right hand whereas the reverse is usually not the case?

Naidoo (1961) matched twenty ambiguously handed children with twenty right-handed and twenty left-handed children. The investigations showed that it was in those tests related to speech and language, speech development, articulation, the verbal section of the WISC and the verbal-visual perceptual tests that the greatest differences were noted between the ambiguously handed and the right-handed, the ambiguously handed having lower scores. In a study of 316 cases of marked reading disability and 245 unselected schoolchildren, Harris (1957) came to the following conclusion: "The ability to distinguish between left and right and a clear preference for one hand developed slowly in a significantly larger percentage of reading disability cases than in unselected children. This suggests the presence of a special kind of slowness in maturation, possibly neurological in nature." Earlier in the study, he states that the reading disability cases show a higher proportion of mixed-handedness (25 percent compared with 8.2 percent) than the unselected group. Strong left-handedness appears in 10.5 percent of the reading disability cases compared with 2.7 percent of the unselected group. In a family study, Falek (1959) found that left-handed fathers tried to train their children to use the right hand more than did left-handed mothers. Concluding this section on hand laterality and its relationship to verbal skills and to possible neurological organization, I would quote Ettlinger (1962), who says, "The strength of lateral preferences is reduced when movements are guided by non-visual cues, according to a recent report on intact monkeys [Ettlinger, 1961]. This finding is in agreement with the proposal of Parson [1924] that hand preference in man is more intimately related to visual rather than non-visual control." It is this latter theme which requires further exploration. A report of the research involving learned and unlearned handedness and other tests is given in Chapters VIII and IX.

Benson (1970) has suggested that left-handed children tend to use mirror writing and inverted writing much more than the right-handed. He goes on to say that mirror writing appears to be a true visuo-motor reversal while inverted writing seems to be an adaptation of left-handed writing to the standard style for the right-handed.

In an analysis of the results of the intelligence tests (WISC) of eighty-seven boys between the age of eight and eleven, David Mosley and I (Bannatyne, 1967b) found that the spatial score (picture completion, block design and object assembly) was greater than a shortened verbal score (comprehension, similarities, vocabulary) in 70 percent of the group who were all reading disability cases. The WISC is standardized so that normal boys would have only a 50 percent incidence of superior spatial ability to verbal ability. *Spatial ability was greater than sequencing ability (digit span, arithmetic and coding) for 76 percent of the reading disability group.* Furthermore, when the three subtests most involving symbolic activity and verbal memory are combined, namely information, arithmetic and digit span, and the result compared with the more visuo-spatial tests, namely picture arrangement, block design and object assembly, we found that 82 percent of the reading disability group achieved higher scores in the visuo-spatial tests than they did in the verbal-symbol memory tests. If the verbal tests are thought of as operating out of the left hemisphere whereas the visuo-spatial tests operate out of the right hemisphere, the implication is one of *a more dominant visuo-spatial right hemisphere ability.* In a study entitled "A Comparison of WISC Sub-test Scores of Pre-adolescent Successful and Unsuccessful Readers," McLeod (1965) summarized the results of previous research into the diagnostic use of the WISC and reading disability cases. Five of the eight studies found that *the reading disability cases were stronger in block design* and the only subtests in which they were weaker were information, arithmetic, coding, digit span and vocabulary. Incidentally, only four of these studies used a control group and in all four cases, the reading disability group was the same as the control group or superior to it in block design. In McLeod's own study, the reading disability cases obtained higher scores than the successful readers on the spatial subtests, namely, picture completion, block design and object assembly, but because his criterion of significance was at the 0.01 level, the significant differences were limited to picture completion only.

Taking the evidence into account from a large number of reading disability studies, it would seem that the majority of the cases are visuo-spatially quite competent or even superior. Very frequently on audiometry tests (Wolf, 1967), the *hearing is normal.* It is difficult to believe that these visuo-spatial boys, who may comprise up to 2 percent of the school population (Gorton, 1964), have almost identical lesions in the left parietal area preventing them from performing these verbal symbolic tasks; it is much more credible that they have a generalized language disability (related to neurological organization) which is a part of the normal distribution of language abilities in the population in general, and which is an opposite, or bipolar, function to spatial ability as documented by I. M. Smith (1964). Drake and Schnall (1966) report that dyslexic boys produced an average of 10.4 different designs as compared with 7.7 in the normal group in a toothpick design test in which the children had to create as many closed-figure designs as possible with six colored toothpicks in three minutes.

More evidence is available to support the above statements. Sperry (1964) has tested human patients who for various reasons do not have an intact corpus callosum. He says, "When the literate hemisphere and right hand fail in a block-arrangement test—one of the few things that the left hand and nondominant hemisphere generally do better—impatient twitches and starts occur in the left arm which may have to be restrained to keep it from intercepting the right." It should be mentioned in passing that block arrangement and block design tests in factor-analytic studies are highly loaded with spatial intelligence. Penfield and Roberts (1959) say, "In the non-dominant hemisphere the area of cortex which corresponds to the posterior speech area has a function also. Removal produces the syndrome of apractognosia. The patient loses awareness of body-scheme and of the spatial relationships about him." In a study of size discrimination in brain injury patients, Weinstein (1962) found that the group with right hemispheric lesions was significantly inferior to controls and to the group with left hemispheric lesions. Mention has already been made that words are better recognized in the right visual field. Geometric figures are recognized equally well in both visual fields according to Terrace (1959).

In a study relating tachistoscopic recognition and cerebral dominance, Bryden (1964) confirmed that alphabetical material is more accurately identified in the right visual field, but an even more interesting finding was that when it came to identifying geometric forms, only 47 percent of left-handers were right-field superior whereas 60 percent of right-handers were right-field superior. For single letters, which are somewhat like geometric forms, left-handers were 43 percent right-field superior whereas 71 percent of right-handers were right-field superior. For all types of stimulus material, 49 percent of the left-handers were right-field superior and 73 percent of the right-handers were right-field superior; this figure is significant at the 1 percent level. Thus, visual field superiority is almost equally balanced among left-handers while 73 percent of right-handers seem to be superior in the right visual field.

There is a great deal more evidence for visuo-spatial activity taking place in the right hemisphere and particularly in the parietal areas there. Even some kinds of superior (nonskill) verbal activities may occur there. Critchley (1962) has found that lesions in the right hemisphere may obstruct creative literary work demanding a particularly high level of performance, cause blocking on word finding, restrict the learning of novel linguistic material or limit an understanding of the ultimate meaning of pictorial matter. Out of fifty-nine cases of unilateral spatial agnosia, Hecaen *et al.* (1952) found that in fifty-one instances the cause was right-sided lesions, in four instances bilateral lesions and in four other instances left-sided lesions. They also stated: "As for those disturbances bearing on topographical relationships (inability to orient on a plan, geographical map, or drawing of a labyrinth), these depend principally on parieto-occipital lesions situated for the most part in the minor hemisphere." Disturbed spatial relationships of a visuo-constructive nature are thought to be caused by right-sided lesions by McFie *et al.* (1950). Several authorities (Mountcastle, 1962) state that constructive apraxia is more often found in association with right-sided lesions than with those in the left hemisphere. It is probably not a coincidence that Barbara Hepworth, the sculptress, calls her left hand her "thinking hand." Reitan and Tarshes (1959) have found that right-sided lesions seriously impair performance on their trailmaking tests which involve an understanding of spatial configurations. Injuries to the right hemisphere also lead to an inability to recognize human faces or cope with body image information (Milner, 1960).

The neurological and psychological evidence presented thus far all supports the hypothesis stated at the beginning of this section that in the visuo-spatial brain, while language functioning remains relatively dominant in (usually) the left hemisphere, and while both hemispheres actively participate in all behaviors involving spatial tasks, *there is a spatial ability "executive control" center in the spatially oriented right hemisphere which dominates the whole brain including language functioning.* In other words, the left hemisphere language functions subserve the more dominant right hemisphere spatial functions in spatially competent people.

Benton (1966), after reviewing the literature on the problem of cerebral dominance, says,

The crucial question is whether the right hemisphere plays a special role in mediating these non-verbal performances of a spatial, visuo-constructive, visuo-perceptive, audio perceptive, and motoric nature. In essence, three types of interpretation have been advanced to account for the observed association between these deficits and the presence of disease of the right hemisphere. One interpretation asserts that the right hemisphere does indeed play a special role in mediating these performances, a role which is analogous to that served by the left hemisphere in mediating language performances. In short, the interpretation says that the right hemisphere *is* dominant for these non-verbal performances of a perceptual, constructional or motoric nature.

The other two interpretations cited by Benton assign a lessor role to the right hemisphere, but it should be noted that none of these positions assert, as I have done on the evidence presented above, that the right hemisphere is in certain visuo-spatial people relatively permanently dominant in terms of total brain functioning and that language in the left hemisphere *subserves* the spatial right hemisphere is a subsidiary role.

The Corpus Callosum, Transfer of Training and Mirror Imaging

One particular problem that constantly crops up in young children, in reading disability cases and in some mature adults is that of the mirror imaging of unit-letters while writing, or the reversal of sequences of letters. Teuber (1962) makes the following statements:

As a paired organ the vertebrate forebrain with its conspicuous cerebral hemispheres poses questions of origin and present function. The evolution of this twin structure is undoubtedly related to the bilateral symmetry of the body itself; the widespread decussation of neural pathways, connecting one half-brain with the opposite half of the body, reflects the need for controversive movements in any bilaterally symmetrical organism as it strives to maintain its course and posture in water, air, or on the ground. . . . As far as is known, all infra-human forms have cerebral hemispheres that are mirror images of each other—both in structure and function. It is only in man that we have to face the additional problem of hemispheric differentiations.

Tschirgi (1958) suggests that man is becoming more and more asymmetrical in his hemispheric functioning; he can now distinguish right from left *even though he makes many mistakes.* Presumably because animals are limited to mirror-image responses to identical left and right stimulation (a rare event in nature), man, too, occasionally confuses the concepts of right and left or he may even emit mirror-image responses when directionality is important (see p. 391). It would seem then that there is still a very large component of visuo-spatial symmetry in the brain of man and that of course this will vary with individual differences. Some confirmation comes from the work of Myers (1962) who, after an experiment with split-brain monkeys and control groups, states:

> As may be seen the solution of the [experimental] problems was achieved equally rapidly by the two groups . . . it is concluded that sensory experiences, transmitted to one hemisphere through the afferent touch pathways, result in the establishment of memory trace systems in both hemispheres. These trace systems of the two hemispheres thereafter enjoy the potential of separate existence apart from one another, as witnessed by their continued expression subsequent to total commissures section. The memories induced vicariously, through corpus callosum in the hemisphere not receiving the afferent stimulation, seem less well defined than those induced directly in the receptive hemispheres. Yet it may be noted that the vicariously induced memory systems suffer little apparent decrement after being split off from the directly induced systems by severence of corpus callosum.

I would only add that the traces in the respective hemispheres are mirror images of each other since the "external" two halves of the "motor" body are mirror images, as are the two hemispheres of the brain in animals and very largely so in man. It is reported in Mountcastle (1962) that von Bonin has said that anatomically the two hemispheres appear simply to be mirror images.

Sperry (1962) has put forward two projection systems of the corpus callosum as possibilities. One he calls a simple homotopic projection principle of cross-connections through the corpus callosum in a very simple mirror-image pattern (see Fig. 12), and the second he calls "supplemental complementarity." Although the present evidence tends more and more to support the mirror-image principle, Sperry says,

> It may still be possible, despite the trend of the evidence, that something of the sort depicted on the right is really involved, i.e.,

that the callosum is not mainly or primarily so much a symmetrizing influence, as it is a means of supplementing the activity of each hemisphere with different and complementary information about what is happening on the other side. It appears there is something special and non-symmetrical about the cross connection between the visual areas (Bremer *et al.*, 1956; Myers, 1960). In the semantic cortex, where contra-lateral and ipsi-lateral points tend to be pretty much in register, the two alternatives shown here would be difficult to distinguish from the data now available. The scheme on the right accords better also with the development of lateral dominance in the human brain.

Commenting on his experiments, Sperry suggests that each hemisphere seems to have its own independent perceiving, learning and memory systems. Further confirmation of this is given by Downer (1962), who has also experimented with split-brain primates using visuo-stimuli. He says,

It would seem that central transfer occurs between extra-striate areas. This suggests that the visual memory trace is laid down in the "untrained" cerebral hemisphere, without the primary visual projection area of that side being involved. What little evidence is available suggests that there is no back discharge from Brodman's Areas 19 and 18 to Area 17 (von Bonin *et al.*, 1942; McCulloch, personal communication). Yet, when the visual primary projection area of

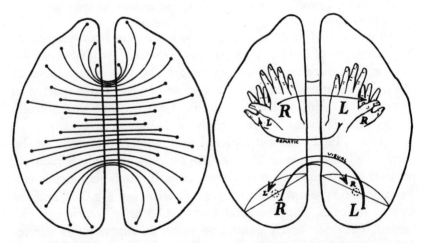

FIGURE 12. Projection of corpus callosum. Simple homotopic projection principle on left compared with that of speculative "supplemental complementarity" on right. (*From Sperry, 1962, p. 47.*)

this side is used for the first time, there is immediate recognition of the correct stimulus-object. If sensation depends upon the primary projection areas, this raises the anomalous situation that the animal recognizes something that it has never seen.

Ebner and Myers (1960), experimenting with monkeys, say, "Normal monkeys recognize immediately with one hand, discrimination learned with the other." Severing the corpus callosum abolishes this transfer.

Mishkin (1962) concludes that the right temporal lobe in man is dominant for visual functions, because visual perception in man is impaired by right temporal lobectomy and by right temporal epilepsy. He suggests that the right temporal area integrates the visuo-spatial functions of both the left and right visuo-spatial areas and that this explains the ability to perform complex preceptual tasks presented in the central visual field. Much depends on what Mishkin means by *integration*. That visual material can be stored or at least processed in both temporal lobes has been established by Penfield and Roberts (1959) and it may be this "stream of consciousness" visual material which, being sited in an impaired right temporal lobe, causes perceptual difficulties. However, all the evidence cited above tends to indicate that just as "symbolic-intellectual" language functions are regulated primarily through the parietal areas in the left hemisphere, so the visuo-spatial-constructive areas are sited, integrated and regulated in the right parietal area. Although it is feasable that some visuo-spatial integration may take place in the right temporal area, it is probably minor; Milner (1962) has found, "Patients with temporal lobe lesions show, for example, no consistent deficits in reasoning or problem-solving, or in the maintenance of prolonged attention." This in no way conflicts with the strong possibility that these visuo-spatial-constructive concepts may be manipulated intellectually (e.g., mathematically, architecturally, etc.) by the centrencephalic system described by Penfield and Roberts.

It would seem that visuo-spatially the human brain still makes considerable use of the two hemispheres and that this is because man must still use two visual fields except in the highly artificial process of reading (two-thirds of mankind still does not read or write). From the work of Downer (1962) we know that visual memory traces *may* not be immediately transferred from one hemisphere to another but that the untrained side, so to speak, utilizes the trace of the trained side via the commissures. However, with color, there is little doubt that at least in primates the memory traces are formed in both cerebral hemispheres during the original learning process. Even if the memory trace of the left hemisphere is merely utilized by the right without the trace itself being laid down in the latter hemisphere, there is still no reason why its operation should not be in the nature of a mirror image. Of course, there is also no reason why the transfer of information from one hemisphere to the other should not occur as both a direct "carbon copy" and a mirror image. Add to these Sperry's "supplemental complementarity" images and the transferred memory traces could be of three different kinds. Manually, although there is a lateralization of handedness to some extent, it is self-evident that almost everybody learns certain finely skilled tasks with their left hand. And the central transfer of training or the availability of training information from one hemisphere to the other for motor purposes is well established.

Turning to auditory sensation, the localization of sound in space obviously involves both hemispheres, but it has been well established that auditory verbal functioning takes place mostly in the left hemisphere in the vast majority of people. We know language and verbal activities in the literate individual have two aspects—one auditory/vocal and the other visual/symbol/manual. The auditory/vocal aspect which is well lateralized will not usually involve mirror imaging or hemispheric transfer of images. However, since reading and writing involve visual and manual tasks, there is no reason why these particular aspects of language processing should not involve *both hemispheres,* particularly if the person concerned is a highly visuo-spatial individual. Even more important, since reading is an almost unique visual activity which directly involves only one visual field, namely the right, and since the left parietal and occipital areas will be mainly involved in the registration of those memory traces (see above), *it is not unlikely that there would be a mirror transfer of this visual and manual information from the left to the right hemisphere.* (If it is not immediately transferred, it may be available to the right hemisphere in a mirror-image configuration.) Furthermore, if the individual concerned, being visuo-spatially dominant in modality, utilizes information from the right hemisphere for motor output, these there is every likelihood that *when such a person writes, the visuo-spatial and even motor pattern mirror images within the right hemisphere will be utilized.* This model is an elaboration of Orton's (1937) and Kettlewell's (1964) neurological model for explaining mirror imaging and reversals in writing, particularly in reading disability cases. It is interesting that Leonardo da Vinci habitually used mirror-image writing in his diaries.

Mirror imaging in writing, which is frequent in young children learning the skill, gradually disappears with age, presumably as right hemisphere visuo-spatial output is suppressed during the processing of language in a writing situation. This does not mean that visuo-spatial right hemisphere output is suppressed in other types of situations which are nonverbal. The problem of mirror imaging in writing is most acute in those letter symbols and words which, when they are reversed, have a separate directional meaning; this characteristic will be investigated in the next section.

Object Constancy, Letter-Design Constancy and Directionality Concepts

As an infant develops, he very quickly learns to recognize objects from any angle so that they retain their visual identity. This permanence of identity is called *object constancy* and presumably all animals up to man have it as a part of their visuo-spatial object-to-memory matching process, and for purposes of orientation. Young children also possess object constancy and normally have no problems with it until they reach an age when two events may occur, either together or separately. The first event occurs when they are introduced to certain visual symbols involved in reading; while most alphabetical symbols have an object constancy which is relatively unambiguous, some do not. The second event occurs when children find that they must attach verbal labels to concepts of direction, such as left and right, east and west.

When a child begins to learn to read, specific letters of the lower-case alphabet cause problems of mirror imaging or reversal phenomena. The most notorious letters are *b* and *d*. We teach the child to recognize the configuration of the letter *b* and to associate it with the sound /b/. This reading process probably takes place in the right-of-midline visual field and therefore the "ganglionic equivalent" of the visual letter *b* is memorized somewhere in the left parieto-occipital area. If visual transfer of training or availability to the right hemisphere occurs in the form of a mirror image (as seems likely from the evidence presented in this chapter), then the letter *b* will be seen, so to speak, from the right hemisphere as a *d*. This would not matter because object constancy would remain and the child would still associate the sound /b/ with this mirror image of the letter *b*, namely *d*. Unfortunately, though, we then take the configuration of the letter *d* and associate it with the sound /d/ and this, too, is learned in the right visual field and also recorded in the left parieto-occipital areas. It is then transferred or made available to the right hemisphere in a mirror-image capacity. There it becomes a *b* and the confusion is complete. The only means the child has of differentiating between the two configuration is by knowing whether the circular part of the letter points to the right or left of the vertical line as seen from the midline of vision in a plane parallel to his face (the sheet of paper being read). If the child climbs over to the other side of a table, it remains a table and object constancy reigns, but if he climbs over to the other side of the letter *b*, then that letter becomes a *d* (Gillingham, 1952).

Evidence that such a mirroring mechanism is in operation comes not only from the neurological findings presented above but also from a recent study of mirror imaging, laterality, motor abilities and spelling (Bannatyne and Wichiarajote, 1969b). Thus, the child, when it comes to the alphabet, has to discard the principle of object constancy and learn a new highly specific letter-design principle, namely, the law of directional-configuration constancy; if the circle in the *b* points one way, it means the sound /b/, whereas if it points the other way, it means the sound /d/. When the young child also senses these letters in the left-of-center visual field, (and this may easily occur in the unlateralized eye movements of young children), then the two respective memory traces may also be laid down in the right hemisphere parieto-occipital areas. If these two then transfer their traces or make them available to the other hemisphere, a four-way tangle results and the child is doubly confused. Children who find it difficult to develop this directional-configuration constancy, will when they write, produce either of the two configurations for either of the sounds /b/ and /d/. Fortunately, if the child should reverse an *s* or an *n* or most other letters, which not infrequently happens in young children, object constancy still holds and we are able to recognize the letter and associate it with its sound, merely commenting that it has been turned back to front. Obviously, symmetrical letters are the easiest to handle as they have no mirror image. It should be pointed out that these children have no visuospatial confusion in the environment at large. Rather to the contrary, *it is because they are so wedded to object constancy and know exactly where they are in normal three-dimensional life, that they become confused in the almost unique situation generated by the written alphabet where object constancy is tossed aside for an arbitrary man-made (and very inefficient) directional letter-to-sound-meaning system.* Some of these points have been examined in detail from slightly different viewpoints by Money (1966b).

Left-Right Labeling and Directional Orientation

This brings us to the other problem area, namely, differentiating left from right. *Left* and *right* are sound-word-labels associated with a pair of directional *concepts* which are essentially mirror images of each other, at least in the bodily sense. The left half of the surface of the body is more or less a mirror image of the right half, and it is a man-made convention that leftness is that area on one particular side relative to a vertical plane bisecting the body from front to rear in a standing position. If the child does an about-face, everything in the environment that was left now becomes right and vice versa. Therefore, in their own way, the concepts of left and right have no object constancy. Left and right directionality is an abstract, arbitrary, conventional system relative to the midline of the body. The difficulty which some people have in remembering which is left and which is right is not that of understanding what the concepts of direction in this context are all about. The major problem is the transgression of object constancy, because left and right as mirror-imaged halves of the body surface are identical under the law of object constancy. Not only is it the same object viewed from a different angle, but apart from the mirror image, the features are equally identical. It is as if the person who has left-right directional problems asks why two labels are given to one and the same thing; of course, he *does* know that there is a difference dependent on the way the body is facing and he strives to fit in with convention, which runs against his own visuo-spatial tendency to see and label things as they are, whatever his or their position in space.

Therefore, in a sense, we can say that the dyslexic child, or other people who have directionality problems related to the concept of left and right, are more immersed in the three-dimensional realities of their environment and in their relation to objects which are constant in that environment. To hypothesize that there is something neurologically abnormal in the form of lesions or impaired neurological dysfunction is unnecessary and misleading unless other coincidental strong evidence is available. Certainly left-right labeling confusion cannot be considered an indicator of neurological dysfunction. I know of several dyslexic children who could move about one of the largest cities in the world without any problems of reality orientation in three-dimensional space, but in their work, they constantly reversed letters, and in their conversation confused left with right. This does not mean that there are not people with lesions who exhibit the same symptoms, but rather that one should not generalize from such people to those who cannot achieve directional-configuration constancy for quite other reasons. That a proportion of dyslexic children does have problems with identifying left and right has been established by several authors, many of whom are listed by Benton (1962).

The person who is visuo-spatially inclined, and in whose brain the language functions are subservient to the visuo-spatial functions, may have a left visual field preference inasmuch as he uses the right hemisphere to interpret the environment he scans. This would mean that he would have at least an equal tendency to move his eyes from right to left, which is the reverse of the movement required in reading. Even if, as is more likely, he uses both visual fields equally, the tendency of the visuo-spatial person will be to scan the environment in three dimensions, one of them being depth, in a more or less random fashion (dependent on salient features) which is contrary to the highly lateralized visual process in one dimension and in one visual field required in reading and writing. The research findings of Lesevre (1966) tend to support such a viewpoint. This unidimensional lateralization of the gaze is by definition more easily acquired by those with verbal ability, a fact which can be established by observing the children in any first-grade reading group. It may be that children with a strong "literate" left hemisphere find it easier to inhibit and retrain the more natural three-dimensional random scanning which we all utilize during most of our waking life. The word *random* is used relatively because I realize that there are patterns to scanning the environment in most three-dimensional life situations.

Neurological Sets

Another important element in the verbal versus visuo-spatial types of brain dichotomy is the development of neurological "sets" (as the child grows into adulthood) which may enable him to switch from one modality to the other. When one indulges in concentrated verbal activity, one's brain is very likely to restructure itself neuronally for the purpose of efficiency; one works oneself into a verbal set when reading, and a visuospatial set during fast driving. People readily able to do this would fall into Walter's (1953) *R* or responsive group, whereas those having difficulty in changing sets would be *P* or *M* individuals (see the next section, "Electronencephalographic Evidence").

In concluding this section, I would like to sound a note of caution. Intelligence is a great compensator for very minor inefficiencies related to a specific skill or learning situation, for example, reading. In my work, I have come across a sprinkling of professional scientists, engineers, designers and artists who were slow learning to speak in infancy, slow learning to read and who even today are slow when working in the medium of language. Most have also had difficulty learning foreign languages. All these problems have been related to the acquisition of automatic linguistic *skills,* not to an appreciation of the content once the code has been interpreted. All can now read fluently but have problems of slow reading and spelling inaccuracies; engineers, in particular, tend to have these problems more than most. In the less intelligent dyslexic, the acquisition of these automatic linguistic code-breaking and fluency skills comes even more slowly, but except in severe cases, eventually and usually these skills are acquired. Exactly how many children in the community have these problems is unknown but I would emphasize that only a small proportion of intelligent visuo-spatial males have any *long-term* serious problems in the acquisition of their native linguistic skills and only a small proportion of these problems will originate from visuo-spatial neurological sets. The nature of the disabilities these kinds of children have will be further discussed in later chapters, particularly Chapter IX.

Electroencephalographic Evidence

The findings of studies determining the relationship between EEG variables and spatial and verbal abilities are not yet very clear-cut or consistent. I.M. Smith (1964) has summarized some of the research results in this area. The conclusion he draws is that there may be a tendency for spatial ability to be associated with a low alpha index and a high alpha frequency whereas verbal ability is associated with the converse. Mundy-Castle (1958) was the main person responsible for this finding, a result which has been confirmed by some investigations but not by others. The person who has probably done the most work in this area is Walter (1953). In EEG studies involving light flicker, he has come to the following conclusion: "It suggests that the alpha rhythms are a process of scanning-searching for a pattern—which relaxes when a pattern is found," and he has isolated three types of people with various alpha rhythm patterns with the eyes open and the eyes closed. Individuals with persistent alpha rhythms (type *P*) which are hard to block with mental effort whether the eyes are open or closed *tend to auditory, kinesthetic or tactile perceptions rather than visual imagery.* The second group (type *M* for minus) is composed of persons whose "thinking processes are conducted almost entirely in terms of visual imagery." The third group, the *R* group (the responsive), whose alpha rhythms disappear when they do an arithmetic problem or open their eyes, are intermediate between the other two groups. They may not habitually use pictorial imagery but they can evoke it when necessary to thought. In passing, it is worth noting that Walter suggests that the theta rhythm may be "a scanning for pleasure, a supposition well supported by the mental experiences accompanying its evocation." On a later page, he says,

> The other particular was the limitation of speed imposed on our sensory and mental reactions by the rate of alpha rhythm. A fast rhythm has unquestionable survival value in a way of life calling for ever speedier decisions and actions. The action difference between an alpha rhythm of 8 [cps] and one of 13 [cps] can be estimated for instance, in the emergency of stopping a car; at 50 miles an hour, a driver with a faster rhythm would stop his car five feet short of the point reached by a driver with a slower rhythm. Similarly, pedestrians and cyclists with a faster alpha rhythm have a better chance of escape.

It would seem from Walter's work that the highly visuo-spatial person would be an *M* type with an alpha frequency of 11 to 13 cycles per second and an alpha rhythm which is constantly flattened into rapid activity because of a continuous scanning internally or externally, with eyes open or shut.

More recently Hughes (1968), working with dyslexic children, examined their EEG records both before and after clustering the children in various groupings. Some of the groups were chosen on the basis of the EEG records, others on the psychological tests which were given to the children. In the first analysis of the data, Hughes found that the children with normal EEG's were superior to those with abnormal EEG's in Block Design and Comprehension on the WISC, while the abnormal group was superior in Picture Completion and Oral Reading. The computer was then asked to classify the children into normal and abnormal groups on its own analysis of the EEG records and many of the children in both groups were found to be misplaced. After further computer sorting of the sample, a best-fit clustering into four groups was found: the normal group, the occipital group (excessive slow waves in the occipital areas), the positive spike group (fourteen-per-second positive spikes) and those with other abnormalities (other slow waves or epileptiform short waves on the frontal or temporal areas). In a simple analysis of variance, the WISC Coding subtest was the only variable to be significant, the occipital group performing best, followed by the positive spike group, the normal group and finally the other abnormalities group, which had the lowest score. This one result in twenty-two could have occurred by chance alone. In a third grouping analysis, the normal and other abnormalities cases were combined into one group and contrasted with the positive spike and occipital cases. A multiple discriminant analysis showed the most distinctive separation of the groups. Hughes states his results thus:

> The two tests which scored highest in the discriminant function were Verbal I.Q., which was relatively low for the positive spike and occipital classification, and Spelling, which was relatively low for the normal and other abnormalities classifications. Block Design was a significant variable in the comparison between normal and abnormal cases and Coding was significant when the four different groups were treated separately. Oral Reading or Spelling are shown to be significant on all three comparisons.

In his conclusion, Hughes states:

> Nevertheless, excessive posterior slowing is frequently seen in a number of conditions including learning disabilities. The other wave form which must be implicated in studies on learning disabilities is the 6-7 and 14/second positive spike phenomenon. This pattern can be seen in approximately ½ of dyslexic children and with a similar incidence in a group of scholastic "underachievers."

Hughes does not attempt any further interpretation of the significant results. Examining the results, it can be seen that those with occipital and positive spike abnormalities do best on the Coding, Spelling and Oral Reading tests, all of which require high automatic language sound sequencing and processing in the speech and language sections of the brain which by and large are not occipital. Perhaps this is an overcompensation in the auditory language areas for occipital shortcomings. The normal and other abnormalities groups were superior on Block Design and WISC Verbal IQ. The Block Design may indicate superior spatial ability but in conjunction with Verbal IQ and the superiority of the normal group in Comprehension (on another analysis of the results given by Hughes), it is much more likely that these scores are caused by the overall higher IQ of the normal and other abnormalities groups. Hughes does not indicate how the children were selected, if they are a representative sample and whether or not they are matched in pairs. He does not mention sex differences. The results of his research must be treated with great caution and they do, as Hughes notes, indicate a need for a great deal more research. This is an excellent pioneering study which in an elaborated version should be carried out afresh on a much larger representative sample, with all the variables carefully controlled. Perhaps the most outstanding and valuable contribution in the above study is that the computer was used to cluster the children on complex criteria, which is a procedure I would recommend in nearly all psychological and educational research involving numerous psychological variables.

The Right Temporal Lobe

Several comments have been made in foregoing sections about the possible functions of the right temporal lobe. It will be remembered that Mishkin (1962) had suggested that the right temporal lobe in man may be dominant for visual functions. Certainly, Penfield and Roberts (1959) found a stream of consciousness interpretive cortex in both temporal lobes; the analogy they used was that of an auditory-visual film sequence. Today, we might call it a video tape record of events in time.

The person who has carried out most of the work on the laterality effects in audition is Milner (1962) who, like many others, found that the left temporal area is largely concerned with the processing of language sounds and related data. However, she states that she and her co-workers have not found any deficits on any verbal task after right temporal lobectomy when that hemisphere is nondominant for speech, and that lesions in the right hemisphere do cause a variety of visual *memory* defects in face recognition, nonsense figure recognition and a delayed recall for geometric figures. In the latter case, the designs can be correctly reproduced at the time of the original presentation. Patients with right temporal lesions are slow and inaccurate in detecting incongruities in sketchy cartoon-like drawings (Milner, 1958) and although they do not easily recognize groups of dots tachistoscopically presented, they can perceive objects to which a name can be attached. In each of these reports, there does not seem to be any indication of a *distortion* of the visual material but rather a memory recognition defect of a kind in which present perception does not match up with, or even connect with, previous experience of an object or configuration. In other words, it is *visual memory through time which is disturbed* rather than the distorted central vision in the present often found in occipital and occipital-parietal lesions, particularly in the right posterior hemisphere.

Milner (1962) gave the Seashore measures of musical talents to thirty-eight patients with temporal lobe lesions. There were no changes in these musical tests for the appreciation of time, rhythm or pitch, even though in every case the right temporal lesion people had more errors than the left. In the case of loudness, there was a barely significant difference between the two groups, the right temporal group making more errors. *In the timbre and tonal memory (melody discrimination) subtests, the error difference was most marked and highly significant.* Therefore, it would seem that the discrimination of tonal memory or melodies, and differences in timbre, are much more functions of the right temporal lobe than of the left. (It is interesting to compare these results with those of Wolf, 1967, in which he found significant differences on many of the Seashore tests between normal children and a group of dyslexic children without detectable neurological dysfunction. Note that the significant tests in Wolf's study were rhythm, timbre, tonal memory and loudness, in that order of significance. However, one should not jump to the erroneous conclusion that a large proportion of poor readers in our schools have right-sided temporal lesions.) It is worth noting again that Milner found no deficits in reasoning or problem solving in patients with temporal lobe lesions on either side—a similar result to all other equivalent research.

It would seem on the evidence that the right temporal area is partially concerned with a video tape type memory for nonverbal visual and auditory events, and that this occurs in the temporal interpretive cortex of both hemispheres in line with the work of Penfield and his colleagues. But just as there is an area demarcation for the interpretive cortex and the primary and secondary auditory language areas in the left temporal area, it would seem likely that the same division of function occurs in the right temporal lobe but in this case with *nonlinguistic*, more tonal musical data. This does not mean that when the primary and secondary auditory areas in the right temporal lobe are stimulated, the patient will hear words or music or anything that represents a memory. Penfield and Roberts make it quite clear that there is no overlap between the interpretive cortex with its memory functions and the other temporal sensory areas. In fact, they state that these experiential hallucinations or interpretive illusions were only produced by stimulation of certain areas in both temporal lobes. Note that one major key to temporal lobe activity in terms of sound sensing and memorizing is an appreciation of *time*.

RELEVANCE TO NEUROLOGICAL DEFECTS IN CHILDREN

Although much of the work described in this chapter used samples of children, there is a wealth of neurological information collected from adult patients, and workers with children usually ask how this can be meaningfully interpreted. Do adult findings have any relevance to the psychoneurology of childhood? Childhood aphasia is in many ways different from adult aphasia and there is little doubt that the psychoneurological development of children with lesions may be very different from that of most normal children. Sperry (1964) mentions the case of a boy without a corpus callosum who developed language in both hemispheres. The ability of the intact hemisphere to take over from damaged or ablated areas in the other hemisphere is well documented (Penfield and Roberts, 1959).

It is very likely that most of the adults who are operated on for a variety of brain lesions have all had only minor localization of function displacements which are different from those possessed by a majority of normal individuals. In other words, the heterogeneity of the cases itself is a guarantee that the localization of function described by a large number of authorities is reasonably characteristic of the distribution of localization in the brain in normal individuals. Furthermore, many of the lesions in many of the patients no doubt developed *after* childhood and consequently the localization of function in their brain will be that of the majority of normal adults. All these adults were once children and nobody has ever suggested that there is a sudden neurological mutation which takes place with the onset of adulthood. Therefore, we can be fairly sure that the general localization picture documented in this chapter is characteristic of most school-age children. I would not like to generalize too far back into early childhood or babyhood, during which time distinctive developmental features and patterns may cause temporary maturational variations, neurologically speaking. Most authorities such as Luria and Penfield, although they usually mention whether or not a particular subject is a child or an adult, do not bother to separate out groups of school-age children from adults; they seem to assume automatically that there is a developmental continuum in terms of localization and therefore they cluster together children and adults when making localization statements.

Chapter VII

MEMORY, MODALITY AND MATURATION

TYPES OF MEMORY AND DEFINITIONS

Almost all research into memory has been concerned with a verbal, usually visual language content, one of the most complex psychoneurological systems possible. Also, in most instances, the subjects used for the experimentation have been university students who come to the laboratory with a wealth of personal knowledge and established intricate learning systems. It seems that memory researchers (mostly through a traditional legacy) have unwittingly chosen the most difficult conditions to investigate basic memory theory and its laws.

Even so, from the point of view of the student of language, it is rather fortunate that this situation has existed because there now exists a body of research findings and formulated memory laws which allow some insight into the acquisition of language and its operational functioning in differing types of learning situations.

The various types of memory, their dimensions and broad definitions, are elaborated below. These definitions will be followed by a discussion of memory research, its findings and its attempts to isolate and formulate constant laws.

Memory in Terms of Storage and Association

That some sensory perceptions are recorded by the brain and stored there for shorter or longer amounts of time, nobody denies. Likewise, almost everyone is agreed that these stored sensory perceptions can be linked or associated together in complex clusters. It has been useful to have a word-label to tag one sensory perception memory unit and the most popular is the word *trace,* usually associated with some qualifying word such as *stimulus* or

243

memory. The word *engram* used to be current many years ago as a synonym for *memory trace,* and it is still used by some people such as Sperry (1964) in some of his neurological discussions. For example, in talking about hemispheric dominance, he says, "In man, where one hemisphere is nearly always dominant, the single-engram system tends to prevail, particularly in all memory relating to language." In this chapter, as the words are interchangeable, I shall use the word *trace* in all contexts. Sensory and perceptual traces can be stored in the brain as units, in associated clusters or as a connected series, the interconnections or associations of the latter two categories being either logically or arbitrarily associated. When these clusters or series are very firmly associated or remembered, they may form a habit or skill which has some degree of automatization as, for example, in speech. Some of these points will also be elaborated in more detail below.

Ways of Reinforcing Memory

The word *reinforcement* is another of those interdisciplinary terms which requires some clarification of meaning since operant conditioners use the term in one way, memory theorists in another and the dictionary in still another. In order to distinguish between the three, I have resorted to the use of mnemonics, using the initial letters of key words in the three definitions.

M-reinforcement will be the label used to describe the use of *motivational drives* and their satiation in the process of operant conditioning to raise learning performance levels. For example, if one rewards a child with candy after each successful learning operation, M-reinforcement is being utilized, and in this case, hunger is the motivational drive.

T-reinforcement will be used as the memory theorists mostly use it, namely, to indicate *trial* repetition, a procedure used in much rote and semantic learning. The subject repeats the words to be learned on a list, or in the form of paired associates or repeats the multiplication tables until an acceptable degree of learning is apparent to the experimenter. In most cases, the criterior of performance is one successful, perfectly remembered run-through of the list, pairs or tables.

A-reinforcement is that traditional kind of reinforcement defined by the dictionary; it is most apparent in the term *reinforced concrete*. Much of the strength of reinforced concrete is imparted by the steel bars or netting which lends its support or assistance to the concrete itself. Thus, A-reinforcement occurs when there is *assistance* from another agent in the same "generic" class, e.g., steel and concrete are both constructional materials. A-reinforcment is a valuable concept to educators who will talk about reinforcing auditory-visual reading processes by utilizing kinesthetic tracing of enlarged writing. The generic class here is "sensorimotor processes or modalities."

Memory in Terms of Time

Traditionally, two types of memory form the basis of experimentation: short-term memory and long-term memory.

Short-term memory (STM) is concerned with retention over a period of seconds or at the very most a few minutes. As will be seen, the amount that can be stored in STM over short periods is very limited; at most, several pieces of information, or bits or chunks, as they are called, may be held at one time but unless they are T-reinforced, either explicitly or through inner rehearsal, forgetting will be rapid.

Long-term memory (LTM) is the expression used to indicate the storage of learned material over hours, days or years. The storage capacity of LTM is immense and this very fact has led to a great variety of hypotheses about its nature.

T-reinforcement, in particular, and other reinforcment procedures in general, shift trace information from STM to LTM with varying degrees of permanence.

Memory in Terms of Sensory Modalities

It is self-evident that memory traces of either kind can occur in each of the sensory modalities. We can remember visual, auditory, kinesthetic, haptic, olfactory and visceral experiences either separately or in various combinations. Thus, verbal behavior can be either auditory or both auditory and visual, as in the case of reading; or auditory, visual and kinesthetic, as in the case of writing. Actually, motor-memory must be in large part dependent on the kinesthetic patterns of past motor experience, patterns which one can use to encode motor activity in the present. Additionally, one can use the same kinesthetic patterns of movement for cerebral feedback matching purposes. For example, in writing, kinesthetic feedback will allow us to correct automatically and instantly for deviations from the habitual pattern. In the case of writing, vision will also contribute feedback information to be matched against established visual patterns and it is not unlikely that the traces of all this visual, kinesthetic and haptic sensory information are totally integrated in habitual pattern sequences in the parietal areas (see Chapter VI).

Memory in Terms of Stimulus Information and Cues

If a subject is presented with data to be learned and does so to a required level, the memory can be tested or evoked in two clear-cut ways. He can recall the data "out of the blue" in the absence of the original material, or he can identify the original data which is presented to him, usually along with other similar data. The former process is called *recall* and the latter *recognition.*

Recall, then, can be defined as remembering the criterion response in its original form and reproducing it accurately on demand in the absence of the original stimulus.

Recognition, on the other hand, can be defined as remembering a criterion response to the performance level of being able to identify the original stimulus accurately on re-presentation, as having been experienced before exactly in that form.

The distinction between recall and recognition is somewhat blurred when definite cues and other mediation or materials are used to facilitate recall. For example, if words are learned in pairs and one of the pair (the stimulus) is presented to cue the recall of the other (the criterion response), the reproduction of the response would seem to be easier than if the cue word was not supplied. The difference is that the cue word is *recognized* and this very recognition of the cue word in paired associate learning very probably introduces recognition pathways which would not be used in pure recall. If the cue word (or action, or design) of the pair originally learned has structural or content elements in common with the criterion response, partial response recognition may occur along with the recall process. This occurs particularly when the subject builds in a mediational recognition "bridge" from cue to criterion response in order to facilitate the recall of the latter. For example, if on the cue *car* one has to recall the criterion response *night,* one could use as a mediator the word *star,* the letters *ar* being the recognition bridge. Thus, although recall and recognition may be separate neurological and psychological processes (and it is by no means certain that they are), in the laboratory they may be very closely interwoven.

Forgetting

A great deal more can be learned about memory if its converse is investigated, namely, forgetting. Everyone has been in the situation of not being able to remember essential information in a moment of need, and the question which memory theorists and researchers ask themselves is, What happened to the memory trace of the data which had been previously experienced and learned at least in some degree? The answer is in some doubt, as there are two major theories of forgetting, neither of which have been decisively proved or disproved.

The first of these is *spontaneous trace decay,* where the memory trace atrophies over time because it is not being used. In other words, it is in the neurological nature of memory to rid itself of unnecessary and unused information, keeping in store only those items T-reinforced through frequent use or initial overlearning. While there is no direct evidence against the theory of spontaneous trace decay, experiments by Jenkins and Dallenbach (1924) have shown that when subjects sleep between learning nonsense syllables and recalling them, they can do twice as well as if they spend their waking hours engaged in other activities. The authors conclude that forgetting is largely a function of interference and inhibition of the old traces by the new. This result has been supported in experiments on prose learning by Grissom *et al.* (1962), who deprived their experimental group of almost all everyday stimuli for twenty-four hours. The experimental group without any rehearsal actually improved their recall of the test passage.

Thus, the second main theory of forgetting is that new material being memorized *interferes* in some way with the previously learned material. This interference, which can only come from the registration of traces laid down by new stimuli, can be accounted for in two different ways, each way forming an alternative subtheory.

The first subtheory suggests that the interference resulting from new traces causes a *decay* (which is not spontaneous, but occurs through an agent, namely, the new trace system) of the original memory trace, particularly when it is not reinforced by any method. Exactly how the new trace system causes decay in the old has not been indicated by the proponents of the theory but this is not surprising as it is more a neurological question than a psychological one.

The second subtheory of interference as a cause of forgetting is that the new incoming trace system being laid down forms a *barrier* or has an isolating effect on the old memory trace, tending to partially or completely seal it off from *availability* to the volitional consciousness of the individual concerned. A major implication of the barrier interference theory of forgetting is that memory traces are never truly forgotten because they do not disappear from the storage systems of the brain. To the degree to which we have paid attention to, and learned, information, so must it be recorded and stored, and if the trace barrier theory has any validity, our problem is one of how to retrieve memories rather than how to stop forgetting what we have learned.

The active processes which cause decay or barrier forgetting are termed *inhibition* or *interference*, and memory theorists and researchers mostly seem to use the two words interchangeably.

A third main theory of forgetting which has been promoted by the gestalt theorist Koffka (1935) is that the trace interference takes the form of restructuring the original trace by the new one. This blending of the two traces tends to form a more "perfect or ideal" resultant memory than either of the two traces would have had independently. The theory implies an affinity between similar "bits" of data which coalesce as the successive memory traces are laid down. Most of the work of the gestalt psychologists has been in the area of visual configuration identification, particularly with respect to closure, the process in which the brain supplies or fills in the missing bits when the data are not quite complete.

The gestalt theory of forgetting has been criticized by J.A. Adams (1967b) in his excellent book on human memory as follows: "And, the central notion that dynamic brain forces urge a figure towards an ideal configuration was a doubtful hypothesis attractive only to the in-group of the gestalt movement. Whatever merit the notion might have had, it fell decisively under the strong experimental attack by Hebb and Foord [1945]." While it is true that the theories of the "old-line gestalt views" are not currently very acceptable, this is mainly because of the failure of the gestalt psychologists to integrate their ideas on closure and preception with other theoretical movements in the mainstream of psychology. The concept of closure is too valuable to be thrown away without further consideration. It is almost self-evident that we continuously utilize past experience of a conceptual coalesced kind to close on inadequate perceptual incoming data. The entire probability "matching" theory of perception (R.L. Gregory, 1966) which has resulted from the study of the preception of illusions is fundamentally a "new-look" theory of gestalt closure, experimentally well founded. But closure occurs not only in the field of vision; it also operates in the auditory areas. When we listen on a noisy telephone line, to a strange accent or to someone speaking rapidly, we continuously close or fill in the unheard or distorted fragments. These psychological closure experiences, which we have all had in the area of language, dovetail neatly with current neurological theories of matching (Chapter VI) and current psycholinguistic theories (Chapter II).

Several points need to be made about a modern theory of closure. First of all, it is a theory of input perception and has little to do directly with output or encoding except inasmuch as the changes in output can occur as a result of continual closure. When we listen to, and interpret, scrambled or strange speech in our own language, we still match it with our existing personal extensive inner receptive language but once this is done, thinking and output utilize processes other than closure. Thus, closure is a process of matching incomplete perceptions against long-term previously learned integrated experience. Closure is an aspect of LTM, and novel perceptions (held in STM) will only transform strongly established LTM traces if they are continually perceived over long periods of time. For example, if an individual lives in a part of the country for many years where his native language is spoken with a particular accent, closure usually causes definite changes in his traces and output accent, these changes ranging from minor to major variations. In children, such changes of accent are often considerable. Quite apart from auditory, visual or other sensory percepts, trace transformation theory, perhaps in a modified form, can account for *concepts* of classes of objects or ideas. When I think of the concept *dog*, it is very unlikely that my brain scans every individual memory of every dog I have ever perceived (although such a state of affairs is not impossible). Even if one does neurologically scan every instance which has gone into building up a concept, it is quite likely that the concept itself is also stored in the brain and that it has been successively, modified or transformed by successive individual experiences. The successively modified concept trace would become more and more centralized and generalized as the individual experiences impinged on it over the years. Furthermore, individual memory traces (to use an analogy) could also be stored like satellites around the concept trace.

It can be shown that concepts exist because, for example, when someone is presented with a picture in a magazine of a new-model car he has never seen before, he recognizes it as a car without any doubt. One can also draw a picture of a car which one has never seen before. The same is true for language functioning where many linguistic utterances appear to be original in their selection of words and sentence structure. Rather than dispense with the concepts of gestalt psychology, a careful reevaluation of them should be made with a view to integrating closure and matching research findings into our wider knowledge of memory and learning.

The theories of forgetting which have been outlined above are not necessarily incompatible. It is difficult to experimentally test the hypothesis of spontaneous trace decay but this does not mean that it is an incorrect one. In some experiments, traces are inhibited or interfered with in some way by newer stimuli, but this does not invalidate the hypothesis that other traces may decay spontaneously. It is equally possible that overlearned material is permanently stored and never decays but that it can be "fenced off," so to speak, by inhibitory barriers which prevent recall or recognition.

The Efficient Causes of Interference

Memory traces can be interfered with either retroactively or proactively. *Retroactive inhibition* is said to occur when material we have previously learned is interfered with (forgotten) by material which has been subsequently learned. The new material in some way blots out or seals off the old.

Proactive inhibition is the reverse situation, in which the newly learned material cannot be remembered when tested because material (usually of a similar kind) which has been learned on an earlier test interferes with or in some way inhibits the new material's retention.

Both retroactive and proactive inhibition experiments have been carried out to test interference theory in both STM and LTM and the conclusions will be reviewed later.

Extinction and Reminiscence

If a habit has been learned, it is possible to extinguish it by eliminating any survival value the act or activity may have for the individual. Thus, extinction occurs in operant conditioning research when M-reinforcement is eliminated after a habit has been learned. A cat can be taught to open a box to get food but if, after the habit is established, the food is then eliminated, the box-opening behavior will slowly decline until it is entirely extinguished. However, if the cat is taken away and later put back in the same situation, it may open the box a few times as if it had remembered that once upon a time food was in there. This slight spontaneous resurgence of memory for behaviors which have been previously extinguished is called *reminiscence*. In some ways, such experiments tend to indicate that the habit is in some degree permanently remembered but that it is inhibited from being activated because of a lack of motivation. Presumably, the hungrier the cat is, the more likely his reminiscent investigation of the box is to occur. Reminiscence may cause problems in dyslexic children when previously overlearned incorrect spellings or pronunciations spontaneously reappear even after considerable extinction has taken place. In situations involving reminiscence, it is possible that the extinguishing experiences are subject to proactive inhibition.

The Permanence of the Trace

The extreme position with regard to trace permanence is that every single stimulus impinging on our senses is indelibly recorded in the brain. Few workers would identify with this viewpoint but according to J.A. Adams (1967b) most learning theorists seem to consider LTM permanent, the strength of the trace being increased by any type of reinforcement. Only one's *performance* (in a given trial) can be lowered by poor motivation or work inhibition. There is no definitive experimental evidence to test and confirm the hypothesis of the "fundamental" permanence of memory. If there were, it would shift research efforts to the principles of retrieval from interference rather than the prevention of forgetting (J.A. Adams, 1967b).

VERBAL LEARNING—LTM

Interference

Most verbal learning studies seem to support the hypothesis that both proactive and retroactive interference cause the extinction of the memory trace rather than putting a barrier around it (Adams, 1967b). This is certainly true of retroactive inhibition since most experiments have been devoted to an exploration of its effects. The more practice a subject has on the original material, the more it resists the extinguishing action of interpolated learned material (retroactive inhibition). The more interpolated material is learned, the more it extinguishes the original material. The experiments from which these laws were built were directed at investigating long-term semantic memory. Some of the evidence supporting this general viewpoint was presented above in the section on forgetting.

Similarity

Osgood (1949) has set down three laws of transfer and retroaction as follows:

1. Where stimuli are varied and responses are functionally identical, positive transfer and retroactive facilitation are obtained, the magnitude of both increasing as a similarity among the stimulus members increases.*

2. Where stimuli are functionally identical and responses are varied, negative transfer and retroactive interference are obtained, the magnitude of both decreasing as similarity of the responses increases.†

3. When both stimulus and response members are simultaneously varied, negative transfer and retroactive interference are obtained, the magnitude of both increasing as the stimulus similarity increases.

The implications of these laws for children learning to read are considerable. When reading, the child is presented with a visual stimulus (grapheme) with which he has to associate a given sound response (phoneme). Owing to both the irregular orthography of the English language and the importance of the *sequencing* of the letters composing graphemes and phonemes, both stimuli and responses are *extremely variable,* thus causing laws 2 and 3 to operate very actively. The variability is aggravated because through reversibility, many grapheme stimuli may elicit a particular phoneme, and one grapheme may elicit many phonemes. Laws 1 and 2 also operate because many graphemes

---

*In other words, the more alike the stimulus words, the easier it will be to remember the single response word.

†This means that it is difficult to remember a set of response words of different meanings as replies to a single word used to elicit each one in turn.

are identical and elicit, or are elicited by, different phonemes. Therefore, any individual child with a poor memory system will be at a distinct disadvantage learning to read; interference operates continuously. In the process of writing or spelling, an identical situation holds true and the very fact that the system has to work from both ends of the complex phoneme-to-grapheme sequences of associations merely adds to the confusion.

Part Versus Whole Learning

In a series of experiments on the topic of part versus whole memorization of material, Postman and Goggin (1964, 1966) have found that on a wide range of materials "The results show consistently that total learning time under the two conditions of practice is either identical or shows only a minor advantage in favor of the part method" (Quote from Postman, 1965.) However, in the *repetitive part method,* parts learned earlier continue to be practiced as new ones are added and this reduces interpart interference and retroactive inhibition: "Total learning time by the repetitive part method is significantly less than by either the whole or the pure part method."

Therefore, any teaching of reading, writing or spelling should operate on this repetitive part, integrative method rather than on a whole or pure part technique. New phoneme-grapheme associations to be learned should be successively added to the previously learned ones while the latter are still being continuously used.

VERBAL LEARNING—STM

Relationship of STM to LTM

Broadbent (1958) has suggested that incoming sensory information is held for brief periods of time in an STM storage system (S-system). Associated with this storage system is a filtering device which in the light of past experience selects relevant information which can then be either fed back into the STM store or passed on to other areas for long-term storage. The short-term store recirculation process of the S-system enables one to keep that particular STM to the forefront of attention for immediate utilization. Any practice or rehearsal (T-reinforce-ment) assisting LTM registration would take place in this feed-back STM loop.

Broadbent's psychological model corresponds rather neatly to Luria's (1966) neurological sensory analyzers which screen in-coming information actively in the light of past experience. Both theories also fit well with the closure model described above. In this context, the screening out of unnecessary information in the light of past experience would have the quality of a useful "nega-tive" action, whereas the effect of closure in the screening ex-perience would be a pulling in or positive attraction of the relevant data for the information already learned. If one does not postulate some kind of experiential dynamic selection of relevant stimuli coming from the brain itself, one must ascribe the sensory flow into the subject as originating only in the stimulus field, a passive role which Luria justifiably criticizes. It is very likely that the motivational pressures on the organism in terms of survival-value drive states do operate internally (in the light of experience) more as a "pulling" action which actively selects preferred stimuli even to the point of seeking them out. An animal will seek the trail to the water hole when it is thirsty, actively selecting the learned chain of stimuli which will lead to slaking that thirst. Therefore, I prefer the word *analyzer* to the word *screen* as a term for the device which selects relevant stimuli on either a positive or a negative basis. This active role of seeking relevant stimuli is also described by Broadbent (1958) under the heading of "vigilance tasks." Thus, the terms *screening* and *filter* are perhaps too passive in denotation compared with the more active word *analyzer* used by Luria.

STM and Serial Recall

Peterson and Peterson (1959) examined the rates of forgetting in STM by presenting subjects with three-consonant units and then preventing rehearsal by having the subjects count back-ward in threes or fours. The curve of forgetting was rapid, the subjects remembering 80 percent of the original data after three seconds but less than 10 percent after eighteen seconds. Hellyer

(1962) found that if the subject is allowed to practice using T-reinforcement, the degree to which the stimulus series is retained is a direct function of the number of repetitions. Many other researchers have shown that *the degree of practice increases the degree of retention.* The only question in all these findings is whether or not LTM is playing a part. If the material can be remembered the next day, it is hardly correct to call the process STM, even if the actual period of direct memorizing practice occurred in less than forty seconds. Once again, the distinction between STM and LTM becomes blurred.

The Role of Interference in STM Recall

That STM forgetting is more a function of interference from other material learned than of "spontaneous" decay was demonstrated by Keppel and Underwood (1962). They found that three-consonant (trigram) test patterns are almost perfectly remembered when there is no proactive inhibition from other learned material.

The Capacity of STM

The span of memory in terms of the number of units which can be retained is essentially invariant. This was determined by G.A. Miller (1956) when he found that the number of chunks or units which an individual can remember is approximately seven, whatever the amount of relatively homogeneous information in each chunk. Thus, the only way to expand one's memory span is to increase the information within chunks organizationally through some mediation process. Thus, as Postman (1965) puts it, "The practical implication is that the most effective method for increasing the capacity of immediate and short-term memory is not necessarily practice on the memory task itself, but instruction in recoding, i.e., in the grouping and categorizing of the environmental sequences which can become functional units in the reception and immediate storage of information." The idea of recoding in the form of grouping or categorizing to form memorable chunks of information is particularly important for children who are having trouble learning to read, write or spell. For example, I have found in teaching practice that color coding greatly assists children to remember phoneme-to-grapheme associations by categorizing them in a regular system. Also, if children see and hear words as syllables, many of which are interchangeable from word to word, they will have less difficulty spelling than they will when they see words as series of single letters. These and other suggestions for grouping and categorizing are elaborated in Chapter XV.

Interference by Acoustical or Semantic Similarity

R. Conrad (1962, 1964) conducted experiments to discover first which letters of the alphabet when listened to are most confused by subjects, and second which letters of the alphabet were confused when seen by subjects. In both cases, the confusion was greatest for letters which *sounded* alike. This experiment is a striking part-confirmation of the hypothesis that *reading and spelling are essentially auditory processes.* Conrad's experiments were confirmed by Wickelgren (1965), who used digits as well as letters of the alphabet. In all cases, items which sounded alike were the most confused. Visual similarity played a minor role.

That *acoustical similarity* interferes more with STM than does semantic similarity was demonstrated by Baddeley (1966) in a series of experiments.

It is interesting to note for long-term verbal memory *semantic* interference is far more important, but in neither STM nor LTM verbal experiments does visual interference seem to play a very active role. In the case of STM, acoustical similarity causes the greatest interference with retention. Once again, this would seem to confirm that language processes, even when visual as in reading, are at the immediate sensory level mostly auditory and non-semantic, a finding which supports the neurological model of speech perception outlined in the previous chapter. Only when the memory of the words is more permanent (LTM) does the meaning of the word become an important variable. This is rather obvious when one considers that an incoming word must be analyzed and identified as a sequence of sounds before one has any experiential chunk or gestalt to which the meaning can be associated.

Recently Chall (1967), after an extensive evaluation of reading research, has suggested that phonic code breaking is the most effective way of teaching reading and that this technique does not lead to any dissociation from the meaning of the words. Her conclusions are completely in accord with the research results quoted above, namely, that acoustical interference is a key variable in STM while semantic interference is important in LTM. In other words, STM is mainly sensory and LTM is mainly meaning-oriented.

STM acoustical interference has implications for the learning of spelling. Efficient teachers have long known that children are confused by lists of words having the same vowel phonemes but differing graphemes. The visual discrimination is overridden by the identity of sound. The best method is to list words with similar sounds and vowel spellings, comparing lists only after learning is complete.

MEDIATIONAL LEARNING IN MEMORY

Mediation and Short-Term Recall

Mention has already been made above (Postman, 1965) that the capacity of STM is approximately seven chunks. However, by grouping or categorizing the content of chunks in mediational ways, the ultimate capacity of STM can be considerably extended. For example, by grouping numbers in threes, or letters into syllables, which are seen as chunks, many more basic items (letters or numbers) can be remembered. In either case meaningfulness will A-reinforce the memorization process; furthermore, if the subject can add his own language mediation associations to the inherent meaningfulness of the stimuli, the short-term recall will be further increased (Groninger, 1966). When a subject creates his own verbal mediators to assist him in recalling stimulus material, the expression *natural language mediators (NLM)* is used (Adams, 1967b). Most people seem to use NLM's (see below) as A-reinforcement to assist in recalling both STM and LTM items.

Mediation and Long-Term Recall

The way in which subjects use NLM's to assist recall has been explored by Adams and Montague (1967). They found that the NLM methods used in paired-word associations are as follows:

1. Sentence association—the two words are used together meaningfully in one sentence.

2. The two words are associated by a single link word of a generic or like nature. This is a form of categorizing.

3. The two words are linked by a sound association; a common rhyme is found between sounds in the two words.

4. The initial letters are associated and remembered.

No doubt other types of NLM's operate not only in paired word associations but also in other types of material. Adams speculates that there are three possible ways in which NLM's may facilitate recall. The first suggests that NLM's are predictors of associational strength between words but have no intrinsic part in that association. The second hypothesis is that NLM's may occur toward the end of the memorizing process and are more a result of it than a facilitator. If the first hypothesis is a "before" correlation, this second one might be called an "after" correlation. The third possibility could be called a "during" hypothesis inasmuch as the "subject capitalizes on the relationship between elements of a pair and integrated sequences in his language repertoire and brings these sequences to bear on the learning of the pair" (Adams, 1967b). Adams calls this "the transfer-of-training view in that verbal units are learned in relation to a vast matrix of existing language habits." Once again, I would suggest that these three hypotheses are not mutually exclusive as processes (unless one deliberately hypothesizes them as mutually exclusive). However, I find it difficult to conceptualize what "associative strength" (first hypothesis) can mean as an experimentally founded variable which by definition has nothing to do with the elements or attributes of words. It is apparent that even a seemingly simple association between two words is almost certainly an extremely complex system of linkages between elements which exist or can be built on an equally wide variety of levels, all the way from distinctive features (Chapter II) to full semantic meaning.

This complexity is being investigated experimentally as in the work of Amster, *et al.* (1970). They found that children memorized highly associated letter pairs more quickly and retained them better over one week than they did low-strength pairs. The results support the importance of the role of letter-sequence interference in the forgetting of letter pairs. Thus it would seem that the more common letter-associated pairs were better remembered through the mediation of meaningful units which the children tended to build from the high-strength pairs (FI, CA, YR, AB, etc.). By contrast the low-strength pairs did not lend themselves to such mediational measures.

Montague *et al.* (1966) have shown that provided they are correctly remembered, NLM's are a powerful aid to accurate recall. But, to date, little is known about the "technology" of mediators apart from the few findings mentioned above, namely, grouping, categorizing, rhyming, using initial letters, clustering conceptually and creating meaningful sentences. All attributes of language which have already been learned by the subject have the potential to be used by him as NLM's in the appropriate learning situation and with appropriate material as stimuli.

Trained Mediation

Adams (1967b) makes the statement,

Natural language mediation is fallible. Not all subjects have freely available mediators for all items and some have inefficient or weak ones. A much better scheme is the teaching of an efficient mediator. We have yet to appraise thoroughly the variables for teaching effective mediators, but the practical implications of this method are large. There is no reason why schoolteachers of future generations should not show students ways of learning materials that will result in their high recall.

This is very true, although, of course, many teachers and their students have long resorted to the intermittent use of a variety of types of NLM aids to memory. There is a great need for research on NLM's and a translation of the results into classroom techniques.

Very few psychologists, psycholinguists, memory theorists or learning theorists seem to interest themselves in the basic research problems of learning to read and spell. While the work of R. Conrad (1962, 1964), Baddeley (1966) and Wickelgren (1965) mentioned above in small part confirms my contention that the reading process is almost entirely an auditory/vocal one, with visual processes (or fingers in the case of the blind) contributing a much smaller, albeit essential, part. This is particularly true for phoneme-grapheme matching in reading, frequently a fundamental problem for a large number of children with reading disabilities. Elsewhere (Bannatyne, 1966e), I have suggested how color coding can act as an A-reinforcer or mediator in serial phoneme-grapheme associations but although this and many other helpful memorization techniques exist, most are rather unsystematized and pragmatic. For example, motor-kinesthetic tracing has long been used to A-reinforce phoneme-grapheme matching in reading (Fernald, 1943), but the most effective method of carrying out this training is not known. The repetitive part method (in which parts learned earlier continue to be practiced as new ones are added) is known to be superior to other methods of rote learning (Postman and Goggin, 1964, 1966) and it should help considerably in the learning-to-read situation, especially when A-reinforcers such as color coding or kinesthetic tracing are used.

One study which has contributed to our knowledge of the development of grapheme-phoneme associations is that of Gibson *et al.* (1963). They tabulate their results concisely as follows:

(1) Familiar three-letter words which have been practiced as units were read more accurately by all the first-graders tested and by the third-grade boys than were non-word trigrams (three consonants in series). (2) Pronounceable trigrams were read more accurately than unpronounceable ones by the same children with both letter and trigram frequency controlled. (3) Third-grade girls read all three-letter combinations with high and equal accuracy resembling adult readers. (4) Span (length of word which can be read under these conditions) increased from first to third grade. (5) As span increased, a difference in reading accuracy also developed between longer pronounceable and unpronounceable pseudo-words. (6) Tentatively, it is concluded that a child in the early stages of reading skill typically reads in short units but has already generalized certain

consistent predictions of grapheme-phoneme correspondence so that units which fit these simple "rules" are more easily read. As skill develops, span increases and a similar difference can be observed for longer spans. The longer items involve more complex contingency rules and longer vowel and consonant spelling so that the generalizations must increase in complexity as the span increases. Thus, the second hypothesis suggested in the introduction is supported. Even though a child is presented with "whole words" and encouraged to associate the printed word as a whole with the spoken word, he still begins to perceive some regularities of correspondence between the printed and written terms and transfers these to the reading of unfamiliar items. This generalizing process undoubtedly promotes reading efficiency and could be facilitated by presenting material in such a way as to enhance the regularities and speed up their incorporation.

It is true that most of these findings, if not all, are already incorporated in the better phonics or linguistics reading programs, but the information may be new to some people and, therefore, it has been reiterated here. This study is an example of the type of detailed research of which there is a great need. The exact order of acquisition of memory (associational) phoneme-grapheme generalizations in the process of learning to read would greatly help in planning reading coursework. This acquisition should be examined under conditions of both deliberate phoneme-grapheme matching training and spontaneous generalization.

RECOGNITION

Definition

It will be remembered that earlier in the chapter, recognition was defined as remembering a criterion response to the performance level of being able to identify the original stimulus accurately on re-presentation as having been experienced before exactly in that form.

Many people have discovered for themselves that the recognition of immediately re-presented material is almost 100 percent accurate under normal circumstances and this has been confirmed in experiments (Shepard, 1967). However, if the stimuli are re-presented days later, the ability to recognize previously presented stimuli falls off markedly (Shepard, 1967).

Other Variables of Recognition

The term *familiarity* has been used by Noble (1953, 1954) as a different variable to meaningfulness and he has empirically defined it as an increasing, negatively accelerated function of stimulation frequency. Put the other way around, this means that the more often one sees an object, the more rapidly one becomes familiar with it, even if one does not know its meaning (purpose). However, Gorman (1961) and Shepard (1967) found that almost exactly the opposite held for word recognition familiarity. In general, words which occur most frequently in the language tend to be less well recognized than unfamiliar words. The above authors separately suggest that there is less interference between rare (but understood) words than there is between frequently used words. This may be true but it seems that motivation has not been considered by the authors and there may be some truth in the old adage that "familiarity breeds contempt," whereas novelty makes one sit up and take notice. It would be easy to run a crucial experiment using high-interest, familiar words against low-interest, rarely used words, and vice versa. Letter (con-figuration) shapes would have to be held constant in such a research project as some shapes seem to be more memorable than others.

Recognition versus Recall

Experiments by Luh (1922) which have been replicated and confirmed by Postman and Rau (1957) have demonstrated that recognition is a very much superior form of retention to recall, whatever form of recall is used.

One way of reducing the performance of subjects in recognition experiments is to increase the number of alternatives from which they have to choose. Postman (1950), using a multiple-choice technique with syllables, found that subjects performed poorly when there were ten or more alternatives from which to choose. A similar result using larger lists of letters or numbers was obtained by Davis *et al.* (1961). The implication for children learning the alphabet, graphemes or lists of words is that not too many alternatives should be presented for recognition during the learning process. It is possible that the limits of span of attention in STM may be a cause of these poor performances.

Interference in either proactive or retroactive inhibition does not seem to be a very important factor in recognition experiments except perhaps as a concomitant of the number of choice alternatives (Adams, 1967b). Little work seems to have been done on similarity as an interfering variable in the recognition process. It would seem highly likely that the more similar the multiple-choice items were, the greater would be the difficulty in determining which item was the original stimulus. In a research of my own on a sample of fifty children using a multiple-choice-answer, visuo-spatial memory-for-designs test, the mistaken alternative most frequently chosen was the design which most closely resembled the original stimulus design (Bannatyne, 1969). Thus, it is likely that letters of similar shape being scanned at speed will be more often confused than dissimilar letters. This may account for some of the confusion of *b* and *d*, *u* and *n*, etc., by dyslexic children.

THE RETENTION OF MOTOR BEHAVIOR

Short-Term Motor Memory

Adams and Dijkstra (1966), in lever-moving experiments, found that rapid forgetting occurred over seconds and that retention was a direct function of the number of reinforcements. This finding was confirmed by Posner and Konick (1966), who varied the experiment by introducing interpolated activities. The latter did not have any significant interference effect on the results and neither, incidentally, did the trials. In commenting on these results, Adams (1967b) suggests that because interference theory cannot explain the STM forgetting of motor functions, spontaneous trace decay is the only alternative hypothesis. As this finding is at variance with STM in other modalities, perhaps motor functioning has a qualitatively different memory system with its own STM and LTM divisions. These findings collectively help explain how kinesthetic tracing over large cursive writing

(Fernald, 1943) may A-reinforce spelling and reading in some dyslexic children.

Long-Term Motor Memory

Continuous motor responses, once they are learned, are retained at a very high level and this is a common experience for most people. In commenting on this as a puzzle, Adams (1967b) says,

> Experimental psychologists have not worried enough about continuous motor responses and why they are retained so much better than verbal responses. There is a good scientific cause to puzzle the problem because large discrepancies of this kind can represent the action of special variables or mechanisms of significance for memory theory. On the other hand, the design and uses of continuous motor tasks may contain uncontrolled variables which operate in behalf of high retention, and if these variables could be defined and controlled, the retention of verbal and motor responses might be the same.

Adams goes on to suggest four possible reasons for this high retention of motor habits (memory): overlearning, lack of interference, strongly resistant traces and method of error measurement.

Of these four reasons, I suspect the third one to be the major key to motor retention. In the following discussion, I have inserted the word *memory* in parentheses to affirm that habits are memorized. At least three large areas of the brain are largely devoted to habitual (memory) motor functioning: the frontal areas of the cortex, the cerebellum and the postcentral areas of the parietal lobe (Luria, 1966; Walsh, 1964; Woodburne, 1967). Indeed, some areas of the cortex are specifically organized and localized to cope with, for example, habitual (memory) eye movements, articulation and the numerous built-in automatic muscular activities which are programmed to keep the body functioning, e.g., heartbeats, breathing, alimentary canal, etc. If the CNS has been programmed with these automatic innate motor "habits" (memory), neurons or sets of neurons must exist which have, so to speak, a relatively permanent memory capacity. There is no reason, then, why, in the interest of survival value, one should not be able to program these types of cells or similar ones from environmental motor training. After all, *all* output from the human body cannot be other than motor at the final stage of the human process, whether it is voice, writing, action or expression.

If every act had to be a purely volitional one, life would not exist. In order to function at all, all animals must have a hierarchy of motor functioning which ranges from the purely innate automatic actions to the purely acquired volitional ones. In any output activity, usually large proportions of the *hierarchial* habitual motor system come into operation in an extremely complex, integrated, interdependent way. For example, handwriting involves letter-shape patterns, letter-sequencing patterns, head and trunk orientation (posture) and several types of eye movements. Luria (1961a) has detailed the development in childhood of voluntary movement and its psychological control systems. See also M. Bannatyne and A.D. Bannatyne (1970).

THEORIES OF MEMORY

Broadbent's theory (1958) of the relationship of STM to LTM has already been described and commented on earlier in the chapter. The concept-model of a filter was felt to be too passive and static to explain the stimulus-seeking behavior of organisms when utilizing their past experience (memories). Otherwise, the theory corresponded neatly with current neurological models which suggest an active sensory analysis of incoming data.

Another theory is that of Ellis (1963) with his constructs of stimulus trace (St) and CNS integrity (Ni). The stimulus trace is a neural response which records, so to speak, the intensity, meaning and duration of the stimulus. CNS integrity is just that, the adequacy or efficiency of the stimulus trace recording apparatus as determined by the attributes of the CNS, particularly as they are manifested in behavioral phenomena such as IQ or mental age. On the basis of his theory, Ellis has predicted that when a subject learns a series of items through the anticipation method to a given level of errorless performance, he will later make more errors in the middle items of the series than in those at either end. Additionally, more errors will be made at the end of the list than at the beginning. Butterfield (1968), in a review of the research literature, showed that Ellis' predictions have not been supported. He says,

> It has been predicted from Ellis' stimulus trace theory that retarded subjects should learn serial lists less quickly than non-retarded subjects and that both retarded as compared to non-retarded subjects and fast as compared to slow learners should make relatively more errors at the middle positions of serial lists. Furthermore, these differences should be greater for lists with longer inter-item intervals. A review of the research literature showed that these predictions have not been supported.

Of course, as Butterfield points out, it may be Ellis' predictions from his theory which are incorrect rather than the theory itself.

Spitz (1963) suggests that poor memory is quite simply a deficit in neural functioning. The electrochemical processes in the neurons of the CNS which are responsible for recording stimuli do not function correctly in four ways. First, it takes longer for stimuli to produce the necessary changes in the cells, themselves; second, once temporarily stimulated, it takes longer for the cells to return to their previous state; third, once a permanent trace has been laid down, it will repetitively attract similar stimuli, making it more difficult to establish new traces for the similar items, and fourth, there is less spread of electrochemical activity from stimulated cells into the surrounding cortical fields. It should be noted that Spitz had in mind mentally retarded children, most of whom he says are neurologically unable to organize incoming material because of the above CNS limitations (Spitz, 1966).

Thus far, the above theories of memory or forgetting are all stated in terms of material causes, specifically the malfunctioning or inadequacy of the CNS. On the other hand, the interference theory of forgetting elaborated by Postman (1963) is expressed as a behavioral model and therefore (unless one is a spiritualist) must be compatible with *some* neurological model though not necessarily the ones outlined above. It will be remembered that two alternative theories were postulated earlier in the chapter as to exactly how interference could cause forgetting. The first hypothesis was that the stimulus trace gradually decayed under the

influence of interference whereas the second maintained that
the interference merely built a barrier around the permanently
established trace preventing everyday recall. The term *everyday*
is used because there is evidence that under hypnosis, in dreams,
under drugs and through the direct electrical stimulation of brain
cells, reactivation can occur of memories which the subject had apparently permanently forgotten. As was noted earlied in the chapter, the two theories are not incompatible and indeed it is possible
that not only do memories fade from interference but other
memories can be built up around them, inhibiting access.

Recognition

There are two theories of recognition which, although they
appear to be directly in opposition to each other, may not be if
they are examined in a neurological context (see the next section).
Postman, *et al.* (1948) consider recognition and recall merely
different manifestations of the same psychological and neurological process, the distinction being in *degree*, with respect to threshold sensitivity and performance. If this theory is correct, then
both recall and recognition responses must emanate from a common memory trace. One gets the impression that the proponents
of the single memory trace theory are considering memory very
much in terms of verbal responses.

By contrast, advocates of the perceptual trace hypothesis
postulate that recognition emanates from a perceptual trace separate from, but associated with, a recall memory trace. The perceptual trace theory of recognition, which has a long tradition, is
more easily discussed in the context of the visual modality, even
though one author (Mowrer, 1960) explicitly states that images
can occur in *any* sensory system. The S-perceptual trace is utilized
or activated when we recognize an environmental stimulus, the
"S" standing for *stimulus*. J.A. Adams (1967b) says,

> The S-perceptual trace is specifically designated with the "S" for
> environmental stimulus to distinguish it from the R-perceptual
> trace from response-produced stimuli and the SR-perceptual trace
> from joint actions of environmental and response-produced stimuli.
> . . . As far as memory is concerned, the S-perceptual trace is reacti-
> vated by the original stimulus at the recognition test and causes

the subject to identify it as old. A capability for recalling a response associated with the stimulus need not be present for the identification response to occur, although it may be in some cases. If so, the recall of the response is assumed to be based on a different memory state which is being called the memory trace.

It seems to me that using associated memory traces from two quite separate stimuli, as in the case of the paired-associate learning, unnecessarily complicates the situation, particularly as NLM's and other kinds of memories may form a chain or network between each pair of memory traces. The response of the subject to the recognition (identification) of a previously experienced stimulus on its re-presentation may be a simple articulatory or motor output, such as saying "that one" by either voice or gesture. Admittedly, this kind of simple response *is* a response from another memory trace (namely, affirmation) but it is qualitatively very different from the elaborate memory trace of an equivalent but different word to the stimulus word. The two types of responses would seem to require separate explanations. Later in his book, Adams criticizes perception psychologists because very often experimental items such as words or even configurations may have

> . . . confounded situations in which S-perceptual and memory traces are formed concurrently. The seemingly meaningless forms and shapes that are often their stimuli may uncritically be considered non-verbal and be taken as the basis for a pure S-perceptual trace. This assumption is false in many cases. The human being has the ubiquitous capability for attaching verbal symbols to stimuli that impinge on him. A subject might be shown a seemingly meaningless shape in a recognition experiment and, if asked, might say that it reminds him of a soaring eagle.

The implication behind this statement is that S-perceptual traces are essentially meaningless, thus making those memory traces with a "recall potential" by implication meaningful. Also by implication, meaning is often verbal, or mediated by words. Thus, added to the mix of recognition-recall is the dimension of meaningfulness, recognition being an awareness of previously perceived nonmeaningful sense data whereas recall is the main memory store which is to a greater or lesser extent rich in meaning. If we cross-reference this with a third variable, namely, STM and LTM, and superimpose on them chains of so-called discrete memory traces such as paired associates or serially learned items, the analysis becomes extremely complex.

If, in constructing a psychological model of memory, we insure that its elements do not deviate from known neurological data, it will be safer than speculating without regard for the nature of the neurological substrate.

THE NEUROPSYCHOLOGY OF MEMORY

It is hoped that the following account of the neurological facets of memory, the descriptions involved and the attempts to bring together some of these findings with current psychological theories will enable us to take a fresh look at the nature of memory. According to Melton (1963), the study of memory is concerned with three theoretically separable events: trace formation, trace storage and trace utilization.

Biochemical Trace Storage

In a paper entitled, "The Molecules of Memory," Rose (1967) makes the following statement about memory and its survival value:

> Evolutionary success amongst animal species has to a considerable extent gone to those organisms which have been able to expand their ability to store records of past experience so as to make increasingly sophisticated comparisons of "now" and "then" and act accordingly. So much is this the case that for humans a very large proportion of the brain has become involved in this mechanism of recording, storing, sifting, and comparing information; relatively smaller portions of the brain are involved solely in the immediate processing of new information or the issuing of commands for present action. It is this sifting process, continually occurring within the brain, which we refer to as consciousness and memory.

One might substitute the term *neurological scanning* for *sifting*.

It was hoped by many scientists that the key to memory storage had begun to be unraveled when Hyden (1961) suggested that because a giant molecule of RNA or protein could accommodate a great many different pattern-shapes by different impulses, it might be the memory store capable of producing complex behavior. As Hyden points out, "The shape of a triangle for example could hardly be recorded in a single configuration of RNA and protein, but would have to be represented if storage is molecular, by a multiplicity of coded molecules at every step in the visual system extending from the retina to multiple projection areas in the cerebral cortex." The only experiments with RNA and protein which have been substantially confirmed by replication are Hyden's in which he found that various kinds of stimulation of cells significantly increased their RNA and protein content. Whether or not the *composition* of the RNA is significantly different is still very much open to doubt. Rose (1967) in reviewing the evidence states that it seems "very probable" that the stimulation of brain cells causes biological changes, some of which include changes in the amount of RNA synthesized. Rose himself leans to the more traditional viewpoint that memory is established by "a change in the probability of a particular nerve cell firing, caused by alteration in the biochemical state of the cell."

These biochemical changes most likely occur in and around the synapse and Eccles (1966), whose work on synapses is definitive, is also doubtful about Hyden's theory of molecular memory with its RNA and protein coding. He points out that an RNA increase in a learning situation is a necessary postulate of *any* closed theory of learning, without the necessity of hypothesizing coding functions to it. Turning to the synaptic theory of learning, he says,

> Common to all these synaptic explanations of learning is the general concept that a given sensory input results in a uniquely patent activation of central neurons; and, according to this explanation, a subsequent representation of this input would tend to be channeled along the same pathways because of the increased efficacy of the synaptic actions exerted by all those neurons that were activated by the initial presentation. There would thus be a further reinforcement of the synapses responsible for the unique pattern of activation and response, with consequently a more effective channeling; and so on cumulatively for each successive application of that sensory input. Necessarily, the postulated changes in synaptic efficiency must be of very long duration—days or weeks. There is no way in which relatively brief durations of synaptic change for each synapse in a serial arrangement can sum to give a more prolonged change.

Eccles notes that it has not yet been possible to demonstrate any changes experimentally but these have usually been performed on the spinal cord. He then lists four ways in which cerebral neurons and synapses differ from their counterparts in the spinal cord. These are frequency potentiation, inhibitory postsynaptic potentials, neuronal complexity and dendritic spine occurrence. Thus, the ability of cerebral cells to greatly increase their effectiveness when stressed by high frequency of stimulation, their postsynaptic inhibitory potentials which are much larger and longer than those of spinal neurons plus the complexity and the number of dendrites and dendritic spine synapses all suggest that cerebral cells are more amenable to learning (on a synaptic basis of facilitated pathways) than are the neurons of the other parts of the CNS. Eccles concludes by saying, "We may summarize this discussion of the structural basis of memory by stating that memory of any particular event is dependent on a specific reorganization of neuronal associations (the engram) in a vast system of neurons widely spread over the cerebral cortex."

Eccles (1966) has also investigated excitatory and inhibitory synaptic activity. He presents three diagrams of Fessard's (1961), one of which shows purely excitatory synapses cooperating in an increasingly selective response network and the other two illustrating the action of feed-forward and feedback inhibition in increasing the specificity of the output. The nature and chemistry of excitatory and inhibitory synapses is summarized in some detail by Gray (1967) but there is little point in discussing or illustrating pictorially their detailed structure and biochemistry here. The points to be stressed are that these excitatory and inhibitory junctions *do* exist, and that they may combine in networks with feed-forward and feedback mechanisms to produce more or less permanent pathways which are the result of learning; however, it is stressed by Gray that a great deal of neurological and biochemical research has still to be done on this hypothesis before it can be given the status of definite fact.

In a recent work, John (1967) has put forward a complex neurological theory of memory—one which is difficult to summarize adequately. He proposes an alternative, a more elaborate viewpoint than the usual theory of memory as established pathways within networks of neurons. Starting from the fact that *time* is required to consolidate the registration of experience, he suggests that some neurons maintain an "altered discharge rate over a prolonged period following a stimulus. . . ." This continuous discharge causes an alteration in the concentration of a critical substance which activates a chemical reaction. The product is an effector which activates a repressor-substance and this, in turn, releases a previously repressed operator, "and nuclear DNA [produces] a new mRNA." This enters the cytoplasm, keying the synthesis of a new protein which operates (a) as a feedback loop maintaining the synthesis and (b) to alter the cell membrane responsiveness "to particular temporal sequences." During this consolidation of memory, the above sequence of events occurring in "a representational subset of neurons" would suggest "that the average activity over the whole ensemble should be an oscillation with a characteristic wave shape." The permanent chemical changes would increase the probability "that the ensemble might subsequently enter the same mode of oscillation." This "achieves the representation of past information which affected the ensemble." John cites many studies "of the changes in electrical activity of the brain during conditioning to indicate that these changes occur in widespread anatomical regions."

John later suggests that input and readout from memory are two components of different polarity at the cortical level. These, he says, "suggest two different anatomical origins for these processes." Other evaluations of electrical events indicate

> . . . that various brain regions may subsume the general functions of transmission, storage and evaluation of information. Detailed examination of the form and latency of the readout process activated during release of a previously acquired behavior by a neutral stimulus also showed that this process arises with approximate simultaneity and identical form in cortical, thalamic and mesencephalic regions. . . .
>
> In the face of this body of fact and logic, it seems reasonable to conclude that learned behaviors are mediated by systems which are anatomically extensive and involve many brain regions . . . . The salient feature of the model . . . is that information in the nervous

system is conceived of . . . as the spatiotemporal patterns of organization in enormous aggregates of neurons.

John drew inferences for his theory of information processing from "the frequency characteristics observed in the electrical waves recorded from various brain regions during conditioning to various intermittent stimuli." His hypotheses seem to combine the electrical wave scanning mechanisms proposed by Walter (1953), probability closure on experience (R.L. Gregory, 1966) and the synaptic modification changes of Eccles (1966). Certainly, the problem of establishing the material cause of memory is an extremely complex one and John's theory of the processes involved accounts for much of the electrical wave forms, biochemical processes, RNA protein syntheses, synaptic changes and broad network hypotheses, each of which is in some way an observable entity of brain activity.

As a result of experimentally studying the visual cortex of the brain, Hubel (1963), after assuming that the human visual cortex works in much the same way as a cat's or a monkey's states that if a person looks at a black square on a white ground,

> . . . the near edge of the square will activate a particular group of simple cells, namely, cells that prefer edges with light to the left and dark to the right and his fields are oriented vertically and are so placed on the retina that the boundary between "on" and "off" regions falls exactly along the image of the near edge of the square. Half the populations of the cells will obviously be called into action by the other three edges of the square. All the cell populations will change if the eye strays from the point fixed on, or if the square is moved while the eye remains stationary or if the square is rotated. In the same way, each edge will activate a population of complex cells, again cells that prefer edges in a specific orientation. But a given complex cell, unlike a simple cell, will continue to be activated when the eye moves or when the form moves, if the movement is not so large that the edge passes entirely outside the receptive field of the cell, and if there is no rotation. This means that the populations of complex cells affected by the whole square will be, to some extent, independent of the exact position of the image of the square on the retina. Each of the cortical columns contains thousands of cells, some with simple fields and some with complex. Evidently, the visual cortex analyzes an enormous amount of information, with each small region of visual field represented over and over again in column

after column, first for one receptive-field orientation and then for another.

Hubel's work complements that of Penfield and Roberts (1959), who found that single-point electrical stimulation of both the primary and secondary visual (occipital) areas in patients causes them to see colors, lights, stars and shadows, but never complete scenes. In the light of all the above information, it is reasonable to assume, as do some authorities, that the secondary areas are association areas where simple bits of information are stored to be scanned and retrieved, perhaps in the manner suggested by John. If Lashley (1950), Eccles (1966), Hebb (1949), John (1967) and the other authorities who subscribe to one kind or another of network theory of cortical activity are correct (and no other explanation satisfactorily accounts for the fact that when large sections of the secondary areas are removed very often memory is retained), then a system of perceiving, conceptualizing and remembering something like that described in Table IX is likely to operate.

Table IX is largely self-explanatory but it should be stressed that the type of process set down is one of the simplest kinds and even then it is very much oversimplified. The table describes those simple stimulus situations in which one suddenly and perhaps unexpectedly "notices" a particular stimulus-object, fixates on it, recognizes it and starts to associate to it. Therefore, the matching cortical pattern has not pre-formed, so to speak, as would be the case if one were indulging in searching behavior.

If instead of noticing an apple, I am hungry and feel like having an apple, I will actively seek out in goal-directed behavior the food in question, carrying in my mind an image of an apple until I find something external resembling that image as a match. In such a case, the whole process would be almost entirely feedback from the conceptual areas back through to the entire matching situation. Stage V would be ready and waiting for stage III to occur and stage IV, the actual matching process, would be almost instantaneous. Continuous feedback from stages VI, VII and VIII would also be screening and rejecting all stimulus-objects other than the apple being sought.

TABLE IX

A Model of Sensing, Perceiving, Conceptualizing, Associating and Memorizing Processes

Stage and Process	Explanation	CNS Functions	Schematic Process	Feedback
I External Stimulus (E)	Pattern or arrangement of bits in the environment. (*Note:* For the purposes of this illustration, V1, V2, V3, A1, K1 and K2 will be the finally perceived object, which is to be differentiated from the total stimulus situation.)	Not applicable.	Total External Stimulus Situation Vision — (EV1) (EV2) (EV3) (EV4) (EV5) (EV6), etc. Auditory — (EA1) (EA2) (EA3) (EA4), etc. Kinesthetic — (EK1) (EK2) (EK3) (EK4), etc.	

II
Sense Organ Reception and Projection
	Preliminary receptor analysis and restructuring of wave phenomena or proprioceptive input into "coded" neuronal impulses. Projection to cortex in precise point-to-point manner. (*Note:* Some reflexive reactions may operate at subcortical levels directly to motor output at this stage, e.g., eye blink.)	Neuronal "code" equivalents of bits (N). (The double strokes indicate a lack of direct association.)	(NV1)//(NV2)//(NV3)//(NV4)//(NV5)//(NV6), etc. {Hues, Shades, Colors, etc.}
			(NA1)//(NA2)//(NA3)//(NA4), etc. {Phones, Distinctive Features, etc.}
			(NK1)//(NK2)//(NK3)//(NK4), etc. {Eye Movement Data: Size, Hand: Size, Weight, etc.}	

III
Primary Registration of Sense Data
	Arrival and registration in the primary sensory area. Projection can be maintained only during *direct* sensing of the environment.	Primary (P) cortical cells activated in *neurologically* equivalent pattern to stage I.	(PV1)//(PV2)//(PV3)//(PV4)//(PV5)//(PV6), etc. {Hues, Shades, Colors, etc.}
			(PA1)//(PA2)//(PA3)//(PA4), etc. {Phones, Distinctive Features, etc.}
			(PK1)//(PK2)//(PK3)//(PK4), etc. {Eye Movement: Size, Hand: Size, Weight, etc.}
			
			Each unit in this column may involve immense numbers and networks of neurons (Eccles, 1966; John, 1967).	

If the word *apple* is *heard,* stages I through VI would still occur but in terms of verbal stimuli and a verbal matching process, which would then "pull out" the concept at stage VII (possibly beginning at stage IV). From there, the process would continue as

Stage and Process	Explanation	CNS Functions	Schematic Process	Feedback
IV Scanning and Selection	Scanning of secondary areas for selection of separate, discrete bits for the purpose of matching against (stage III) incoming array of bits. Visuo-spatial process probably involves alpha rhythm. Bits may be grouped in chunks if already subassembled in secondary areas from habit.	Primary areas plus secondary areas most closely connected to primary areas. Note cycling feedback. (S) stands for the scanning and sorting process.	Bits Separated and Sorted But as Yet Unassembled. Chunk	+ I
V Matching (Gestalt) Organization or Reorganization of Bits or Chunks (If auditory-verbal, will involve sequencing)	Almost simultaneously with stage IV, active organization or reorganization occurs of bits or chunks into a whole, matching the stimulus pattern arrangement of stage III. If stage-III data prove inadequate, this leads to best-fit closure, trial-and-error feedback, probability matching, etc., at stage IV (e.g., illusions). Also cycling assembly hypotheses and verdicts fed back from stages VI and VII on partial assembly attempts. Minimal percept attribute recognition required.	Matching involves secondary areas on wider basis. Feedback cycling essential to assembly of associated bits of *relevant* object.	Irrelevant Suppressed Bits or Clusters	+ I

indicated. If the word *apple* is *read,* stages II through VI would occur visually, establishing the letter configuration of the word, but the process would then loop back to stage IV. If von Bonin *et al.* (1942) and Downer (1962) are correct when they say that

Stage and Process	Explanation	CNS Functions	Schematic Process	Feedback
VI Image Stability (If auditory-verbal image will be a formed sound-label after, closure)	Matching pattern is stabilized as an integrated whole image (or set of images) but is, as yet, without much "meaning," e.g., like strange object or unknown foreign language. Cross-association with other bits, chunks, images, percepts and/or concepts may sometimes occur at this stage (e.g., higher reflex).	Wider secondary areas.		
VII Definitive Percept or Concept Meaning Associations (If auditory-verbal, word will "pull out" associated concepts)	Almost simultaneously with stage VI, definitive "incoming" concept associations occur with well-established (from experience) percepts and concepts to establish present meaning. This is really a two-way feedout and feedback process to establish full experience-rich conceptual meaning as a psychological focal point or a conceptual gestalt of identified, synthesized, relevant experience – a focal center. If no strong associations exist, weak ones will be tried as matches (e.g., illusions of the "which is it?" type). The feedback involved may ask for more incoming information or attempt to reorganize the data as at stage V. Usually with familiar objects or words there is a final acceptance of the percept-concept meaning as a good match and the image is recognized as being meaningful.	Ranges through entire cortex.	Incoming Concept-Contributory Associations	

the visual memory trace is laid down in the untrained cerebral hemisphere without the visual primary projection area of that side being involved (although Downer is referring to split-brain transfers of information), it would seem highly likely that *no*

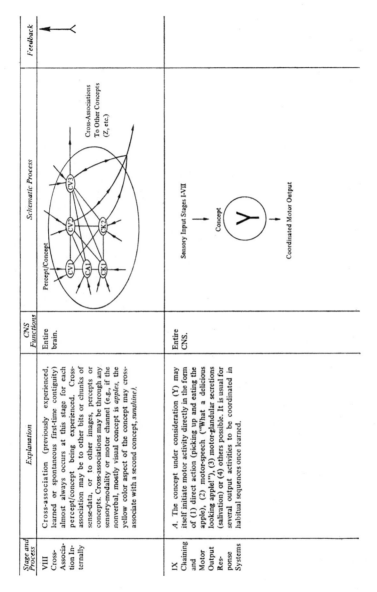

Stage and Process	Explanation	CNS Functions	Schematic Process	Feedback
VIII Cross-Association Internally	Cross-association (previously experienced, learned or spontaneous first-time contiguity) almost always occurs at this stage for each percept/concept being experienced. Cross-association may be to other bits or chunks of sense-data, or to other images, percepts or concepts. Cross-associations may be through any sensory-modality or motor channel (e.g., if the nonverbal, mostly visual concept is *apples*, the yellow color aspect of the concept may cross-associate with a second concept, *sunshine*).	Entire brain.	Percept/Concept / Cross-Associations To Other Concepts (Z, etc.)	Feedback
IX Chaining and Motor Output Response Systems	A. The concept under consideration (Y) may itself initiate motor activity directly in the form of (1) direct action (picking up and eating the apple), (2) motor-speech ("What a delicious looking apple!"), (3) motor-glandular secretions (salivation) or (4) others possible. It is usual for several output activities to be coordinated in habitual sequences once learned.	Entire CNS.	Sensory Input Stages I-VII → Concept (Y) → Coordinated Motor Output	

internal process would need to involve the primary projection areas when outside stimuli do not do so. Therefore, the auditory word would be assembled at stages IV through VI and stage VII would pull out its concept equivalents. It is important to note that

Stage and Process	Explanation	CNS Functions	Schematic Process	Feedback
IX(cont'd) Chaining and Motor Output Response Systems	B. The concept (Y) under consideration (e.g., *apple*) may cross-associate with another, technically separate concept Z (e.g., *orange*), as when one sees an apple but preferring to eat an orange (1) *actively seeks* one of the latter which are not in sight, (2) speaks ("I'd like an orange"), (3) salivates or (4) takes some other alternative possible. C. (1) The concept (Y) under consideration may initiate a chaining or network chaining of cross-associated concepts, percepts, images, chunks and/or bits; (2) the end result may on occasion have no motor response of any kind, as stimulation does not invariably produce a response; (3) concepts participating in cross-associated chains may also be separately stimulated (stages II-VIII); (4) in listening to speech or reading there is a continuous *verbal* stimulus elicitation of continuously chained concepts (stages II-VIII); (5) the chains of cross-associations may be directed by *thought* (centrencephalic) manipulative programs modeling external relationships (e.g., *this* and *that* together equal *these*) to solve a problem, and outputs (like inputs) may occur along the chain to facilitate the final activity or to shape the environment motorically in stages. These inputs and outputs, like some chained concepts, may *mediate* the ongoing conceptualizing process in a variety of ways (e.g., NLM's in STM or LTM).	Entire CNS.		

apart from stages VII and VIII and some aspects of stage IX, quite *separate cells* are likely to be involved at each stage. If paired-associate learning is taking place, the cross-association for consonant trigrams and such nonmeaningful stimuli would occur at stage VI, but if some kind of meaningful mediation occurs, this would then involve stage VII and possibly stage VIII. Certainly, associations of normal words will always involve stage VIII.

If we limit the term *recognition* to nonmeaningful stimuli, even if it progresses on to conceptual meaning subsequently, the recognition process would terminate at stage VI and could only cross-associate on a simple letters-of-the-alphabet, bit or chunk level. This would be the kind of definition of *recognition* which Adams (1967b) seems to be suggesting, at least at the perceptual trace level. Recall in the paired-associate situation would involve recognition at least to stage VI if not stages VII and VIII at one or more of which points cross-association to the response word would occur. The associated word-image and/or concept would then pull out the appropriate word from store, assemble it and articulate it. Tip-of-the-tongue behavior (Adams, 1967b) would occur because of weak concept cross-associations or chaining at stages VIII and IX. It is also possible for tip-of-the-tongue behavior to occur at stage IXB between the second (Z) concept and its motor output; the concept will be present but its association with articulemic word-assembly systems may be weak. Most current models of memory and perception can be fitted into this table in appropriate ways and on various levels. It would seem that *recognition* must always be an *input process* right to the conceptualizing stage where it meets and mingles with the beginning of *recall*, which is almost entirely an *output process*. If we use a prompt or cue (e.g., a paired associate) to enable a subject to recall a particular word or concept, recall will not begin until the process of recognizing the prompt or cue is almost complete. Even so, *response* recognition can occur during recall, a complicated process requiring a detailed explanation.

THE RELATION OF STM TO LTM, RECOGNITION AND RECALL: A WIDER VIEWPOINT

Short-term memory fulfills several distinct psychological functions which can be set out as follows:

1. To hold temporarily incoming signals (arrays of bits) in (presumably) the primary sensory areas *while* experiential match-

ing (on one or more stage levels) occurs. This utilization of the term *short-term memory* is questionable because tachistoscopically we cannot remember what we have not recognized (identified) except perhaps eidetically. This is true even of so-called meaningless stimuli such as configurations or trigrams. But these *do* have minimal experiential meaning inasmuch as they are identified through matching as lines or letters. This type of STM, if it exists, has little to do with the types of STM which follow.

2. To hold temporarily in *focus of attention, for any matching purposes, incoming data* on any stage-level from V through IX (bits, chunks, images, percepts, concepts, relational program concepts or any mixture of these). This can be labeled *data-matching STM (MSTM)*.

3. To hold temporarily in focus of attention paired or chained associates (of bits, chunks, images, percepts, concepts, relational program concepts or any mixture of these) on any stage-level from V to IX, the *association linkages* being the essential task-content of the STM. The material against which the incoming data is to be matched will usually come from LTM storage. For example,

	X, B, K	with	T, L, C	(bits)
or	1234	with	ABCD	(series)
or	an apple	with	a carpet	(percepts or images)
or	fruit	with	astronomy	(concepts)

This type can be labeled *associational STM (ASTM)*.

4. To hold temporarily in the focus of attention any internally neurologically activated concept (probably a need-state aroused through biochemical/metabolic somatic activity, e.g., hunger) while selective search behavior proceeds in the environment for objects offering satiation, i.e., an internally evoked percept or concept to the externally object-matching process. This is a *vigilance* task process (see Broadbent, 1958) and this type can be labeled *vigilance-data STM (VSTM)*. An example of this type is when an individual is hungry and without any external stimulation "realizes" that he wants to eat an apple and so goes in

search of one, vigilantly screening stimuli until he perceives an apple to match (stages I through VII) his internal apple image.

5. To hold temporarily in the focus of attention any material or informational data which is being, or is about to be, centrencephalically manipulated (with other data, or chunks, or concepts, etc., also held in the span of attention) utilizing *relational* programs. These data may be in the form of abstract concepts. This type can be labeled *RSTM*.

6. To hold temporarily in the focus of attention any incoming informational data (matched or not) while it is being transferred to and *consolidated* in LTM storage *(CSTM)*. This is not meant to imply that additional consolidation processes cannot take place elsewhere, especially in the LTM functioning itself.

If we disregard the possibility of sense-data registration STM (see item 1 above), then the other types of STM described above (items 2-6) are really a partial synonym for *focus of attention* if the term is defined as a neuropsychological state and *is not limited to the perception of external stimuli.* If (apart from rare first-time learning situations involving completely strange material) matching as a psychological process is a key two-way process (sensorially, or internally and associationally initiated), one or more sets of informational data must be *held in consciousness* (attention, awareness) for the variety of purposes described, namely, matching of incoming images which are held in STM (MSTM), relational reasoning manipulation (RSTM), association (ASTM), vigilance (VSTM) and LTM consolidation (CSTM), all of which usually and eventually lead to some output mechanisms (see stages IXA-IXC).

These five types of STM (2-6) are not to be considered as being functionally separate. It is the identity, and possible origin or source, of the material content (or informational data being held or processed) which is the definitive label. The STM *focus of attention* is most likely one aspect of the centrencephalic system which holds material or data while they are being relationally processed or are about to be processed. The material or data can originate from any of the described sources but once in the focus of attention, they are centrencephalically held in STM for a variety of purposes, such as input matching, association, vigilance (output matching), relational processing or LTM consolidation.

STM is *the holding mechanism of and for the continuously operational conscious focus of attention with its limited capacity span.* The temporary *holding* of STM data most likely occurs within the centrencephalic system (or wherever "conscious" reasoning takes place) along with reasoning and other functions or processes, the data being returned to LTM store if it has been internally evoked. The hippocampus may, or may not, act as a *secondary* temporary storage hold in the above situation. (For example, if 456 is divided by 6, the first figure of the answer, 7, must be held in STM while the carrying figure is calculated and combined with the units figure to obtain by division the second figure of the answer, 6. From the evidence (see p. 287), it would appear that the hippocampus does act as a secondary temporary storage hold (for the more primary focus-of-attention holding system) into which incoming data can be shunted for a few seconds while the focus of attention briefly concerns itself with other relevant matters, or while the incoming data are being memorized in LTM. There is no reason why temporary shunt-data holding by the hippocampus (or anywhere else) should not also be a continuously operative device.

This would mean that STM is a different psychological process from LTM because STM is the holding mechanism for the processes concerned with the selection of attentionally required incoming data for the centrencephalic manipulation system or for the retrieval of data from LTM storage for the same purpose. This suggests that STM is one anchor end of, and for, those scanning processes of incoming data, and of internal LTM material. STM is not a scanning process itself; neither is it a manipulative program. It merely holds data temporarily in the interests of other processes and programs. At this point, there is a need to differentiate between several types of scanning:

1. *Scanning for image assembly* (of parts to whole) which

occurs when one scans the secondary areas to match incoming sense data bits with stored experiential (LTM) information. This is probability matching on a perceptual level as suggested by Broadbent (1958) and Gregory (1966). Bits and chunks and "part" images may be assembled in the matching process in a hierarchical way—levels of prefabrication, so to speak. The final matched (and recognized) image may then be held in STM for other subsequent processing.

2. Internal LTM store *associational scanning* for the selective evocation of informational data usually in whole percept or concept form to be used in focus-of-attention reasoning manipulation or associational chaining. Selected units are held by STM temporarily while being utilized in the focus of attention in a manipulative or associational way. Matching must occur in a closure-type way—the missing piece fits the program or chain, the solution piece fits the puzzle, or the link joins the chain. This matching also occurs or recurs in the light of previous experience —often experience with relational programs, e.g., language syntax processing.

3. *Vigilance scanning* is the converse of image-assembly scanning. The drive-need evokes the concept and perhaps a particular percept which generates an active perceptual-motor (feedback-integrated) searching behavior, seeking environmental matching stimulus-objects. Many recognition tests involve vigilance scanning.

We are now in a position to define *recognition,* which is any of the above matching processes at the moment the closure-match occurs. Recognition, then, is a process end result, an awareness that matching has occurred. Thus, we can recognize a spontaneously seen and assembled object, a unit-memory out of LTM or an object actively sought in the environment. Note that relational manipulative programs can also be stored in LTM as relational *concepts* and therefore can be matched and recognized, e.g., one can multiply 6 times 5 and recognize the program as having been previously experienced. LTM is a "passive" store which has to be scanned and has to have its selected units fed into the STM focus of attention before they are activated in some program. *Recall* of information-data occurs only as an internal end result of an associational or manipulative process (which includes association) and is essentially the first stage of a possible output response. For example, if the pair *apple-carpet* is learned as an association and put into LTM storage, the cue *apple* presented later, will be held in STM (after *its* LTM assembly matching) while LTM is scanned associationally (by the focus-of-attention scanning mechanisms) for the word *carpet*. This occurs as type 2 associational scanning for chained (single-link) best-fit closure. Provided the learning was sufficient and interference is noninhibiting, the word *carpet* will be scanned, pulled out, matched in terms of linkage closure and *recognized* as the best-fit match while being held by STM in the focus of attention, then fed out through the appropriate motor functions as "recall." Therefore, the process of recalling is an associational one which involves the associational scanning, matching, recognition, STM and motor output mechanisms.

Interference occurs when STM focus-of-attention activities are interrupted or diverted by and to other stimuli. This includes interference with any hippocampal STM side-store data activity. Because STM and other focus-of-attention activities have a limited capacity span of, say, six to nine chunks in the normal adult, interference occurs when input exceeds capacity. The data selected to be retained in the focus of attention and held there will be those most appropriate to various drive-needs, to stimulus intensity, etc. Similarity interference would seem to be a discrimination difficulty in determining which of the alternatives presented during the scanning and matching processes (types 1, 2 or 3) is the best fit.

T-reinforcement and rehearsal maintains STM focus-of-attention holding on stimulus data, which right from the outset through all trials will automatically lay down or consolidate the LTM trace systems (probably through synaptic modification) until interference with STM focus activity (usually a shift of attention) terminates that particular data-trace long-term registration. This LTM registration may range from being abrupt, intense and interference-resistance (as in trauma), to drawn-out, weak and interference-prone (as in learning nonsense syllables). If Eccles (1966) and others are correct about more or less permanent synaptic facilitation within networks being the basis of LTM, then LTM item registration will occur in a progressive buildup through time.

A major factor in all the above operations is that LTM storage is a major "passive" source of experiential information which can be utilized through scanning to supply data (held in STM) for any of the above purposes—input matching, association, vigilance (output matching) or relational processing. It is worth reemphasizing that even the programs utilized in relational processing can themselves be stored as concepts (principles) in LTM. STM holds a limited amount of any type of data from LTM or other input sources to the forefront of consciousness (attention) while they are being processed in one or more ways. All children and particularly learning disability children can be trained to facilitate all these holding and scanning processes.

The Hippocampal Zone and Memory

Milner (1965) has found that patients with hippocampal lesions retain a considerable amount of knowledge concerning jobs, skills, understanding and use of language and memories of earlier experiences, but that if their attention is diverted during the process of short-term recall (e.g., digit repetition) the information is lost. Milner, in describing this state of affairs, says,

> The evidence from our patients is that this attentional process (digit span) is also independent of the hippocampal system. Any proposition, number series, or word association to which the patient can give attention at one time is retained and available for recall, provided attention has not been diverted elsewhere before this recall is required. In other words, the essential condition for recall is that the trace be kept ceaselessly active. In the normal individual, however, many experiences are retained for a time at least, without any need to keep them constantly in mind. Whether or not any stable trace will ultimately be formed will depend on many factors, such as the nature of the material, the frequency of rehearsal, and so forth. But it is this short-term storage which makes the more enduring change possible. The fact that in our patients with bilateral hippocampal lesions, forgetting appears to take place the instant

their attention is diverted shows that this consolidation process involves hippocampal and not merely cortical cells. . . . The removal of the hippocampal region will leave these well established associations between cell assemblies essentially intact, but will make it very difficult for new associations to be built up and those not yet independent of hippocampal activity will be lost. The fact that some motor skills may be acquired independently of the hippocampal system suggests that this defect is less general than we supposed at first.

Milner also notes that ". . . the acquisition of visual-motor skills may prove to be independent of the hippocampal system." Thus, it would seem that the primary modality to be affected by the short-term storage disorders associated with hippocampal lesions is *the auditory one.* Milner reports that maze learning also proved difficult but the maze to be learned was of the nailhead variety with *no* visual guidelines, the only cue being a buzzer which sounded when the patient erred from the correct path. It is also likely that memorization of counted nailheads would be an important auditory mediator in learning to trace the maze correctly. There is some indication from Milner's work on the relationship of hippocampal lesions to STM storage *that auditory memory functions may be somehow different in subtle ways from motor and, separately, visual memorizing* (see Bannatyne, 1966c).

In concluding this section, it is interesting to note that the idea of a hippocampal STM storage gives some neurological support to Broadbent's filter model of a feedback holding system for STM before it is transferred (if it is to be transferred) to LTM storage. In my own model, such transfer would proceed automatically, although at a variety of rates depending on the activity of several variables, e.g., T-reinforcement, interference, span, etc.

Penfield and Roberts' View of Memory

Penfield and Roberts (1959) classify memory into three separate mechanisms within the brain: memory for experiences, memory for concepts and memory for words. They also add skills which they say some might call memories, such as piano playing or driving an automobile. Under skills, they include speaking and writing.

1. *Experiential* memory arises from the record of the stream of former consciousness which is stored in the interpretive cortex of the temporal lobe. Penfield and Roberts say, "Thus the experiential record serves a man for subconscious interpretations and for the recollection of occasional memorable events."

2. *Conceptual* memory is nonverbal, except perhaps in a transitory way, being a building up of experiences associated with particular types of objects or events.

3. *Word* memory is separate from concept memory. Penfield and Roberts say, "As time passes, there is formed within the brain the ganglionic equivalent of a word and the ganglionic equivalent of a concept. Experience over the years continues to reinforce the back and forth neuronal interrelationship between the two." Later the authors say that the connection between *speech mechanism* and *concept mechanism* is evidently reflexive and automatic.

Penfield and Roberts also comment on the neurological nature of memory:

> The nerve cells and nerve branches of some parts of the brain, or perhaps the synapses which join the branch of one cell to the body of another cell, are altered by the passage of a stream of electrical potentials. This is what makes permanent patterns possible. This is the basis of all *memory*. Thus, man is able to find, in his ideational speech mechanism, four sets of neuron patterns; the sound units of words employed when listening to speech, the verbal units followed for speaking, the visual units for reading, and the manual units for writing.

This work by Penfield and Roberts supports my use in Table IX of separate neurological structures from stage II through stage IX, where the coding for these separate systems is the initial letters preceding the sensory letters in the schematic diagrams.

Memory in Space and Time

Pribram (1962), expanding on statements by Nauta (1962), suggests that there is a difference between brain mechanisms that provide stability in space and those that provide stability in time. Memory enables us to maintain stability through time because we can orient the present in terms of the past. In fact, Pribram suggests that we have four brains.

One brain, our "perceptual" brain, we might call it, maps at the ever-changing *spatial* array of our external environment from some of its constant features. A *second* brain is involved in managing our behavioral economy in the face of changes that take place over time. This is our "homeostatic" brain. Each of these brains, the "perceptual" and the "homeostatic," has, in primates, an associated brain. These associated brains, classically called the "association areas," serve to code the neural events involved in perception and homeostasis: Alternatives and Plans thus become possible.

With respect to plans, Pribram, like Luria, suggests that the frontal association cortex is critically involved. Pribram also suggests that coding behavior over *time* must involve a digital memory mechanism in the secondary association area. Pribram's separation of our spatial and time-oriented brains lends some support along with Penfield and Roberts' statements to the hypotheses put forward below.

Previously, I have suggested (Bannatyne, 1966c) that eventually it may be found that the neurological functioning and storage systems of *auditory* material in the temporal lobes and their associated areas are quite different from those concerned with *visual* recording and matching in the occipital lobes and their associated areas. Even visual processes recorded in the temporal lobes (interpretive cortex) were found by Penfield and Roberts (1959) to be much like a moving film whereas those in the occipital lobes were simple flashes of light of varying intensities. Hubel's work (1963) also indicates that in the visual cortex groups of cells seem to operate on an on-off light-to-dark basis. The work of Walter (1953) and the conclusions of R.L. Gregory (1966) support the view that visual perception is neurolgically a scanning and matching process, the matching involving some kind of "digital memory mechanism" (Pribram, 1962). Spatial perception and a spatial memory of objects and scenes, etc., is, in a sense, static or constant. Even when we see a moving object we track it with our eyes to keep it relatively static in our line of vision. All visual mechanisms seem to concentrate on holding an image steady at the focus of the gaze long enough for us to recognize it by matching it against our prior experiences. It is well known that this occurs even in reading (Lesevre, 1966). Although our eyes have evolved to detect movement, once that movement is detected we endeavor to identify the moving object by tracking and holding it static. Thus, vision is more concerned with the static perception of space and less concerned with the detection of data primarily concerned with time, even though, of course, time is intimately involved.

By contrast, auditory data appear to be handled in a quite different way. It is impossible to have complex sounds which are meaningful unless they are sequenced relatively slowly (compared with tachistoscopic visual thresholds). Brief or compacted sound cannot be understood by the listener. Whether the sounds are meaningful noises, words or music, the sequence in which they occur is an essential factor in our appreciation of the content. One is tempted to alter Penfield and Roberts' analogy of a moving film for the interpretive cortex to that of a video tape. The sequencing of sounds of any kind through time would then occur not so much on a yes-no digital basis as on a quantitative analogue basis. If these elements were scanned for memory-matching purposes, sequences of "tape" could be run over intervals of time, the result being music, noises or words strung together in meaningful shorter or longer series. The continuously sequenced memory-process program quite feasibly could also scan the other association areas of the brain including the visual area, and could reassemble and integrate them as time sequences of whole memories from several sensory modalities, the result being much like Penfield and Robert's stream-of-consciousness findings (temporal lobe), which resulted from eletrical stimulation.

Thus, there would be two types of visual memory—the regular static object and circumstance identification matching process, essentially visuo-spatial in nature, and the continuous video tape time-sequenced processes which continuously pull out and reassemble the relevant digital visual data and other sensory data as the tape is run. The interpretive cortex, then, would consist of this kind of a master integrational memory system of a multisensory type. This master interpretive memory data system could possibly be one integrated basis for concept storage as well as accounting for stream-of-consciousness sequences as described by Penfield and Roberts. Mishkin's (1962) suggestion that the right temporal cortex may integrate activity from both striate areas (that is, both visual fields) is in keeping with the above hypotheses. However, I would include the interpretive areas in both temporal lobes within the multi-sensory master memory system but would exclude active relational reasoning programs except inasmuch as they had formed a part of the original memories when they were first experienced. After all, we remember relational principles and programs as well as utilizing them when we think.

If we relate the above hypotheses to I.M. Smith's (1964) verbal ability and spatial ability dichotomy, it would seem that the visuo-spatial type of person would tend to operate more on a digital yes-no memory basis (which may or may not be continuously recorded by the master memory), whereas the auditory-verbal type of person would utilize the more time-oriented sequential analogue type of memory recording system.

In Chapter III, the numerous conventional aspects of language were discussed in some detail. These arbitrary characteristics of language (and for that matter, emotionality and mores) should be contrasted with the three-dimensional logico-spatial relationships of visuo-spatial information. Also in Chapter III in a section on thinking, reasoning and language, I put forward the proposition that thinking processes model those relationships in space-time which involve active change wrought by some physical or biological agent or agents in the wider sense of those words. These internalized models of the changing space-time relationships of external objects (or rather the internal equivalent of the latter, namely, images, percepts, concepts) when processed by the human brain *are* thinking and reasoning. *Visual* imagery, whether evoked by environmental stimuli or from memory, must change and shift in infinite variety, even if our cognitive logical manipulations of that imagery (through the laws of thought) are by comparison very limited. By contrast, verbal memory, and for that matter most *auditory* memory, to be efficient, must be indelible and inflexible, its conventionally determined content being fixed in memory. One could go even further and say that the ganglionic equivalent of a spatial or a verbal concept is determined by the neurological characteristics of its particular sensory modality; in other words, verbal thought remains *qualitatively different* from spatial thought even though both may take place in an integrated centrencephalic reasoning system linked to the respective cortical areas. The abstract thought of a Newton or Einstein is very different from that of a Shakespeare or Ibsen.

NEUROLOGICAL MATURATION RATES AND OVERLEARNING

Several authors have discussed the hypothesis that some children with reading disabilities appear to be handicapped by a "maturational lag" (Bender, 1963; Critchley, 1964; de Hirsch, 1965). Bender was one of the first to put forward this theory and she quotes in evidence symptoms such as weak cerebral dominance, immature EEG records and other signs of delayed maturation. It is as though the whole pattern of maturational development is slower in some children. The etiology, Bender claims, is not one of structural defect so much as a congenital pattern. Cases are cited in the literature in support of the hypothesis, and I have personally worked with several children who have exhibited symptoms associated with slow maturation. De Hirsch (1964, 1965) and de Hirsch *et al.* (1966a, 1966b) have worked with premature children and found them lagging in several areas including reading ability. Kellmer Pringle *et al.* (1967) also found premature children inferior in seven out of fifteen tests. These were tapped patterns, language comprehension, word finding, number of words used, mean of the five longer sentences, sentence elaboration and definitions; articulatory defects were not found to be characteristic of premature children. De Hirsch (1965) reviews three cases with verbal disabilities who show some of the "plastic behavior Bender describes as characteristic of schizophrenic youngsters." She goes on to say,

Plasticity might be observed along a continuum. There are at one end children in whom plasticity is pervasive, ego-organization is diffuse, ego-boundaries are fluid, and there is trouble with reality testing. At the other end, there are those youngsters who are in no way bizarre or deviating, who are able to form meaningful relationships and whose plasticity shows mainly in inability to stabilize perceptual experiences and to maintain a "linguistic gestalt."

The dyslexic boys with whom I have personally worked have some times been in the latter category, being quite capable visuo-spatially, with a good spatial score on the WISC (Bannatyne, 1967b—see research report) and good physique and motor skills, who, nevertheless, seemed less able to register associated auditory-to-visual memories in the area of language. As has already been noted, Wolf (1967) found these children to be poor at skills involving music and, in particular, the sequencing of notes. In other words, their memory for sounds in sequence was *not* "indelible and inflexible," certainly in terms of STM discrimination. The fact that music does not involve vision, that these boys are often visuo-spatially capable and that, as Baddeley (1966) showed, the main interference in STM experiments is acoustical even with visually presented words pinpoints the difficulty of this type of dyslexic boy as being in the *auditory* area. However, much more research will have to be carried out before these hypotheses are fully investigated and explored in detail although some research has already been completed (Bannatyne and Wichiarajote, 1969b).

The overlearning of any kind of material is known to be necessary if that material is to be retained in LTM without being affected by semantic or other interference. This is stressed both by Underwood (1964) and Postman (1962). In the more educational context, Frostig (1966) stresses the need for repetition and overlearning, which is a process of continuing to learn the material in question for several more trials after it can be perfectly reproduced.

Levels of Automatization, Habituation and Fluency of Output

As material or informational data are increasingly registered through any type of reinforcement in LTM storage, their recall or reproduction tends to become more and more automatic in operation. The process of learning (memorizing) a task or series of tasks must, in some way, be deliberate and conscious, at least for the duration of the initial learning process. However, very often the aim of memorizing is to render the memorized tasks instantly and automatically available as subsidiary skills to those other tasks which must be conscious, such as reasoning processes. Reading is such a skill. When we learn to read (and unlike speaking, reading is an artificial process not naturally learned), the objective is to reduce the visual-auditory code-breaking processes to the level of a habitual skill which we can conveniently leave to operate automatically while we concentrate on conceptual meanings and imagery of content. The way in which reading involves automatic skills in several modalities will be discussed in the next chapter; suffice it here to say that it is an old notion in psychology that habits form a hierarchy inasmuch as simpler, more basic habits can be organized into higher-order habits in complex output operations. The term *habit* is usually restricted to sequential motor responses; therefore, many aspects of almost all output phenomena can be included under this heading. Habits as one aspect of output tend to become more and more automatic over time since they are used from day to day as tools subserving other ends, in this instance, communication.

Many other neurological processes may occur in the brain before a habitual response ends them as a series of events. A detailed description of some which occur in language processing was given in the previous chapter. One key factor in language production is the necessity for the brain to get complex sets of skill sequences out of store on several hierarchical levels at the same time. To achieve this, there must be continuous automatic monitoring feedback on every level which will cue in each automatically elicited piece of the sequence of neurological events in its correct position. The more one dwells on this point, the more incredible the operation of the neurological machinery seems, especially since almost all of it is fully automatic once learned. For example, if one writes a sentence, all the movements of one's eyes, hands and body must be smoothly coordinated through time along with the neuropsychological processes of reasoning, recalling, syntax generation, visual processes, kinesthetic motor pattern programming and so on. If our focus of attention can only hold between seven and nine bits or chunks of information at the most, it is LTM and the habituation of motor-kinesthetic responses coalesced into complex skills which, being automatized, allow us to attend to a few key items in consciousness.

Cognitive Structure and Hierarchical Concept Systems

The difference between logical meaning, psychological meaning and rote learning processes has been clearly defined by Ausubel (1963). Meaning for him always implies "some form of representational equivalence between language (or symbols) and mental content." However, there is another type of meaningfulness in which, for example, deaf children *know* the use or purpose (meaning) of many objects in the environment without necessarily knowing the auditory symbols or printed labels we attach to them as communicative tabs. It may even be possible to understand nonsymbolized concepts by having a generalized image of a class of objects or events. Of course, abstract concepts such as mathematics three or four levels removed from the concrete will not be able to be manipulated relationally without the use of symbols. Ausubel's criterion for *logical* meaning is to be found, he suggests, in the attributes of objects themselves and in their nonarbitrary relationships, and his point of view here coincides with the one I have elaborated for visual phenomena. However, for Ausubel, logical meaning is independent of any individual person, although of course individuals can be logical. He defines *psychological* meaning as the subsuming of logical propositions within a particular person's cognitive structure and thus psychological meaning is always idiosyncratic. Meaningful tasks, whether logical or psychological, are relatable and "anchorable to relevant and more inclusive concepts in cognitive structure." Thus, although Ausubel does not word it this way, the content of meaningful material is subject to the laws of thought even if these are imperfectly interpreted by an individual person for whom these meaningful relational associations form a complex, hierarchically organized, conceptual system. Therefore, as we learn meaningful new material, it is fitted neatly into the percept/ concept hierarchical jigsaw of knowledge, which is all relationally organized. This system is presumably a major aspect of LTM, the associations being facilitated by logical relationships and permeated by reasoning programs.

Ausubel suggests that it is this very interrelatedness which allows us to greatly extend our temporal span of retention. In other words, if our seven or so chunks in the focus of attention are hooked up to vast relationally associated conceptual memory stores, the range of material to which we can attend over seconds will be quite large. By contrast, *rote learning* is arbitrary and nonmeaningful; fundamentally, it is a very different kind of learning and retention process. Ausubel says, "Rote learning tasks can only be incorporated into cognitive structure in the form of arbitrary, intramaterial associations, that is, as discrete, self-contained entities organizationally isolated, for all practical purposes, from the learner's established conceptual systems." He concludes that since the human brain is not efficiently designed for long-term, verbatim storage of arbitrary, intramaterial associations, retention span for rote learnings is relatively brief. A memory theorist would put this in another way, saying that rote memory which is not facilitated by natural or acquired language mediators is more subject to interference and is thus more difficult to learn and more easily forgotten. Even so, since the basic material to be learned is not meaningful, it would be more easily forgotten than data with a meaningful content.

Language Learning Disabilities, Motivation and Memory

It would seem that the whole problem of logical, psychological and rote learning is far more complex than the above paragraph would indicate. The learning of language, itself, is a rote task inasmuch as the associations of words to objects are quite arbitrary and conventionally determined. It is fairly certain, according to Penfield and Roberts (1959), that words may even be stored in areas separate from images, percepts and concepts and any hierarchical logicality which the words possess is, so to speak, lent to them by the independent nonverbal cognitive structure.

The degree of imagery and conceptualizing associated with any material or data which have to be learned by rote will vary along the continuum from the completely nonmeaningful (if it exists) to an almost completely meaningful content expressed in absolute symbols (as in mathematics). Nevertheless, there is little doubt that meaningfulness does facilitate rote learning, particularly in circumstances in which one can refer to higher-order principles for assistance. Meaningful learning deals in concepts and associations between logical concepts whereas rote learning, at least in everyday life, is very often a process of memorizing the symbols associated with concepts and systems of concepts. We may very well understand the logic of multiplication but the rote learning of multiplication tables is still a long and tedious task for children. One may understand historical events in considerable sociological detail but the memorizing of names, dates and places will still take hours of concentrated repetition.

The principal difficulty for learning disability children is to remember which graphemes are associated with which phonemes, particularly as the orthography of the English language is so irregular. Alwitt and Bryant (1963) found that the immediate memory traces of reading disability cases do not decay at a faster rate than do those of normal readers, but they do have *a lower memory span.* The authors suggest that perhaps dyslexic children are unable to attend to the task at hand. While attentiveness is no doubt a factor, the short memory spans of these children could be attributable to a *poor auditory sequencing ability* in keeping with inadequate melody discrimination (Wolf, 1967; Drake and Schnall, 1966). Therefore, if dyslexic children have difficulty in sequencing sounds, any meaningful mediator which would extend their memory span would seem highly desirable. Two ways of recoding the irregular orthography of the English language into a more systematic series of associations are using a set of phonetically regular letter symbols (as in the initial teaching alphabet) and color-coding the phonemes so that one color stands for one sound.

With respect to the types of STM described earlier in this chapter, the dyslexic child would have most trouble with ASTM.

If he were of the type who had little difficulty with visuo-spatial problems (e.g., Picture Completion on the WISC), then we would say his VSTM was above average. Some severe cases of dyslexia will not remember phoneme/grapheme associations in reading or spelling after several hours have elapsed, even though their STM for the associations was excellent. Just as with Milner's patients with hippocampal lesions, it is almost a case of out of sight, out of mind. This inability of *some* dyslexic children to transfer associational material from STM to LTM satisfactorily and permanently is possibly caused by powerful interference between lessons. This interference, which may occur in only a few cases, can be compensated for by A-reinforcement which may use the techniques just mentioned. If motivational factors are causing interference and the children are suffering from anxiety, M-reinforcement will be necessary, a technique which will be investigated further in Chapter XIII. Repetition or T-reinforcement is a normal and essential part of any rote learning process; all language learning as a skill is, in the final analysis, rote memorization.

Chapter VIII

READING, SPELLING AND WRITING AS NEUROPSYCHOLOGICAL PROCESSES

READING, SPELLING, WRITING AND OTHER PROCESSES

A possible model of various psychological processes which may be involved in object/concept recognition, reading, listening, spelling and writing is set out in Table X. The table centers around column C, which is labeled "Stimulus (Nonsymbolic) Object/Sounds, etc."; this is essentially a condensation of Table IX. It tends to follow the sensing processes and the internal scanning or analyzing and matching processes implied by Luria (1966), R.L. Gregory (1966) and, in a different context, Broadbent (1958), which were discussed in detail in Chapter VI. Column B outlines the process which occurs when the incoming stimulus is a single word to which the subject is listening. Up to stage V, which parallels stage V in column C, the word has a nonmeaningful stimulus quality, the process being one of assembling the sound-match against previous experience. Stages VI and VII do provide meaningful feedback to assist in the final matching process. Although the whole system works on feedback and probability, some of it semantic, the full association with the percept or concept meaning occurs between stage VII in column B and stage IV in column C. However, because in this particular instance only an internal image is being evoked in column C which is initiated from column B, the image is assembled directly from stage IV to stage VI without matching against an outside perception.

When we read a word, as in column A, the visual processes have to assemble and match the visual impression of the word just as if it were an object without meaning. This process is detailed in column A. At stage IV, there is probably a continuous

300

TABLE X
POSSIBLE MODEL OF OBJECT/CONCEPT RECOGNITION, READING, LISTENING, SPELLING AND WRITING PROCESSES

A. Stimulus Word Reading	B. Stimulus Word Listening	C. Stimulus (Nonsymbolic) Object/Sounds/etc.	D. Oral Spelling	E. Word Writing
I Printed word	I Speaker's voice (word)	I External object (directly sensed)	I Concept or percept isolated	(From DV)
II Visual (eye) reception and projection	II Ear reception and projection	II Sense organ reception and projection; acuity	II Phonemes (sounds) scanned and collated into sound-word gestalt as an associational feedback to DI and feed-forward to all subsequent numbers	VI First grapheme letters encoded in motor pattern in writing
III Primary area registration of letters in sequence, individual-letter discrimination and closure. Assembly into visual graphemes (chunks?)	III Primary area registration, distinctive features, phones, etc., in sequence assembly into phonemes. Discrimination?	III Primary area sensory registration of data, external discrimination	III Phonemes separated out again	
IV Scanning and selection of matching graphemes in secondary areas. Discrimination and sequencing	IV Scanning and selection of matching phonemes or word parts. Discrimination and sequencing	IV Scanning and selection of bits or chunks in secondary areas. Internal discrimination	IV First phoneme in word selected for modality transfer: Recorded into its equivalent grapheme image (visual)	VII Recycle to BIV to pick up second phoneme for letter writing, then third phoneme, etc.
	AIV to BIV: Reading. Continuous grapheme/phoneme matching cycle			

V Matching process, visual closure. Graphemes possibly clustered into conventional units (morphs or syllables?)	V Matching process, closure from phonemes heard, syntax cues, other context-meaning, lip-reading gesture	V Matching process—establishing gestalt organization of bits or chunks into whole. Sensory closure on probabilities	V First grapheme transposed into individual letter names. (For writing, proceed to EVI)
VI Stabilized visual pattern of configurations	VI Word or morphs stabilized as previously heard sequence of sounds	VI Image-to-stimulus match stabilized	VI First grapheme letters articulated on motor plan
BV to AV: Feedback	VII Association with its percept/concept meaning (Proceed to CIV to continue verbal stimulus of imagery process	VII Meaningful percept/concept associations scanned and synthesized. Meaning closure (nonverbal) utility established. (For spelling only, proceed to DI)	VII Recycle to DIV to pick up second phoneme, then for articulation, third phoneme, etc.
	BVI to AVI: Feedback	VIII Cross-associations to other concepts	
		IX Chained associations, sequencing of percepts or concepts (nonverbal)	
		X Motor output or to DVIII	
		VIII Continuous speech: Recycle DII-DVII continuously, superimposed on CIX. Vocal output or may proceed to EVIII	VIII Continuous writing: Recycle DII-EVII, superimposed on CIX

grapheme/phoneme-matching cycle which occurs when one fixates on a particular word. For literate adults, this may last a few milliseconds. Of course, the scanning referred to here is internal and does not involve eye movements, at least within a single fixation. (It is true that minute eye movements do occur continuously to prevent image fading, but these are not especially relevant here.) It will be noticed in column A that stages V and VI may be necessary for feedback purposes, in that the stabilized visual pattern of configurations (letters) merely confirms that the cycling process of continuous grapheme/phoneme matching has been correct from the probability point of view. Thus, if one reads *t-a-b-l-e-s*, the visual closure at the end helps confirm that the word was neither *table* nor *tableau*. Thus, the visual word which is read scans and selects matching phonemes at stage IV in column B and then the inner listening process continues from stages V through VI and VII until it finally moves through the column C sequence to complete the chain of meaning. Column C can run through the processes of sensing, scanning, matching and establishing meaning, through cross-associations and chained associations, to motor output (direct action) which in this case would be nonverbal. If the output or encoding is to be articulated as in oral spelling (and, in a very rapid sense, speaking) the column C process moves at stage VII across to oral spelling (column D, stage I). The stages in column D are self-explanatory, except that in normal speech, the process would be so rapid that continuous speech would be articulated. If handwriting is involved, the transfer occurs at stage V where it transfers to column E, stage VI. Stages IV-VII in columns D and E keep recycling to transpose the grapheme images into letters which can be individually encoded as handwriting motor patterns.

One of the most important aspects of this model is the way in which the various facets of language decoding and encoding are all interconnected. The most complex activity is the one which involves all five columns—that is, the situation in which one is reading for meaning and making original notes from the content. In another context, Osgood (1963) has described a probability model for sentence construction in speech which would take the content of Table X into the dimension of word selection and syntax sequencing. This would all take place in column D, stage VIII, under the heading of "Continuous Speech," which, itself, could be encoded into stage VIII, "Continuous Writing," in column E. In my own previously described model (Chapter III), much of this syntax sequencing would be predetermined by the nonverbal sequences of thought (manipulated concepts, images, etc.).

Much has been said in previous chapters, particularly Chapters III and IV, concerning the development and characteristics of normal speech. In Chapter III, many of the conventions associated with the orthography of the language were discussed; of course, orthography involves the visual aspects of verbal processes which have been described in this section. However, I estimate some 80 percent of reading disabilities to have their origins in an inadequate auditory/vocal language functioning and therefore in the sections which follow it should be realized that the associative (memory) problem area tends to be on the auditory/vocal side of the memory link between phoneme and grapheme rather than on the visual side.

READING AS A COMPLETELY LEARNED PHENOMENON

In Chapter II, a case was made out for language potential being a largely innate characteristic of the human race which, given a stimulating environment, developed naturally and spontaneously in all intact human beings (see also Chapter IX). Lenneberg (1967) has devoted a whole volume to establishing the biological foundations of language. In Chapter IV, the possible ways in which this natural language development progresses in infancy and childhood were described, and the contributions of several authorities in this area were presented and discussed. All these sections were almost entirely concerned with the spoken word and few references were made to the written language.

Whereas a child will spontaneously develop spoken language in a suitable environment, even to the extent that it is considered abnormal if he does *not* develop speech, two-thirds, of the world's population still cannot read and write. Moreover, almost all children have to be actively taught reading in a quite deliberate way through structured lessons in school if they are to acquire the requisite skills. To my knowledge, it is an extremely rare and gifted child who will develop the ability to read and write spontaneously without *any* formal tuition. A parallel illustrative situation would be walking (speech) as opposed to driving a car (reading).

Figure 1 (page 23) showed that to move from the object or concept image to the written word, one has to move through the auditory language process. This claim and the claim that reading is very much an auditorially based process are supported by the work of R. Conrad (1962, 1964) and of Conrad and Hull (1964), who found that whether letters are presented visually or auditorially, any confusion of perception usually occurs on the basis of letters which sound alike. Baddeley (1966) went on to confirm these findings using words. Whether they were printed or spoken, the words caused confusion in the auditory modality. My own research investigations with Wichiarajote (Bannatyne and Wichiarajote, 1969a) indicate that *even an encoding task such as written spelling is largely an auditory/vocal process* (see the report later in this chapter).

When children go to school at the age of five, six, or seven to learn to read and write, most already have a considerable store of spoken and auditory language rich in meaning. The alphabets of most Western languages are phonetic, which means that the written symbols more or less represent the sound symbols; they do not represent the objects or concepts concerned directly. Thus, when children enter school, they already possess the characteristics described in columns B and C of Table X, and the formal process of learning to read and write systematically associates the characteristics of column A with those of column B and the characteristics of columns D and E with those of columns B and C. To further confirm that reading and writing are largely auditory processes, it should be remembered that blind children can learn to read dispensing with vision altogether; they can substitute their fingertips for their eyes. By contrast, as anyone who has taught deaf children knows, it is extremely difficult to teach these children adequate language and still more difficult to teach them to read and write. (It may be possible at a later age to teach some deaf children to read and write on a direct visual symbol-to-object meaning association basis, eliminating the auditory element, but this is a very special case far removed from the usual educational situation.)

AREAS AND LEVELS OF OPERATIONS IN READING

There are four main levels of operations in the processes of reading, spelling and writing: the sensory, neurological and physical level; the motivational/emotional level; the cognitive/memory level, and the academic level.

On the first level, the *sensory neurological and physical level,* it is obvious that, if the sensory organs are intact, if the child has the capacity to lateralize its gaze in saccadic movements with training, if eye-hand coordination is efficient, if LTM and STM operate efficiently, if the brain wave profiles are normal and if the bodily or physiological support for all these operations is adequate, then the child in question will have a satisfactory basis for learning to read, write and spell on this first level.

On the second level, the *motivational/emotional* one, the child must have some motive for learning to read, write and spell. If the child's home background is, or was, inadequate from the language point of view (see Chapter V), the child may not only have no linguistic basis for learning to read but may also lack the motivation to do so. Alternatively, personal conflicts or other pre-occupations may so interfere with the child's attentional processes that STM and LTM may be rendered powerless to habituate the incoming verbal stimuli to a satisfactory skill level. More about the motivational/emotional aspects of language development will be considered in Chapter XIII.

The third level is that of *cognitive/memory operations.* Any fundamental inadequacy in any of the memorizing processes and their related activities (Chapter VII) may cause a degree of failure in the acquisition of reading, spelling and writing skills. Additionally, any neurological dysfunction in any of the primary or secondary sensory areas of the brain, the centrencephalic system or the integrations of any of these will usually result in a degree of illiteracy. Aspects of these neurological dysfunction disabilities will be discussed in Chapters X and XI.

The fourth level is the *academic* one, under which we can include such things as the teaching procedures and techniques used to present to the child, in a systematic program, the relevant information which will result in his acquiring reading, writing and spelling skills. In other words, are the curricula to which the child is exposed efficient in their teaching of the language skills which are their educational objective?

Some of the more important of the processes involved on each of various levels are discussed in more detail below.

READING AS AN AUDITORY-LABEL/VISUAL-LABEL MATCHING PROCESS

The point that reading is a phoneme/grapheme matching process and that the English language has an irregular orthography hardly needs to be made again, but it should be stressed that these auditory/visual associations need have no meaning attached to them in order for them to operate in a habitual way. Thus, we can read words fluently without understanding what we read. Reading as a skill is a matter of associating sounds to visual (or tactile) symbols, and even though it may be a very complex process neurologically speaking, at its best it is a high-speed, purely automatized, completely memorized, habitual skill.

Meaning, on the other hand, is a component of auditory/vocal language, a point clearly made in Chapter II. To discover the meaning of a printed word or sentence, a person must first decode that printed set of symbols, transposing it into auditory/vocal signs even if only as an inner language.

Discrimination of Phonemes

In order to identify graphemes, one must first have experienced phonemes as discrete items in auditory language. Liberman *et al.* (1962), using synthetic speech sounds as stimuli, evaluated discrimination along an acoustical continuum to find that listeners could discriminate sounds only as well as they could identify them absolutely as phonemes. Although many consonants appear to have a discrimination peak at phoneme boundaries, vowels are quite different, with no increase in discrimination at the phoneme boundaries. Thus, the perception of synthetic vowels tends to be continuous. The authors go on to say that there is considerable feedback from one's own articulation which assists in the discrimination of phonemes of all kinds. However, since vowels acoustically run into one another without discrimination peaks or stops, it would seem that they are the most difficult to discriminate. It is for this reason that only the vowels have been color-coded in the Psycholinguistic Color System (Bannatyne, 1968b).

Fortunately for most people, the spoken word is acoustically redundant in that there is a superfluity of distinctive features through which phonemes and sequences of phonemes can be identified at least as parts of words (Chapter II). We do not have to be consciously aware of phonemes as units for this automatic speech perception process to take place efficiently.

That articulation is important in other language processes has been demonstrated by Nazordva (1952), who found that when articulation was not permitted, the number of mistakes in writing made by pupils in the first and second grades was increased between five and six times. The second confirmation was made by Sommers *et al.* (1961b), who found that training in articulation administered to a group of first-grade children with many articulation problems resulted in a significantly higher reading factor and reading comprehension score for the experimental group. Shriner (1968), in reviewing the literature, notes that Menyuk (1964) and Vandemark and Mann (1965) have separately demonstrated that articulatory defective children have associated syntactical problems. These studies suggest that training in articulation will provide children with an accurate discrimination of phonemes, helping them learn to read and write more effectively.

In yet another paper on auditory discrimination and articulation, Weiner (1967) has thoroughly reviewed the field. His one major finding was that there is a positive relationship between poor auditory discrimination and the more severe articulatory difficulties at the age levels below nine years. The author quotes Wepman (1960) as follows:

First, there is evidence that the more nearly alike two phonemes are in phonetic structure, the more likely they are to be misinterpreted. Second, individuals differ in their ability to discriminate among sounds. Third, the ability to discriminate frequently matures as late as the end of the child's eighth year. Fourth, there is a strong positive relation between slow development of auditory discrimination and inaccurate pronunciation. Fifth, there is a positive relationship between poor discrimination and poor reading. Sixth, while poor discrimination may be at the root of both speech and reading difficulties, it often affects any reading or speaking. Seventh, there is little, if any, relation between the development of auditory discrimination and intelligence as measured by most intelligence tests.

Almost anyone who has had experience remediating children with reading disabilities knows that it is not uncommon to find a history of poor speech development in many cases.

Auditory Sequencing and Melody Discrimination

Although sounds have to be discriminated when they are sequenced (Liberman *et al.*, 1962), a sequence of sounds is far more than a series of individual discriminations. Several times in previous chapters, the work of Wolf (1967) and of Drake and Schnall (1966) has been quoted with respect to the melody discrimination difficulties which some poor readers have. Wolf, in particular, carefully screened out boys who had observable signs of neurological dysfunction and all his group had normal audiometry records. The work of Milner (1962) suggests that the right temporal lobe is strongly associated with performance on tests of musical talent, whereas the left temporal lobe is known to be associated with speech perception functions. The fact that children who are poor readers (left hemisphere) have difficulty discriminating sequenced melodies (right hemisphere) strongly suggests that there is a generalized "lack of talent" in *both* temporal lobes. Furthermore, with respect to Wolf's research, it is inconceivable that a group of boys of the same age in one area of one town who have been screened to eliminate neurological dysfunction should have lesions in two hemispheres in roughly identical very specific locations; that would be stretching chance too far. Once again, the inescapable conclusion is that the auditory deficit in genetic dyslexic children is a generalized discriminatory and sequencing one, probably involving memory, which is a part of the normal distribution of temporal lobe auditory functioning in the population as a whole. This could mean that the efficient cause could be genetic or environmental, and evidence will be presented in the next chapter which suggests that in a considerable proportion of dyslexic children (but by no means all) the efficient cause is genetic in nature. Wolf's own findings certainly suggested that a genetic factor was present.

An analysis of the psychoneurological functions underlying melody discrimination tests suggests that several variables are in operation. The first of these is memory span, that is, the number of sounds which can be retained in STM and held there so that comparisons of pitch can be made. A second factor would be the rhythm or beat, which mediates the sound. Wolf found that on the Seashore measures of musical talents, rhythm was one of the best discriminators between the experimental and control groups. Loudness thresholds also discriminated between the two. These results indicate an all-around lack of auditory skills. However, in the melody discrimination tasks, the importance of STM, attention span and interference should be given careful consideration. Many research studies (McLeod, 1965) have shown that large numbers of reading disability children obtain a low WISC Digit Span score, which, in the ITPA (Illinois Test of Psycholinguistic Abilities), is called auditory sequencing. Wolf obtained similar results on the WISC digit span subtest. In a study of my own with Wichiarajote (Bannatyne and Wichiarajote, 1969a; also see p. 362 and Chapter IX), while no difference was found between poor and good *spellers* (not readers) on an auditory discrimination test, there was a significant correlation of $r = 0.314$ between left-handedness (right hemisphere) which is not trained, and success in melody discrimination (right hemisphere). The representative sample was composed of fifty third-grade children.

In a study of eighty-seven Lancashire boys between eight and eleven years of age with reading quotients less than 80 (Bannatyne, 1967b), Moseley and I found the "sequencing" score on the WISC (in this instance Digit Span, plus Picture Arrangement, plus Arithmetic) to the main area of deficit. Other research studies which show this *lack of auditory discrimination and/or sequencing memory disability in poor readers* are Forrest (1967), Steiner (1967) and Kass (1962).

Phoneme/Grapheme Matching and Sequencing in Reading and Spelling

Chall (1967) in an extensive review of the research and other literature on methods of teaching reading between 1910 and 1965 comes to the firm conclusion that ". . . the experimental correlational and clinical evidence indicates that a code emphasis is the better way to start [reading]." By "a code emphasis" she means, of course, the use of phonic methods of teaching reading. Several pages later, she says, ". . . evidence from the clinic indicates that inhibiting oral and articulatory responses and other secondary aids such as finger pointing and whispering retards rather than fosters the development of meaningful reading." In other words, speech sequencing aided by manual pointing will mediate progress in reading successfully. Bateman (1967a), in a study comparing different methods of teaching reading to children who had been classified as auditory or visual modality subjects, found, "The auditory method of reading instruction was superior to the visual method for both reading and spelling; the auditory-modality-preferred subjects were superior in both reading and spelling to the visual-modality-preferred subjects; and, there was no interaction between subjects' preferred modality and the method of instruction used." In the study by myself and Wichiarajote mentioned above (Bannatyne and Wichiarajote, 1969a), the poor spellers and good spellers (on a split-group basis) had significantly different means on the ITPA (Kirk *et al.*, 1968) sound-blending subtest, but not on auditory sequencing, auditory closure, visual sequencing and visual closure. The ITPA sound-blending subtest's correlation with spelling ability was $r = 0.40$ (0.01 level of significance). Thus written spelling would seem to be more related to sound-blending ability (articulemic-vocal sequencing) than to ITPA auditory sequencing, auditory closure, visual sequencing or visual closure. Written spelling is also not correlated with a simple melody discrimination xylophone test ($r = 0.06$). An explanation of these results in the light of other statistics is given in the section on spelling below. It would seem, then, that reading and spelling cannot be completely equated in terms of cognitive or language functions generally. While reading contains, so to speak, a large element of auditory (digit-span) sequencing, this may be less important in the processes involved in spelling.

Irregular Orthography and Mediational A-Reinforcers

There has been frequent mention throughout this book of the fact that the orthography of the English language is highly irregular, in that many phonemes can be represented by one grapheme and many graphemes can be represented by one phoneme, particularly for vowels. That this is a considerable handicap to children in learning to read has been proved by Downing (1968). Using the initial teaching alphabet, he has demonstrated that a regular orthography will help children learn to read at a significantly faster rate. Of course, the gain considerably decreases and is *not* significant if the child has to transfer back to the traditional orthography, but as Downing points out, this only reconfirms that the latter is a considerable stumbling block to beginning readers.

Fortunately, whether the child is learning to read or is already an accomplished reader, many mediational variables assist him in deciphering the visual code into the auditory code and finally into its contextual meaning.

The shape of the letters and the shape of the word assist the experienced reader because, as Downing points out, it has long been known that subjects can read the top halves of words far more fluently than the lower halves, presumably because the top sections of letters have many more visually distinctive features. These features tend to be recognized automatically by experienced readers because as we read, we are unaware that we are recognizing shapes as we "lock on to" the meaningful content of the passage.

The meaning of the content, itself, enables us to predict on a probability basis what is likely to come next in any one proposition. Osgood (1963) has elaborated a probability-based theory about sentences which states that words which follow can be, to some extent, predicted from those which have gone before.

This probability prediction element has other bases besides meaning. Different languages sequence words in terms of syntax in a variety of different ways. It is true that the commonalities of syntax between languages are greater than their differences (Lenneberg, 1967) and that the conventional sequencing of words within a particular language is sufficiently standardized for us to predict which type of word—e.g., noun-phrase—is likely to occur next; in some cases, even the meaning of the following words may be known. As Goldman-Eisler (1964) has pointed out, the more conventional our statements or utterances (e.g., a greeting), the more predictable and fluent they are; conversely, the more original the content, the less predictable and more hesitant they become.

The morphology of our language, that is, the meaningful units (words and part-words) of which it is composed, including prefixes, suffixes, declensions, etc., also enables us to predict the likelihood of what is to follow. For example the suffix *ly* is most likely to occur on words following verbs, namely, adverbs.

All the other conventions of language sequencing which were listed in Chapter III contribute to the predictability of sequencing in both words and sentence structure, but only the main ones have been mentioned here. All these sequencing patterns are monitored by memory systems which have been spontaneously learned and automatized in the experienced reader, who, by and large, is unaware of their operation except as a subject of special study. Together with the distinctive features of speech perception, which probably operate in terms of inner speech during the reading process, these sequencing patterns form a highly *redundant* memorized (automatized) system, one which is necessary to achieve very fast rates of reading.

The specific content of the above characteristics of reading is arbitrary because each culture and subculture evolves its own sound utilization systems. In almost every respect, English as a communicative medium is in some degree irregular with the one exception of meaning; and ambiguity even exists there. In words which sound the same and which are spelled in the same way, only the meaning in context can satisfactorily identify the intended sequence (e.g., *bow, charge*).

The Time Factor in Reading and Closure

The reading process, when taken from the time the words as stimuli first enter the visual field until the time when the meaning is fully understood, is functionally a continuous (stochastic) one, but it can be separated into three distinct stages which may occur only milliseconds apart. The first phase occurs when the eyes run ahead in fluent reading, differentiating and registering the pure, *visual* stimuli through visual discrimination and visual closure, utilizing saccadic eye movements which feed the data into the occipital areas. The next phase concerns what Luria or Myklebust would call "inner speech." During this phase, we translate the visual stimuli through a process of phoneme/grapheme matching, auditory closure and sequencing probability into the *auditory* word. The third phase, in time, occurs while we scan internally for the *meaning* of the auditory word and relate this to the context of the previously read content (see Table X). Here, too, there is a type of closure onto the most likely meaning, given a particular word in a particular context. While for the experienced reader all these successive processes tend to occur automatically, the beginning reader and the dyslexic child do not possess them, at least to any reasonably efficient degree. It is the acquisition of all these time-based functions which may prove difficult *at the learning stage,* that is, during the acquisition of reading skills. For example, a child may have to be taught quite deliberately to let his eyes *run ahead* of the words he is "thinking" and, if he is reading aloud, even farther ahead of the words he is speaking.

From what has been said above, it will be seen that *closure,* in a variety of guises, is of key importance to this acquisition of reading skills. Visual closure will be considered in more detail later, and closure onto meaning has been explained in both this and previous chapters (see Table IX). Auditory closure, however, requires examination in more detail.

Auditory Closure

When we listen to a foreign accent or to someone mispronouncing a word and yet recognize the sounds in the word as a gestalt and can interpret it in terms of meaning, we are exercising auditory closure. For example, if someone pronounces the word *automatic* incorrectly by laying stress on the second syllable, *tom*, we might still recognize it by relating it directly to our own personal version of the pronunciation. A child who is learning to read (and this includes many learning disability cases) may sound out a word incorrectly as a kind of "near miss." The child who is more verbally gifted will immediately close on his own slightly incorrect blending of the sounds and be able to identify the word in question fairly quickly. However, it is a common experience to all teachers of dyslexic children to hear a child who is reading slightly mispronouncing (and sometimes even correctly pronouncing) a given word, unable to close on the correct pronunciation and its meaning. This may occur even though in general conversation the child knows the word extremely well. In such cases, it is almost as if the inner language associated with reading is not associated with the inner language generated from speech perception. In the research mentioned above, a significant correlation of $r = 0.43$ was obtained on the ITPA between the auditory closure subtest and the sound-blending subtest. The correlation between auditory sequencing (digit span) and auditory closure was low and not significant. The correlation between auditory sequencing and sound blending was even smaller.

Thus, auditory closure and sound blending have a lot more in common than either does with auditory sequencing, at least if the latter is defined as a memory for digits. (Letters can be substituted for digits because we obtained a correlation of $r = 0.66$ between the ITPA auditory [digit-span] sequencing subtest and the parallel-consonant letter-span test of our own construction, which merely substitutes consonants for digits. This consonant letter-span test also had low correlations with auditory closure and sound blending on the ITPA.) These results would indicate the importance of training children in blending techniques while they are learning to read, and to associate these blends with the inner language which they have developed from early childhood. This theme is further developed in the section below, "Spelling as an Encoding Task."

ROTE MEMORY, RECOGNITION AND RECALL IN READING, SPELLING AND WRITING

It is useful to summarize here the main points which emerged from the previous chapter on memory as important to reading, spelling or writing. Most of the reference credits will not be reiterated here.

Reminiscence or the spontaneous return of deliberately extinguished behavior, such as incorrectly spelled words, can occur in dyslexic children long after those words have been subsequently learned in their correct format.

The implications of Osgood's (1949) three laws of transfer and retroaction for children learning to read or spell were found to be considerable. Because one grapheme may elicit many phonemes and one phoneme many graphemes, particularly with reference to vowel sounds, considerable negative transfer and retroactive interference will occur. Therefore, any child with a poor memory system will be at a disadvantage learning to read or spell. The ideal solution to the problem is to make the orthography of the language regular and yet somehow retain the original spellings of the words in the language. The only technique known which can achieve this is color-coding the troublesome phoneme/grapheme matches while retaining the original spelling. Since the vowels are the main problem, in terms of irregularity, only they need be color-coded (Bannatyne, 1966e, 1968b).

Postman (1965) states that the learning time taken by the repetitive-part method is significantly less than learning by either the whole- or the pure-part method separately. Therefore, when children are learning phoneme/grapheme matching or lists of spelling words, they will learn them more quickly and more efficiently if each time a new item is added, the whole list is repeated. There is almost no need to restate the extremely well-known fact that the degree of practice increases the degree of retention; *overlearning*, that is, repetition of the words after a perfect performance, is the secret for insuring the automatization of language skill processes.

The number of units or chunks which can be retained in STM is, in the average individual, approximately seven, but in many dyslexic children, the number tends to decrease to five or fewer. Almost all the research results on the WISC digit-span subtest, when given to dyslexic children, indicate this. Therefore, any grouping, chunking or categorizing in a logical way, such as breaking groups of similar words into syllables, prefixes, morphs and suffixes, or again, color-coding, will assist in the spelling memorization processes. Sequences or phoneme/grapheme matches in sizable word groupings must be retained long enough in STM for an effective transfer to LTM to be established.

Acoustical similarity interferes with STM retention whether the words are heard, written or read. Therefore, in any memorization tasks, an effort should be made by the teacher to insure that words which sound the same but are spelled differently are not included in the same list or passage. Of course, this does not apply to words which have exactly the same phoneme and grapheme equivalents; therefore, it is quite advantageous to include in the same list similar-sounding words with similar spellings such as *bean, leaf, seal,* etc.

Any mediational devices which will help establish the link between two words or a word and a particular series of sounds should be used. A deliberate training in the use of efficient mediators has been advised by J.A. Adams (1967b).

Both short-term and long-term motor memory systems are less subject to interference than is the case in auditory or visual memorizing. This confirms that kinesthetic tracing and activity methods of teaching reading which involve a considerable amount of writing should A-reinforce the retention of words in reading and spelling. They are strongly recommended.

In any discussion of memory, one cannot ignore motivation and attentional processes. Obviously, if a child is not concentrating on the task in hand, there is no basis on which retention can proceed. Ways of motivating the child to attend to this and other types of tasks will be discussed in some detail in Chapters XIII and XV.

SPELLING AS A SKILL

A Research Report on Spelling

A research on a representative sample of third-grade children was carried out by the author and a brief summary of the results which relate to spelling are set out below. The research is reported in more detail elsewhere (Bannatyne and Wichiarajote, 1969a; see also Chapter IX).

The significant correlations between spelling in the form of a written word spelling test and other test variables are set out in Table XI. Some variables which were not correlated with spelling, but which one might expect to be correlated with it, are also included. These ten variables have been selected from a total of forty-seven included in the survey as a whole.

A brief explanation of the variables reported in Table XI is required. More detailed test descriptions are set out in Chapter IX.

1. The written word spelling test was from Schonell and Schonell (1960).

2. The BVSMT (Bannatyne Visuo-Spatial Memory Test) is a multiple-choice-answer, memory-for-designs test constructed to eliminate the design-copying *motor* factor. This particular score is the choice-design which slightly simplifies the original stimulus design. It is one of eight possible designs from which the subject could choose his answer after a four-second presentation of the original stimulus design.

3. The balancing test required the child to stand on one leg with his eyes open, arms folded, for as many seconds as possible. A second balancing test of standing on tiptoe using both feet with the eyes closed supported the above finding by increasing the total balance correlation (which was significant) although its separate correlation with spelling was not significant.

TABLE XI

CORRELATIONS BETWEEN WRITTEN SPELLING AND SELECTED VARIABLES ($N = 50$)

	1	2	3	4	5	6	7	8	9	10
1. Word Spelling (written)	1.0									
2. BVSMT Simplification	−0.29*	1.0								
3. Balancing on One Leg	0.33*	0.00	1.0							
4. Unlearned Ambidexterity	0.42†	−0.14	0.28*	1.0						
5. MFD Test (very accurate design score)	0.33*	0.01	0.08	0.03	1.0					
6. Sound-Blending ITPA	0.40†	−0.15	0.16	0.25	0.37†	1.0				
7. Auditory Closure ITPA	0.11	−0.05	0.08	0.05	0.13	0.37†	1.0			
8. Auditory Sequencing ITPA	0.21	0.07	0.27	−0.14	−0.13	0.02	0.22	1.0		
9. PERC Auditory Discrimination	0.25	0.21	0.19	0.05	0.19	0.02	0.20	0.26	1.0	
10. Letter-Span Memory	0.17	0.11	0.24	0.09	0.02	−0.01	0.16	0.66†	0.24	1.0

*$r = 0.273$ (0.05 level of probabiltiy).
†$r = 0.354$ (0.01 level of probability).

4. The unlearned laterality tests included three items: the thumb which is placed on top when the hands are clasped, the hand which is placed on the upper arm when the arms are folded and which hand is used to touch the left ear on command. This unlearned handedness was not significantly correlated with any variable (right, left or ambilateral) from an orthodox trained handedness test.

5. The children's hand-drawn copies from the Graham-Kendall Memory-for-Designs Test were judged by two people for "very accurate reproduction of the original," and this score was used here.

6. The sound-blending subtests from the ITPA revised version (Kirk *et al.*, 1968) were used for this score.

7. This score came from the ITPA auditory closure test in which the children have to correctly pronounce words which have been presented vocally with a phoneme or two missing.

8. The ITPA auditory sequencing test is a digit-span task similar to that on the WISC but using different timing. The child has to listen to a series of numbers and repeat them back to the experimenter.

9. The auditory discrimination test from the Perceptual and Educational Research Center is similar to the Wepman auditory discrimination test. Similar-sounding word pairs have to be discriminated.

10. The letter-span memory test was devised to parallel the digit-span test using consonants instead of numbers; hence the high correlation with item 8 (digit span).

Discussion of Results

There was a significant tendency (using t-tests) for poor spellers (the lower spelling half of the sample) to choose a simplified version of the original stimulus design of the BVSMT. There were no significant differences between poor spellers and good spellers on the choice of mirror-image designs, rotated designs, fragmented designs, disproportionate designs, complicated designs or designs which had been made more symmetrical. Rotation was the next in line but the difference between the means was not significant.

The ability to balance on one leg with the eyes open is positively correlated with spelling achievement ($r = + 0.33$), a result which tends to suggest that overall coordinated motor control and eye-motor coordination is a concomitant of good spelling. Note that the quality of the writing was not scored.

A fascinating result was the significant correlation ($r = + 0.42$) between unlearned ambidexterity and spelling achievement. In the whole survey, the unlearned and learned laterality tests were separately significantly correlated with many of the other test variables; the results are reported elsewhere (Bannatyne and Wichiarajote, 1969b). The smaller but significant correlations ($r = + 0.28$) between unlearned ambidexterity and balance (the only laterality score correlated with balance) would seem to indicate a superior motor coordination between the two sides of the body and between these two variables and the eyes. In other words, the inference is that the superior speller possesses superior visuo-motor coordination; it is not stretching the evidence too far in the light of Luria's (1966) remarks on motor planning, to suggest that spelling as an encoding function is very *heavily* dependent on automatized motor/kinesthetic/praxic/visual sequencing processes.

Certainly, the memory-for-designs unit when *motor*-encoded as a drawing is reflected in the significant correlation between the very accurate reproduction score of the Graham-Kendall Memory-for-Designs Test with the word spelling test. The nonmotor BVSMT original design choice was not correlated with spelling to any extent.

The sound-blending test (ITPA) is significantly correlated ($r = + 0.40$) with the spelling test. It is interesting that sound blending is also correlated significantly with the memory-for-designs very accurate score. This suggests that sound blending has in it, so to speak, a considerable element of the motor/kinesthetic/visual aspects of reading and writing, even when the stimuli are presented orally. This result would seem to support those educators who claim that reading is best learned through an active writing and spelling curriculum (e.g., Fernald, 1943; Spalding, 1970).

Although the ITPA auditory closure subtest is significantly correlated ($r = 0.37$) with sound blending, it is not itself significantly correlated with spelling. This would suggest that auditory closure is far more of an auditory-input, temporal-lobe type of test than is sound blending, a conclusion which fits in with auditory closure being largely a recogniton sensory decoding operation (one aspect of reading) rather than a visuo-motor recall encoding task (one aspect of spelling).

Variables 7, 8, 9 and 10 were included in the above matrix to illustrate that they are of less importance in spelling (encoding), even though they are obviously highly auditory in modality. Of course, this does not mean that they are not important in the *reading decoding* process. Even the letter-span memory test (variable 10) was not correlated with spelling ability even though it was highly correlated with the auditory-sequencing digit-span subtest on the ITPA. A factor analysis of the data by and large confirmed the above correlational analysis.

The general conclusion from the above results is that spelling as a written test, and probably as an oral test (because of the importance of sound blending), is very much determined by the efficiency of the vocal-motor/kinesthetic/praxic/visuo-spatial output processes, the pattern memory influence in these processes and the degree of automatization or habituation which has or has not been achieved in that output. In particular, it would seem from the research *that articulemic sound-blending (vocal-motor) sequencing training is all-important to correct spelling from the sequencing point of view while visual sequencing is incidental.* While the unit designs (configurations) of letters and graphemes must be *separately* reproducible as units from visual memory, they are apparently strung together on a "string" which neuro-psychologically is a *vocal-motor patterning.* The implications of this articulemic sequencing for teaching children spelling will be discussed in Chapter XV. It would seem likely that the vocal-motor sequencing and the handwriting sequencing of the elements of words would be highly integrated vocal-motor functions. From personal experience, I find it extremely difficult to *say* one word while I *automatically write* another—it takes considerable conscious concentration. Normally one pronounces a word to be spelled while writing it; one does not spell it letter by letter.

It is worthwhile to compare the above results on spelling with those found by Kass (1962) in her investigation of the psychological correlates of severe reading disability. She found the sample of twenty-one reading disability cases to be similar to normal readers in understanding questions (auditory decoding, ITPA), describing familiar objects (vocal encoding, ITPA), digit-span memory (auditory/vocal sequential, ITPA), conceptual communality picture association (visual-motor association, ITPA) and answering with gestures (motor encoding, ITPA). That these reading disability cases did not have low scores on the digit-span test is at variance with most of the WISC studies on learning disabilities, some of which have been summarized by McLeod (1965.) In Kass' study, the reading disability cases had significant deficits in a controlled-association analogies test, e.g., "Father is big, baby is ———" (auditory/vocal association, ITPA); memory for a series of pictures or geometrical designs (visual-motor sequential, ITPA); sound blending (Monroe); memory for designs (Graham-Kendall); mazes (WISC), and perceptual speed (Primary Mental Abilities Reasoning Test [PMA]). Perceptual speed is a rate-of-recognition test.

Although the children had no known auditory or visual impairment, Kass does note that the tested deficiencies may be related to neurological dysfunctions which limit symbolic storage. The results indicate that disabled readers are deficient in seven out of eight abilities at the *automatic-sequential* psycholinguistic level but in only one of six representational-level abilities (see Figure 5). Some of Kass' results (e.g., normal auditory/vocal sequential scores) do not tally with other findings, such as those of McLeod (1965) and Wolf (1967), and her sample was almost certainly heterogeneous. (In Chapter I, in an overview of many different possible types of learning disability cases, I advocated the need for clustering research to help identify homogeneous groups of children in the area of learning disabilities. In my own research with Wichiarajote reported above [Bannatyne and Wichiarajote, 1969b], the children were a representative sample of local third-grade children attending public school. Wolf's group was carfully screened to exclude neurological dysfunction cases and McLeod's review covered many research studies and samples.) Nevertheless, one main conclusion which Kass has come to and which many other authors have noted is the number of reading and spelling disability cases who fail on tests involving automatized functions in the various sensory modalities. Whiting *et al.* (1966) carried out research on thirty dyslexic children and thirty normal children to test the automatization skills of the two groups. They developed a group of automatized tests and nonautomatized tests, but, unfortunately, most of the former are highly verbal or involve arithmetic skills while the latter are almost all spatial. On all the verbal and arithmetic tests, the normal group scored significantly better, whereas on the nonverbal tests, there was usually no difference between the groups. Anyone reviewing the literature on reading and spelling disabilities can hardly help but come to the conclusion that the inability to automatize (or rote memorize) auditorially, visually, motor-kinesthetically or praxically is central to the problem. This inability also extends to cross-modality association, e.g., auditory-visual integration (Birch and Belmont, 1965c).

Spelling as an Encoding Task

When we write a letter to someone, it is our conceptualizing and thought processes which are the major stimulus of the content, which means that the words we must spell have to be sequenced solely from recall. Usually, in such a situation, there is no external cue which acts as a stimulus to facilitate the spelling. Thus, the spontaneous composition of prose is a slightly different spelling situation from the one in which the child is cued by a list of words dictated to him orally which he must then reproduce correctly in writing. This slight cueing which comes from hearing the spoken word can help the more verbally able child because it discriminates the phonemes which comprise the various words, and through the habitual phoneme/grapheme sequencing associations, automatically sequences the written symbols in the correct order. From the above research results, it appears that *it is the voice as a motor function which determines sequencing in the spelling process.*

In a like manner, even when the child is working from conceptualizing processes and not from the spoken word, he must hear his phonemic inner vocal language in order to encode the correct graphemes which are associated with the internalized auditory word. Almost invariably the child has firmly established many of the associations between objects and concepts and their auditory/vocal word symbols before he enters school or learns to read or write. When he does eventually learn to read and write in school, the new visual symbols and their sequences are *associated with the extensive auditory language which is already present.* It would seem highly likely that those children who have auditory shortcomings of one kind or another (not necessarily always caused by neurological dysfunctioning) may not be able internally to "hear" or process phonemic elements of words in a sufficiently discriminatory and analytical way to provide the inner speech cues for satisfactory spelling output. It is highly likely from the above research results that the problem is poor sound blending resulting from a lack of phonics training or an inability to profit from it. From Table XI, it is apparent that sound blending is a much more important variable than auditory closure, auditory sequencing or auditory discrimination. It will be remembered that in Kass' (1962) study of reading disability, sound blending and auditory/vocal association were the only two auditory/vocal types of tests which significantly discriminated between the two groups of readers.

In a study on the influence of certain reading methods on the spelling ability of elementary school children, Peters (1965) came to the following conclusion:

> The implications of this research for remedial teaching are that for children who are finding spelling difficult, those taught to read by a look-and-say method are restricted with visual, but no rational reference. Those taught to read by a phonic method are able to make a reasonable attempt (possibly a homophone) while i.t.a. children because of their economy and systematic control of output are free to

learn correct spelling conventions which for them it is essential and practicable to be taught. It is concluded that though spelling attainment is not affected, perceptual training is transferred to spelling techniques, with important implications for remedial teaching.

Peters found that children who were taught by the phonics method, although equal to the other children in many categories of error, were superior in the remaining categories of fewest transpositions, fewest substitutions of vowels and greatest number of reasonable phonic alternatives. Since phonics training includes or should include a large amount of sound blending and articulation training in synthesizing words from their phonemic elements, it would seem that the synthesis which is involved in blending sounds during the reading process in some way assists in the reverse situation, namely, the analysis of a unit word in inner speech into its component parts, which are then encoded (spelled) either vocally or in handwriting. This is an interesting confirmation of the study by Sommers *et al.* (1961b) which concluded that training in articulation significantly improves the performance of children in reading comprehension. Thus, the facilitation process between reading and spelling is a two-way one.

The Nature of Sound Blending

The fusion of sound into a smooth utterance, or the analysis of an utterance into its component sounds (phonemes or distinctive features), is rather obscure. The spectrographic analysis of speech (Fant, 1967) demonstrates how complex the speech waves are. He says,

> Distinctive feature analysis applied to speech does not require an initial stage of segmentation in terms of sharply time limited portions of the speech wave. Some features appear and fade out gradually, and the tendency of segmental structuring to be observed in spectrograms is such that one phoneme is often characterized by cues from several adjacent segments and that one segment may carry some information on the identity of two or more successive phonemes.

Although much more work will have to be done on the nature of speech and speech perception in terms of their elemental units before the nature of sound blending is fully understood, Fant quotes Penfield and Roberts (1959) to support the notion that the brain has two separate locations for motor units (for words) and sensory units (for words). Penfield and Roberts say, "This strongly suggests that the motor units for words and phrases are separated somehow, spatially, from the sensory units. But it is also clear that they are both located in the general region of the cortico-thalamic speech areas of the left side, where they are closely inter-related in function."

This work has led Fant to construct a hypothetical model of brain function in speech perception and production (see Fig. 13). The model closely follows the work of Luria and the many others previously quoted in this book. It also parallels the psycholinguistic diagrams of Osgood, Wepman and others (see Chapter II) inasmuch as the distinctive features correspond to unit automatism, whereas the phonemes, syllables, words and prosodemes correspond to sequencing automatism. In spelling, however, we may regard phonemes, graphemes and articulemes as the basic units. From the sound-blending aspect, the important part of Fant's model is the two-way feedback or rather the "feed-around *K F D K* and *K D F K*, which would account for the A-reinforcement that articulatory motor patterns lend auditory patterns and vice versa. In the spelling situation E F G H I, the loop F K K D F, if automatically activated, would A-reinforce the breaking down or analysis of the motor patterns into phonemic and unit letter or

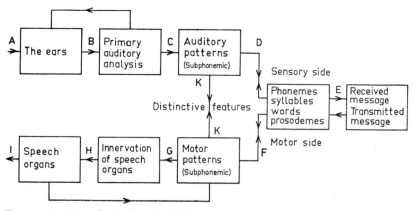

FIGURE 13. Hypothetical model of brain functions in speech perception and production. *(From Fant, 1967, p. 112.)*

328 of the chapter. Even so, on Fant's model, the blend-

grapheme sequences. However, Fant's model is of the neuro-psychological functions in speech perception and production and is not primarily intended to hypothesize the mechanisms involved in reading, spelling or writing, which are outlined in Table XI at the beginning of the chapter. Even so, on Fant's model, the blending of separate phonemes would take place in the *F G* box of motor patterning.

This takes us back to Luria's work (1966) in which he says,

> Expressive (motor) speech always requires the presence of a kinetic system (or chain) of articulatory movements with constant inhibition and modification (depending on the order of the sounds to be articulated) of preceding articulation. . . . The pronunciation of any sound or syllable is possible only if an articuleme can be inhibited at the right time and the articulatory apparatus can be transferred to the next articuleme. It follows that a disturbance in the kinetic system (or the specific motor programs) of the whole word and the inability to promptly inhibit each link of this system inevitably leads to a profound impairment of the pronunciation of words.

Luria goes on to describe how patients who have lesions in Broca's area (area 44)

> . . . cannot pronounce a syllable or a whole word, for the ability to inhibit individual articulatory impulses and to shift from one articulation to another is extremely limited. The patient has to make a separate, special effort for each sound and therefore cannot articulate a complete word smoothly. As a rule, the pronunciation of an articuleme reveals pathological inertia, and the patient cannot move on to the next sound.

Such patients have similar difficulties when they try to write because the integral kinetic structure of writing is disturbed.

If, as Luria suggests, the motor patterning and innervation of speech organs (as in Fant's model) depends on Broca's premotor area, it is reasonable to suggest that children who find blending difficult in reading, or letter sequencing difficult in spelling, have a less efficient encoding motor patterning (probably involving Broca's area) than do their peers. It should be made clear that this statement in no way implies lesions or neurological dysfunctions. The assumption is that almost all "normal" physiological and neurological functions in the intact population as a whole can be ranged along a relatively normal continuum with many intact individuals falling at the lower end of the distribution. Thus, many persons, particularly males (Morley, 1965), will exhibit articulatory hesitancies, slight mispronunciations, etc., even though their speech production falls within normal limits. That boys are significantly poorer spellers than girls is reported by Maccoby (1966) in her review of spelling research. Such children can no more be said to be brain-damaged than can those millions of individuals who have IQ's of under 90. Broca's area, while it may regulate the facilitation and inhibition of articulemes, is not necessarily responsible, so to speak, for assembling kinetic distinctive features into those articulemes, but this is of minor importance here because blending is essentially a process of fusing the articulemes from the template originally presented by a phoneme analysis from the word as represented in inner perceived speech. One must have experienced hearing a word to pronounce it. The child who cannot blend when reading may sound out the phonemic units of the word successfully but be unable to run these sounds together in the conventional pattern. If the inner speech hypothesis is correct, the child's problem is one of (a) running the sounds (articulemes) together smoothly enough to approximate a normally spoken word and (b) matching this word approximation against both the *auditory* patterns and the already learned relevant *motor* (articulemic) patterns of inner speech. The quality of the two latter patterns will determine the quality of the reading. In the case of spelling, the articulemic motor pattern will be of paramount importance.

The conclusion to be drawn is that children who have specific difficulties in the sound blending of words or in the spelling of words will require intensive training in careful listening, in phoneme analysis (phonics training) and in clear sequential articulation as well as in a variety of blending exercises.

Rhythm and Syllabification

Children with blending problems will also be helped by separating words into syllables and by exaggerating the accented rhythm of the phonemes (or articulemes) within each syllable. Words should be said quickly as a whole word at the beginning of an exercise and then should be gradually broken down into their component phonemic parts in a reverse process to blending so that the child understands how words may be analyzed. Thus, when he comes to put them together again in a blending process, he will be helped by this understanding of word analysis. One useful method for blending initial consonants with a following vowel is to shape the vocal apparatus in an exaggerated position ready to say the consonant but instead the *vowel* is pronounced. This technique usually produces a perfect blend.

Written Errors in Spelling

The usual way to categorize spelling errors is in terms of omissions, substitutions, additions, interpolations and reversals. This rather mechanical approach to the problem has its limitations from both the theoretical and practical teaching standpoints. From Peters' work quoted above and from that of Kinsbourne and Warrington (1964), it is apparent that the type of error is likely to be correlated with either, or both, symptomatology or method of teaching. It is quite possible that the term *symptomatology* is also valid in this context for normal children, in the sense that individual differences in verbal, spatial and other abilities may have an effect on the types of spelling errors produced by any one child.

Apart from methods of teaching reading and the effects of individual differences, spelling errors can also result from the reversal of two letters in the word or from the mirror imaging of one particular letter. The reversal of two letters or even a whole word is not always caused by the neurological consequences of a poorly lateralized hemispheric verbal dominance in the brain as described in Chapter VI. As Peters (1965) points out, children who have been trained in phonics methods (and I would add to this group many dyslexic children), when faced with a word they do not know, attempt to spell it in a phonetically regular way. In many irregular English words, the conventional spelling is a reversal of what would be phonetically logical; therefore, the child will spell the word *little*, for example, as *littel*, the latter being the more sensible rendering. This and numerous other instances may be incorrectly interpreted as a neurological reversal. Another way in which two-letter reversals may occur is through conventionalized spelling patterns which are contravened by the particular word to be spelled. For instance, a child may habitually write words ending in *ing* and become so used to the sequence that when he spells the word *sign*, it is automatically written as *sing*. Superficially, this would appear as a reversal. It is also likely that a proportion of two-letter reversals will occur by chance, particularly when the child is completely ignorant and guesses a sequence in the reverse order. These problems are further elaborated in Chapter XIV in the section "Spelling Tests."

There is no way of insuring that the correct sequence of letters will be reproduced on each occasion the word is spelled. Some individuals, particularly gifted linguists, have such an excellent rote memory for phoneme/grapheme associations that the automatization of encoding vocal-motor and written spelling patterns is rapid and reliable. For the less fortunate, there are various procedures and memorizing techniques which may be of help; a review of these is presented in Chapter XV. One point should be noted here, namely, that graphemes, blends, diagraphs, diphthongs and triphthongs should each be kept as a unit when the word to be learned (spelled) is presented to the child. This is usually best achieved by breaking the word into syllables as a first step in the analysis. Above all, it should be remembered that the research evidence suggests that articulemic sequencing is of key importance to correct spelling.

EYE MOVEMENTS

As has been previously pointed out, there is little doubt that the eyes evolved to scan the environment in three dimensions, mainly for the purpose of detecting movement (of food or predators) and to track fixated objects in the interest of survival. Reading and writing are the only regular tasks which demand that the eyes *move from left to right in one dimension and one direction* in a series of quick saccadic (jerky) movements. Even the direction in which one reads is conventionally determined; while most Western languages are read from left to right, Arabic and Hebrew are read from right to left while Chinese is scanned vertically. The development of eye movements in reading and the pattern of those movements has been thoroughly investigated experimentally by Lesevre (1966). She studied a group of seventy-seven subjects (including eleven adults) and a group of twenty-two dyslexic children. Other children who were educationally or culturally backward or who suffered from spatial disorientation formed yet a third group. Lesevre studied the oculomotor reaction time required to fixate an isolated stimulus, and, separately, the ability to scan systematically a series of visual stimuli in a given sequence and direction. For normal children, she found a twofold development of oculomotor activity. The first developmental progression concerned the efficiency of the gaze's activity whatever the direction imposed on that activity. This development occurs steadily from six to twelve years after which it slackens off into adulthood. (The youngest children were six years of age.) This increasing efficiency is demonstrated by (a) a progressive lessening of the length of the oculomotor reaction time (to move from one stimulus to the next), (b) a progressive decrease in the number of *adjusting* eye movements during the switch from stimulus to stimulus required to locate and fixate a series of irregular stimuli and (c) a progressive improvement in ocular stability or fixation time, that is, a slight decrease in the number of minute irregular *verifying* movements while fixating.

Taken overall, the actual average length of *the time of accurate fixation of the static gaze when it is used to perceive and verify information remains remarkably stable from six years to adulthood.* In other words, as the child grows older, the time required to perceive and interpret a given stimulus during one fixation remains fairly constant, but the number of random eye movements and the number of brief unusable or unused fixations gradually decreases. The time taken for one saccadic movement also decreases or alternatively the length of the movement increases for the same amount of time. The second progressive development concerns the existence of a preferential direction of scanning. The ability to direct the gaze from left to right increases in efficiency with increased age, being nonexistent at six years (in France). This right lateralization seems to establish itself between the ages of seven and eight and goes on increasing slightly until adulthood. Efficient left-to-right lateralization is accompanied by a decrease in the number of uncertain or irregular movements and unusable fixations but this correlation does not hold for right-to-left movements. In other words, the left-to-right lateralization of the gaze is a unidirectional, automatized motor habit which is not reversible (unless deliberately trained to be so).

Most of the dyslexic children studied by Lesevre showed greater oculomotor instability, a slow oculomotor reaction time and a higher number of short pauses when compared with their normal counterparts. Lateralized scanning was equally poor in both directions. This absence of lateralization appears in a most spectacular way on the oculograms when, having been instructed to scan in a given direction, the dyslexic subject opens his eyes and is only able after very pronounced hesitation to follow the required direction. Lesevre points out that those authorities who consider dyslexia only a disturbance of symbolic functioning are incorrect since this definite visual scanning "disorder" does exist experimentally. However, there are children who, although bad readers, show a normally developed oculomotor scanning maturity, including a well-established lateralization of the gaze. Lesevre shows that these children's difficulties are more related to such areas as speech, socioeconomic deprivation, or inefficient teaching. Even more surprising is her discovery that there exist children who are competent readers but who have a poorly developed oculomotor stability and a weak lateralization of scanning. I suspect that these children might be intelligent genetic dyslexics who have learned to read in spite of lateralization difficulties. It should be remembered that reading is the only activity in life calling for left-right lateralization of the gaze and it is probably an artificial, acquired development occuring only in literate societies.

Note that scanning disorders in *reading* can occur (paradoxically) in physiologically normal, genetic dyslexic children who possess excellent vision (see Chapter IX).

One can only interpret Lesevre's results on the principle of multiple causation and possibly on the degree of severity of any particular handicap. Thus, a child with severe oculomotor developmental problems, even though he may have an excellent reading teacher, may still have trouble learning to read efficiently. A socially disadvantaged child with only slight oculomotor inefficiency but with a good teacher may be similarly handicapped. Certainly, it would seem very necessary that one essential part of the diagnosis of any learning disability case would be an electro-oculographic measurement of eye movement; and excellent paper on the techniques of eye movement recording by electro-oculography has been written by Shackel (1967). The techniques used by Lesevre and Shackel are far superior to the eye camera method.

Two research workers who have used the eye camera and whose work in some measure confirms the above results are Calvert and Cromes (1966). Out of their total sample of dyslexic students, they found a small group of students resistant to oculomotor training and all these subjects possessed an oculomotor characteristic *uncommon* to those subjects who made adequate progress. This characteristic ". . . was a very fine eye tremor occurring approximately at intervals of 18 seconds, with a duration of one to three seconds in the focussing phase of the test, or in the actual reading phase, or in some instances in both phases." This tremor was not a nystagmus but rather a sporadic tremor. The authors claim that these oculomotor spasms have been found in over 90 percent of the reading disability children who did not respond to specialized reading training and that it is a condition associated with short attention span, poor memory, temper outbursts, hyperactivity and occasionally reported dizziness. They found that these subjects responded to small doses (50-150 mg per day) of primidone, with the result that the subjects responded favorably to training in reading, and many of their behavioral symptoms were reduced or disappeared altogether. Even after the primidone was discontinued, one or two months later, there was no reappearance of the oculomotor spasms.

The handicaps of erratic eye movements and poor discrimination may be counteracted remedially by using large-sized print, finger or pencil-point tracking along the line, a moving card with a slot cut in it and letter cancellation exercises in old magazines (e.g., cross out every *a* and *n* on the page, tracking left to right as in normal reading). In passing, I would like to suggest that visual fixation difficulties are perhaps aggravated by having the child read intense black print on startlingly white paper. Workbooks and textbooks in *clear* print on high-quality newspaper seem to facilitate reading by not "dancing" before the eyes.

Visual Fields

Very little work has been done to investigate the role of the visual fields in reading. Hebb (1949) reports a tachistoscopic experiment by Mishkin and Forgays. He reports their experiments thus:

> . . . reading does not train all parts of the retina in the same way, even when acuity does not enter the picture. . . . Fluent readers of English used to reading from left to right, are able to recognize words to the right of the fixation point between two and three times as well as words to the left of the fixation. Readers of Jewish (in which the words run from right to left) recognize more words to the left of the fixation. These results can be obtained when the subject does not know whether an English or a Jewish word is coming next, or when it will fall to the right or the left of fixation—that is, with a random order of left-right, English-Jewish presentations.

These results have been confirmed by Bryden (1964) and Bryden and Rainey (1963). The right visual field is the one predominantly used for reading English, because the words "track" across the field from the periphery to the macular area as the eye proceeds from left to right in saccadic movements along the line of print. It is possible to test this for oneself, using a card to blot out half the field of vision while reading. When the card covers the right visual field on the page, reading is hesitant and slow, being limited to word-by-word recognition. However, when the card follows behind the point of focus, there is no hesitation and a normal speed of reading can be easily achieved.

In an advertising billboard study known to the author, it was discovered that persons studying the billboard, while they tended to read the written copy with their right visual field, tended to locate points of interest on the billboard using their left visual field. It is certainly obvious that when one is reading English prose, the left visual field must locate the beginning of the next line. One aspect of visual field phenomena that has never been investigated is visual field dominance. In Chapter VI, I suggested that on the basis of the evidence presented, some highly visuospatial people may have a dominant right hemisphere which is subserved by the nondominant verbal left hemisphere, and that such people would tend to use the left visual field preferentially when scanning the environment. (As has been pointed out, this left visual field scanning also occurs when viewing billboards or locating lines on pages.) However, a person with a dominant left visual field might show a tendency *to move the eyes from right to left in order to move objects to be viewed into the center of the visual field.* The conventional left-to-right reading movement would be unnatural to such a person. This may be one of several reasons why certain visuo-spatially competent people have found it difficult to learn to read. It is also possible that the natural tendency to move objects in the left visual field into the center of vision by scanning from right to left may account for the slow left-right lateralization of the gaze experimentally established in some dyslexic children by Lesevre.

It is pertinent to the dyslexia problem that visuo-spatial children would prefer to scan the environment in three dimensions at random rather than discipline themselves into lateralizing their gaze in one dimension for the purpose of reading. From this hypothesis, one would predict that these visuo-spatial dyslexic children would obtain higher scores on the WISC subtests involving three-dimensional scanning such as picture completion, block design and object assembly. As has been stated previously, the review of the research literature on the WISC in terms of reading disability cases by McLeod (1965) confirms this prediction. I would suggest that the great majority of these visuo-spatially competent, poor gaze-lateralizers fall within the group of genetic dyslexic children described in detail in the next chapter. Once again, it should be emphasized that most samples of dyslexic children are drawn on an unselected heterogeneous basis and definitive research is difficult under such conditions. Lesevre is to be commended for her cluster analysis of the groups within her sample.

Visual Discrimination and Mirror Imaging

Many children have no trouble perceiving configurations and it is self-evident that any child who has learned to read efficiently must be able to discriminate shapes above a certain proficiency threshold. Earlier in the chapter, I quoted a statistic from my own research with Wichiarajote (Bannatyne and Wichiarajote, 1969b) in which a low but significant correlation was found between spelling disability and choosing a simplified design in the place of an original. This research is described in some detail in this and the next chapter.

The Bannatyne Visuo-Spatial Memory Test (BVSMT) was devised to investigate in a systematic multiple-choice way (which eliminates motor drawing) the correlations between "pure" visuo-spatial memory and other psychological or physical characteristics. One choice (out of eight possible) was the rotation of the original design through 90 degrees to the right. The frequency with which this rotated design-answer was chosen was significantly and negatively correlated with auditory sequencing ($r = -0.308$) and sound blending ($r = -0.295$). Sound blending was also significantly negatively correlated ($r = -0.304$) with the design-answer choice in which the original design had been made more symmetrical. Therefore, rotating designs and making designs symmetrical would seem to be possible indicators of poor sound blending.

One of the tests administered to the representative sample of third-grade schoolchildren was the Simultaneous Writing Test, in which the child has to write the numbers 1 to 12 down the page in two columns, using the left and right hands simultaneously. The number of mirror reversals of numbers made by the dominant hand were counted and this score was found to be correlated ($r = +0.43$) at a significant level with the BVSMT design-answer choice in which the original stimulus design was selected as a mirror image. The correlation with dominant-hand mirror imaging of numbers in simultaneous writing was not significantly correlated with any of the other design-answer choices, namely, simplification, rotation, fragmentation, disproportion, complication or symmetry.

Even more startling were the correlations between the BVSMT visuo-spatial multiple-choice memory-for-designs test, and handedness. The frequency of the choice of the *correct* (original stimulus) answer design was highly and negatively correlated ($r = -0.44$) with unlearned right-handedness. The unlearned handedness test is a composite of arm-folding, hand-clasping and ear-touching. Unlearned right-handedness was also significantly correlated in a positive way ($r = +0.30$) with the frequency of choice of the *rotated* answer design. As would be expected, unlearned left-handedness was even more highly correlated with the choice of the correct original stimulus design-answer ($r = +0.50$), a striking confirmation of the hypothesis that unlearned left-handedness and visuo-spatial ability uncontaminated by trained motor activity (i.e., writing or drawing) are closely related. If one re-reads the appropriate sections in Chapter VI, this finding can only mean that the right hemisphere is visuo-spatially dominant, even though there is little doubt that the left hemisphere contributes to visuo-spatial activity in many ways. Unlearned left-handedness is negatively correlated with the choice of *rotated* designs ($r = -0.42$) and with the choice of the *fragmented* designs ($r = -0.31$). Only one correlation was significant between learned handedness and the BVSMT, namely, learned left-handedness and the choice of the *mirror-imaged* design-answer ($r = +0.31$). This finding helps confirm the correlation between the mirror imaging of numbers in the simultaneous writing test and the choice of the mirror-imaged designs on this multiple-choice memory-for-designs test.

Two sex differences were discovered on the test. The girls chose, with a significantly higher frequency, the rotated answer design, while the boys tended to choose more frequently the complicated design choice. The rotation of designs, particularly with block designs and with the execution of design copying or memory-for-designs tests, is traditionally and with some slight experimental evidence associated with brain damage, but it is difficult to believe that in a representative sample of schoolchildren a significantly higher proportion of the girls are brain-damaged than are the boys, if indeed one could believe so many were brain-damaged. There is a hypothesis which is current with some authorities that dyslexia is almost always a manifestation of neurological dysfunction, yet even though it has been established that a significant majority of dyslexic children are boys, here we have the *girls* in a representative sample of schoolchildren exhibiting this supposedly major sign of neurological dysfunction. The hypothesis is further negated by the fact that the girls did much better than the boys in the spelling test, even though the difference between the means is not quite significant ($t = 1.937$, boys: $\bar{x} = 24.62$, girls: $\bar{x} = 34.36$).

The major conclusions of the research (Bannatyne, 1969; Bannatyne and Wichiarajote, 1969a, 1969b) was that mirror imaging and the simplification of designs are probably indicative of a maturational lag and/or right hemisphere activity, whereas a poor layout of designs and a disproportionate drawing or selection indicates some neurological dysfunction. Rotation is linked with right hemisphere activity.

Visual Closure and Word Pattern Recognition

Form perception, visual closure and the retention of sequences of patterns all involve the operation of a complex set of factors, some of which have already been discussed in both this chapter and Chapter VII. Frostig (1964) has tests and teaching programs for the assessment and remediation of visuo-spatial disturbances which may interfere with reading and spelling processes. The main areas investigated in these tests are figure-ground discrimination, orientation, closure, spatial relations and sequencing. These visuo-spatial functions will be defined briefly.

In figure-ground discrimination, the child has to be able to recognize a given shape against a confusing background. Orientation can involve mirror imaging, reversals, rotations and similar changes of position. Closure occurs when a figure is not complete and there is a tendency on the part of the viewer, in the light of his past experience, to complete or "close" that figure. A manipulation of spatial relations in the Frostig test involves recognizing the position in space of a configuration of dots and the lines drawn between some of them. Visual sequencing is more of a memory task as in the ITPA subtests, in which a demonstrated series of designs has to be reproduced in the same order from memory. In all of these processes, form, directional constancy and speed of recognition are essential elements, particularly in the reading process.

The implication of disturbances in geometric form perception for reading disabilities will be more fully discussed in Chapter X.

COMPARISON STUDIES IN READING METHODS

Comparative research into the efficacy of methods of teaching reading is fraught with difficulties. The number of variables which have to be controlled or accounted for are numerous. For example, children in the experimental and control groups have to be equated in terms of intelligence, sex, age, grade, socioeconomic status and overall representativeness; schools have to be equated for size, area, urban-rural location and previous reading policies; teachers have to be equated for teaching skills, training, favorite teaching methods, motivation, sex, age, reward-giving and reinforcement systems and lesson preparation time; the research design has to take into account Hawthorne (halo) effects to insure that the control groups and their teachers are as highly motivated and active as are the experimental groups with their (usually) novel curriculum. Ideally, the experimental design would rotate schools, methods, teachers and children through time to insure valid comparisons. To date, I do not know of one study that even roughly approximates these criteria. In a study which is better than most, Bleismer and Yarborough (1965), after a detailed investigation of ten different reading methods on some 484 pupils in four schools, came to the following conclusion:

> A criticism frequently made of synthetic programs is that the rather close attention given to word elements may lead to inadequate development of comprehension skills. In the present study, however, there was only one instance (out of twenty-five) in which mean

Paragraph Meaning scores favored an analytic program; and this difference was not significant. Conversely, twenty comparisons reveal all significant differences in favor of synthetic programs. It would appear, therefore, that beginning reading programs which give attention to sound-symbol relationships prior to teaching of words, or which involve a synthetic approach initially (pupils actually building words from sounds), tend to be significantly more productive in terms of specific reading achievement in grade one (as measured by the criterion test) than do analytic reading programs which involve the more conventional approach of going directly from readiness procedures (using pictures) to the reading of whole words before either letter names or the sounds the letters represent are taught.

In a study comparing two phonics methods, Duncan (1964) found that the "phonics first" approach, which introduced vowel sounds at the beginning of instruction, was superior to the technique which did not introduce vowel sounds until a sight reading vocabulary had already been established. Once again, the synthetic approach in which the elements of words, taught phonically, are studied first was found to be superior with first-grade children. This latter experiment included testing of the two groups at the end of the third year.

Once again, it is necessary to mention the work of Chall (1967) who, in her review of methods of teaching children to read between 1910 and 1965, came to the conclusion that code-breaking methods of teaching reading are the most effective.

INTELLIGENCE, COMPREHENSION AND READING

That intelligence is highly correlated with global reading ability has been demonstrated many times, but usually the term *reading* is an all-embracing one in that it includes a large element of *comprehension* (intelligence), thus making the argument circular. Mention has been made in earlier chapters that reading skills of an *automatic* or *habitual* nature should be sharply distinguished from intelligence, comprehension and conceptualizing, which are characteristics of language as a whole—in fact, it is probable that meaning and conceptualizing are nonverbal in essence (see Chapter II).

Not only are many unintelligent children able to read (code-break) more fluently than some of their more intelligent peers, but also one sometimes comes across a quite intelligent child (nonverbally) who finds it difficult to learn to read and spell even up to his grade level. In a study by the National Foundation for Educational Research in England and Wales (Pidgeon and Yates, 1956), it was found that an unexpectedly large proportion of children had reading ages well in advance of their mental ages. This casts some doubt on the practice among teachers and psychologists of using the child's mental age as a maximum standard against which to measure reading and spelling competence. Kline and Lee (1970) record that one of their research findings in a transcultural study of dyslexia was that reading disability is not related to intelligence above a certain baseline.

These findings suggest that educators need to revise their assessment techniques when evaluating reading skills, and, even more important, they should not assume because a child cannot read and spell competently that the child is unintelligent. Another assumption which many teachers make quite erroneously is that because a child cannot read a word, he cannot understand it. Vocabulary-building lessons and comprehension exercises are best carried out in the *absence* of the printed word, preferably during some enrichment program involving group discussion and an exchange of ideas. If a teacher wishes to discover which words in a passage of reading are not understood by individual children, she should ask them orally what the words mean before the reading lesson begins. Meaning is more associated with the auditory/vocal modality than it is with the visual/reading one. Chall (1967) reports that children who have been taught through phonics techniques are just as quick to understand the meaning of the passage they have read as are children taught by other techniques. Therefore, the evidence indicates that there is no truth in the old adage about phonics methods teaching children to "bark at print."

Reading disability cases are no exception to the above rule, except when, for the moment, they have to concentrate so much on the code-breaking skills that they are unaware of the meaning of what they have read. However, this is more an indicator of the difficulty of deciphering the code passage than it is of an inability to comprehend. Many dyslexic children have so much difficulty code breaking that the process has to be just that much more concentrated if they are ever to learn to read competently. It is a useful practice first to read aloud difficult passages which the child will have to attack, so that he understands the meaning *before* he attempts to read. There seems to be a kind of break-through threshold in terms of fluent reading skills at about the age of eight (or the end of the second grade), at which time the average child masters the basic process. For a variety of possible reasons, dyslexic children, even when intelligent, may find it difficult to reach that threshold and will only come to break through it when they are taught to read using special techniques. One such group of dyslexic children will be discussed in the next chapter. Even when these and other children have been taught to read quite fluently, there is often a residual problem of not being able to spell competently. It is for this reason that the teaching of reading through phonics should always involve copious amounts of phonetic articulation and writing. The principle is that if a child can write and spell a word, he can certainly read it.

SUMMARY OF LANGUAGE PROCESSES

Table XII summarizes most of the sensorimotor skill processes involved in listening, speaking, reading and writing (including spelling). It complements Table X by presenting the information in a different format which can be directly adapted for methods of teaching listening, speech, reading, writing and spelling to all kinds of children.

A very important point to be stressed is the cumulative aspect of the processes involved as one moves down and across the table. This cumulative effect in terms of functions can be examined in the light of Osgood's psycholinguistic model (Osgood and Miron, 1963) or neuropsychologically (Luria, 1966).

TABLE XII
SUMMARY TABLE OF LANGUAGE PROCESSES

Functions	I. "Letters" Auditory: Single Phonemes Vocal: Single Articulemes Printed or Written: Single Graphemes (One or More Letters)	II. Sequences of Letters—Words and Part-Words (Morphs) Sequences of Phonemes Sequences of Articulemes Sequences of Graphemes	III. Sequences of Words—Sentences Heard Sentence Spoken Sentence Printed or Written Sentence
Listening (Auditory Decoding) Hearing I, II or III, plus understanding I, II or III, namely, auditory decoding through recognition-memory	(a) Involves: auditory identification (recognition) of each single phoneme. Also involves discrimination from other phonemes	(e) Involves: 1. auditory sequencing and closure-recognition of series of phonemes, e.g., tea, tea/eat 2. auditory series discrimination from other series, e.g., tea/eat	(i) Involves: 1. auditory sequencing of series of words in conventional strings, 2. word-meaning association, 3. understanding relations between concepts expressed
Speaking (Vocal-Motor Encoding) Speaking I, II or III, plus understanding I, II or III, namely, vocal encoding through recall-memory	(b) Involves: 1. Auditory identification and discrimination as above in (a), with 2. vocal-motor imitation of single articuleme through auditory and visual (looking at face, lips, etc.) input	(f) Involves matching of: 1. auditory sequencing and closure recognition as in (e), with 2. vocal-motor imitation of series of articulemes through auditory and visual input	(j) Involves: 1. sequencing of thought-concepts, 2. matching (association) of these with auditory words, 3. matching of these with vocal-motor strings of patterns

	(c)	(g)	(k)
Reading (Visual and Auditory Decoding)	Seeing I, II or III, plus understanding I, II or III, namely, visual (and auditory) decoding through (a) auditory recall memory, (b) visual recognition memory	Involves matching of: 1. visual identification and discrimination of graphemes, 2. auditory identification and discrimination as above in (a), with 3. some vocal-motor reinforcement as in (b)	Involves matching of: 1. visual sequencing and closure-recognition of a series of graphemes plus discrimination of differing series, with 2. auditory sequencing, etc., as in (e), and with 3. some vocal-motor reinforcement as in (f)	Involves: 1. all in (j) above, plus 2. visual recognition of sequences and visual closure on series of words in meaningful context

	(d)	(h)	(l)
Writing (Digital-Motor Encoding)	Writing I, II or III plus understanding I, II or III, namely, motor (limb) encoding through (a) auditory recall memory, (b) visual recall memory, (c) motor/kinesthetic pattern recall memory	Involves matching of: 1. motor/kinesthetic configuration patterns of graphemes (and of course their component letters) originally imitated, 2. all processes outlined in (c)	Involves matching of: 1. motor/kinesthetic sequential recall of previously imitated series of grapheme patterns, with 2. all above processes in columns I and II	Involves: 1. all the other sections of the chart, plus 2. motor/kinesthetic sequential recall for series of words

Chapter IX

INHERITED FACTORS IN LANGUAGE ABILITY AND GENETIC DYSLEXIA

THE EVIDENCE FOR INHERITED FACTORS IN LANGUAGE DEVELOPMENT

T here is sufficient doubt felt by some social scientists, psychologists and educators as to the part played by genetic factors in language development (and some other aspects of human psychology) that it would seem necessary to set down in detail the evidence which has accumulated over the years. The skepticism seems to derive from a feeling that any variable not attributable to environmental learning is somehow unalterable or untrainable and that we are helpless to do anything to modify any presented problem with a genetic basis, an attitude which is unfounded in fact. (Incidentally, many people have the same kind of attitude about ameliorating deficits resulting from neurological dysfunction.) The answer to the pure environmentalist is twofold. First, to ignore or wish away genetic factors is an unscientific, head-in-the-sand policy which can only do more harm than good, if only because the techniques which might have to be used in cases with a genetic etiology may be quite different from those used in environmentally caused cases. Second, special techniques may be able to be developed (and have been) which will help genetically less well-endowed individuals to achieve a sufficiently high performance in a given area of functioning to enable them to operate in a relatively normal way. The specialized assistance may come from prophylactic devices, mediational techniques, intensive programs or any combination of these. A child who cannot learn to spell but who carries a pocket dictionary is not so much worse off than the excellent speller; as will be seen, spelling in particular is an ability which, in potential, is largely inherited.

One's inherited endowment and one's environment are in constant interplay, so much so that one cannot exist without the other. Jinks (1964), in an introduction to his paper entitled "Behavior Is a Phenotype—The Biometrical Approach," says,

> My purpose is to examine the experimental and analytical consequences of accepting the premise that behavior, like any other property of an organism, is a phenotype, determined jointly by inherent causes (usually referred to as nature or genotype) and external agencies (nurture or environment). Thus, individual differences in behavior may have a genotypic, environmental or a joint origin, and we cannot assess their relative contributions merely by measuring the differences. These must be investigated empirically by a breeding test or by examining familial relationships.

Jinks goes on to point out that few behavioral differences are of the relatively simple, classical Mendelian type:

> Typically, they are small, continuously varying differences that require careful quantitative measurements to reveal them, even though the extremes of the continuous range often differ in a major way. A familiar example is the distribution of I.Q. in man. For such characteristics the approach and techniques of biometrical genetics (Mather, 1949) are necessary to partition the variation between heritable and environmental causes, and to analyze their nature and interactions.

Connolly (1966) suggests that the neglect of genetics in experimental psychology was largely caused by the behaviorist influence of Watson (1924), because of Watson's assertion that there was no real evidence for the inheritance of traits. Connolly also makes the point that behavior is a phenotype. He says,

> An organism's genotype, that is its genetic constitution, interacts with its environment to produce the resulting phenotype, for example, emotionality, intelligence or height. The number of genes is large; in man, for example, each cell is thought to contain 40,000-80,000 and each gene may produce effects both individually and in interaction with others. From what has been said it should be clear that genes and not phenotypes are inherited; a gene can, of course, only act within an environmental framework. This is an important point, and failure to appreciate it has often led to faulty reasoning. . . . Most of the characteristics which are of interest to the psychologist are of the quantitatively variable kind; that is to say not the all-or-none variety, but those producing "more" or "less" effects. These polygenes as they are called have individually minute effects, but cumulatively produce differences in stature, emotionality, intelligence

and many other important traits. Because of these polygenes an organism will possess an enormous amount of genetic variability, and most of the phenotypic variability we observe will be a function of these systems.

Three categories of evidence are presented below. First, there is the evidence for the inheritance of language functions in general; second, the evidence for genetic factors in specific language functions, as, for example, in spelling, and third, those research studies which indicate familial inheritance patterns in some kinds of dyslexic children.

It should be mentioned that to date, *I have been unable to find one study which supported the environmentalist point of view that genetic factors play a minor or negligible role in language functioning.* On the other hand, there is much evidence available which demonstrates that genetic factors *are* important. Although it is impossible to reiterate it all here, much of the evidence and many of the points presented in previous chapters are very relevant to this one, so much so that the information presented in them was partially intended to provide a detailed background against which this and subsequent chapters could be interpreted.

The Inheritance of Language Functions

Although the points made at the end of Chapter II in support of genetic factors operating in language functioning were summarized in Chapter VI, it is pertinent to review them briefly yet again.

It will be remembered that seven sets of evidence were presented, namely, (a) the morphological characteristics of vocal organs and brain devoted to speech; (b) the evidence that intelligence (and its component abilities), at least in its degree of maximum potential, is inherited; (c) the evidence that language development occurs in early infancy in an automatic way, provided the environment is satisfactory; (d) the definite sex differences that occur which cannot be entirely or easily attributed to training; (e) the fact that language acquisition is a universal and spontaneous event common to very nearly all human beings; (f) the evidence that spoken human languages have many elements in common across approaches and time scales; and most important of all, (g) the fact that twin and family pedigree studies have presented hard evidence for the inheritance of verbal traits. Some of these sets of evidence are taken from Lenneberg (1967).

Inheritance Factors in Specific Abilities

Maccoby (1966), in discussing sex differences and identification or modeling of parental behavior by children, points out,

Not all aspects of intellectual functioning are susceptible to modeling. Vocabulary and verbal fluency are aspects of a parent's intellectual equipment that a child can copy. Normally, his spelling is not. Yet, girls maintain superiority throughout the school years in spelling and fluency, though not in vocabulary. Much of a parent's quantitative reasoning is done covertly, so that it is not accessible for copying, and very little spatial thinking is communicated from parent to child. Yet it is in spatial performance that we find the most consistent sex differences. . . . Sex differences in verbal ability decline during the age period when the rise of identification and differential modeling ought to increase them. And consistent sex differences in quantitative ability do not appear until adolescence, long after the time when boys and girls have begun to prefer same-sex models.

The implication of the above passage for learning theory models of language acquisition is considerable. It is likely that, insofar as infants obviously do acquire a particular sound-sequencing language *content* environmentally, the learning theory models put forward by Woolman (1965) (see Chapter IV) or by Jenkins and Palermo (1964) are on the right lines. Thus, the investigation of language acquisition now becomes a matter of ascertaining how much is environmental content learning (and to that extent, what is the correct model), and how much is attributable to genetic endowment; even more important is ascertaining how the acquired content and endowed form of language are *interlaced*.

Verbal intelligence could be considered to be a predominantly "form" aspect of language acquisition and development if only to the extent that the earlier the automatic skills of verbal behavior are "learned" (or able to be learned) and the more efficiently they are able to be utilized, the more superior verbal intelligence functioning will be, all other things being equal. Therefore, any evidence that intelligence of either a verbal or a spatial kind (its bipolar counterpart) is inherited will also support the hypothesis that verbal skills are, in some degree, inherited. The most reliable evidence for estimating the relative contributions of heredity and environment to verbal ability, spatial ability, automatized skills within both those abilities, and intelligence (logical reasoning) comes from twin studies. Acceptable twin studies compare monozygotic (single-egg) twins who have been reared together with monozygotic twins who have been reared apart. Preferably, these two groups will also be compared with dizygotic (two-egg) twins, one group being reared together and the other group being reared apart. This makes possible a four-way statistical analysis using chi-square tests, analyses of variance or even multiple abstract variance analyses (Cattell, 1960). The latter technique may include groups of adopted children.

In a now famous study, Newman *et al.* (1937) carried out a twin study comparing monozygotic twins reared together with those reared apart. One of the intelligence tests used was the Stanford-Binet Scale and the results for this test show much more variability for the DZ (dizygotic) group. The intrapair correlations for the MZ (monozygotic) group reared together were $r = 0.88$, with $r = 0.77$ for the separated MZ twins. The correlation was only $r = 0.63$ for the unseparated DZ group. The Stanford Achievement Test results were quite different. The MZ and DZ unseparated twins had very similar correlations of $r = 0.95$ and $r = 0.88$, respectively. However, the separated MZ twins' correlation was $r = 0.51$. Of course, in an achievement test, most of the content is "environmentally learned," whereas intelligence tests are supposed to be constructed to eliminate environmental learning as much as possible.

Eighty-eight pairs of MZ twins, of whom forty-four were reared apart, were studied by Shields (1962). When comparisons were run on both verbal (Mill Hill Vocabulary Scale) and non-verbal (Dominoes) intelligence tests, the differences between the MZ groups were found to be small, but both of the MZ groups differed considerably from the DZ group. Shields notes that there was not much variation in the cultural and educational backgrounds of most of the separated MZ twins. On the personality measures of introversion and extraversion and neuroticism, the MZ twins in both groups were much more alike than were the members of the DZ group. Shields concludes that heredity is a much more important factor in intelligence and personality than had hitherto been thought. However, in both studies, the authors comment that even monozygotic twins reared together can differ widely in intelligence and personality in individual cases. It would seem that most human variables could be placed along a continuum ranging from an almost 100 percent contribution by heredity at one end to a 100 percent contribution by environment at the other; physiological factors would tend to fall toward the heredity end, whereas some few psychological factors might tend to fall near the environmental end. On the evidence of twin studies, however, most of the psychological characteristics measured in both cognition and personality tend to fall above the halfway mark toward the heredity end.

Stafford (1962) has suggested new techniques for analyzing parent-child test scores for evidence of hereditary components. He has applied these to twin data and parent offspring for the purpose of identifying single locus effects (of dominant-recessive modes of action) underlying a phenotypically continuous trait. By applying his methods to twin data, he found evidence for single locus effects in the scores from the Seashore Pitch Discrimination Test, Koh's Block Design Test, Primary Mental Abilities Reasoning Test, and a spelling test. These particular tests should be well noted as they will appear again in studies outlined below. In particular, the recurring importance of *spelling* and *fluency* becomes apparent.

Vandenberg (1966) has surveyed methods used in human behavior genetics and reports on some research results from the Louisville Twin Study which he is conducting. He notes that B. Price (1950) has reviewed pregnancy and birth factors which may affect identical twins more than fraternal twins. Price concludes that such factors would cause traditional twin studies to underestimate the role of heredity. R.C. Johnson (1963) and

Vandenberg (1966) found no increase in IQ differences for twins separated early compared to twins separated later.

Vandenberg used multivariate analyses to determine whether the same (probably very large) set of genes determined the scores on the six subtests of the Primary Mental Abilities Reasoning Test. To do this, he considered the covariants of twin differences; DZ differences are caused by hereditary as well as environmental influences but MZ differences are only caused by environmental influences. Vandenberg reports,

> Inspection of the columns of the colution (the "eigen" vectors) led to the impression that the four independent sources of hereditary determination were concerned with (a) knowledge of words as in vocabulary tests, (b) the use of words as in word fluency and verbal reasoning tests, (c) spatial ability, and (d) number ability. The precise identification of the relative contribution of variables to these roots is a problem that has not yet been solved. These results have been confirmed by a Finnish twin study [Bruun et al., 1966].

In a later section, Vandenberg makes a comparison of four separate studies with the Primary Mental Abilities battery, one by Blewett (1954), one by Thurstone et al. (1955), and two by Vandenberg himself. As Vandenberg (1966) says, the results show an encouraging amount of confirmation:

> The evidence for an hereditary component in word fluency is significant at the one percent level in all four studies, for verbal ability (as measured by multiple choice tests) the results are at the .01 level in three studies, and at the .05 level in the fourth study. For spatial ability, which is the ability to manipulate in one's mind spatial patterns in two or three dimensions, there is evidence for an hereditary component at the .01 level in two studies, for reasoning only the British study [Blewett] found significance (at the .01 level), and in the two studies where the memory subtests were used, no significance was reached.

In the Differential Aptitude Tests, the verbal reasoning subtest with its mixture of verbal ability and simple reasoning evidenced a hereritary component significant at the 0.01 level. Similarly, a multiple-choice spelling test contained a hereditary component at the 0.01 level. Clerical speed and accuracy, which is a kind of perceptual speed, also gave evidence in both studies at the 0.01 level of a hereditary component. Perceptual speed is a kind of automatized ability. Vandenberg reports that only one study was available at the time of his writing on the hereditary components in the Wechsler Adult Intelligence Scale (WAIS). All of the tests showed a significant hereditary factor except picture completion and object assembly. Similarities, digit span and picture arrangement were significant only at the 0.05 level.

In a summary of significant levels for ratios between DZ and MZ within-pair variances on subtests of three intelligence tests in seven studies, Vandenberg lists various abilities and their degree of significance. His conclusion is as follows:

> There is, in addition, rather convincing evidence for differences in the importance of heredity for various important abilities as shown in Table 8 by a decrease in the importance of the hereditary component, as we go down the table. The order, if actual values of *F* are also considered, seems to be word fluency, verbal ability (including spelling and grammar), spatial ability, clerical speed and accuracy, reasoning, number ability and memory.

Number ability, reasoning and memory were not significant on several studies. It should be noted that the ability which was significant beyond the 0.01 level on several studies was the PMA *word fluency* subtest. *Verbal ability generally, spelling, grammar and spatial ability were also mostly significant at the 0.01 level* except that the WAIS object assembly subtest was not found significant. The main conclusion is that word fluency, verbal ability, spelling, grammar and spatial ability are, on the strength of the seven research studies quoted by Vandenberg, the ones with the largest hereditary component.

In still another large twin study in progress in England, Mittler (1968) has also found evidence that heredity makes a considerable contribution to the acquisition of various linguistic abilities.

All the above statements and research results have come from observations of subjects without language disabilities. Taken together, they present almost irrefutable evidence that genes play a large part (very probably between 50 to 80 percent, according to most investigators) in the determination of various language skills, particularly verbal fluency, spelling and grammar (syntax). It is now incumbent on anyone who wishes to deny that inherited factors play a *considerable* part (but not complete) in the acquisition of language to examine all the reported evidence, demolish it scientifically *and* present concrete research findings that prove heredity plays little or no part. It is not sufficient to demonstrate that environmental factors are involved in acquiring language, for that is self-evident.

The heredity component in verbal ability helps explain why reading ages at all IQ levels sometimes far exceed mental ages (Pidgeon and Yates, 1956, 1957) and why even severely mentally defective children can sometimes read fluently (Houghton and Daniels, 1966). It also partly explains why some people are "born linguists" who can rapidly learn many languages to the habitual skill level and it also accounts (in part) for the word-finding skill of poets, novelists and playwrights. Of course, many other factors also contribute to these talents.

Research Studies on Genetic Factors in Dyslexic Children

Several research studies have now been carried out on dyslexic children and collectively they make up a considerable body of evidence for the inheritance of dyslexia. It is necessary to repeat here that there are many types of dyslexia (see Table II, page 00) and the one which I suggest is the concern of most of these particular research studies is genetic dyslexia; the original authors do not use the word *genetic*. If many language skill functions are distributed throughout the population, then there will be a group of otherwise intelligent people falling at the lower end of the distribution who will have a lack of linguistic skills. This group no doubt will include, among others, many people who have simply not inherited enough language ability to fulfill certain demands made on them our educational system. These points will be further elaborated later in the chapter after the research evidence has been presented.

Lenneberg (1967) has reviewed the evidence from family history studies and some twin studies for the inheritance of language potential. With respect to familial occurrence, he says,

The familial occurrence of congenital language disability is well documented through a number of published pedigrees [Luchsinger and Arnold, 1959; Arnold, 1961; Brewer, 1963]. . . . After a survey of all published cases, we may well agree that Brewer's conclusion that congenital language disability is probably a dominant, sex-influenced trait with at least fair penetrance. . . . Of particular interest are the extremes of the normal range. Both global language-facilitation and global language-difficulties may be attributed to inherited factors. Transitions from borderline normal to borderline abnormal appear as delayed onset of speech, protracted articulatory difficulties in childhood, congenital expressive disorders, or conversely, hyperfluency resulting in cluttering or pathological talkativeness.

In his review of eight papers devoted to the study of language in twins by various authors, Lenneberg concludes, "All studies agree that fraternal twins are much more prone to differences in language development than identical twins."

One of the studies referred to by Lenneberg is that of Hallgren (1950). In a monograph on specific dyslexia, Hallgren surveys the literature and presents data from several of his own studies on clinic groups, school groups and twins. The research is presented in considerable detail. The number of twins studied was too small to give reliable results, but Hallgren came to some clear-cut conclusions on the basis of 276 cases of specific dyslexia which were studied on both a clinical and a genetic basis. His results showed that at least in boys, there is a direct association between speech defects and specific dyslexia. Hallgren stated:

> . . . the genetic-statistical analysis shows that specific dyslexia, with a high degree of probability, follows a monohybrid autosomal dominant mode of inheritance in groups I and II in the present series, the manifestation being practically complete. In some of the families in Group III, the mode of inheritance is presumably also monohybrid autosomal dominant.

The groupings used by Hallgren indicate the number of people in the child's immediate family who were also affected with specific dyslexia.

In his study of thirty-two carefully selected dyslexic boys without brain damage or severe personality problems, Wolf (1967) found a significant difference between the experimental and normal control groups, in that the experimental group "evidenced a history of reading and spelling disability in their fathers and history of reading disability in their brothers, but not their sisters, and their mothers had directional disorientation."

In yet another twin study, Norrie (1954) found a 100 percent concordance of dyslexia in monozygotic twins but only a 33 percent concordance among dizygotic twins.

More recently, a large study was carried out in California by P.A. Adams (1967), S. Fisher (1967), Forrest (1967), and Owen (1967). These authors separately studied seventy-six educationally handicapped (EH) children and compared them with (a) seventy-six of their same-sex siblings, (b) seventy-six matched same-sex children who were successful academically (SA) and (c) seventy-six of the siblings of the latter children. Almost all of the mothers and fathers of the EH and SA children were interviewed and their high school records taken. The findings were as follows: Owen (1967) found that the ordinal position within the family was not significantly related to learning disability in this sample. If the ordinal position was important, genetic factors could be ruled out. SA parents had significantly higher grades in English courses at the high school level than did EH parents. EH mothers were significantly poorer in mathematics than SA mothers.

Forrest (1967), working with the same sample, found many differences between EH and SA subjects after a comprehensive neurological and medical examination. It is worth noting that some of the children in the samples were neurological dysfunction cases, but no attempt was made to screen out such cases prior to the statistical calculations. The historical factors differentiating EH and SA subjects were irritability during infancy, colic, decreased sound production during prelingual development, poor listening skills after age two, ease of mother-child communication (the EH child was more difficult to talk to than his sib) and temper tantrums. Examination and test score factors which differentiated EH and SA subjects are as follows: In each case, there were strong similarities between each group and its siblings for tapped rhythmic patterns (which were closely correlated with digit span on the WISC), right-left discrimination, double simultaneous touch, fast alternating finger movements and fast alternating hand movements. Forrest found no differences in measures of hand, foot and eye preference (laterality), adventitious overflow movement, arm extension test scores or walking on a balance beam. He states in the text,

> We did not find that possible prenatal, neonatal or postnatal complications were significantly more frequent in the EH population. Our population had very few premature births and no relationship to birth weight was found. However, in individual cases, the direct relationship of such complications to neurological abnormality is apparent. . . . In our study of the 264 subjects examined, only four children were found to have definitive signs of neurologic abnormality. Three were EH children and one was a SA child. . . . The present effort to define factors which underlie learning problems in children is based on the hypothesis that neurological organization is a result of genetic and environmental factors. Therefore, it is not surprising that familial similarities are evident. We anticipate that future analysis of factors within subgroups of our population will show interesting patterns and relationships.

It is worth reiterating this research conclusion that *children's learning problems seem to be based on genetic and environmental factors rather than neurological abnormality except in a few cases.*

Using the same children, P.A. Adams (1967) compared the groups on various tests. On the WISC, the EH children had significantly greater differences between their verbal and performance IQ's than did the SA children, the EH children having significantly poorer WISC verbal abilities than performance abilities.* Adams found the EH and EH siblings to be significantly lower than the other two groups on the information, arithmetic, coding and digit-span subtests. The EH children had significantly higher scores on the picture completion subtest and Adams concludes that therefore, as a group, they do not suffer from a perceptual deficit of a visual nature. Also, the EH and SA subtest scores were highly correlated on comprehension, similarities, object assembly and coding. The achievement test findings indicated that there were significant differences between the EH children and the SA children in both reading and spelling. There were similar tendencies in the EH and SA siblings. Adams sug-

---

*This confirms my own WISC findings on genetic dyslexic children.

gests that *spelling* is a more sensitive indicator of language disability than is reading because there are fewer and apparently less effective methods for compensation. Adams also gave the children a Draw-A-Person Test and found that for all groups, the scores correlated significantly with the performance scale IQ's and the full scale IQ's. The Draw-A-Person scores failed to correlate with the verbal scale IQ's. The high correlation with the performance skills scales showed specifically that the abilities involved in the Draw-A-Person Test are closely related to the skills required by the block design and object assembly subtests.

On the same sample, S. Fisher (1967), in analyzing the Draw-A-Person scores, found that the drawings made by the EH children were markedly inferior to the drawings made by the SA children even though four different scoring systems were used. On the Bender-Gestalt Test, the arrowhead on card 3 produced the greatest difference between the EH and SA children and distortion was the only type of error that yielded a significant difference between the two groups. Fisher goes on to say that both groups were able to discriminate the errors they had made and, considering the performance of the EH children on the picture completion subtest of the WISC, Fisher indicates that although EH children ". . . may not use their ability well, apparently they do not lack the ability to discriminate forms accurately when their attention is drawn to the problem." *Therefore, I would suggest, it would seem likely that the inferior drawings may result from a maturational lag of a motor kind rather than a visuo-spatial deficit* (see Bannatyne, 1969, and research report later in this chapter).

Michal-Smith *et al.* (1970) found learning problems in four siblings of middle-class background. On my own breakdown of the WAIS and WISC subtests these students are noticeably poor in sequencing skills (digit span plus coding plus picture arrangement) as compared with their verbal conceptualizing and spatial abilities. The authors conclude that the data point to a hereditary factor as the underlying cause.

The familial patterns of expression of specific reading disabilities in a population sample have been investigated by Walker and Cole (1965). The selected sample included all the families with three children in grades 2 through 12 in a suburban public school system. Any family unit in which any one of the three siblings had an IQ of below 90 was eliminated. Seventy-five family units were studied; the units were made of equal sibship size for ease and accuracy of analysis. The families were of a high income and cultural level. In the sample of siblings, there were 117 males and 108 females. In this study, specific reading disability was defined as spelling performance below certain standards in subjects with normal intelligence. One of the many reasons for selecting spelling was that it was the most mechanical of language tasks. Using a chi-square to test significance, the authors found that specific reading disability (spelling) was aggregated in families beyond chance at the 0.005 level of significance. According to Walker and Cole,

> Familial aggregation was further supported by considering the presumably unaffected siblings in specific-reading-disability families. Since 83 percent of the males in these families were affected, the unaffected siblings were predominantly female. Seventy-six percent of these siblings were females compared with 46 percent females in the total normal families. Median spelling rating for females in our total sample was 1.21 years above that for males. Yet, the predominantly female siblings of the SRD cases showed a median spelling rating more than a year below the median for the total normal-family siblings.

The authors conclude that using the spelling criterion, there is a remarkable prevalence of specific language disability in certain families, and that the genetic hypothesis is the most compatible with the presented findings.

The research findings presented so far in this chapter are collectively irrefutable evidence that a considerable genetic factor is operating in the area of language ability, particularly in the complete absence of contradictory research. In reviewing the literature, I have been unable to find any research study which has not found a genetic factor operating in the area of language skills. This is important because to counter the large number of positive findings presented above, the "pure" environmentalist would either have to produce at least a few twin or family studies indicating that language abilities in the general population were randomly distributed on a nongenetic basis or explain how environmental factors cause genetic-like patterns of variable clustering. For instance, some of Vanderberg's *nonlanguage skill* results do *not* have a genetic basis on the research findings.

It can be concluded, then, on the totality of the evidence presented, that language abilities in general and word fluency, spelling and grammatical abilities in particular are inherited to a considerable degree, as is their disability aspect, namely specific language disability or dyslexia. It should be emphasized yet again that there is no suggestion that environmental factors do not play any part. Environment and learning are both very important contributors to language development processes. What one inherits is a potential or a structural (neurological and physiological) set. Most of the content of a language is contributed by environmentally learned conventions. Another environmentally determined factor in the acquisition of language is the skill with which the child is taught language in both the home and the school. Chapters V, XII, and XIII deal specifically with problems relating to various environmental causes of language learning disabilities. The environment is also extremely important in the remediation of all learning disability children and language disability cases in particular. Even those children called genetic dyslexics (Bannatyne, 1967b) can be remediated by using highly individualized educational methods. It is appropriate here to quote Thoday (1965), who says, "Genotype determines the potentialities of an organism. Environment determines which or how much of these potentialities shall be realized during development."

In a study by Kline and Lee (1970), the authors say the data suggested that (a) subcultural factors are not important in this instance, (b) the incidence of disability appears to be related to the difficulty of the language and to the patterns of association needed for learning the language, (c) visual perception as emphasized by Frostig is not a significant factor in learning to read, (d) body image is not related to reading disability, (e) functional neurological factors may play a role in some cases of reading disability, (f) the teaching method appears to be basically important in learning to read, with a multisensory approach favored, and (g) reading disability is not related to intelligence above a specific base line.

All my own field and desk research confirms the validity of the above points but to be fair each point needs to be qualified to place it in the right interpretive context. Subcultural factors may be important in other types of subcultures. Genetic factors (which were not mentioned in the above study) are a very likely original cause of associational learning problems connected with the orthography of the language and these may well have an auditory/vocal basis as a material cause, a hypothesis which is almost certainly valid in the light of all the evidence presented throughout this book. Visual perception might have been more important than this study suggests if a broad sample of learning disability children were used, but I agree that by and large visual perception is a much less important factor in reading disabilities than has traditionally been supposed. Goldberg (1970), a Johns Hopkins ophthalmologist, has said, "The experiments performed demonstrate that it is the degree of comprehension that produces the type of ocular movement and not ocular motility that determines the degree of comprehension [in reading]."

Body image may not be directly related to a child's level of reading under conditions of broad sample research, but some groups of neurologically immature children may produce poor body image drawings and have reading disabilities. The younger the children in the sample and the more efficiently they are subcategorized, the more likely they are to exhibit such a correlation (which should not be interpreted as a causal relationship, since the two "symptoms" may have a common etiology, namely a maturational lag). "Functional neurological factors" should be interpreted in the widest sense and should not be equated with brain damage. That multisensory teaching techniques are the most effective is very true and can be extended to include code-breaking methods (Chall, 1967); these are all incorporated in the Bannatyne Psycholinguistic Color System (Bannatyne, 1968b). However, this should not be interpreted as stating that dyslexia is the result of poor teaching or inadequate methods because the vast majority of children *do* learn to read under such inadequate conditions. Why, therefore, in countries which have languages with a highly irregular orthography, do some children *not* learn to read even moderately well in small groups in specialized reading centers with the guidance of specially qualified teachers; and why does so much research repeatedly show neurological and/or genetic factors to be present in such children? (Note that the above assessment of Kline and Lee's excellent study is my own.)

In passing, it is pertinent to note that Rice (1970) and the I.D.E.A. (1969) found that minor visual problems are of very little significance in causing reading failure. Teachers and parents should be very careful about investing large amounts of time and money on vision training or neurological motor patterning.

A RESEARCH REPORT

A research was carried out on a representative sample of normal third-grade schoolchildren to investigate whether or not there were any meaningful relationships between spelling ability, handedness, visuo-spatial ability (independent of motor activity), mirror imaging, balance and various auditory skills. Three hypotheses which were to be tested were (a) Orton's (1937) suggestion that mirror imaging in dyslexic children was the result of right hemisphere activity, (b) my own assertion that the right hemisphere might, in some people, dominate the *whole* brain visuo-spatially, with verbal activity in the left hemisphere subservient to the visuo-spatial right hemisphere, and (c) my assertion that sequencing in spelling was less a visuo-spatial activity than an auditory/vocal-articulatory one. The evidence of the research supported all these hypotheses (on a "normal" population). Further research is required to explore and confirm the details. These hypotheses are especially relevant to my contention that genetic dyslexic children are visuo-spatially capable (in terms of their overall intellectual ability), but that this does not help them to process spelling because sequencing in spelling is not a visual task of any consequence—it is an articulatory vocal process. The research results with respect to spelling were reported in the previous chapter. (For a detailed description of the research, see Bannatyne and Wichiarajote, 1969a, 1969b; Bannatyne, 1969.)

The Sample

The sample consisted of a representative group of fifty third-grade children comprised of thirty boys and twenty girls. Although the sample contained one or two learning disability cases, it is to be emphasized that the vast majority of the sample more or less coped with regular third-grade schoolwork. A few of the children may have been socially disadvantaged and very few could be classified as upper middle class.

The Research Design

The design was of the simplest kind: the fifty children were given a battery of tests, the scores of which were intercorrelated. Other results were obtained by finding out whether or not there were significant differences (t-tests) between the mean scores for (a) boys versus girls and (b) good spellers versus bad spellers. Some of the t-test results are reported in Chapter VIII.

A Varimax factor analysis largely confirmed the correlational and t-test analyses presented below.

The Tests Used

The battery of tests used is briefly described as follows.

The Bannatyne Visuo-Spatial Memory Test was devised to assess a person's visuo-spatial memory for designs in a "pure" way without involving motor activity. Each of fifteen separate stimulus designs is presented in turn for four seconds. Next a blank page is turned, an operation taking one second. This reveals a page of eight designs, from which the subject is required to select one design as the exact equivalent of the original stimulus design. The eight designs, which are randomized on the page, include the original design, a simplified version of it, a mirror image, a 90-degree rotation, a fragmentation, an out-of-proportion version of it, a complicated design and a symmetrical version. The subject is told beforehand that one design is the same as the original design and that he must select that particular one. On the above sample of fifty eight-year-old third-grade schoolchildren, the distribution of correct answers and the scatter of item difficulty were normally distributed.

The Revised Illinois Test of Psycholinguistic Abilities (Kirk *et al.,* 1968) cannot be described in detail here. The visual closure subtest requires the subject to search for and identify objects and parts of objects within a series of pictures. The auditory sequencing subtest is a digit-span memory test similar to that in the WISC but with half-second intervals between digits. The subject is required to repeat back the series of numbers which have been dictated by the experimenter. The visual sequencing subtest requires the subject to remember the order in which a series of almost nonmeaningful geometrical designs on little cards have been placed, the subject having to sequence the designs in the correct order from memory. On the auditory closure subtest, the subject is requested to say words which have been spoken by the examiner, but which have phonemes or even syllables missing from them. For example, on the stimulus word *ingernail* the subject must reply *fingernail.* The sound-blending subtest requires the subject to synthesize into normal speech words which are presented with intervals of silence between phonemes.

The spelling test was a simple graded word spelling test ranging from very simple three-letter words to quite complicated ones (Schonell and Schonell, 1960).

The balancing test requires the subject to stand on one foot with his eyes open for as long as possible. The score reflects the number of seconds this posture can be maintained without undue wobbling.

The mirror-writing score was obtained from the simultaneous writing test in which the subject has to write the numbers 1 through 12 down the page using both the left and right hands simultaneously. The mirror-writing score was obtained by counting up the number of mirrored numbers in the column written by the dominant hand.

The unlearned handedness test consisted of three items: folding arms, clasping hands together with meshed fingers and touching the left ear with a particular hand. A very careful analysis was made of the results of these three subtests to insure that there was a commonality of handedness across all three in terms of laterality. An ambidexterity score was obtained if an item was performed in an ambidextrous way or if one item was performed with the right hand and the other with the left hand. The latter preferences were still used to contribute to the right and left scores. When both measures of ambidexterity occurred, the results were combined.

The learned handedness test consisted of finding (a) with which hand the child could best write, (b) which hand could pile ten cards more quickly and (c) which hand was uppermost when the child clapped hands. It could be argued that the latter is untrained but I think it is a reasonable assumption that most children are deliberately taught to clap hands in infancy by parents and siblings. Ambidexterity was calculated in the same manner as for the unlearned handedness test.

Results

Table XIII presents some of the findings of the research. It

TABLE XIII
UNLEARNED AND LEARNED HANDEDNESS AND
CORRELATED VARIABLES*

Unlearned Handedness	Significant Variables†	Correlation†
U Right Hand	BVSMT Accurate Original Designs	−0.44
	BVSMT Rotated Designs	+0.30
	Revised ITPA Visual Closure	−0.31
U Ambidexterity	Written Spelling—Graded Words	+0.42
	Balance—One Foot, Eyes Open	+0.28
U Left Hand	BVSMT Accurate Original Designs	+0.50
	BVSMT Rotated Designs	−0.42
	BVSMT Fragmented Designs	−0.31
	Revised ITPA Auditory Sequencing (Digit Span)	+0.31
Learned Handedness	Significant Variables†	Correlation†
L Right Hand	Mirror Writing with Dominant Hand	−0.33
L Ambidexterity	Nil	Nil
L Left Hand	BVSMT Mirror Imaged Designs	+0.31

*Sample: 50 third-grade children (30 boys and 20 girls).
†$r = 0.273$ (0.05 level of significance); $r = 0.322$ (0.02 level of significance); $r = 0.354$ (0.01 level of significance).

indicates that unlearned right-handedness (left hemisphere activity) is correlated significantly with a tendency to select rotated designs on the BVSMT. Traditionally, the rotation of designs is considered an indicator of brain damage, but here it may be regarded simply as a particular type of visuo-spatial inefficiency. Unlearned right-handedness (left hemisphere) is significantly *negatively* correlated with the selection of accurate original designs on the BVSMT. The fact that a significant *negative* correlation was also obtained with the revised ITPA visual closure subtest confirms that these results are not a test artifact. It is to be stressed that none of these tests involve manual dexerity of any kind; in other words, the motor performance factor has been eliminated as a confounding variable from the visuo-spatial task situation.

The implication is that unlearned right-handedness and left hemisphere activity is associated with poor visuo-spatial ability insofar as it is measured by these tests. It will be remembered that the right hand is largely controlled from the left hemisphere and that this hemisphere is less concerned with the control of visuo-spatial functions. In fact, most of the relevant authorities quoted in Chapters VI, VII and VIII are in little doubt that the vast majority of people process language functions in the left hemisphere, and visuo-spatial functions predominantly in the right hemisphere. Visuo-spatial functions also involve the left hemisphere and the right temporal lobe in specific ways (Sperry, 1962; Hecaen and de Ajuriaguerra, 1964; Benton, 1966; Zangwill, 1962; Milner, 1962; Teuber, 1962; Weinstein, 1964; Luria, 1966; and many others).

Unlearned ambidexterity showed a high positive correlation with graded word spelling. Other research results previously discussed in Chapter VIII indicated that spelling along with sound blending has a visuo-spatial *unit* (not sequencing) design element in it, a statement which is also supported by the spontaneous occurrence of mirror-imaged letters in the written spelling of some children. An implication of this correlation with unlearned ambidexterity is that both sides of the brain may contribute visuo-spatially in a unit-design way to written spelling. The correlation of unlearned ambidexterity with balance supports this view; it is perhaps not surprising that skill with both hands correlates with the ability to balance, the neurological implication being that a fine motor-kinesthetic feedback control of equal quality in both hemispheres would seem necessary for the precise maintenance of a balancing posture.

Unlearned left-handedness is highly and positively correlated with the selection of the accurate original designs on the BVSMT Test. Unlearned left-handedness is *negatively* correlated with the selection of rotated and fragmented design choices. This would help confirm the hypothesis that the right hemisphere has as one of its primary concerns visuo-spatial processing, particularly when these results are compared with those for the right hand.

Another surprising result in terms of the overall hypothesis that language functions take place in the left hemisphere is the significant correlation between unlearned left-handedness and the revised ITPA auditory sequencing test score. This subtest is a digit-span memory test and one explanation of the correlation may be that in a rote memory test such as this, the dictated numbers have little or no numerical value and are processed more on the level of musical notes than of words. On this hypothesis, digit-span memory would, at least in part, take place in the primary auditory sensory areas and related secondary areas in the *right* temporal lobe. Milner's (1962) work suggests that music is processed largely in the right hemisphere temporal area.

Support for a partial temporal lobe "control" of digit-span auditory sequencing memory comes from two research studies. Spreen *et al.* (1965) found that defective identification of *meaningful sounds* within the settings of adequate hearing for pure tones is also shown more frequently by patients with right hemisphere disease. In other words, some meaningful sounds are processed in the right hemisphere and the numbers in a digit-span test are meaningful sounds. Boshes and Myklebust (1964), in a study of learning disability children (in which 46 percent of the sample had no detectable neurological abnormalities), found *auditory blending* scores to be positively correlated with WISC verbal IQ, vocabulary and object assembly (a spatial subtest) for the neurologically abnormal group. The correlation, however, was a very low, negative, nonsignificant one for the normal group. Another explanation, not incompatible with the one just given, is that unlearned ambidexterity or unlearned left-handedness is indicative of a brain with overall superior neurological functioning —one which balances the body well and does not rotate or fragment designs as occurs in neurologically dysfunctioning brains. According to some authorities (see Chapter X), this efficient (unlearned ambidextrous or left-handed) brain, in verbally competent subjects such as those in this sample, would process certain automatic language functions reasonably efficiently in the left hemisphere as well as processing spatial material in the right.

Turning to learned handedness, we find that learned right-handedness is negatively correlated with mirror writing with the dominant hand. In other words, the more one has been trained to use one's right hand and the more firmly this is established, the less likely one is to exhibit mirror writing with that right hand on a simultaneous handwriting test. The implication is that mirror writing occurs more in ambidextrous or left-handed people (right hemisphere activity), a statement supported by the trend of the correlations which, probably because they are divided between the two variables, were not quite significant. Learned ambidexterity was not significantly correlated with any of the variables, which is not surprising, but learned left-handedness (right hemisphere) was significantly correlated with the choice of mirror-image designs on the BVSMT. This also in a sense confirms the negative finding about mirror writing with the right hand. This conclusion supports Orton's hypothesis that mirror imaging in dyslexic children is the result of right hemisphere activity.

All the correlations in Table XIII connected with handedness, visuo-spatial memory for designs, mirror writing and balance support the hypothesis that mirror writing and mirror imaging occur less frequently in right-handed children. The results also support the hypothesis that visuo-spatial material is processed in the right hemisphere, and that additionally, although alternative explanations are equally acceptable some types of verbal material *may* also be processed there, at least in part. Note that auditory closure and sound blending were not significantly correlated with any handedness variables on this representative sample of fifty third-grade children.

Table XIV sets out the correlations of some of the variables with the sex of the child. The sex of the child over the whole sample was correlated significantly with only two variables, namely, the choice of rotated designs or complicated designs on the BVSMT. Since girls were given the higher value for the purpose of calculating the correlations, the results suggest that girls chose the rotated designs more frequently than did boys. On the other hand, the boys tended to complicate designs more often than girls did. Both these results were confirmed by t-tests. The boys had a tendency to choose mirrored designs and to mirror-write with their dominant hand but neither result was quite significant. The girls had a tendency to spell better than the boys but this result was not significant either. These nonsignificant correlations, as well as the significant ones, are set out in the table to indicate that the hypotheses that boys tend to mirror-image designs and girls tend to spell better than boys are not contradicted by this particular set of data, which is all in the "right direction." It is well known that although "right direction" trends are almost always evident in sex difference studies, it is somewhat difficult to obtain significant statistics without very large samples (Templin, 1957; Maccoby, 1966; Morley, 1965).

An important point to remember is that the BVSMT does not involve motor-kinesthetic activity; otherwise, the visuo-spatial

TABLE XIV
CORRELATIONS OF SOME VARIABLES* WITH SEX OF CHILD†

Sex (girls higher value), and		
BVSMT Rotated Designs	+0.29	Sig (0.05)
BVSMT Complicated Designs	−0.28	Sig (0.05)
BVSMT Mirrored Designs	−0.25	N. Sig
Mirror Writing with Dominant Hand	−0.25	N. Sig
Spelling-Graded Words	+0.21	N. Sig

*These variables were the five with the highest correlations with sex out of a total of 47 variables.

†Sample: 50 third-grade children (30 boys and 20 girls).

results might be very different. This point is supported by the results obtained on this same sample of children with the Graham-Kendall Memory-for-Designs Test which was administered at the same time as the BVSMT. There is little doubt that the motor element complicates the whole picture; a detailed analysis of the results has been published elsewhere (Bannatyne, 1969). Further evidence on this point comes from Ames and Ilg (1964), who administered a battery of tests which included the Gessell Incomplete Man Test. In all the tests, the responses of the girls were superior to those of the boys, the superiority and greater maturity of the girls being most clearly and consistently seen in the Incomplete Man Test. The authors report: "Present findings confirm those of earlier investigators in suggesting that the test performance of girls in this age range appears to be considerably advanced over that of boys." These results tend to support the hypothesis that boys have a maturational lag which may cause a slightly less efficient motor functioning when they are compared with girls en masse. Thus, boys' results on tests involving motor activity such as a memory-for-designs test, a draw-a-man test, the Bender Gestalt Test and the Oseretsky Test may be inferior to those of girls, even though their "pure" visuo-spatial functioning may be superior in some ways. That boys are superior to girls visuo-spatially in some ways is attested to by the research reviews of Maccoby (1966), I.M. Smith (1964) and P.E. Vernon (1961). On the other hand, Dykstra (1966) found girls superior to boys auditorially, a result indirectly supported by most of the verbal ability research projects reviewed by Maccoby.

Table XV sets out the correlations of unlearned and learned handedness tests. These correlations are not significant, a fact which should give pause to all concerned with the measurement of laterality. They indicate that even within such a narrow field of study as handedness, a functional split-half reliability check, so to speak, suggests that certain unlearned items may be measuring very different laterality functions (in terms of the brain) from those tasks which test learned laterality. This would seem to make an item analysis, in the interests of homogeneity, oblig-

TABLE XV
CORRELATIONS* OF UNLEARNED AND LEARNED
HANDEDNESS TESTS†

Unlearned	Learned		
	Right	*Ambidextrous*	*Left*
Right	+0.12	−0.23	+0.06
Ambidextrous	+0.06	+0.02	−0.22
Left	−0.19	+0.27	+0.04

*$r = 0.273$ (0.05 level of significance).
†Sample: 50 third-grade children (30 boys and 20 girls).

atory in the formation of all laterality tests. One thing is certain —we can no longer automatically assume because a test item involves some form of laterality that it measures the same thing as the next item.

The above statements concerning laterality tests also apply to other tests; the BVSMT was constructed for the purpose of eliminating motor functioning from visuo-spatial activity and it produces quite different results from a parallel test which involves drawing. It would seem a profitable exercise in most psychological and neurological research to purify our test items along sensory or motor dimensions, with considerably more attention to detail than has been usual in the past. Multi-modality tests may be useful for general educational or intellectual assessment purposes but they blur research findings.

The overall conclusion from the above research results is that they support the general hypotheses concerning laterality of hemispheric functioning, visuo-spatial ability and sex differences put forward in previous chapters. Although the picture is by no means complete, there is sufficient all-around evidence from this and the other studies quoted to warrant a much more detailed investigation of the hypotheses put forward concerning the psychology, neurology and physiology of genetic dyslexia.

The positive correlation between digit-span memory (revised ITPA auditory sequencing) and unlearned left-handedness, and an even higher correlation ($r = + 0.37$) between ITPA sound blending and drawing accurate designs from memory on the memory-for-designs test (Graham-Kendall), plus many of the other significant correlations *argue for a "general factor" of effi-*

cient neurological functioning equivalent to general intellectual ability. This postulated general efficiency of the brain may be the material cause of the factor of general intelligence (*g*) found in almost all of the factor analyses which have been carried out on intellectual functioning (P.E. Vernon, 1961). It will be remembered that the sample for the above research was a representative one of fifty normal third-grade schoolchildren and there is every reason why their verbal ability should be correlated with other psychological skills. The bipolar factor of verbal versus spatial ability described by P.E. Vernon (1964) and I.M. Smith (1964) in their reviews of numerous research findings are almost always the second and third factors to be extracted from a factor analysis, their bipolar nature only becoming evident after the general intellectual efficiency (*g*) factor has been extracted. One important point which emerges from the results reported above is that the hypotheses concerning handedness, mirror imaging, visuo-spatial ability, balance and sex differences (to name but a few) are also significantly discernible in a representative sample of normal children.

The way in which these characteristics (handedness, mirror imaging, etc.) are manifest in genetic dyslexic children is examined in detail in the remaining portion of the chapter.

GENETIC DYSLEXIA

The description of genetic dyslexia which follows comes from a variety of sources. Much of it comes from the many research studies which have been quoted previously throughout this book; some comes from my own research findings and some from my clinical evaluation of a large number of individual children suffering from learning disabilities. When it is necessary to support a statement with evidence, the particular research will be quoted again. The term *genetic dyslexia* is my own (Bannatyne, 1966f, 1966g, 1967b), and in the light of the research findings quoted above, it seems a particularly apt label for those children who may inherit a specific language disability. Most of the research reports so far mentioned did not attempt to screen out of their sample population neurological dysfunction children and, in a way, the strength of the clear-cut genetic findings is increased by this fact. However, the heterogeneous samples used to tend to blur the particular symptom characteristics of all dyslexic groups whether they consist of "pure" genetic dyslexic children, communicative dyslexics, culturally disadvantaged children or neurologically dysfunctioning children. For example, Lesevre (1966) found several of these types in her sample. Additionally, most of the above samples included many girls and my personal experience with genetic dyslexia is that, in accord with research findings, it tends to be mostly a male affliction; the relatively few girls with learning disabilities tend more to neurological dysfunction or emotional disturbance as the cause. Very occasionally, one does come across a genetic dyslexic girl. It should be clearly stated that none of the authors of the research studies mentioned use the term *genetic dyslexia* nor are they responsible for any of the statements made below unless their names are specifically mentioned.

The Characteristics of Genetic Dyslexic Children

In Table II (page 18), a hierarchical classification of the causes and types of dyslexia was presented. Four groups of dyslexia were mentioned: genetic dyslexia, primary emotional communicative causes, minimal neurological dysfunction and social or cultural or educational deprivation.

I suspect that different types of institutions have a way of attracting particular categories of learning disability children. For example, a hospital unit with a neurologist in charge will probably have referred to it a preponderance of neurological dysfunction cases, whereas one with a psychiatrist heading the unit will see many emotionally disturbed learning disability cases (many of whom may also have neurological dysfunction). Speech therapists will obviously have referred to them more children with primary language disorders. However, the genetic dyslexic child, unless he has severe emotional problems as well, is not often referred outside the public school system; if he is seen at all, it is usually by school or educational psychologists who will recommend a remedial reading program, if one exists, within the school system. Of course, many other types of dyslexic children are also not referred outside the public school system, but the point to be made here is that the genetic dyslexic boy is less recognizable and less likely to be referred to outside agencies than almost any other type of learning disability case. This situation is reflected in the various research projects which have been referred to in this and preceding chapters. Those studies which report a high proportion of familial dyslexic symptoms have samples which either have been carefully screened to eliminate neurological dysfunction or have been drawn from the school system directly with implicit or explicit screening for intellectual capacity, cultural background and a specific academic deficit (e.g., spelling).

In the light of these points, I consider that the time has come when learning disability research should no longer be carried out on heterogeneous samples of schoolchildren or clinic cases without first making some attempt to cluster the attributes and symptoms presented by the children before, during or as a part of the findings of the research project, depending on its objectives. There are now several computerized statistical techniques for clustering attributes or specific variables, quite apart from the traditional statistical ones. One complicating factor in clustering research is the frequency of compounded typologies; because the etiologies of the groupings of symptom types are not mutually exclusive, children can and do suffer from two or more types of dyslexia.

Visuo-Spatial Ability

Genetic dyslexic children, most of whom are boys, tend to have a competent visuo-spatial ability in terms of their overall intellectual performance. The evidence for this statement comes from many research studies which will be mentioned below (some of them have also been mentioned above), but first, it is necessary to establish that children who perform capably on several of the WISC performance subtests have none of the conventional signs associated with neurological dysfunction or brain damage. A study by J. Holroyd (1965) makes this very point. Twenty children with at least a 25-point difference between verbal and performance IQ's on the WISC were compared with twenty control subjects from the same hospital. Where verbal IQ's were 25 points higher than performance IQ's, significantly more indications of brain damage were found by the various other diagnostic techniques used. *Where performance IQ's were 25 points higher than verbal IQ's, no difference was found in brain damage signs between these children and the control subjects.* The Oseretsky Test of motor performance offered the highest significant correlation with the various neurological examination ratings.

In a study of eighty-seven boys with learning disabilities, aged eight to eleven years, with WISC IQ's between 85 and 115 and reading quotients less than 80, Moseley and I (Bannatyne, 1967b) found that 70 percent of the sample had a spatial score (picture completion plus block design plus object assembly) greater than their verbal conceptualizing score (comprehension plus similarities plus vocabulary). As the WISC is standardized, only 50 percent of normal children would have a spatial score greater than their verbal conceptualizing score. This research was reported in more detail in Chapter VI.

McLeod (1965) has summarized numerous studies of the subtest profiles of the WISC among reading disability cases, and has also contributed a study of his own. Most of the findings indicated that the reading disability cases were strong in picture completion, block design, and comprehension and sometimes on object assembly. These children tended to be weak on the information, arithmetic, coding, digit-span and vocabulary subtests. Similar results were obtained by P.A. Adams (1967). Wolf (1967) found that his group of dyslexic children (from which had been excluded obvious neurological dysfunction cases and emotionally disturbed children) was superior to the normal control group in picture completion, and he attributes this to the children becoming picture readers. However, this would not account for the competent block design performances found in the many studies reviewed by McLeod, and Wolf himself did not find any differences between his two groups on block design scores. It is known (Maxwell, 1959) that picture completion, object assembly and block design have strong loadings on the spatial performance factor of intelligence, which is the reason why I have separated out these three WISC subtests as a spatial ability score. In the light of the work of I.M. Smith (1964) and P.E. Vernon (1961), who have established verbal and spatial abilities as bipolar factors in intellectual performance, one can only conclude that a considerable number of dyslexic children, in terms of their own overall ability, are strong on visuo-spatial tasks and weak on automatic verbal skills such as digit span. (Note that in the WISC, the arithmetic subtest is largely a verbal test involving a memory for numbers.)

Additionally, all the research and other contributions reviewed in the first section of this chapter indicate that these verbal skills and spatial ability have a large hereditary component.

The remainder of the chapter will be devoted to a detailed analysis of the nature of genetic dyslexia.

Sex Differences in Dyslexic Children

That dyslexic boys outnumber dyslexic girls by a considerable proportion is widely known. These sex differences and those in language abilities in general were discussed in Chapters II and VI. Bentzen (1966) has extensively reviewed the topic in language and other areas. From my own review of the literature and personal experience in schools, clinics and centers, I have found that the proportion of boys to girls may range from 3:1 in cases of mild disability up to 10:1 in cases of severe disability. Therefore, much depends on the cutoff point in terms of the mildness of the disability, with the sex difference proportion changing accordingly. In personal discussions, the principals of several high schools have estimated that up to 25 percent of boys of average intelligence or above have some considerable difficulty in learning foreign languages to the rote skill level. In my opinion, this is also the operation of a mild genetic language disability.

It is almost certain that the sex difference proportion is completely reversed with respect to spatial ability in the light of the evidence presented in the review of the research by Maccoby

(1966). This confirms the conclusions on sex differences and spatial abilities by I.M. Smith (1964) and P.E. Vernon (1961). It is interesting that in the research studies reviewed by Maccoby on the topic of perceptual speed (a perceptual-motor sequencing test), eight of the studies showed the girls to be superior whereas the other two studies showed no sex difference. The tests used in these studies were usually the WISC or WAIS coding and digit symbol tests.

Motor-Kinesthetic Performance

Very few studies have thoroughly examined large samples of dyslexic children to ascertain their overall motor performance. Bryant (1964) found that two-thirds of reading disability cases in a clinic population obtained motor development scores completely below the normative distribution for their age, which leaves one-third with normal motor functioning. He used the Lincoln-Oseretsky Scale to ascertain the degree of impaired motor development (see Chapter X). Forrest (1967) found no significant differences between his learning disability cases and their control group for "adventitious overflow movements and arm extension" (variations in posture and motility which are observed when a child is asked to close his eyes and maintain arm extension for a given period of time). Note that Forrest's group was a school-based population. In my own work, in centers for learning disabilities, like Bryant, I have found that at least one-third of the children have not had any measurable motor-kinesthetic deficit; indeed, one of my many eventual criteria for making a differential diagnosis between neurological dysfunction and genetic dyslexia was the presence (MND) or absence (genetic dyslexia) of motor-kinesthetic disabilities. The whole topic of motor-kinesthetic performance will be investigated in much more detail in the next chapter.

The conclusion is that a considerable group of dyslexic children are at least average or above average in motor performance (J. Holroyd, 1965) and I strongly suspect that the great majority of these are genetic dyslexic cases.

Intellectual and Conceptualizing Abilities

Technically speaking, a genetic dyslexic child may have an IQ at any level on the scale. Thus, it is possible for a mentally retarded child with an IQ of below 70 also to suffer from genetic dyslexia, insofar as it tends to run in his family. In my work, I have found boys in classes for mentally retarded children who, on tests, had a WISC verbal scale IQ of 75 points or less, and a spatial ability IQ (picture completion plus block design plus object assembly) of which any professional engineer or architect would have been proud. One boy had a spatial ability IQ of 145— he was described by his teacher in that most condescending of phrases as "being clever with his hands." Of course, genetic dyslexic children are scattered throughout the normal population in terms of intellectual ability (Walker and Cole, 1965), but as has been repeatedly stated, the type of intelligence they possess tends to be more nonverbal, or visuo-spatial.

Most genetic dyslexic boys go into trades and professions which utilize their visuo-spatial skills, becoming designers, mechanics, engineers, farmers, surgeons, dentists, architects, chemists, factory workers, builders, physicists, transport drivers, pilots, artists and sculptors. My evidence for this comes from two sources: (a) the large number of ex-dyslexic adults whom I have met in several countries and (b) the occupations of ex-dyslexic fathers with dyslexic sons. Many of them have university degrees and all tell the same tale, which always includes several of the following characteristics: somewhat slow speech development in early childhood, difficulty with auditory sequencing, closure and blending, difficulty in learning to read initially and a residual problem in spelling which usually persists into adulthood. Most of these men have clear, logical, scientific minds which can create, plan, organize and develop visuo-spatial materials and processes in a highly competent way (see Chapters II and VI). They can also handle *absolute* symbols, such as those used in chemistry, and are very able to cope with abstract reasoning. One person, for example, is a professor of physics who did not learn to speak until he was three or read until he was eight. However, in spite of this slow start, he became an excellent scientist in school and today is a highly original and excellent physicist. This is only one of many such cases known to me personally.

Genetic dyslexic boys, provided they are not too emotionally disturbed, have a *logical* quality to their intellectual reasoning which seems to be one aspect of spatial ability. Spatial ability was defined in Chapter VI as the ability to manipulate objects and their interrelationships intelligently in multidimensional space, the latter including any number of dimensions from two to infinity. The nonverbal intellectual manipulation (spatial) may be theoretical, symbolic or abstract, may utilize body-extensional tools (radar, telescopes, instruments, cranes, cars, etc.) or may be directly manual. If males are less adequate than females in overall verbal *skills,* then genetic dyslexic males possess this inadequacy to a much greater degree. The reader is referred back to the first few sections of Chapter VI for more information about sex differences in verbal and spatial ability, the nature of these cognitive abilities and possible evolutionary explanations for their existence. (Deficits and disabilities referred to in this and other chapters do not refer to sensory or motor *organ* defects unless explicitly stated.)

Auditory and Speech Symptoms

The speech perception and production characteristics of genetic dyslexic children are many and varied and there is no constant pattern or profile of auditory characteristics across the group apart from a real tendency to be less able to discriminate melodies (Drake and Schnall, 1966; Wolf, 1967). Musical perception and perhaps some aspects of musical ability generally seem to be localized in the right (verbally nondominant) temporal lobe in the great majority of people (see Chapter VI and Milner, 1962). Speech perception is almost always represented in the left temporal (and surrounding) areas. *As it is most unlikely that approximately 2 percent of the school population, mostly male (Gorton, 1964) have almost identical "mild" but specific lesions in the same areas of the temporal lobes of both hemispheres, the only possible conclusion is that the etiology is not one of brain damage.* No research in any discipline, including neurosurgery, has ever even hinted at such a possibility.

The major alternative hypothesis, which has very strong support from the research studies quoted earlier in the chapter, is that of a hereditary disability or lack of talent in the discriminative perception of sequences of sounds. It would seem that the poor melody discrimination of genetic dyslexic children (Wolf, 1967) in the right hemisphere (Milner, 1962) is accompanied by an equally inefficient left hemisphere appreciation of the sounds which are sequenced in words. After all, words are composed of a series of noises called phonemes which could be classified as complex notes or chords. I have been told that in Sweden some educational institutions use music tests to screen students for courses in foreign languages. Many dyslexics have histories of *slow speech development* and *poor listening skills* during babyhood and infancy (Forrest, 1967). In my own work with genetic dyslexic children, slow or mildly unusual speech development is more often found to be a symptom than not.

One striking and subtle speech development symptom which may continue even into adult life is *the inability to discriminate between vowels which sound alike,* particularly the short or neutral vowels. To test this symptom effectively, auditory discrimination tests should present the vowels in similar sounding words, preferably using the same consonants, e.g., *pen* and *pin.* Most consonants are not a problem to genetic dyslexic children. A possible explanation is that consonants have a wider range of distinctive features and other characteristics than do vowels (see Chapter II). Certainly it would seem that training in the articulation of phonemes may help in sharpening the dyslexic child's perception of them.

Auditory closure and sound blending are significantly correlated as verbal factors in a representative sample of third-grade children ($r = 4.3$—see Chapters VIII and IX), and the genetic dyslexic child has difficulty with both. Kass (1962) found that a mixed group of severe reading disability cases showed deficits on the Monroe Sound Blending subtest when compared with the control group. Many genetic dyslexic children at a certain point in their reading progress will be able to sound out phonically the phonemes in a word while reading but will be unable to blend them to the point where they recognize the word as one in their established auditory/vocal vocabulary. Strangely, and not infrequently, they may correctly blend the word and still not close on their previous experience with that word as an auditory/vocal concept. Most people have a problem of auditory closure when they hear a person with a strong foreign accent pronouncing words in an unfamiliar way. Note that auditory closure is the auditory or listening equivalent to sound blending, which is concerned with speech output.

Phoneme/grapheme matching, which is an aspect of *auditory sequencing memory*, is another problem area for genetic dyslexic children and, for that matter, for other types of dyslexic children. They seem to find it extremely difficult to remember which phoneme is associated with particular graphemes within a word-letter context. Additionally, they frequently find it difficult to remember the sequence of phoneme-to-grapheme matches within a particular word. The problems associated with sequencing memory, blending and closure are as much a problem in spelling as they are in reading, if not more. In the case of spelling, the problem is probably a retrospective one in the sense that the child has not previously memorized sequences of phoneme/grapheme matchings during the reading process (including word reading); therefore, very frequently the main effort during the remediation of genetic dyslexics is the memorization of phoneme/grapheme matches within words as sequences of sounds.

Genetic dyslexic children almost certainly have a maturational lag of the type described in Chapter VII, which may be a formal cause of their difficulties in memorizing to an automatized level the above auditory-visual associations. Some of the implications of maturational lag for genetic dyslexic children are discussed both below and again in Chapter XIII.

To say that genetic dyslexic children are less fluent than are other children, while it is true, it is too generalized a statement to have much empirical meaning. Dyslexic children generally cannot learn some language skills to a highly *automatic* or habitual level as easily as other children, a fact which has been demonstrated in several researches (Kass, 1962; Whiting *et al.*, 1966), but even these studies do not define the nature of fluency or linguistic automatization to any degree. Clues as to the nature of fluency may be found in the work of Rogers (1952) and Murphy (1933). Rogers, in a factorial study of verbal fluency, found that girls were superior to boys (in a high school population) on correctly sorting disarranged words (e.g., *iragffe* = *giraffe*) and on form naming, the latter being a simple test in which sequences of shapes such as stars, squares, circles, crosses, etc., have to be rapidly *named* in sequence, the stimuli being the designs themselves in sequence. Other significant correlations between sex and fluency skills were obtained for handwriting, unfinished stories, naming things to eat, spelling and rate of reading, the girls being superior in all of these. Murphy found that the good readers (IQ-controlled) were faster in word association tests, were better at definitions of the sentence completion type, had a higher accuracy score in a vocabulary test and were better at choosing which of a number of statements best illustrated the meaning of a given word. There were no differences between good and poor readers in the amount of imagery produced in association to a word, the type of imagery produced, the amount of abstract or concrete imagery produced, the types of association in a pre-association test, the number of associations per word, the richness of these associations or the number of associations to an ink-blot test. These studies tend to confirm that it is the *automatic, habitual types of verbal association* as against other types of association or content which best define *fluency* as the term is used in this reading disability context. Once imagery concepts are produced (particularly in terms of the amount, type, abstractness, richness or number of images), automatic fluency no longer operates as a decisive factor.

Mention should again be made of the work of Goldman-Eisler (1964), who found that once an original (nonautomatic) element crept into the content of thought, the fluency of the speech expressing that thought decreased. In her words, "Fluent speech was shown to consist of habitual combinations of words such as are shared by the language community." Goldman-Eisler says that her experimental results are

> . . . incompatible with the assumption of statistical determination of speech as the only factor in its generation. . . . The assumption [is] that hesitation pauses in speech are the delays due to processes taking place in the brain whenever speech ceases to be the automatic vocalization of learned sequences, whether occasioned by choice of an individual word, by construction of syntax, or by conception of content. . . .

The implication is not that genetic dyslexic children indulge more in original thought content, although that might be true; the deficit seems to be less on the conceptualizing-imagery aspect of language than on the speed of association, accuracy of association and verbal-label association side of the word-to-concept linkage. Thus, thoughts or concepts flow relatively well in genetic dyslexic children (my own inference from Murphy's results), but verbal-labels and all the sensorimotor components of verbal-labels— speed, accuracy and availability—are somewhat "hesitant." The latter sentence is important because the speed, accuracy and availability of verbal-labels, whether they are heard, spoken, read or written, are dependent on the efficiency with which the brain assembles from storage the components of words on any level, from recognition of distinctive features to the almost instantaneous recognition of phrases in the experienced reader.

In a recent paper, Kolers (1968), after discussing the nature of bilingualism and information processing, suggests, "The results [of his research] show that the concept is the decisive factor in recall and that two languages increase access to concepts." It is the fact that *language must communicate the concept* that requires a search for verbal-labels and these too have to be recalled in their own right. This can lead to tip-of-the-tongue can't-think-of-the-word behavior, a common phenomenon with genetic dyslexics. Thus, the nature of memory and the remedial techniques which best facilitate memorizing to an *automatic* level of functioning are tremendously important in the remediation of genetic dyslexic (and other types of dyslexic) children. These aspects of the problem are discussed in Chapters VII and XV. The essential basis for much of this memorizing process is to be found in the auditory areas of the brain and their functioning, together with the other speech and language areas which may provide considerable feedback facilitation of the memorizing processes, even if they are not absolutely essential to language perception (see Chapters II, III and VI).

To summarize, the main *auditory/vocal* problems of the genetic dyslexic child lie in the area of auditory vowel discrimination, auditory sequencing memory, auditory closure and sound blending, poor speech development and feedback, and a poor memorization for verbal associations, particularly in terms of the speed, accuracy and labeling aspects of all linguistic skills. These manifest themselves in the mechanics of reading, spelling and writing as an inability to memorize phoneme/grapheme associations and the sequences in which they occur in specific words.

The Genetic Dyslexic and
Orthography, Memory, Reading and Spelling

Because the traditional orthography of the English language is extremely irregular—that is, the particular association of each auditory symbol to each visual symbol is only accurately identifiable in each single sequential context (word)—the task of reading or spelling largely becomes one of rote memory associations, each cued by several conventional contexts: the sequence of sounds, the sequence of letters in a word, the number of letters in the word, the sequence of words in the sentence and the conceptual content of the passage. The difficulty is increased when one realizes that the visual symbols must also be sequenced *separately* from the phonemes in a word-context. In short, the sequences of sounds and their multiple arbitrary associations with sequences of letters and graphemes must always be learned by rote, because there is no logic to them. It is this rote memorizing of thousands of arbitrary, orthographically irregular, phoneme/grapheme associations which the genetic dyslexic child finds extremely difficult. By contrast, spatial concepts are amenable to "first principle" conceptual logic as in, for example, geometry, and the spatially capable person prefers a logical structure of principles from which he can work in any applied field, such as architecture or engineering. Spatially capable genetic dyslexic children being part of the group also prefer the logic of applied principles. On the other hand, the verbally able person can more easily memorize arbitrarily associated or unsystematically linked material, such as objects or concepts and their linguistic symbols. Languages are founded on a variety of nonlogical arbitrary conventions, most being somewhat unsystematic in their coding conventions. There are reports that languages which are phonetically "logical" are less of a problem to dyslexic people (Makita, 1968). With this in mind, and with the additional burden of the eyes wanting to move in all directions and mirror images frequently cropping up, the task of reading becomes well-nigh impossible.

If the major problems for the genetic dyslexic are auditory sequencing, auditory discrimination and associating auditory symbols to sequences of visual symbols, the central emphasis in any training program must be auditory sequencing, a training in careful listening, with the whole approach phonic in nature.

Compulsory Education for Literacy

One of the final causes of genetic dyslexia is culturally determined by the relatively recent law of the land which demands universal literacy. Except for very rare isolated cases (e.g., a king in Germany), genetic dyslexia could not exist and did not exist 250 years ago because nobody *had* to learn to read, write or spell and very few people did. Even today, two-thirds of the world's population is illiterate so most genetic dyslexic children go completely undetected and indeed are completely *normal* members of the population in their cultures. The human race does not mutate observably over thousands of years, let alone one or two hundred, and *the human race did not evolve to learn to read.* Of course, the human race did evolve to learn to communicate vocally and as has been previously and frequently stressed, spoken language is, to a large extent, a natural inborn human function (see Chapters II-VI and Lenneberg, 1967). Language is a natural potentiality only at the vocal/auditory level of sensorimotor functioning. Whereas a child will *spontaneously* learn to speak and to understand language in a favorable ecological environment (and it is considered highly abnormal when a child does not do so), all children, with the possible exception of a few prodigies, have to be taught *explicitly* in a rather formal fashion to read, to spell and to write. If they do not have such deliberate education, they simply do not learn these skills, though nobody would attribute their illiteracy to any cause other than the lack of tuition. A good analogy between auditory/vocal communication as opposed to reading and writing is that of walking as opposed to driving a car. Walking is innate and provided the environmental ecology allows it to develop, it will occur naturally and spontaneously to the extent that if a person does not walk, he is considered to be highly abnormal; indeed, one can walk in one's sleep. However, driving a car has to be learned in a slow, formal way, even if it is self-taught. It does not occur naturally any more than cars do and, by analogy, reading does not occur naturally any more than books do.

Once the law of the land demands that everyone must learn to read in the interests of the final cause of social survival, a new ecological niche is created and some children will be found who quite simply *do not have the talent* to acquire the new "artificial" reading and spelling skills required of them. This point will be better understood if another example is given. If tomorrow the government passed a law saying that everybody should learn music, that is, learn to perform, read and write music to the level of simple waltzes, there would be many musical dyslexics in the community who, at present, go unnoticed. These people merely suffer a lack of musical talent but since music is not essential to social survival, musical "dyslexia" is a minor matter. Nobody suggests because a person cannot write or play a simple waltz, draw the likeness of a human face or run a mile in five minutes, that he is brain-damaged, seriously emotionally disturbed or the possessor of abnormal recessive genes. Genetic dyslexia, then, occurs because very *recently* in human history a new ecological criterion for communication has been introduced as a "universal" social necessity, namely, reading and writing. A person must be endowed with a large variety of cognitive and sensorimotor abilities which can be functionally integrated above a certain threshold level of attainment in order to reach the eighth-grade level in reading, which is the lowest acceptable level of reading achievement. Numerous official educational research findings attest that there is a broad cutoff area at about the seventh percentile in the normal distribution of literacy in the population (plus or minus 5 points depending on environmental circumstances), below which dyslexic children of all types will find it difficult to learn to read, spell and write. They cannot easily adapt to the new social verbal ecological environment with its demand for high literacy.

The proportion of these who are genetic dyslexic cases is not known but a rough estimate is that about one-third of all reading disability cases of average or above-average intelligence are genetic dyslexics. Based on published research studies, particularly that of Gorton (1964), this would be about 2 percent of the normal school population. This is my own opinion, not Gorton's, but the screening symptom variables he used are very akin to those of genetic dyslexic children as I have found them. The expression "average or above-average intelligence" is used to eliminate mentally retarded children from the distribution. This is not meant to imply that mentally retarded children do not suffer from genetic dyslexia or indeed any other type of dyslexia. They may very well do so but any occurrence of genetic dyslexia in such children is not caused by mental retardation per se. The two conditions may coexist but neither one can be attributed to the other. In carrying out research on genetic dyslexic children or other kinds of reading disability cases, it is always wise to limit the study to children of average or above-average intelligence in order to simplify the research situation and reduce the number of contributing variables. Of course, a quite separate valuable exercise would be to investigate the incidence of genetic dyslexia among mentally retarded children. It is also worth reiterating that some genetic dyslexic children are misdiagnosed and erroneously placed in schools for the mentally retarded or deficient.

Genetic dyslexic boys (and some few girls) would have no distinguishing characteristics in a nonreading society such as existed in most countries two hundred years ago and still exists in large areas of the world today. With their good visuo-spatial abilities and low verbal skill ability, genetic dyslexic boys would go unnoticed in a nonliterate community of an agricultural, forest-dwelling, or simple artisan type. Their spatial skills would be at a premium. Unfortunately for such children, the cognitive ecology of society has changed abruptly and it now puts a high premium on complete reading and writing competency. The ecological niche has changed from a male spatial one without reading to a male spatial one with reading; genetic dyslexic boys are *maladapted* to the new environment.

Genetics, Heredity, Polygenes and Evolution

Genetic dyslexia is almost certainly a polygenic factor. Connolly (1966) describes polygenes in the following way:

> Most of the characteristics which are of interest to the psychologist are of the quantitatively variable kind; that is to say not of the all-or-none variety, but those producing "more" or "less" effects. These polygenes as they are called have individually minute effects, but cumulatively produce differences in stature, emotionality, intelligence and many other important traits. Because of these polygenes an organism will possess an enormous amount of genetic variability, and most of the phenotypic variability we observe will be a function of these systems.

It is to be stressed that genetic dyslexia is a resultant in the area of reading of a large number of normal physiological and psychological characteristics and that it occurs at the lower end of the normal continuous distribution curve of basic language skills. Although it is predominantly a male characteristic, this does *not* mean that it is caused by a single sex-linked gene as is baldness. Because genetic dyslexia is a multifaceted complex set of sensorimotor and cognitive characteristics, it must be a widespread pattern across many genes (polygenic) or characters, all of which contribute their part. A physical analogy would be height. Height is normally distributed in the population and males are generally taller than females, the difference in the means being significant. Many genes determine height: the genes which program the development of glands, bones, muscle tissue, metabolism, etc. Some short males will fall at the lower end of the distribution but will be normal in every other respect; they are not dwarfs with an abnormal genetic inheritance, nor are they short because of "damage" during pregnancy, birth or disease. They are short because their fathers were short and probably the generations before them. Similarly, all those sensory, motor and other neurological characteristics, which are each patterned by specific genes, combine to produce a resultant potentiality in the infant for the acquisition of linguistic skills. The various short-comings of the necessary characteristics in the auditory-speech-language areas of human functioning are the efficient cause (polygenic) and material cause (neurological functioning) of genetic dyslexia. The formal or developmental cause is a generalized neurophysiological maturational lag.

The evolutionary reasons for genetic dyslexia are, in a sense, nonexistent because as has been pointed out the condition is largely the result of a very recent social and legal (societal survival-value) demand for literacy (the final cause). Even so, while most people can learn to read relatively easily, the genetic dyslexic does not and the origins of this state of affairs need to be examined. In Chapter IV, an evolutionary explanation was given for the sex differences found in verbal and spatial abilities and this explanation also serves for the existence of genetic dyslexia, particularly in males. It was suggested that there is a premium, in terms of family survival value for females, in possessing adequate communication skills whereas the equivalent premium for males lies in spatial abilities. Since verbal and spatial abilities are very likely to be a bipolar factor (I.M. Smith, 1964; P.E. Vernon, 1961), the greater the possession of one in any individual the less likely the other is to appear as a comparable talent, given a specific overall level of intellectual functioning.

Spatial Ability, Visual Fields, Reversals, Mirror Imaging, Symmetry and Hemispheric Lateralization

The very fact that a genetic dyslexic boy tends to be spatially competent in terms of his overall intellectual ability can itself be a handicap to the reading process in several ways. First of all, he finds it difficult to learn to scan print in one dimension as required in rapid reading; second, the hemispheric balance of functioning which results from good spatial ability *may* be the cause of confusion in reading through the mirror imaging of letters and possibly the reversal of words; third, the fact that some letters of the alphabet contravene the law of object constancy may also cause visuo-spatial problems in reading. A detailed neurological background was given to these characteristics in Chapter VI, and although many of the details will not be reiterated here, a further discussion from another viewpoint is appropriate. It will be appreciated that many of the statements which follow have been documented in previous chapters and any reader wishing to review the research evidence should reread the appropriate sections.

Problems in Gaze Lateralization

A good appreciation of spatial relationships demands a fairly well-coordinated motor system and an acute three-dimensional vision in *both* visual fields. These call for the equal use of the visual and motor areas of the brain in both hemispheres. This neurological state of affairs—that is, the equality between the hemispheres in people with a reasonable or high degree of spatial ability—tends to make them left-handed or ambidextrous in certain tasks and skills. It also tends to make them scan the whole field of vision very rapidly in all directions as is necessary in a three-dimensional world. For example, the pilot, surgeon, dentist or sculptor would be very inefficient if he did not possess these attributes. Reading, on the other hand, calls for the discipline of scanning in one direction only, and a person with a natural tendency to scan the environment rapidly in all directions will probably find one-dimensional scanning habits in reading difficult to acquire. The genetic dyslexic boy, along with his auditory language skill problems in learning to read, will find the discipline of one-dimensional eye-scanning training an added difficulty. It is very likely that some of Lesevre's (1966) sample of dyslexic children with poorly lateralized gaze were genetic dyslexics. In a sense we can say that the eyes of genetic dyslexic children are too competent and efficient at the job they were designed or evolved to do, namely, three-dimensional scanning, to be habitually limited to the new and very artificial visual task of one-dimensional reading.

Reversals

Genetic dyslexic boys have a tendency to reverse the order of the letters in a word or reorganize them in such a way that they spell a different word. Instances of this are as follows: *on* for *no; was* for *saw; felt* for *left*. These reversals, taken from the first three sections of the Gates-McKillop Reading Diagnostic Test (Form 1) Oral Reading I subtest, are by an eight-and-a-half-year-old boy with severe genetic dyslexia. A likely reason for these reversals of letter sequence is the right-to-left scanning of the gaze which in genetic dyslexic children may be mixed in with conventional left-to-right scanning. The words are read backward in part. This phenomenon may also account for some mirror imaging of individual letters, both symptoms being the outcome of a right hemisphere visuo-spatial dominance. Ilg and Ames (1950) found that reversals tended to persist in normal children until eight or nine years of age. Genetic dyslexic children, I suggest, are the more severe cases in this group.

Mirror Imaging and Symmetry

An appreciation of space in terms of survival value, particularly with respect to vision, demands peripheral stimuli to be rapidly recognized and interpreted in both the left and right visual fields and hence in both the left and right visual areas of the brain. Moreover, nature probably invented the two hemispheres to work in terms of symmetrical mirrored sensory and motor functions (see Chapter VI; Teuber, 1962; and others). Most external bodily functions, particularly those involving the motor and visual areas, require mirrored neurological impressions because one side of the body surface is very much a mirror image of the other (Tschirgi, 1958). Since men have learned to read, this ancient requirement for other purposes has been a slight handicap. When we read, convention demands that our eyes move from left to right, at least in the European languages. Quite apart from the fact that reading demands training the eyes to move in one dimension in one visual field, there are many problems connected with such a muscular training. In reading, only the right visual field is dominantly involved and this means that almost all the visual information is fed into the left occipital lobe from which it is probably internally transferred in its mirror image to the right occipital lobe. In visuo-spatial people with hemispheres having an equality of dominance, it is very likely that these transferred mirror images (letters) in the right visual field can be fed *out* when writing or even when reading almost as easily as the correct one in the left visual cortex (Bannatyne and Wichiarajote, 1969b). As both are almost equally associated with a particular sound, either one can be fed out in response to that sound. The mixup is increased when the mirror image of the one letter is also the primary image of yet another letter-sound combination. Therefore, the visual letters *b* and *d* and the phonemes for *b* and *d* become a four-way tangle (see Chapter VI; Orton, 1937; Kettlewell, 1964).

In short, mirror imaging and the poor lateralization of eye movements in one dimension are probably caused by a competent spatial ability which itself results from a relatively "superior" development of the visual and possibly the motor cortexes, in contrast with a relatively inferior development of the auditory areas. Good visuo-spatial ability demands an equality of hemispheric dominance, even though, as has been pointed out previously, there seems to be some kind of control center in the right hemisphere; however, such a requirement often causes inferior auditory-language functioning, the brain being poorly lateralized for verbal purposes. This latter statement is based on the fact that younger children, with presumably less well lateralized verbal brains, tend to produce mirror images (and a variety of rotations) more often than do older children (Benton, 1958; Wechsler and Hagin, 1964). That younger children produce more mirror images than do older children is well documented (Newson, 1955).

Another mirror-image factor which may add to a genetic dyslexic's reading and writing problems is that automatization of the alphabet in spelling requires specific letter exceptions to the law of object constancy which operates in the wider environment. Thus, a *table* as an object is a *table* from any angle but a *b* is not a *b* from any angle—it becomes a *d* or a *p* or a *q*. Thus, directional-configuration constancy must take the place of form constancy for some letters, particularly those which have a changed denotation with a change in direction or orientation; e.g., *d, p, b, q* (Money, 1966b).

However, this directional-configuration inconstancy shown by genetic dyslexics does not explain why they hardly ever seem to reverse other letters such as *c, f, k* and *r*. Many small children will reverse *S, Z, N, h, m, n* and *u*. Most other letters of the alphabet are not symmetrical and hence are irreversible. It is as if some letters have an unambiguous configuration constancy which renders them less susceptible to being reversed. Newson (1955) in her research summary on the development of line-figure discrimination in preschool children suggests, "This disability is particularly pronounced when the line figures concerned fall into a certain category as to symmetry, viz: that category which includes the letters "S," "N" and "Z." Other characteristics of the figures (such as length/breadth ratio, meaningfulness, etc.) appear to have no affect on the operation of this disability." Newson found that training significantly decreased the number of mirror images and that the "disability" derived from a lack of experience in the practice of the directional discrimination of troublesome letters. A similar straightforward training will help genetic dyslexic children, many of whom will outgrow mirror imaging or at the least show a decrease in its frequency of occurrence with age.

In the recent research already described (Bannatyne and Wichiarajote, 1969a), a significant negative correlation ($r = -0.30$ at the 0.05 level of confidence) was found between choosing a symmetrical version of an original stimulus figure in a multiple-choice visuo-spatial memory-for-designs test and sound blending on the revised ITPA. In other words, the more able a child was to sound-blend, the less likely he was to choose the (incorrect) symmetrical version of the original stimulus design. In a roundabout way, this tends to confirm Newson's conclusion that "there is some evidence . . . for a positive relationship between ability in discrimination of the mirror image and previous experience in writing." Obviously, children who have had previous experience in writing will also have had previous experience in reading and sound blending. Newson's findings for five-year-old children in no way suggest that the persistence of a mirror imaging or reversal deficit in a few dyslexic children is caused by a lack of training, even though this may be a contributory factor.

Implications of First-Grade Screening

There is little doubt that suitable screening and training procedures for dyslexic children during the first months of first grade would eliminate the need to remediate nine out of ten dyslexic children in later grades. Not only is the remediation of dyslexic children expensive, but very often a great deal of unlearning of incorrect knowledge and habits has to be effected, frequently a tedious procedure for all concerned. Mirror imaging may be one of several valuable diagnostic indicators in kindergarten or at the beginning of first grade which may be used in a screening battery for the detection of dyslexic children; all kinds of dyslexic children may mirror-image letters but I suspect that genetic dyslexics do so more than most.

At the opposite extreme, in terms of age, is Leonardo da Vinci who wrote all his diaries in mirror writing. He was left-handed and unable to learn Latin competently despite years of effort. Yet his spatial genius was only matched by his supreme dexterity and unparalleled creativity.

CODING DEFICIT GENETIC DYSLEXIA: A NEW HYPOTHESIS ABOUT A POSSIBLE SECOND TYPE (CLUSTER) OF GENETIC DYSLEXIA

Over years of assessing learning disability children of all kinds I have gradually been becoming more aware of a second group of children in whom the characteristics may be both genetic and "normal" in the sense that they may run in families and be one end of a normal continuum of ability or lack of it in the population as a whole. Again the condition seems to occur much more often in boys than in girls, and it is also a dysfunction of automatized fluency which has poor memory as a basis (probably having as its formal cause a maturational lag). The memory deficit in question undermines the ability of these children to *code rapidly* on the WISC coding subtest, and quite often their block design score is also low. Yet I have found none of the conventional signs of neurological dysfunction (brain impairment) in these students. Their representational drawing ability is frequently poor to mediocre and their memory for designs is usually only fair at best.

Very tentatively, I have suggested that this coding disability (which I have found to run in two families) is an inherited dysfunction of visuo-spatial *praxic memory* which renders the child or adult both slow and inaccurate in coding speed tests. Such children not only find it difficult to learn to read but their handwriting is very irregular and their spelling is bizarre until they learn to read and spell out of their acquisition of code breaking through training in phonics. Then (unlike the spatially competent genetic dyslexic) their spelling improves rapidly.

GENETIC DYSLEXIA, MATURATIONAL LAG AND SECONDARY EMOTIONAL PROBLEMS

Toward the end of Chapter VII, maturational lag, a hypothesis put forward by Bender (1963) as a contributing formal cause to reading disabilities, was discussed at some length. Some dyslexic boys exhibit signs of maturational lag which (in some respects) are similar to those described by Bender (1963) and de Hirsch (1965). I have classified these particular children as genetic dyslexics because in spite of a slow maturation in speech, handedness and language generally, they are quite competent visuospatially, and from the motor-kinesthetic aspect they function relatively normally even though they may be a little clumsy and slow. Yet there remains an overall "plasticity" of physique, personality and, above all, cognitive processing, somewhat difficult to define. These observations now require some clarification and further objective support.

It is important to realize that neurological dysfunction resulting from brain impairment, biochemical imbalance or some genetic *abnormality* can also be associated with a maturational lag. The two types of maturational lag then have different efficient causes but have many characteristics in common. A differential diagnosis between the two calls for considerable experience, skill and training on the part of the examiner.

Children with coding deficit genetic dyslexia also have a maturational lag which is genetically determined (a hypothesis at this point in time), but the deficit seems to be more in the area of praxic abilities than in the auditory/vocal language areas of the more frequently encountered type of genetic dyslexia. A poor memory within the respective sensorimotor modalities seems to be the cognitive material cause of each type.

Sex Differences in Maturation

In a convention paper given by Schiffman (1965), he quoted Nelson (1959) on the onset of skeletal ossification for males and females. For seven bones mentioned, the girls were at least a year ahead of the boys and sometimes much more. I have been told there is evidence—but I have no reference—that the onset of myelination of nerve fibers occurs earlier in girls than in boys. It is also known that girls develop many verbal functions earlier than boys and frequently at an early age (Maccoby, 1966).

As a part of the author's research project, reported earlier in the chapter, t-tests were run between boys and girls on the balance tests. It was found that there was a significant difference between boys and girls in their ability to balance on their toes with their eyes closed. It is difficult to attribute this entirely to environmental learning, particularly as the girls were far superior to the boys. Bentzen (1966) has posed the possibility "that a causal relationship exists between the uneven sex distribution in pathologic conditions and both the biophysical vulnerability of the male organism and the fact that males generally mature at a slower rate than females of the same chronological age, for which there is considerable evidence." Bentzen refers to Burke (1898), Espschage (1940), Greulich (1955) and Bayley and Jones (1955) in support of her hypothesis, one with which I would concur. She summarizes by saying,

It appears from live-birth records that, although approximately the same number of male infants as females are born, the male infant is biologically more vulnerable to the impact of stress than is the female. It can also be concluded that, among school-age children, boys tend to be biophysically less mature than girls of the same chronological age, and that, finally, sex ratios reported in studies of a wide range of learning and behavior disorders include a significantly higher proportion of males than females.

Therefore, we can conclude that there is a considerable amount of evidence that maturationally boys lag behind girls and since the characteristic is almost certainly normally distributed, some boys will lag more than others. Maturational lag is genetically determined as it is primarily physiological in its basis, e.g., bone ossification. It is suggested that genetic dyslexic children have a maturational lag (that is, an overall *slower* development) as one formal cause of their slowness in learning to read. Moreover, it would seem that a maturational lag with its effect on neurological plasticity of functioning may also boost creativity, especially of a visuo-spatial kind.

Neurological Plasticity and Creativity

Along with all the cognitive and behavioral disorders, which seem to occur in males far more frequently than females, on the other side of the coin in the wider fields of achievement it seems that males are far more creative and productive than females. Sears and Feldman (1966) state that artistic production is not expected of boys. In such circumstances, it seems strange that the number of women artists and sculptors who achieve fame is very limited, especially when compared with the women who attain distinction in the field of letters. This suggests the hypothesis that at least in visuo-spatial activities the male brain with its maturational lag may be not only more plastic (or neurologically immature), but as a result also more creative and flexible and that this in turn may be caused by a less indelible memory apparatus. It is interesting that Drake and Schnall (1966) found that a group of dyslexic boys were able to make more designs out of colored toothpicks than were an equivalent group of competent readers. If the recording of auditory stimuli and, in particular, language requires a reasonably indelible memorizing system, it is not too speculative to suggest that this may inhibit the kind of free-ranging, unusual associations that may be required for creativity, particularly in the visuo-spatial aspects of life.

In the auditory areas, and throughout the brain, the genetic dyslexic seems to have a greater plasticity or flexibility of functioning with its implications for less psychoneurological structuring and a poorer memory system. This inherited plasticity is in contrast with a dominant, highly structured auditory functioning with its implications for an excellent rote memory, a good sense of rhythm and superior processing of sequences of sounds and even musical notes. On the other hand, plasticity may lead to a fluidity of reasoning and a more original "creative" processing of experiential data. It appears then that genetic dyslexia is an end result of a particular pattern of neurological inheritance which happens to be reasonably good in certain visual aspects and rather poor in the above auditory characteristics. Quite a large number of normal genes must be involved in the inheritance of a pattern of this sort. The material cause of neurological plasticity would probably be some biochemical facilitation at the synapse, less myelination or some other such state.

Secondary Emotional Problems, Plasticity and Maturational Lag

Brendtro (1965) in his study of affectionless boys came to the following conclusion:

> A significantly greater proportion of affectionless than control subjects manifested school learning disabilities. There was suggestion that the verbal impairments of affectionless subjects were counterbalanced by increased facility in certain non-verbal areas. This is supported by the significantly better performance of affectionless than comparison subjects on the WISC picture completion sub-tests. This study indicates that affectionless subjects are generally impaired in verbal intelligence, vocabulary, and time conceptualization and tend to display learning disabilities. These verbal impairments are quite pronounced in a few affectionless subjects, but among others are only slight.

Elsewhere in his summary, Brendtro uses the term *psychopathic personality disorder* to describe the boys in the experimental sample, the entire sample being composed of boys. He suggests that remedial reading programs might serve to help these boys. The similarity of the educational and cognitive profile of these children to that described in this chapter with respect to genetic dyslexic boys is striking. Not all of Brendtro's experimental groups had learning disabilities and it is not even remotely suggested here that the psychopathic personality and the genetic dyslexic developmental pattern are intrinsically linked. On the contrary, I agree with Brendtro's findings that a large majority of the affectionless subjects had distorted child-mother relationships. The most common is characterized by a lack of parental affection accompanied by neglect, physical brutality or the condoning of the boys' negative behavior. However, the reading disabilities of these boys can be accounted for in several ways which are not mutually exclusive. First, because of their emotional disturbance, the boys have obviously not profited from academic instruction; second, those with neglectful and angry mothers can, in all probability, be included in the primary emotional communicative dyslexic group, and third, because they have competent spatial ability and poor sequencing ability, it is quite possible that a proportion of them have been born into families with a tendency to genetic dyslexia.

A rather speculative hypothesis which I wish to put forward is that genetic dyslexic boys have a greater vulnerability and are more susceptible to emotional disturbance than are verbally competent children. The hypothesis in detail would run roughly as follows: Almost all girls (and they have a superior verbal functioning in language skills), when compared with boys, are less delinquent, commit fewer crimes and appear to be less extreme in almost every aspect of emotional disorders (Bentzen, 1966). This could be attributed to their less plastic, more rigid mode of psychological functioning which, in its turn, would have as its material cause faster rates of biophysical maturation. The neurological indelibility and rigidity of language functioning is reflected in the superior verbal fluency and spelling ability of the female, both of which are strongly inherited (Vandenberg, 1966). Many males also having these qualities would also tend to be less susceptible to extreme emotional conduct and personality disorders of a nonpsychotic type. Such people tend to be socially conforming even in rebellion. By contrast, the slower maturing, more *plastic,* less verbal, less rigid, more emotionally unstable (male) person is particularly vulnerable because he has greater difficulty in absorbing conventions of any kind, whether they are linguistic or social. Such a mind will be more attuned to the three-dimensional logic of the physical world with its absolute laws and principles rather than to the conventional rules and regulations which are arbitrarily set up and which have to be indelibly memorized in the interest of social and tribal survival. (Obsessionally tendencies in this context would be indicative of instability, not rigidity.)

Although genetic dyslexic boys may have an increased susceptibility to emotional disturbance and even delinquency, many of them do not. However, in almost every case, they certainly develop an inferiority feeling and a poor self-concept with respect to their scholastic achievements. This poor self-concept can cause a great deal of trouble in the regular school, particularly if the educational program is a very inactive sedentary, auditory one. Genetic dyslexic boys require a very active program which employs visuo-spatial *aids* even in reading and other language lessons. Of course, these language lessons have to be auditory/vocal and phonically oriented in content and structure.

POSSIBLE MATERIAL CAUSES OF GENETIC DYSLEXIA

While the original or efficient cause of genetic dyslexia is (almost certainly) a polygenic inheritance, while the formal (pattern) or developmental cause is almost certainly a maturational lag involving various kinds of memory (the cognitive material causes) and while the final cause is a law of the land which has demanded universal literacy in very recent times, the neurophysiological material cause is very possibly a *biochemical imbalance,* a factor which has been stressed by Drake (1966b). Note that this biochemical imbalance does not necessarily imply some strange abnormality in the children concerned, nor should these children be confused with other types of dyslexic children including those with neurological dysfunction which results from lesions of the brain. Drake comments that these children who may have a biochemical imbalance are both hyperactive and hypoactive (daydreamers) at different times of the day and that Dexedrine® has been found useful in mitigating the condition.

McGlannan (1970) and her co-workers have been investigating glucose levels in the blood and a family history of diabetes. She has had success putting children on a protein-rich snack diet morning and afternoon. She also notes that many dyslexics seem to have red or red-blond hair and freckles. One is again reminded of the statement by Richardson (1966), who said,

> Secondly, it must be remembered that many of these disorders can occur in generation after generation of apparently normal children. For example, slow speech development and specific difficulties in reading and writing often associated with ambidexterity or poor lateralization of handedness are relatively common in the families of Campbell and Maclean in Scotland. Are we then to assume that all Campbells and Macleans have brain abnormalities?

THE WIDER IMPLICATIONS OF SPATIAL ABILITY FOR EDUCATION

It would appear from the work and research reviews of P.E. Vernon (1961) and I.M. Smith (1964) and the data on genetic dyslexic children reviewed in this chapter that large numbers of boys have intellectual abilities of a visuo-spatial nature which are not being recognized, allowed for or trained in the orthodox school curriculum. In particular, elementary and junior schools, which are largely staffed by women teachers, tend to be highly verbal and sedentary. The emphasis in the curriculum is on a linguistic rather than a visuo-spatial education. This overemphasis on passive, verbal subject matter frequently achieves exactly the opposite of its intended objective by turning every boy with a slight tendency to genetic dyslexia into a reading disability case (although not necessarily a complete nonreader) who underachieves throughout his school life. If the school curriculum were balanced, with more activities in language subjects, more aids, more apparatus and, above all, an increase in nonverbal subjects, the lot of the visuo-spatial child would be much happier. For example, I know of no program in constructional activities which runs through the junior and senior schools. Montessori activities stop at the end of nursery school or kindergarten and are not taken up again until the student enters the engineering college, or school of architecture at a university. There is a real need for someone to program constructional activities and related subjects as a part of the school curriculum rather than leaving both boys and girls to acquire what little knowledge they have from a few childish constructional toys.

SUMMARY OF SYMPTOM VARIABLES PRESENTED BY GENETIC DYSLEXIC CHILDREN

The following list is a summary of the symptoms presented by genetic dyslexic children. No one of these symptoms is absolutely essential to the occurrence of genetic dyslexia, but a reasonably high percentage of them should be present if a sound differential diagnosis is to be made. Of course, some of the characteristics also occur in other types of dyslexia and therefore an extensive analysis of many test results and other variables is diagnostically essential (see Chapter XIV). These symptoms, and even the types of dyslexia themselves, are usually not mutually exclusive. It should be remembered that compounded or multiple disabilities are not infrequent, and their intensity may range from mild to strong. The numbers refer to the schematic diagram of the brain in Figure 14:

1. The auditory discrimination of vowels is often poor in genetic dyslexic children, usually far more so than discrimination of consonants.

2. Genetic dyslexic children have inadequate auditory phoneme/grapheme sequencing memory, both independently as paired units, and when these auditory and visual symbols have to be matched in word processing during reading, spelling or writing.

3. Sound blending when reading, and auditory closure when listening, are rather poor. Genetic dyslexic children

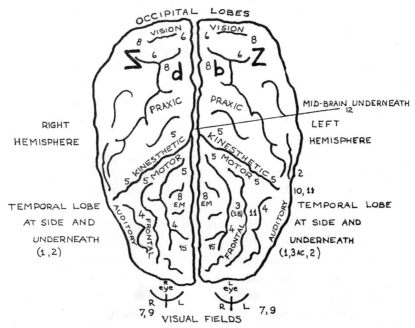

FIGURE 14. The characteristics of the genetic dyslexic child. This is a schematic diagram without depth and is not intended to be an exact indicator of the neurological areas involved.

do not seem to make as much use of past experience in these areas as do their more linguistically normal peers.

4. Genetic dyslexic children often have mildly deficient speech development, and speech feedback (both internally and externally) may be inadequate. These conditions usually begin at birth or shortly after and tend to persist into late childhood if not adulthood. Even so, a number of these children have an apparently normal speech development as reported by parents.

5. Genetic dyslexics suffer from a maturational lag in many language functions. It is as if the usual maturational lag in males, both biophysical and neurological, is exaggerated in genetic dyslexic boys. This would also account for *slight* physical clumsiness in these boys in *some* cases. This lag

decreases with age and the boys may become very co-ordinated and competent when older.

6. Genetic dyslexics seem reasonably efficient in their visuo-spatial ability, congnitively speaking, relative to their overall intellectual ability. However, motor performance (e.g., drawing designs) must not form part of the assessment of this visuo-spatial right hemisphere capacity because it will confuse two often contradictory variables.

7. Genetic dyslexics learning to read tend to have difficulty in lateralizing their gaze in one dimension and even read slowly once that skill is established. They prefer scanning the environment in three dimensions.

8. Genetic dyslexic children tend to mirror-image letters when reading and writing. It is probable that this may partially stem from an equality of hemispheric visuo-spatial functioning in the brain, the mirror images being the result of right hemisphere activity; it may *also* occur as a result of right-left scanning eye movements during the reading process. The latter condition may also cause two-letter reversals in spelling.

9. This mirror imaging of letters in reading and writing may *also* result from directional-configuration inconstancy which contravenes the law of object constancy. These three causes of mirror imaging are *not* alternatives; they are three compatible aspects of a single efficient cause, namely a right hemisphere visuo-spatial brain "set."

10. Genetic dyslexic children may have difficulty in associating *verbal labels* to directional *concepts* but have *no* visuo-spatial disorientation of any kind in terms of the environment. In other words, they are fully cognizant of true direction in actual space but may not know the linguistic labels for those directions such as *right-left, east-west,* etc.

11. Genetic dyslexic children tend to have a residual spelling disability even after they have been taught to read with fluency. This residual spelling difficulty may be extremely difficult to remediate. Articulatory/vocal-blending

training in spelling sequencing is recommended (Bannatyne and Wichiarajote, 1969a).

12. Provided that they have average or above-average intelligence, genetic dyslexic children usually have little difficulty in comprehending spoken language when listening intently. However, a lack of interest in auditory stimuli and distracting visuo-spatial and auditory events in the environment may seem to impair comprehension.

13. Genetic dyslexics are vulnerable to secondary emotional disorders for a variety of reasons. A likely one is the neurological consequences (in terms of memory and communication) of their own maturational lag. In particular, a poor self-concept tends to develop, and such motivational techniques as M-reinforcers and high-interest techniques can help change the self-concept into one of self-respect (see Chapter XIII).

14. The fathers of genetic dyslexics are rarely in highly verbal occupations in terms of subject matter; more usually they are in spatial occupations.

15. The ability of genetic dyslexics to organize words and plan syntax in sentences may be somewhat inefficient.

The characteristics of coding deficit genetic dyslexic children are as follows (the list is to be regarded as a hypothesis):

1. These children have a marked deficit in their ability to code on the WISC coding subtest.

2. They have only a limited ability to draw representationally.

3. In memory-for-designs tests their performance is below average.

4. Their auditory/vocal and overall verbal ability is usually average or slightly above average compared with their total score.

5. The other males in the family may have similar deficits.

6. Three-dimensional constructional ability using blocks is poor, particularly if the constructions have to be built from a memorized model made by the examiner.

7. In younger children (kindergarten, first and second grades), handwriting and spelling are particularly inept but these improve rapidly when code-breaking techniques of reading are taught.

Case Histories of Genetic Dyslexia

Two case histories of genetic dyslexia are presented, each from a different point of view. The first case gives an overall picture which includes a description of both the test data and the tuition. The second case emphasizes the course which tuition took and the type of problem presented to the teacher. A third case of possible coding deficit genetic dyslexia is also presented.

Michael (Diagnosis: Genetic Dyslexia)

Chronological Age: 14 years, 2 months

WISC Scores:

Verbal IQ	108
Performance Scale IQ	125
Full Scale IQ	117

Scaled Scores:

Information	11	Picture Completion	18(SpA)
Comprehension	11(CA)	Picture Arrangement	12(SeA)
Arithmetic	11	Block Design	16(SpA)
Similarities	13(CA)	Object Assembly	14(SpA)
Vocabulary	10(CA)	Coding	8(SeA)
Digit Span	8(SeA)		

Spatial Ability (Total, SpA): 48

Verbal Conceptualizing Ability (Total, CA): 34

Sequencing Ability (Total SeA): 28

Previous Tests, 1964

Chronological Age: 13 years, 10 months	*Arithmetic Age:* 10 years, 6 months

Reading Age		*Spelling Age*
Sep. 64—6 years, 10 months		7 years, 0 months
Sep. 65—7 years, 6 months		7 years, 6 months
Dec. 65—8 years, 0 months		8 years, 6 months
Mar. 66—9 years, 0 months		9 years, 0 months
Jul. 66—9 years, 10 months		9 years, 0 months
Mar. 67—		9 years, 7 months

Neale Test:

Sep. 1964—Speed:	7 years, 6 months	Jun. 1966—	7 years, 6 months
Accuracy:	7 years, 9 months		8 years, 5 months
Comprehension:	9 years, 6 months		9 years, 3 months

Initial Tester's Comments: Michael was described as very hesitant and partially slow. Unsure even when right. Seemed depressed.

Report from School: Described Michael as an intelligent boy of many interests. Very friendly and reliable. In a special backward group of fifteen.

Psychological Report: Sounds not known: *b, q, g*. Does not always link word with meaning. Reverses *b* and *d*. Confuses *b* and *p*, *r* and *t*. No spatial difficulties. Blending and sequencing difficulties. No signs of any neurological dysfunction.

ITPA, Oct. 1965—Chronological Age: 14 years, 6 months.
Above norms for all items except:

Auditory/Vocal Sequencing (Digit Span): 6 years, 3 months
Visual-Motor Association: 8 years, 3 months
Vocal Encoding: 8 years, 11 months

Templin—Auditory Discrimination Test: 6 errors.
Monroe—Auditory Discrimination Test: 2 errors.

Home: Two younger sisters. Hard-working family with good standards. Basically emotionally secure. Father likes anything mechanical. He works as a salesman selling farm machinery and equipment. Mother had reading and spelling difficulties and a slight lisp. Not worried over Michael's difficulties, but anxious for them to be overcome so that he can train for a career.

Infancy: Normal milestones except for speech. Left-handed.

Walked unaided at fourteen months. Dressed himself at three years. Told the time at ten years. No severe illnesses in infancy. Later measles and mumps. Is color-blind. Talked late. Had difficulty in pronunciation. Speech clear at 4½ years.

Michael was always timid and nervous; afraid of the dark and wanted company. Used to wet bed if emotionally upset.

Had intensive coaching at school and home for reading disabilities.

Interests: Scouting, boating, fishing, model making, swimming, shooting. Likes to tinker with farm machinery.

TUITION

High-Interest Project: "The River." Michael drew an accurate chart-map of the river in considerable detail. This was used as the basis of his written work; over 2½ years, this has developed into hobbies and interests, wildlife on the farm, scout badges, etc. His interest never flags and he has learned many words through this.

Sep. 1964: Michael learned words as a whole through the Fernald technique. Was not found to learn a word by just looking at it, but by writing, looking and saying. Very great spelling difficulty. His enthusiasm for life and work carries him along. Seems to be learning through phonetic help.

Nov. 1965: Systematic phonics approach used. Rules help Michael to spell. He has great difficulty in blending letters even when he knows them individually. Some errors—read *fell* as *fl;* wrote *pr* for *dr, belog* for *belong; groing* for *growing; olddest* for *oldest; sug* for *sung; unbrocen* for *unbroken; sboil* for *spoil; sgin* for *skin.* Much over-learning needed for spelling. Stott sentence cards used as an aid to speeding eye movements. Edith Norrie letters used for building words. Phonic fluency now excellent for speeding blending.

Science: Michael says that at school he knew all the answers in his science exam but he could not spell a word.

Sep. 1966: Michael makes notes at home, brings them, learns his errors. Types out his work correctly himself, often spelling aloud as he types. Rules are inserted as they arise naturally or else an opportunity is created to teach one.

Jan. 1967: Intellectual approach gradually being introduced. Prefixes, suffixes, roots, games with suited meanings. Spelling book being screened slowly—twenty words every two weeks. Michael's reading is speeding up now as is his sounding out of letters (ten-year level). Have often had to chase him along lines with a piece of paper to make him look ahead and not hang on to words he has read or regress.

Audiometric Test: No deficiency. Michael often omits *n* and *s* when spelling.

Brick Wall Game (Stott): Seven minutes allowed. In Dec. 1965, twenty-one words built—gradual progression and speed with this. In Mar. 1966, fifty-three words built.

Present Great Spelling Difficulty: To remember when to use *tch, dge, ck.* Confuses the rule. Michael will leave school in July, 1967. Hopes to be apprenticed.

Paul (Diagnosis: Genetic Dyslexia)

Chronological Age: 12 years, 6 months

Background: Paul was a "normal" baby, brought up in a comfortable middle-class home. His speech may have been late and he was a little clumsy, but otherwise his parents do not recall any signs of retardation in infancy.

He was a happy boy during his first two years at school, despite his lack of progress in reading and writing. In his third year, however, he was ignored by the Head, who ridiculed him and accused him of laziness. No longer happy, Paul would not join in any games unless he was the leader. He started taking home small articles belonging to other children.

His parents referred him for psychotherapy. It was revealed that he had a Verbal IQ of 104 and a Performance IQ of 145 (WISC). This failure in reading and writing was attributed to frustration and lack of confidence. For several years, he was given both psychotherapy and orthodox remedial reading lessons, with no improvement resulting.

Admission: At the age of 12½ years, Paul was diagnosed as suffering from genetic dyslexia and accepted for tuition. It was revealed that there was a family history of difficulties relating to reading and spelling. It was realized that, because of the severe nature of Paul's dyslexia and his secondary emotional difficulties, he would be extremely difficult to teach. He was now at a new school, and the Principal was most cooperative.

Tuition: When tuition started, Paul had a reading age of 9 years and a spelling age of 7 years. Here is an example of his work at that time:

> Sudnley I sore a figr. In the darcknes, I faid. A hoge monster, I noow may anchort histrey wayl. I thort it was a Bronlesarus-meges, a very pqler monster in dead. It past mey and weny fethr in the kave. I qikley idvonst in the kave I ran. And I flall, I had faln over a karks of a foage gopponckr-aramus. It was a vedgabl eater. I fobld along. Sudnley I sor a prmitif man. He soor mey and fang a sper it gust sist my. I ran and ran I was on to the moor I fell. I must have nocket myself out, bucks wen I wock I was in bead. I tould my mother and father, but they gust larft. That night I lacked out ve my wino, I sore a hoag shape lack a monster.

It can be seen from this that Paul was *trying* to spell the words, but that he had little understanding of the conventional composition of words. He was completely lacking in confidence and initiative, but he *wanted* to improve and was cooperative and conscientious during lessons.

During his first year, Paul was taken right back to the beginning. He was taught that a word is not a meaningless jumble of syllables, but a collection or sequence of *sounds* represented by visual symbols. He learned the sounds of letters, and digraphs, and how a word was built up from them. He began to *listen* to words and to *understand* them. He gained confidence in his ability to apply his knowledge to new words, his ability to *read* the sounds in a word, instead of being expected to remember, by sight, a meaningless jumble of unrelated symbols. He was trained in auditory discrimination and sequencing, and realized that by *listening* and analyzing, he could get these sounds in the right order. Rhythm and accentuation was used to help him grasp syllabification. By the end of the year, he had improved his reading, mostly through coping with a large diversity of phonic written work. As recognition is easier than unprompted recall, quite typically his spelling had not improved so rapidly. This became the target for Paul's second year at the Center.

Fortunately, at the beginning of this year, Paul had the advantage of knowing he had done well in his other school subjects during the previous year. His confidence increased, and very soon he could read and comprehend adult material. He now had only the usual residual spelling problem. His main difficulty here was "unlearning." Being a conscientious and very intelligent boy, he had for many years produced written work containing many wrong but consistent spellings. His task now was to realize firstly which words were incorrect, and secondly how to put them right. In this, he was handicapped by poor retention and a lack of sequencing recall. The task again was going to be difficult. He learned, and applied, spelling rules. Most of his lessons were spent *writing;* constant practice was essential to make the application of all he learned automatic. Sometimes he checked all spellings before he wrote them. At other times, he would bring a composition completed at home, find as many of his own mistakes as possible, and analyze them. Then he would do the same with mistakes found by the reader that he had missed, until he understood why a word was incorrect, and until he had the necessary knowledge to put it right. He made several years' progress in his spelling, but is even now still below average.

A specimen of his later work reads as follows:

It was a cold windy night. The wind was ice cold and it had blown a thonder cloud over the Downs. It was a night to be in frunt of a blasing fire. But meny people had ventured out to the fair in spite of the wind and the forecast of torrential rain. Hundreds of people had come to the first day of the fair. Meny people were on rides or on the amusements, the shooting gallery, the coconut shies or the hoop-la stalls. A strong smell of onions and hamburges floated round the fair. All was going well until it started to rain.

His main improvement over his two years' tuition was in attitude. All his written work now shows interest and initiative, his style is much improved and his syntax is now quite good.

Conclusions: Paul is leaving the Center so that he can gain full benefit from his last compulsory year at school. He intends to stay on after fifteen, and would then like to train either as a draftsman or in electronics. He seems a much happier boy and is now an active Boy Scout. During his holidays he "caddies" at the local golf course. Paul is extremely kind and generous. He is interested in his future, and now has confidence in his ability to cope with reading and to help himself continue improving his spelling. With the cooperation he gets at school, he is sure to progress steadily.

The way Paul has overcome his extreme difficulties shows great strength of character; it was hard work, but he persevered. Had his dyslexia been diagnosed earlier the task would have been considerably lightened. It is probable he would not have experienced any emotional difficulties, and with his superior spatial intelligence, he should by now have been in a high school on his way to the university. As it is, he will now probably have to content himself with being a technician, instead of being a professional person in a spatial occupation.

Malcolm (Diagnosis: Possible Coding Deficit Genetic Dyslexia)

Chronological Age at Initial Assessment: 7 years, 0 months (grade 2)

TEST SCORES

WISC Scores:

Verbal IQ	115
Performance Scale IQ	100
Full Scale IQ	109

Scaled Scores:

Information	15	Picture Completion	16
Comprehension	11	Picture Arrangement	8
Arithmetic	10	Block Design	9
Similarities	15	Object Assembly	13
Vocabulary	11	Coding (checked twice)	4
Digit Span	9		

Spatial Ability (16 + 9 + 13): 38
Verbal Conceptualizing Ability (11 + 15 + 11): 37
Sequencing Ability (9 + 8 + 4): 21
Acquired Knowledge (15 + 10 + 11): 36

(Note poor block design, coding and sequencing skills.)

PERC Auditory Discrimination Test: 3 incorrect out of 60 (normal)

Memory-for-Designs (Graham-Kendall): 9 incorrect out of 15 (poor)

Simultaneous Writing:

Left-hand mirrored numerals: 4 out of 11

Right-hand mirrored numerals: 7 out of 11

(Note: It is very unusual for this result to happen.)

Draw-Your-Family: Very immature drawing of stick figures.

ITPA: Low scores in Verbal Expression, Visual Closure, Auditory Sequential Memory and Visual Sequential Memory

(Note: Auditory Closure and Sound Blending were not administered.)

Birth history and pregnancy: These were by no means clear of mild trauma, but no more so than for most children. He was a good baby, very active and alert, with rapid motor development and average speech development. Had ear infections, tonsillitis and chicken pox, but no abnormal fevers. Brother has handwriting problems and was poor at arithmetic but eventually scored in top 5 percent in College Board Examinations; very high verbally.

Malcolm is painfully slow in all his skill subjects but given time he scores well.

Pre- and Post-Academic Test Scores (note that tuition was still in progress at the time of the second testing): The Psycholinguistic Color System Reading, Writing, Spelling and Language Program plus the Miami Linguistic Readers were the main method of tuition.

	Pre-Academic (November)	Post-Academic (May)
WRAT:		
Reading grade	1.3	2.3
Spelling grade	1.1	2.2
Arithmetic grade	1.8	3.9
Neale Test:		
Rate of Reading	Did not score	6 years, 10 months
Accuracy	Did not score	7 years, 5 months
Comprehension	Did not score	8 years, 5 months

The above results are set down here in the hope that they will stimulate other clinicians and research workers to look for other similar cases, particularly where there are two or more members of the family with like problems. In the above case the WAIS given to the elder brother had a similar configuration of scores to that of Malcolm. It should be noted that Malcolm was trained in the logic of mathematics using the Cuisenaire rods.

Chapter X

MINIMAL NEUROLOGICAL DYSFUNCTION DYSLEXIA (MND)

INTRODUCTION AND DEFINITION

If authorities have some continuing difficulty agreeing as to a satisfactory definition of learning disabilities, the same situation does not hold when it comes to a definition of minimal neurological dysfunction, or minimal brain dysfunction as it is more often called. The U.S. Department of Health, Education and Welfare published in 1966 a definitive document on the terminology and identification of minimal brain dysfunction in children (Clements, 1966). The project director of this operation, S. D. Clements, has elsewhere elaborated on the definition given in the above-mentioned monograph (Clements 1967):

> Minimal brain dysfunction as a diagnostic and descriptive category, refers to children of near average, average, or above average intellectual capacity and potential with learning and/or certain behavior abnormalities ranging from mild to severe, which are associated with subtle deviant functioning of the central nervous system. These may be characterized by various combinations of deficits in perception, conceptualization, language, memory, and control of attention, impulse, or motor function. These individual differences may arise from genetic variations, bio-chemical irregularities, perinatal brain insults, and/or illnesses or injuries sustained during the years critical for the development and maturation of the central nervous system or from other organic causes as yet unknown. During the school years, a variety of special and often specific learning disabilities is the most prominent manifestation of these conditions. The early recognition and adequate evaluation of such children is imperative because they require special forms of management and education if they are to develop to their fullest potential.

This is a broad definition but I would add one or two provisos. First, educationally mentally handicapped children can suffer from brain dysfunction. Second, although it may be semantic quibbling,

413

I prefer the wider term *neurological dysfunction,* which refers to the nervous system as a whole rather than to that part of it arbitrarily defined as the brain. Another point to be made is that the word *minimal* means what is says (not major) and qualifies the term *dysfuction,* not the word *neurological.* The latter word is an adjective but *brain* is not, hence causing confusion. The phrase *minimal neurological dysfunction* does *not* necessarily suggest damage or lesions and the term is *not* synonymous with minimal brain damage or any variation of it. It can include *genetic or biochemical abnormalities.*

The fact that some minimal neurological dysfunctions do have their *major* dysfunction equivalents has been made in the Public Health Service Monograph already mentioned. The author (Clements, 1966) suggests that the impairment of fine movement or coordination may have its major equivalent in the cerebral palsies; subclinical seizures as reflected in EEG abnormalities may have a major equivalent in the epilepsies; deviations in attention activity, level impulse control and affect may have their equivalent in autism and gross disorders of mentation and behavior; intellectual deficits may be the equivalent of major mental subnormalities, and nonperipheral impairment of vision, hearing, haptics and speech may have their equivalents in blindness, deafness and severe aphasias.

In the above definition, Clements uses the term *genetic variations,* a phrase which requires clarification from my own viewpoint. Under the heading of minimal neurological dysfunction (MND), I include only those children whose neurological functioning is *abnormal* in the sense that they are qualitatively dissimilar by reason of, for example, dead cells, malfunctioning cells, an absence of cells, malformed areas, etc., which are *not* found in the mass of the normal population. Certainly, I would agree that there is a fringe area between what could be considered normal in the CNS and what could be considered abnormal. Under the heading of genetic causes of MND, I do not include the genetic dyslexic group described in the previous chapter. Children whose brains are abnormally malformed or damaged for genetic reasons are in the MND category, however. This is rather a subtle distinction, but it is a real one which can be seen more clearly, for example, in height: dwarfism may be caused by abnormal genes but shortness may be a family characteristic. Abnormal genetic causes will be discussed in a little more detail later.

In this chapter, once again there is no suggestion that the peripheral sensory or motor organs and their immediate pathways are not intact; on the contrary, the assumption is that the vocal organs, ears, eyes, motor-kinesthetic-tactile organs and other sensory organs are operating in a clinically normal way. Of course, this may not mean that vision, hearing or muscular control, etc., is functionally normal—if it is not, the implication is that this must stem from some malfunctioning of the CNS and not from the organ itself.

Criticisms of the MND Viewpoint

In a study of minimum cerebral dysfunction, Paine *et al.* (1968) reviewed the literature and carried out a factor analysis on eighty-three children suspected of having a minimal organic cerebral dysfunction of some kind. The factor analysis of historical and neurological data yielded seven factors, symptom complexes or dimensions. The authors found four factors which seemed to have a CNS basis; perceptual deficits, motor incoordination, abnormal EEG and abnormal reflexes. The first two were thought to be the most accurate and important but it should be emphasized that there are four patterns of neurological abnormality, each by definition unrelated to the others. The authors conclude, "Thus, minimal cerebral dysfunction is not a homogeneous diagnostic entity, but rather a way of describing a variety of unrelated minor dysfunctions, some neurological, some behavioral and some cognitive, which could get a child into difficulties with his social and familial environment."

From my own experience with MND children, I would very much agree with the conclusion that minimal cerebral dysfunction is not a "homogeneous diagnostic entity," although I do not consider factor analysis a satisfactory clustering technique for the above purpose, particularly when the factors are "by definition" at right angles and uncorrelated. A factor analysis such as this tends to cluster test variables in terms of the sensory modalities or motor functions they sample. Therefore, it is not surprising that the first factor is essentially a visuo-spatial one and the second factor a motor incoordination one. The use of the term *perceptual* to describe factor 1 is a misnomer as none of the tests involve auditory perception. None of the tables have high loadings on language items, a fact which goes to confirm the impression that the factor analysis has isolated sensory functioning rather than analyzed the data *across modalities* in a search for several syndrome dimensions. No doubt a large number of auditory/vocal verbal tests of a highly specific nature may have yielded another factor of auditory/vocal functioning. Strictly speaking, the factor analysis, by grouping symptoms and characteristics into "homogeneous" clusters, does not prove that MND children are not all roughly alike in terms of the presenting syndrome. The authors have only demonstrated that the syndrome is a complex one with many modality characteristics, but the syndrome itself may be fairly constant, as it is, say, in migraine.

If the term *minimal neurological dysfunction* and its equivalents are accepted as generic terms which cover several, or even many, clusters of variables, we are in the same logical (hierarchical) situation as when any generic term is used, e.g., *virus diseases* or *creative children*—measles are not mumps, and musicians are not sculptors. As has been pointed out in previous chapters, there is a need to use and even devise new computerized, attribute clustering techniques which test the validity of syndromes on a direct empirical basis rather than to use a statistically artificial one such as factor analysis which utilizes preconceived ideas about the structural relationships between clusters and variables.

Neuropsychological Testing

Herbert (1964) has reviewed the literature on the psychological testing of brain damage in children and rightfully comes to the conclusion that they are woefully inadequate. He calls for the ". . . development and application of tests which describe the various psychological deficits resulting from brain-injuries and which have implications for the academic and social training of the child, rather than by evolving diagnostic tests of dubious clinical value." Herbert also suggests that it is essential to bear in mind Wortis' (1957) statement: "There is, in short, no 'brain-injured child,' but only a variety of brain-injured children whose problems are quite varied and whose condition calls for more refined analyses than some of the current generalizations on the brain-injured child provide."

Luria (1966) has shown how valuable highly specific psychological tests can be when they are directed narrowly at one particular modality and sample it in as "pure" a fashion as possible. I have attempted, in developing a visual-spatial recognition memory test, to eliminate both motor functioning and recall from the traditional memory-for-designs test. In this chapter, *visuo-spatial* refers to a nonmotor visual understanding of objects and their relationships in space without the immediate involvement of motor functioning. *Visuo-motor* is the term used for a combined visual and motor functioning. Human neuropsychological functioning is incredibly complex and its intricacies can never be analyzed in detailed neurological, psychological or even behavioral terms if the measuring instruments are not pure, precise and specific.

Neuropsychological examinations in cases of learning disability are valuable in many ways, particularly in the area of differential diagnosis and the writing of prescriptions for remediation. The training of eye lateralization, for example, in cases of CNS-caused muscular tremor, may be very different from the eye-movement training of genetic dyslexic boys. The former may require large-print text, whereas the latter will be helped by a card with a slot in it with which to scan the lines of standard print.

Academic Variables

Because neurological dysfunction may range from a specific impairment to a very generalized one, through an infinite variety of "mosaic patterns" of function and malfunction, the variety of academic disability is equally varied. Certainly, the basic skills and their components in reading, writing, spelling and arithmetic are very often affected in one or more combinations. Since other academic pursuits involve these skills to some degree, they, too, are likely to be impaired; for example, science lessons are well-nigh impossible without some reading, writing and calculation. Additionally, the child's work habits may be affected by untidiness, slowness and disorganization. Many of the academic problems described in other chapters are evidenced by these children.

Prevention

Perhaps the greatest hope for the future arising out of research studies into MND will not be improved diagnosis and remediation, valuable though they may be; it will be prevention. The long-term aim must be to uncover the multiple *etiology* of these CNS dysfunctions in the hope that at least for some of them, a way will be found to prevent the disorder arising in the first place. It is in the interests of encouraging future research in the prevention of neurological dysfunction, by all disciplines, that the following sections are presented.

ETIOLOGY AND TYPES OF CAUSALITY

While neuropsychology may be in its developmental infancy, great advances have been made in the last decade, with the publication of such works as Luria (1966), Mountcastle (1962), John (1967), Penfield and Roberts (1959), Eccles (1966), Hecaen and de Ajuriaguerra (1964) and the series "Developmental Medicine," published by the Spastics Society, London. Innumerable journal publications supplement these. Taken together, this is a considerable body of knowledge which cannot be lightly ignored or set aside—rather it should form the basis of expanded research in our quest for a fuller understanding of neurological impairment and learning disabilities.

The Original Efficient Causes of MND

The term *original causes* applies to those events, situations and conditions which, through some abnormal circumstances, affect or cause material changes in the neurophysiological state of the body including the brain—changes which, in their turn, may become material causes of sensorimotor and behavioral malfunctions. The original efficient causes are listed and discussed in the hope that their mention may help stimulate further investigation with a view to eliminating or reducing their occurrence. While that is the primary purpose, a knowledge of original etiology can also help the diagnostician and remediator, if only by providing a few more relevant pieces of information, background knowledge or experience which may play their part in the total pattern of diagnosis and prescription of remediation. The wider and deeper our experience, the more accurate and beneficial our work will be with, and for, particular MND children.

Prematurity

A significant association between prematurity and oral language performance has been established by de Hirsch *et al.* (1966a). The research showed that in seven of the fifteen areas tested—patterns, language comprehension, word finding, number of words used, mean of the five longest sentences, sentence elaboration and definitions—the premature group's performance was inferior to that of children born at term. It is suggested by the authors that these results come from the premature children's lingering neurophysiological immaturity.

Anoxia

In a comparative study of boys from birth to five years of age, one-half described as asphyxiated at birth and one half nonasphyxiated, Ucko (1965) could find no differences in either the intellectual or general emotional development of the children. It is to be noted that the children had not begun school and so no comment on reading disability was possible. This study did show, however, that the asphyxiated group was significantly distinguished from its nonasphyxiated counterpart by specific "temperamental characteristics," namely, unusual sensitivity, overreactivity and a tendency to disequilibrium when normal routine was broken. As the Stanford-Binet Scale was used to assess intelligence, it would seem to indicate there was little fundamental difference between the two groups (each composed of twenty-nine boys) with respect to language skills development. Commenting on the lack of cognitive impairment in this study, one eminent physician suggested that it is just possible that some anti-anoxia biochemical mechanism may come into operation to prevent damage to the infant's brain during the transfer period from dependence on the placenta until it breathes.

Other Pregnancy and Birth Difficulties

There are now many suspected or known causes of neurological dysfunction which may operate during pregnancy or birth.

Bleeding during pregnancy was found to be a key indicator by Rodin *et al.* (1964) and separately by Paine (1965).

Since the thalidomide problem, other drugs, x-rays and excessive amounts of vitamins, particularly during the first trimester of pregnancy, are suspected of causing major or minor defects in some children. James *et al.* (1967) quote statistics which, although not significant, strongly suggest that these agents may cause defects.

A faulty diet, particularly one too low in proteins, is suspected of having a deleterious effect on the brain and subsequent intelligence. This has been reported by Churchill (1966) as the outcome of a twin study at the Lafayette Clinic, Detroit.

Febrile illnesses (fevers) during pregnancy, particularly in the first trimester, are known to sometimes affect the fetus. Rubella or German measles can certainly cause disorder, and now mumps and chicken pox are also very much suspect. According to White (1966), in a study of one thousand pregnant women he found forty mothers who had mumps and twenty who had chicken pox during pregnancy. Significant abnormality occurred in about 40 percent of the babies of the chicken pox mothers and about 35 percent of those born to the mothers who had had mumps. The main symptoms were impairment of general health, abnormalities of the liver and, in some instances, mental retardation.

Toxemia during pregnancy was found in many of the case

history reports given by parents in a study by Prechtl (1962) of children having choreiform movements.

During the birth process, a long, hard labor of up to, say, forty-eight hours, abnormal presentation, difficult delivery and the child being held back at birth for thirty-five to forty-five minutes are all mentioned by Paine (1965) as causing possible brain insults. The usual result in such cases is anoxia, but Paine stresses that they are merely *potential* causes of damage to the brain, a qualification amply supported by the research by Ucko (1965) referred to above.

Wolff (1967) compared the obstetric histories of one hundred primary school children referred to psychiatric department with one hundred matched controls. No significant differences were found between the groups in maternal age, birth weight, factors suggestive of an abnormal fetus, complications of pregnancy or delivery and the postnatal condition of the child. The author concludes that children who have sustained damage from prematurity or birth constitute only a minority of the children with behavior problems who come forward for psychiatric care.

Abnormal Genetic Factors

In a speech on the genetic bases for intelligence, Reed (1967) suggested that there were at least 114 gene pairs (loci) which could be responsible for some form of mental deficiency. He pointed out that intelligence is a multigenic trait and even a few random genes in the gene pool could cause a wide variation of intelligence. He assumed that intelligence is inherited because it steadily increases as the evolutionary ladder is climbed and the phylogenetic scale matches exactly with degree of intelligence.

Once again, it should be pointed out that genetic dyslexic boys should not be included in the genetically *abnormal* group (see Chapter IX). It is possible for genetic dyslexic children, as well as for children with *abnormal* genes which "prevent" subsequent learning, to form a part of the normal continuous distribution of the population in language skills. Nevertheless, a real and theoretical distinction must be made between the two genetic groups.

I would predict that within a decade or two *abnormal* genetic factors will be found to be one of the *major* causes of neurological dysfunction—probably far more important than pregnancy, birth and neonatal considerations.

Neonatal Complications

These are listed by Paine (1965) as subdural hematoma, cephalhematoma, convulsions and cyanotic spells. They may affect the brain in various direct ways which need not be elaborated here.

Other Original Efficient Causes During Infancy and Childhood

Various diseases such as meningitis, encephalitis, measles, mumps and perhaps others, are sometimes thought to cause MND to a sufficient degree to cause language and possibly other learning disabilities.

Severe head injuries or concussion are always suspect inasmuch as the brain may be damaged by them directly or as a result of cerebral hemorrhage. Lead poisoning from eating paint may cause damage to the nervous system (Schwachman and Kopito, 1968).

There may be other original efficient causes of MND which have not been mentioned above; indeed, the list is by no means intended to be complete, but it will suffice to indicate the tremendous variety of causes of MND and the even greater amount of research and social awareness required to reduce their influence and incidence to an absolute minimum.

Developmental Timing of the Original Cause

It has been pointed out by several authorities in the symposium *Childhood Aphasia* (West *et al.*, 1960), that the date of the onset of a brain injury during babyhood, infancy or childhood is an important factor in the prognosis of cognitive functioning. All other factors being equal, the more functions which have been developed, learned or otherwise established before the onset of impairment, the more chance the child has of eventually functioning with some degree of competency. Of course, much depends on the site, the type of damage and the extent of the lesion. One wonders if Helen Keller would have been able to compensate and develop her potentialities so excellently if she had not had twenty months of normal infancy before being struck down by her damaging illness. On the other hand, if the insult to the brain has occurred during pregnancy or perinatally, provided the lesions are not in crucial locations and are not too extensive or severe in effect, compensation may occur through other areas taking over or because the brain makes the best use of what is there. In this respect, Hecaen (1962) says, "Functional restoration takes place equally in astonishing proportions whether it is due to the 'taking over' of functions by the other hemisphere or by zones of the same hemisphere which had not so far had an activity of capital importance but potentially, capable of carrying out this function."

Neurophysiological Conditions or States (Material Causes of MND)

Mention has been made of some of the various types of lesions which can occur as a result of the original causes just described. These require further elaboration.

Brain Lesions

Renfrew (1962) notes, "Some lesions are spread profusely throughout the cerebrum while others are focal, that is to say, they are restricted to a part of the cerebrum. The terms 'diffuse' and 'focal' have obviously opposite meanings but their definitions are nevertheless difficult." Renfrew goes on to describe in detail the inferences of cerebral lesions which can be made from clinical evidence and suggests that usually focal organic lesions are caused by neoplasms, abscesses and cerebral vascular causes and accidents, whereas diffuse organic lesions are caused by various diseases. It is not appropriate here to discuss further the determination of the site of a specific lesion, a topic which is more the concern of the neurologist. However, it is important to point out that generalized diffuse lesions present quite different manifest symptoms from those which are apparently caused by highly specific foci. Although some children may have highly specific handicaps, I am of the opinion that there is also a small clustering of children who do present a syndrome of diffuse or generalized dysfunction characteristics. They will be described below.

Biochemical Causes

Several people have suggested that there may be biochemical causes of MND and the implication is that in such cases, there is no lesion. Smith and Carrigan (1959) have put forward a theory which accounts for reading disability in terms of the biochemical nature of the synaptic transmission of neuronal impulses. They suggest that the chemical acetylcholine (ACh) facilitates nerve impulses and that the enzyme cholinestrase (ChE) inactivates the ACh causing a synapse which has just fired to revert to a resistant state. However, if some biochemical imbalance causes an excess of ACh over ChE, then cells will tend to keep firing and this may cause a continuing fixation on a particular stimulus. An excess of ChE will have exactly the opposite effect, that is, the fixation time will be limited and, for example, reading will be inaccurate. Smith and Carrigan speculate that thyroid malfunction causes a high concentration of ChE and that excessive activity of the pituitary gland causes an excess of ACh. They also suggest that quite apart from ChE, epinephrine and norepinephrine (both secreted by the adrenal medulla), by suppressing acetylcholine, inhibit impulse transmission at the synapse. Thus, anxiety can inhibit fluency in reading. All that can be said by way of comment on Smith and Carrigan's theories is that it will be some years yet before the biochemistry of neurology progresses sufficiently to test their hypotheses.

E.C. Gray (1967) says, "Suspected excitatory transmitters such as acetylcholine, nor-adrenaline, and glutamic acid, and inhibitary substances such as y-amino butyric acid can be isolated and studied. . . ." The symposium on the human brain in the *Science Journal*, May 1967, indicates that our knowledge in these areas has a long way to go, yet. Drake (1966b) also suspects that many children are being misclassified as brain-damaged when, in reality, they may have biochemical imbalances. He says,

This would suggest an alternative to the brain damage hypothesis—that those children who have been thoroughly tested by a neurologist without positive findings may possibly be suffering from biochemical imbalances or inborn metabolic defects rather than from brain damage. . . . Psychogalvanic studies indicate that these [hyperactive] children showed an unusual drop in body tension levels when they sat for any period of time. The administration of Dexedrine tended to mitigate this hypoactivity and to maintain normal tension levels in order that the child might perform.

These biochemical theories should be taken very seriously, particularly in the light of the work centering around the nature of synaptic transmission, memory, storage and the interaction between the regulatory functions of the brain on our endocrinological and hormonal systems. One can even speculate that genetic dyslexia, although at one end of the normal distribution in certain memory and language skills, might well be at the lower end of a normal distribution in some such biochemical "situation" as that described above. McGlannan (1970) and her co-workers are investigating this possibility in some detail.

The Need for Caution

As Birch (1964) points out,

Given the complex matrix of behavioral disturbance which children designated as "brain damaged" present, it is clear that no single scientific discipline and no simple research strategy can possibly provide knowledge that will result in adequate understanding or effective planning for the children with whom we are concerned. To approach the problems meaningfully requires the pooled resources, skills, and techniques of, at the very least, such disciplines as neurology, psychology, physiology, psychiatry, education, epidemiology, sociology, pediatrics, and obstetrics. Working together, these disciplines can approach the questions of etiology, pathology, pathogenesis, and developmental interaction which emerge in any serious consideration of children with brain injury.

To illustrate the care one must take in diagnosis, Lorber (1965) provides us with a particular instance. He describes one little boy, aged twenty-one months, as "an alert, playful boy, able to say many words, liked to look at picture books, pretended to 'read,' and named some pictures. He liked playing with toy cars and building toys. He could feed himself with a spoon and fork. He was running about all day with occasional falls. He was toilet-trained during the day but had occasional accidents." This child was a case of hydroencephaly and repeated attempts to find any residual cortical tissue by appropriate examinations met with failure. As far as could be detected, the child had no cortical hemispheres to speak of, even though the EEG showed some activity.

CHARACTERISTICS, INDICATORS AND SYMPTOMS OF MND

The list of symptoms and variables associated with MND in the literature are almost never-ending and even if we keep to the neurophysiological characteristics, the list is formidable. Clements (1966) lists as developmental variants frequent lags in the developmental milestones, a generalized maturational lag, possible physical immaturity, frequent reflex asymmetry, mild visual or hearing impairments, strabismus or nystagmus, high incidence of left and mixed laterally and confused perception of laterality, hyperkinesis and hypokinesis, general awkwardness and poor, fine visuo-motor coordination.

It is to be stressed that this is not a syndrome and no correlations or clusterings are implied by the above list. A large-scale and expensive research would be required to investigate in detail the symptomatology of MND with a view to clustering the symptoms, not in a factor analytic sense, but into predicted diagnostic patterns, if, indeed, any exist.

One of the most prominent authorities in the area of learning disabilities was A.A. Strauss (Strauss and Lehtinen, 1947). Strauss defines the brain-injured child as one "who before, during, or after birth has received an injury to or suffered an infection of the brain. As a result of such organic impairment, defects of the neuro-motor system may be present or absent; however, such a child may show disturbances in perception, thinking, and emotional behavior, either separately or in combiation." These disturbances, particularly those of perception, hyperactivity and distractability, frequently result in reading disabilities. Strauss put forward from his own observations of children almost all the characteristics of MND which have subsequently been stressed by many others. He described problems in visual and auditory discrimination, closure and integration, including sound blending, perseveration and a discrepancy between the maturation of the separate psychological functions necessary for perceptual organization and competent reading ability. For remedial training, Strauss suggests exercises in spatial relationships, and figure-ground discrimination. In the reading process itself he stresses pointing a finger at the word being read.

The Strauss syndrome or its equivalent, which is very similar to that described above in the section on diffuse impairment, has been critically examined by many authors who feel that Strauss and others have promoted it as a single, homogeneous entity within which all MND children could be grouped. Whether or not Strauss really put forward such a rigid viewpoint is open to question; however, the current trend is almost diametrically the opposite, viewing each MND child as having a unique set of characteristics. Thus, all MND children are by implication scattered more or less at random over all possible permutations and combinations. My own viewpoint mentioned earlier is that there *is* a small but identifiable cluster of cases (within the total MND group) who can be categorized within a syndrome, the material cause of which is a diffuse impairment of the brain. With respect to other reading disability cases suffering from MND, there may also be clusters, smaller in number and more heterogeneous in characteristics, whose attributes are determined by localized lesions impairing a specific cognitive function or functions. For example, the Gerstmann's syndrome cases may form a small group. Of course, many children *will* be unique in the particular symptom profile they present and such children collectively may even form the majority of the total MND group. That is one reason why the reading disabilities set out in Table II were classified in terms of symptoms or characteristics, not children.

The Diffuse MND Syndrome

I feel rather diffident about postulating even a limited MND syndrome at a time when many authorities, some with factor analytic research evidence, are asserting that no syndrome exists.

However, I have examined several children who have exhibited signs of mild clumsiness, poor memory for designs, spidery handwriting, speech deficits in the past or present, mild auditory deficits and emotional lability. Two such cases had IQ's over 120. Of course, all the usual academic disabilities were present in these cases. One example follows.

Peter was brought to me at the age of seven by his parents, who were both doctors. The other five children in the family were all highly intelligent, the eldest being in postgraduate school and the youngest a baby. The family were very well adjusted and Peter was a living example of how learning disability children can and should be raised. Although he had a full scale WISC IQ of 125, and his verbal score was much higher than his performance score, he was finding it extremely difficult to learn to read, write and spell and to cope with numerical calculations. During the last three weeks of pregnancy, his mother had suffered a placental deficiency. Peter was "different" from birth, being slower to develop than any of the other children in almost every sphere. At the age of seven, he was still mildly uncoordinated physically and was finding it difficult to cope with regular school from most aspects of his life, although he remained emotionally stable and was constructive in outlook. As his WISC record indicated "flashes" of intelligence at an IQ level of 145, it was decided to put Peter on a straight phonics reading program involving a great deal of writing. His innate verbal ability, although patchy, stood him in good stead and within a few weeks he was reading above his grade level. The point to be made is that after an extensive psychoeducational diagnosis, it was found that, metaphorically speaking, the cream had been taken off the cortex. Almost every sensory and motor function was uneven and qualitatively irregular.

EEG Studies

An account of an excellent EEG study into reading disability (Hughes, 1968) was outlined at the end of Chapter VI, the results of which were rather inconclusive. Freeman (1967) has surveyed the literature as to the effectiveness of the EEG as a diagnostic tool in various neuropsychological areas of controversy such as headaches, nightmares and reading disabilities and comes to the following conclusion: "The marriage of convenience between the EEG and special education has never been a very happy one. The available evidence suggests that until more definitive information is available, a mild separation, or at least a platonic relationship, would be more appropriate."

In reviewing some two dozen references in my own files which link EEG findings with learning disabilities, I have found none that give conclusive results which would be diagnostically useful and therefore I would completely agree with Freeman's verdict. Perhaps as EEG research progresses and as equipment improves, the day will come when EEG records will provide reliable indicators of specific sensorimotor deficits. As matters stand, only very occasionally can the EEG record be interpreted as a clear indicator of neurological dysfunction, and, excluding epilepsy, an accurate EEG specification of its nature is rare.

Other Research Projects

Rubin *et al.* (1967) studied a sample of abnormal children which included three groups: the neurologically impaired, the emotionally immature and the neurotic or emotionally disturbed group. They found that the main indicators of impairment were the perceptual tests; the Frostig Developmental Test of Visual Perception, subtests 3 and 4, were the best indicators (form constancy and position in space). Next was gross muscular incoordination followed by fine or precise motor incoordination. The fourth main indicator was the Bender Visuo-Motor Gestalt Test, in which perseveration was a key symptom. Early feeding problems, except for vomiting, were also excellent indicators of neurological impairment. An analysis of EEG records indicated that the emotionally disturbed group had the most abnormal records.

In another research report from the Lafayette Clinic in Detroit, Rodin *et al.* (1964) factor-analyzed a large array of data on fifty-nine boys and thirteen girls. The children were referred for undesirable classroom behavior or for poor academic progress. The first factor seemed to be a motor factor. The highest loadings were on impaired finger, hand, toe and foot rapid movements. The second factor was one of intelligence, but the third factor was most interesting. The loadings on this factor were an older chronological age, a normal Bender test, a diagnosis of psychoneurosis with internalization, fast activity in EEG and a chief complaint of reading disability. Internalized psychoneurosis refers to shy, anxious or withdrawn characteristics in the child. The authors do not name this factor except to say that it is essentially one of age. I would suggest that within the limits of factor analysis, it is suspiciously like the profile presented by many genetic dyslexic boys. Factor four was found to be an EEG factor, standing mostly in isolation, while factor five was a clear-cut one concerned with hyperactivity. This factor was loaded with high background voltage in the EEG record, and may be associated with MND.

At the very least, the above research would tend to confirm that the *contents* of these factors do exist in children exhibiting undesirable classroom behavior or having poor academic progress. However, as usual, the factor analysis has tended to cluster together variables with functional identity or similarity, rather than clustering *profiles* common to homogeneous groups of children.

Another factor-analytic study by Ayres (1965) on patterns of perceptual-motor dysfunction in children is presented in the section below devoted to motor disorders.

Gerstmann's Syndrome

In adult patients, any injury or disease in area 39 of the parietal lobe in the dominant hemisphere may interfere with the patient's ability to read or otherwise process symbols. It has been suggested by several authors that "specific developmental dyslexia" may be caused by a maturational lag or other lack of development in some children of these symbol-handling parietal areas of the brain (Hermann, 1959; Eames, 1960; Kinsbourne and Warrington, 1963c). The classic adult symptoms of Gerstmann's syndrome are dysgraphia, dycalculia, right-left disorientation and finger agnosia.

Few would quarrel with the location hypothesis, or indeed, the fact of the existence of a syndrome in some dyslexic children not unlike that exhibited by adult patients suffering from Gerstmann's syndrome. Kinsbourne and Warrington (1963) actually provide a detailed case report of seven children with such symptoms. The essential problem is to discover how the symptoms of this syndrome were caused in the first place and how many such children exist in the population; the percentage is probably very small. I have found finger agnosia to be rare.

Indicators of MND Characteristics in the Classroom

The types of indicators for which teachers can be on the lookout in the classroom are as follows: The MND child may not be able to draw very well or may produce very immature drawings; his handwriting is inclined to be erratic, malformed and possibly spidery in appearance; he may be awkward and clumsy, particularly with respect to precise movements such as paper folding; he may be tone-deaf, singing out of tune; his articulation may be noticeably slurred or imprecise, and emotionally he may be labile. A child may only exhibit one of these symptoms to a severe degree or any number of them may exist in varying degrees of mildness or severity. Other kinds of dyslexic children may have very untidy handwriting; therefore, taken alone, this is not a reliable indicator of MND.

Maturational Lag

Children with MND often have a maturational lag which in many ways may be similar to that of genetic dyslexic boys who are neurologically intact. The differential diagnosis of the two types of dyslexic syndromes is difficult, though it can be done with sufficient training and experience on the part of the examiner. Note that the MND "syndrome" is actually a multiplicity of complex syndromes.

The Prognosis for MND Children

Hecaen was quoted above for his statement that the brain has many ways of achieving functional restoration, either through the action of the other hemisphere or by other zones in the same hemisphere. The brain seems to have a considerable capacity for accepting training or retraining, even when impaired, although special techniques may be required to achieve this. Some spastic children can be artificially trained to walk much as the rest of us learn to drive a car.

Several factors contribute to a good prognosis for MND children. These criteria, which are rather obvious, have come from my own experience in working with learning disability children. The milder the impairment, of course, the more likely the remediation is to meet with success. I have also found that success is more likely with diffuse mild impairment cases than with those children who appear to have localized foci characterized by specific deficits. The younger, the more intelligent and the more emotionally stable the children are, the greater is the likelihood that their learning disability problem will be ameliorated. Children with severe neurological dysfunction in the auditory areas are the most difficult to treat because these areas are essential to language development. A child with a high verbal scale score on the WISC is usually a better prospect, remedially speaking, than one (MND) with high performance and low verbal scale scores. Of course, an exception to the latter is the highly intelligent genetic dyslexic boy who would not be classified as MND in any case.

SENSORIMOTOR MODALITIES

Frequent reference has been made, particularly in Chapter II, to psycholinguistic models of communication and the remarkable similarity the models have to each other, especially those of Morley, Osgood and Wepman. In Chapters III, VII and VIII, some of the major processes involved in perception, conceptualizing, thinking, listening and reading were described. The tables in these chapters are quite compatible with a psycholinguistic approach to language. Essentially, the simplest elaboration of the composition model is one of sensory input and projection, automatized decoding (both unit and sequential) and representational-level conceptualizing with thought processing or concept manipulation, all of which is followed by an elaborate encoding motor output system wholly integrated with the sensory and cognitive systems described. The neurology of language and communication was outlined in Chapter VI and further details are described in Chapter XI.

The conclusion to be drawn from all these approaches is that the most optimal and profitable way of investigating MND (as a sensory/cognitive/motor system) is to analyze it, first across the various individual sensory modalities, thinking processes and motor output functions and second in terms of their *integrated* relationships. A considerable amount of research has been carried out along these lines by research workers (e.g., Birch and Belmont, 1965b, 1965c; Luria, 1966) and in general, this modality research approach has yielded more valuable information than has, for example, factor-analytic studies. Therefore, each of the subsections which follow has as a topic one particular sensory modality, motor functioning, cognitive processes or integrational systems.

Attention, Distraction, Motivation and Hyperactivity

Ayres (1965) found a factor of "tactile defensiveness" in a study of one hundred children with suspected perceptual deficits. She describes it as follows:

> Most clearly represented by hyperactive, distractible behavior this factor was interpreted as a previously unrecognized syndrome characterized by deficit in tactile perception, a defensive response to certain types of tactile stimulation and hyperactive behavior. The fact that hyperactive behavior appeared with significant loading on only one factor suggests that, in this group, disinhibited behavior might be linked with one particular neurological mechanism.

Ayres' viewpoint is considered in more detail later in the chapter.

Birch *et al.* (1964a) hypothesize that short attention-span perseveration, etc., derives from altered patterns of relation between the processes of excitation and inhibition. They say, "Short attention span may be viewed as the result of relatively weak excitation and/or weak surrounding inhibition; perseveration, as the result of excessively strong or persistent excitation and/or strong surrounding inhibition; distractability as the product of relatively short-lived excitation and/or weak surrounding inhibition resulting in ineffective insulation." These authors have taken the first steps in a research investigation of these hypotheses.

It will be remembered that Ucko (1965) found that his group of boys who were classified as asphyxiated at birth were significantly different from their control group on the following characteristics: unusual sensitivity, overreactivity and a tendency to disequilibrium when normal routine was broken.

Broadbent (1962) presents evidence to support the hypothesis that when the rate of pulsing, or modulation, is the same for two sounds, the hearer perceives them as one sound. Broadbent says,

> It seems reasonable to suppose, therefore, that a man can listen to one person and ignore another primarily by selecting from the mass of sounds entering his ears all those frequencies that are being modulated at the same rate. Since it is most unlikely that the vocal chords of two speakers would vibrate at exactly the same rate at any moment, modulation would almost always provide an important (if not the sole) means of separating a pair of voices.

Broadbent quotes other research which suggests that attentionally, the content of speech takes precedence over its physical characteristics. His overall conclusion is that the brain in all probability has two attention mechanisms for aiding listening to speech, one of which is a continuing content and the other the pulsing or modulation of the voice. The actual pitch or frequency of the voice is far less important.

I would suggest that Broadbent's findings about attentional processes are helpful in understanding the short attention span and distractability of MND children. If the "locking-on" modulation listening mechanism has been impaired, not only will two or more voices be receptively unseparated, but more "primary" stimuli than language will also attract the children's attention almost reflexively (the startle reflex). Of course, the child is not necessarily startled or frightened by extraneous noises or sights— the term *startle* is used because this turning toward unusual stimuli is present in all of us and it is reasonable to assume that it is a differentiation of the startle reflex present at birth. To combat this, I have found that headphones with large earmuffs like those used by airplane pilots not only cut out extraneous startle stimuli, but they also present the voice being listened to, within one inch of the eardrum. If, additionally, the volume is turned up to compensate for volume impairment, the child can do little else but fixate on the voice. Zelder (1966) has shown that auditory stimuli are more distracting to MND children than are extraneous visual stimuli.

As for the content of the passage, which is the second attentional mechanism mentioned by Broadbent, the major consideration would be its *meaningfulness* to the MND child. Because I am of the opinion that language in the narrow sense is an automatized skill medium, the main use of which is to transmit mostly nonverbal thoughts, concepts and relationships, I suggest that the content we "lock onto" is composed of the continuing meaningful thought processes and their theme. If one watches a sophisticated science program on television, for example, much of the meaningful content is transmitted directly and nonverbally. Thus, the content of passages presented to MND children must be well within their understanding while they are learning reading skills.

However, it is equally true that one may be motivated to watch some science programs and not others, to listen to some lectures and not others. Thus, interest motivation with its final-cause needs is an important factor in the attention a person pays to a particular theme or content. Most normal children are motivated to attend in a listening, reading or even watching situation because their training has made a variety of their need-satisfactions contingent upon the success which can only come from a satisfactory attentional behavior. These various needs may be internalized as in novel reading for amusement, or dependent on external satisfactions as when we receive praise or material rewards. These need-satisfactions are not mutually exclusive and, therefore, to help distractible MND children with attentional problems to lock onto content in their academic work, I recommend high-interest curricula (preferably founded in their own continuing interests), lavish praise and some checkmark or visible reward system through which they can measure their success directly.

Attentional Factors and Cognition

The effects of MND on the development of cognitive structures have been summarized by R.W. Gardner (1966a, 1966b). Drawing on information from his own and other research studies, he suggests that MND has the following effects. The child has a limited span of attention and memory for separate items and cannot easily organize the material. Because the child is unable to screen out distractions, this also affects his selective recall of memories. Sometimes, however, the MND child may have surges of attention of longer duration, and while the causal agent is unknown, it is not necessarily motivational in nature. Because the child cannot screen out distractions, this affects his selective recall of memories and his limited attention span also restricts the number of stimuli which can be scanned before making decisions or adjustments. If the structural cognitive mechanisms are faulty in operation, so is the processing of data. MND may also impair the capacity to categorize, and to abstract conceptual items in detail in effective ways. It may also cause the child to focus on isolated elements or result in a fragmented approach to concept formation.

Another effect may be the poor quality of the interaction between new percepts and memories of all their related percepts. Gardner uses the term *leveling* and suggests that normal people level their old experiences up to new ones but neurological dysfunction increases leveling down to old memories resulting in less new adaptation and less shaping through experience. Memories may be fewer and of poor quality. Gardner goes on to suggest that MND children have a literalness in their reality perception and understanding, but are unwilling to experience uncomfortable events. Their liking for the literal is counterbalanced by a dislike of novel organizations of stimuli with consequent limitations on abstraction, imaginativeness, creativity and self-organization. Gardner's account of the possible effects of neurological dysfunction on cognitive structures and their development is so thorough that further comment is unnecessary. His remarks on motoric responses are given in the appropriate section below.

Conceptualizing and Reasoning Disorders

Dyslexic children, by definition, are not mentally retarded (even though some mentally retarded children may be dyslexic). But intelligence is not a unitary homogenous ability and therefore it is usual for dyslexic children to give an extremely patchy or uneven record on the subtests of the WISC or ITPA. Although there are numerous exceptions, it is usual for MND children to have a verbal score which is superior to their performance score. Some of these MND cases may exhibit Gerstmann's syndrome (Kinsbourne and Warrington, 1963), but on the whole, consistent patterns of test results are hard to find. Diagnosing conceptualizing disorders in neurological dysfunction cases is a complex task which will be described in part in Chapter XIV.

Considerable numbers of dyslexic children, whether MND, genetic, communicative, socially disadvantaged or otherwise, do not have conceptualizing problems in the sense that their fundamental ability to reason is not impaired. Very often, their poor performance on reasoning tests stems from the fact that they do not have the automatized skills, verbal labels or perceptual-motor peripheral equipment to grasp the nature of the presented problem. Frequently, the lack of automatized skills causes them to work slowly, and so timed tests fluster and confuse them. Once these skills or mechanisms have been trained or supplied, dyslexic children are usually able to tackle logical problems with considerable competence.

MND children often seem to have difficulty with relational concepts, that is, concepts which acquire their meaning relative to some standard or reference point. Many such systems are "abstract" and culturally determined, which makes it doubly difficult for MND children to remember them. Note that this relational category includes our measurement systems, e.g., time, length, direction, weight, distance, etc. Other relational systems which may confuse MND children are family relationships, mathematical systems and rules and regulations related to specific situations (as in school). Any remediation should include a screening of these relational systems so that the child can be taught that which he does not know.

I.M. Smith (1964) has hypothesized that logical reasoning is primarily founded in visuo-spatial ability, a point of view with which I concur (see Chapters II and III). Neurologically, this would imply strong linkages between the occipital and parietal areas and the centrencephalic system (Penfield and Roberts, 1959). If these assumptions are correct (see Chapter VI), then impairment of these regions should cause deficits in logical reasoning ability. It would be difficult but not impossible to prove this hypothesis with direct evidence because it would be necessary to design, construct and standardize special intelligence tests for the purpose. Certainly, a poor performance on the WISC block design and object assembly subtests is traditionally an indicator of neurological dysfunction, particularly in cerebral palsied children (M.L.J. Abercrombie, 1964). Kinsbourne and Warrington (1963c), in an examination of seven children with Gerstmann's syndrome, found that the children performed very poorly on block design and object assembly subtests; it is worth reiterating in this context that their verbal IQ was at least 20 points higher than their performance IQ. There is a need for more research into the precise cognitive deficits of MND children, preferably in terms of the rationale put forward by R.W. Gardner, previously outlined. Graham *et al.* (1963), Ernhart *et al.* (1963) and Reitan (1966) have all produced concrete research findings in this general area.

Minimal Autism

Very occasionally, one comes across reading disability cases who, on extensive examination, appear to have all the symptoms of autism in a very mild form. Although slightly thin and pale, they give the impression of being "well-made" children of the type described by Rimland (1964). Speech development has usually been slow and their ability to emotionally relate to people has usually been tenuous. Temperamentally, they are inclined to be rather flat. Although their sensorimotor abilities seem to be intact, their reasoning ability in the sense of problem solving is usually weak. Therefore, on the WISC, they tend to get low comprehension and block design scores, whereas picture completion subtests or those in which items are sequenced tend to be carried out competently. Not infrequently the parents are intelligent and the siblings normal. These children should profit from a training in logical problem solving, particularly in mathematics.

Even with training, conceptual and reasoning disability cases tend not to outgrow their dyslexia as rapidly as do perceptual disability cases, as indicated in a research study by Silver and Hagin (1966).

Visual CNS Dysfunctions

Three separate groups of research workers have found visual or visuo-motor factors to be important indicators of CNS dysfunction: Rodin *et al.* (1964), Paine *et al.* (1968) and Werry and Sprague (1967). The test most frequently used to assess this ability was the Bender Visuo-Motor Gestalt Test. In an investigation of rotated designs on the Shapiro Rotational Test by brain-damaged adults, Shapiro *et al.* (1962) found that the brain-damaged group with visual field and oculomotor defects rotated far more than did the other groups. An interesting finding was that patients with frontal lesions, temporal cortical lesions and occipitalparietal lesions all rotated little compared with patients with cerebellar and diffuse lesions. All the nine oculomotor cases and those with field defects were also high rotaters when compared with the other brain-damaged group. Nevertheless, it should be remembered that in my own research reported earlier, I have found that normal third-grade girls tend to choose the rotated designs in a multiple-choice visuo-spatial memory test significantly more often than do boys. There is no indication that these normal nine-year-olds are brain-damaged, psychotic or suffer from any psychological abnormality. It would seem then that the rotation of designs as a differential diagnostic indicator of neurological dysfunction requires much more detailed investigation before it can be considered reliable or valid.

The Frostig Developmental Test of Visual Perception isolates five visual perceptual abilities, relating them to specific mistakes in reading: eye-hand coordination; figure-ground perception (losing one's place on the page, skipping words, substituting letters, having difficulty in scanning); form constancy (differentiating among similar matters, words of similar configuration, different scripts); perception of position in space (letter and number reversals), and perception of spatial relationships (scrambling letters in words, and words in sentences). In a research with experimental and control groups composed of kindergarten children, Linn (1968), using the Frostig Training Program for Visual Perception, found a significant difference between the means of the two groups when they took the Frostig Developmental Test of Visual Perception as a post-test. Subsequently, children who had problems in reading in the first grade were found to be those who had not received training with the Frostig program and who had earned low perceptual quotient scores the previous year. Children who had had the Frostig program encountered very little difficulty in word discrimination, reading and arithmetic learning.

In serious cases of visual CNS dysfunction, the shapes of the words and letters may be distorted, fragmented, rotated, complicated, simplified, disproportioned, mirror-imaged or made symmetrical. The order of the letters in a word may be reorganized, so to speak, by the addition, omission, reversal or combination of the individual letters.

The problem of directional-configuration constancy (mirror imaging, etc.) also comes to the fore (as it does in cases of genetic dyslexia) as a problem for visuo-spatially impaired MND children. However, in the latter case, the cause is a very different one, namely, neurological dysfunction. MND children, in order to outgrow mirror images and reversals, have to mature visually beyond form constancy to a state of learning where the direction in which a letter is facing (relative to one's face) signifies a particular sound-meaning. CNS impairment seems to cause a maturational lag in some children in this respect (Bender, 1963). Some MND children do not even attain a visuo-spatial mastery of form constancy, a fact sometimes attested to by the results of the appropriate subtests on the Frostig Developmental Test of Visual Perception (Rubin *et al.*, 1967).

R.L. Gregory (1966) indicates that most research, particularly into visual illusions, points to visual recognition as being a matching process in which perceived data are matched for similarity or even identity with a vast store of accumulated visual experience. Perhaps this is why some adults can read complete sentences with one or two saccadic movements of the eyes, the material being visually compounded into very familiar chunks which are easily matched. The opposite holds true for visually impaired MND children; many of the visual disturbances listed above can, on the simplest level, be accounted for *by some distortion in the matching process.* The distortion could occur at any stage of the psychoneurological process, whether it is sensory projection, visual cortex registration or its possible final storage in permanent memory. In almost all cases, a distortion somewhere along the line will result in a defective permanent registration of visual imagery. Therefore, subsequent experiencing of the established (distorted) images can cause faulty perception on two possible counts: a distorted input and a distorted permanent memory trace against which to match it. Thus, frequently the subject has no criterion for knowing that a stimulus is distorted apart from having this communicated to him through another channel such as descriptive language or guided kinesthetic tracing. Maximum use of both these alternative channels should be made in remediation.

Eyedness and Laterality

Forness and Weil (1970), in a precise study of thirteen MND children retarded in reading, found eight of the subjects to be left-eyed. In view of what has been said earlier about visual fields, it is possible that the left eye is a little less efficient in sensing the right visual field, which is the one in which reading occurs. This hypothesis should be investigated ophthalmologically. Note that (as is usually the case in laterality research) these authors found these MND subjects little different from unselected children in handedness.

Visuo-Motor and Constructional Apraxic Disorders

Constructional apraxia has been defined by Drever (1963) as "the inability to manipulate, or deal intelligently, with objects, as a result of brain lesion." This is conceptually similar to my own definition of visuo-spatial ability as the ability to manipulate objects and their relationships intelligently in multidimensional space. Therefore, I would define apraxia as the inability to manipulate objects intelligently in two- or three-dimensional space, using the hands or other body muscles. Money (1962) in his glossary defines apraxia as "the loss of ability to perform purposeful movements, in the absence of paralysis or sensory disturbance; caused by lesions in the cerebral cortex."

Hermann (1964) mentions the occurrence of some kinds of apraxia in MND dyslexic children; in particular, dressing apraxia in a mild form sometimes occurs in that such children have difficulty getting into clothes or in fastening their ties or shoelaces, but a unilateral neglect of one-half of the body or of "extra-personal" space occurs very infrequently.

The point is made by Benton (1962) that "a patient may show relatively severe perceptual impairment as expressed in defective performance in writing, drawing, and constructional praxis tasks and yet show no noteworthy dyslexia." Benton has found many apraxic patients who have difficulties performing such constructional tasks as stick arranging and block building, and who have poor writing ability.

The difference between perceiving a pattern correctly and copying it correctly is stressed by M.L.J. Abercrombie (1964). She points out that visuo-motor activity is guided movement under visual control. Also, there is little evidence as far as visual perception is concerned that cerebral palsied children see things in a distorted manner but they may see them in an immature way without the differentiations which might be expected of their mental age. Abercrombie *et al.* say, "They can therefore be described as suffering from developmental lag in their perceptual skills." They go on to point out the need for very highly differentiating tests which can be used diagnostically with MND children.

Two hypotheses have been put forward to explain constructional apraxia. One suggests that apraxia is primarily a result of faulty perceptual functioning, a viewpoint expressed by Mayer-

Gross (1936) and Denny-Brown (1958). A similar viewpoint is that of Kleist (1934), who postulates that constructional apraxia results from a faulty linkage between visual perception and motor performance. A third possibility, hinted at by Abercrombie *et al.*, is that the difficulty in constructional apraxia may be more "toward" motor-kinesthetic malfunctioning. Admittedly, this is a rather artificial three-way split, but the outcome of any research investigating these hypotheses is likely to have beneficial implications for the training of children suffering from constructional apraxia. One research which investigates two of the alternatives, namely, the perceptual versus the linkage alternatives, has been carried out by Domrath (1968). Domrath administered the Benton Visual Retention Test, the Draw-A-Man Test, the Block Design Test and other tests to 143 second-grade children. He found that good perceivers tended to show a higher level of visuoconstructive performance than poor perceivers; the implication is that constructional apraxia is a reflection of poor perceptual ability rather than of intact perception with a poor linkage to motor functioning. However, Domrath does not rule out the possibility that a small proportion of cases may fall into the latter category.

In my own recent research, the details of which are given in Chapters VIII and IX, correlations were run between the Bannatyne Visuo-Spatial Memory Test and the Graham-Kendall Memory-for-Designs Test. The former is a multiple-choice recognition memory-for-designs test which, from the motor point of view, involves only pointing. The multiple-choice answer designs include the original design and the following variations on it: simplification, mirror image, rotation, fragmentation, altered proportions, complication and making it symmetrical. Each of the fifteen designs is separately exposed for four seconds, with a further second being allowed to elapse before the subject selects a particular design answer. The Graham-Kendall Memory-for-Designs Test also involves fifteen designs, each of which is separately presented for five seconds; the subject is then required to reproduce the design from recall-memory by drawing it manually on a piece of paper. In the research, the Graham-Kendall responses drawn by the children were analyzed by two judges into the same categories used in the multiple-choice answers to the BVSMT: the original, a simplification of it, a mirror image of it, etc.

The correlations between the two tests were mostly low. The correlation between the BVSMT choice of original design and the number "reasonably correctly drawn" on the Graham-Kendall test was $r = +0.37$. The only category which was correlated with itself across the two tests was mirror imaging and that was a barely significant *negative* correlation ($r = -0.27$). However, the manual rotation of designs on the Graham-Kendall test correlated significantly ($r = +0.35$) with the choice of the mirror-image design on the BVSMT. Also correlated with the BVSMT mirror imaging was a simplification of the design when drawn manually ($r = +0.33$). By contrast, a manually drawn complication of the design on the Graham-Kendall test correlated positively with the choice of the rotated designs on the BVSMT ($r = +0.36$). One other correlation is interesting; the drawing of mirror images was positively correlated ($r = +0.28$) with the choice of the correct original design on the BVSMT, indicating that drawing mirror images is associated with accurate perception in a recognition memory-for-designs context. By contrast, all the other categories of manually drawn designs of a distorted kind (simplification, rotation, fragmentation, etc.) are negatively correlated with the choice of the original design on the BVSMT and most of them are not significant.

These results suggest that *both* visual and motor functioning play their part in the distortion of designs, both independently and together. Mirror imaging, when manually linked, cannot always be classed as a "distortion," but rotation on each test is significantly and negatively correlated with an accurate performance (or selection) on the other test. Drawing rotated designs on the Graham-Kendall test was positively correlated with the selection of the mirror image design on the BVSMT ($r = +0.35$). Remembering, too, that the girls selected a rotated design significantly more often than did the boys, one is prompted to suggest that many factors other than neurological dysfunction appear to be operating in the reproduction or selection of designs from memory. Certainly, the whole "problem" is much more complex than a breakdown into gross visual or motor-kinesthetic functioning. A factor analysis of the results suggested an MND grouping in which drawing disproportionate designs (Graham-Kendall), selecting them (BVSMT) and distributing MFD designs poorly on the page were key items. Rotation was *not* in this grouping, but fragmentation was (Bannatyne, 1969).

It would seem that Luria's viewpoint, that constructional apraxia is a complex integrational system involving motor-kinesthetic, vestibular and visual components, is a more likely one than simpler versions.

The Spiral After-Effect Test and MND Children

When a black-printed spiral is rotated in front of the eyes for a short time, it may appear to continue rotating after the spiral itself has been stopped. Davids *et al.* (1957) found that the Spiral After-Effect Test differentiated fifteen spastics from normal and maladjusted children, the after-effect being shortest in the cerebral palsied children. There was no correlation between spiral after-effect and IQ. In another research, Blau and Schaffer (1960), using the Spiral After-Effect Test with 420 normal children, found a selected group of forty-six children who did not perceive the effect. The authors predicted that this group of forty-six would have abnormal EEG records. In fact, 86 percent of the forty-six children did have an abnormal EEG record, whereas none of a normal control group of twenty children who did perceive the effect had abnormal records. Mann *et al.* (1963) found that the Spiral After-Effect Test successfully and significantly discriminated between first-grade children who were competent on reading readiness, reading achievement, intelligence and draw-a-person tests and those who were not. This result did not hold for number readiness or achievement tests. These research results suggest there may be a link between spiral after-effect, MND and reading disability.

Motor, Kinesthetic and Vestibular CNS Dysfunctions

One of the most frequent comments in the literature on learning disabilities is the number of children who exhibit symptoms of clumsiness, poor muscular coordination, restlessness and slow motor development in infancy. In the three factor-analytic studies by Rodin *et al.* (1964), Paine *et al.* (1968), and Werry and Sprague (1967), the first or second major factor to emerge was one of motor incoordination. In a research study into impaired motor development among reading disability cases, Bryant (1964) administered the Lincoln-Oseretsky Motor Development Scale to thirty-two consecutive cases of reading disability coming into his clinic. All the boys had WISC verbal or performance IQ's of 90 or above and had relatively severe retardation in a basic academic skill. Bryant's findings were as follows:

> In the reading disability cases, about two-thirds obtained motor development scores completely below the normative distribution for their age, and most were far below the lower end of their age norms. Age and I.Q. were not correlated with deviation from the mean normative age on the test. Of the cases below the norms, about one-third were identified as showing some motor difficulty in an examination by a pediatric neurologist. A careful pediatric examination identified motor difficulty in only 10 percent of the below norm cases, but a careful medical history coupled with the pediatric examination identified about one-third of the cases. Using all examinations and histories, over half of the cases scoring below the normal distribution were *not* identified.

Bryant concludes that neurological and pediatric examinations are *too gross* to pick up many cases with motor impairment; among the severe specific reading disability cases there is a high percentage with motor impairment and "this suggests a neurological dysfunctioning that involves both language and motor functions."

In my own research, a positive significant correlation was found ($r = +0.33$) between balancing on one leg and spelling ability. This finding was supported in a research by Cooke (1968), who gave balancing tests of various kinds to 293 fourth-, fifth- and sixth-grade children, correlating the results with the California Mental Maturity Test and the Iowa Test of Basic

Skills. He found low significant positive correlations (ranging from 0.15 to 0.32) between most of the verbal scores on these tests and most of the balancing scores. As balance requires considerable motor, kinesthetic, visual and vestibular sensing integration, these correlations would seem to lend some slight support to the hypothesis of those research workers who claim that a well-developed and integrated set of motor generalizations is necessary for a full cognitive development which, of course, will include academic skills such as reading, writing and arithmetic. Several people have elaborated such a viewpoint and each of these will be considered separately below.

Kephart and the Perceptual-Motor Match

Kephart (1966) postulates a very systematic development in a child's learning, founding it in the two basic realities of space and time. He says, "The great majority of brain-injured children have difficulty in making the adequate observations necessary to the development of a space-time structure and even more difficulty in organizing these observations into a comprehensive schema." Kephart suggests that in early infancy, a child's information is primarily motor-supplied by his body moving in space. These movements build into motor skills for the accomplishment of a specific objective and motor patterns which, though less precise, permit the development of consistent information about the body and the environment. Walking, for example, is a motor skill but locomotion is a motor pattern involving many skills. Combinations of motor patterns lead to a motor generalization. According to Kephart, "The motor generalization involves an initial datum which is elaborated through variation, the integration of these variations, and abstraction from this integration of a generalized principle. Thus, locomotion, in addition to being a pattern, may become generalization." Motor activities, he suggests, are usually completely subservient to exploratory behavior which requires the extensive use of motor generalizations.

There are four motor generalizations, the first of which is balance and the maintenance of posture; these functions maintain the child's relationship to gravity. The second locomotor generalization enables the child to observe relationships *between* objects in space—he locomotes from one object to another, thus acquiring an appreciation of structural relationships between objects. The third generalization is contact, one through which the child manipulates objects. Contact has three basic stages, namely, *reach,* by which he makes contact with the object; *grasp,* for maintaining contact, and *release,* for terminating contact. The fourth and final generalization is that of receipt and propulsion, both involving moving objects, the former making contact with them and the latter imparting movement to an object. Through this final generalization, the child establishes a structure involving movement in space and the impression of a figure moving in front of a ground. Kephart goes on to say, "This initial body of motor information is extremely important to the development of a consistent space structure involving the three dimensions of euclidian space. For the development of such information, motor generalizations are required." He is careful to stress that no specific movement or exercises are essential to the development of motor generalization; what is important is a "flexibility of motor performance which provides for variation and, hence, the abstraction of a generalization." Thus, Kephart separates himself from the ideas of Delacato and Doman (see the following section).

In discussing the "perceptual-motor match," Kepart stresses that perceptual information is only meaningful if it is correlated with previous motor information. This process entails a perceptual-motor match which enables a consistent body of information to be formed that can be translated back and forth between motor and perceptual abilities. If such a match is not made or is made inadequately, the child will live in two worlds, one sensory and one motor. Kephart suggests that form constancy, the distortion of which is a common problem with MND children, arises from the contribution of motor exploration. For normal people, round objects are known to be round because they are felt as round, even though from an angle they may be seen as elliptical. (Personally, it seems to me that form constancy could arise solely from *seeing* a series of round objects change through time into elliptical ones as they turn in space.) Even so, Kephart is right to stress the importance of the perceptual-motor match and its contribution to our sensorimotor generalized experiences from which we abstract an appreciation of such concepts as size constancy and form constancy.

The "time structure" aspect of space-time is learned and generalized through a developing appreciation of three concepts, according to Kepart. The first is synchrony, in which the child is unable to appreciate separated events unless he appreciates simultaneous or synchronous ones. Rhythm, the second aspect of the temporal dimension, enables the child to appreciate equal temporal intervals betweens units. The third aspect or concept is sequence, which involves the ordering of events on the temporal scale. Kephart points out that sequencing is a frequent problem for some children in the classroom.

Kephart integrates all these concepts into a master one which he calls *veridicality*, "by which is meant the child's organization in response to the fundamental physical laws of the universe."

Kephart goes on to suggest three major principles for teaching brain-injured children. The teaching should be (a) developmentally oriented, (b) directed toward the development of generalization and (c) directed toward the establishment of veridicality within the child's existing body of knowledge.

The criticism of Kephart's point of view will be presented later along with that of the other authorities with related approaches to the problems of learning disability children.

Delacato and Doman

Delacato (1954, 1964), in collaboration with Doman, has put forward a theory of neurological organization founded in the assumption that individual development, ontogeny, closely recapitulates species development, phylogeny. Delacato traces this development through all species and parallels it with an anatomical development in human beings beginning with the spinal cord and medulla and progressing through the pons and midbrain to the cortex, where development terminates in mature human beings in the form of hemispheric dominance. An essential part of the theory is that if any stages or phases of individual neurological development are missed out in any motor or sensory modality, then some degree of immaturity or impaired neurological organization will result. Delacato stresses that although *mobility* is the key function throughout development, neurological organization with its hemispheric lateralization cannot be fully achieved without an integrated development of visual, auditory and tactile senses as well as a development of language. The neurological organization of mobility results from a development through the following stages: movement of arms and legs in isolation; crawling and cross-pattern crawling; creeping on hands and knees and cross-pattern creeping; walking, using arms for balance; walking; walking and running in cross patterns, and using a dominant leg in a skilled way. With respect to language, Delacato suggests that such disorders as aphasia and reading disability result from weak neurological organization. To help such children, one must assist them in progressing up through the various phases of neurological development, preferably in all sensorimotor modalities.

This treatment is achieved by first evaluating the subject on Delacato's neurological schema; then, "those areas of neurological organization which have not been completed or are absent are overcome by passively imposing them upon the nervous system in those with problems of mobility, and are taught to those with problems of speech or reading. When the neurological organization is complete, the problem is overcome." Since language functioning is largely the result of a well-lateralized brain, Delacato hypothesized that if the brain can be lateralized by moving the child through the lateralization effects of an orderly motor development, language and reading disabilities will largely disappear. Therefore, he promotes a program of physically manipulating the child into cross-patterned crawling, crawling, creeping and walking. Included in this is the sleep position which also facilitates lateralized neurological organization. A crucial point in Delacato's system is his belief that if outside agents such as parents and friends move the limbs of the otherwise passive child in the correct patterns, there will be a feedback to the brain which will passively, so to speak, result in increased neurological organization. Thus, the child will have his limbs manipulated in a sequence of cross-patterns, crawling and creeping and he may be taught to sleep in a particular position. More closely related to reading remediation is Delacato's recommendation that laterality can be increased by not allowing the child to listen to music, by having him read orally in whispers, by making him use only his dominant hand, by occluding the nondominant eye (this ignores the fact that the retina of each eye is connected with each hemisphere), by training a dominant foot and by altogether discouraging use of the nondominant side of the body except in cross-patterned motility situations.

Delacato has not produced any evidence, other than anecdotal, to support his far-ranging hypotheses. The one study which set out to test the theory was carried out by Robbins (1966) on three groups of second graders who were not suffering from MND. The results of this study did not support any of Delacato's hypotheses about laterality and reading development.

Ayres: Reading as a Product of Sensory Integrative Processes

Ayres (1965) carried out a factor-analytic study into types of perceptual-motor dysfunction in children. The sample consisted of one hundred children with suspected perceptual deficits and fifty without. The results of the analysis led to a hypothesis of five syndromes characteristic of dysfunction. These were (a) developmental apraxia (deficits in motor planning, tactile perception and finger identification); (b) tactile, kinesthetic and visual perceptual dysfunction in form and position in space; (c) tactile defensiveness demonstrated by hyperactive-distractible behavior, faulty tactile perception and defensive responses to tactile stimuli; (d) deficits of integration of the two sides of the body identified by difficulty in right-left discrimination, avoidance in crossing the midline and incoordinate eye lateral hand movements, and (e) deficits of visual figure-ground discrimination. A sixth factor considered unworthy of syndrome status was best represented by one-legged standing balance and it appeared in matrices of both dysfunction and control groups. Unfortunately, among her variables Ayres did not include either sex or a language score such as spelling. Two such scores would have contributed little to the variance and so would have preserved the intent of the study, yet at the same time would have yielded a wealth of information about these vital areas. Ayres' factor-analytic study, unlike most others, does not show individual sensory modalities; it is more "expressive of rather specific mechanisms by which inter-sensory and (sometimes) motor information is coordinated to permit development and manifestation of perceptual-motor ability." However, it should be remembered that no auditory tasks of a specific nature were included in the study.

Ayres (1967) has put forward theories concerning the phylogenetic and ontogenetic development of sensory integrative processes which culminate in the neurological organization necessary for learning to read. Under the heading, "How the Brain Developed the Ability To Learn To Read," Ayres makes the following statement, "Man's brain has developed over millions of years. Everything that occurred over those years to influence its evolution toward a more effective structure is in some way related to each child's individual development. In turn, each child's ability to master reading, as well as other academic subjects, is dependent upon his development." This premise is incorrect because man's brain did not evolve to learn to read. Reading is an artificially learned unnatural integration of separate sensorimotor faculties which developed in terms of survival for quite different and possibly separate purposes. That most of us can learn to read is a happy accident; most of the world's population cannot yet read and only two hundred years ago probably over 99 percent of people were unable to read. Of course, spoken language, which has tremendous survival value, is a product of evolution and has occurred spontaneously in the human race for many tens of thousands, or even hundreds of thousands, of years. However, much of what Ayers says applies to language and speech in general and is therefore valid. Although reading is no more innately programmed than is, say, learning to drive a car, the "happy accident" of being able to learn to read does (like learning to drive a car) depend on a certain degree of sensorimotor integration.

Ayres lists the neurological correlates of reading disability as "insufficient inhibition of the primitve tonic neck and labyrinthine reflexes, deficiency of equilibrium reactions, difficulty in moving the eyes across the mid-line, inability to coordinate simultaneous motor activity on the two sides of the body, and (tentatively proposed) defective visual perception of the horizontal sequence of objects in space." She then suggests that the centrencephalic system, as proposed by Penfield and Roberts, may possibly be responsible, along with other neurological areas, for an overall integrating function including that of the two hemispheres. Apraxic problems are a second type of disability Ayres considers to contribute to reading disability; she conjectures that they may be a malfunctioning of the frontal areas of the brain which are concerned primarily with motor planning and perhaps other intersensory integrations. The third sensory integrative mechanism subserving reading is a visual form-in-space perception. This mechanism includes not only the visual, but also the tactile and kinesthetic perceptions of form in space.

As a result of the above theoretical position, Ayers puts forward a series of training programs which directly train the dysfunctioning sensory integrative mechanisms concerned. Postural and bilateral integration are trained by inhibiting the appropriate reflexes. Ayres says, "When the reflexes are sufficiently integrated into the nervous system, the child's inner urge for postural mastery over the gravitational force will almost automatically involve him in the many postural adjustment and balancing activities which encourage development of equilibrium." To integrate the two sides of the body and the two hemispheres, Ayres suggests exercises which Kephart (1960) has developed, and to train eye movements, she recommends specific horizontal tracking exercises. She regards the basic problem in motor planning as a disorder of the tactile system (a result of her research), and this can be normalized "through careful application of touch-pressure stimuli to hands, arms, face, back and legs." Form and space perception are trained not only through visual perception but by integrating this with the "enhancement of kinesthesia and vestibular input." Prolonged contraction of postural muscles and other similar exercises are prescribed for these cases.

As with the other authors, criticism of Ayres' viewpoint will be left till later, but an indirect confirmation of her stress that the tactile system is important in apraxic disorders comes from a research by G. H. Fisher (1963). He found that the children in his sample recognized by touch alone thirty common objects much better than wooden models of those objects, concluding, that texture is therefore more important than shape as a cue for identifying objects. We can conclude from these two studies that more emphasis should be given to the tactile sense in the study of learning disability cases and, in particular, to any defective sensing of objects in the environment. However, relative to vision, it may not be quite so important. Rock and Harris (1967) found that vision completely dominates touch concepts and even helps to shape those concepts.

Barsch

Yet another "global" integrational theory in which movement plays an important part is that of Barsch, who has adopted the term *movigenic* to describe his viewpoint. Barsch (1965) clearly indicates that the Movigenic Curriculum has been devised to help children with special learning disabilities. He suggests that the "intelligence approach" and the "psychological approach" have failed to help these children and proposes a third approach to their education which can be designated as the "physiologic approach." This is described by Barsch as follows:

> In broad terms, this approach regards the child as a sensory-perceptual-motor organism confronted by a variety of energy forms which somehow must be converted into meaningful systems of information if he is to achieve full efficiency as a learner. The learner is a space oriented being with a physiologic makeup designed to travel through "educational space" processing information to his progressive advantage.

Many learning disability cases, says Barsch, have not become efficient listeners in their preschool life, although their auditory system is intact; they have not become efficient visualizers, although their sight is adequate, and their other basic equipment is there, "but the five years of basic training to prepare them to meet the curriculum demand have emphasized other objectives than the critical developments necessary for academics." The Movigenic Curriculum was set up to achieve a state of physiologic readiness that would enable learners to achieve a level of total organization so that they might profit from the existing academic curriculum. The curriculum was derived from a series of eight constructs which serve as a nucleus for the theory of movement. Briefly, these eight constructs, which Barsch spells out in some detail, are (a) that all living organisms must survive in an energy surround; (b) that survival in that surround is contingent upon movement; (c) that gravity is the major force to be resolved in developing patterns of movements in the interest of survival; (d) that the human organism is a "homeostatic, adapting, bilaterally, equating, dynamic, multi-stable system designed as an open energy mechanism so as to promote its survival in an energy surround"; (e) that coordination, which is the relating of coordinates, is necessary; (f) that there must be sensorimotor organization of movement within space; (g) that movement has survival value to the human organism, and (h) that communication is "an interchange of 'space worlds' between speakers, writer and reader, etc." From his eight constructs, Barsch, after reviewing the literature, found that there were twelve dimensions which might "serve as areas of developmental concern in building a unique curriculum." Four dimensions were grouped together under the heading of "Postural-Transport Orientations," namely, muscular strength, dynamic balance, body awareness and spatial awareness. Four more were grouped under the heading of "Percepto-Cognitive Modes"; these were tactual dynamics, kinesthesia, auditory dynamics and visual dynamics. Under the heading of "The Degrees of Freedom," Barsch grouped his final four dimensions, bilaterality, rhythm, flexibility and motor planning. The Movigenic Curriculum defines these twelve dimensions in detail and gives details of all the exercises, tasks, activities, etc., in which the children participate to assure their physiologic development.

In an experimental "run" of the Movigenic Curriculum, which was informally assessed using observational techniques, Barsch concluded that the most significant improvements were noted in dynamic balance, kinesthesia, rhythmic movement, bilaterality, flexibility and motor planning, while less dramatic gains were noted in the other areas. Whether or not successful participation in the Movigenic Curriculum will assure an improvement in children with learning disabilities has yet to be decided in future experiments of a more quantitative nature. However, teachers will find detailed descriptions of an excellent collection of activity exercises in Appendix 1 of Barsch (1965), but there are noticeable gaps. For example, under dimension 5 (visual dynamics), although there are many exercises for visual tracking, none of them involve lateralized saccadic movements of the eyes such as are involved in the reading process, a training which is easily achieved by cancellation tests using old magazines (the child draws a line through, say, all the *a*'s or *t*'s or any other selected letters on the page).

In research into the effect of a rhythmic and sensorimotor activity program on the perceptual-motor-spatial abilities of kindergarten children, Painter (1964), having designed the activities in accordance with "the theoretical constructs of Kephart and Barsch," found that the experimental group's gain was superior to the control group's gain in all expected areas: the Goodenough Draw-A-Man Test, the Beery-Buktenica Developmental Form Sequence Test, the Illinois Test of Psycholinguistic Abilities Motor Encoding subtest and a sensorimotor-spatial test devised by the author. The experimental group also significantly exceeded the gain of the control group in the ITPA Auditory-Vocal Association subtest. The differences between the other subtests were not significant and could be attributed to a Hawthorne or halo effect. While these findings lend support to Barsch's movigenic theory, and for that matter all sensorimotor training theories, it should be remembered that Painter's children were not learning disability cases and they did not improve significantly over the control group in many important subtests of the ITPA.

Comments on the Above Theories

At the University of Illinois, students who are paraplegic or who suffer from other types of paresis (often of a severe kind) are welcomed. Although many of these students have never crept, crawled, balanced or, for that matter, participated in comprehensive physical education programs, all can obviously read well and the majority successfully attain higher degrees. In a hospital school not long ago, I watched a cerebral palsied boy, who could not control any of his continuous movements, type out an essay at his high school grade level, using his big toe. Although he could read and write very well, he was unable to articulate any words at all.

Forrest (1967) found no differences between his educationally handicapped children and an academically successful control group on a balance test involving walking on beams. However, Forrest's group of EH children may have included many genetic dyslexic boys whose balancing ability would be normal. Clustering children into various categories of dyslexia on a symptom basis is essential in all learning disability research, and this is nowhere more true than when the research involves an investigation of physiological data. Rutter *et al.*, (1966) carefully selected an experimental group of eighty-nine children with choreiform movements and compared them with three other types of control groups. Their findings were as follows: No consistent relationship was found between the presence of choreiform movements and other abnormalities on the neurological examination. In those children where there did seem to be an association, no specific pattern was found. Whichever tests were used and whatever severity of reading disability was demanded, no relationship could be found between choreiform movements and abnormalities of behavior as measured by a teacher's questionnaire. Incidentally, no association was found between pregnancy complications and choreiform movements. Of course, this does not prove that choreiform *eye* movements do not cause reading disability as the authors (see Lesevre, 1966) did not take oculomotor factors into account. Stemmer (1964) has found an association between choreiform movements of a marked kind and writing problems.

One could go on citing numerous research studies illustrating the point that children with specific or even generalized sensorimotor defects may very well learn to read and write. Many children who have lain on their backs in bed all their lives have achieved academic success.

The Specificity of Sensorimotor Functioning

The above theories do not take into account several important principles, both physiological and psychological in nature.

The first is that *specificity* of functioning, in terms of *muscular activity*, has tremendous survival value and is a phylogenetic concomitant of intelligence. The more intelligent a species, the greater its adaptability to specific or novel ecological situations, and human beings are the most intelligent, the most adaptable and the most able to utilize specific functions in isolation from others. Thus, people born without eyes or even without hearing may come to learn to read using other senses.

The second point is that although there may be some limited generalization of movement, by and large, specific sensorimotor skills and activities each have to be taught separately. Transfer of training is a much smaller element in the aquisition of skills than is specificity of the training required. Learning to balance on a galloping horse will contribute only a little to acquiring the skills of skiing; learning to balance on a beam (Forrest, 1967) or how to creep on the floor (Robbins, 1966) has little to do with the acquisition of reading. Of course, this does not apply to the training of highly specific sensorimotor functions which are actively employed in the reading or writing process (e.g., eye movements, hand movements or even articulation).

A third point to be made concerns the use of the word *learned*. This word is very ambiguous in meaning and each meaning may involve many quite different separate physiological and/or psychological processes. Examples of learning which are largely unrelated are rote memorizing; visuo-spatial problem solving; auditory differentiation of stimuli; habituating "unnatural" complex movements (e.g., writing); the spontaneous maturation of innate programs such as babbling, walking or sucking, and so on. Thus, to say one "learns" movement in space, balance, creeping or any of the other "generalizations" which occur spontaneously in children before the age of, say, five years, is to confuse two types of learning. In fact, I would go so far as to say that the term *learning* should not be applied to such functions as the development of sucking, walking, creeping, crawling, biting, chewing, scanning, listening, talking, running, laughing, crying, clinging, hitting, climbing, throwing, etc., because no formal training is necessary and it is a rare environment which does not allow the *spontaneous emergence* of each of these functions at the appropriate stage of the child's psychophysical development. In other words, these functions will emerge spontaneously in almost all environments provided the specific equipment within the child is separately necessary to each of these functions is intact. For example, the child who physiologically or even neurologically is unable, through damage, to develop spontaneously its locomotion capabilities will, if intact in other areas, learn to talk and to read quite normally and on time. Of course, it is true that children with generalized impairment will have a maturational lag in all these automatic developments but such a generalization is also highly specific in operation and the various impaired area functions will each require highly specific training programs.

Even area integration training is, in this sense, highly specific. As far as intact children are concerned, it should be remembered that some American Indian children used to be bound to boards during infancy, yet when released, they walked on schedule. It would seem, then, that the word *generalization* must not be substituted for the term *automatization*. Motor habits, particularly continuous ones, once memorized (and I refer here to nonspontaneously occurring motor habits), are retained much better than most other skills, particularly verbal ones (Adams, 1967b). What actually occurs is that simple gross motor skills are habituated at first, and these may subsequently be incorporated (through frontal motor planning, according to Luria, 1966) into subsequent more precise, complex functions. Also, "bits" of previously automatized, quite separate skills may be recombined in new sequence structures, but this does not contravene the principle of specificity of action, and cannot be called generalization—it is a specific integration for a particular purpose.

The final point to be made is that the phylogenetic "motor

activity" scale is not quite as continuous in its development as the above theories would make out. Most species have highly specialized functions in specific areas which in many cases are far in advance of human capabilities, provided, of course, that the latter do not use aids. Humans cannot jump from tree to tree or navigate under the sea like eels; they cannot balance balls like seals, nor do they communicate as rapidly as does the dolphin. On some problem-solving tasks, the canary is far more intelligent than the cat or the monkey (Stettner and Matyniak, 1968).

In stressing the specificity and automation of motor functioning, I wish only to strike a balance with the concept of generalization, not to eliminate it. However, perhaps the words *general efficiency* as an attribute of the neurophysiological structure provide a better concept than *generalization*. In my own research (see Chapter IX), balancing on one leg was significantly correlated with spelling and unlearned ambidexterity and almost correlated with auditory sequencing. Balance was negatively correlated with the drawing of inaccurate designs on the Graham-Kendall Memory-for-Designs Test. Height and weight were consistently correlated with intelligence scores; the correlation coefficient was approximately 0.20 on large-scale studies (Stroud, 1956). Cookes' (1968) results correlating balance with verbal skills were usually low, with correlations of around 0.20 in most cases, although for grades 3 and 4 the total balance/language correlation was 0.32. In the light of all these findings, one can postulate a vague generalized neurophysiological efficiency "quality" in terms of which individuals can be scaled. To be accurate, such a scale would have to partial out maturational growth factors and allow for a variety of talents, a formidable task. Even if the hypothesis were to be confirmed, the correlations between overall efficiency of functioning and the results of specific skill tasks would be so low as to make accurate prediction impossible. Furthermore, this overall sensorimotor efficiency is almost certainly inherited to a high degree and provided the environment is ecologically favorable, the genic potential will be realized spontaneously and automatically as normal maturation.

Intersensory Development and Integration

The work of Birch and his colleagues has been highly specific in the investigation of intersensory integration. Birch and Lefford (1963) investigated the relationships among visual, haptic and kinesthetic sense modalities for geometric form recognition on 145 children from five to eleven years old. The results showed that the ability to make the various intersensory judgments clearly improved with age, and that the differences between subjects tended to decrease with age. It was also found that it was generally more difficult to make intersensory judgments of identical forms than of nonidentical forms. There were no differences in performances made with the preferred hand as compared to the nonpreferred hand in twenty-two left-handed children, but for the whole group, fewer errors were made with the preferred hand under all conditions. *However, when judging identical forms, it was found that fewer errors were made when the nonpreferred hand was utilized.* This would be left-hand/right-hemisphere functioning in most of the children. Could it be that one cannot verbalize differences between identical forms and must make purely right hemisphere spatial judgments? (See also Sperry, 1964; also quoted in Chapter VI.) In another study, Birch and Belmont (1964a) compared control and brain-damaged groups with reference to their intersensory and intrasensory functioning. It was found that although the two groups did not differ significantly from one another in their intrasensory abilities, a significant deficiency in the utilization of intersensory information existed in the brain-damaged group. They conclude that the ability to analyze complex patterns of visual stimulation into subgroups may involve a different integrative system from the one that is required for the performance of tasks based on intersensory integration. These systems, say the authors, are correlated in the normal person but are dissociated in the brain-damaged patient. Ayres (1965), in the study mentioned previously which investigated patterns of perceptual-motor dysfunction in children, also found that "perceptual deficits in children show affinities resulting in symptom arrays or syndromes which are not found in children from a random population. The syndromes . . . seem to be expressive of rather specific mechanisms by which inter-sensory and (sometimes) motor information is coordinated to permit development and manifestation of perceptual-motor ability."

In another study of 200 children, Birch and Belmont (1964b) found a significant difference in auditory-visual test performance between reading disability children and normal readers. They interpreted the results as indicating that the development of auditory-visual integration has specific relevance to reading, although it is not the sole factor underlying reading incompetence. In the study, the incompetent readers were significantly less able to make judgments of auditory-visual equivalence (patterns and visual dot patterns) than were normal readers. Unfortunately, Forrest (1967) found a significant difference between dyslexic and educationally normal children on a tapped-pattern rhythm test so the Birch and Belmont results must be considered "not proven." The results may reflect an intra-auditory deficit.

These studies are only a beginning, and much more research work is required in the investigation of specific sensory and inter-sensory functioning.

The Specific Training of Deficits

In my experience with learning disability children, I have found it advantageous to remediate directly specific neurological or psychological deficits where they exist. To date, research correlations between most purely physiological deficits and cognitive abilities, particularly those involved in reading, are low (Robbins, 1966; Forrest, 1967; Stroud, 1956; Cooke, 1968; Bannatyne and Wichiarajote, 1969b). Training in physical activities will improve children in the area of physical activities but there will be little transfer to language skills, unless some kind of instructional language program is devised. No one other than Painter (1964) has yet demonstrated that any of the physical training programs recommended by Kephart, Delacato, Ayres or Barsch have any significant effect whatsoever on oral language development and, more specifically, reading, except inasmuch as language may be used instructionally in the programs. Painter's research on kindergarten children demonstrated only one significant language

(ITPA) gain after motor training, namely, auditory/vocal association, an analogies test. The experimenter suggests that some other gains might be caused by a halo effect. It would be a valuable exercise to compare a physical training program and a language training program on two reasonably well matched groups of third-grade learning disability children. It would be very surprising if on pre- and post-testing the language-trained group had not improved in language significantly more than the physical education group. A control group should be included whose activity would be lessons in painting.

A New Approach to Sensorimotor Development

The importance of *communication through language* has been very much neglected in physical education programs. This is rather strange when one considers that psychophysical development in humans is very different from that in other animals, a difference that I would suggest has been largely brought about by the *evolution of language* in human beings. Even chimpanzees use a large number of sounds to signal each other about conditions in the environment, while dolphins may have a quite sophisticated language through which they can inform each other about environmental and even internal conditions such as the need for air (Lilly, 1968). Almost all animals have their musculature directly "wired" to noise so that, for example, a sharp sound in the environment will frequently spark them into immediate motor flight; in fact, both fight and flight reactions are closely linked to sound stimuli.

Human beings have a *phonetic* language with interchangeable sounds and this has vastly increased the number of complex noises, called words, which we can make as compared with other animals. Thus, whether we look at the long period of training through which the human child and adolescent must pass to learn how to avoid physical danger, or at the other myriad survival-value activities in which we must all engage (food gathering and eating, car driving, etc.), it is self-evident that language communication and motor activity are not just inseparably linked— they are *indivisible* aspects of the human psychophysical whole.

The essential and central importance of language to human motor development has been very much neglected to date, probably because it has not been generally realized exactly how extensive that interdependence is. In the following section, research material is presented to clarify this dependence of motor development on human communication.

The Development of Learned Voluntary Movements in Infancy and Childhood

In a paper entitled, "The Genesis of Voluntary Movements," the eminent experimental psychologist, A.R. Luria (1961a), sets out in considerable research detail the nature and stages of the development and interdependence of language and voluntary movement. He says quite unequivocally,

> It has been established that voluntary activity does not originate from any primordial properties of an internal life, but from the relations between a child and an adult. The adult at first describes certain tasks to a child, who is later able to carry them out in response to his own verbal instructions. L.S. Vygotsky indicated the basis of a child's development when he pointed out that, "A function which is first divided between two people later becomes a method of organization of the activity of a single individual."

It is important to realize that the *inhibition of movement* on an internal or external *command* is the true state of voluntary movement control.

Summarizing Luria's research, we can say that the development of *self-controlled voluntary movement*, particularly of an *inhibitory kind*, is very largely determined by the following:

1. Direct environmental signals other than adult speech such as a bell or other noise; this takes place up to and around two years of age. Of course, many children can *initiate* movements to an external command at much earlier ages.

2. The developmental state of the child's own speech which is acquired from adult "instructional speech." In other words, the child is able to *inhibit* (control) his own actions on the commands of adults at around three years of age. At younger ages he often tends to *perseverate* his

actions, although brighter children may do this less.

3. The increasing building up of *internal language* inside the child which accrues from listening to adult commands as described in item 2. This buildup of internal command language takes place from approximately four years of age onward.

4. The last stage of development occurs when the child no longer obeys the actual internalized adult instructions to carry out an action but *operates directly from his own thoughts* which have developed from all the previous external and internal instructional training and memory.

In other words, he has now "got the idea" of performing the inhibiting action which at this stage is fully under his own control as a *voluntary movement*. Until this final "thought control" idea is developmentally achieved, the child is really under the control of adult instruction (even if internalized) with respect to the specific actions involved. Of course, the above sequence is followed on different developmental activities for many years throughout childhood, from the infant's learning how to stroke a cat to the older child's learning to skate.

The above account of the importance of language communication in the development of voluntary movement in infancy and early childhood in no way contradicts the proposition that *some* voluntary movements are not doubt learned on a *nonverbal* trial-and-error basis. However, the latter system would seem to be a much less efficient way, in terms of (a) the actual learning process and (b) the ultimate efficiency with which the specific voluntary movement is performed. For example, a child who is instructionally taught how to handle equipment will learn much more rapidly and be much more efficient than a child who is left to find out on his own.

If the above sequence of events from external instruction to an internalized thought control of movement occurs in normal children, it is apparent that the educational process should be even more deliberate in those children who show signs of psychophysical impairment or evidence of maturational lags. Obviously, these children will require a psychophysical developmental program which has as its ideal objective a "perfect" thought-constructed body image—one which has been deliberately built by adult-mediated verbal communication in the form of instructions. It should always be remembered that the only way "out of" our bodies for any purpose is through motor activity, and that includes the voice and eye muscles along with other muscular functions. Movement is a *tool* through which we achieve non-motor purposes, mostly for survival in the widest sense. It is imperative, therefore, that young normal and handicapped children be given systematic training through a program which has been very carefully thought out from both the instructional and developmental points of view. Such a program must have as its foundation principle the *command internalization process*, and must tune its verbal instructions to that objective. This present program (see below) has been deliberately constructed to achieve as its objective that the child will come to internalize all the verbal instructions associated with the psychophysical education program until all the complex motor actions involved are under the direct voluntary thought control of the child.

In addition to the internalizing of adults' instructions and their transformation into thought-controlled motor system in the child, other facets of the nature of psychophysical development have to be considered in some detail, and these are discussed below.

Motor Skills and Memory

In his book *Human Memory*, J.A. Adams (1967b) says,

We all know from personal experience that the forgetting of continuous motor skills like ice-skating and riding a bicycle is trivial over long retention intervals of weeks, months, and years. These anecdotal observations are supported by controlled laboratory investigations. There is no doubt that continuous motor responses are retained very much better than verbal responses and very frequently continuous motor skills are retained perfectly over very long periods of time whereas discrete ones of brief duration are usually frequently forgotten.

It would seem important, therefore, that in any training program the activities in which the children are to participate should be as *continuous and repetitive* as possible rather than discrete and brief.

It should also be noted that verbal material, as compared with motor responses, is easily forgotten. Therefore, any verbal instructions which the child is eventually to internalize should be succinct, to the point and repeated frequently by both teacher and children. In this context, Adams says, "Great overlearning was discussed as a reason why continuous motor skills are retained so well. Discrete motor responses, like verbal responses, may be poorly retained because their level of learning is low." The implication is that overlearning is essential both verbally and motorically.

The purpose of the *overlearning* of voluntary movement is to render the muscular coordination of skills involved more and more *automatic* in response over time, once the brain has decided that the stimuli in the environment require that specific response. Thus, we practice tennis strokes deliberately and clumsily at first but with more and more skill until they can be produced instantaneously and correctly. Handwriting training is another example of automatic coordinated learned muscular operation subservient to environmental demand, cognitively interpreted.

The Body Image and Its Elements

THE ACTUAL PHYSICAL BODY: We all possess a physical body which is the original "reality template," so to speak, out of which, through which and of which the child gradually becomes aware consciously and unconsciously. (I say unconsciously because it would seem that even when we are asleep, we are very "aware" of our bodies and their psychophysical activity as, for example, when we dream of falling and the body tightens up.) The physical body feeds back information from the muscles through the kinesthetic/proprioceptive end organs but, of course, many of these may operate automatically, particularly in small children. This automatic operation (which may even be on a reflex arc through the spinal cord in some instances) means that the child is not *conscious* of the particular muscles which are in operation even though in another sense, the muscles have been moved "voluntarily." Note also that the actual physical body is directly sensed to a greater or lesser extent through vision, hearing, the tactile senses, pain and even smell and taste. This brings us to the second aspect of the body image.

THE PERCEIVED BODY: As has just been indicated, the child uses almost all his senses to be *aware* of the parts of his body when they are in motion; theoretically, this includes the static state. Perception is, as any artist or scientist knows, largely a matter of training and certainly little children do not use particular senses to perceive their bodies, or if they do, the degree of perception may be minimal. This body perception can be trained.

THE BODY SCHEMA: This facet of the body image is founded in the child's awareness of the relationships that the various parts of his body have to each other. In other words, how do the trunk, limbs and various organs interrelate to form an *operational system?* Thus, the body schema might by analogy be described as the *mechanical system* aspect of the body image.

THE BODY IMAGE ITSELF: The key to the body image as a gestalt or whole is to be found in full sensorimotor coordination and a complete psychological *awareness* of the parts of the body as they perform fully integrated activities. The body image may be very incomplete and it is only in a rare person that it is a mirror of fully coordinated function at the conscious level.

THE BODY CONCEPT: The body concept is a much wider psychological construct than the body image. The body concept would develop from life-space experiences and related conceptual training in the widest sense. Thus, the body concept might include such self-attitudes as hypochondria/health, passiveness/activeness, weakness/strength, lack of stamina/a lot of stamina, full coordination/high uncoordination, no ability to learn skills/great ability to learn skills and so on. While the body concept is crucial, it does feed back and influence the body image in various ways; it may improve that image, bringing it closer to a healthy realistic ideal, or it may distort and fragment the image until it is a twisted and remote replica of reality.

The Body Image and Handicapped Children

Many books and papers have been written on the body-image drawings of handicapped children and one of the most useful and complete is the one by M.L.J. Abercrombie (1964). She quotes several research studies which have been carried out on cerebral palsied children and illustrates how they distort the body image in drawings and various popular visuo-motor and visuo-spatial tests. She summarizes her conclusions by saying,

> It would seem that as far as perception is concerned, there is little evidence that cerebral palsied children see things in a distorted manner, though they may see them in a primitive or immature way, that is, they fail to make differentiations at the level of complexity which might be expected from their mental age. They can therefore be described as suffering from *developmental lag* in their perceptual skills. The bizarre drawings and other constructions which some of them make may seem to be unlike what normal children produce at any age, but it is possible that these also may be explained by a mixture of immature and more mature way of performing.

A New Program for Psychophysical and Body-Image Development

It would seem that what is required is a very precisely constructed, *communication-based*, psychophysical developmental program which will bring all children to a mature level of psychophysical operation for their chronological and mental ages. Such a program has been devised by M. Bannatyne and A.D. Bannatyne (1970). It is fully programmed for use by teachers and has been demonstrated to bring about real changes in the body-image and psychophysical development of young mildly handicapped learning disability children. The Body Image/Communication Program trains the child in (a) body-image appreciation, (b) voluntary movement control, (c) auditory sequencing memory, (d) physical development, (e) attentional and listening skills, (f) motivation to succeed and (g) laterality.

Specific Motor, Kinesthetic and Tactile Deficits

Particular types of deficits which directly influence language functioning and, in particular, reading may each be directly trained. In fact, in those cases of dyslexia requiring it, a fine motor/kinesthetic training of the fingers and eyes and of speech (articulation) can be carried out immediately without any protracted program of neurological lateralization, perceptual-motor generalization or matching or training in gravity-oriented physical development. Such programs would almost certainly benefit the physiological growth and integration of many afflicted MND children and are recommended for that purpose. Their influence on reading, if any, is very likely to be minimal and much faster progress will probably be made by directly training such children in those motor, kinesthetic and tactile skills necessary to linguistic communication, spoken and written.

Kinesthetic/Haptic Training

Fernald (1943) has stressed the importance of kinesthetic tracing as a part of a high-interest, cursive writing program for teaching reading. However, the Fernald kinesthetic technique assumes that the kinesthetic function of the child is intact and the method is used primarily to A-reinforce other defective sensory areas, usually auditory memory or auditory-visual integration. But the method is useful, too, with MND children who have defective kinesthetic feedback and the technique should be supplemented with largescale chalkboard writing and tracing with eyes open and closed.

The symptom of finger agnosia has been investigated by Kinsbourne and Warrington (1962, 1963b, 1963c). These authors as well as Benton (1959, 1962, 1966) have researched the related problem of finger differentiation. Kinsbourne and Warrington constructed three tests for evaluating finger differentiation and finger agnosia (one an ingenious finger block test) and used them to investigate seven cases of children who were suspected of having "the developmental Gerstmann syndrome." All the children had spelling difficulties and all but two were significantly retarded in reading. All the children had verbal IQ's on the WISC at least 20 points higher than their performance IQ's—their intelligence was in the average range. (Note that with this WISC pattern of scores, these children could not have genetic dyslexia.) All the children failed the finger block test and the in-between finger tests and only one succeeded on the finger differentiation test. The authors report that a strong familial tendency was *not* a feature of these children's backgrounds. They conclude that the Gerstmann syndrome exists in some children and may occur with a wide variety of symptoms. Rodin *et al.* (1964), Paine *et al.* (1968) and Werry and Sprague (1967) all found impaired finger movements to be a definite motor incoordination symptom.

Children having finger agnosia may be helped by any manipulative activities which involve writing, and they should be encouraged to pay attention to what their fingers are doing. This can be achieved by asking them to vocalize their finger activity. They may mold individual letters and words in modeling clay or playdough, they may sort heaps of large plastic letters into separate piles with their eyes blindfolded or they may trace textured letters with their eyes closed. These kinesthetic/tactile exercises should form only one track among several in any lesson and should be phased into a program of cursive writing in due course.

Eye-Movement Dysfunction

As the topic of eye movements has been discussed in some detail in Chapter VIII, mention here can be limited to noting that malfunctioning eye muscles are a common cause of reading disability (among others) in many MND children (Lesevre, 1966; Calvert and Cromes, 1966). The MND child with choreiform eye movements may need considerable training in moving his eyes saccadically along a line of print, and a part of his difficulty may be an inability to recognize quickly the shapes of letters and words; such children will require training in the recognition of these shapes. This should be followed by reading practice using books printed in large print-type.

Speech (Articulation)

Much has already been said about the motor aspects of speech production and more will be said in Chapter XI. Although speech is not absolutely essential to the acquisition of language (see Chapter II), the MND child whose articulation is uneven, slurred or otherwise impaired frequently has difficulty in learning to read adequately. Certainly a training in articulation helps children learn to read (Sommers *et al.*, 1961a). I suspect that clear articulation helps one to delineate more clearly and consciously the phonemes and other sound units in our language, so that when it is time to decode them during reading or to encode them when writing, the increased discrimination facilitates rapid recognition or production.

When autistic children are trained to articulate specific sounds their imitation or modeling of the mouth movements of the instructor can be of key importance. Likewise, one suspects that some MND children as infants have found it difficult to imitate or model the articulatory movements made by their parents. The implication is that while the speech apparatus may be intact, the real deficit is the child's *inability to copy or imitate* the mouth movements of the person from whom he is learning. This may entail training a child to imitate before embarking on an extended training of articulation itself.

In a discussion of sensory, motor and central defects and their influence on language acquisition, Teuber (1964), quoting a case described by Richard L. Gregory, suggests that the cross-modality transfer of learning may be much more feasible than had previously been supposed. This would mean that a child learning to write through a kinesthetic/tactile program would considerably A-reinforce his visual understanding of the language.

Teuber also has something to say about sensorimotor coordination. Quoting his own work, along with that of von Holst, Sperry, MacKay and Held (each working independently), Teuber suggests that the motor system may be able to "inform" the sensory systems directly via a central discharge without invoking the notion of feedback through reflexive peripheral loops. These direct neural communications he calls "corollary discharges." Thus, as the central motor system signals effector muscles, there is concomitantly a discharge directly from the motor system to the sensory system within the CNS and prior to any return signal from the CNS periphery. This discharge represents the expectation and anticipation of a normally occurring change in afferent (return) patterns. This enables us, says Teuber, to explain such classic problems as why the world stands still when we move our eyes voluntarily. (See also Gregory, 1966.) There is much anatomical evidence in the form of fibers of the pyramidal tract for this corollary discharge and this gives us a physiological basis for distinguishing voluntary from involuntary movement. Teuber states:

> A voluntary movement now would be one in which there is a corollary discharge, by which I reset my central sensory mechanisms for the anticipated change. An involuntary or passive movement would be one in which no such corollary discharge meets with the ascending input. Incidentally, these notions do not fit at all into current S-R theory, and that's why I think these notions may bear on studies of speech and language. After all, it is in the approach to language learning that S-R theory fails so utterly, and S-R theory—as Lashley never tired of pointing out—is only traditional reflex-physiology "psychologized."

Teuber suggests that through direct corollary discharges, the articulatory control systems in the brain may be able to directly "inform" the other sensory systems, particularly (in the context) the auditory one, without the necessity of hearing oneself speak.

One implication of Teuber's statement is that some children with neurological dysfunction may have their direct feedback discharge impaired, a state which would prevent a central cross-checking comparison on any voluntary movement articulations they are about to make. Stuttering, which can be induced through delayed external feedback, may also possibly be caused by impaired central feedback. Of course, the remarks in this paragraph, which are my own, are very speculative and should not be confused with Teuber's main statement, for which there is some neurological evidence (see above).

Rhythm

Although the topic of rhythm crops up from time to time in the literature, it is usually mentioned in passing or as an adjunct to some other more easily defined subject. Rhythm, as measured by the Seashore tests (Seashore and Lewis, 1960), was found by Wolf (1967) to be an excellent discriminator between dyslexic boys and their normal counterparts. The dyslexic groups who were rhythmically inferior did not contain children with detectable neurological dysfunction of any kind and were much more likely to be cases of genetic dyslexia. In another study by Birch and Belmont (1965c), the auditory-visual integration of brain-damaged and normal children was investigated using auditory tap patterns and equivalent visual stimuli. The authors found the cerebral palsied children to be significantly poorer than the normal children in their auditory-visual integrative capacities. Although Birch and Belmont found that digit-span memory was unrelated to auditory-visual integrative performance, they did not test the efficiency of the two groups on duplicating auditory tap patterns *independently* of the visual stimuli. Forrest (1967) found a significant difference between educationally handicapped children and academically successful pupils on a test that repro-duced tapped patterns (which *was* correlated with the WISC digit span). This suggests that Birch and Belmont's results may be a single (auditory)modality defict. Therefore, I am not con-vinced that a cross-modality integrative function was exhaustively tested in the Birch and Belmont study; it could be that the capacity to "remember" auditory rhythms is inferior in many cerebral palsied children, just as it is in dyslexic children (Drake and Schnall, 1966; Forrest, 1967; Wolf, 1967). I strongly suspect that a sense of rhythm is one of the more important factors under-lying verbal ability.

Rhythm can be appreciated in each of the sensorimotor modalities equally well but, of course, its main dimension is *time* and its major input-output mode of expression, musical beat, is *auditory-motor*. If an appreciation of time and of musical tonality is at least in part a function of the right temporal lobe, these functions are almost certainly embedded, though perhaps to a lesser degree, in the language functioning of the left temporal lobe. Beating drums or dancing probably involves the frontal lobes because motor planning is strongly suspected of taking place there (Luria, 1966). Luria also suggests that speech planning takes place in these premotor areas, and speech rather obviously has a considerable if complex rhythmic component—it is not just noise. Therefore, it is not unreasonable to suppose that if for some reason the temporal and frontal areas are not functioning as well as they might, input and output musical and motor rhythms will be of poorer quality in the right hemisphere, while heard and spoken language will suffer in the left hemisphere. Of course, these various functions are not entirely confined to a particular hemisphere. One thing is certain, that complex rhythmic abilities of an auditory-motor nature require a great deal more research investigation, particularly with respect to the part they play in speech perception and production. One remedial teacher, who is a talented musician, found that children improved more rapidly in reading and spelling when the accent and beat of words and phrases was clarified and overemphasized.

Auditory/Vocal Defects in MND Children

Neurological dysfunction can cause many types of defects in the auditory or vocal functioning of impaired children, any one of which may be a material cause of their reading or spelling disability. Frequently, these dysfunctions are multiple.

One intelligent girl, fifteen years of age, who suffered from centrally caused auditory deficits, was able to describe them. Sometimes, speech sounds seemed to wax and wane as if the volume were being turned up and down in an irregular way. Sometimes there might be temporary deafness in some frequency ranges. The overall impression was of an inefficient telephone line which may also have been quite "noisy" on occasions.

MND children may have poor auditory discrimination and poor auditory closure on gestalts of sound, particularly for words in which phonemes are blurred or slightly mispronounced. The auditory memory of many MND children is often inadequate in both recognition and recall forms. Poor recall of sequences of phonemes is often reflected in low digit-span scores on the WISC or ITPA. Memorizing phoneme-to-grapheme association may be a difficult task, as might be remembering sequences of those associations.

Many of the auditory problems mentioned in the previous chapter in connection with genetic dyslexic children also apply to MND children, but it must be stressed that the efficient and material causes are quite different for the two groups.

In reading, spelling and speech, the sound-blending abilities of neurological dysfunction cases are frequently inadequate. Some of these children are extremely resistant (in spite of their best efforts) to the learning of sound-blending skills. As a result of having some or all of these deficits, auditory word-labels (vocabulary) and auditory concepts are not "built." In other words, there is a general paucity of functioning in the whole auditory-verbal area.

Another deficit possessed by most MND children is their inability to automatize verbal fluency skills. They do not seem to be able to integrate and synthesize auditory language with motor/kinesthetic planning and visual scanning input in rapid habituated ways. In such cases, overlearning is an important remedial technique.

MND children suffering from auditory deficits not infrequently exhibit mild aphasic symptoms. It will be remembered that most dyslexic children have problems in associating the auditory word and the spoken word with the written or printed word, whereas in this context, aphasic children have difficulty associating auditory and spoken words to objects and concepts. Aphasic children, like most deaf children, may also have considerable difficulty acquiring words in the first place. As aphasia will be discussed in detail later in the chapter, it will not be further elaborated here.

A slow, uneven speech and language development with speech deficits (not attributable to organ malfunctioning) which persist into later childhood is one of the main indicators of auditory/vocal neurological dysfunction, and many of the above symptoms will be found in such children.

Emotional Problems in MND Dyslexia

This aspect of MND symptomatology will be dealt with only briefly at this point because the topic will be covered in some detail in Chapter XIII. Much of the neurological regulation of the emotions is centered in the hypothalamus (Woodburne, 1967) and impairment in this area must surely lead to unstable or "lopsided" emotional reactivity. If the cortex is diffusely or locally impaired, it would therefore follow that emotional reactions to stimuli may be either excessive, distorted, inappropriate or inhibited, depending on the extent and site of the lesions, and the types of cells damaged. This would account for the great variety of emotional and social behaviors which have been reported as being characteristic of MND children (Clements, 1966).

Anxiety and Motivation

Although these topics will be dealt with in much more detail in Chapter XIII, a brief discussion of the effects of anxiety on attention and motivation when learning to read is relevant here. Boxall (1962), using his own School Anxiety Test, which he successfully validated against other tests of anxiety, showed clearly that children with high or low anxiety tend to fail in reading. Girls of high anxiety read either very poorly or at an average standard, while for boys high anxiety correlates with good reading and low anxiety with poor reading. The sample was composed of 117 boys and girls in their second and third years of junior school. Lynn (1955), in a similar study on a similar group, obtained significant positive correlations between the results of an anxiety test and reading test scores. Though the literature correlating academic performance and anxiety is vast, it is inconclusive because the anxiety measures are invalid and rarely sample dyslexic children. There is an urgent research need for a thorough examination of the role anxiety plays in all types of learning disability children, because I strongly suspect that a high degree of underlying anxiety is strongly correlated with very poor academic performance, especially in MND children, including boys. This hypothesis does not mean that low anxiety cases are good readers; therefore, the sample would have to be carefully chosen and the research design rather subtle. Present anxiety "tests" (or questionnaires) are inadequate and some new way of evaluating the quantity and quality of the anxiety would be necessary. Even more importantly, the nature of the objects and situations which actively stimulated the anxiety would have to be delineated.

Concluding Remarks

There are numerous case histories to be found in the literature

(Frostig and Hart, 1965; Kirk, 1966; de Hirsch, 1965; Jansky, 1965; Association for Children with Learning Disabilities *Selected Conference Papers*, 1966). Therefore, none need be appended to this chapter by way of illustration. Also, apart from the diffuse impairment syndrome, each MND child is unique and to be representative, one would have to select dozens of illustrative cases.

Chapter XI

APHASIA

INTRODUCTION

There is little doubt that aphasia is the most interesting and most complex of all languages disabilities. A very large number of experts have written on the topic of aphasia during the past century, and some of those workers had an amazing insight into the problem inasmuch as subsequent research has repeatedly confirmed their early findings. Hughlings Jackson was one of these pioneers who felt that speech in terms of single words was rather a meaningless process and consequently for him the sentence or proposition was the essential aspect of language. It was as if he was emphasizing the sequential processes, both of word selection and of its concomitant, sequential meaning. For the sake of theory, he distinguished between the intellectual and emotional aspects of language and noticed how in aphasic cases these two functions of communication might become separated. In other words, in some individuals, speech is often rather flat and unemotional, while in others, although excitement may be present, the propositions themselves may lack full meaning. Jackson tended to approach the study of aphasia as a clinician, particularly from the psychological standpoint. For example, he realized that there were levels of behavior and that voluntary behaviors, when they ceased to exist in the individual, might free involuntary ones. He also noted that the behavior of some aphasics tended to be abnormal, and that other nonlanguage factors might be disturbed. One of his greatest insights was to realize that thought and language were not one and the same thing even though for most communication purposes they were inextricably bound together. Furthermore, he recognized that the language processes in the brain were not confined to one

479

specific area. Altogether, Jackson made a remarkable contribution to our knowledge of aphasia.

Henry Head took up Jackson's ideas in the early 1900's and elaborated on them in many ways. Head was fortunate in that he was able to examine many casualties from World War I using tests which he had developed to investigate not only language disturbances but also other kinds such as those in mathematics and music. For him, aphasia was "a disorder of symbolic formulation and expression." Head classified the speech symptoms of aphasics into four groupings. The first was *verbal aphasia,* which seemed to be largely a speech condition; the second was *nominal aphasia,* which was characterized by the inability to label objects with the correct words or to understand their meaning in the absence of the object. The third group was composed of such symptoms as jargon speaking and telegrammatic language; these were classed as *syntactical aphasia. Semantic aphasia* was the name given to those cases who could not appreciate the full meaning or significance of a statement or proposition.

Before continuing with a deeper discussion of aphasia, it is necessary to outline the kinds of problems the aphasic child has to cope with internally in his struggle to communicate through language functions.

SYMPTOMS AND DISABILITIES

The aphasic child may exhibit any clustering of the following list of symptoms, each of which is briefly described at this point as a basis for discussing how these various facets may be meaningfully organized.

Auditory Discrimination and Recognition of Speech Sounds

Even at the perceptual level, the aphasic child may appear to have difficulty discriminating heard sounds from background noise. This is an auditory figure-ground problem which may also be linked with problems of attention and distraction. These two characteristics, in turn, may be either emotional (with a neurological dysfunction basis) or caused by poor discriminatory screening between complex sets of incoming auditory stimuli. Inasmuch as these discriminatory functions take place through time, the aphasic child may find it difficult to receptively track continuous incoming speech with any degree of accuracy. By analogy, a telephone line may be noisy and, in terms of volume efficiency, it may be unpredictable.

Central Processing of Auditory Perceptions

Even for those words and sentences which are successful in "reaching" the central integrative and conceptualizing areas of the brain (including the centrencephalic system of Penfield and Roberts, 1959), there are difficulties which may arise. The various experiential memory systems of the brain may be more or less defective and, because of the resulting lack of information with which to compare the incoming material, the latter may be meaningless. Even if the information is superficially understood on a "concrete" level, the aphasic child may find it difficult to manipulate the information intelligently. In other words, he will not understand or appreciate interrelationships between concepts. The neurological causes of such a disability, which borders on aspects of autistic symptomatology, may be quite varied.

Context Problems

Sometimes aphasic children may be unable to relate the information (which they seem to have received and "interpreted") relevantly to their immediate environment. For example, even though they may understand instructions and even the purpose behind those instructions, they may be incapable of reacting appropriately. In fact, there are many ways in which the central cognitive functions of aphasic children may function inadequately; of course, all of these may involve any facet of cognitive activity.

Speech Problems

Almost all aphasic children rather obviously will have trouble with spoken language, but the speech, or rather the speaking problem of the aphasic child should not be confused with the specific speech disabilities of the child whose only problem is a peripheral difficulty in articulation. Of course, by the laws of chance, some aphasic children also have problems of peripheral articulation. More often their speech symptoms take the form of perseveration, peculiar noises and "parrot" imitations, all of which seem to emanate from some form of complex cerebral dysfunction. The term *cerebral dysfunction* in this context includes possible genetic factors which do not normally occur in the population as a whole.

In the light of the above summary of the kinds of symptoms which occur in aphasic children, it becomes possible to examine more closely the psychoneurological and psycholinguistic nature of this complex disorder.

DEFINITIONS AND CLASSIFICATIONS

Before discussing some current definitions of aphasia, one should note that the disorder is almost always complicated by other difficulties, some primary and some secondary in nature. Speech defects have already been mentioned and to these we can add central (perhaps partial) deafness and some types of mental retardation. Occasionally, one may find a case of minimal autism or slight cerebral palsy. In almost every aphasic child, there is an overlay of primary or secondary emotional disturbance.

One of the first distinctions to be made is that developmental aphasia is almost always qualitatively different from acquired aphasia. The term *developmental aphasia* merely means that the disorder probably has been in existence from birth or shortly after, so that the child has developed from the outset with a disturbance of language functioning. In the case of acquired aphasia, the brain has been impaired by some disease or trauma subsequent to the acquisition of a degree of language. The language which was acquired prior to the disease or accident will then be distorted and disturbed in ways which may be quite different from the case where true language never existed. Many adult aphasias are of the acquired kind, whereas the vast majority of aphasic cases in early childhood are developmental in nature.

So complex is the symptomatology of aphasia that some authorities consider clear-cut cases extremely rare and therefore throw doubt on the idea that aphasia may be a collection of disorders with several common elements; hardly anyone in the field would suggest that aphasia is a homogeneous entity. Louis Dicarlo (1960) has reclassified sixty-seven children previously diagnosed as having "congenital aphasia" into five groups. Seventeen children had IQ's between 18 and 58 and were placed in one of the retarded mental develoment groups; eleven children with IQ's between 60 and 75 were placed in another retarded mental development group; twenty of the children were classified as emotionally disturbed, although in the normal-to-bright range of intelligence, and another fifteen had defective hearing, although their IQ's ranged from 60 to 117. Only four of the children could be classified as having aphasoid characteristics. Dicarlo points out that while all these sixty-seven children were characterized by severe inabilities to relate and communicate, a careful appraisal of them strongly postulates the concept of multiple deficiencies.

In a report (West *et al.*, 1960) of the proceedings of an institute on childhood aphasia held at Stanford, the Professional Advisory Committee of the California Society developed the following statement as a tentative definition of childhood aphasia:

> It is an impairment in language function (expressive and receptive) resulting from maldevelopment or injury to the central nervous system, pre-natally or post-natally. (Post-natally means anytime within the first year of life.) The language deficiency may or may not be associated with other cerebral or neurological pathology or dysfunction. Excluded are language problems associated primarily with: (1) mental deficiency, (2) hearing impairment, (3) central nervous system damage affecting the peripheral speech mechanisms, (4) emotional disturbance, (5) delayed maturation in language development resulting from social and emotional factors or physical factors not primarily due to central nervous system involvement.

The authors note that emotional factors include the schizophrenias.

As one examines aphasic children or reads the cases in the literature, it will become apparent (and Dicarlo's statement becomes more validated) that the number of aphasic children who fall within the above definition is small. In other words, a clear-cut case of "pure" aphasia is rather rare. At this point, it is necessary to clear the problem of central deafness and distinguish it from aphasia. Worster-Drought (1957) distinguishes clearly between the inability to hear resulting from central deafness and the inability to comprehend language. He suggests that central deafness results from lesions affecting the transmission of sound within the brain, whereas the inability to understand, comprehend or interpret intact incoming auditory information may be caused by lesions of the interpretive cortex. Almost all workers would agree with Worster-Drought's distinction. The problem which confronts the clinician is to eliminate central deafness as a possibility, particularly in severe cases. E.N. Taylor, reporting to an institute on speech and language held in England in 1963, described his work on this problem. It may be that the disorganization of the central word schema in aphasia is related to the inhibitory effects of visual stimuli which interfere with a normal auditory monitoring feedback. By recording the EEG in the waking state and during sleep, the differences in the child's responses to various sound stimuli help detect whether or not the problem is one of central deafness or aphasia. Using a similar technique, Neil Gordon reported to a conference in London during 1966 that such testing must be very carefully carried out, particularly because the records at different levels of sleep, and with different input stimuli, may vary greatly. A child may react to the word *Mommy* but not to other stimuli. Also, the responses may vary depending on whether the audiogram is ascending or descending. Even so, if the child reacts to meaningful whole words but not to incidental sounds, then, as Gordon says, "This selectivity must surely involve the cerebral cortex although it may not be essential for the production of an arousal response in a sleeping subject." It is to be hoped that EEG techniques will will become more sophisticated and that a great deal may also be learned about the nature and probable location of the problems facing any individual aphasic child.

The traditional and most usual classification of the symptoms presented by developmental aphasics is to divide them into the receptive or sensory aphasias, and the expressive, executive or motor aphasias. Aphasic symptoms involving conceptualizing or integrational problems are usually merged into the receptive group or the expressive group according to whether one is primarily concerned in one's professional work with hearing and communication disorders or with speech and language production problems. In other words, some workers think of language as being almost entirely input and interpretation, thus relegating speech to a kind of simple motor articulation printout stage, whereas speech correctionists and pathologists tend to think of reception as a relatively simply process of detecting sequences of sounds. The true language functions are those of formulating words into meaningful sentences which are then produced as spoken language or, for that matter, written language. Wepman (1960) says, "We have concluded that aphasia, the language disorder, is best considered as a defect of the integrative processes only, while the agnosias and apraxias can be considered as defects limited to the nonsymbolic function of transmission into and out of the system." Monsees (1957) quotes Myklebust, who gives a definition similar to Wepman's: "Perhaps the most fundamental problem confronted by the aphasic child is his reduced capacity for normal integration. He sees, hears, and feels; but he cannot integrate this sensory information into an experienced pattern which is logical and reliable for purposes of understanding his environment. . . ."

Monsees goes on to say that she does not believe the aphasic child to be deficient in these integrative processes but rather places more emphasis on the diagnosis of the nature of the language disability itself. She believes ". . . that the main characteristic of the aphasic child is the weakness in memory for speech sounds and for the sequence of sounds in a word or of words in a sentence." She goes on to quote Hardy (1956), who says, "What is most obvious is that they [children with this type of language disorder] cannot naturally listen, understand, store and recall symbolic structures involving a time order and a stress pattern." Next she quotes Broughton and further amplifies her contention that aphasia is primarily a defect of memory for symbol patterns. Monsees suggests that those children who do not learn language graphically when fitted with a hearing aid and taught with methods commonly used with the deaf and hard-of-hearing form a distinct group and that

> . . . these children exhibit the weakness of memory for speech sounds and for the sequence of sounds in words which C.I.D. (Central Institute for the Deaf) emphasizes as the crux of the problem of aphasia. In our opinion, diagnosis of aphasia cannot be properly given until after a period of diagnostic teaching which clearly reveals such memory weakness for speech sounds and sequence.

The reader will see from the first sentence quoted above that aphasics, at least in the experience of Monsees, have areas of auditory deficit very like those found in genetic dyslexic children and for that matter other types of dyslexic children with auditory problems. This concomitance of symptoms will be explored in more depth later.

Wepman (1960) has classified the types of aphasia in accordance with his five stages of language development. Although these categories have been identified in studies of adult impairment, they do have relevance for childhood aphasia. Global aphasia is the first kind and is at the first prelanguage stage of development characterized by speechlessness. Jargon aphasia at stage two of the developmental process is also prelanguage, and is characterized by meaningless autistic and echolalic phoneme use. The third stage is pragmatic aphasia, which has as its symptoms poor verbal comprehension and the oral expression of words and neologisms largely unrelated to meaning. Semantic aphasia, at the stage-four level, is characterized by the inability to use substantive language; one or two word groupings often form complete expressions. Syntactic aphasia (stage five) is characterized by the abnormal use of grammar or syntax in oral expressions. Wepman describes these categories further:

> The first two types, global and jargon aphasia, are described by the related stages of development in infancy, while the last three types are represented by an absence or dysfunction of their related stages

on the developmental side of the table. Thus pragmatic aphasia is an inability to comprehend or form a clear, meaningful statement and therefore, the speech used is unrelated to meaningfulness; the semantic aphasic cannot use the process of substantive word formation, while the syntactic aphasic lacks the syntax of the language.

Sheridan (1964) suggests that children can be clustered into five major groups for purposes of treatment and training. Group one is composed of those children whose primary difficulty is severe or partial deafness. Group two has in it those children who hear and can interpret spoken language but cannot use it themselves. They can, however, communicate effectively in other ways such as organized mime, drawing, finger spelling or writing; i.e., they possess good "inner language" and use symbols. Group three includes those children who hear and comprehend simple language when addressed in short sentences, at a slow rate and in familiar situations. They may possess a limited spoken vocabulary which they help out with gestures; i.e., they possess a primitive "inner language" which is usually effective only in the "here and now." Group four is composed of children who hear and may repeat words or sentences in parrot fashion, but who do not comprehend their meaning. They may also recall musical themes and enjoy playing with noise-making toys but they do not use any symbolic forms. They show some awareness of their environment and communicate with other people in prelinguistic fashion by pulling, pointing, clinging, pushing away, screaming, etc. Group five has in it those children who hear but pay no attention to speech or to other meaningful sounds. Their prelinguistic communication is reduced to a minimum. They may by hyperkinetic or completely immobile, but in either case they are more or less inaccessible. Although Sheridan does not label these groups, the symptomatology would suggest that those in group five are noncommunicating cases, autistic children or perhaps children suffering from childhood schizophrenia. Group four would be the receptive aphasics and group two the expressive or executive aphasics, while group three could perhaps be labeled a mild mixture of groups two and four. Group one by definition consists of the partially or completely deaf.

Wood, speaking at the California Conference on Childhood

Aphasia (Wood *et al.*, 1960), looked at the problem of classifying aphasic children in quite a different way. His classification groups more by original causes than by a functional "What is going on in the brain now?" type of grouping. He suggested three types of aphasia. The first originates from organic problems. The second group is composed of those children who are unable to use the spoken word as a symbol on either an emissive or receptive basis or a combination of both. Several experts including Wood do not think that there is such a thing as true expressive aphasia because speech as a printout function is always permeated, so to speak, with more "central" processing such as understanding and organizing information linguistically. Wood felt that this symbolic type of aphasia might be developmental, but it was rare for such children to catch up and develop normal language processes. The third type of aphasia is one with a large familial element; that is, it would seem to be genetically based.

Bender (1963) has suggested that aphasia is a disorder in the developmental processes of language and that it is likely there are a number of different areas of developmental lag which may also be seen in motor functions and personality organization. Aphasia may also be seen in space and time perceptions and in cortical functioning which is so plastic that "the pattern is at a level which has been inadequate." The problem is how to increase the adequacy of this pattern. In order to solve this problem we also have to think of neurological etiology.

THE NEUROLOGY OF APHASIA

The above definitions and classifications have led steadily toward a more neurological viewpoint, and it is here that the problem of aphasia becomes even more complex. Apart from the wide range of language symptoms, aphasic children often present disorders in other functions such as a distorted body image, an inability to copy designs, directional disorientation, poor coordination, clumsiness, hyperactivity, poor attention span, emotional disturbances and finger agnosia, not to mention various other agnosias, apraxias, etc. An extensive list classifying many of these disorders and those more directly related to language was drawn up many years ago by Anderson (1944). Her list, the essentials of which are set out below, is in remarkable agreement with Luria's categories described later in the chapter.

I. Expressive manifestations
    A. Implicit (probably caused by a parietal lesion)
        1. Ideational aphasia
        2. Ideokinetic aphasia
    B. Overt (probably caused by a frontal lobe lesion)
        1. Spoken language
            a. Broca's aphasia (third left frontal convolution, cortex)
            b. Subcortical aphasia (subcortical Broca's region)
            c. Transcortical aphasia (questionable)
        2. Written language: Agraphia (Exner's writing center, second frontal convolution)
II. Receptive manifestations
    A. Auditory (superior temporal convolution)
        1. Agnosia (Heschl's convolution)
        2. Aphasia (posterior part of superior temporal convolution)
    B. Visual (temporoparieto-occipital area)
        1. Agnosia
            a. For linguistic symbols
            b. For objects and colors
            c. Geometric-optic
        2. Aphasia
            a. Alexia
            b. Agraphia
            c. Anomia
    C. Other sensory media
        1. Tactile
        2. Cutaneous
        3. Kinesthetic
III. Associative manifestations
    A. Aphasia on lower levels
    B. Aphasia on higher levels

IV. Combinations of manifestations
  A. Wernicke's aphasia
  B. Total aphasia
  C. Other combinations of aphasic manifestations

It should be noted that the above list is a classification of "aphasic manifestations" or, to word it another way, those variables found in aphasic children; it is not a classification of aphasic children and so it is a much more precise categorization than most.

As the neuropsychology of language has already been discussed in some detail, it will not be recapitulated here. However, there are several points made by various authorities which are worth reiterating at this juncture. It is much more profitable to consider the function of the brain and body as complex integrated systems "vertically" established, rather than as levels, since the cerebral cortex does not work in semi-isolation from the rest of the brain or sensorimotor organs. A second neurological point is the importance of both internal and external feedback, particularly in the monitoring of speech. Although as Lenneberg has pointed out, at least one child has developed a complete inner language without vocal feedback, it should be noted that an absence of feedback and a distorted feedback are two different things. It is well established experimentally that delays and disruptions of external feedback through laboratory apparatus cause speech difficulties (Yates, 1963). Webster *et al.* (1970) have confirmed that stuttering can be induced by delaying auditory feedback, and Dinnan *et al.* (1970) have found that male stutterers have a 0.95-second difference in time delay over normal speakers. This reaction time difference is interpreted as resulting from possible minute imperfections in the auditory/vocal feedback loop.

Templin *et al.* (1960) have commented that real deviations in language behavior are more frequent in boys than in girls and that this sex difference is true of most other deviant behavior. They point out that these differences are very slight in the developmental pattern of the normal population but that girls do tend to attain accuracy in the articulation of surnames, achieve a higher level of grammatical structure and begin to talk a little earlier than do boys. On the other hand, boys may have larger vocabularies and a wider range of information, and may talk more rapidly than girls do at the same age. All these differences tend to be slight and Templin *et al.* suggest that they may be culturally determined. Nevertheless, most aphasic cases tend to be boys and this follows the sex difference pattern in dyslexia, in other language disabilities and in much other research on normal children. *I suspect that a basic genetic factor is operating here (in combination with many other possible factors) and that this factor is identical to the one I have described in some detail to explain such sex differences in Chapters VI and IX on genetic dyslexia and the neuropsychology of language.* Certainly this sex difference in aphasic cases would have to be accounted for in terms of the neurology of the brain one way or another. It is to be stressed that I do not consider "normal" genetic factors a primary cause of aphasia as in dyslexia. The inherited predisposition of an inability to cope easily with verbal skills *aggravates* aphasia, which may result from a large number of causes singly or in combination.

Yet another "neurological" symptom is the lack of handedness, or rather the poorly defined laterality of handedness, in aphasic children. While there is no doubt that this can be explained to some extent on the maturational lag theory that aphasic children tend to be neurologically organized at a younger age than their actual chronological age, it can also, in part, be attributed to the organizational nature of the more visuo-spatial type of brain (see Chapters IX and X). Of course, these two aspects of development are *not incompatible;* in fact, it may be highly likely that almost all aphasic children suffer from a multiple handicap inasmuch as they have a severe maturational lag, a visuo-spatial type of brain organization and some neurological impairment as well.

Hardy (1960) mentions several categories of clinical observations which must be made when assessing the aphasic child. The first of these is investigation of the detail of auditory discrimination and recognition relative to sensitivity; this can be checked with an auditory discrimination test and an audiogram. His second category is that of foreground-background auditory perception, which is largely a function of attention. The third category is that of fixation of attention through time; in other words, the child must rapidly and competently process successive stimuli. The fourth consideration is the ability of the child to relate the incoming information appropriately to the context of events in the environment, while the fifth need of the aphasic child is the ability to *track*, that is, the capacity to process multiple bits of information in a meaningful way. Any child who cannot cope with the complexity of a sentence will have a disability in tracking complex data. Hardy points out that all these conditions may be trained and even reorganized through learning.

Agranowitz and McKeown (1963) have equated several areas of the brain with various language defects, presumably caused by lesions. The first of these is auditory verbal agnosia, in which the recognition of spoken language is impaired; this they say is caused by lesions in Wernicke's area of the brain, which is in the superior temporal area, while motor aphasia, a deterioration of the memory for the motor patterns of speech, is related to lesions in Broca's area. Anomia and amnesic aphasia—the inability to recall names, words and language—are caused by lesions in the lower part of the junction between the temporal and occipital lobes. The inability to handle the symbols for reading (alexia), writing (agraphia) and arithmetic (acalculia) is caused by impairments of the angular gyrus in the parietal area. Agraphia as a motor function—that is, an agnosia of how to make the movements of the hands and fingers in writing—would appear to involve the motor cortex, the part called the "writing center," which normally subserves the functioning of hands and fingers. When visual perception and the recognition of shapes are disturbed (visual-verbal agnosia without agraphia), the lesion is thought to occur in the primary visual areas and possibly in the association areas of the visual cortex in the occipital lobes as well. Many of the above functions would appear to be located in the left hemisphere of the brain in the majority of individuals. These locations have been largely confirmed by many research workers, notably Penfield and Roberts (1959), Luria (1966) and Hecaen and de Ajuriaguerra (1964).

Another contributor to our knowledge of the neuropsychology of aphasia is K. Conrad (1949), who in studying soldiers with brain injuries compared the hemisphere in which the lesion occurred with the handedness of the patients. Ninety-four percent of the cases of aphasia occurred in the left hemisphere of right-handed people. However, in the left-handed patients, 59 percent had lesions in the left hemisphere and 41 percent in the right hemisphere. It is clear that aphasia which is the result of lesions in the right hemisphere is far more frequent in left-handed subjects than in right-handed subjects. Conrad's work suggests that in left-handed people there may be a tendency for language to be represented in both hemispheres, but caution should be exercised in interpreting these results in terms of childhood aphasia, since all Conrad's subjects were adults. Another point of interest is that left-handers *may* not have any more language representation in the right hemisphere than do right-handed people; there is at least a theoretical possibility that the increase in aphasic symptoms for left-handers with damage in the right hemisphere could occur because left-handed people may have more dominant *motor functions* in the right hemisphere and the aphasia may be the result of vocal-motor disturbance rather than an inability to handle auditory symbols.

Ingram and Reid (1956) noted a marked lack of consistent hand reference in 71 percent of a group of patients diagnosed as having developmental aphasia. This study also tended to suggest that vocal-motor functioning is well represented in the right hemisphere at least at the same level as it is in the left hemisphere. After researching the subject of cerebral dominance and handedness, Subirama (1958) found that aphasia which follows injuries to the left hemisphere tends to disappear more quickly and completely in left-handed people than in the right-handed. This certainly seems to suggest that the symbol or sign represented in the language at least on an auditory level is to some extent represented in the right hemisphere, although once again the finding could be attributed to vocal-motor functions. It is worth noting at this point that dyslexic children tend to have reversals in reading and spelling and that these, according to Orton (1937), *may* be caused by mirror-image symbol representation in the right hemisphere. Some experimental confirmation of right hemisphere symbol mirror imaging has recently been published by Bannatyne and Wichiarajote (1969b). In a clinical study, Brown and Simonson (1957) found that thirteen of one hundred aphasic cases with predominant reading disability had lesions which were definitely posterior at the end of the sylvian fissure in the region of the angular gyrus. It would seem that we can safely conclude that the visual symbolic aspects of language are definitely represented in the parietal areas of the cortex. Critchley (1964) has written extensively on this subject.

THE CONTRIBUTION OF A.R. LURIA

One of the giant figures in the investigation of language, particularly from the neuropsychological aspect, is the Russian psychologist A.R. Luria. In his volume entitled "Higher Cortical Functions in Man," (1966) he says that there are several kinds of aphasia which he names as acoustico-amnestic, efferent kinesthetic, efferent motor, optic, semantic and acoustic temporal or sensory. Luria criticizes the traditional breakdown of disturbances of the higher cortical functions into three independent groups: agnosia, apraxia and aphasia. He suggests that all recent work indicates that a much more profitable approach is to regard all three as aspects of a complex interrelated system of neurological functioning. In particular, he suggests that the agnosias and apraxias are frequently difficult to separate as contributors to a particular malfunction. He also remarks that recently neuropsychology has rejected the idea that sensory and motor processes are isolated functions. Motor components are involved in many sensory processes; that is, both afferent and efferent components are fully integrated in most sensory or motor "acts." Luria says,

> Many clinical descriptions of aphasic symptoms are given without proper analysis, and the classifications of these disturbances are based either on hypothetical schemes, in which patterns of "conduc-

tion" or "transcortical" aphasia (usually unconfirmed by clinical psychological investigation) are identified, or on purely linguistic descriptions of "nominal," "syntactical," and "semantic" aphasias, which do not reflect the true richness of the clinical syndromes and their relationship to their underlying physiological mechanisms.

Luria adheres to the point of view that the perception of speech is dependent on the analysis and synthesis of the elements in the flow of sound and that this work is carried out by "auditory and kinesthetic analyzers." He suggests that the pronunciation of words, which essentially is a complicated system of articulatory movements, has as its basis the same kinesthetic and auditory analyzers involved in the perception of speech. (Some research doubts about this hypothesis were presented in another context in Chapter II.) It should be noted that *each* sensory and motor function has its specific analyzer, which is a functional area of the brain devoted to discriminating and interpreting the stimulus from its background "noise." On this theory, sensation is an *active* process which selects the signal components of stimuli while it inhibits the other components. Luria says, "Sensation incorporates the process of analysis and synthesis of signals while they are still in the first stages of arrival." He goes on to say, "According to this view, from the very beginning the sensory cortical divisions participate in the analysis and integration of complex, not elementary, signals." The auditory analyzers and the integrational functions involved in interpretive listening to speech are processed in the secondary areas of the auditory cortex. This work is also carried out in close collaboration with the inferior regions of the frontal area which have special speech functions.

Luria points out that if one is ignorant of a foreign language, one does not even discriminate the phonemes of that language whereas when listening to one's native language, almost every phoneme can be heard and interpreted at least in the gestalt sense; thus the auditory analyzer and integrator is the result of specific learning from infancy. Furthermore, Luria claims that articulation is essential to language development generally, so much so that the interpretation of speech is considerably determined by past articulatory experience. As has been previously stated, the word *essential* in the above sentence is now in some doubt on the basis of recent research (Lenneberg, 1967). It is worth noting that Weiner (1967), in a review of the literature, has found that the auditory discrimination of phonemes and the articulation of phonemes are closely correlated, at least as disabilities.

LURIA'S NEUROPSYCHOLOGICAL CLASSIFICATION OF APHASIA

Temporal Acoustic Aphasia

This is a disturbance of discriminative hearing, that is, a disturbance in the analytic-synthetic activity of the auditory cortex. The lesion usually occurs on the superior temporal region of the left hemisphere and the resulting acoustic agnosia is a cause of speech disturbance. The main symptoms are as follows:

1. *Literal paraphasia:* This is the inability to pronounce a word the subject has heard. Quite often the subject will distort the sound composition of the word or replace it with a word that sounds something like it and that very often has a similar meaning.

2. *Disturbed motor speech:* Disturbances of the motor aspect of speech may occur because the phonemic quality of the word is not immediately available to the subject.

3. *Verbal paraphasia:* This is the substitution of a word with the same meaning as the stimulus word and, of course, it may also have a similar sound. Verbal paraphasia is most clearly seen when the subject substitutes a description of the term for the term itself.

4. *Word salad:* In severe cases, the patient's speech may resemble a word salad; that is, it just does not make sense. This is not a disturbance of intellectual functioning; it is part of the inability to process phonemes. However, speech disturbances are not always present and often the availability of habitual words and strings of words is not impaired in any way.

5. *Writing, spelling and blending:* Obviously if the ability to process phonemes is impaired, the ability to write prose, to spell words either orally or in writing and the ability to

blend given phonemes into words will be seriously disorganized. Luria points out that kinesthetic epigrams such as the initials of countries (U.S.A.) or organizations (U.N.O.) can be written, as they are visual forms.

6. *Reading:* Although in the milder cases of acoustic failure patients may be able to understand the general meaning of what is written in papers or books, they will fall down on understanding unusual reading material. However, these subjects will not be able to make out the letter syllables or even the structure of familiar words. Luria says, "When the sound (phonemic) structure of speech is disordered, the system of word meaning based on this structure must also be disordered."

7. *Conceptual/comprehension impairment:* As a corollary of item 6, in severe cases of acoustic aphasia there may be an almost complete disintegration of the conceptual structure of speech, but if the object (e.g., a chair) which is to be named is pointed out to the subject, quite often this limitation of the choice of visual alternatives assists in fixing the meaning of the word for the subject.

8. *Anomia:* Although Luria does not use the term *anomia,* his description of the next symptom is very akin to descriptions of anomia made by other people. He describes the typical speech of subjects with acoustic aphasia as being almost bereft of substantives, consisting mostly of smaller auxiliary words, e.g., conjunctions, prepositions, adverbs, etc., that form a semimeaningful unity of intonation. Thus, speech may be comprehensible to some extent even when there are few nouns in it.

9. *Speech memory:* Lesions in the superior temporal region result in an impairment of the ability to memorize and reproduce words phonemically; with respect to the flow or fluency of speech, this may be termed *speech amnesia.*

Luria points out that patients with an impairment of the left temporal lobes are quite able to visually analyze images. They can appreciate the spatial organization of shapes and have no spatial apraxia; indeed, their intact view of spatial functioning may be used to compensate for auditory defects. Another important point is that melodic hearing and musical appreciation may not necessarily be disturbed in any way although there is some suggestion that lesions in the right temporal region may affect musical skills. It will be seen that on examining all the above symptoms, the key deficit is "a disturbance in the analytic-synthetic activity of the auditory cortex" in the form of a disturbance of the differential system of speech sounds. The disturbances of the conceptual aspects of acoustic aphasia arise *directly* from the disturbances of the *phonemic* aspects of speech.

Acoustic-Mnestic Aphasia

Luria suggests that this type of aphasia, which presents a clinically different picture from acoustic aphasia, is caused by lesions occurring in the middle segments of the convex portion of the left temporal lobe, that is, the extranuclear portion (areas 21 and 37). These areas are in part connected with the visual analyzer, the auditory analyzer, the limbic lobe, the basal segments of the temporal portion of the cortex, the hippocampus and the amygdaloid body. Luria quotes Penfield and Roberts (1959) who, on stimulating the convex surface of the temporal lobe, induced complex hallucinations, memory images and changes in the state of consciousness. They attributed mnestic or word memory functions to the area, regarding it as interpretive in function.

The symptoms which follow are those which Luria has found in patients suffering from acoustic-mnestic aphasia:

1. *Phonemic hearing:* Phonemic hearing is completely or partially preserved. The subjects are able to repeat closely related phonemes without confusion unless the problem is more complicated.

2. *Word sequencing:* Subjects have *difficulty in reproducing series of words* and will occasionally replace them with repetitions of earlier words. In sentences with multiple phrases, the patient very often forgets those coming at the end of the sequence.

3. *Delayed memory:* If the subject is asked to wait several seconds before repeating a presented word sequence and

the interval is filled with unrelated speech, the subject cannot remember the originally presented items.

4. *Word order:* The inability to remember series of words is further indicated by the fact that the subject cannot usually reproduce the correct presentation sequence of a stimulus series.

5. *Perseveration:* Patients will tend to repeat mechanically series of words which have been previously learned rather than a set of new stimulus words, particularly if the first sequence was thoroughly learned previously.

6. *Visual signs:* The retention of visually presented signs such as geometrical figures is much superior to the retention of the traces of words presented orally.

7. *Word-object association:* This is somewhat akin to anomia in acoustic aphasia. In this symptom the patient when presented with several objects will *mix up their names,* for example, calling an eye an ear. However, if objects are presented singly the patient can usually name them satisfactorily; in this, he is different from the person suffering from acoustic aphasia. Luria calls this "the inhibitory effect of one word on another" and suggests that it is a clear indication of the pathological stage of the cortex in the temporal region.

8. *Word seeking:* The speech of these people usually contains many instances of *word seeking* and paraphasias but these are more verbal than literal in character.

9. *Writing and spelling:* Usually providing the language situation is a relatively simple one, these patients are able to write and spell fairly accurately. They do not have "gross disintegration of the sound structure of language (phonemic substitutions, difficulty in sound analysis of words, writing disorders, etc.)."

It is apparent from the above descriptions that whereas the first type, temporal-acoustic aphasia, tends to have as its basis a disintegration of the phonemic aspects of word and sentence formation, the problem in acoustic-mnestic aphasia tends to operate on a *whole-word basis;* it is the word *gestalt* which is "lost" or misassociated. It would seem that in the first type of aphasia much more of an analyzer and phoneme integration function is involved than in the latter type. In acoustic aphasia words seem to be lost because the phonemes cannot be correctly or adequately processed, whereas in acoustic-mnestic aphasia, the phoneme processing is intact but the words as a whole are dissociated from their objective meanings wherever and however these are stored in the brain. As frequently the visual writing aspects of signs and their visual meanings are retained, presumably the difficulty is largely in the acoustic word storage (temporal) area.

Intellectual Functioning in the Two Aphasias

The manipulation of visual material in an intellectual way is usually intact in patients with lesions in the temporal lobe. Any intellectual exercises involving spatial relationships, spatial analogies, geometrical problems and even some forms of arithmetic can be carried out accurately. However, these problems have to be executed on paper as the subjects seem to be unable to carry through series of successive operations in which some of the results have to be mentally processed. Of course, any activity involving the more complex requirement of speech associations as a mediation process are performed inadequately. As Luria says, "These patients are incapable of performing discussive operations necessitating the participation of a system of differentiated verbal associations with well-established traces." He then goes on to suggest that this presents a problem which he poses thus:

> How can this peculiar preservation of the direct comprehension of spatial, and in particular, of logical relationships in patients with such severe disturbances of speech be explained? There can be no doubt that a system of abstract logical relationships grew and took shape on the basis of speech. Can this system remain intact in speech disorders? In our attempt to interpret this fact, we should not fall into the error typical of the idealistic doctrine of the Wurzburg School, according to which intellectual activity is quite distinct from speech and is a primary and independent function.

Luria goes on to suggest that lesions of the temporal region do not destroy speech completely and that the dependence of reasoning on the *original kinesthetic aspects of speech* has been dispensed with neurologically, thus giving intellectual functioning a kind of maturational independence of operation.

This seems a rather circuitous explanation. In the light of recent evidence (see Lenneberg, 1967; MacNeilage *et al.*, 1967; and discussion in Chapter II), it is very probable that the speech production and speech perception areas are *not essentially* interdependent for the successful maturational development or everyday functioning of each. This is true even though each can and usually does assist in the development of the other in normal people. Another important point is that concepts are almost entirely nonverbal in nature whether these concepts are auditory, visuospatial, motor/kinesthetic or of any other kind (Penfield and Roberts, 1959; see also Chapter III); deaf children can reason very well visuo-spatially (Furth, 1966).

Temporal-Parietal-Occipital Left Hemisphere Lesions or "Optic Aphasia"

A difficulty in remembering the meanings of words, an extinction or amnesia of word meaning, is seen in patients who have a lesion of the temporal-occipital portion of the left hemisphere. All other auditory tasks can be adequately performed by the subject, even correcting words which have been incorrectly pronounced. Such patients can accurately *copy drawings* presented to them but are unable to *remember* drawings which are removed; these cannot be reproduced. These symptoms seem to suggest that there is a severe disorder in the association interface areas of the temporal, inferoparietal and occipital regions.

Afferent (Kinesthetic) Motor Aphasia

Luria defines this group of aphasic people as those who have a disturbance in the ability to articulate words and to use speech despite the preservation of elementary oral movement. This type of aphasia has been included by others in the overall category of expressive or executive aphasia. Luria says,

Lesions of the inferior divisions of the postcentral region of the left hemisphere (adjacent to the operculum Rolandi) do not lead to motor aphasia as an isolated phenomenon. As a rule, the disturbance appears as a series of apraxic disorders in the working of the oral apparatus. These defects are reflected particularly clearly in the most complex forms of movement of speech apparatus composing the system of speech articulation. In many cases, these defects of articulation constitute the chief symptoms of this form of motor [kinesthetic] aphasia.

People with this type of aphasia find it extremely difficult to articulate words or sounds quickly and without concentration, because the patient is unable to manipulate his vocal organs, tongue, lips, etc., into their correct positions. It is the kinesthetic afferent supply which is affected to the extent that *the subject is unable to analyze and integrate the kinesthetic signals which are the basis of speech.* As Luria points out, writing and reading are sometimes involved in this type of aphasia because *articulatory movements play an important part in the analysis of phonemes during the early stages of learning how to write.* Thus, subjects will make articulatory substitutions and write down the wrong graphemes. With respect to reading, older people suffering from this type of kinesthetic aphasia who could already read well can usually read established words and phrases, especially if they are read silently. It is reading *aloud* which is a problem because it involves disturbed articulation.

Efferent (Kinetic) Motor Aphasia I (Superior Premotor Zone, Left Hemisphere)

This type of motor aphasia is caused by lesions of the superior areas of the left premotor cortical zone. Luria says that the speech of these patients is "deautomatized and tense" and the articulation of every word requires a special effort. Grammar may be only slightly affected, if at all, and patients can readily pronounce individual words correctly and name objects successfully. These speech difficulties stem from a disintegration of "highly automatized skilled movements" of the speech processes. The subject must make a deliberate effort in order to attain any semblance of normal, rapid, continuous speech.

Efferent (Kinetic) Motor Aphasia II (Inferior Premotor Zone, Left Hemisphere)

Lesions of the inferior areas of the premotor zones of the left hemisphere (Broca's area) cause a very different set of symptoms from those of the superior areas. Their central problem is "the disturbance in complex consecutive synthesis, encompassing [the] inability to construct complex systems of articulations and difficulty in inhibiting preceding articulations for smooth transfer from one articulation in a series to a next." Luria suggests that this is the essence of true Broca's aphasia. Subjects who are not too profoundly disturbed may be able to articulate isolated sounds but not syllables or words because of their *inability to inhibit specific articulatory impulses*. The inability of the person to move onto the next articulated sound is described by Luria as a "pathological inertia." While patients will find it extremely difficult to write syllables or words, they may be able to write separate letters correctly. Additionally, they will incorrectly order the letters in a word. The reason for this is that the integral kinetic structure behind word articulation is disturbed. There may be perseveration of letters or parts of letters in writing, and an inability to reproduce presented phrases or sentences is very apparent. In other vords, there is a severe disruption of the flow of fluent spontaneous speech which is caused by "a gross disintegration of the kinetics of speech movement of the dynamic schemes of the expression as a whole. . . . As a rule, *the pronunciation of an articuleme reveals pathological inertia and the patient cannot move on to the next sound.*"

Yet another symptom is that of the telegraphic style of speech in which the patient will condense the usual full, rich speech to the type used in a telegram, although very often the words will not be in a correct order. It should be noted that many of these people who suffer from kinetic motor aphasia will usually lose the *melodic structure of speech,* which of course is an aspect of fluency. This is not the case in the kinesthetic types of aphasia. It is interesting that many genetic dyslexic boys exhibit this syndrome in an extremely mild form. It is well within the bounds of genic possibility that the efficiency of Broca's area is partially determined by polygenic inheritance.

Lesions of the premotor region will result in an intellectual impairment which is more caused by the disturbed dynamics of the intellectual process than by a defective content. Luria claims that intellectual activities, synthesized over time, develop mentally through the mediation of *internal speech,* becoming to some extent automatized and, even more important, synthesized. It is this automatic synthesizing component of intellectual operations which facilitates a fluency of intellectual operation which in its turn can be disorganized by lesions of the premotor sections of the cerebral cortex. Luria, however, stresses that these patients *do not have difficulty in understanding the meanings of words;* they also have no extinction of meaning, and do not find it difficult to grasp spatial and logical relationships. Their main difficulty is in "realizing the significance of complex logical grammatical structures. They can grasp a problem only after prolonged, detailed, and deliberate operations." Therefore, fundamentally it is a verbal *skill* rather than a cognitive function which is under discussion. This retardation of understanding, Luria suggests, may be the result of impaired internal speech because it is difficult for such patients to understand the meaning of a passage if they are told to work it out silently in their heads.

Frontal "Dynamic" Aphasia

This type of aphasia is the result of lesions of the frontal lobe in the left hemisphere situated anteriorly to Broca's area. Although the kinetics of speech articulation *may* not be disturbed in this type of aphasia, there is a disturbance of "speech initiative." The sequential elements of series of phonemes, words or phrases may be disorganized in these people, but the predominant symptom is their inability to engage in a meaningful dialogue. Their problem lies in an inability to *formulate* spontaneous, originally developed speech which will complement the stimulus question or sentence. While they may be readily able to engage in the more *habitual* forms of speech such as reciting the days of the week or perhaps giving routine answers, they are helpless if required to recount a story they have just read, or to develop a presented plot. Luria suggests that frontal dynamic aphasia may be an attenuated, more complex variant of kinetic aphasia.

In frontal dynamic aphasia, lesions of the frontal lobes seem to impair the ability of people to plan their verbal actions, particularly with regard to immediate intentions, and therefore there is no regulating effect on their overall behavior. Such subjects tend to perseverate a particular aspect of a motor function, most usually those which the patient has learned some time in the past. Luria sums up his section on the influence of lesions of the frontal lobes on actions and speech as follows: "It seems that what are most severely affected in patients with a lesion of the frontal lobes are the systems of preliminary syntheses, formed with a participation of speech connections and determinants of the subsequent course of nervous and mental processes."

Applicability of Luria's Work to Childhood Aphasia

Luria's work has added tremendously to our knowledge of childhood aphasia even though, as is the case with Penfield and Roberts, his work has been carried out largely with patients who have lost the power of normal language functioning because of subsequent lesions in the brain. The extent to which his findings are applicable to developmental aphasia in children (who have never experienced language) is arguable, but many of the symptoms mentioned by Luria have rough parallels in developmentally aphasic children. Certainly the specific functioning of the various areas of the brain would not seem to be as diffuse or diverse as some writers have suggested; it would seem at least plausible that children with specific brain impairments would present symptoms which would be the "developmental equivalent" of those mentioned by Luria. For example, children with impairment of the frontal lobes would tend not to develop a synthesizing foresight or planning ability of their actions and speech in the immediate environment. Of course, if the child were suffering from a generalized mild impairment throughout the whole cortex, most of the symptoms mentioned by Luria would be presented by the children in this "not developed equivalent" sense.

Later in the chapter, I have tabulated the various types of aphasia suggested by Luria and others such as Anderson in a systematic way, with a view to an organizational structuring of the field.

PSYCHOLINGUISTICS AND APHASIA

The one major source of information about psycholinguistics and its relation to aphasia comes from a book edited by Osgood and Miron (1963), which consists of the report of an interdisciplinary conference held in Boston in 1958. At this point, the discussion will be confined to a consideration of their systems of classifying cases of aphasia. Osgood's model of behavior was described previously in Chapter II (Figure 4). Osgood summarizes the grouping of aphasic cases on his model by saying,

> This [psycholinguistic] conception leads one to expect aphasic patients to be differentiable into (1) decoding versus associative versus encoding disturbances and (2) interdisturbances reflecting mentally semantic or meaningful versus grammatical or skilled aspects. Thus, although we would expect many patients to display complex types of disorders, we should also expect to find some who have trouble mainly with semantic decoding, some who have trouble mainly with grammatical and skill aspects of encoding, and so on.

The congruity between Luria's descriptions of specific types of aphasia caused by neurological lesions and Osgood's psycholinguistic grouping is quite remarkable. This congruity would seem to arise because both Luria and Osgood had, as a major foundation for behavior, the overriding importance of speech and language. Patients with temporal acoustic aphasia (with their symptoms of literal paraphasia, disturbed motor speech, word salads, difficulty in writing, spelling, blending, reading and anomia problems), because their basic difficulty is one of processing phonemes on an automatic and integrational basis, would be classified on Osgood's system as suffering from integrational decoding problems. Obviously, these disturbances will tend to distort subsequent psycholinguistic processes so that to some degree (and Luria indicates this) associational and decoding operations will also be impaired as a consequence. By contrast, temporal acoustic-mnestic aphasics who have word-seeking problems, word sequencing problems, delayed memory, word-object association difficulties and relatively intact writing and spelling can be classified on Osgood's psycholinguistic model as having representational, decoding and association disabilities. Patients with optic aphasia would fall right into the category of representational association disorders. The psycholinguistic areas in which the afferent motor aphasia group (which has difficulty in complex forms of movement of the speech apparatus composing the system of speech articulation) would best seem to fit are the decoding, integrational and projection categories. Patients in the efferent kinetic motor aphasia group would also be in the encoding, integrational and projection categories but elements of the integrational and projection association systems would also seem to be partially behind their difficulties. Patients with frontal dynamic aphasia, who have problems synthesizing planned action and speech, would best be placed in the representational, encoding and possibly predictive integrational encoding segments of the chart. This is about the limit to which the two systems, the one neuropsychological and the other psycholinguistic, can be matched; as Osgood admits, this is mainly because the chart is not intended to match the extreme complexity of neurological interconnections. Instead it is intended to clarify an abstraction from all behavior, particularly language behavior.

Olson (1960) made a comparison of receptive aphasic, expressive aphasic and deaf children on the Illinois Test of Psycholinguistic Abilities. This test was originally developed by Kirk and McCarthy (1961) from both the Wepman (1960) and the Osgood (1963) psycholinguistic models. In Olson's research, the receptive aphasic group did poorly on all the decoding, association and encoding tests which involved auditory or vocal channels. However, they were superior to the expressive aphasic group in motor encoding (pantomiming the uses of everyday objects). The major areas in which the expressive aphasic group was poor were the two tests involving encoding, both vocal and motor. By contrast, almost all the deaf children were superior to both the receptive aphasics and the expressive aphasics across most of the tasks. These results are very much in keeping with the ones Olson predicted for the various groups. As a comment on this study, it is worth noting that on the strength of this ITPA analysis, these two broad groups of aphasic children fall into symptom patterns very similar to those described by Luria. Presumably the receptive aphasics are poor at auditory decoding, auditory/vocal association, vocal encoding and auditory/vocal sequencing and automatisms because their phoneme discriminating and integrating equipment in the temporal and related areas is impaired. On the other hand, the expressive aphasic group has problems of vocal and motor encoding which may originate from the poor development of motor synthesis and, in particular, of speech-motor synthesis in the premotor areas of the frontal lobes.

In passing, it is perhaps worth suggesting that a set of tests of aphasia could be constructed from the combined knowledge imparted by Luria and Osgood. Such a set of tests would make the differential diagnosis of childhood aphasia much more accurate and reality-based as well as indicating treatment which would remediate or train the deficit areas while reinforcing through the intact areas. For example, action miming might be a useful approach with receptive aphasic children.

A NEW, INTEGRATED CLASSIFICATION OF THE TYPES OF APHASIA

In Table XVI, I have sorted the categories of aphasia into a formal classification system, each type of aphasia having its own distinctive title. All seven classes are defined in three separate ways. In the first column is the major process which defines the essential language characteristic of the particular aphasic disability. The middle column indicates the sensorimotor modality, and the third column lists the cortical areas in which lesions or maturation lag can occur. In any discussion of the various types of aphasia, one need only use the first two columns to clearly identify which type of aphasia is being considered.

It will be seen that Luria's types of aphasia and Osgood's psycholinguistic categories can be readily spliced into this table if one takes into account the various sensorimotor channels. It will be noted, however, that except perhaps for items 3 and 7,

TABLE XVI
A CLASSIFICATION OF THE TYPES OF APHASIA

Process	Sensorimotor Modality	Cortical Area
1. Phonemic identification	Auditory discrimination and sequencing	Superior-temporal aphasia
2. Lexical memory	Auditory sequencing and closure	Convex-temporal aphasia
3. Semantic	Auditory-optic	Temporoparietal-occipital aphasia
4. Oral-apraxic	Kinesthetic speech (possibly also motor)	Inferior-postcentral aphasia (also precentral motor)
5. Deautomatized (conscious effort required)	Motor speech	Superior premotor aphasia
6. Articulemic (possibly syllabic)*	Motor speech—sequencing	Broca's inferior premotor aphasia
7. Dynamic	Integrational—syntactical planning	Frontal aphasia

*According to Osgood (1963), the syllable may be the basic unit in the expressive speech of linguistically competent individuals.

the classes of aphasia are nonrepresentational in psycholinguistic terminology. Although most of these classes of aphasia are at the integrational or projection level, it can be seen that as one works around the psycholinguistic curve (Figure 4) from input decoding to output encoding (or moves down Table XVI from item 1 to item 7), each type of aphasia will tend to exhibit some of the symptoms belonging to the succeeding types of aphasia. This is especially true for cases of childhood developmental aphasia in which the child has never had adequate linguistic experience. Incidentally, semantic optic aphasia as a language disorder corroborates the hypothesis that the word-labels (which represent specific meanings, namely percepts and concepts) are a quite separate system from those percepts and concepts even though labels and meanings must be closely associated (Osgood, 1963; Bannatyne, 1967c).

APHASIC AND SCHIZOPHRENIC LANGUAGE IN CHILDREN

De Hirsch (1967) has set down the criteria for making a

differential diagnosis between aphasic and schizophrenic children in terms of their language functioning. She points out that whereas in aphasic children it is only the perceptual, motor and linguistic functions which are primarily unstable, in schizophrenic children the instability is much more pervasive, involving the organization of the whole personality. In the latter group, the "boundaries between self and non-self are blurred." She also notes that the auditory memory span of aphasic children is extremely short whereas that of schizophrenic children may be very long; however, the relevance of the material may be questioned. Furthermore, communication with schizophrenic children is difficult because they cannot ego-relate or "tune in" to the sender's message, whereas the aphasic child does not seem to have the processing and organizational equipment to receive and interpret the message. Other symptoms of schizophrenic children are that their speech tends to be bizarre, mechanical, high-pitched and monotonous. For them, words are objects in their own right, not symbols which refer to other things. Aphasic children, on the other hand, to the extent that they do have speech language, usually relate it, however inadequately, to their environment. It can be seen, then, that the language and the motivations for producing speech are qualitatively very different in the two types of children.

TRAINING, THERAPY, TREATMENT AND REMEDIATION

Many words have been used to describe the work which has to be done to help aphasic children. Of them all, I prefer the word "training" because this suggests that one is teaching the child something new, whereas most other terms suggest the child has already learned something which has to be unlearned and replaced with new or modified information. Developmental aphasic children by definition have not acquired many aspects of language and consequently they will need training in the deficit areas.

Two major methods of training aphasic children have been suggested, one by Myklebust (1957) and one by McGinnis (1956).

Myklebust first suggests that one should not always be demanding speech from the aphasic child; rather one should encourage language. Sounds which the child makes should be reacted to as if they were verbal communications. Encouraging the child's gestures can be a great help to him but even more important is the development of the aphasic child's inner language. Myklebust suggests that the child should be given every opportunity to associate the spoken word with concrete objects. This may be facilitated through play and other school activities and it should be persevered with in order to broaden the child's experience. The order of the developmental training is that experienced by the normal child during normal growth. The first stage is that of gaining meaningful experience of objects and people; the second stage is relating words to these experiences, the words the child hears from other people.

The third stage is that of building up inner language; that is, the aphasic child will have a meaningful inner vocabulary through associating heard symbols with their objects. Once the child's inner language has developed sufficiently, it is time to begin training him in receptive language. The therapist continues naming not only objects but actions and descriptions which must exactly fit the activity in which the child is engaged. Throughout this time, no demands are made on the child to use speech. Myklebust says that if the child has no problems of expressive language but suffers only from *receptive aphasia*, he will develop speech quite naturally once an inner and receptive langauge have been developed. The final stage is to develop complex conversational intercommunication by making frequent use of questions, requests, instructions, etc. Orthodox speech training may be necessary for those children who have expressive problems, the amount of training corresponding with the extent of the difficulty.

McGinnis, with her well-known association methods, approaches the problem of teaching receptive aphasics very differently. The method is founded on several principles which are as follows: First, a phonetic approach is used when teaching words. Second, the emphasis is on the articulatory sequence of each phoneme. Third, each phoneme in its appropriate sequence is firmly associated with its grapheme in cursive script. Fourth, vocalization is a very important starting point in building language and is encouraged from the beginning. Finally, there is a systematic sensorimotor association program which will be described shortly. Returning to the first point in the association method, McGinnis emphasizes that the phonemes are taught singly and a very accurate articulatory production is required. Before a child is allowed to blend the individual phonemes into a word, he must first be able to articulate each separate phoneme. Smooth blending is not required until the child can accomplish it naturally without loss of clear pronunciation. The child is taught to write at the same time, using cursive script, but the child with receptive aphasia is not expected to know the meaning of any word until he is capable of pronouncing it clearly.

There are several steps employed in teaching the child the use of nouns. Together these make up the sensorimotor association method. The aphasic child must learn to pronounce in sequence the phonemes which make up the stimulus word and must learn to match a picture of the object with the printed word. The child should be able to copy the word; he must articulate each sound as he writes the corresponding grapheme. When the teacher articulates the word, the child is asked to repeat the word aloud and to match the object itself (or a picture of it) to the written form of the word. He must be able to say the name of an object and to write the word from memory, again articulating each sound as he writes the graphemes. A variation on the last technique is for the teacher to speak the word directly into the child's ear so that he cannot observe any facial or articulatory expressions on the teacher's face. McGinnis emphasizes this intersensorimotor association, a technique which builds up from the simple "bits" of language, namely, phonemes and graphemes, and the memorizing of these associations.

The reader familiar with the remedial methods of Gillingham and Fernald for use with dyslexic children will see many parallels with the McGinnis technique. It has been realized increasingly in the last two decades that phoneme/grapheme association training is very successful in the remediation of learning disability cases, particularly for genetic dyslexia, and this is also true for cases of receptive aphasia. As McGinnis says,

Our observations of the children we have classified as receptive aphasic lead us to believe that their problem is more an inability to communicate verbally about their daily experiences than it is a lack of understanding of those experiences. For this reason, our approach to teaching aphasic children emphasizes the development of skill in the use of the tools of communication.

It is interesting that the method of training *receptive aphasic children* which McGinnis has found the most successful, namely, one based on phoneme/grapheme sequencing, *exactly corresponds with the neuropsychological findings of Luria in cases of temporal lobe aphasia.* This group, it will be remembered, has great difficulty in the sequencing of phonemes as a skill, and it is quite logical that this should be the main problem area in developmentally aphasic children who have not experienced true language. It is also interesting that McGinnis finds the problem essentially one of language *skills* rather than one of meaningful content. This also seems to be the case with almost all dyslexic children whose problems lie more in the area of spelling and reading than with heard speech.

Stark and others (1968) have recently outlined a trained program for teaching structural language to children whose difficulties range from relative mutism to mild articulatory semantic and syntactical disorders, problems which the authors attribute mainly to *word and sequencing memory failure.* The individually administered training program involves a maximum use of the visual modality to generate correct verbal responses together with minimized motor responses (e.g., eliminate writing and substitute responses matching a caption and pictures), and a carefully graded task-analyzed presentation in which failure is rarely experienced. Distractions are eliminated and the learning environment is highly structured. The program begins linguistically first with nouns and then with verb phrases; prepositions and conjunctions are added gradually. One verb in the present progressive form is used in any one set of part-lessons. This program, like Myklebust's, tends to teach an inner language first, utilizing linguistic structure. The authors claim that many of the children come "to generate novel utterances once they are provided with language units consistent with basic grammatical relations." It would seem, however, that most of these children had considerable word-speech before training commenced, as their main difficulties were with structural syntax.

APHASIA AND DYSLEXIA

Having worked with a variety of learning disability children and some aphasic children, I have noticed that some of the former group present aphasic-like symptoms. Others have thought likewise; for example, Eisenson (1963) has said, "We have repeated instances of children who began their experience with us with a diagnosis of delayed speech and who continued or returned to us over two or three years later with a designation of reading disability." He goes on to note that many of the characteristics of dyslexic children parallel in a milder way those of some aphasic children; for example, they may have a poorly established laterality and there may be an excessive number of boys. Other aphasic children show signs of MND inasmuch as they may have weak motor skills, some left/right disorientation and spatial disorganization.

The aphasic child has problems in *associating the meaning of a word with the phonemes which make up the spoken word* and it would seem that most of the problem lies in the child's inability to associate those phonemes in sequences into composite words. The dyslexic child may have a reasonable vocabulary of spoken words but he has difficulty *associating the phonemes which comprise the spoken word with the appropriate graphemes of the written word.* In both aphasic and dyslexic children, the problem often seems to center around the rapid processing of phonemes into blended gestalts of articulated sound. It is worth repeating that it is mainly the skill which has not been learned, namely, the skill of sequencing sounds and of associating those blended groups with either objects (that is, concepts or "meanings"), as in aphasia, or with their printed word equivalents, as in dyslexia. In either case, the problem is one of automatic unit and sequencing memory associations of the type defined by Osgood in his psycholinguistic model of language behavior. It is very interesting that teachers of aphasic children and teachers of dyslexic children have separately come to the conclusion that, as Frostig (1966) says, *overlearning* is extremely important in all training programs if they are to be successful. Yet another parallel in the treatment of aphasic and dyslexic children is that of speech training. Both types of cases usually profit immensely from training in precise articulation and in blending sequences of phonemes fluently.

Generalized impairment of the cortex is a not infrequent neurological state in aphasic children just as it is in children with learning disabilities. In such cases, the lesion is not specific to an isolated area as is usually the case in tumors, accidents or war wounds. Therefore, it is important to realize that many cases of developmental aphasia will exhibit a composite symptomatology. Aspects of most or all of the types of aphasia listed in Table XVI will usually be present, in which case a multiple-track training program will be required. Initially, each track will be aimed at an area of specific deficit but as the treatment proceeds and the child begins to develop real communication skills, the tracks will converge into a single broad language program. The principles of such a training system are outlined in the chapters on remediation and although the subject under discussion there is learning disabilities, the details are in principle applicable to developmental aphasia. In fact, many aphasic children may be helped to learn language by being taught to read at the same time. This gives them a visual symbol system (graphemes) with which to associate and consolidate phonemes and articulemes; Good (1968) has used color coding for this purpose. The Psycholinguistic Color System (Bannatyne, 1968b) should prove a very useful teaching technique for this purpose.

Chapter XII

SOCIAL, CULTURAL AND EDUCATIONAL DEPRIVATION DYSLEXIA

THE PROBLEM

Not infrequently, children are referred to learning disability centers, particularly those in large cities or backward rural areas, who have all the characteristics of the socially disadvantaged child. Exactly what these characteristics are in terms of physiology, cognition, personality, family relationships, emotional disturbance and education is difficult to determine because hard, clear-cut research data is difficult to find.

In essence, the social problem itself nowadays mostly centers around school failure which, in turn, results from some basic inability to profit from the orthodox school program, usually even in first grade. Most investigations or research studies have suggested that this basic material cause of the child's lack of success in the educational system arises from a cultural deprivation, one main component of which is language. Several authorities have stressed these cultural and language aspects of deprivation and many agencies have set up preschool programs to investigate ways of counteracting the effect of deprivation on the personality and cognitive development of disadvantaged children. Some specific projects will be discussed later below, but first one must mention the traditional enrichment programs.

Schemes such as the Head Start program have usually been organized along traditional kindergarten and nursery school lines with the intention of providing the culturally disadvantaged child with the material sensorimotor and language experiences most middle-class children have in their home and nursery school environment. Many toys and activities are provided; the children learn nursery rhymes and participate in many group games. They

516

will paint, model clay, converse together and play house but later, in the first and second grades, when they learn to read and to calculate, they will have almost as much difficulty as their less enriched peers. Almost from the beginning of life, they seem to be at a disadvantage which steadily widens as they grow older. Since culturally deprived children are behind their peers to begin with, a truly successful program will *accelerate* their progress, at least until they become as successful achievers as their middle-class counterparts.

Even though language may be the central problem in both cases, the socially disadvantaged child differs from the primary emotional communicative dyslexic by reason of the all-around poverty of the social, cultural and emotional experiences to which he is subject; he usually suffers in many areas of his personal development because his whole neighborhood is ecologically inadequate. Usually, the deprivation of a communicative dyslexic child is restricted to one facet of life, namely, language, and this occurs in the context of his family, not its cultural or social environment.

LANGUAGE-ASSOCIATED FACTORS
The Viewpoint of Bernstein

Many of the experiences the socially disadvantaged child does have do not enable him to communicate meaningfully with teachers who operate from middle-class standards of education in schools organized on middle-class lines. Bernstein (1961a) makes this point clear when he adopts Goldman-Eisler's (1958a,b,c) concepts of highly coded utterances (conventional sequences which have a high frequency of usage, e.g., "Isn't it a beautiful day?") and now-coding utterances (individuated sequences of words with a low transition probability involving analytical thought processes). Subculture language content seems to abound with highly coded *standard* utterances and these Bernstein calls *public language,* as opposed to ". . . a system which permits and encourages now-coding utterances, or one where they may be frequently signalled and elicited, the pure type of *formal* language." Public language ". . . is a form of condensed speech in which certain meanings are restricted and the possibility of their elaboration is reduced." By contrast, in a formal language, (a) grammar and syntax regulate meaning, (b) logic and stress are mediated through complex sentence construction, (c) prepositions indicate relationships, (d) impersonal pronouns are frequent, (e) adjectives and adverbs are used frequently and discriminatively and (f) expressive symbolism discriminates between meanings within speech sequences.

Bernstein adds several other characteristics to the above list and then presents the opposing characteristics of a public language—that is, the reverse of the qualities expressed above. In discussing the educational implications of his work, Bernstein suggests that there is an inherent resistance on the part of the public language speaker to change to a more formal mode of communication. This may be caused by a lack of flexibility occurring after the critical period of language learning in infancy has passed: "Such language change may involve for the speaker the experiences of isolation, bewilderment and defenselessness; whilst the structure of the 'teaching' situation may well be felt as persecutory." In the case of public language, the socially disadvantaged child is the recipient from adults of communications which are concrete, immediate, terse and authoritative. As a rule, emotions and feelings remain undifferentiated and guilt is seldom aroused, although loyalty and responsibility to the local group are implicit. On the other hand, formal language is used by the middle classes and tends to indicate logical relationships, to arouse guilt, to make use of symbolism and concepts and to stress intent rather than consequence. The public language speaking child tends to learn mechanically and forget easily, and because he finds formal language quite bewildering, more often than not he withdraws from the learning situation. In other words, he lacks "the receptive schemata or if he possesses them, they are weakly organized and are unstable." Public language, according to Bernstein, ". . . symbolizes a tradition where the individual is treated as an end in himself, not as a means to a further end."

Bernstein suggests that any educational situation should try to preserve the public language tradition in which the individual is treated as an end in himself but at the same time it should make available the possibilities inherent in a formal language. This would mean that socially disadvantaged learning disability children who have language associations which are essentially concrete, personal and immediate must gradually be shown the conceptual and causal uses of words in a suitable context which is within their personal experience. By Piaget's criteria, such children are still at an early age, or stage, of logical development and they should be led slowly through successive stages toward logical causality as learning proceeds.

Bernstein stresses that the intimate personal contact between child and teacher is an essential factor if the learning process of public language speaking children is to be successful. One principal of a high school in the East End of London always tries to employ qualified teachers who have lived all their lives in the local area because, he claims, they are the only ones who can "get through" to the dockland children.

Bereiter and Engelmann—Direct Academic Instruction

Bereiter and Engelmann (1966) point out that disadvantaged children frequently score 5 to 15 IQ points below average. Because intelligence tests have a cultural bias and at least to some extent measure the impact on intelligence of middle-class scholastic and cultural values, they are quite good indicators of cultural, social and educational deprivation. Bereiter and Engelmann say,

> Compared to this overall average of three to nine months' retardation [in intelligence] disadvantaged children of pre-school age are typically at least a year behind in language development—in vocabulary size, sentence length, and use of grammatical structure. *Indeed, in practically every aspect of language development that has been evaluated quantitatively, young disadvantaged children have been found to function at the level of average children who are a year or so younger* (Weaver, 1963).

The two authors point out that the socially disadvantaged child may be a year or more retarded in logical development or reasoning ability, and in this respect, they are in accord with Bernstein. In some areas of psychological functioning, disadvantaged children are well up to the average of the wider community or even above it. For example, their performance on immediate memory-span tasks and certain rote-learning tasks is usually very adequate, *something which distinguishes them from most mentally retarded children and other kinds of dyslexic children.* Therefore, Bereiter and Englemann conclude, "Performance of this kind comes closer to demonstrating raw ability to learn. It would appear from this that what disadvantaged children lack is learning, not the fundamental capacity to learn."

Hess and Shipman (1965) asked groups of middle- and lower-class Negro mothers to teach their children various tasks, but the lower-class mothers did not seem to have any of the instructional techniques which would enable them to teach their children quickly and efficiently. Bereiter and Engelmann, commenting on the work of Hess and Shipman, point out that American middle-class society passes on many of its cultural activities, standards, etc., through deliberate teaching, much of which obviously involves language: "The child spends his early childhood in an environment where teaching does not take place and where the language with which teaching is carried out is not used; therefore, he may not even learn how to be taught, and when he is exposed to teaching, he may behave much as if he were mentally retarded or devoid of language altogether." Bereiter and Engelmann stress the separation and manipulation of words in sentences, but even more important is the development, through self-questioning, of the ability to engage in an internal logical dialogue through which complex problems can be solved. Much of their teaching program is directed toward actively training children to use small connective words and other structure words, the absence of which prevents a flow of meaning. They also train them to separate words clearly and, above all, to utilize their newfound meaningful sentence construction ability in outward forms of the internal dialogue which they must acquire to be academically successful.

The teaching in the Bereiter-Engelmann preschool involves a direct instruction approach which calls for regular lessons and lesson plans, opportunities for practice and feedback, corrective procedures and definite criteria for the children to meet, particularly in reading and arithmetic. Specific goals and detailed objectives are planned and the teaching procedures are intensive, but the children do not seem to suffer from this. The authors point out that disadvantaged children are characterized by "an unhealthy lack of stress concerning all things intellectual or academic," and they feel that it is essential to produce a certain degree of stress and anxiety, always insuring that it is no more than the children can comfortably handle. At the beginning of the program, the stress is applied externally through exhortation and reward systems, but these are soon replaced by the newfound desire of the children to solve problems, enhanced by the repeated experience of having successfully solved previous problems. The whole program is characterized by having a well-structured curriculum, the teaching being direct and to the point. If possible, there is a complete absence of irrelevant interference from any source.

The Bereiter-Engelmann method of teaching disadvantaged children in the preschool has not yet been in operation long enough for follow-up studies to be completed. It will be interesting to see if the children taught by their method maintain the progress and new skills they have learned, in the regular public school programs and even on to the university.

A Comparative Study of Two Preschool Programs

Karnes *et al.* (1966c) and her colleagues carried out a comparative study of two preschool programs for culturally disadvantaged children: a highly structured program and a traditional nursery school program. The highly structured curriculum was designed to develop the basic language processes as well as knowledge in the areas of mathematics, language art, social studies and science. The development of language skills was given high priority as it is the area of greatest academic weakness among culturally disadvantaged children. Pre- and post-tests were carried out on both groups using the Stanford-Binet Intelligence Scale, the ITPA, the Peabody Picture Vocabulary Test, the Frostig Developmental Test of Visual Perception and the Metropolitan

Readiness Test. The results showed that the IQ (Stanford-Binet) gains manifested by the experimental group were statistically superior to those of the comparison nursery school group. Both groups gained considerably, but the highly structured program group gained more. On the ITPA, both groups made considerable gains in psycholinguistic abilities but there were no significant differences between the two groups. Similarly, although both groups gained considerably on the Peabody Picture Vocabulary Test, the difference between the gains was not significant. After completing a visual perceptual development program, the highly structured group made gains which were greater than those made by the nursery school group but the difference between the gains was again not significant. The hypothesis that at the end of the treatment period the experimenal subjects would score higher on tests of school readiness than the comparison group was confirmed in the areas of number skills, reading readiness skills and total readiness. Taken overall, this study confirms the contention that a highly structured curriculum, squarely aimed at improving academic skills in a direct manner, is superior to one using traditional nursery school techniques.

In a more recent paper, Karnes *et al.* (1970) report that out of four different programs tested on four-year-old disadvantaged children, the results clearly favored the highly structured preschool situation. Risley *et al.* (1970) obtained similar results using behavior modification along with the structure.

Language and Psycholinguistic Skills

Several studies have been carried out investigating the psycholinguistic skills of socially disadvantaged children. In addition to these, there is one study on the structure of language which will be reported below. The first studies, however, make use of the ITPA to investigate language.

Weaver (1963)

Using the ITPA as a pre- and post-test, Weaver found that two experimental socially disadvantaged groups on separate training programs were significantly higher after training than the control group on visual decoding, auditory/vocal association and the total ITPA score. The auditory/vocal subtest scores were lower than the visual-motor subtest scores in all three groups; all three had language ages significantly lower than mental ages, the two variables correlating at $r = 0.88$ for the girls and $r = 0.81$ for the boys. Apparently, even in socially disadvantaged children, the language superiority of girls exists. All three groups were weak in auditory/vocal automatic skills such as grammar, but at the same time, all three groups were quite competent in auditory/vocal sequencing (digit-span memory).

Deutsch (1967)

In a research design similar to the others which involved an experimental group in a training program, Deutsch gave the ITPA to both the experimental and control groups as a check on progress over three separate years. The experimental group improved much more than the control group, but of much more importance were the ITPA profiles averaged over the three years. The culturally disadvantaged children showed less ability in auditory decoding, auditory/vocal association and auditory/vocal automatic skills (grammar), while they showed superiority in vocal encoding and on the auditory/vocal sequential test (digit-span memory). Thus, not all language skills are depressed in the culturally disadvantaged—they have a good short-term auditory memory span and can vocally encode (by describing several objects in detail) quite competently. It would seem therefore that the educational problem of socially disadvantaged children involves more than just language deficits.

Shriner (1968)

In an investigation of morphological structures in the language of disadvantaged and advantaged children, Shriner, on comparing the morphology scores between the groups, found *no* statistically significant difference. The morphology test was constructed to measure both the receptive and expressive aspects of morphology, the tasks being to apply morphological rules to unfamiliar situations. The two groups of preschool children, each consisting of twenty-five subjects, were matched by mental age. Between-group comparisons were made which looked for differences between males and females, subtest items and receptive versus expressive abilities, but no significant differences were found here either.

I suggest that the ubiquitous presence of the television set in culturally disadvantaged homes may account for an all-around morphological competence, given average intelligence potential. In descriptions of the homes of culturally disadvantaged Negro children, S.W. Gray (1967) commented that the television set was likely to be switched on from early morning until late at night. It would seem, then, that the parents may no longer be the main source of language experience for preschool socially disadvantaged children. Note that I am *not* suggesting that all language skills or content are acquired from television; only a few basic ones, such as morphology, may be so learned.

THE MOTIVATION TO LEARN

Several studies have been carried out which strongly indicate that language is not the only key factor causing the socially disadvantaged child to remain academically handicapped. In fact, there are indications that language may not even be the main contributor to the situation. If preschool children have a competent auditory memory, motor encoding ability, morphological knowledge and vocabulary (all findings of the above-mentioned studies), any residual language dysfunction would have to be extremely large and serious to account for the failure of socially disadvantaged children in their academic schoolwork. The research evidence presented below suggests that motivation is also a major factor, both variables probably being compounded into a serious social handicap.

Motivating and Training the Mother

In a second study, Karnes *et al.* (1966a) used the approach of working with the mothers of culturally disadvantaged children in a pilot project. Two groups of fifteen preschool Negro children were matched and tested on the Stanford-Binet and ITPA tests.

Eleven weekly sessions of two hours' duration were held over a twelve-week period for training the *mothers* of the children in the experimental group. Three teachers with experience in teaching preschool children separately conducted small-group meetings. The participant mothers were paid for the training sessions they attended. The mothers received no remuneration for the working sessions at home with their children, which were scheduled twice a month. The teachers helped the mothers and assessed the appropriateness of the instructional materials. The mothers and children in the control group received no treatment.

Significant pre- and post-test gains were recorded in the intelligence of the experimental group children over the controls on both the Stanford-Binet Intelligence Scale and three subtests of the ITPA (Visual Decoding, Auditory-Vocal Association and Auditory-Vocal Sequencing). The growth in Total Language Age was significantly beyond that of the increase in chronological age as was also true for Auditory Decoding, Visual Decoding, Auditory-Vocal Association, Vocal Encoding, Auditory-Vocal Automatic, Visual-Motor Sequencing and Auditory-Vocal Sequencing. Thus, working with and training the mothers in a teaching-learning program can foster the intellectual and linguistic development of their children. However, Karnes does not use or involve the family and its motivational dynamics as a whole.

Motivating and Training the Teacher—Teacher Expectations

Rosenthal and Jacobson (1968) have conducted experiments in schools located in socially disadvantaged areas which suggest that the *teachers' expectations and attitudes* may have a lot to do with the poor academic performance of culturally deprived children. The authors discovered that the preconceived attitudes teachers have about children so permeates their teaching activities that a kind of self-fulfilling prophecy occurs. If children are presented to teachers as bright and adventurous, the teacher expects and predicts that the children will succeed in their academic life, and without fully realizing it, she handles and tutors them in such a way that her predictions are fulfilled. Conversely, if children are presented as dull, deprived and disinterested, her attitudes and teacher techniques are unintentionally modified so that the children remain just that—socially disadvantaged. It is to be emphasized that in their research project, the experimental treatment of the children involved nothing more than giving their names to their new teachers as those of children who could be expected to show unusual intellectual gains in the year ahead. Thus, the difference between these children and the undesignated children who constituted the control group was entirely in the minds of the teachers. There was no crash program to improve reading ability, no extra time for tutoring, no trips to museums or art galleries— only the fact that the teachers *thought* the children were potentially eager and intelligent. Rosenthal and Jacobson compared their results in terms of IQ gain with another "total-push" program which had taken place elsewhere.

> It is interesting to note that one "total-push" program of the kind devised under Title I led in three years to a 10-point gain in I.Q. by 38 percent of the children and a 20-point gain by 12 percent. These gains were dramatic, but they did not match even the ones achieved by the control-group children in the first and second grades of Oak School. They were far smaller than the gains made by the children in our experimental group.

It would seem from this study that the motivational attitudes of adults play a far greater part in the degree of suscepibility that socially disadvantaged children (and probably all children) have to profiting from academic work and, indeed, from all education in its widest sense. The next section illustrates this point further.

Achievement Motivation and the Role of the Father

In a review of the literature, Swift (1966) suggests that oversimplified, stereotyped assessments of social class academic motivations should be avoided. Many research studies present conflicting results, but Swift, by integrating the conclusions, extracts a general hypothesis about academic success. It is that regardless of the actual social class (or subculture) the

> . . . academically successful family was one in which mobility-pessimism about job advancement prospects was high and discipline was traditional. Commitment to education was "high" but of a very different nature to the high commitment expressed in the ideal-type

middle class family where it is valued for its liberating qualities for the individual. . . . [The parent] is also likely to understand what is involved in schoolwork and will not be burdened by the idea that the people who get into higher classes represent a different sort of person to himself.

This hypothesis was put to the research test by Swift in a 10 percent random sample of a local education authority division. He found that *the father's dissatisfaction with his job and its prospects* (mobility-pessimism) related significantly to the likelihood of his child's success on the secondary school entry examination. In the sample, only one out of nine lower-middle-class fathers of successful children did not have high mobility-pessimism. Swift notes that Argyle and Robinson (1962) have suggested (and in the light of the above results, correctly) that introjection or projection of parental ambition is important in parent-child relationships, particularly in the family attitudes to schoolwork.

Confirmation of the important role of the father is to be found in a review paper by Biller (1970). He concludes by saying that a high degree of father absence in black families repeatedly crops up in research studies and that the lack of a meaningful continuous relationship with an adult male is a serious situation that must be corrected if children's growing social and educational opportunities are to be realized.

ACADEMIC FAILURE IN SOCIALLY DISADVANTAGED CHILDREN SEEN AS A MULTIPLE MOTIVATIONAL PROBLEM

There is little doubt that language is an important factor in the lack of progress shown by socially disadvantaged children, but perhaps it has been overstressed; the motivational attitudes of the child, the teacher and the family have traditionally been somewhat neglected. I do not wish to imply that there should be no language training or that highly structured programs in language, reading, writing and arithmetic should be neglected; much the opposite. Every training program, preschool or otherwise, should include a reasonable element of academic work, but education is more than the content which is learned and even more than learning how to learn; it is also the instilling of a desire to learn and to want to continue learning. I have a suspicion that not a small amount of the increase in IQ shown by the children in the Karnes' *et al.* (1966c) and Bereiter and Engelmann programs is attributable to the enthusiasm of the teachers, their expectancies and the authoritarian parent-role implicit in the method.

The motivation of each of the adults involved in the child's total environment requires detailed analysis.

The Child and His Self-Concept

Small children who are physically healthy and neurologically intact have a natural liveliness and curiosity, but if it is undirected from the outside, learning will be spasmodic and motivational energy will be dissipated. Therefore, the models presented by the adults in the environment are all-important because the child will spontaneously align himself with the motivational goals laid down for him in both structure and content. Naturally, as Bereiter and Engelmann point out, the material and social rewards have to be forthcoming and give the child satisfaction. These rewards, however, come (ideally) not only from the teacher but also from the parents, the siblings and the child's peers in school. Only through such a comprehensive program will the child's self-concept become motivationally favorable. Therefore, in any school program for the disadvantaged, a systematic check should be made to insure that all these rewards exist, and if they do not, they must be established. A considerable degree of success in motivating socially disadvantaged children has been achieved with a classroom kit of behavior management materials called Motivation Management Materials, by A.D. Bannatyne and M. Bannatyne (1970).

The Motivation and Expectations of the Teacher

It is almost trite to say that the teacher should be enthusiastic and regard her children as bursting with potential and eager to learn. Unfortunately, many socially disadvantaged children do not have these characteristics, at least to a reasonable degree. It takes a lot of effort on the part of the teacher to reward children, praise them, set up high-interest lesson programs, develop her talents as a "personality" to whom the children cannot but attend, counsel the parents on praising and otherwise encouraging their children's scholastic efforts and, at the same time, monitor her own expectancies of what the children can do. Yet she will have to do all these things if she wishes to work successfully with socially disadvantaged children.

The Mother

Karnes *et al.* (1966a) have shown that working directly with the mother is not only feasible but necessary. She has to be trained in many child-handling techniques which, in effect, aim at turning her into a middle-class mother. The mother in a socially disadvantaged family may thus have to be taught how to play with children, how to talk *with them* rather than *to them,* how to teach them and how to train them in many social skills which even she may not initially have. Above all, she must come to *praise* her children frequently for even the tiniest academic success.

The Motivation and Training of Fathers

It is an accepted truism that many socially disadvantaged families are run on a matriarchal system, the father fulfilling a passive and sometimes independent role, somewhat disconnected from the family. These men have few of the characteristics of the middle-class father who is frequently the final arbiter in family matters and who controls the finances, sets the wider standards and limits and, above all, sets the social, moral and academic expectations of the children. In such families, the mother's role may be mistaken as matriarchal, but in effect, she is usually interpreting and fulfilling patriarchal mores and standards of achievement implicit in the community.

Therefore, the father of socially disadvantaged children very frequently requires rehabilitation in his orientation to both his family and his job. These aims may require extensive counseling and even training as a skilled worker, the goal being to produce a socially mobile family.

One program which is attempting to fulfill many of the above motivational aims is Project Know-How, attached to Florida State University in Tallahassee. The staff there works with whole families, training the fathers and finding them jobs, and training mothers in social skills and household and childhood management. The children participate in an enriching kindergarten program. Although it is too early for any concrete results, the program is very promising.

DISADVANTAGED CHILDREN WITH LEARNING DISABILITIES

Lesevre (1966), in a research into the ocular-motor patterns associated with visual exploration, makes the following comment:

> Children who are bad readers, but who have a normally developed spatial function as well as a completely established lateral dominance, show a completely normal behavior of the gaze for their age, when tested for the efficiency of their ocular activity in general and also for right lateralization. These children are the dyslexics whose predominant difficulties are related to the area of speech, and the poor readers whose low level of reading or even sometimes total failure to read is due to such socio-economic reasons as a lack of education or deficiency of teaching.

These research results seem to indicate that children who are educationally or perhaps culturally disadvantaged do not suffer from the motor scanning problems which other dyslexic children appear to have. This is an important point, because it would seem to indicate that there *may be no neurological or physiological reasons* hampering culturally deprived children who have not learned to read. Incidentally, this ease of development of left-right lateralization of the gaze, together with an average or above-average digit-span memory score on the WISC or ITPA, enables one to *differentially diagnose* socially disadvantaged children from genetic dyslexic cases.

By the laws of chance, some socially disadvantaged children will have specific sensorimotor deficits, conceptualizing problems or genetic dyslexia. These children will not only require deficit-matched remediation to help them with their learning disabilities, but will also need an active motivational program which, if possible, should include the counseling of both parents.

SUMMARY

Any effective comprehensive program designed to help socially disadvantaged children must take into account the following factors:

1. Early formal academic language training is desirable and is not incompatible with other creative education.

2. Teacher expectations about the child are crucial and must be positive and optimistic. The teacher must *know* that the children are bright and lively.

3. The mother requires training in child handling, communicating and praising academic success.

4. The father must have a need for self-improvement which permeates the whole family in terms of motivation.

5. The child's self-concept must be trained to be positive and academically oriented.

6. Long-term follow-up support of the family and school is essential for continued all-around progress.

Chapter XIII

EMOTIONAL AND MOTIVATIONAL PROBLEMS

INTRODUCTION

Many remedial and other reading teachers are not familiar with the research, theories or techniques of emotional disturbance and one of the objectives of this chapter is to "block in" this information in an overview. In the process I will present my own view of the nature of emotional disturbance, one which I have developed over many years of teaching groups of emotionally disturbed children in mental hospitals and special schools. More than in any other aspect of educational practice, emotional disturbance must be theoretically understood (as one prerequisite) if the teacher or psychologist is to help disturbed children with their problems.

Estimates of the degree of emotional disturbance in learning disability cases ranges from 100 percent down to 75 percent (Hake, 1969). Personally, I feel that many of these estimates may be too high because undemonstrative conforming poor readers may be overlooked in class and because none of the incidence figures quoted is the result of statistical research with control groups. However, I suspect that the majority of learning disability children are emotionally disturbed in varying degrees compared with other children; the complexities of the problem are investigated below.

THREE USES OF THE TERM "EMOTIONAL"

Emotional and motivational factors come into learning disabilities in three separate ways. Each of these ways requires a detailed explanation to obviate diagnostic confusion.

In *primary emotional communicative dyslexia,* the word *emotional* is used to indicate that an emotional relationship between mother and child does exist or should exist. In this type of dyslexia, something about the emotional relationship is not as it should be and this directly inhibits mother-child communication during the critical phase of language development from birth to four years. In other words, *the emotional facets of the relationship are a primary efficient cause acting directly on the language processes themselves, causing the latter to be inadequate or distorted in some way.* The disinterested mother is not concerned with her child and this lack of concern deprives the child of actual speech training. The depressed mother does not relate positively and this directly inhibits the growth of language in the child. The angry mother conditions her child in a classical way, so that he comes to associate language with fear in himself and with angry attitudes in adults. Such a child will come to avoid words in authoritarian situations because they are associated with punishment. In all these cases, the emotional relationship between mother and child interferes in a direct primary way with the child's *linguistic communication,* with the result that he has an insufficient language background. Later, this will prevent him from learning to read competently at his expected level. These children are not *necessarily* emotionally disturbed—in fact, many are quite motivated and stable from the personality point of view (see Table II, Chapter I; and Chapter V). In school subjects, other than language, their performance is sometimes up to standard.

A *second* quite different way in which emotional factors can operate in language development occurs when the child is *genuinely emotionally disturbed* without language being necessarily involved. Such children are not usually afraid of words and their language milestones may be quite normal and their vocabularies adequate. On any *oral* language test, they would not be far below expected levels on the basis of overall intelligence. However, they may be a long way behind their potential in reading, spelling and writing and possibly arithmetic, a discrepancy which is the result of the educational deprivation which in turn is the *result* of their emotional disturbance. Thus, very frequently, emotionally disturbed children are too preoccupied with their personal emotional problems to concentrate on acquiring *academic* skills or knowledge. Usually, they are unable to pay attention, they have a poor relationship with the teacher, they may find restrictions irksome, and their anxieties about their own physical and ego preservation may be so high that even when they do attend to lessons, comprehension eludes them and short-term memories are not consolidated into long-term memory. Emotionally disturbed children such as these quite simply do not have the excess energy to concentrate on *any* schoolwork (including reading) any more than do most adults when they are going through emotional crises—unless work is their habitual method (mechanism) of escape.

The *third* type of link between emotional disorders and learning disabilities is usually termed *secondary emotional disorders*. These arise out of the learning disability itself. In other words, the child is relatively well adjusted even after he first enters school but gradually, as his learning disabilities disrupt his normal progress through the school curriculum, he finds himself in deeper and deeper conflict with the school system and possibly with his home. The result is increasing anxiety, avoidance behavior and possibly more extreme forms of conduct disorder, disturbances or tantrums. In these cases of secondary emotional disturbance, the emotional problem is usually cleared up fairly rapidly, once the child makes sufficient real progress in learning to read to fulfill the final-cause expectancies laid down by his school and home.

Many learning disability cases do not exhibit any symptoms of emotional disturbance other than perhaps mild anxiety and an impatience stemming from their frustration at not being able to learn to read fluently. They may also show signs of embarrassment when with their peers, and may underestimate their real competencies in other fields of study.

RESEARCH STUDIES ON EMOTIONAL AND MOTIVATIONAL FACTORS—A REVIEW

In a research study of juvenile delinquency, Pierson (1964) came to the following conclusion: "Well over 80 percent of the variance of school achievement is accounted for by motivation alone, suggesting that certain aspects of educational philosophy are in urgent need of re-thinking or revision, at least insofar as that philosophy affects delinquents and predelinquents." In another research study into motivational factors in reading, Schrock and Grossman (1961) gave visual training to twenty seventh-grade poor readers of average intelligence, for two fifteen-minute periods a week for four weeks. The purpose of the visual training was only to provide motivation through special attention, and was designed to accomplish nothing from a visual standpoint. The experimental group averaged a significant improvement in reading of seven months over the four-week period, while the control group averaged a loss of one month.

As an incidental aspect of this study, many of the students in both groups were found to have a variety of visual defects which called for optical correction.

In an interesting study of the educational aspects of childhood maladjustment, Yule and Rutter (1968) found a strong association between poor reading attainment and antisocial disorder but little association between reading attainment and neurosis. The authors felt that the findings did not suggest that psychiatric disorders as such lead to reading failure directly. *Emotionally disturbed poor readers had much the same developmental delays in language, and much the same social characteristics and perception as dyslexic children who were not maladjusted.* By contrast, the poor reading disturbed group did not share many of the family characteristics of the maladjusted children who were making normal school progress. The authors conclude, "It appears probable that *either* the reading difficulty is the primary handicap which then leads to secondary antisocial problems *or* that both the psychiatric and educational difficulties stem from a third group of factors evident in the child and his family from an early stage in the child's self development."

In agreement with the work of Yule and Rutter, Schroeder (1966) found that the emotionally disturbed group with the highest achievement scores in reading consisted of the neurotic and psychotic personalities. The "school difficulties" category had the lowest mean achievement level in both arithmetic and reading. While there was no evidence that intelligence was a significant factor, both age and sex were found to be significant variables. These two research projects tend to confirm the hypothesis that reading disability, even in emotionally disturbed children, tends to be associated with conduct disorder personalities. It will be remembered from Chapter IX that Brendtro's (1965) work associated psychopathic (conduct) tendencies in children with reading disabilities; the work of Krippner (1963) also points this way. Spache (1957) found that retarded readers ". . . were inclined to be more aggressive and defensive than children of their age, less insightful, and are relatively poor in knowing how to handle situations in conflict with adults."

Other behaviors and emotions apart from antisocial ones play their part in reading disabilities. Two studies on anxiety were mentioned in Chapter X and the conclusions were that girls with high anxiety are not good at reading, while boys of high anxiety are good readers. Boys of low anxiety tend to be poor readers. Similar results were found using the Children's Manifest Anxiety Scale in two separate research studies, one by Cowen *et al.* (1965) and the other by Frost (1965). Conduct-disorder or acting-out children do not usually manifest anxiety in the way that is measured by these tests, which use self-evaluation systems.

Muller and Madsen (1970) found that children with anxieties and reading problems were equally well desensitized by having stories read to them and by muscular relaxation. Although it was not mentioned by the authors specifically, the desensitizing agent may well have been the warm friendly reinforcing contact with empathetic adults. (See the conclusions at the end of this chapter.)

Most studies investigating the relationship between anxiety and reading have used samples of normal schoolchildren rather than groups of emotionally disturbed children, and the latter may well exhibit very different symptom variables compared with those of normal children. The anxiety of affectionless children (psychopaths, sociopaths, conduct disorder cases, acting-out children) may not be elicited by conventional anxiety testing scales because it is overlaid by a surface "don't care" attitude and aggressive behavior. It is their avoidance behavior when faced with academic work or other person-to-person situations of an intensive kind which suggests that a deep anxiety is present. There is a real need for more subtle measures of anxiety which do not rely directly on a child's awareness of anxiety-producing situations. If the hypotheses suggested later in this chapter have any validity (and they should be thoroughly researched), then ways will have to be found to desensitize these aggressive conduct-disorder children with respect to the anxiety aroused in them by the prospect of success, new knowledge, positive attachment and concentrated work.

One research which found a significant relationship between reading failure and anxiety was that carried out by R.E. Gregory (1965). Using the Bristol Social Adjustment Guides to measure many variables including anxiety, he found a significant connection between reading failure and restlessness throughout the school (the whole sample) and (among the older children) between reading failure and an anxiety for the approval of other children. This type of anxiety is more related to a child's self-concept than to the deeper types of anxiety referred to above. The study does indicate that anxiety is not a unitary entity inasmuch as it can be manifested in different ways in various situations and in association with different kinds of people.

Maturational Lag

Not a few emotionally disturbed children are very well able to cope with academic work (Yule and Rutter, 1968). It is those who are unable to achieve because of their preoccupation with more basic survival-value emotional problems with whom we are mainly concerned in this chapter. Even so, many of this latter group may *also* be dyslexic and in some cases, both the emotional and reading disorders may very possibly have a maturational lag as their formal cause (see Chapter IX).

Family Relationships, Self-Concepts and Academic Success

A child acquires attitudes toward himself from birth onward in the same way in which he acquires attitudes toward other people and things. He listens to what other people say about him either when they speak directly to him or when they speak to others about him in his hearing. If he *repeatedly* hears that he is a naughty boy, or lazy, or clumsy, or dirty, or inefficient, or rude, or any other derogatory term, he soon comes to *believe* it and instead of changing (an impossibility in such nonreinforcing circumstances), he begins to fulfill the negative role prescribed for him. In other words, he develops a negative self-concept because he believes what adults tell him about himself. On the other hand, a child who is praised, appreciated and firmly attached in a positive way to his parents and family, develops a very sound, stable and positive belief in himself which will give him a fundamental confidence in himself, always provided his abilities and successes are *realistically* presented to him. Such a child has a very positive self-concept.

It is obvious that this positive self-concept must include healthy, enthusiastic attitudes to school and academic work. Both parents and teachers should frequently and appropriately praise, reinforce and reward both *effort* and *success* in all academic activities. If this is true for normal children, it is doubly true for learning disability children and the emotionally disturbed.

The term *attachment* is very crucial in any discussion of reinforcement (see below). It can be defined as the environmentally modifiable innate bond which attaches children to mothers (and later, to other adults) for both their own survival and society's. Attachment is observable in almost all animals including the primates. Without a teacher-child attachment built on praise, encouragement and personal contact, learning will occur, if it occurs at all, only as an avoidance of punishment.

In a large study in England, Douglas (1964) found that children tend to work well when their parents are interested in their academic progress. This rather global finding is amply confirmed in more detailed studies. This theme, which was a major finding or conclusion in terms of the motivation of socially disadvantaged children in the previous chapter, will be seen to be equally crucial in the remediation of emotionally disturbed children with learning disabilities.

In a study of *self-esteem*, Coopersmith (1968), using a sample of normal middle-class boys, found no consistent relation between self-esteem and physical attractiveness, height, early trauma, the size of the family, breast or bottle feeding or the mother's occupation. In the group studied, the boys' self-esteem depended little on family social position or income level: "Our subjects tended to gauge their individual work primarily by their achievements and treatment in their own inter-personal environment rather than by more general and abstract norms of success." Boys with high self-esteem had a close relationship with their parents. This relationship took the form of an interest in the boys' welfare and concern about their companions, problems and activities. Both the mother and father regarded the boy as a significant person who was worthy of their deep interest. Thus, the boy came to value himself in a similar favorable way. These parents of children with high self-esteem were less permissive than parents of children with lower self-esteem. The parents

> . . . demanded high standards of behavior and were strict and consistent in enforcement of the rules. Yet their discipline was by no means harsh; indeed, these parents were less punitive than the parents of the boys who were found to be lacking in self-esteem. They used rewards rather than corporal punishment or withdrawal of love as disciplinary techniques and their sons praised their firmness.

These results should make every teacher pause to reconsider her role as a parent-figure in the eyes of her students and the immense value of praise and reinforcement rewards, not necessarily of a material kind, which can assist them to value themselves more highly.

Success is an essential key to progress but success is only intrinsically meaningful if it signals emotional satisfaction to the individual. Otherwise, the successful response is nonmotivating. As will be seen, success may even seem dangerous to the child if it brings with it the threat of insecurity.

Hake (1969), in a research comparing poor and above-average readers, found significantly more negative covert motivations in the former group. These were as follows: First, the poor readers saw their home and parents as more threatening and less warm and comforting; second, the poor readers tended to identify more with story characters who had punishing teachers; third, poor readers told more stories of children who did not like themselves; fourth, they told stories of children who solved personal problems through defense mechanisms rather than by facing reality; fifth, the poor readers identified with children who solved personal problems aggressively, and sixth, poor readers told more stories of children who were held in dungeons, beaten or even killed by the hero.

Vorhaus (1952) examined the Rorschach configurations associated with reading disabilities in 309 children attending a reading clinic. All the children were submissive and appeared eager to learn. They came from privileged homes, felt guilty about their disability, but lacked enthusiasm and responsiveness. None of the cases were psychotic or neurologically damaged. Four groups of cases emerged, each having its distinctive personality characteristics:

1. The first type of child was constricted in personality, its growth potentials being stifled by a covert rejection of the child concealed behind a facade of a "good home." Spontaneity and naturalness had been repressed, though the prognosis was often good.

2. For the second group of children, the pleasure drives had been turned inward, becoming a source of compensatory gratification on a primitive level. They had not become a source of emotional growth outwardly expressed in positive (attachment) relationships. These children withdrew from their frustrating environments and became detached from socially valued activities such as reading. Vorhaus pointed out that inner resources still existed in these children and if they were turned outward, the prognosis was good.

3. In this group there was an appearance of conformity as

distinct from any definite attempt to conform. Behind the facade was a concealed, stubborn, silent resistance, and a determination on the part of the child to preserve his creative drives as his personal secret pleasure. Reading ability became a symbol of participation in cultural (parental) demands, and as these threatened the ego, such participation became intolerable. This can be called the "leave me alone" group, which was very passive-aggressive in outlook.

4. The typical child here agreed that he was unworthy (poor self-concept) and became self-persecutory. His mother and father must be right, because they are always right, and if they call him bad or lazy, he must be these things; therefore, he must be punished. This group had a thread of parental love left intact, but because it was so valuable and fragile, success (by altering the whole situation) might have severed it. *The teacher and parents must reassure the child that success will not damage future relationships.*

In all these cases, improvement can only come about by building a strong, warm, continuing relationship between teacher and child, one which devolves from a strongly reinforcing task-oriented positive behavior in the remedial situation. Only in this way will success eventually come to bring personal satisfaction.

It is possible for reactive aggression to develop in some children as a response to punishment or excessive authority control in areas other than reading. In these cases, refusing to learn to read is a retaliatory attack on that authority (parents or teacher), because the child knows that it would give pleasure to the adults concerned if he did learn to read. Only when such a child comes to *like* (attach to) the teacher will progress be possible.

The self-concepts of boys may be differently structured from those of girls. Academic achievement was found by Fink (1962) to be significantly correlated with self-concept in boys but not in girls. Bayley and Schaeffer (1964), in an analysis of the data from the Berkeley Growth Study, found that in general a boy's "intelligence" is strongly related to the love-hostility dimension of maternal behavior, while in girls it is related primarily to the educational level of the parents. However, girl-achievers tended to have more ambivalent feelings about themselves than did the boys, whose feelings were mainly negative (Shaw, 1960). Hake (1969) found a strong trend for girls to evidence more covert maladjustment than did boys in both poor- and good-reader groups. These sex differences suggest that straight M-reinforcement in all its aspects may operate more successfully with boys than with girls.

In a study of 300 adolescent girls, Orme (1970) found a significant correlation between emotional instability and left-handedness. This is an interesting finding in terms of right hemisphere activity and plasticity of brain functioning, mentioned in previous chapters.

Reading achievement and its relation to maternal behavior has been investigated by Della-Piana and Martin (1966). These authors found that the mothers of overachieving girls exhibited significantly more positive social-emotional reaction and more total warmth than did the mothers of underachieving girls. In his book on the subject of the "self," Hamachek (1965) repeatedly stresses the importance in the first year or two of life of the development of the self-image, an image which he feels is essentially completed before adolescence. The infant has the broad foundation of his self-concept laid down by the parents and those around him at a time in life when he is most vulnerable to *training in feelings of acceptance or rejection.*

If the built-in aspects of attachment (smiling, caressing, etc.) are able to be fulfilled in a favorable environment, the child will be reinforced in his feelings of being accepted by his mother and the family in general. Such a child will later feel himself to be a worthwhile individual, even at a young age. However, many socially disadvantaged children, while they have a worthy self-concept stemming from infancy, do not necessarily extend this to the academic sphere, unless the parents themselves reinforce this. Sensitivity to praise and other reinforcements by the parents *for scholastic achievement* have to be transmitted quite specifically as social-cultural values. While attachment is still the major bond facilitating this process, the transmitted attitudes built into the child are a complex combination of aggression (competition), anxiety (of failure), curiosity (about the content of books) and imitation (in the form of identification).

Sometimes one hears clinicians stating that a child cannot learn to read easily because the parents are "pressuring" him too much. Except in extreme cases, overpressuring is usually only an important cause when the child is unable to cope with schoolwork for quite other reasons, such as neurological dysfunction, genetic dyslexia or primarily emotional disturbance. Most intact, stable children are able to keep up with the competitive pressures brought to bear on them by parents and teachers, a situation which brings with it a degree of anxiety. Of course, excessive pressure is undesirable, but of itself it does not cause learning disabilities except in rare cases; it does, however, aggravate other more basic causes.

Although mothers have been the parents mentioned most thus far, as with the socially disadvantaged child, the role of the father is frequently a key one. Children, if they are to develop both self-respect and a healthy academic self-concept, will have that development facilitated by a father who sets standards and who takes a lively interest in their progress. A boy's masculinity and a girl's femininity are to a large extent determined by the father's attitudes and encouraging acceptance of these qualities in his children. Both masculinity and femininity have considerable elements of *differentiated* positive aggression built into them and the father of the boy or girl in part determines the quantity and quality of that positive aggression. Positive aggression will be discussed in detail later in the chapter; it can take the form of determination, ambition, competitiveness, study-stamina or problem-solving tenacity. A son may be weak and uncompetitive or positive and full of ambition, with many possible variations between the two. A daughter can work to please her father as an expression of her femininity, particularly if he reinforces that aspect of her achievement. Therefore, for both sexes, a male teacher may elicit motivations which it may be difficult for a woman teacher to stimulate. Of course, the mother (or a woman teacher) also fulfills her particular and differing roles for developing masculinity and femininity in boys and girls, respectively. The point about male teachers has been made because there are so few in our schools and even fewer in learning disability centers.

MOTIVATION AND ETHOLOGY: A NEW THEORY

As a subject of study, motivation comprises a whole section of psychology, and one of the most controversial. My own viewpoint is an eclectic one in that I endeavor to synthesize major aspects of the various theories, most of which have a considerable body of research evidence behind them. The various theoretical standpoints on motivation are not mutually exclusive and the arguments between, for example, the learning theorists and the psychoanalysts (both environmental theories) are more concerned with defining limits to the universe of study and to what is admissible as testable hypotheses or proof than they are about getting down to researching issues in mutually common ground, particularly events in the first few years of life.

Motivation is a term which for me combines the categories of emotions and drives. The idiosyncratic ways in which I use each of these words will become clear later in the chapter. However, it is important at this point to say that I regard emotions (feelings) as an awareness, in any organism, of a *drive* in operation in the interests of some survival-value need. We *feel* hungry (emotion) when the metabolism of our bodies operates on the endocrinological system by having a physiological "need" for *food* (a drive, or species-specific instinct pattern, e.g., sucking). The term *partly innate patterned drive* is used in this and other chapters to represent a *continuum* of possible patterns of drive operation in organisms, ranging from the most highly structured species-specific innate behavioral programs, in which only a comparatively modest amount of "learning" takes place (e.g., sex), to broad unstructured developmental programs which, although basically genetically determined, are largely "content-filled" through environmental training and learning (e.g., fear). *There is no such thing in primates as a drive, instinct or emotion which is entirely innate or completely learned;* as will be seen in the next section, the innate aspect of any drive *must* have its ecological niche, the one to which the drive adapted in the first place. For example, a baby's sucking mouth with its attendant hunger is meaningless without an environmental nipple. An attachment smile is pointless without a face to smile at.

Psychobiological Survival Needs

The body and brain of all animals function as a unity in an *evolving* natural world. That world is still largely competitive because, as Darwin pointed out, the prize of continued evolution for a species goes to the one which can best survive in terms of having its key needs fulfilled. A "need" is a psychobiological drive in a state of disequilibrium and as such, it seeks and requires some form of satiation or discharge in the interests of survival. Thus, an important element in survival is the fulfillment of needs. Human beings, like all animals, have psychobiological needs and if these needs are not positively fulfilled, the opposite of survival occurs in some degree, namely, stultification, degeneration or death. Obviously, humans and animals must have the right kinds of foods in the right quantities; they need to explore and to be curious, not only to obtain food (in forest, field or laboratory) but also to fulfill other survival-value needs such as improved transportation. The hypothalamus has in it control centers for body water balance (including thirst), appetite and hunger, temperature changes, blood pressure and the emotional reactions of rage or fear. The hypothalamus also regulates the activity of the anterior lobe of the pituitary gland which, in its turn, regulates the secretions of the adrenal medulla's gonadotrophic secretion, thyroid activity, etc. These glands, in their turn, regulate many bodily functions including aggression and sexuality (Woodburne, 1967). Very often these bodily need functions, as developing behaviors, become highly differentiated or distorted in various ways, depending on how powerful influences in the environment, such as parents or school, have molded or trained need-fulfillment behavior patterns.

However, not all of these behavior patterns are necessarily

100 percent trained or learned, and this is where learning theory in its broadest sense becomes extremely complex. Over the last twenty years, the research work of a group called ethologists has been gaining increasing recognition (Lorenz, 1952, 1963; Harlow, 1959; Thorpe, 1963; Hinde, 1966; Bowlby, 1957; Klopfer and Hailman, 1967). These scientists have found that many of the behavioral patterns of need fulfillment exhibited by organisms in their response to a psychobiological need-state are innately determined, so much so that extinction through training is well-nigh impossible (Breland and Breland, 1961; Harlow, 1959). Psychologists are beginning to realize more and more (something which geneticists and biologists have always accepted) that behavior is a complex mixture determined by an *interplay* of hereditary (genic) and environmental influences. In any one psychobiological-environmental situation, the proportions of heredity to environmental influences have been largely predetermined for that species through past evolutionary survival-value behavioral contexts (ecological niches). For example, I suggest that fear, including anxiety, is largely unprogrammed in man, behaviorally speaking, because dangerous situations, predators, etc., vary considerably from place to place around the world. Each child has to learn in an *undistorted* way, from his parents and local culture, the objects he should fear in the interest of survival. By contrast, sexuality is highly programmed, comparatively speaking, because it has a relatively narrow survival-value objective, namely, reproduction. As is well known, even sexuality can be somewhat *distorted* through environmental influences. These psychobiological, species-specific, innate, partially learned need-fulfillment patterns, which I will henceforth call *partly innate patterned drives,* will be further discussed in a later section.

Inasmuch as a learning disability child lacks the motivation to learn, some partly innate patterned drive is not operating in a conventional way; there would seem to be several factors contributing to such a state of affairs.

The reader should be aware that the theories and hypotheses which follow have been very much abbreviated. It is not possible in a short chapter to do more than outline the broad themes of my position.

Attachment Drive

Shortly after birth, all primate babies, like most other animals, become strongly *attached* to the mother, the bond thus formed gradually loosening and broadening throughout infancy and childhood. In humans, this attachment rapidly comes to include other members of the family; subsequently, it broadens to those adults and peers important to the child, including his teachers. Harlow (1961, 1963); Harlow and Suomi (1970); Bowlby (1958, 1961), and Ambrose (1960) have investigated aspects of attachment. Harlow's work with primates strongly suggests that the attachment bond is quite separate from food needs and that in one of its aspects it operates strongly in the presence of fear. Ambrose's work has shown how the "smiling response" of the baby from the second month of life reinforces the mother's attachment to the child. The mother's face (or a plate with two dots for eyes and a mouth) will elicit an attachment smiling response from the child. I suggest that this cycling process of simple attachment between mother and child, if continuously reinforced, differentiates into a complex affectional relationship system between mother and child which later expands to other people as suggested above. Thus, contrary to Skinner's (1953) environmental hypothesis, the implication is that *the "social reinforcement" of behavior systems is really the attachment bond in operation, which is innately predetermined to a considerable extent.*

It is not suggested for one moment that the environment and learning do not also play an important part in this differentiating process. Instincts or drives with their partly built-in behavior patterns (precise or loose) were evolved for species survival rather than for personal survival. Therefore, the innate response patterns are keyed to match an *expected* environmental or ecological niche, a match which has been maximized for species survival. Evolution *is* the genetic adaptation of behavior to *a specific experiential environment*. This match, in terms of the members of the species, is never exact. There is a double distribution of inexactness: one covers the imperfections or deviations within the individual members of the species with respect to inherited gene-pool patterns; the other is the changes in the environmental circumstances of any one individual, the environment being slightly different from person to person. To illustrate from the animal world, a gazelle may be killed by a predator because it did not inherit the capacity to run quite as fast as the remainder of the herd (an innate difference), or it may die because a particular water hole was newly poisoned. Children, too, may suffer from the effects of inherited individual differences as happens in genetic dyslexia, but they may also suffer when the instinct-drive behavioral patterns have been *unable to develop normally* and satisfactorily because an *unusual* environment (usually the home) does not permit the development of the pattern to proceed and differentiate in the *intended* built-in survival-value way. *I hold that these environmental distortions of the partly innate patterned drives are responsible for most nonpsychotic emotional disturbance and conduct disorders in children and adults.*

It is important to realize that the "expected" environment which the partly innate behavioral pattern (however structured or unstructured) is to match may quite well be a *learning* situation of a stereotyped kind. Thus, all relatively normal children seem to progress through a somewhat standardized infancy which can be discerned across cultural differences if they are not too extreme. Nature makes do with roughly 90 to 95 percent survival of the members of a species. Most psychobiological developmental behavior patterns seem universal wherever children live. Sucking, smiling, tears, walking, tantrums, speech, attachment, sexuality and many other programs all clock in and develop in roughly predictable stages. Pigaet has investigated numerous cognitive developmental schedules which seem dependent on a nice coincidence of innate readiness and necessary environmental fulfillment, and there is an urgent need for a meticulous equivalent investigation in the area of behavioral drive programs.

Another important point to be made is that the impact a

normal expected (learning) environment has in developing and differentiating the partly innate patterned drive can facilitate and accelerate that differentiation if the environment is *especially favorable*. Thus an excellent teacher or mother can effectively promote development.

The Distortion of Behavioral Patterns

If a broody hen is prevented from obtaining the materials to build her nest, she will pluck out her own feathers to do so (Thorpe, 1963). An infant or young child who is separated from his mother or home for some time may emotionally detach from the mother and remain that way even when she returns, a situation thought to be one basis of depression; or the child may re-attach with clinging behavior a few hours or even days after the reunion, a personality state which may last through life (Bowlby, 1961). In like manner, curiosity can be warped, sexual patterns can be distorted and phobias of harmless objects or ideas can be conditioned. All these abnormally distorted, partly innate patterned drives result from an incompatibility of training, rearing or education (formal or informal) which is environmentally determined, with the pattern which is to a degree inherited. The natural body, including the endocrine glands, the hormones, the brain with its regulating centers and the whole differentiating plan of behavioral life-growth, requires specific *positive training* in the same direction as the instinct-drive programs, whereas unusual environmental influences may train, mold or even re-mold the child *against* nature. This clash of environment and built-in pattern can occur both in the home and at school, in community institutions or through unusual chance circumstances. Of course, these environmental influences are rarely entirely either negative or positive. Most often they are a blend of both, depending on the extremely complex attitudes and emotional problems in the home, the school and the community.

The programs of the partly innate patterned drives may operate in varying degrees and ways throughout childhood and adolescence and even adult life. Sex is an obvious instance, especially in its programmed patterns of puberty and adolescence. Positive training in terms of sex education is necessary to differentiate the drive in its natural development.

An organism rarely makes its peace with an environmentally disorganized, partly innate patterned drive. Such an organism will usually make an effort to put matters right, that is, to find compatibility with its natural genetically determined behavioral programs, even though that attempt, by community standards, may be as distorted as the patterns it attempts to set straight. Children, even the intelligent ones, are dependent on the adults in their environment for setting patterns straight. The behavior of disturbed children, even in its most destructive phases, is usually a disarranged plea for the malfunctioning environmentally trained, partly innate patterns to be reorganized or even integrated into a harmonious forward-growing organism. It is impossible even for children reared in the most enlightened homes and communities to be without some conflict. Our bodies and minds, with their multitude of environmentally trained, partly innate behavioral patterns, evolved for the ecology of a natural jungle or plain, desert or waterside setting. The children of ancient communities, and even of similar communities today (e.g., the Australian aborigine), could be active all day without much physical restriction. They had their aggression channeled in conformity with local custom (Mead, 1950). They were often considered adult by the age of ten, and married and had children shortly after puberty. The variety of customs allowed by the local environment, physical or cultural, was tremendous and had to be that way in the interest of survival; however, in spite of the variations, the natural developmental patterns of human growth were almost invariably recognized and integrated into the social milieu. This occurred because in such cultures food seeking, reproduction and the conservation of resources against natural catastrophes or enemies were basic to everyday life. Of course, although myths and legends may suggest it, life was no Garden of Eden. However, it was a natural one very unlike that of today. We no longer have to hunt for our food; it waits for us in the supermarket. We no longer participate in fertility rites to make all things grow well, nor do we marry at puberty, because sex means babies and babies prevent our students from receiving an education. It is a peculiar incompatibility that as our children become healthier, the age at which puberty occurs becomes earlier, yet the "nonsexual" period required for educational and vocational training becomes prolonged into the twenties. Sexual problems, though they may lead to much unhappiness in adolescence and adult life, are perhaps not so serious in our society as the maladaptive "training" of attachment, fear and aggression.

Inherent in the parent-child partly innate patterned drive of attachment is the emotion of affection or, in behavioral terms, the act of positively relating through smiling, conversing and caressing. Affection usually means an absence of attacking behavior (aggression). Attachment evolved in almost all species to hold the infant close to the mother during that period of dependency when it is particularly vulnerable to accidents, predators, strangers, etc., but attachment also has reinforcing qualities because affection rewards the child while he is being trained during the long developmental phases of the first fourteen years of life. Through attachment and its use as an affectionate reinforcer, the mother, the father, other children, the teacher and others in the community can usually provide an adequate but far from ideal training for the child which is not too incompatible with the partly innate patterned drive programs that must be environmentally developed for the child to survive in a competitive world.

Aggression and Attachment

Aggression, if properly differentiated through positive training in such a way that it is able to follow through the natural developmental program from birth to the end of adolescence, is probably the most valuable and creative patterned drive man possesses. Through differentiated well-trained aggression, we can fight disease, effect social change, cut down crime and even create works of art which make a social contribution. Research into the partly innate patterns of the development of aggression and into the training required to differentiate them into those of a mature, forthright adult is long overdue. I suggest that "infantile omnipotence," "temper tantrums," "gangs," "pecking orders" and "adolescent rebellion" may prove to be partly innate patterned drive developmental aggression programs if they are properly researched. Undifferentiated, literally infantile aggression—that is, violence, sadism and persistent animosity—take a great toll in murder, mutilation and misery around the world, and the only way these problems can be ameliorated is to understand the innate drive patterns of development and restructure them through appropriate counseling, molding and training. The affectionless child, the psychopathic boy, the antisocial delinquent and the conduct-disorder case, if the hypothesis is correct, are the result of environmentally perverted, innate developmental patterns of aggression.

According to Berkowitz (1962, 1967), aggressive behaviors are largely learned. Ideally, then, all infant environments would facilitate the differentiation of the partly innate patterned drives by providing a positive training in an *appropriate* favorable ecological niche. Learned maladaptive partly innate developmental patterns of aggression *prevent the formation within the personality of those satisfactory attachment reinforcement-needs which will motivate the individual to learn academic subjects.* This is because aggression and attachment appear to be bipolar counteracting primary drives when they are both associated with the one person. Furthermore, because in these children the aggression is usually warped from early training experiences, it cannot easily be differentiated in the regular school programs into the competitive, ambitious drive which will please parents and teachers and eventually, in adult life, produce more goods and services for the wider community.

Fear and Aggression

It may seem paradoxical, but (despite the popular assumption) innate drive patterns may be largely unstructured in the interest of survival. Fear is a partly innate patterned drive which, as I have already suggested, may be somewhat unprogrammed. This is because the people, animals and things about which children must be made anxious or afraid vary so much from one place to another. Even so, built-in patterns such as a fear of falling, loud noises, bright lights or pain almost certainly exist, some perhaps before birth. Their physiological basis is the startle reflex, a reaction which any of the above trauma will elicit automatically in the neonate. Once the baby begins to be aware of his environment, it becomes possible for the mother to condition him to be afraid of people, objects, actions or even ideas. Much more important than these factors is the power of the parents to make their children afraid of their own natural drives and their partly innate developmental behavioral patterns. Sexuality seems to be socially evolving away from the traditional silence and negative or nontraining attitudes. The situation with respect to aggression is worse. The nationwide confusion about aggression may arise (and on Berkowitz's findings must partially arise) from learning. Too often, well-intentioned but misguided training regards anger in children as a "sin," potentially destructive and murderous. In a strange contradiction, the partially built-in drive which is to be extinguished utilizes itself in that training act. The parents or teacher in a variety of ways may punish (be aggressive to) the child who displays open aggression, until he learns through fear to shut it off. Being a partly innate patterned drive, it continues to develop in more differentiated forms, some of them open and acceptable such as "healthy competition" and "ambition." However, some aggression may become distorted into a variety of behaviors such as bullying younger children (rather than protesting upward to the feared authority), damaging property, stealing or turning anger inward in the form of guilty self-punishment.

When undifferentiated or "shut-off" aggression is expressed in these ways, attachment and fear combine to create guilt toward the figures of attachment, usually the parents or teacher. Guilt further cripples the expression of aggression because it often operates even in the absence of the parents. When the parents' prohibitions are an expression of those of the whole culture, individual guilt and its avoidance take a communal form of condemnation. In such a community, "conscience" operates through guilt to inhibit or censor various aspects of various patterned drives which it considers threatening to social survival. Films are banned, books forbidden and social protest crushed. Sometimes, such a course seems fully justified, but often it is based on a false psychological premise, and a new generation, realizing this, may adjust the social structure accordingly. Distorted communal aggression arising from fear takes many forms such as racial hatreds; a national disregard for those who are sick; the neglect of babies, including a lack of medical care; crime; a dislike of strangers, particularly the "enemy"; dislike of the Establishment or innovators of social change, and so on.

If, in a child's life, parental aggression has been substituted for attachment, guilt which depends on the presence of the latter cannot exist, and the result is an affectionless child, a potential psychopath. This type of individual has "nothing to lose" and his undifferentiated aggression can burst forth in reminiscent situations, fulfilling distorted motives. Other patterns exist. When the parent is mostly loving (attachment) but with sufficient aggression to frustrate the child frequently, positive rebellion may ensue, a strangely differentiating role which some people play throughout life. Again, if parental love is present much of the time but with an undercurrent of constant slight interjections of aggressive control, the child becomes obedient and conforming with perhaps occasional weak protests. Large amounts of attachment-love combined with threatened anger tend to produce a child who is meek, overobedient and even withdrawn. Thus, attachment-love combined with a parental demand for a considerable degree of conforming behavior can do as much damage to a child's personality as parental aggression, particularly when those conforming behaviors are themselves trained distortions of still other drives such as sex or aggression. The resulting internalized conflicts are relatively obvious. If one wants love, one denies aggression; if one wants sex, one denies love, because the loved child is taught by the loved mother that sex is forbidden. Curiosity must be confined through fear to topics prescribed by the family as socially acceptable. All too often children are raised in a bewildering illogical array of complexly distorted, partially innate patterned drives, leaving many aspects of them in crude, undifferentiated, guilt-laden states.

Attachment, fear, sexuality, curiosity and aggression interact in a large variety of ways from birth onward. Fear seems to appear first as a startle reflex immediately after birth, but aggression in its most undifferentiated form soon follows, usually as a response to frustration. Attachment and curiosity tend to build quickly from four months onward but as Ambrose (1960) has implied, the smiling response may be an attachment pattern which appears as early as the sixth week.

Curiosity

Curiosity is probably an outgrowth of the desire to explore which itself may grow from the baby's early delight in following dangling toys, etc., with his eyes. It is a partly innate patterned drive which motivates problem-solving cognition. Curiosity is probably only slightly programmed developmentally.

Imitation

One other partly innate patterned drive needs mentioning because from the point of view of the parent or teacher, it is essential for training children. After a thorough examination of the literature and a close observation of numerous children of all ages, I have come to the conclusion that a key partly innate patterned drive is one we call imitation, mimicry or modeling. In studying the development of language in children, I am convinced that one very important aspect of its acquisition is the innate ability of the infant to imitate sounds spontaneously in a correct sequence; furthermore, it seems almost impossible to extinguish the growth of language in children whose speech and hearing equipment is intact. Certainly, as we have seen in primary emotional communicative dyslexic children, language acquisition can be somewhat impaired by a distorting environment, but in general, such children can communicate clearly in their native language. Emotionally caused aphasia or mutism in children is rare, and it probably stems from a detectable neurological dysfunction. Imitation or modeling also uses the drive of attachment, particularly in its reinforcement aspects (smiling, cajoling, etc.), in the overall process of the environmental training of the child by parent or teacher. This may include training in language, or in the differentiation of partly innate patterned drives or of cognitive structures and their contents. While all the drives contribute to *training* a child in the home or at school, attachment, curiosity and imitation by natural design play the largest part. Some aggression, fear and anxiety may be necessary for the purpose of negative reinforcement or punishment. In my opinion, the five partly innate patterned drives of attachment, curiosity, imitation, anxiety and aggression together form a basic structure for behavioral learning theory.

Behavioral Learning Theory

Learning theory as a body of knowledge has developed rapidly in the last few years, mostly from the work of Skinner (1953). The way in which learning theory can best be applied by the teacher to the classroom or remedial situation has been described by Madsen and Madsen (1970), who point out that if we wish to modify behavior, we must discover in what kind of motivational situations the children will work best; these situations may be (a) obtaining rewards in the form of things they want, (b) seeking or receiving adult approval to fulfill acquired needs, (c) avoiding unpleasantness (punishment) or (d) acting in certain ways from habit. Negative behavior, or for that matter all behavior, fulfills some need in the child and so before one can extinguish negative behavior, one must find the satisfactions or "payoff" the child obtains from that behavior. Once this payoff is consistently eliminated, while the negative behavior may increase for a while, in time it will be extinguished. According to Madsen and Madsen, we can shape the behavior of children by organizing stimuli and events in their environment so that the student "receives approval/disapproval reinforcements contingent upon appropriate/inappropriate behavior. Therefore, reinforcement teaching is the structure of approval and disapproval reinforcers, through time, which shape desired behavior toward specific goals."

Madsen and Madsen mention five techniques which can be used for the structuring of contingencies. The first technique involves approval which is associated with "happiness." This may involve giving the child food, candy or toys, or even tokens which can be traded for these things; children who are more *mature* will accept praise, personal attention, smiling, etc. (It can be seen that approval is an aspect of attachment and it may take some time and much effort on the part of the teacher to "attach" the child to her. This is why she may have to start with small toys as rewards, or even with candy.) Approval can be withheld once the positive reinforcer is established and if this is done only occasionally, the child will continue to hope for an approval reward if his behavior improves the next time around. The unhappiness anxiety or fear which comes from disapproval or punishment is a traditional motivator. Physical punishment can add pain to a temporary breaking of the attachment bond.

I suggest that the instinct drive operating in the case of disapproval or punishment is aggression of an active kind, whereas the mere withholding of approval could be described as aggression of a passive kind. Psychological punishments may be forms of direct aggression, the operative partly innate patterned drive in the child being fear. His behavior will be modified because he will fear the pain which he knows will come from the punishment of the next transgression. There are emotionally disturbed children who invite punishment regularly. Usually, these children have become inoculated against pain, even though by normal standards the punishment may be quite severe. Once he is inoculated against punishment, the "payoffs" for the child may be considerable; first of all, he may have obtained a direct satisfaction as a result of the negative behavior or act itself, e.g., he enjoyed the candy bar he stole from the teacher's desk. Second, he may enjoy the act of aggression itself; expressing one's aggression is usually a satisfying experience. Third, the child may be rewarded by the attention the whole incident receives from both the teacher and other children; and fourth, he may be M-reinforced by his own feeling of having *control* of the situation while all the teacher can do is react with ineffective punishment. To modify the behavior of these children, each of these reward-satisfactions has to be reduced or eliminated. Task-contingent rewards and an effective punishment system must be substituted. The punishment side of the operant balance should always be less than the positive reinforcers. Once a new punishment system is operating effectively, the threat of disapproval, if it arouses a modicum of fear in the child, may be sufficient to bring him into line. If the main purpose of the child's misbehavior is to attract attention, studiously ignoring him or isolating him may have the desired effect. This cuts off the reward system so that, after a few stepped-up attempts on the part of the child to keep the old pattern going, the attention-seeking behavior slowly fades away. The best results are obtained from programs of behavior modification in which the child knows exactly what is required of him and what is not; this is best achieved by establishing a set of simple rules with standard rewards and punishments which he can use as guidelines.

Many of the child-rearing and controlling techniques which have been used by parents and teachers since families and schools began are summarized neatly and accurately in the principles and techniques of learning theory and behavior modification. Traditionally, parents and teachers have tended to be somewhat unstructured and intuitive in their application of behavior learning principles and for a normal healthy family such an approach is highly desirable. Gifted teachers may also work in an intuitive way. Most of us, however, as parents or teachers, are not in this category, and behavior modification through enlightened operant reinforcement systems will relieve tension, reduce anxiety and move everyone concerned in a constructive direction, even though the initial "breaking-in" period of establishing the new system may sometimes be unsettled. However, *there is one important proviso, namely, that the behaviors must be modified in a way that is completely compatible with the partly innate patterned drives which the child has inherited.*

Just as Breland and Breland (1961) found it almost impossible to extinguish innate behavior patterns in subhuman species, so it is equally difficult in humans. I have heard young counselors talk of extinguishing a child's sexual behavior and of establishing a reinforcement schedule to achieve that objective. While it is possible to modify a child's sexual behavior by substituting one outlet or set of outlets for another, it is very doubtful that all of them could be "extinguished" (that is, be not observable) without causing considerable stress to the personality. The same is true of aggression or any other so-called primary drive. *Behavior modification used wisely is invaluable as the environmental training counterpart of the partly innate patterned drives; these two aspects of learning are quite compatible.* If they are not used too rigidly or interpreted in too narrow a context, reinforcement techniques can bring stability to the lives of both normal and disturbed children. Even more valuable is the use of behavior modification for *realigning with the partly innate behavioral drive patterns those deviant or inappropriate behaviors which have already become environmentally established.*

One pitfall which a parent or teacher may be led into, when adopting an operant learning approach to children's problems, is to oversimplify situations which may be very subtle. The computerlike complexity of the human mind and body not infrequently causes traditional *simple* behavior modification to be inadequate in the face of the presenting problems. This is particularly true with regard to the interplay of innate and environmental factors which impinge on a child within a family and school setting. One complicating factor is the innate tendency for most behavior to become more and more established and habitual through time. When we first learn to drive a car the operations are difficult, but after twenty years we can run on "automatic pilot" for hours at a time. In a parallel manner, it would seem that the environmental modifications of our partly innate behavior patterns, once they are established in adaptive or maladaptive patterns, slowly harden through the years. At least three factors contribute to the degree to which a particular behavior has "set" in a particular individual. A primary variable is the age of the person, and the younger he is the better the prospect for retraining. A second important factor is the intensity and duration of the original training, both of which contribute to the degree of behavior habituation; this factor causes great resistance to modification.

The third contributor is the extent and structure of the innate instinct-drive pattern which is embedded in the behavior. The more structured the innate pattern (e.g., puberty and adolescent sex), the more specific is its survival objective (e.g., reproduction), and the greater the contribution of the genes to its program the more solidly fixed or set that behavior will become, whether environmental training has been compatible or distorting. (This is equally true of what we might call cognitive programs such as language, and motor programs such as walking, but of course, one usually desires to modify these through training only by speeding up and improving on the innate pattern.) Partly innate patterned drive programs that have been trained in a way which, although in line with the innate programs, are at odds with society's standards, may be very difficult to modify. For example, a boy might be trained by his father to box and battle out his differences with other boys directly with his fists, a pattern that is difficult to modify. Parents may encourage open active sexual behavior in young children which, although quite natural in other cultures, is not so in Western societies. A mother can cause her children to cling to her by strongly reinforcing the natural attachment pattern in infancy, thus making the children overdependent. Later the natural breaking of the mother-child attachment relationship during adolescence may be stormy and difficult. For convenience of discussion, I have tended to overstress the role of the mother in the upbringing of children; the father is equally important, and teachers also play a powerful role in training children in the ways described.

The Motivation To Learn in a Classroom Setting

In the final, much oversimplified analysis, a child lacks motivation to learn academic work for any or all of the following reasons:

1. Because the attachment instinct-drive is distorted,

he is unable to attach strongly enough to the teacher with a positive bond to understand or need the reward systems such as praise, affection, smiling and caressing, which are normal attachment behaviors.

2. The child's anxiety levels are so high and so bound up with success at impossibly high achievement standards that he becomes confused and distraught when confronted with academic tasks.

3. For a large variety of past situational reasons, he may be frustrated to the extent that his aggression dominates his relationships with people. This not only distorts his attachment relationships but also makes the refusal to do academic work an aggressive act in its own right.

4. The child's capacity to imitate or model (as a partly innate aspect of learning) may be disturbed or reduced below a minimal functional level by the operation of more urgent emotional needs, for example, an extreme attachment need for affection characterized by clinging behavior. Aggression, too, can reduce the effectiveness of imitation in an academic setting. Of course, the modeling of aggressive behaviors may be operating very efficiently.

5. If the child's curiosity has been repeatedly dampened or forbidden expression in infancy, reading may later become included among the forbidden items through stimulus generalization. The knowledge which the child is told will come from books when he can read may also threaten the preferred security of the status quo since knowledge implies change. Many adults forbid children certain books for this reason.

All these disturbed facets of behavior may carry with them fear, anxiety, confusion, a lack of confidence, a sense of frustration, an active or passive rebellion and, perhaps more permeating than all, the boredom which comes from the resultant extinguishing of study-motivations.

EDUCATIONAL THERAPY AND REMEDIATION

Although it is not primarily the job of the learning disabilities teacher to treat emotionally disturbed children, one has to be pragmatic and to face the fact that there are now nowhere near enough teachers of emotionally disturbed learning disability children anywhere in the world. Very often a particular type of center or clinic (e.g., the child guidance clinic) in the local area is the only one available and it has to "handle" handicapped children of all kinds simply because no others exist within driving distance. Thus, a speech and hearing clinic may find itself working with emotionally disturbed children who have a slight hearing problem while elsewhere a teacher of the emotionally disturbed will find herself helping a child develop clear articulation along with his mild emotional disturbance. In the face of these practical difficulties, a strong case could be made out *for training special teachers across all three disciplines: speech and hearing disorders, emotional disturbance and learning disabilities* (tridisability teachers) (see Chapter XVI).

For reasons of space, the following comments and techniques have to be presented in a very much summarized form. Further information should be sought from the following references, some of which are quoted in this chapter: Long *et al.* (1965); Redl and Wineman (1957); Haring and Phillips (1962), and Knoblock (1964, 1966).

Physical Therapy and the Use of Drugs

The possibility of using specific relaxation exercises to reduce stress in emotionally disturbed children so that they can come to concentrate better on academic schoolwork has been suggested by Hirshoren (1968). As yet, a program has not been worked out in detail, but most of the tasks would involve relaxing specific muscles and eventually the whole body in a relatively stimulus-free room just prior to the remedial lesson. Particular attention would be paid to neck and face muscles. It might also be possible to take two-minute breaks during the lesson itself when the child felt too tense to continue working efficiently. The whole program would be "sold" to the children as Eastern yoga. However, relaxation procedures should only be used as a very secondary aid and should not interfere directly with the program of academic work. It should be mentioned in passing that Redl and Wineman (1957) in their excellent book, *The Aggressive Child*, recommend a system of relaxation and quieting down before bedtime for emotionally disturbed children in residential care. Recently, Muller and Madsen (1970) have tested the muscular relaxation hypothesis on anxious children with reading problems and found that story reading by the teacher to the children was just as effective in reducing reports of behaviors generally called "anxious" as was planned group desensitization which included much muscular relaxation. No control for motivation was used and it may be that the story reading made the children ambitious to read for themselves.

Drugs are sometimes referred to in the literature (Paine, 1965), but in my conversations with psychiatrists, neurologists and pediatricians the effectiveness of drugs seems to be a very hit-and-miss affair. Bradley (1958) says, "We still need a great deal more information regarding the precise mode through which various tranquilizers alleviate certain specific behavior symptoms. Until this is available it will be impossible to select accurately a particular drug for use in a particular clinical problem." Nine years later, Freeman (1967), in an extensive review of the past thirty years, concluded, "Until better longitudinal studies of children with and without different handicaps are available and more meaningful diagnostic schemes are developed, it remains difficult to draw firm conclusions about the influence of drugs on learning and behavior." Thus it would seem that at present, anxiety-reducing drugs and drugs which modify hyperactive or conduct-disorder behavior have to be prescribed on a trial-and-error individual basis, switching to placebos occasionally as a check.

The Identification of Emotionally Disturbed Children

Ordinarily in the school system the emotionally disturbed child is indirectly almost self-selecting inasmuch as he is a specific problem to the classroom teacher or the school as a whole. Most often, therefore, those emotionally disturbed children who are referred to psychologists or psychiatrists for further assessment are the behavioral problem cases whose symptoms are aggressive in one form or another. The "odd" child whose cognitive or emotional behavior is very unusual or bizarre also tends indirectly to be self-selecting. The kinds of children referred to clinics will depend very much on the personality and outlook of each teacher because she will tend to select children whom she finds to be a problem in the classroom. Frequently, the withdrawn child and the overconforming child are overlooked, even though they may be quite emotionally ill. The genetic dyslexic boy may also escape referral, not so much for his emotional disturbance, which may be minimal, but because he is frequently considered to be "lazy" and "not interested" with respect to academic work.

Until elementary school children are regularly screened for emotional disturbance and learning disabilities, one will have to continue to rely on the classroom teacher for their identification. Therefore, teachers should acquaint themselves with the symptoms exhibited by emotionally disturbed and learning disability children and should not have too much pride in being able to cope with any child. Inadvertently they may be doing that child a disservice. In particular, they should not regard a conduct disorder student as a disciplinary challenge because he may be in urgent need of professional help.

The teacher is still the best person to identify emotionally disturbed and learning disability children. Maes (1966) found that a teacher's rating scale was the best predictor of all. Behavior checklists such as those devised by Stott and Sykes (1958), Quay and Peterson (1965) and Bower and Lambert (1965) can assist the teacher, principal or psychologist in the selection of emotionally disturbed children. Quay *et al.* (1966) and Quay (1968) have suggested dimensions of classification and a conceptual framework within which to classify these children.

Educational Therapy in a School Work Setting

Over the years, like many other people, I have come to the conclusion that not only is the school (not necessarily the regular school) the best place to help emotionally disturbed children, but that the most help can be given in a work-oriented school program, the curriculum of which must be not only enlightened but extremely wide-ranging in subject matter. From 1954 to 1958, I helped organize one of the first day schools for emotionally disturbed children. It operated on a class basis, the children being divided according to their degree of emotional disturbance and ability to concentrate on schoolwork. The organization, even in those early days, provided for a kind of "crisis teacher" who took care of emotional emergencies, and a "time-out" room where an acting-out child stayed with a teacher until he was sufficiently calmed down to return to his classroom. The mornings were devoted to academic school subjects and the afternoons to activities such as watching films, participating in plays, film-making, woodwork-shop, swimming, gardening, art and crafts, etc. During these afternoon periods, the children were allowed to choose two activities to participate in, each lasting an hour. The afternoon classes were heterogeneous in every way. Thus, a boy or girl or group making a go-car in the workshop would continue working on it for an hour each afternoon until it was finished. Discipline was maintained on the basis of a few simple rules which all the children knew. They also knew the punishment for breaking the rules, which was either deprivation or time out. Socially acceptable behavior was rewarded with privileges. Although life in the school was by no means always peaceful and there were many "teething" problems in the first year or two, the basic organization seemed sound.

Hewett's "Engineered Classroom"

The efficacy of a strongly structured classroom organization together with a programmed curriculum, with the whole system functioning on an operant behavior modification basis, has been demonstrated by Hewett (1967a). His work in the education of emotionally disturbed children is among the most advanced and excellent anywhere in the world today, and it is unfortunate that no more than the barest outline can be given here. Basic to Hewett's "engineered" classroom are two concepts: the learning triangle, which affects the child through task, reward and structure, and the hierarchy of educational tasks. These tasks are arranged in the form of a "ladder" at the base of which is the lowest level, attention. Moving up the ladder, the other tasks are, in ascending order, response, order, exploratory, social, mastery and achievement. The curriculum is programmed on cards— one card per lesson—for each topic on each of these levels and the room as a whole is organized to facilitate the usage of these cards; there is a time-out room, a mastery center, an order center and an exploratory center (with a science area, communication area and art area). An essential person is the teacher's aide who can carry out much of the routine organizational work. Each student has a work record card and as he completes tasks throughout the day checkmarks are given on a fixed ratio basis every fifteen minutes. Two checkmarks are given for starting the assignment (attention level), three for following through (response level) and a possible five bonus marks for being a *student* on the order, exploratory, social or mastery levels, depending on the child's learning deficits. Much of the work is highly interesting, involving the child in activities and games which call for child-operated equipment.

The basic goal of the engineered classroom is to keep every child functioning as a student. Hewett has devised an intervention scale which corresponds to the educational task hierarchy, the object of the intervention being to change the child's assignments when he begins to display signs of maladaptive learning behavior (e.g., intervention, daydreaming, boredom, disruption). According to Hewett,

> The teacher may select any intervention seen as appropriate or may try the student at each intervention level until his behavior improves. As long as the child is able to stabilize himself during any of the student interventions, he continues to earn checkmarks on a par with those students successfully pursuing mastery level assignments. He is in no way penalized for the shift in assignment.

This does not seem to worry the other children, who accept the teacher's explanation that the student in question needs a different kind of assignment to help him learn. The checkmarks are exchangeable for tangible items such as candy, toys, etc., but the desire for these "soon gives away to the satisfaction of succeeding in school and receiving recognition as a student from peers, teachers, and parents." These last few words have a familiar ring, being the prime attachment motivation for emotionally stable children and one objective in building motivation in socially disadvantaged and learning disability children.

Other Behavior Modification Learning Disabilities Classrooms

An Experimental Education Unit was set up at the University of Washington* to provide opportunities for the study, assessment and remediation of educational retardation in eight students of junior high school age who were admitted to the unit on the basis of having serious learning and behavior disorders. Task-analyzed individual programs were arranged for each child and activities known to be highly interesting were established as reinforcement contingencies to reinforce the academic activities of the students. Over a period of approximately one hundred days all the students made functionally significant academic gains. In reporting on the project, Nolen *et al.* (1967) state that one of the most welcome by-products of the use of high-strength activities to reinforce a low entering level of responding was the personal pride in achievement evidenced verbally by students. Pride is obviously a social reward and it seems as if the students were moving from more material gratifications to human relationship ones.

Graubard *et al.* (1970) found token economies much more effective with disruptive children than traditional methods. Discrepancies between the token economy classes were accounted for by various aspects of teacher behavior. The authors found group reinforcement to be more efficacious than individual reinforcement and it was the conduct problem children who appeared to profit most from the token system.

The Learning Disabilities Research Project and the Use of Reinforcement

Recently, in the Learning Disabilities Research Project, we found that dyslexic children are much more attentive when some system of "external" recognition of their efforts is used. This may

*Seattle

take the form of tokens or perhaps the gold and silver stars which teachers have used for generations. As with Hewett's and Nolen's groups, we found that reinforcement tokens, checkmarks or stars are best given for small units of work completed. With hyperactive, easily distractable children a checkmark should be given for every reply or written answer. Children who have great difficulty concentrating or comprehending can be given one mark for trying and a second for succeeding. If a child is not able to think of the tokens or marks as symbols of achievement which bring praise from adults and peers, then they may be traded daily or weekly for some small toy or candy.

The lessons should proceed rapidly, moving quickly from task unit to task unit, lavish praise accompanying the tokens or marks as they are given. Because the praise is contingent upon success and the recognition tokens or checkmarks are used as material awards, the child to whom personal relationship reinforcers are at first meaningless, or even feared, will slowly come to appreciate the praise rewards.

The usefulness of operant material reward techniques as behavior modifiers lies in their ability to establish a simple relationship of a positive kind which will eventually bring the child into a strong personal attachment relationship. Behavior modification using rewards first binds the child to the adults on a basic acquisitive need or drive until the learning situation slowly changes the nature of the bond (to attachment) and possibly its strength.

It is my personal viewpoint that much of the literature and published research in learning theory is partially incorrect because it *opposes* positive reinforcement to punishment (including disapproval or aversive conditioning). Too many people have adopted this "either/or" approach on the basis of quite subjective prejudices and of course their research results almost invariably prove that when the two are *contrasted*, a purely positive reinforcement system is significantly superior to a purely negative system. However, I believe that a combination of positive and aversive conditioning procedures in the proportions of 80 percent positive and 20 percent negative will prove to be by far the most effective behavior regulation system, particularly during the initial stages of any program.

Traditional Techniques in Educational Therapy

The traditional alternative to operant conditioning behavior modification is essentially one of reinforcing on an informal basis the tenuous bonds which exist between the emotionally disturbed child and his teacher. In a complex intricate adult-child relationship the teacher strives to clarify values in the child's mind centering the restructuring process in the remediation itself. Academic objectives and motivational changes occur side by side in small steps within the framework of the educational medium. Some teachers are extremely skillful at using this technique, of which the one essential ingredient is that both teacher and child must genuinely like each other even if the child's liking is somewhat mixed with other emotions. A successful teacher can remediate several children on this basis as a group.

Giving the children personal responsibility, introducing a degree of humor into the lessons and using high-interest materials and content (see Chapter XV) can all contribute to a lively lesson which will help build a strong attachment bond between child and teacher. The respect of a child for a teacher always contains some *slight* element of anxiety, usually in the form of a fear of the withdrawal of affection. The teacher will get far more cooperation from a child when she is genuine about withholding praise (or tokens) when they have not been earned. Every opportunity should be given the child to gain more success, and so the steps in the lessons should be well within the child's ability to achieve them if he concentrates. Thus, a fair criterion for task failure rates would be no more than one failure in twenty successive items. Occasionally, if it is used sparingly, a friendly challenge to the child through mild teasing may help. Teacher and child should sit side by side during the lessons. Many techniques for remediation are suggested in Chapter XV.

THE IMPORTANCE OF SUCCESS

Earlier in the chapter a brief mention was made of the importance of success, particularly in the building of a sound self-concept. In fact, a child's attitudes to success may make up a large proportion of his feelings about himself. Therefore, a considerable amount of praise and encouragement should be lavished on all learning disability cases—and, for that matter, on most other children. Telling a child that he is intelligent or clever or even successful may bring dramatic changes. However, as Skinner and other learning theorists have pointed out, the learning tasks as units should be small, logical, noncomplex, linear (or hierarchical) and immediately rewarded. Work which has been carefully programmed into easily achieved discrete units will bring much more rapid progress than large chunks. If the teacher praises or otherwise rewards each attempt and each success, the child will forge ahead. If the material content of the lessons is also inherently interesting, he may leap ahead.

PARENT COUNSELING

Several separate and often complementary approaches to counseling or involving the parents of learning disability children are possible whether the children are emotionally disturbed or not. The following list may serve as a brief guide to those who wish to explore parental involvement.

Direct Counseling

In my work with parents I have gradually moved from a mild indirect type of counseling to a straightforward and frank statement of what I have diagnostically found the child's problems to be academically, cognitively, emotionally and neurologically. Almost invariably parents have risen to the occasion with compassion for their child, asking what they can do to help. One very bright adolescent boy recounted a Thematic Apperception Test full of death and depression which had the parents weeping. Within three months after my suggestion that the mother communicate much more with her eldest son and that the father take his sons riding, camping, hunting, diving and skiing (he hardly ever saw them previously), the boy in question was a changed person, full of the excitement of a rich, natural life and achieving academically as well.

Operant Reinforcement with Points at Home

Several times I have placed boys on a behavior modification economy at home to reduce tensions, aggressive abuse and negativism in the family. This is more successful when the mother is seen every week or two to monitor her progress with the system and to help her straighten out stray ends. Of course, praise and encouragement are an essential part of any points economy system.

Parent Discussion Groups

In some locations it is possible to organize regular meetings of parents during which they discuss the problems they have and share possible solutions. These groups call for considerable skill on the part of the group counselor.

Parents Remediating Children

If parents are brought in as aides to help with the remediation of the children, it is wise to insist that they work with children who are not their own. Also, the teacher must give them clear directions on every detail of each exercise to be taught. Positive reinforcement helps here.

Bedtime Stories

Usually the only direct reading contact I allow parents to have with their own children is to read them bedtime stories and I emphasize that the children are *not* to do the reading.

Wartenberg (1970) has suggested that (a) parents should act as reading models, (b) parents should read to their children, (c) parents should provide a variety of reading materials and (d) parents should stimulate their children's interests.

THE IMPORTANCE OF ATTACHMENT

From the motivational standpoint, all of the methods mentioned in this and the previous chapter depend very much upon the partly innate patterned drive of attachment. While many other factors also contribute to both motivation and academic success, the common bond is a warm feeling between the teacher and child which is in many ways similar to the bond between the parent and child. If that bond does not exist, motivational substitutes have to be found which will hold the child's interest either from curiosity or acquisitiveness until the attachment bond can be firmly built. Of course, even if there is a strong positive relationship, other motivators such as curiosity and personal interests can and should be used.

Once a firm attachment is established, there is a basis for continuous learning, and that learning occurs in accord with principles of both the partly innate patterned drives and environmental learning theory (in the widest sense), even when it takes place on an informal and flexible basis.

A MOTIVATION MANAGEMENT MATERIALS CLASSROOM KIT

A classroom kit of behavior modification and shaping materials which operate both on the children's work output and on their emotional behavior has been developed, tested and published by A.D. Bannatyne and M. Bannatyne (1970). These motivation management materials work by developing strong positive self-concepts, responsibility, industrious work attitudes and pleasant feelings. Negative behavior is effectively reduced by a system of withdrawal of reinforcements. The kit has been used successfully with regular elementary school children, the socially disadvantaged, emotionally disturbed classes and other special classes.

Chapter XIV

DIAGNOSIS AND TESTING

DIAGNOSING LEARNING DISABILITIES

Diagnosis is a concept with many labels, and people in different disciplines or with different viewpoints may choose a particular term to their liking. Some part-synonyms used for discovering what is wrong with fellow human beings are *assessment, evaluation, task analysis, investigation, checkup, finding out, observing behavior* and *problem solving*. We will not be far away from a satisfactory definition of *diagnosis* if we accept Webster's three versions and slightly modify them. On this basis, a diagnosis is the act or process of deciding the nature of a disorder or disability by examination and through the examination making a careful investigation of the facts to determine the nature or basis of the problem. Diagnosis is also the decision from such an examination or investigation.

It is a little less easy to give a satisfactory definition of *learning disabilities* (see Chapter I). One essential aspect of a learning disability is the *discrepancy* between the child's apparent potential and his performance in practice when he has to carry out some essential learning process. The learning disability itself is not primarily caused by inadequate mental ability, emotional disturbance, or sensorimotor organ defects. Of course, it is quite possible for a child with learning disabilities to *also* have defective sensory apparatus (for example, defective eyesight), to be mentally retarded or to exhibit some form of emotional instability.

Almost always the remediation of learning disabilities will require specialized teaching techniques. Learning disabilities usually manifest themselves in disturbances of global end-result complex behavior, such as reading, and like the iceberg, they are nine-tenths hidden. Just as there are hundreds of reasons why a person may not be able to walk, so there are hundreds of possible discrete causal "states" which can result in the inability to learn to calculate, read, write or spell well. This is equally true for most other academic studies in which the child may engage. Specific deficits are rarely mutually exclusive and not infrequently several separate deficits may combine in a multifaceted disability to make diagnosis and remediation quite complicated (see Chapter I).

Team Diagnosis

To insure an unbiased accurate diagnostic examination, a team of specialists should work together with the child. The key members of the team, some of whom may help part-time, are an educator, a psychologist, a speech correctionist, a pediatrician and a social worker. It will be obvious from the account of the diagnostic procedure below which team member investigates and supplies specific data and information. Either the educator or the psychologist should be the executive director of the team (both of whom should have been trained in the field of learning disabilities) since remediation is almost always a psychoeducational process. Other experts such as an EEG specialist, a psychiatrist, an ear, nose and throat specialist, etc., may be consulted as the team thinks necessary. In fact, an EEG, electropolymyographs, a physical checkup and vision and audiometry tests should be obligatory in all cases. The team should be able to converse together about children rather than working separately and sending in isolated reports. The word *team* implies teamwork and a free exchange of opinions. If the pediatrician and neurologist can remediate a case or two under the direction of the teacher, it will improve their diagnostic capabilities.

The Purpose of Diagnosis

The diagnostic objective must be to prescribe precisely for the remediation of the deficit areas and the guiding rule should be: *Remediate the deficit areas and A-reinforce through the in-*

tact areas. For example, if a boy has an auditory discrimination problem, one would thoroughly train him in phoneme discrimination, and if his writing ability is intact, he would be asked to write down for record purposes the mistaken (and corrected) words in which the difficult phonemes were presented auditorially, thus A-reinforcing the corrected discriminations through motor/kinesthetic activity. The word *reinforce* is used here in its original meaning of a strengthening agent and not an operant reward.

From what has been said, it will be apparent that it is essential not to miss any area or facet of the child which might be contributing to the end-result learning disability either on the surface or manifest level, or on any of the other supporting levels which are less obvious. I shall describe each of the four major levels which require diagnostic analysis, indicate the types of tests and information used on each level and explain how to cross-analyze the data for the isolation of deficits. The following descriptions of the various levels are meant only to be illustrative and therefore detailed descriptions of tests and diagnostic procedures will be found in later sections.

The Academic Level

This is the area in which most teachers and many psychologists usually investigate the child's problems. Almost any of the major better-known achievement tests are valuable as an overall screening of the academic attainment of individual children or groups. It is very important to note the school subjects in which the child does well or poorly, and also his areas of success and failure within each subject. Even on achievement tests, indicators can be found as to which sensorimotor or cognitive skills are tending to lower the child's performance. Obviously the child's reading capabilities require a thorough examination and details of some useful reading tests are given later in this chapter.

There is a great need for a standardized comprehensive spelling test which examines the child not only orally and in writing, but also on words which have a regular orthography and words with an irregular orthography. The child's handwriting can be assessed from his written spelling, but he should also be given the opportunity to write as well as he is able.

If learning disability children make a concentrated effort, many can produce quite good work, possibly near the class average; however, it should always be remembered that this may require a very special effort whose equivalent is not demanded of most normal children on an everyday basis. Within all these tests on the academic level, one can make quite a detailed diagnosis of the specific points with which the child needs help. However, it is quite possible that intensive instruction only on the academic level may not result in the rapid progress expected, simply because more fundamental deficits underly the child's problems with his schoolwork.

Cognitive and Sensorimotor Ability Level

There are several major tests which should be given on this level and the Wechsler Intelligence Scale for Children is an essential one. The WISC subtest scores can be profitably analyzed in a special way which is set out later in the chapter. The Stanford-Binet Intelligence Scale is far too verbal and unstructured in content and presentation for the assessment of learning disability cases.

The next major test in the cognitive and sensorimotor abilities level is the Illinois Test of Psycholinguistic Ability. A revised version, which has also been published (Kirk *et al.*, 1968), contains twelve subtests which are described later. A profile drawn in accordance with the instructions in the handbook will indicate immediately many of the child's deficits and strengths. The third major test is the Frostig Developmental Test of Visual Perception. The Frostig Test has five subtests: Eye-Motor Coordination, Figure-Ground, Form Constancy, Position in Space and Spatial Relations. This test is valuable for a quite detailed analysis of a child's visuo-spatial ability and visual perception in two dimensions. Another test which should be part of a complete diagnosis is the Graham-Kendall Memory-for-Designs Test which investigates just that—the child's memory for designs.

A useful auditory discrmination test is the one by Wepman

(1958) or one issued by the Perceptual and Educational Research Center (Drake, 1966a). Here again, most normal children should attain an almost perfect score. Also included in diagnosis on this level are such tests as melody discrimination, visual discrimination, direction sense laterality and so on, all of which are described in more detail later.

Personality, Emotional and Motivational Level

One of the most useful sources of information on this level is the Family Information Form, which the parents have to fill in at home. The questions on the form cover a large number of topics such as the number and order of siblings, "milestones," speech acquisition, mother-child separation, symptoms of neurosis or other emotional disturbance, family language background, the child's physical development, the incidence of learning disabilities in other members of the family and the number of schools and types of classes the child has attended. The mother is also asked for a full pregnancy, birth and subsequent medical history of the child and, if possible, this should be cross-checked with medical informants.

A psychologist should be asked for a personality assessment of the child, and I have found the Bene-Anthony Family Relations Test to be of value in assessing the child's attitudes to the members of his family. Some assessment of the amount of anxiety exhibited by the child is also useful. Other orthodox projective techniques can be administered by experienced clinical psychologists.

A careful search for the child's genuine interests in life will help in the remedial planning of high-interest work programs and literature selection. A lengthy checklist combined with a conversational approach should prove effective here.

Neurophysiological Level

On this level there is a need to investigate the electrical functioning of the brain and a full EEG is necessary. Even more important than an electroencephalographic record is an investigation of the child's motor functioning. It is now possible, as Prechtl has done using a portable electroencephalograph, to obtain electropolymyographs which will help determine any muscle dysfunction which is attributable to neurological dysfunction.

The muscles of the eyes can be evaluated for normal functioning by using electrodes to obtain oculomotor tracings. By this means, any choreiform (twitching) or irregular eye movements will be detected (see Shackel, 1967). On the broader motor level there are various motor performance scales, but I have found that if one gives a few impromptu tests of body balance and finger coordination one achieves the same diagnostic objective.

Along with the above tests, assessments of the child's vision and hearing should be made by competent professional people. Apart from the usual thorough audiometry examination, a speech and hearing expert should evaluate the child's articulation, recheck his auditory discrimination and even administer a language assessment scale. Learning disability personnel can utilize the services of suitably trained speech and hearing people, particularly in the diagnosis and remediation of articulation and listening-auditory deficits. If possible, one such person should be on the staff for the dual purposes of diagnosis and training.

The Technique of "Funneling In"

Although each child will probably require up to ten hours of testing and other examinations, there is no need to extend the procedure indefinitely. It is a useful practice to look at the information yielded by the Family Information Form, the WISC, the ITPA, the Frostig Test and the Auditory Discrimination Test with a view to discovering those areas in which the child functions well and those in which he appears to have broad deficits. For example, if he successfully completes the Frostig Test and the spatial items on the WISC and ITPA, there will be no need to give him any further visuo-spatial tests. However, assuming his auditory functioning to be poor, there may be a need to investigate the problem in more detail using such tests as Melody Discrimination, Articulation Assessment, etc. Referral to the speech and hearing clinic might be advisable. When funneling in on a deficit, it is better to give too many tests than too few.

Cross-Analysis and Consistent Patterning

Once all the test results and other information are at hand, all should be written up on a large chalkboard in separate chalk-drawn "cells" until the board looks like a vast mosaic. One then cross-analyzes all the figures and information, searching for *consistent patterns and profiles* which will precisely delineate the, areas of both dysfunction and sound performance on each of the four levels. Usually two or more people from the team, including the psychologist and educator, should carry through this cross-analysis.

The Diagnostic Report Form

The diagnostic coordinator next draws up a rather precise summary of these deficits for each of the four levels: the academic level, the cognitive and sensorimotor ability level, the personality, emotional and motivational level and the neurophysiological level. Underneath these is a space for further comment on etiology, interlevel complications, suspected compound deficits and any other important special points in the child's background such as, for example, parental or sibling suicide, *known* brain damage, multiple births, etc.

Writing Remedial Prescriptions

The sheet which is used for setting out the remedial prescriptions follows closely the one used for the diagnostic report. In other words, a prescription is written for *each of the several levels* in which defects have been identified; if there is no prescription for any particular level a brief explanation should be entered in its place of why remediation is not necessary. As on the diagnostic sheet, there is space under the various remedial prescriptions for further comment, in which can be entered detailed explanations of the choice of remedial topics, techniques and other teaching ideas and devices. Thus, remediation which is multitrack follows the remedial prescription; a fuller description of the process is given in the next chapter. *Diagnostic remediation* will also be discussed there.

THE FAMILY INFORMATION FORM

This form, which is sent to the parents so that it may be filled in by them in their own home and with plenty of time to remember the necessary details, should include questions or spaces which will allow the following information to be recorded:

1. Full name of child, date of birth, sex, present age, address, telephone number, etc.

2. Full names of parents, ages, date of marriage, father's occupation in detail, rank or position; mother's occupation (if working) and past occupations, particularly before marriage.

3. Name of family doctor, address and telephone number.

4. The names of all siblings in descending order of age, with dates of birth, sex and relationship to the patient.

5. A space for details of adoption of any of the above, including date of adoption. (The patient should appear in the list of siblings and should be clearly marked as the "child referred.")

6. The name, address and telephone number of the present school the child is attending, the name of the principal and the name of the class teacher.

7. The type of class, in some detail, that the child attends at present.

8. A list of all previous schools the child has attended with grades and special classes.

The second section of the form deals with the pregnancy, birth and postnatal complications or diseases up to two weeks of age. Here it is not sufficient to leave large blank spaces—numerous prompts or checklists should be presented to the parents to jog their memory. Wherever possible the obstetrician or maternity hospital is contacted for detailed information, but cross-checking is always a profitable policy, hence the information from the mother as well. The name and address of the maternity hospital should be included and, if possible, the name of the doctor who attended the birth.

The third section of the form deals with infancy and includes subsections, complete with checklists, inquiring after the usual milestones and training periods. Motor development, physical development, toilet training and details of early feeding are all inquired about. Speech and language development comes later on the form. Space is always provided to elaborate on any unusual developments in the child's history during infancy in each of these areas.

Childhood from about the age of three or four years onward is the concern of the fourth section. Any abnormalities of development are asked about. Details of all childhood illnesses from two weeks of age onward are requested here, with particular reference to virus diseases. A checklist of a large number of childhood diseases is given with space for the parents to write in detail about the severity and the dates of onset and duration. Any accidents which the child has had are to be reported in the next subsection, and here a checklist of locality (e.g., school, home, road) can be given as an aid to memory.

The fifth section to be dealt with is that of psychosomatic and neurotic disorders, behavioral symptoms and any other relevant "symptomatic" information. Once again, a long and detailed checklist is presented to the parents. The section and the list should be headed only with the word "Symptoms," together with a brief sentence saying simply: "If the child has had any of the following symptoms, please check and insert dates of onset and the duration." An example can be given to the parents to follow.

Mother-child separations are then inquired about. Any separations for any cause from birth to five years are to be listed, together with the reason for them. A checklist is provided, e.g., sibling births, illnesses of the child, illnesses of the mother, business, holidays and any others, asking for dates, duration times and details of where the child stayed and who looked after him. Of course, this information is intended to check the possibility of separation-anxiety which may have led to personality defects. Also in this section is a brief inquiry as to whether the mother has worked full-time or part-time and if so, who looked after the children and where they were looked after. The point here is not what the mother did as much as how the mother-child relationship was handled during the hours she was at work. Communicative dyslexia may be hinted at.

The language background of the child is the next topic. Here we are concerned with both speech, articulation and language development in infancy and environmental factors in the child's language development, particularly in terms of those languages spoken by any members of the family household and, in particular, by the mother. Sometimes, during the critical period of a child's language development from birth to four years, the child was cared for by someone who did not speak English to any degree or he may have been reared in a non-English-speaking country. All these influences may aggravate the poor language development of a dyslexic child.

The next main section is concerned with the development of miscellaneous key activities which, examined carefully, may indicate neurological disturbances or psychological inadequacies. Questions are asked, for example, about the age at which the child learned to tell time, rode a bicycle, did up buttons, used eating implements correctly and ceased to be clumsy. While these "home activities," as they are called on the form, are all subject to environmental training, delays in several of them do indicate at least that further investigations are necessary. This is one of those situations where, if the answer is normal, nothing need be done, but if the answer is abnormal, the matter must be pursued further. Not all questions are initially asked to obtain a final answer. If a mother cannot remember an answer to any question, it usually means that development was normal, whereas abnormalities are often remembered.

At the end of the form, a page is left for the parents to write down what they think is wrong with the child, how it came about and the continuing reasons for the child's disability. In other words, a full statement of the problems the child has as they are seen by the parents is obtained and frequently it is a very illuminating document. When completed, the form should be signed and dated by the parent who filled it in.

WECHSLER INTELLIGENCE SCALE FOR CHILDREN

At the present stage of intelligence test development, the WISC is an essential part of any diagnostic battery. Although it has several shortcomings, it can be quite useful as one of many indicators of the various types of dyslexia. Before proceeding to describe a new way of analyzing the test for diagnostic purposes, it is useful to examine the psychological variables underlying each subtest.

Information

Because this subtest depends so much on acquired knowledge which in its turn depends on a large number of educational and cultural factors, not too much notice should be taken of the child's score in this area. If the score is high, then the child is likely to be very intelligent; a dyslexic child who can pick up a great deal of general knowledge (through listening in class, or perhaps watching television) without being able to read easily must have an excellent comprehension.

Comprehension

Although this test also appears to depend to some extent on experience, and certainly on the acquisition of middle-class cultural factors, the degree of problem solving involved is sufficient to indicate to the examiner the child's ability to work out or appreciate the commonsense reason for a situation. It is a pity that there is such a cultural bias with such words as *check* and *charity*. The Comprehension subtest is mainly one of conceptualizing, and because it is included in the Verbal Scale, we assume that the child will solve the problems verbally. It is also true that solutions can be found by *visualizing* the scene, projecting oneself into it as in a moving film, and then describing the outcome. In other words, the child can conceptualize many of these problems visually and resolve them pictorially with a minimum of verbalization. Therefore, the genetic dyslexic child with a superior ability to conceptualize visuo-spatially will often solve these comprehension problems successfully.

Arithmetic

This subtest is almost solely dependent on educational factors. Although it does assess the child's ability to manipulate serially numbers as concepts, the knowledge required for its successful achievement is without doubt almost entirely picked up in school. In my experience, the subtest is a reliable indicator of scholastic failure but not of dyslexia, because arithmetic is affected by anxiety (Biggs, 1962) and tends to reflect work attitudes. However, there is an auditory sequencing element in this verbal type of arithmetic.

Similarities

This is another test of conceptualizing which assesses the child's ability to abstract a generic category from two related instances. It would seem to be a much more verbal test than the Comprehension subtest, but it also has a visuo-spatial conceptual content. Verbally, it depends on rather sophisticated oral vocabulary responses, many of which the dyslexic child may not know simply because his difficulties with "attentive listening" and reading may prevent him from acquiring many abstract words, e.g., *alcoholic, musical instruments, carbon fuel.*

The Similarities test lacks clarity in its instructions, the prompts being unfair to the child who initially gives answers scoring 1 point. Obviously, the child who scores 2 points has got the idea of generalizing abstractly, and the child who scores 0 points on the first item is told, "Oh, yes, they are both fruit," which, unless he is particularly stupid, immediately suggests to him that generalizations are required. But the child who says, "Both have a skin," scores 1 point and is *not* told the generic word (fruit), is therefore under a handicap and is likely to score only 1 point per item throughout. Thus, I always give the full prompt to *all* children on item 5 (*plum* and *cherry*). Most of the questions have a scholastic or scientific quality, and as many genetic dyslexic boys are interested in science, they have learned the appropriate words and may score well.

Vocabulary

Vocabulary is as much an understanding of the meaning, or the operational-context-in-experience of words, as it is the ability to associate and remember auditory labels for objects or concepts. Wechsler states quite categorically in the manual that the "general rule for scoring Vocabulary is that any recognized meaning of the words is acceptable, eloquence of range and precision being itself disregarded." When testing dyslexic children, I adhere strictly to this ruling. As long as the child convinces me that he has an adequate idea of the meaning of the word, he gets a score of 2 points. Thus, both verbally able children and genetic dyslexic children may score quite well but for quite different reasons: the former use their excellent verbal memories and the latter their superior visual imagery.

Digit Span

This subtest assesses the child's immediate memory for auditory/sound sequences. The series of sounds (numbers) are spoken reasonably quickly in a definite order and the series must be accurately reproduced in speech at the child's own speed. No visual processes are involved, except perhaps the possibility that the child may "image" written number symbols as a part of the memory processes. Therefore, the Digit Span is a test for memorizing automatic/auditory sequences. Kirk and McCarthy (1961), in a digit span test in the ITPA, classify it as an automatic auditory/vocalizing sequencing test. Neurologically, the digits have to be played back in the same order in which they were put in, the child being in a position somewhat akin to a tape recorder. It should be noted that this is a very different kind of memory from (a) the random playback of the separate items dictated, (b) the sequential playback of meaningful material, (c) a memory for principles, ideas or concepts quite apart from the language in which they are expressed and (d) a logical sequence of numbers, all of which can be deduced by remembering the first few.

Perhaps an even better test of automatic auditory/vocal sequencing would be a series of discrete nonsense sounds rather than numbers. Most dyslexic children find the Digit Span subtest especially difficult, presumably because it comprises two separate memorizing abilities: the ability to recall separate items of sound which have no meaning as a group, and the ability to remember their specific sequence through time. There is little doubt that both of these functions among others underlie good verbal ability (see the previous chapters).

WISC PERFORMANCE TESTS

The motor coordination of the child partially determines his ability to succeed in all the tests which follow, and MND immediately reveals itself in the results. I would separate visual processes from motor ones, because visuo-spatial elements are not equally present in each of the Performance subtests (Maxwell, 1959). Another important consideration in the tests is that several of them enable the child to *learn* the appropriate skills as he proceeds. This is particularly true of Block Design, Object Assembly and Coding and Mazes, tests in which the ability to profit immediately from insight and practice is an important factor. Most of the Performance Tests are timed—that is, the child has to work at speed—and this may be a handicap to many dyslexic children, *particularly where automatic processes are involved.* It is therefore best when testing dyslexics not to lay too much stress on speed, as this may arouse anxiety.

Picture Completion

Genetic dyslexic children find this test extremely easy. The test itself is one of a simple visual perception of detail, but three separate techniques have been introduced by Wechsler which the child can use to work out what is missing in the cards. The child must depend directly on his previous experience or familiarity with objects in his own environment, although some of them may have been seen only in books. However, the principle involved is to generalize the child's experience, e.g., "As most animals have two ears, this animal has two ears." The second principle which they can use with some of the cards is to recognize that the object is asymmetrical (e.g., the rooster has only one spur); in a way, these cards test attention to detail and observation of visual clues. Finally, the child may have to appreciate how the objects work or move in order to discover the missing piece. Scissors must be hinged to cut, and a screw must have a slot for a screwdriver. In all the Picture Completion items, there is a visual gestalt closure factor operating to the extent that the picture does not look right, or appears to be all there. It will be interesting to correlate it with the visual closure subtest of the revised ITPA (Kirk *et al.*, 1968). Personally, I believe it is the tendency which genetic dyslexic children have to rely on visuo-spatial perception and imagery which enables them to do well in this particular subtest.

Picture Arrangement

This is rather a complex subtest, and it is difficult to discern which of the several possibilities is dominantly operating. To make a success of arranging the pictures correctly, the child must (a) have an understanding of events as temporal sequences, (b) know the conventions of storytelling, (c) be reasonably familiar with cartoon strips, (d) be familiar with cartoon drawing conventions (some children see the policeman as an Army officer) and (e) be able to integrate several separate events as a whole story. If the child does not think in the conventional story mold, he may announce an equally valid version. He may have to choose between stories if he is bright and so it is wise to ask the child who has an incorrect answer why he has placed the cards in the order he has. Wechsler has provided a quite extraneous series of clues in the series "Gardener" (the position of the sun in the sky), and it is possible for a child to sequence the cards correctly by using this evidence alone.

This test would seem to be not so much a performance or spatial test as an auditory/verbal one, simply because it is intimately tied to the temporal and sequential aspects of storytelling. If one adds to this the left-to-right conventional placement of the individual cards, it is seen to be even more verbal. Maxwell (1959) found that Picture Arrangement had a lower loading on his Space-Performance factor than did Comprehension.

Block Design

This subtest would seem to be one of the farthest removed from verbal skills as only spatial relationships seem to be involved. Memory is not involved. The spatial "puzzle" has to be solved by analyzing the model design into parts, finding those parts and synthesizing them to form a whole identical to the model. The sequence of events can be in any *random order* in both analysis and synthesis stages. The child supplies very little information from experience, although it is true that training in spatial relationships will help. This is demonstrated by some children who, although they start quite poorly (perhaps from inexperience), subsequently seem to learn the technique and go on to complete all the designs with increasing efficiency. Incidentally, on one or two rare occasions I have *limit-tested* a child by asking him to continue after two failures, only to find that he was able to complete the whole series correctly. Maxwell (1959), in his factor analysis of the WISC, found the Block Design and Object Assembly tests most loaded with a space-performance factor. The loading of Block Design was 0.35 and the loading of Object Assembly 0.54. Genetic dyslexic children usually achieve quite a high score on the Block Design test—one such child completed all the items in record time, but constructed an exact mirror image of the last design without realizing it.

Object Assembly

Maxwell's analysis found that this subtest is also highly loaded with spatial ability. The child has to organize the relationships of objects and part-objects into meaningful wholes, which is one definition of spatial intelligence (see Chapter II). Object Assembly is not as pure a spatial test as Block Design, because the objects the child has to assemble are real ones. Therefore, the results are heavily dependent on his past experience with these objects. The child must recognize the parts of the objects, and this takes two forms: first, he must recognize each section as an object in its own right, and second, he must recognize each part as a section of the whole object. Each assembly can be tackled either as a trial-and-error operation, or as a "best fit" operation founded in his own past experience. Theoretically, the trial-and-error method should take longer; therefore, the score will be lower. It would seem logical that the same perceptual factors operate in Object Assembly and in Picture Completion. I have noticed that the initial stage of identifying the object is usually accomplished almost immediately, even by many neurologically impaired children. It is the *unusual angle* from which the Horse, the Face and the Automobile are portrayed which many children find baffling. One characteristic which spatially capable children possess seems to be the ability to recognize common objects from unusual angles—the principle of object constancy is no problem to them.

From the purely practical point of view, children who have had a great deal of experience with jigsaw puzzles seem to do much better than those who have not. As an extension to the test, I have on several occasions explained to children who were completely baffled by one or two of the items, how one could match edges and the ends of lines. After this, they completed the puzzles very quickly. Rigidity and plasticity of thought or attitudes also has an effect. One boy said, "That is the back of the car, because it is the back axle," pointing to the front bumper, and he refused to try the piece in any other position. Therefore, the child who, being less rigid, is able to experiment freely has a distinct advantage, and I suspect that if spatial ability is linked with plasticity of functioning, this flexibility is one reason why genetic dyslexic boys do quite well on this subtest. Visual experience and visual memory also contribute to success, whereas perseveration, or a narrow visual "set," will result in failure. For example, a child who had the whole face puzzle almost correct in thirty seconds insisted on trying to fit the chin as a second ear, because "The man must have two ears."

Coding

Although it is included in the Performance section of the WISC, there is little doubt that Coding makes use of a large number of practical skills, which underlie verbal processes. On Maxwell's Verbal-Intelligence factor, it had the highest loading of all, 0.49 (as compared with 0.32 for the vocabulary scale). The skills embodied in the Coding subtest can be listed as follows: (a) the ability to memorize symbols, (b) the ability to understand that it is possible to memorize symbols, (c) the ability to memorize arbitrary associations at speed, (d) the recognition of small designs as symbols which have been previously experienced (several of the designs can be meaningfully interpreted), (e) the motor proficiency and previous experience of the eyes to return to the appropriate place on the guide key (children used to reading should have a greater facility for doing this), (f) rote knowledge of the sequence of numbers from left to right, (g) eye-motor coordination and precise finger (motor) control of the pencil (as in writing), (h) the capacity to sustain a concentrated attentional effort on a meaningless routine task at speed and (i) auditory skills which may be involved, not only in the identification of the designs, but also in internal vocalizing.

It can be seen from the above list that a large number of psychological, sensory and motor skills are mutually involved in performing the Coding subtest. Almost all of them are *automatic* in their operation, or nearly so, the only randomized element being the presentation of the designs, which can be memorized. Perhaps the most important point of all is that the associations which the child is required to identify, or even memorize, are quite arbitrary and sequentially irregular, and therefore, the subtest closely parallels language in both its arbitrary and visual-symbolic forms. It will be remembered that in almost all languages, there is no logical reason why a particular series of sounds or series of letters should stand for a particular object (see Chapter III). Genetic dyslexic children and, for that matter,

MND children, find the Coding test particularly difficult. Genetic dyslexic children find it difficult because of the arbitrary associations and the rapid sequencing involved. The MND children are slow because of poor visuo-motor coordination, whereas a third group, the emotionally disturbed children, may find this subtest difficult because they cannot sustain a satisfactory motivation, particularly as it comes near the end of the WISC battery.

Mazes

I do not usually administer the Mazes test when examining dyslexic children, and therefore, I have no observations to make on its usefulness. Wolf (1967) found that his group of dyslexic children did poorly in the Mazes test.

SUGGESTED PROCEDURE FOR REANALYZING THE WISC RESULTS OF DYSLEXIC CHILDREN

I have found it diagnostically useful to group the Scaled Scores of the WISC in the following way.

Spatial Ability

Picture Completion ⎫ Average Scaled Scores
Block Design   ⎬ Total = 30 points
Object Assembly   ⎭

Genetic dyslexic children usually obtain a high score in this group when the three scaled scores are added together. Of course, the "high" score is relative to their own average score over all the WISC subtests. It is not suggested that the children who do well are necessarily gifted. These three subtests all involve the manipulation of objects (and parts of objects) in space without sequencing. MND children often do very poorly in terms of their total Spatial Ability Score.

Conceptualizing Ability

Comprehension ⎫ Average Scaled Scores
Similarities   ⎬ Total = 30 points
Vocabulary   ⎭

Apart from Coding, these three subtests had the highest loadings in Maxwell's analysis on the verbal factor. I have suggested above that these three subtests can be answered at least in part by manipulating spatial images conceptually. Genetic dyslexic boys of high intelligence do reasonably well at these three tests as a group, but the combined score will not usually be as high as their Spatial Ability score. There is no consistent conceptualizing pattern for MND children.

Sequencing Ability

Digit Span   ⌠Average Scaled Scores
Picture Arrangement ⎨Total = 30 points
Coding   ⎩

For genetic dyslexics, the results of these three tests added together are usually poor and almost invariably fall below both the conceptualizing and spatial scores. Digit Span and Coding usually vie to achieve the lowest place. Picture Arrangement is not really similar to the other two, but genetic dyslexic children frequently find the sequencing difficult. The three sets of total scores for genetic dyslexics usually fall in the same pattern—Spatial Ability highest, Conceptualizing Ability in the middle and Sequencing Ability lowest of all. With MND children, the pattern may vary considerably, but often the Sequencing Ability score is the lowest of the three. Sometimes in verbally talented MND children, Sequencing Ability is highest. Additionally, if an MND child has a visuo-spatial disability it is fairly obvious that the spatial score will fall in the middle or will be lowest. The conceptualizing score is not infrequently highest in MND cases.

Another grouping is a child's Acquired Knowledge score, which provides an estimate of educational attainment.

Acquired Knowledge Score

Information   ⌠Average Scaled Scores
Arithmetic   ⎨Total = 30 points
Vocabulary   ⎩

Other WISC Studies

McLeod (1965) has examined eight previous research studies into the diagnostic use of the WISC in reading disability and some of his findings have been discussed in Chapter IX. Note that he does not indicate the statistical significance of the results for the other earlier studies. Seven of the studies found groups of mixed reading disability cases to be weak on Coding, and three to be weak on Digit Span. In almost every case, the children were weak on Information and Arithmetic, but these two tests are educationally loaded. Three of the studies found reading disability children to be weak on Vocabulary, but as stated above, it depends very much on how this subtest was scored. On the other hand, the dyslexic children were strong on the following subtests:

Picture Completion:	3 studies
Picture Arrangement:	4 studies
Block Design:	5 studies
Object Assembly:	2 studies
Comprehension:	4 studies
Similarities:	3 studies
Vocabulary:	2 studies

In no cases were the children strong on Information, Arithmetic, Digit Span or Coding. McLeod himself (1965), in his own research carried out on 116 reading disability cases and 177 competent readers, obtained the following results. The retarded reading group scored considerably lower than the controlled group on the Information, Vocabulary, Arithmetic, Digit Span and Coding subtests. They scored significantly higher than successful readers on the Picture Completion subtest. The retarded reading group also scored significantly lower on all verbal subtests, as well as on the Coding and Picture Arrangement subtests. McLeod states, "There are grounds for believing that the coding, and perhaps picture arrangement sub-tests might be more meaningfully grouped with the sub-tests which comprise the present verbal scale." This statement supports my own findings that genetic dyslexic children score lowest on the Picture Arrangement, Digit Span and Coding subtests (excluding Information and Arithmetic as educationally influenced). It should be noted that the reading disability groups in the studies quoted by McLeod, and those in his own studies, probably contain MND cases and communicative cases, as well as genetic dyslexics.

Schiffman (1965) gives a table of the intercorrelations of the subtests of the WISC for 240 clinically retarded readers. On comparing these with Wechsler's intercorrelations, one finds that the retarded readers almost invariably produce nonsignificant correlations of a low order. In fact, only six intercorrelations were above ±0.3, and if the Information subtest is excluded, only three intercorrelations above ±0.3 remain. Vocabulary and Comprehension correlate at $r = +0.47$. The correlation of Block Design and Object Assembly is $r = +0.58$, and that of Coding and Picture Completion is $r = -0.40$. Thus, a pattern can be seen in these results that supports the grouping of subtests I have suggested above. Maxwell's (1959) factor analysis results, which also support the WISC subtest clustering, have already been discussed.

WISC AND MND CHILDREN

Annett *et al.* (1961) found WISC and other test patterns in MND children which were similar to those found in studies of children with unilateral lesions and EEG foci. Those with left hemisphere unilateral EEG foci had deficits on language tests, particularly on the Vocabulary subtest. However, they did quite well on nonlanguage tests. Conversely, children with right hemisphere foci had severe deficits on Picture Arrangement, Block Design, Object Assembly and Coding. While Arithmetic was poor, their Vocabulary (left hemisphere) scores were similar to those of the control group. Visual-perceptual deficits are found more often in cerebral palsied children with left hemiplegia (i.e., right hemisphere dysfunction) than in those with right hemiplegia (Wedell, 1960). These studies are in line with almost all other lateralized hemispheric function research (see Chapters VI, VIII and IX).

Digit Span and Similarities subtest deficits are associated with left hemisphere involvement and Picture Arrangement and Block

Design deficits with right hemisphere involvement according to McFie *et al.* (1950) and McFie (1961a, 1961b). Picture Completion is not associated with lesions in either hemisphere. A deficit on the Vocabulary test may be linked with lesions in either hemisphere in MND children.

As is implicit in my own classification of MND children, I would suggest that there is no fixed pattern of WISC results, *except* that in the basic linguistic sequencing skills, MND children will often do poorly on Coding and Digit Span. However, I have had isolated cases of poor readers who have done quite well on these two subtests. It is unwise to rely solely on the WISC for a differential diagnosis between the different kinds of MND children, or for that matter any other types.

READING TESTS

I do not intend to cite the hundreds of reading tests available for assessing the attainment levels of reading disability cases. Any well standardized test which gives a fairly reliable reading grade or age is useful. It is preferable to sample with two tests, rather than relying on just one. None of the tests which are available are first class, and to my knowledge, none have been constructed which allow for and measure regular and irregular orthography performances. I suspect that dyslexic children would be much more incompetent on reading tests with many irregular words than would normal readers. The Gates-McKillop Reading Diagnostic Test (Gates and McKillop, 1968) is very long and the following sections may be left out if time is short: Words Flashed, Phrases Flashed, Recognition and Blending, Naming Capitals, Recognizing Nonsense Words, Recognizing Initial Letters, Recognizing Final Letters and Vocabulary Syllabification.

The Neale Analysis of Reading Ability (Neale, 1964) has three scores: Accuracy, Comprehension and Rate of Reading. The implications of each of these three scores in the final analysis of the data should be taken into account, although the Comprehension score is in reality (as are so many comprehension scores) mostly a test of verbal memory. Genetic dyslexic children, when given the Neale Analysis of Reading Ability, usually have a very slow Rate of Reading score, an average Accuracy score and a high Comprehension score.

The Wide Range Achievement Test (Jastak *et al.*, 1965) is an essential achievement test for establishing performance levels in word recognition, spelling and mechanical arithmetic.

It is rather difficult to discover whether or not a child is reading as well as he might, simply because we as yet cannot measure his "innate" reading potential. Some people compare the child's reading age with his chronological age or grade, while others set it against his Verbal IQ. Both often give false results (Pidgeon and Yates, 1956, 1957).

Problems of maturational lag also confuse the issue. In the child who is a late developer, potential reading ability would be maturing at a later age. Note that these children require special tuition to realize their potential abilities.

My own practice is to try to raise the reading and spelling age at the very least to the level where the child's reading ability subserves his other talents. If, for example, he wants to be an engineer, he must be able to read and write engineering documents, but he will never have to write a novel. Sound competence is the aim. Of course many reading disability children who are efficiently tutored (see the next chapter) are rapidly brought up to grade level or even higher in a few weeks or months.

SPELLING TESTS

As has been seen, spelling is frequently a residual problem which remains after the child has learned to read, but it is also a problem from the beginning of school. Usually, words having an irregular orthography cause the most trouble in spelling tests and free writing exercises. Many spelling tests are available, but as with writing tests, none have separate lists for words which are regularly and irregularly spelled. Such a test having four categories of word types ranging from the very regular to the extremely irregular would be very useful diagnostically. I suspect that whereas genetic dyslexic children would do *very* poorly on an irregular spelling test, MND children with visuo-spatial disorders would do equally poorly on each section of the test.

Several people have attempted to analyze the spelling mistakes made by reading disability cases or poor spellers, but even if very great care is taken, this is not a very fruitful line of investigation, mainly because it is extremely difficult to classify the vast majority of errors (see Chapter VIII). This is true whether the classification is practical or psychological.

Most dyslexic children of all types tend to spell words with phonetic logicality when they are stumped for the true sequence. For example, they will write *torc* for *talk*. Other actual examples of phonetic spelling are set out below; they demonstrate how a research worker could "falsely" classify them:

Correct Spelling	"Incorrect" Phonetic Spelling	Incorrect Sequence Analysis
Spare	Spaer	Reversal
Adjacent	Ajacent	Omission
Liquid	Likwid	Substitution
Readily	Readirly	Addition

Kinsbourne and Warrington (1964) found that patients with aphasic speech make extraneous letter errors in spelling, whereas patients having finger agnosia make more sequential errors.

READING SKILL TESTS

The following tests can be used diagnostically for the isolation of individual problem areas rather than for "etiological" clues.

Phoneme/Grapheme Recognition and Association

A full list of the graphemes used in English are presented to the child on cards one at a time and he is required to pronounce each in turn. Where alternative pronunciations are possible, he is asked to say as many as he knows. The graphemes are all listed in Spalding (1970), in Gillingham and Stillman (1960) and in the Psycholinguistic Color System (Bannatyne, 1968b).

Blending

The child is asked to blend separate sounds which (a) are

orally read out separately and slowly to him, e.g., *p-a-t*, and (b) are presented on cards as simple nonsense syllables which follow linguistic conventions, e.g., *th-ir-lp*. (See the Gates-McKillop Reading Diagnostic Test, the ITPA and the Roswall-Chall Auditory Blending Test.)

Phonics Survey

See later in this chapter for a brief description.

Psycholinguistic Color System Flash Cards Checklist

These cards can be used for diagnostic purposes because they not only cover every usual phoneme in English (and each spelling of each phoneme) but also have a sample key word printed on each of them. By asking the child to read these words, the examiner can quickly assess which phoneme/grapheme combinations he does not know.

Letter Discriminations

A list of thirty paired words ranging from simple to complex spelling are presented to the child who has to indicate which pairs are *not* spelled identically; for example,

cat		scissors	x
cat		scsisors	x
dog	x	pencils	
dag	x	pencils	
ruler		assosiation	x
ruler		association	x

If such a test is constructed not only so that the paired words with one word misspelled are randomized, but so that various types of mistakes are systematically "planted" (and later analyzed), useful information about corrective measures is obtained. A child does not have to read or spell beyond the first-grade level to make these word comparisons.

VISUO-SPATIAL AND VISUO-MOTOR TESTS

Normally, genetic dyslexics do quite well on visuo-spatial and visuo-motor tests, whereas MND cases tend to do poorly, unless, of course, their visuo-motor functions are neurologically intact. The primary emotional communicative cases also do well on spatial tests.

Bender Visual-Motor Gestalt Test (Bender, 1938)

This test, as its title implies, is as much a motor test as a visual one. Certainly children with either visual or motor CNS disturbances do it poorly. There is a wealth of literature on the Bender Visual-Motor Gestalt Test to which I would refer the reader, particularly to Koppitz (1964). Genetic dyslexic children are generally successful on this test.

Memory-for-Designs (Graham and Kendall, 1960)

For this test, the children have to copy in succession from immediate memory each of fifteen separate simple designs. According to I.M. Smith (1964), memory-for-designs tests are the most highly loaded with spatial ability, and genetic dyslexic children usually do quite well on them; however, the memory element can be a problem for them. Some MND children may remember the designs but their *drawings* may have a very poor quality of line, angle, etc.

Bannatyne Visuo-Spatial Memory Test (Bannatyne, 1968c)

This test has been devised to assess a person's visuo-spatial memory for designs. Many of the visual memory or copying tests already in use do not measure "pure" visual functioning of a neurological nature because they invariably involve motor activity. It is known from studies with spastic children (Abercrombie *et al.*, 1964) that frequently the distortion of the reproduction of the Bender designs is caused by motor dysfunction and not by visual impairment.

To obviate this difficulty, the Visuo-Spatial Memory Test was constructed. The subject does not involve his motor functions other than to point or verbally indicate the correct design. This is achieved through a multiple-choice technique. The test booklet is constructed in such a way that the subject examines the stimulus design for four seconds, then during a period of one second he is presented with a turning blank page interleaved between the design stimulus and the multiple-choice sheet. The idea of the blank sheet is to eliminate retinal or neurological after-images and any eidetic imagery which would lead to spurious results. After a total of five seconds the subject is presented with a sheet of eight designs, only one of which is an exact replica of the original. The other seven designs have been slightly modified in the ways indicated below. Naturally, the placing of the eight choice designs has been randomized from item to item to prevent a perseverated selection of the correct design. Every effort has been made to insure that the eight designs are unambiguous in terms of the modifications made to them.

1. Original—exact reproduction of the original stimulus design.
2. Simplified—has a small "piece" deleted.
3. Mirror—literally a mirror-image reversal.
4. Rotation—the design is rotated clockwise 90 degrees.
5. Fragmented—a small piece is "broken away" from the design.
6. Proportion—the original proportions are altered slightly in such a way that the resultant design is not similar to other choice alternatives.
7. Complicated—a small piece is added to the original design.
8. Symmetry—the original design is made symmetrical in some way so as to avoid ambiguity with other choice alternatives.

A failure is recorded on the child's record form when he fails to respond, or says he does not know, or will not respond.

Some of these modifications are founded in the time-honored indicators of various types of symptomatology. Whether or not these diagnostic links such as rotation with "brain damage," or mirror images with specific dyslexia, actually exist is part of the reason why this test was devised. The seven variation designs can be used in visuo-spatial memory research to discover if there are any group differences within populations or correlated variables from other tests.

The BVSMT test has already been given to fifty eight-year-old schoolchildren and the distribution of correct answers and the item difficulty scatter are normally distributed. This result was expected because the designs were originally selected in accordance with the visuo-spatial developmental work of Vereecken (1961). The BVSMT is not yet standardized.

Benton (1963) Visual Retention Test

This is another memory-for-designs test, which is a little lengthy and cumbersome when working with children.

Since memory-for-designs tests introduce a memory factor, these tests cover a broader spectrum of disabilities than does the Bender, and so when time is short, memory-for-designs tests are more economical, so to speak. It is interesting that Wolf (1966) has found that a longer short-term memory for designs (over fifteen seconds delay) gives trouble to reading disability cases, who do not have any neurological symptoms—presumably, genetic dyslexic children. Therefore, it would seem that genetic dyslexics, while able to successfully manipulate spatial material, cannot cope as well with long-term visual memories. Since the designs are arbitrary and mostly meaningless, I suspect that even in the visual area genetic dyslexics find it difficult to make and remember arbitrary associations. This poor memory functioning should not apply when genetic dyslexics work with conceptually logical spatial materials, as, for example, geometrical theories. Obviously, any research on this point would have to allow for optimum learning situations, and not rely on ordinary achievement tests in school subjects for validation. Note that genetic dyslexic children may mirror-image designs on visuo-spatial tests.

Frostig Test of Visual Perception (Frostig, 1964)

Frostig has constructed an excellent test involving visuospatial and visuo-motor functions, and has standardized this for eye-motor coordination (line drawn between points), figure-ground (tracing over interlocking figures), form constancy (finding the common element in several complex designs), position in space (multiple-choice matching or selection of drawn objects) and spatial relations (joining dots conforming to a given pattern). This test is extremely useful for the diagnosis of visuo-spatial and visuo-motor problems in MND children, but unfortunately, its ceiling age level is too low (eight to nine years).

The Spiral After-Effect Test

Blau and Schaffer (1960) found that this test successfully screened out from a normal group of children those who had abnormal EEG records. The reading skills of this latter group are not indicated but the results suggest that this is a promising test for diagnosing MND children. More research is called for to investigate the types of deficit this test detects.

OTHER TESTS OF VISUO-SPATIAL ABILITY

There are many other tests which have been developed to assist the ability of the child to manipulate objects and their relationships intelligently in two- or three-dimensional space. Several of these are summarized by M.L.J. Abercrombie (1964) and even more tests are mentioned by I.M. Smith (1964) in his book on spatial ability. The only one which I would single out for particular mention is the Marble Board (Strauss and Lehtinen, 1947). Both these books also suggest various other perceptual tests, particularly those which combine two or three sensorimotor functions.

Memory-for-designs and design copying tests have been quoted in research papers more than any other kind of test as indicative of neurological dysfunction when the child obtains a very poor score. As *one* indicator of MND, I find these tests extremely valuable. Genetic dyslexic children often do them well and therefore the tests can be used as a part of a battery for differential diagnosis.

Tests of Finger Agnosia and Finger Discrimination

If a child is unable to identify which finger has been touched by an examiner when the child cannot see it, this would seem to indicate that the neural pathways are not functioning adequately, at least in terms of the sense of touch, or the haptic sense. Several tests have been developed to assess such a disability, the details being set out below. A defective haptic sense may cause severe handwriting problems or may be indicative of Gerstmann's syndrome (see Chapter X).

Finger Localization Test

Benton (1959) has summarized several finger localization tests. He utilizes a box like a wide tunnel whose front is draped with a small curtain. The box may be, for example, nine inches high and eighteen inches wide. The back of the box is open, so that the examiner can see the child's hand when he or she pushes it through the curtain, under the box. The child places the hand face up and looks at a drawing of a model hand on top of the box. When the examiner touches one side (half) of a particular finger, the child is to identify the particular part of the finger, as well as the finger itself, with a pencil point, by indicating on the drawing the exact location.

The In-Between Test

Using the box above, the examiner uses his own thumb and forefinger to touch two fingers on the child's hand in such a way that one finger is left untouched between them. The child is to state which is the in-betwen finger. This test is described by Kinsbourne and Warrington (1963b).

The Finger Block Test

Kinsbourne and Warrington in the same paper also described an ingenious test which makes use of two sets of four wooden blocks. The blocks are shaped as in Figure 15. My own administration is as follows. The child places the hand under a large piece of square cloth (say, one square yard). The examiner, without allowing the child to see them, places each block in turn into both the child's hands in such a manner that the fingers are

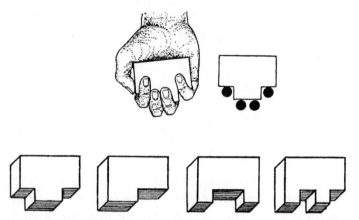

FIGURE 15. The finger block test. Blocks are 2 × 1½ × ½ inches with cutouts ½ × ½ × ½ inches. *(From Kinsbourne and Warrington, 1963b, p. 134.)*

appropriately placed in the cut-out segments of each block. As each block is placed in position, the subject must identify which it is by pointing to the appropriate block of the duplicate set, which is placed in a row in front of him. As two of the blocks are reversible, six alternative positions are possible for each hand. One mistake is allowed by chance factors; three or more mistakes indicate malfunctioning of some kind. Kinsbourne and Warrington (1962) suggest that the symptom of finger agnosia is a part of the Gerstmann syndrome (Gerstmann, 1940) and they have presented evidence from patients with left parietal lobe lesions to support their point.

TESTS OF LATERAL DOMINANCE

The major aspect of theories about dyslexia concerns cerebral dominance and its physical manifestations. Several tests for assessing handedness and eyedness in individuals have been developed and some also assess the dominant foot and ear.

Clark (1957) states quite categorically that in her research on 330 schoolchildren of about eleven years of age, she could find no relationship between preferred hand and preferred eye. Furthermore, she could find no connection between those who were nondominant in tests of handedness and those who were doubtful on the tests of eyedness. She did note that boys showed a greater tendency than girls toward left preference in *all* tests of hand, foot and ear preference.

The Harris Test of Lateral Dominance (Harris, 1947)

The following things are tested:

1. Knowledge of right and left—the subject is asked to show the examiner his right hand, his left ear and his right eye.
2. Hand preference—ball throwing.
3. Simultaneous writing—the subject writes with both hands at the same time.
4. Handwriting—full name.
5. Tapping—making dots with a pencil (timed).
6. Dealing cards.
7. Strength of grip.
8. Monocular tests—the subject looks through a kaleidoscope, a telescope and the sights of a rifle.
9. Binocular tests—cone and hole in card (ABC Vision Tests).
10. Stereoscopic tests—using the Keystone Telebinocular (1968).
11. Foot dominance—kicking and stamping.

All the tests are rated by the examiner on a five-point scale ranging from strong right to strong left. Several of the tests require the subject to use both hands alternately and are timed.

Bannatyne Laterality Tests

The following battery of subtests has been devised to separate learned handedness from unlearned handedness. Most of the tests below can be scored as right, left or ambilateral (note that these tests are not identical to those used in the research reported in Chapter IX).

Learned Handedness Test

1. *Simultaneous Writing:* The subject writes simultaneously

in two vertical columns two sets of the numbers 1 to 12. All instances of mirror writing, of reversals with the dominant hand and the dominant hand itself are noted.

2. *Making Crosses:* The child is required to make as many crosses as possible with each hand separately in twenty seconds.

3. *Dealing Cards:* The child is asked to deal twenty cards from the pack as quickly as possible, using each hand separately. The time taken in each case is recorded.

4. *Turning Pages:* Using a well-thumbed book, the child is required to turn over twenty pages as quickly as possible, first with the left hand and then with the right. The pages must all be turned from the right-hand side to the left-hand side of the book. Handedness is determined by comparing the two times.

5. *Scissors Cutting:* The time taken to cut one length of a standard sheet of letter paper (eleven inches) is recorded for each hand. If the scissors have a large finger-grip hole, the child should be made to hold them correctly each time.

Unlearned Laterality Test

1. *Filing Nails:* The subject is asked to file the nails of each hand, and in both instances, *the hand which moves most* is noted. If the right hand is moved, irrespective of whether the left or right hand is being filed, a score of right is recorded, but if the left hand is moved both times, the child is scored as left-handed. If both hands are moved, then the child can be classified as ambidextrous. One or two trials are held with each hand.

2. *Clasping Hands:* The child is asked to clasp his hands tightly, fingers interlaced, and the thumb which is uppermost is noted. That thumb will indicate the dominant hand (unlearned). Four trials are given.

3. *Folding Arms:* When the child folds his arms, if he is right dominant (unlearned) he will tend to have his right hand on top of the upper left arm and tuck the left hand underneath the right upper arm. Four trials are given. If neither hand is tucked in, the child is classified as ambidextrous.

4. *Touching Ears:* The child is asked to touch the left ear first. Most child will use their left hand for this task but if the right

hand is used, they should be classified as right-handed. Next, the child is asked to touch the right ear and if the left hand is used, he is left-handed. If the left hand touches the left ear and the right hand the right ear, he is mildly right-handed. Two trials of each command are given.

5. *Winding Cotton:* The child winds four feet of cotton onto an empty reel twice with each hand. The child should be rated right-handed, left-handed or ambidextrous depending on which hands move each time. Children are not usually taught which hands to move.

6. *Arms Extended:* With eyes closed and fingers spread level, the child extends his arms fully, hands wide apart. Still with eyes closed, the arms are quickly crossed, the uppermost arm being the dominant one (four trials) (Silver and Hagin, 1960).

Footedness Subtests

1. *Kicking:* It is a good idea in a test of kicking to measure the accuracy with which the child can kick a ball between the legs of a chair placed, say, three feet away—three attempts with each foot.

2. *Stamping:* As in the Harris test, the child is asked to spontaneously stamp out an imaginary fire.

3. *Balancing:* The child is asked to balance on each leg as long as possible (twenty seconds maximum) with arms folded. Two trials are given for each leg, with a rest between all trials.

4. *Hopping on Each Foot:* The child hops, using one foot at a time. The most stable foot is noted.

Ear Dominance Tests

These tests were suggested by Clark (1957).

1. *Head Turning:* A sound is made directly behind the child's head while he is seated squarely in a chair. He is asked to turn his head on hearing the sound. This is repeated five times, with the child being encouraged to turn more quickly each time.

2. *Sound in Box:* With the child seated squarely at a table, hands behind back, a box into which a ticking stopwatch has been inserted is laid centrally on the table in front of him. He is

asked to put his ear to the box, to determine if the watch is ticking. This is repeated five times, the watch being stopped on the first, third and fifth trials. The ears used are noted.

3. *Noise Out of the Window:* The child is asked to stand squarely facing the window, and then is asked if he can hear a faint noise outside (e.g., an imaginary bird, bell or siren in the distance). The examiner notes which ear the child presents to the window. The child is encouraged to listen intently twice more, and any change of ear presentation is noted.

Visual Field Dominance

It is useful to test visual field dominance in dyslexic children. If possible, a tachistoscope should be used. The child is asked to fixate a central point and various types of visual stimuli are presented briefly in each visual field, both separately and simultaneously. Pictures of objects, simple meaningless designs and alphabetical letters should be used. The number of possible visual field tests that can be carried out in this way are numerous and it can be a special subject of study, one which as yet is largely unexplored.

Simultaneous Writing Test

Holding a pencil firmly in each hand, the child writes the numerals 1 through 12 down the middle of each half of a vertical sheet of paper. A vertical guideline is usually drawn down the middle of the sheet and two small "*x*'s" are placed at the top of each blank column to indicate the starting points. The child is verbally harried to make him move quickly and his hands must write the numbers simultaneously. Count the number of mirror-imaged numerals made by each hand. Children with a maturational lag (both MND and genetic dyslexics) will tend to make several mirror images, the number depending on both lag and age.

DIRECTIONALITY TESTS

Dyslexic children are often assessed as having a poor sense of direction. Personally, I have found that in genetic dyslexic children this is caused more by their auditory/verbal memory disability than by a lack of innate spatial ability. Directions are relative spatial concepts which have meaning relative to the front or face of the person concerned, or to a conventional point on a map. All these relative (not absolute) spatial concepts, like everything else, have their verbal labels. If these labels stand for the directions of the compass, or right and left, the dyslexic child will have an additional difficulty because the bodily mirror images involved have no absolute value. Thus, many dyslexic children (and particularly genetic dyslexics) will know perfectly well where an external object is in relation to their bodies if all they have to do is communicate the information in nonverbal language, i.e., by the gesture of pointing. The only trouble crops up when they have to answer directional-label questions or to *verbalize* the direction relative to their own position. Therefore, failure on tests of direction *labels* cannot be considered exclusively indicative of neurological dysfunction. It is possible to hypothesize that high spatial ability in neurologically normal people is negatively correlated with verbal accuracy and speed in labeling directions. Certainly one should distinguish clearly between handedness and directional discrimination. MND children do sometimes have genuine spatial disorientation deficits (Abercrombie *et al.*, 1964).

Benton and Kemble (1960) have also suggested that confusion in right-left orientation may be a function of verbal ability. Belmont and Birch (1965) present evidence that the level of right-left awareness in a retarded reading group may possibly be "a defect in body schema and praxis, rather than one of verbalization as such." Belmont and Birch's findings can be criticized on several counts. First, the retarded reading group and the normal reading group were not matched in any way except on age; second, no attempt seemed to be made to diagnose subgroups within the retarded group as a whole (it is likely that MND children with genuine spatial defects were mixed with genetic dyslexic children with good spatial ability), and third, the WISC performance and verbal scales, according to Maxwell (1959), bear little relationship to verbal and spatial abilities when they are empirically defined. Benton (1959) sets out an extensive schedule for assessing right-left discrimination. He suggests that the ability to consistently discriminate right and left is correlated with a strong dominant hand, and he quotes Elze (1924), who reports that normal adults with a subjective difficulty in right-left discrimination tend to be ambidextrous.

Standardized Road Map Test of Direction Sense

John Money (1966a) has devised this test, which accurately assesses the ability of the subject to label turns in a standardized route on paper.

CONCEPTUALIZING ABILITY

Some dyslexic children find it difficult to conceptualize adequately in certain ways. One of these, of course, is directionality, which has been discussed above; other areas of concept difficulty include comparisons of weight, size, time, etc., the names of colors, days of the week or months. Almost all these concepts are relative ones, their relativity being determined by reference to some conventional man-made reference criterion, e.g., a meter, an hour or a pound. Conceptualizing should not be confused with thinking, which is the intelligent manipulation of concepts (see Chapter III).

Hawthorn Concepts Scale for Children

Rabinovitch (1962) has constructed the Hawthorn Concepts Scale to test this aspect of reading disability; the scale is highly verbal and in many ways involves verbal intelligence. It contains large numbers of questions and directions which the child must understand quite apart from the verbal encoding ability the child must have to make the appropriate verbal responses.

The scale investigates the following areas: Personal Information (e.g., Where do you live?); Quantity and Dimension (e.g., Which is bigger, 80 or 90? About how much do I weigh?); Number Knowledge (e.g., Read these numbers to me—457, 6,923); Directionality (using maps and diagrams) (e.g., In which direction is Mexico from here? In what direction does this arrow point?); Writing (e.g., Write these numbers for me—35, 6,301); Laterality (note that this is not a dominance test but a test of knowledge of right and left from verbal cues) (e.g., Show me your left ear), and Time (e.g., What is the coldest time of the year? What time does school begin each day?).

Personally, I consider that the Hawthorn Concepts Scale mainly tests the child's ability to handle language in terms of relational and arbitrary conceptual systems. The genetic dyslexic child seems to prefer to work with absolute concepts. If MND children cannot handle relational concepts, one of the reasons may be that they cannot keep two things in their minds simultaneously, or they may be unable to think logically (see Chapter X). This will require more extensive testing using the WISC and ITPA.

The Illinois Test of Psycholinguistic Abilities (ITPA)

Kirk and McCarthy (1961) have devised an ingenious composite test which samples the child's abilities across the whole sensory-psychological communication system. The complete test grew from a slightly modified version of Osgood's (1957) original model. For details of the psycholinguistic model underlying the ITPA, see Chapter II.

The Revised ITPA (Kirk *et al.*, 1968) assesses the processes involved through the following subtests, which are briefly described:

1. *Auditory Receptive Process* (Auditory Decoding): This assesses the child's ability to derive meaning from verbally presented material. It is a controlled vocabulary test in which the child is asked questions which require "yes" or "no" answers, e.g., Do dogs eat? Do dials yawn?

2. *Visual Receptive Process* (Visual Decoding): This assesses the child's ability to gain meaning from visual symbols. The subject has to locate among several alternative comparison pictures the one which is perceptually identical to the one previously viewed (stimulus).

3. *Auditory-Vocal Association:* This assesses the ability to relate verbal symbols on a meaningful basis, in this case by analogy. A sentence completion technique is employed, e.g., I cut with a saw, I pound with a ———.

4. *Visual-Motor Association:* Here the child is required to relate visual stimuli on a meaningful basis, by relating pictures of common objects, e.g., Which one of these things (hammer and sock) goes with this (shoe)? The test is slightly more complicated at the upper levels.

5. *Verbal Expression* (Vocal Encoding): This text is intended to determine the number of meaningful ways in which the subject can verbally characterize a simple object, like a ball or block. In a way, this is a verbal discriminative ability, particularly in terms of fluency.

6. *Motor Encoding:* The subject has to supply gestures which are appropriate for the manipulation of given objects, or pictures of objects, e.g., the child should pretend to drink, if shown a picture of a cup.

7. *Grammatic Closure* (Auditory-Vocal Automatic): This test assesses the ability to acquire automatic habits of handling syntax and grammar using a sentence completion technique, e.g., Here is a dog; here are two ———.

8. *Auditory Closure:* Here the child is asked to reproduce a whole word correctly when it is presented with some sounds deleted, e.g., tele–one; auto-o-ile.

9. *Sound Blending:* The sounds of a word are spoken separately at half-second intervals and the child has to recognize and say the word.

10. *Visual Closure:* This assesses the ability to identify partially concealed common objects in four picture scenes, each containing fourteen or fifteen examples of the object being sought.

11. *Visual Sequential Memory* (for Designs): The subject is required to sequence from memory sets of small geometrical figures in the order in which they were set out by the examiner several seconds previously.

12. *Auditory Sequential Memory* (Digit Span): This is a digit-

span memory test, each series of numbers being spoken at a rate of two per second.

Although it is well founded on an excellent theoretical model, the ITPA is also a very pragmatic assessment of the child's abilities, and is extremely useful in determining the child's deficit areas in language functioning. It is a powerful weapon for both the school psychologist and the remedial teacher, when they wish to prescribe a work program for reading disability cases. However, from the purely neuropsychological point of view, the ITPA combines several functions in each subtest and therefore does not measure "pure" sensorimotor functioning. This is in no way a criticism, because the test was not devised to measure either simple sensorimotor performance or intelligence per se, tasks which many of the other tests summarized in this chapter can do. However, the ITPA does measure *verbal* intelligence rather than language skills, the correlation of the ITPA with the median Stanford-Binet Scale across the eight main levels was $r = 0.55$. The standardization sample consisted of "average" children, so the correlation is artificially low because the sample selection was deliberately restricted to the middle range in intelligence and achievement.

MOTOR PROFICIENCY AND PERFORMANCE SCALES

Not until recently have psychologists begun to use tests of motor proficiency which would accurately clarify their subjective judgments about a child's motor proficiency or defects. In almost all psychological tests, the subject is required to move in some way, even if he only uses the speech muscles, and therefore it would seem an elementary precaution to make sure that variances of motor ability are not influencing research results. Bryant (1964) has reported that a sizable proportion of the children going through a learning disability center attained motor development scores well below the normative distribution for their age.

The Oseretsky Tests of Motor Proficiency (Doll, 1946)

This scale, which originated in Russia in 1923, now has six

subtests for each year of age, from four to sixteen years. The method of scoring is similar to that used for the Stanford-Binet Intelligence Test. The six subtests for each age were selected in accordance with the following rationale: (a) tests for general static cooperation, (b) tests for dynamic cooperation of the hands, (c) tests for general dynamic cooperation, (d) tests of motor speech, (e) tests for simultaneous voluntary movements and (f) tests for synkinesia (associated involuntary movements).

Eighteen articles of equipment are required and the whole test takes approximately one hour to administer. Using a revision of this scale, Stott (1965) has found the standardization to be somewhat incorrect for British children.

The Lincoln-Oseretsky Motor Development Scale

Sloan (1955) radically reorganized the whole structure of this test in several ways—in fact, in many respects, it is an entirely new test. The original eighty-five Oseretsky items were whittled down to thirty-six. The whole scale was standardized, each subject being required to complete all thirty-six tests to the best of his or her ability. The scores on all thirty-six tests are totaled, and by consulting the appropriate table, the percentile norm can be read off, relative to the child's chronological age. The disadvantages of the Lincoln-Oseretsky test are that it requires fifteen pieces of equipment and takes approximately one hour to administer.

The Purdue Perceptual-Motor Survey

Roach and Kephart (1966) have developed a survey which has as its basis the "generalized movement" theories of Kephart (see Chapter X). The survey consists of thirty items involving walking a board (three items), jumping, identifying body parts, imitating movement, drawing lines and circles on the chalkboard (four items), body muscle tone and control (two items), ocular pursuits (twelve items), developmental drawing (two items) and rhythmic writing (three items).

The purpose of the survey is to assess deficit areas of perceptual-motor functioning and presumably to take some remedial action about setting them right. The test manual is well illustrated and the scale is simple to administer. It appears to give similar results to the other motor tests, particularly in the key areas of balance, fine motor movement and coordination. However, too many of the items may be testing areas which the child has previously *learned*.

The Bannatyne Motor Proficiency Scale

As it is obvious that motor development is one extremely important indicator of neurological functioning, I felt that there was a need for a motor proficiency scale which was relatively quickly administered and which required very little equipment. Although the scale is still in an early stage of development and is as yet unstandardized, it is sufficiently advanced to be used for research purposes where matched groups are involved. The six pieces of equipment required are universally available in almost every school or household—paper, a tennis ball, a book, a blindfold, a tape measure and a yard of cord. The fifteen subtests were carefully selected on several criteria. All children from four to fifteen years of age inclusively should be able to perform each of the tests in varying degrees of skill. The various parts of the body are brought systematically into the tests, and different types of movement are incorporated in the tests.

Tests 1 to 5 involve the fingers, hands and arms. Tests 6 to 10 involve parts of the head and neck and tests 11 to 15 involve the limbs and trunk. Tests 1, 6 and 11 involve precise movements. Tests 2, 7 and 12 involve precise rhythm and coordination. Tests 3, 8 and 13 involve balance. Tests 4, 9 and 14 involve gross movement (trunk, etc.), while tests 5, 10 and 15 involve gross rhythm and coordination. Each of the subtests contains complete instructions for the examiner, and with practice, the whole scale can be administered in approximately twenty minutes.

AUDITORY DISCRIMINATION, SPEECH AND ARTICULATION TESTS

A proportion of dyslexic children of all kinds have had a poor or slow speech development of one kind or another in infancy, and some of them have retained traces of these defects. The following tests explore these defects.

Language Skill Tests (Templin, 1957)

Templin has investigated the acquisition of speech sounds in childhood, and her research presents several findings in this area. Her articulation and sound discrimination tests are particularly valuable for assessing their respective areas of language development. However, it must be admitted that the articulation test is rather long for everyday use, while the sound discrimination tests are not sufficiently sensitive to screen out some dyslexic children with mild defects in this area. The Templin-Darley Tests of Articulation (Templin and Darley, 1960) are essential for examining defective speech cases.

Wepman Auditory Discrimination Test (Wepman, 1958)

Wepman has devised a test which I have found to have the same basic problem as that of the Templin Auditory Discrimination Test; that is, it does not screen out children with very mild auditory defects. In most discrimination tests, the vowel phonemes are given insufficient attention and many genetic dyslexic boys are not screened out by them. Note that auditory discrimination tests, to be reliable, must be tape-recorded using a woman's voice.

PERC Auditory Discrimination Test

Drake (1966a) has developed a test which is similar to Wepman's but slightly superior to it in some aspects.

Auditory Closure Test

Many dyslexic boys find it difficult to pronounce correctly words which are deliberately mispronounced by the examiner. Furthermore, they often cannot identify words well known to them—for example, *yumbrella* for *umbrella* (changing *u* to *you*) or *achestra* for *orchestra* (see Bannatyne, 1967b). A change in the accented syllable will also puzzle them, e.g., accenting the *u* to *you* in *gradually*. I usually administer this test informally without a set list of words.

In all auditory tests, the child should face away from the examiner, preferably looking toward a blank wall. This avoids giving the child lip-reading clues. The ITPA includes an auditory closure subtest (Kirk *et al.*, 1968).

Voice Production Checklist

If there is a qualified speech therapist available, it is just as well to have all dyslexic children examined for voice production. If such a person is not available, the following list indicates which parts of the vocal apparatus may be inefficient:

1. Nasal airway: Check that the child can breathe easily through his nose for two minutes without noise.

2. Lips: Is there any abnormality or lack of control, e.g., harelip, loose?

3. Tongue: Size, shape and control are important.

4. Front teeth—are there any gaps, or any missing?

5. Other teeth: Fillings, gaps, etc., should be checked.

6. Palate: Check the hard and soft palates—are they normally domed?

7. Uvula: Is it normal size?

8. Velum: Is this present and of normal appearance?

9. Tonsils: Are they infected, enlarged, absent or normal?

10. The voice: The voice should be assessed for variation in pitch, rhythmical qualities, volume control and breath control.

A thorough examination of auditory discrimination, speech and articulation can be very revealing when diagnosing dyslexia. Most genetic dyslexic children, although their initial speech development may be slow, have no actual speech and articulation disabilities. Their slow speech development originates from the rather subtle inability to discriminate certain kinds of sounds, particularly when strung together in rapidly spoken sequences. They tend to be baffled by unusual sounds and by unusual accents in foreign languages, and are confused by noise.

Broadly speaking, the more actual speech and articulation defects that are found, the more likely the child is to have some neurological dysfunction, or something "not quite right" with the voice production apparatus.

Melody Tune Discrimination

Drake (1965) found that when it came to specifying which tone in the second of two melodies was different from the corresponding tone in the first melody, dyslexic boys were inferior to normal readers. The pairs of melody differed from each other in one tone only. It is interesting that both groups performed equally well on a tapped-rhythm test of similar construction. It would therefore seem useful to construct a tune discrimination test on the lines of the one described by Drake, particularly as it may differentiate diagnostically between MND and genetic dyslexic children. Drake's findings have been confirmed by Wolf (1967), who has discriminated between dyslexic boys and competent readers on several of the items of the Seashore Measures of Musical Talent (Seashore and Lewis, 1960), one of which is a melody discrimination test. (See also Bentley, 1966.)

Diagnosing MND Auditory Disturbances

Holroyd and Riess (1968) list several techniques for investigating MND auditory problems. These are as follows:

1. Speech versus nonspeech; in this method the child is exposed to a variety of types of distorted speech (filtered, compressed, etc.), which are compared with one another and with pure tone and noise "nonspeech" sounds.
2. Monaural versus binaural speech stimulation with or without distortion.
3. Threshold versus above-threshold (supraliminal); the minimal intensity required for the signal to be heard or understood.

The authors refer to several research projects in this area. Bocca *et al.* (1954) found that in cases of temporal lobe lesions the threshold of single ear understanding is raised for the ear contralateral to the lesion. Jerger (1960) has shown that in order to balance loudness in the ipsilateral ear to the lesion at suprathreshold levels, some patients need more intensity in the contra-lateral ear. The same threshold sensitivity may be present for the tonal stimulus. Hennebert (1964) reports that dyslexic children differ from deaf and normal children in their speed of recognition of undistorted words in the two ears. Matzker (1959), by passing the verbal signal through filters, feeds low frequencies to one ear and the highs to another. Normal people synthesize the two halves adequately but persons with central lesions may not. In another test, Matzker transmits a succession of pure-tone impulses to the two ears with a difference in the time of arrival at each ear. The greater the difference, the farther from the midline of the head the sound will appear to originate. Normal people correctly estimate the location of the sound in space but neurological dysfunction cases do not. Several frequency ranges should be tried.

PERSONALITY ASSESSMENT SCALES

When one examines a child in a clinic setting, or even at school itself, it is almost impossible to get a picture of how the child acts in the classroom and playground. There is no substitute for *directly observing* the child at school, but if possible this should always be done before the first interview so that the child will be unaware of who the observer is.

Bristol Social Adjustment Guides (Stott and Sykes, 1958)

These guides comprise a large number of scales covering various aspects of the child's life. One scale is particularly valuable for obtaining a standardized account of the child's school life. Various personality scores such as unsettledness, withdrawal, anxiety, hostility to adults, unconcern for adult approval, anxiety for approxal, hostility to children and restlessness can be calculated. These guides are particularly useful for comparisons before and after treatment.

Vineland Social Maturity Scale (Doll, 1959)

This may prove useful with younger children, but in the older age ranges and for genetic dyslexic children with specific handicaps in the verbal areas, it will be of little value.

Other Scales

Other scales which can be administered directly to the child are available, but almost all of them require the child to have a fair standard of reading ability and this tends to rule them out for group administration when working with dyslexic children. Of course, the questions can be read to the child and if there is good rapport, valid results will be obtained. It is a good idea to investigate a child's particular anxieties, but as yet most of the anxiety scales tap only worries of which the child is aware. Sarason *et al.* (1960) have constructed two such scales, the Test Anxiety Scale for Children and the General Anxiety Scale for Children.

Projective Techniques

Many psychologists have favorite methods of assessing personality by means of projective techniques, provided they find them an acceptable idea in the first place. As is well known, the interpretation of tests like the Rorschach or the TAT is extremely subjective and unreliable, though there are people who can obtain a wealth of valuable information from them.

Family Relations Test (Bene and Anthony, 1957)

This test is very useful with younger children, and it can be objectively scored. The Family Relations Test requires the child to place one hundred separate cards, on which various family attitude statements are printed, into small boxes. Each box represents a member of the family. This ingenious system enables one to find out how the child feels about the other people around him in the home.

Draw Your Family Test

Usually I have the children draw their entire families, using colored fiber pens or pencils. They can include the family pets.

The size, position and appearance of the members of the family should corroborate the Family Relations Test results.

PRESCHOOL SCREENING TESTS

One of the most urgent tasks facing workers in the area of reading disabilities is the construction of screening devices or tests which will enable us to identify potential dyslexics, just prior to or immediately after school entry. I feel that such tests should not require any recourse to preschool reading or writing skills, which (a) form a circular argument and (b) are culturally determined.

Slingerland (1964)

Slingerland has devised three sets of language disability screening tests for the primary grades 1, 2, 3 and 4; while they are very useful, they do depend on language skills.

De Hirsch et al. (1966b)

De Hirsch has carried out a preliminary study in the production of reading, spelling and writing disabilities in children from an original battery of thirty-seven kindergarten tests. Ten proved to be very promising in terms of prediction; in fact, this predictive index actually identified 91 percent of the failing readers and spellers in the general sample. These tests were as follows:

1. Pencil use—grasp and control of a pencil.
2. Bender Visuo-Motor Gestalt Test—six of the nine designs were used.
3. Wepman Auditory Discrimination Test—twenty word pairs were used.
4. Number of words—the number of words used in telling a fixed story.
5. Categories—producing generic names for three clusters of words.
6. Horst Reversals Test—matching letter sequences for their order.

7. Gates Word-Matching Test—an abbreviated version was used.

8. Word recognition I (Pack)—picking out two previously memorized words from a pack.

9. Word recognition II (Table)—picking out the two words from nine words on a table.

10. Word Production—writing from memory as much as can be recalled of the two words.

It is worth noting that three other tests met the specified criteria for inclusion in a Predictive Index, but they were left out of the final battery because they correlated highly with the ten tests listed above. These three tests were Tapped Patterns, Name Writing and Letter Naming. Incidentally, girls were significantly better than boys on the Overall Reading Performance Index, on the spelling test and on the writing test, even though the samples were quite small. The Overall Reading Performance Index consists of the combined scores for the two reading tests and was used as a standard against which the thirty-seven kindergarten tests could be correlated.

It can be seen from the above summary of the Predictive Index that the most effective screening tests are those which come to grips with fine motor coordination, visual appreciation of designs, auditory discrimination, verbal recall and phoneme/grapheme association.

The judicial use of a battery like the one above, perhaps supplemented by follow-up tests, would enable the experienced examiner to distinguish between genetic dyslexic children and MND children, particularly if a full Family Information Form were available. Genetic dyslexic children should do fairly well on Pencil Use and on the Bender Visual-Motor Gestalt Test relative to the norms. The battery is a little too heavily weighted on tests utilizing words.

Graham and Ernhart (1964)

These authors have devised an experimental battery of tests for the detection of brain injury in preschool children. These tests were not constructed for group screening, but they can help in the detection of individual MND children, who are likely to have specific language disabilities. The Graham and Ernhart tests are as follows:

1. Vocabulary Scale: These are the picture and word vocabulary scales from the 1937 Stanford-Binet Intelligence Scale.

2. Block-Sort or Concepts Test: Twenty-six blocks in various combinations of three colors, three forms and three sizes have to be sorted in various ways, using formboards by matching and by sorting.

3. Copy-Forms Test: The children have to copy correctly eighteen very simple designs as a motor coordination test. They also have to draw a continuous line between sets of concentric geometrical figures. The two figures on one card are identical, but the width and shapes vary from card to card. This is really a test of tracing between lines.

4. Perceptual-Motor Battery: This is a battery of six subtests, the first being a figure-ground one, where the child has to recognize the figure which is placed against a repetitive all-over design. The tactile localization subtest requires the child to point to objects or parts of the body which the examiner has touched. There are two mark-car subtests, which require the child to mark with a pencil all the automobiles on a page of various drawings, with two types of scoring. In the distraction-variable error subtest, the subject has to place a miniature bowl of flowers in the center of a piece of paper on which sets of toy dishes have already been placed in various successive positions. The plates distract the child, causing him to place the bowl of flowers off-center, the degree of displacement being measured. The distraction-constant subtest is the same as the distraction-variable error subtest, but the method of scoring is different.

5. Parent Questionnaire: An extensive questionnaire is given the parents on a "true, not sure, false" scale. The subscales measure hyperactivity, aggressiveness. emotion-

ality, demandingness, unpredictability, temperateness, inactivity, infantilism, negativism, compulsiveness, fearfulness, inwardness and independence; in addition, there is a buffer scale. The subscales from inactivity onward are designed to measure maladjustments, while the ones before it measure brain injury.

6. Examiner Ratings: Various behaviors are checked if they occur during the examination, e.g., wandering attention, loss of control, babyish behavior and timidity.

The above rather complex battery of tests can only be administered by a psychologist to individual children and therefore cannot be a general screening test. Graham and Ernhart's battery will be of greatest use for determining whether or not preschool children should have already been screened out for some kind of neurological dysfunction. Although the tests have not been published yet, they are available from their author.

SELECTED ITEMS FOR A SCREENING BATTERY OF TESTS

As a result of careful consideration of the available tests for children of all. ages, I would suggest the following tentative list of tests which could be used, not only for screening preschool children, but also for a first "rough" diagnosis of various *groups* of dyslexic children. Schoolchildren would first require academic testing and subsequently more detailed testing.

1. Figure-Ground Recognition Test (e.g., hidden figures) —Frostig, or Graham and Ernhart.
2. Bender Visual-Motor Gestalt Test—Koppitz (1964).
3. Bannatyne Visuo-Spatial Memory Test.
4. Motor Proficiency Scale—Balance and fine coordination items.
5. Fine Auditory Discrimination for Selected Consonants and Vowels—Test to be constructed.
6. Melody Discrimination—Seashore (Seashore and Lewis, 1960) or Bentley (1966).
7. Digit Span—WISC.
8. Coding—WISC.

9. Auditory Closure—ITPA; Blending—Roswell and Chall (1963) or ITPA.

10. Fluency of Form Naming (e.g., twenty-five stars, circles, crosses, squares and dots are named in random order and timed—Rogers (1952).

11. Matching Letter Sequences (e.g., The Horst Test)— De Hirsch *et al.* (1966b).

12. Simultaneous Writing Test—Number of mirror-imaged numerals.

13. Phoneme/Grapheme Association Ability—The ability to recall ten vowel phoneme/grapheme associations learned from flash cards at the beginning of a one-hour testing session, which have to be reproduced at the end of that session. The graphemes are *a (azure), ue (blue), o (copper), aw (fawn), i (lime), ur (purple), oy (royal), o (rose), ar (scarlet)* and *ow (brown)*. Of course, the words are not used; they are taken from the Bannatyne Psycholinguistic Color System.

The genetic dyslexic child will generally do less well on the tests involving auditory discrimination, sequencing and language functions, while the MND children will do poorly on tests which involve their specific deficit areas. MND children with diffuse impairment will score poorly on almost all the tests.

In addition to the above, a completed Family Information Form should be obtained for all the children screened out.

SOME SUPPLEMENTARY DIAGNOSTIC TESTS

The following tests are included for a variety of reasons; for example, they may have a specialized usage, they may be useful "funneling-in" tests or they may show developmental promise.

Wechsler Pre-School and Primary Scale of Intelligence (Wechsler, 1967)

This test is a companion to the WISC. It tests the intelligence of children from three to six years of age. The ability breakdowns suggested earlier for the WISC do not apply to this test.

Serial Order Test (M. Walker, 1965)

The child is asked to continue and complete a series of short strings of beads by adding more in the same order. This is not timed, but mistakes are noted.

Lamb Chop Test of Direction Sense (Wechsler and Hagin, 1964)

This test is designed to investigate tendencies to vertical, horizontal and depth rotation in children by having them match or recall an asymmetric figure in eight different positions. The figure is in the shape of a lamb chop. The test is very promising as the authors found that horizontal rotations (mirror images or reversals of figure) persisted among poorer readers in the third grade. No differences were found between left- and right-handed normal first- and third-grade children.

Learning Methods Test (Mills, 1955)

This test is designed to aid the remedial teacher in determining the student's ability to learn new words under four different teaching methods: (a) visual, (b) phonic or auditory, (c) kinesthetic or tracing and (d) combined methods. It is a series of teaching lessons with testing to determine immediate and delayed recall and the appropriateness of the various methods for different individuals. However, it is to be noted that the best short-term learning method may not be the best long-term one if the child has a specific deficit which requires training for a certain skill level to be reached. This test oversimplifies the complicated changes through time in the process of learning to read.

The Picture/Sound/Symbol Test (Bryant, 1964)

This duplicates the reading act in that the child is presented with pictures of colored, make-believe animals which are given nonsense names; these in turn are printed using strange but consistent symbols. The number of learning trials required for one perfect recall run of both the oral and printed name is recorded. So also is the score from one trial of matching pictures and printed names an hour later. This test successfully discriminates dyslexic children from normal children. It has not yet been published.

Phonics Knowledge Survey (Durkin and Meshover, 1964)

This is a thorough phonics examination covering names of letters; all sounds including blends, digraphs and combinations; special instances, and syllabication. It is very useful for assessing the child whose knowledge of phonics is patchy.

Evaluating Comprehension of Linguistic Structure (Carrow, 1968)

This test permits the assessment of oral language comprehension *without* requiring language expression from the child. Each of a set of plates of one or more line drawings represents referential categories and contrasts that can be signaled by form classes and function words, morphological constructions, grammatical categories and syntactical structure. The plates which test the structural contrasts provide two or three pictures, one of which represents the referent for the linguistic form being tested; the alternate pictures represent the referents for the contrasting linguistic forms. Norms are given for ages three through seven. The test results seem to indicate that one category of form classes or function words does not develop before another but that comprehension varies for items within each category.

The Halstead-Wepman Aphasia Screening Test (Halstead and Wepman, 1949)

As the name implies, this set of tests is used for assessing aphasic children. The Aphasia Screening Test should only be administered by those qualified in this area.

Further references on diagnostic tests include Reitan and Heineman (1966), H.B.C. Reed (1966), Taylor (1961), Buros (1965), Cattell and Warburton (1967) and Money (1962). Naturally, it is impossible to include numerous other useful tests here, but the ones not mentioned are usually intended for use on all children and have no special usefulness for assessing dyslexic children.

MISCELLANEOUS COMMENTS ON DIAGNOSTIC TESTING

The following techniques are not set out in any particular order. They are, rather, random points one should watch for when testing a child psychologically or for achievement. This list can be used as a checklist, both when preparing a room for testing purposes and during the testing itself. Have two tables ready (angled), and use one to lay out all materials systematically. If possible, the auxiliary table should be somewhat lower than the testing table and at right angles to it on the right side. Use a clipboard on your knee to hold the blank test forms—it is much easier to work this way than on the table and the child cannot see the record form. Sit at an angle to the table if necessary. Try to achieve a smooth transition from one subtest to the next; if all the materials have been laid out on the table, it should be a simple matter to pick them up in their correct sequence. Remove used materials (e.g., blocks or cards) and put them out of sight quickly, preferably back into the box provided—they can be rearranged in the box later. Learn all the instructions for each subtest and the layout of the materials on the table by heart. Develop a snappy, bright, thorough presentation which will keep the child working. Be encouraging; say, "You are working hard" or "You are doing a good job." Look, but do not stare at the child when you are the source of the essential stimulus— speak loudly, openly and clearly, particularly when reading numbers. During auditory discrimination tests, have the child face away from you to prevent lip reading. Record all the child's vocal and manual efforts on the tests, including the numbers he gives on the Digit Span subtests of the WISC and ITPA, as you can then note reversals, omissions, substitutions, etc.

Never suggest to a child that he might be tired by saying, "Are you tired?" If you do this, he will probably say "yes," which will depress both of you. Use the child's name frequently. If the child is yawning, allow him to stand up and stretch, but first emphasize that it is a little break, otherwise he might be disappointed to find that he has to begin again. Avoid references to tests as games; it is better to say, "I have some things for you to do [for you to look at]." Alternate active and passive tests. Also alternate verbal and spatial tests, though of course, this does not apply to subtests. Variety and action will keep the child from becoming bored. If you feel that any insight is to be gained, test the limits of a failed item *after* you have been through the whole subtest, e.g., figure-ground problems in the WISC Block Design subtest. However, excessive limit testing will tire out the child for later tests. Normally, no erasures should be made by children on their record booklets. Frostig exclusively disallows erasures. Use pencils without erasers on them. Make your own notes on separate sheets of paper to one side in all those tests where the child uses the record blank or where there is none provided, e.g., in the Memory-for-Designs Test. Put the child's name and the date on all papers. In tests which require the child to attend visually to stimulus cards, etc., it is a good idea to look at his eyes to insure that he is watching carefully, e.g., in the Memory-for-Designs Test. Extraneous noises distract a child from more unwanted stimuli (Zelder, 1966). A quiet room should be selected for testing and any moving visual stimuli should be removed, e.g., a pendant necklace.

If, for some reason, you have to leave the room to collect a forgotten stopwatch, or if in the room itself you have to prepare a test which you had not intended to give, do not leave the child sitting with nothing to do. *One test activity I invented to fill these gaps in a valuable way is the Draw Your Family Test.* The child simply draws everybody living in his household in color on a standard-sized blank sheet of white paper. Quite a lot can be learned of the child's own self-concept and personality in relation to the rest of the family from such a drawing. Do not lengthen the testing procedure with lots of little breaks. Above all, keep things moving in a relaxed, but highly efficient, brisk fashion. In the report, include a physical description of the child, particularly noting slightly unusual features, e.g., very pale, egg-shaped head. These observations may be subjective but they complete the overall test impression for the reader.

CONCLUDING REMARKS ON DIAGNOSIS

This entire book is about diagnosis (among other topics), and this chapter has merely presented some of the formal and informal tests and procedures I have found useful when assessing children with learning disabilities, mental defects and/or emotional disturbances. The techniques mentioned here will only be effective and diagnostically meaningful when administered and interpreted in the light of the content of this volume.

We owe these children the courtesy of a long (though in short sessions), extensive and thorough examination which should be no less efficient than the equivalent diagnostic examination they would receive in a large hospital for an obscure physical disease. As professionals, we all have to progress beyond the "IQ assessment and reading test" approach, which is akin to the doctor taking a pulse and feeling the brow.

DIAGNOSTIC REPORT—TEST CHECKLIST

I. ACADEMIC LEVEL

Neale Analysis of Reading Ability

Gates-McKillop Reading Diagnostic Test

Phonics Survey (Durkin) or Psycholinguistic Color System flash cards

Spelling Test (Ayres)

Wide Range Achievement Test

II. COGNITIVE AND SENSORIMOTOR ABILITIES LEVEL

WISC PLUS BANNATYNE ANALYSIS

ITPA (Rev.)

Frostig Test of Visual Perception

PERC Auditory Discrimination Test (or Wepman)

Memory-for-Designs (Graham-Kendall)

BVSMT

Learned and Unlearned Laterality Scale (see this chapter)

Benton Right/Left Discrimination Questionnaire

Bender Visuo-Motor Gestalt Test

Simultaneous Writing Test

III. PERSONALITY/EMOTIONAL/MOTIVATIONAL LEVEL
Family Information Form
Family Relations Test (Bene-Anthony)
Draw Your Family Test

IV. NEUROPHYSIOLOGICAL LEVEL
Finger Agnosia Test
Lincoln-Oseretsky Motor Development Scale
EEG
Medical/Physical Information (family doctor)

Speech and Hearing
Referral to speech and hearing clinic, if possible
Melody Discrimination Test (Seashore or Bentley)
Articulation assessment
Audiometry assessment
Language assessment

Ophthalmological and Vision Tests
Referral to ophthalmologist or optometrist, if possible
Bausch-Lomb School Vision Tester
Keystone Telebinocular Tests
Color Blindness Test
Other tests, as indicated

Chapter XV

REMEDIATION

INTRODUCTION

The topic of remediation can be approached meaningfully in several ways and this chapter has been organized with each of them in mind. All the previous chapters in this book should be read before this one, otherwise much that is said will not be understood in its context of language development and neuropsychological functioning.

THE REMEDIAL ENVIRONMENT

The teacher, if he is tutoring one child at a time, should strive to develop quickly a warm and genuine relationship with the child, preferably sitting side by side during the lesson. The surroundings should be quiet and free from distractions, particularly moving objects (goldfish or caged pets should be placed behind the child), and extraneous noise should be reduced to a minimum. Zelder (1966) found that auditory distractions were more serious than visual ones. Floors should be carpeted where possible.

The teacher should watch out for signs of stress, irritation, boredom or impatience and should adjust the lesson program accordingly. The lesson plan should provide for the child to be continuously active, which is best achieved by frequent changes of activity during the lesson. In a forty-minute lesson, no one task should run for longer than ten minutes unless the child is completely absorbed in it. In most cases of reading disability a complete break should be made with the child's usual school reading programs, which will tend to be associated with boredom and classroom competition. Remedial reading must be "personalized" as much as possible. The same conditions apply, with appropriate adjustments, when teaching small groups of children.

MOTIVATION AND HIGH-INTEREST TECHNIQUES

If a child is disillusioned about academic work, and in particular reading, it is advisable to take him right off the usual basal reading books as these will perpetrate old attitudes. Often, conversation may take up a considerable part of the first lesson or two, thus radically altering the traditional teacher-child relationship. Incidentally, as the child talks, his ability to construct spontaneous prose language can be assessed. Even direct *counseling,* according to Dolan (1964), can significantly improve the reading performance of "problem readers" over that of a control group.

The Fernald (1943) remedial reading program does not use readers and has as its basis the selection of high-interest words by the child. The kinesthetic tracing aspects of Fernald's system will be discussed below in the section on motor-kinesthetic training. A similar high-interest word-selection program, which has been suggested by Ashton-Warner (1966), may be very useful for socially disadvantaged children.

With boys and girls seven years of age and over, I have found it useful to encourage the child to select a theme or topic in which he or she is extremely interested. This is used as a basis for most of the lessons and on occasion may even be developed into a work project which, of course, will involve a great deal of spelling, writing and reading. Pirates, racing cars, pop music groups and even science topics such as geology are the types of subject matter which might be used. One intelligent high school boy, a poor speller who aimed to be a geologist, read and wrote reams on rocks and minerals. Even though he required much help in reading advanced books, his progress was probably much more rapid than it would have been using traditional readers.

Phonics and Other Language Games

Most children are captivated by a game and it is a good idea to collect and file as many as possible. A box of letters on chips of cardboard (Norrie, 1960; Bannatyne, 1966e) facilitates the invention of many games. Plastic letters fulfill the same purpose. The following "games" are recommended.

Programmed Reading Kit (Stott, 1962)

This kit is an excellent series of thirty teaching aids for use in reading classes; it is the result of ten years' research into the difficulties and defects children meet in learning to read. The material is suitable for children of all ages, and can be used with all children, from those who do not even know what is meant by *sounds* to those with a reading level of about nine years. The kit allows some children to go faster than others, a situation, incidentally, which allows the equipment to be used by more children at the same time. The material is in the form of games which are so simple to play that they need only a few moments of explanation. The learning process is self-correcting and the checking of any written exercise can be done by the teacher at a glance. The children are highly motivated because the games really do absorb their interest, and the material is so finely graded that the children can move easily from one stage to the next without anxiety.

The letter-sound associations are learned in an almost unconscious way, rather than by using the more direct word-building techniques of the traditional phonics approach. Stott places stress on the fact that letter-sound associations should be learned informally, until they can be recognized at sight. The scheme is complete in itself, but it should be used in conjunction with other methods or suitable reading books, and can even be used for playing games outside the regular class reading time. I can strongly recommend Stott's Programmed Reading Kit to any remedial teacher, particularly if it is used as a part of the lesson when the child is able not only to relax but also to learn phonics informally in the process.

Magic Squares (Childs and Childs, 1965)

This game gives the children practice in using the alphabet and helps them learn phonics. The game can be played by one child on his own, competing against his own earlier scores, or by a number of children. A Magic Square consists of nine letters placed in a square pattern in such a way that the patterns of the letters can be sequenced to form many separate words. In each game, the player can start in any square and move from there to any other square that touches the one he is in; he may continue to any number of other squares, provided that they touch the one he is in, always moving the pencil sideways or diagonally. The object is to form as many words as possible, bonus points being allowed for longer words. If the child is using this game in the presence of a teacher, I would suggest that he be asked to *sound out* the letters during word building both as he moves from square to square and when he writes out each completed word on the score sheet. One disadvantage of this game is that it uses individual letters and not graphemes.

Other Games

Many games which are on the market, such as Lexicon and Scrabble, can be adapted for use with dyslexic children. The main consideration is to make these games much easier to play than they usually are if the rather sophisticated rules which come with them are used. In the case of Scrabble, there is no need to use the board, or if it is used, the penalty scores should be ignored. Any games which bring the child into contact with letters and words will be helpful, particularly if the child is asked to pronounce the words carefully and, if possible, to analyze the phonemes of which they are constructed. It is best not to spend too much time on informal games (except for Stott's), as their "productivity" in terms of learning is not as high as more direct programs, though they do temper a formal lesson rather successfully. For further games, see Warburton (1966), Slingerland and Gillingham (1965) and *The Phonovisual Game Book,* by Buckley and Lamb (1960). A search of any up-to-date school and university bookshop will usually yield up to half a dozen books for teachers which contain numerous games for use in the classroom. It is not difficult to invent games using words and sounds, or to modify traditional games for this purpose.

Humor

It is beneficial to inject as much humor as possible into the remedial situation. This applies as much to the pupil-teacher relationship as to the work content. Spelling lessons, particularly, are inclined to be boring and such devices as using the weekly spelling word list in humorous sentences can be helpful (see below). Dr. Seuss' Beginner Books are colorful and very funny to children and should be used occasionaly as light relief (Seuss, 1963). Lessons should be associated with pleasure.

Story Time

We tend to forget, in our concentration on study skills, that reading is a tool or instrument for other ends; it is *not* an end in itself. We learn to read so that we can acquire knowledge, be entertained or follow instructions. Writing is a skill which is learned to communicate these things. Personal entertainment is the primary reason why most adults read and the child who is learning will be very much more motivated if he regularly experiences the pleasures reading brings. Therefore, it is an excellent practice to read the child a brief or serial story day by day for at least five minutes. Choose stories which are exciting and rewarding. The story should never be read by the child and, in any case, it should be much too difficult for that purpose. Boys like the "Hornblower" naval stories, but any which are fast moving and absorbing will do. Many older classics are too slow and verbally complex for dyslexic children. If the story is read for the last eight minutes of a lesson, the children will end the time with pleasant reinforcing feelings about reading which will be generalized to all the previous learning processes and tasks.

Color

Insufficient use is made of color as a motivator in remedial work. Color coding will be discussed below, but quite apart from this, colored pens, illustrations or stick-on papers may be used to advantage. For example, if a boy draws a racing car in various colors, he can also label all the parts in the same colors. Syntax and types of words can be color-coded, but not in combination with phoneme color-coded reading programs (Bannatyne, 1968b).

Themes and Projects

It was mentioned previously that themes and project topics may form the core of highly motivational programs. An example of a successful program is given below. It is in the form of the original first-stage prescription. The boy in question was ten years old at the time.

Relevant information: M. has poor motivation. He has a secret burning desire to learn to read. His aspirations are impossibly high—he demands perfection of himself. He has a severe primary learning disability which has been unresponsive to previous programs. He is very poor on the ITPA Auditory-Vocal Sequential and Visual-Motor Sequential subtests. He is mediocre on the ITPA Auditory-Vocal Automatic, Auditory-Vocal Association and Visual-Motor Association. His IQ (WISC Full Scale) is 110, and he has an intractable personality conduct disorder.

Recommendations: It would seem that M. requires a great deal of phonics memory training but in the past, emotionally, he has reacted adversely to such programs. Therefore, it would seem that the paramount task is to *motivate* M. to work in this area. The following scheme is proposed. A major interest of M.'s should be tapped to form the basis of a project-type series of lessons; hot rod cars are one of his favorites. The program should start by M. making a scrapbook of large paper sheets in which he sticks (in the middle of each page) a picture of a hot rod car cut from suitable magazines, which should be purchased and given to M. by the teacher. The parts of the cars should be labeled clearly with the appropriate words and for a short while M. should be required to read only one or two of these every five or ten minutes, the rest of the time being devoted to a general discussion of racing cars.

After a week or two, a slightly more formal book should be constructed, preferably in looseleaf form; it should follow this sequence:

1. At the top of the page write a printed lower case *a* in two forms (*a* and *ɑ*), a capital A and a cursive *ɑ*. Some way below

write (in cursive writing) the word *car,* and then again the *printed* word *car.* In the center of the page let M. draw in color a rather spectacular-looking hot rod car. Underneath the picture write a very short caption sentence such as "The car races." The rest of the lesson should be devoted to discussing cars in general but once every five minutes M. should be asked to make the sound *ar* as in car.

2. The next day the consonant hard /c/ should be chosen as the phoneme for the lesson. A whole page should be taken, the letter *c* being written in four different ways and the word *corner* being written underneath in both cursive and printed script. The drawing in the center of the page this day can be an aerial view of a racetrack with many corners, each of which will be labeled *corner;* the shorter sentence caption underneath will be "The car races around the corners of the track." At intervals during the rest of the lesson, which will be a general discussion on racing, M. will be required to read the sentence and the words *corner* and *car,* and to sound the phoneme /c/. (Read the racing magazines before giving them to M.)

3. The next letter should be a vowel phoneme, perhaps a short *u,* and a suitable word associated with cars should be printed and read by M. in much the same way as in the previous day.

4. On subsequent days continue, alternating vowel phonemes with appropriate consonant phonemes, all of which can be adapted to words connected with cars and racing. Make up short sentences on each series of the intermixed phonemes which M. has already learned. The number of phonemes learned per day may be increased if no stress is indicated. M. should reread all the previous sentences each day.

5. Buy plenty of racing car magazines for M. to look at and even sneak in, not too frequently, the opportunity for M. to read words or passages in them, particularly to reinforce those he has already learned. For example, get him to underline all occurrences of the word *racing.*

6. Do not introduce M. to any formal readers during the whole of this program, as he has severe negative attitudes toward them. He should make up his own racing stories with your help,

and should write them in his looseleaf book. Suggest simple plots to him if he cannot invent his own.

Other comments: It is possible that many of M.'s tantrums and conduct problems may arise from his frustrations over not being able to read easily. He should be given gold stars on a card and should be liberally *praised* for every success. The steps in the above program should be minimal so that his chances of failure are equally minimal. It is known that M. feels himself to be worthless and therefore any increase in his genuine worthfulness both in his own eyes and the eyes of others will probably reduce his frustrations proportionately. M. is quite an intelligent boy and providing he can be motivated to stay with the program of phonics training, the outlook is fairly good.

Self-Concept Building

As suggested in Chapter XIII, *this is a very importanct aspect of remedial work and success is unlikely unless it is taken into account.* Plenty of praise, rewards and recognition within a warm teacher-child relationship will go a long way in this respect, provided that success is insured in schoolwork. The lesson steps should be sufficiently small and graduated to achieve this process, being tailored to the needs of each child. I always tell boys and girls with an above-average IQ, in the presence of their parents, that they are bright and intelligent. Full remedial prescriptions will explicitly state the motivators which are required throughout the entire remedial program. Always praise all children liberally *both* for attempting the work and for success.

Token Reinforcers

The giving of tokens, checkmarks, stamps, stars, etc., is to be encouraged and those teachers working with large groups are strongly advised to read Hewett's (1964) account of his engineered classroom. He also has an instructional film well worth seeing. Whether or not tokens or checkmarks are traded for candy or toys depends on the emotional maturity of the children. Colored stars gummed onto square-ruled cards are excellent motivators for all children, particularly if five red stars earn a silver one and five silver ones earn a gold one.

Reference should again be made by the reader to the behavior modification and operant reinforcement programs described in Chapter XIII. The only purchasable materials at the time of writing are the Motivation Management Materials Kits by A.D. Bannatyne and M. Bannatyne (1970).

REMEDIATION TECHNOLOGY

It should be pointed out that there is no "cure" for dyslexia. It is not that children do not improve or attain their full potential; it is that the word *cure* is inappropriate because dyslexia is not a disease. It is an end-result condition arising from a variety of causes which can be positively modified or ameliorated with appropriate training and tuition. Usually, but not always, the academic level of the remedial prescription will entail using a phonics programs because these have been found to be most effective in several research studies (see Chapter VIII). Phonics or code-breaking methods are many and varied and one must avoid thinking of them as a single technique. Details of some of the variations are given in this chapter.

Matching Remediation to a Specific Deficit

For effective remediation, the rule is, "*Remediate the deficit areas by matching remedial techniques to specific deficits; these must also be reinforced in every way possible through the child's intact areas.*" This is particularly true of auditory, speech and language deficits.

Diagnostic Remediation, Task Analysis and Programming

Diagnosis does not end once remediation begins. On the contrary, it is essential for the diagnostic process to continue throughout remediation. The teacher must constantly watch for and deliberately isolate the specific task-problems which are holding up immediate progress and find ways of resolving them. This is called *task analysis,* and it is to be thought of as a very precise technique.

If the child's work is programmed in minute steps, the whole being in logical sequence, and if he is a beginning reader of any age, it is a straightforward matter to put him through that program systematically. However, if he already has a considerable smattering of reading and spelling knowledge, it may be much quicker to patch up the weak spots and failure points in his mosaic of knowledge, and this is where task analysis can be extremely useful. For example, the child may have erroneously learned several phoneme/grapheme associations, but these can only be discovered by a close examination of the tasks he has already completed. On the other hand, if a certain amount of work has been allocated to be taught within a given week, it is advisable (for the teacher's benefit) to test the child on the work on Friday to screen out errors which can be correctly learned the following week. In a way, this is what most competent teachers do as a part of their regular classroom instruction, but in a remedial context, task analysis is much more precise in both testing and tuition. If the child makes more than occasional errors, the program is defective. Do not forget that the basic ingredient, so to speak, of task analysis is to insure that the remediation takes account of each unit-step in the work program and the logic basic to it. Therefore, always explain "why" as well as "how."

In the programming of unit-items in a single-skills-learning curriculum, there is much redundancy, and different children will require differing amounts of it. Frequently, bright children can deduce chunks of information from fewer item-bits than other children can. The ideal program will test children initially and assign them an individual track which will move them successfully through that program economically and with efficiency. Loop programs can take care of any rare "snags." If the whole curriculum could be computerized for individual instruction with infinite looping programs yet could be *teacher-administered*, we would have perfection.

Multitrack Remediation and Prescription Writing

Just as diagnosis is carried out on four levels, the academic level, cognitive and sensorimotor level, the emotional and motivational level and the neurophysiological level, so also is remediation multitrack. Remedial prescriptions should be written for each level and should "cover" each deficit the child shows. On the *academic level,* a suitable reading, writing and spelling program is usually required though, on occasions, it may not be phased into operation until more fundamental deficits have been at least partially improved. *Cognitive and sensorimotor* track programs may be necessary; for example, the Frostig Program of Perceptual Development, or a conceptualizing training program may be prescribed. *Motivational* track suggestions have been made above, and those which motivate a particular child should be prescribed in some detail. On the *neurophysiological level,* eye movement training or articulation training may be prescribed. If, on any particularly level, there is no need for a prescription, the reasons for this should be clearly stated. For example, a child may be emotionally mature and not require specific motivations because he is already a keen and diligent worker; this should be made clear in the recommendations. Remediators should follow the broad prescriptions recommended unless there is good reason for departing from them. However, prescriptions need not necessarily always comment on day-to-day tactics, techniques and detailed procedures. For example, a prescription may recommend overlearning phoneme/grapheme matchings, but the way in which the remediator sets about achieving that objective is usually his responsibility. Normally, *several remedial or training tracks of learning will be in motion at the same time* and it is up to the teacher to decide in detail how to remediate on each of these tracks. Some tracks, such as speech training, may be coordinated with other personnel or agencies.

As tuition progresses, the neurophysiological tracks and perhaps some of the others may be phased out or coalesced. The academic track is the mainstream program into which the others are merged. On the motivational level, tokens will be dropped once social or attachment reinforcers become effective. This track convergence should be as rapid as possible, the timing of the convergence being determined by frequent criterion testing.

The phrase "track advancement effectors" describes all those (often unitary) occasions, contingencies, situations, devices, actions, ideas, insights, modifications, rearrangements and inventions which cause the child to move nearer to the academic, psychological, social, personal, neurological and physiological objectives which will have been suggested in the trial prescription for remediation. Track advancement effectors are the key units of remedial change and it is up to the remedial teacher to watch for these so that they can be reapplied both to the child in question and to other children being tutored.

Basic Reading Skills

These have been suggested by Hagin (1967) as perceptual skills, word recognition, fitting meanings and study skills. The first can be either auditory or visual and includes left-right recognition and figure-ground differentiation. Word recognition covers sight words and context cues; fitting meanings covers the comprehension of words, factual comprehension (knowledge) and interpretation of meaning; study skills include the location of material and its selection, organization and retention. When teaching a child, one should not allow the child to slip from his defective channel of learning to his preferred one, e.g., the child may use meaning cues rather than the perceptual ones he is being required to learn. In the latter case, it might be as well to use nonsense words. Hagin also mentions the three stages of learning words, the first stage being recognition of the letters, matching them with phonemes and discriminating between them. The second stage consists of copying the word (letters) in writing, while the third stage is the recall of the sequence both visually and orally in spelling.

Fluency in Reading

Children who are taught by the phonics code-breaking method often reach a point where their analytic-synthetic word attack skills become so ingrained that they can read only in a stilted way. In dyslexic children, this occurs at approximately the end of the second-grade level of attainment. A useful remedial procedure in such cases is to take a page of a reading book which the child has already read once previously and whose words are known to him. A story may be selected from a linguistic reader or the Psycholinguistic Color System which is a grade level below the stories presently being read for accuracy. The idea is to get the child to read the page as quickly as possible against the stopwatch, but he must read every word, though not necessarily correctly, the mistakes being disregarded. The point is *to teach one skill at a time;* if one is teaching fluency, one disregards word accuracy, and vice versa. High-speed reading for fluency, disregarding mistakes, can be introduced as a remedial track for five minutes of the lesson when it appears as a problem interfering with the child's progress. Fascinating novels will also improve fluency—adolescent boys will read the James Bond stories at high speed. Only *after* children can code-break phonemically can one proceed to teach them to read those particular words by visual-auditory-vocal gestalt sensing using flash cards, tachistoscopes and other so-called "sight" methods. Phonics first and sight second is the motto.

USING TEST MATERIAL TO TRAIN DEFICIT AREAS

Most diagnostic tests consist of subtests, each of which assesses a particular narrow area of performance. If a child has a deficit on any of these subtests, the type of material used in the subtest can be utilized in the remediation process. This is particularly true of the ITPA, WISC and Frostig tests. Karnes *et al.*, (1966b) has formulated from the ITPA many activities for developing psycholinguistic skills with preschool culturally disadvantaged children, and some of these activities may be upstaged for use with dyslexic children. Wiseman (1964, 1965) has also devised many remedial ideas based on the ITPA subtests.

THE "IDEAL" REMEDIAL READING TECHNIQUE

Before devising the Psycholinguistic Color System (see below), I began by setting down the various criteria which I felt an "ideal" remedial technique should satisfy on the academic level (Bannatyne, 1966e). The criteria are as follows: It must be firmly founded on a *phonetic* basis. The individual graphemes of the language must be (at least as one part of the program) discrete units so that they can be arranged and rearranged in any order. The regular orthography of English must be sufficiently systematized in some way so that each grapheme can be identified by referring to a logical cue. The technique must allow the child to overlearn phoneme/grapheme associations. The child should be able to move equally easily from the printed word to the sounded word and vice versa. The system should be able to be used alongside other remedial techniques. It should be pupil-oriented rather than teacher-oriented and, if possible, the technique should have a finite definition in space (e.g., a kit of materials and charts) so that practical goals and limited objectives can be presented to the child. He should obtain a feeling of increasing mastery over the material. Children of all ages and ability levels should be able to use it equally well and in a variety of ways. The child must become involved and enjoy working with the materials for their own sake, the material itself being flexible and adaptable. Few remedial techniques meet more than four or five of these criteria.

AVAILABLE OR PUBLISHED REMEDIAL TECHNIQUES

The following techniques have been selected on the strength of their popularity and reported success with dyslexic children over the years. Admittedly, very little comparison research has been carried out on these methods but the reason for this is a valid one. The number of variables which has to be controlled in comparison research is extremely large (see Chapter VIII) and even if in spite of this, the research is done, very limited conclusions can be drawn from the results because of the variety of types of dyslexic children. We still tend to think of old-fashioned panaceas when it comes to remediating learning disabilities, a phase which medicine moved out of a century ago. The problem in remedial education is not which one method is the best but rather how we can effectively carry out research which will *match* all the available techniques with the particular specific deficits they must remediate. In other words, remediation is largely a matter of selecting and prescribing the correct "treatment" for specific disabilities. Therefore, most of the following methods have a particular usefulness in the tuition of dyslexic children.

Regularizing Orthography

There are several color-coding systems for teaching reading and there is evidence that they are successful. Jones (1965) gave 110 nursery school children a pair of matching tests of English reversal letters, one in black and one in color, and this was followed by another pair of matching tests in black and in color of English words transposed into an unfamiliar script. The result showed a much higher score for the colored version, which was also preferred by the children. There were no significant sex differences.

The Psycholinguistic Color System: A Reading, Writing, Spelling and Language Program (Bannatyne, 1968b)

As has been pointed out several times previously in this book, the problem dyslexic children have in associating phonemes and graphemes occurs with vowels. Good (1968) has come to the same conclusion. Therefore, in the Psycholinguistic Color System *only the seventeen vowel phonemes are color-coded, and this is done in such a way that the name of the color itself indicates the sound of the vowel phoneme.* For example, the phoneme /ee/ as in the word *green* is colored green and all the graphemes which are spellings of the sound /ee/ are also colored green, e.g., *field, receipt, bean.* Another example is the phoneme /eye/, which is colored lime, as are all the other spellings of the sound /eye/, e.g., *light, tie.* Altogether, there are only seventeen vowel-phoneme colors in the PCS, and they can be learned quickly by most children. It is far easier for them to learn seventeen logical color associations than to learn several hundred vowel-phoneme/grapheme arbitrary associations which are highly irregular in orthography.

The PCS is designed to be used with all kindergarten or first-grade children as well as with dyslexic children. It is hoped that used correctly, it will *prevent* many children from developing learning disability problems in the first place. It also rapidly remediates dyslexic children, especially those with speech, auditory and memory deficits. The PCS is soundly based in psycholinguistic theory, so much so that at the outset much of the initial program includes articulation and vocal sequencing tasks. The children are also involved in identification, discrimination, sequencing and closure tasks on the sensorimotor and meaning channels used in language processing.

The PCS has a series of fully programmed children's workbooks and teacher's guidebooks. These include words, sentences and stories which are read by the children, the vowels being traced over using a set of colored pencils (only 2 or 3 at a time), thus enabling the teacher to tell instantly whether or not a child can pronounce a grapheme/phoneme association in a particular word correctly. Of course, the color vowel associations are introduced very gradually one at a time in a succession of interesting exercises, sentences, stories and games, and progression through the series can be either individualized or lock-stepped for the group or class. A parallel series of PCS games and supplementary tasks (in preparation) will enable the teacher to reward children who work quickly, or to give supplementary work to slow learners. All the PCS books utilize colored pencils, and the books contain numerous illustrations which the children can color as yet another reward for good work. The goal has been to make the workbooks as entertaining, attractive and smooth-flowing as possible to children. They are fully linguistic.

A part of the equipment is a set of flash cards, the vowels being printed in color, while the consonants and frequently used words are in black and white. These flash cards cover *all* phoneme/grapheme associations including consonants, and are invaluable for training the children in groups or individually. All the graphemes associated with one color-sound are printed on one wall chart, making a total of seventeen vowel color phoneme/grapheme wall charts; additionally, further charts have all the consonants printed on them in black, while another black-and-white chart has popular words printed on it. These wall charts with their pictures and key words teach the children phoneme/grapheme and color matching, which they learn easily in a gradual progression, while the flash cards can be used for both testing and recall training without cues or prompts.

Additionally, it is hoped that the phoneme/grapheme color combinations will also be published in the form of small letters on sheets of cards which can be cut up into small chips and filed in a PCS box which contains numerous tiny compartments. This Grapheme Box and its use with dyslexic children has also been described elsewhere (Bannatyne, 1966e). These small letter cards or chips can be used for sequencing graphemes on the child's desk during individual or class lessons, and for copying words the teacher has written on the board. The idea behind this letter-chip sequencing system is that many children suffer from an inability to remember constantly changing patterns of phoneme/grapheme associations and therefore the simultaneous manual, auditory and visual sequencing of phonemes and graphemes is an essential element in learning to read, write and spell. The letters of the PCS box are useful for systematic word and sentence building, for syllabication practice, for the analysis and synthesis of successive sounds and for various activities and word games. Details of five stages of a teaching program for dyslexic children with these kinds of problems have already been published (Bannatyne, 1966e).

The PCS includes an early reading scheme, a full reading scheme, workbook programs, flash cards, wall charts, etc. It is very simple in operation and easy to learn from both the children's and the teacher's points of view. Almost all children learn to read rapidly, the color acting as an A-reinforcer, M-reinforcer and even T-reinforcer. The children are active almost all the time, the work is fun and the colors are phased out gradually as the child becomes more competent. Another advantage of having the child use colored pencils in the workbooks is that the teacher can carry out instant task analysis; mistakes are immediately obvious and easily corrected.

The PCS evolved out of my research and clinical practice over two decades. It has inherent in it almost all the theoretical and practical knowledge presented in this volume and is recommended for beginning readers, preventive programs and all reading disability children.

Words in Color (Gattegno, 1963)

In this method of teaching the reading and writing of English, color is used as a cue to understanding. All the letters, both consonants and vowels, and combinations of letters representing a single sound are printed on one set of charts in sets of colors; for example, a child recognizes the /k/ sound from its color, though it may be written as a *k, kk, kc, ck, ch, qu, que, cch, c,* or *che.*

An additional twenty-one wall charts with words printed in colors on a black background are also included in the set. The series consists of a large number of English words which gradually introduce the pupil to all the sounds of the language through the phonic color code. As the child works through the charts, so to speak, the complexity of the colors, their sounds and the words they represent increase. Throughout, teaching is subordinated to learning by the "whole" method and to getting the pupil oriented. In addition to the twenty-one wall charts, there are eight classification charts which summarize in lists all the graphemes represented by each single phoneme in the English language. Over forty colors represent the phonemes and graphemes of the English language.

Gattegno's system includes primer books, word building books, worksheets and books of stories, together with a background book, teacher's guide and word cards. Almost all these books, etc., are printed in black on white, because it is part of the system that the color learning is done from the wall charts, the child having to rely on memory when reading printed material. In practice, it is difficult for children to remember the arbitrary color/phoneme associations, to recall all forty or so combinations without cues and to discriminate between the graduated colors in artificial light.

Color Story Reading (J.K. ones, 1965)

This scheme is based on fifty-three color symbols which cover forty-two phonemes. The symbols consist of thirty-five individual letters, nine digraphs and nine color backgrounds. As far as possible, individual letters of similar shape are distinguished by color, so as to assist visual learning. The nine backgrounds, which are round, square or triangular, all represent phonemes, except for the round blue background which represents silent letters. The letters are printed in black on the backgrounds. The use of the backgrounds enables the color symbol code to achieve a wide phonetic coverage with the total of only three colors, red, blue and green, plus black. This permits both easy visual discrimination and economical printing in book form. About one word in ten contains a letter or letters which cannot be given within the color code and these nonform letters are printed in black on white.

The story part of color story reading consists of nineteen stories which the teacher reads or relates to the children. The text and illustrations in the children's colored reading books refer to the characters and events in these nineteen stories. The teacher-read stories provide concrete images for all the forty-two phonemes in the phonetic color code. The colored reading books are stricter. Not only the words, but all the letters are introduced gradually; sentences tend to develop out of each other, and the individual illustrations are linked to the text by the principle of identity. As a medium, the color symbol code is phonetic, not phonic. Phonic instruction relies on a group of black symbols whose inadequacy, as representative of English sounds, is equaled by the irregularity of English spelling. Along with phonics, the children are taught the sounds of the alphabet, but with the phonetic medium of colored symbols, the children learn the alphabet of the sounds. The colored symbols are tailored to fit the child's existing auditory knowledge on a correspondence of virtually one symbol to one sound, and as Piaget has so convincingly demonstrated, young children in particularly require a one-to-one correspondence for effective learning.

Color Coded Sound Symbols (Good, 1968)

This method, like the PCS, color-codes only the vowels and was invented to teach children attending speech and language clinics. However, the colors are not named and therefore no direct cue is available (other than rote memory) for identifying which color represents which sound. Flash cards and word building are an aspect of the teaching program.

The Initial Teaching Alphabet (i.t.a.)

It is to be hoped that by now the i.t.a. need not be described in detail in such a book as this. In brief, it is an alphabet of letter symbols, which although very similar in shape to the traditional English alphabet, has a completely regular orthography built into it. The phoneme/grapheme correspondence is regular and permanent. It is not yet clear how children with reading disabilities of various kinds fare under remedial tuition which is based on the i.t.a. The research studies so far present rather contradictory results. Georgiades (1964) and Downing (1967) have indicated how difficult it is to assess the effectiveness of alternative reading systems using comparison techniques, even in the ordinary classroom.

The major problem that genetic dyslexic children are likely to have with learning to read using i.t.a. is that of transferring back to the traditional orthography once they have become reasonably competent in the original medium. They have so much difficulty remembering the sounds which are correlated with one set of written symbols that to saddle them with an additional set can only make greater problems. But one cannot dismiss a major innovation in the field of reading without giving it a fair trial, and it is to be hoped that more people will carry out research into the long-term effectiveness of the i.t.a. with severe reading disability cases. More specifically, we need to find out which *types* of dyslexic children profit most from i.t.a. An account of the research on i.t.a. is to be found in Downing's recent work (Downing, 1967).

Visuo-Motor and Spatial Training

The methods described in this section do not apply to children suffering from genetic dyslexia. If one looks at Table II, a group of children will be seen to be categorized under the MND heading as having visuo-spatial problems, and it is that group which will require help from the methods described.

Very few visuo-motor and spatial training programs have been published. The best-known program is the Frostig Program for the Development of Visual Perception (Frostig and Horne, 1964). This program is described in some detail in a later section of the chapter. It consists mainly of numerous programmed items similar in format to the ones in the Frostig Test of Visual Perception.

The Cuisenaire Rods (Cuisenaire, 1953) are very useful for giving visuo-spatial disability children an appreciation of what might be called mathematical space. The rods help children gain insight into spatial logic and numerical relationships. I personally also use the Cuisenaire Rods for the remediation of arithmetic and number disabilities.

Direct Phonic Techniques

In the above heading, the word *direct* is intended to suggest that no extraneous prompts or cues are used systematically to help the child work out the phoneme associated with a particular grapheme. Nor do they make extra special A-reinforcement use of other sensory channels, except inasmuch as they are already in the reading or spelling process.

The Gillingham-Stillman Method (Gillingham and Stillman, 1960)

Gillingham and Stillman have produced a program of work for dyslexic children which systematically introduces them to almost all the phoneme/grapheme associations in the English language, and it does this extremely thoroughly and systematically. As in all good phonic methods, this method relies heavily on vocalization by the teacher and child. The child has to associate the visual symbol with both the name and the sound of the letter and get used to the feel of his speech organs in action, while pronouncing any particular phoneme. The entire program is laid out in considerable detail in a large manual. The graphemes are printed on a set of phonic drill cards and the child has to learn the sound-symbol associations by rote. The process is reinforced in many different ways. The grapheme is copied by the child, traced with the finger or pencil, written from memory with eyes averted and written in response to the sound made by the teacher. The cards with their black-on-white letters can be set out to form words, the child blending the sequence of sounds with increasing speed and smoothness. Quite often the child has to echo the teacher's speech before reproducing a sequence of sounds alone; as the child writes the word, he should sound the letters aloud as each is written. Gillingham and Stillman outline programs for daily lessons which, when satisfactorily completed, enable the child to read very simple sentences and stories which are composed of simple, phonetically regular words. A little later in the course, consonant blends are introduced, as is the silent final *e*. Another concept stressed in the technique is the syllabication; games are played by matching syllables correctly. Gillingham and Stillman consider writing and particularly tracing vital for memorizing letter forms and correcting mirror writing. Unlike Fernald, they state that all tracing should be accompanied by "sounding" the phonemes. Dictation is recommended, as it lengthens the auditory span, and the child is encouraged to write original stories occasionally. The children must learn a number of spelling rules to the point where they can be produced adequately.

Sound Phonics (Childs and Childs, 1962)

S.B. Childs, who also uses Gillingham-Stillman techniques in her teaching, has systematically organized the letter-sound connections in the English language so that they can be presented to children in a logical organized way. She suggests that English is much more regular and consistent in its letter-sound association than most people recognize and she says that while estimates may

654   Language, Reading and Learning Disabilities

vary about this, depending on the criteria, an estimate of 85 to 90 percent "regularity" is usual among experts. I personally would disagree with this, because from an orthographic point of view, the vowels in almost every word have many equivalent possible grapheme spellings, e.g., *brown, broun, broughn.* On this basis, there is probably a 5 percent one-to-one regularity in vowel phoneme/graphemes. However, in the absence of a coding system, it is extremely valuable to teach children phonic regularities of pronunciation, inasmuch as they do exist.

Sound Phonics is a handbook for the teacher and the information in it has to be studied and absorbed by the teacher before it can be used with profit in the classroom. Once learned, this organization of phonic analysis can be used indefinitely, along with its companion volume, *Sound Spelling.*

Words are divided into three phonetic groups—the very regular, the systematically irregular and the very irregular. The latter group are taught as sight words. The manual contains detailed instructions for blending, for introducing double letters and for syllabication. There is a lot of material neatly condensed in these books, not only about the application of the authors' techniques, but also about the psychological and practical processes involved in linguistic functions. There are lists of classified words and a rather useful glossary.

Hegge, Kirk and Kirk (1955)

These authors have produced a book of remedial reading drills which they suggest are most effective with children whose reading status is below the fourth-grade level, and with those who have a severe reading disability or any extreme visual or auditory defects which have been corrected. The child must be educable in sound blending, and must be well motivated and cooperative.

They stress that the greatest incentive for children is showing them success at all times, especially at the beginning of training, and the drills have been constructed on the principle that the child should be presented with a task he can readily master. The child is shown the letters *s, a, c, t* and *p,* and is taught these sounds. In a few minutes, the child can repeat the words *cat, pat, tap, mat, at, sap* and *sat*. This quick success shows the pupil that he can learn sounds fairly easily. It is emphasized to the child that he must sound rather than spell words, and he is taught most of the consonants and the short vowel *a*. The child should also write letters on the blackboard from memory, sounding them at the same time.

A method of teaching blending is next described. Single words are written and said slowly. Next, the initial letter of, say, the word *sat* is split off, e.g., *s-at*. Next, the *at* is divided into *s-a-t*. This gradual breaking *down* of the word enables the child to understand how the words are made up of separate phonemes; once this is understood, he is ready to begin practicing the remedial reading drills. The teacher should always begin with the first drill. The child reads the drill at his own rate. It has been found that slow accurate reading of the first drills causes more accurate and more rapid blending of sounds later and, eventually, more efficient reading. All the drills should be read orally and the stress is on accuracy, not speed. It is recommended that the child continue reading from the drills until he shows signs of fatigue or inaccuracy. At this point, the child goes to the board, writes a difficult sound and at the same time pronounces it. He then has to close his eyes while writing it and saying it; this aids retention. The authors emphasize that both the analytical and synthetic processes should be used in the drills—that is, building up words from individual sounds and breaking down known words into individual sounds. Other mnemonic devices are suggested which help the child to associate the sound with the symbol; e.g., for the sound *sh*, the finger is placed over the lips.

Sentence reading is introduced gradually and this may be constructed by the teacher at first. Later, story reading should be introduced, preferably using phonics books. Note that all words which cannot be sounded because they are phonically irregular have to be taught as whole words. If the teacher keeps a record of the most difficult of these sight words, they can be given special drill, using flash cards. When part three of the book is reached, that is, the advanced sounds, the emphasis should be placed on reading and word study rather than on phonics material. About the only criticism to be made of this method is its lack of intrinsic motivational elements. The teacher must use it imaginatively or the child will be bored.

Edith Norrie's Letter-Case (Norrie, 1960)

Although it was originally constructed for use in Denmark, there is an English version of the Edith Norrie Letter-Case. It is arranged phonetically because her method embraces speech training as well as exercises in spelling and reading. The box is divided into many small compartments, in which small cardboard pieces of postage-stamp size are placed, ready for use. The pieces in each compartment have printed on them a particular letter or grapheme. When composing a word, the child selects the pieces and spells that word in sequence on the table. The unvoiced consonants are printed in black, the voiced ones in green and the vowels in red; the pupil learns that there must never be a word or syllable without a red letter in it. In addition, the lip sounds or labials are located in one area of the box, the palatals in another and the gutterals in the third area. A mirror is supplied so that the child can examine his own lips and tongue when sounding words or letters.

Thus, it can be seen that the whole technique depends a great deal on phonics training and sequencing and is particularly valuable for teaching spelling. Norrie herself advocates graded dictation with the words always being built from left to right. She stresses the great importance of praising the child for his successful efforts. The Letter-Case can also be used for exercises in grammar, auditory training, directional training and so on.

Phonovisual Method (Schoolfield et al., 1960)

This is a method of teaching elementary phonics based on the use of pictorial charts together with a plan for training auditory and visual discrimination. There are twenty-six sounds on the consonant chart and seventeen on the vowel chart. In step I, the children are taught to recognize, read, write and say consonant sounds as initial letters of key words and key pictures. They then transfer these skills to the vocabulary in their own books. Final consonants are then added, followed by vowels and blends. Later, these are supplemented by secondary spellings, comparisons of sight and phonetic words, compound and multisyllabic words, and prefixes and suffixes. The whole technique may be used as a parallel teaching system to any established sight method of teaching reading.

Writing and Kinesthetic Techniques

The Writing Road to Reading (Spalding, 1970)

This approach, called the Unified Phonics Method, claims to correct the defects in the whole-word method of teaching reading. It is not so much a remedial method as a preventive measure, because if children are taught the Unified Phonics Method at the beginning of their school life, according to the authors, it obviates the need for remedial teaching later.

Nine teaching procedures are outlined:

1. The phonograms (graphemes) are taught by having the pupils say in unison the one or more sounds of each phonogram while showing them the appropriate phonogram flash cards one after another in various sequences. Each phonogram is written on paper just after they pronounce it. This unites the visual, auditory and kinesthetic functions of the brain.

2. Both child and teacher are to avoid naming the letters. Only their phonic sounds are to be used, so that the child comes to think of the letters as being sounds.

3. A phonogram containing two or more letters should always be called by its sound—never spelled out.

4. Correct legible handwriting and accurate pronunciation are required from the very beginning.

5. Words are dictated from a spelling list for the children to write, but they must say aloud each phonogram or each syllable just before they start to write.

6. The basic rules for spelling, plus their exceptions, are to be taught, as they occur in the children's writing exercises.

7. Only when there are no rules is rote memory to be relied on, and the dictionary is the only authority.

8. Spelling is the basic key to all written language.

9. Reading from a book is not begun until the pupils have completely learned enough common words to understand the meaning of a sentence.

The author goes on to describe exactly how the child should learn cursive writing. This is followed with the spelling rules, which the child will learn in time. Sample pages of how the child's notebook should look are set out, and these are followed by lists of words, which can be used to illustrate each of the spelling rules. The last chapters are devoted to teaching different grades and to the problems presented by children with specific difficulties. Throughout the book the enjoyment that the child must have in his work is stressed.

I have found this book invaluable, even with young adolescent boys who are very backward in reading or spelling. It is rather difficult to fire the children with enthusiasm within such a formal framework, but this is not a criticism of the basic technique; rather it should be seen as a challenge to the ingenuity of the remedial teacher.

Other Writing Techniques

It cannot be emphasized too much that writing and spelling must form the major section of any remedial program. Spalding and Spalding's methods can easily be interlaced with other teaching ideas. For example, the children can write stories around the particular words they are learning at any time, and as long as the stories are fascinating, interest will be maintained and the child will learn with help from the teacher how to construct sentences. It should be remembered that sequencing in writing may have a vocal-motor basis rather than a visual one (see Chapter VIII) and therefore writing should not be isolated from speech activties.

The style and syntax used by the child have not been sufficiently stressed by many authorities, which is rather surprising, because I have found that dyslexics have almost as much difficulty in sequencing words smoothly as they do with letters or phonemes. It is quite possible that this poor syntax may be the result of inadequate experience or illogical thinking, but whatever the cause, the children require a great deal of practice in spontaneous writing. This criticism does not apply to remedial techniques such as Fernald's or Ashton-Warner's, described earlier.

The Fernald Kinesthetic Technique (Fernald, 1943)

Fernald was one of the first to demonstrate that children with severe reading disabilities could be taught to become competent readers.

At stage 1, the child is told that there is a new way of learning words, and he is asked to select any interesting word he wishes to learn, regardless of length. The teacher writes this for him in very large print on a strip of card about 2½ × 12 inches, in cursive writing. With his forefinger, the child traces over the letters, saying each part of the word. He does this many times, until he is able to write the word separately on paper without looking at the original. Several words of his own choice are taught in this way until there are enough for him to begin making his own book about any topic that is of intense interest to him. The child writes a story and while doing so asks for the spelling of any word he wishes to incorporate into it. Each time, the new word is written out on a strip of card for him to trace and learn. His stories have to be typed before the next day so that he can read them back in print while the original is still fresh in his mind. As new words are written, traced and learned, they are filed in an index box to which he may refer at any time.

Stage 2 is reached when the child has a sufficiently larger vocabulary to dispense with tracing. Even so, the child must say new words over to himself and write them without looking at the copy. The pupil continues to write freely and his stories should become much longer. The tracing should be dispensed with gradually but the teacher should make no attempt to simplify the words used or the context written, if only because the child is capable of determining his own level of performance. During stage 2, a small word box file may be used in place of the larger one and, of course, the size of the writing is reduced considerably.

Only at stage 3 are books introduced if the child wants to read them, and he no longer needs to have words written for him as a matter of course. Stage 4 is reached when he has the ability to recognize new words from their similarity to words or parts of words already learned. By now, the child should be eager to read, and the content of the books must be of great interest to him. It is important that he should have sufficient help to make his reading fast enough to maintain his interest in the information of the passage being read.

It is not necessary, Fernald claims, to teach phonics alongside this method, as the child should quickly come to recognize phonemes through experience. The strength of the Fernald method lies in its use of kinesthetic tracing and high-interest motivation. Both these aspects of her work can easily be adapted for use alongside other remedial reading techniques, such as the PCS. In fact, almost all the best remedial techniques incorporate tracing as one of the several methods available for helping the child.

This method is particularly valuable when used with those MND children who have problems of hand-eye incoordination, finger agnosia or poor writing control. The constant tracing over very large cursive letters helps establish fine motor coordination as well as reinforcing the sequencing process. Frostig (1966) suggests that sometimes this tracing should be done with the eyes closed. Note that Hirsch (1963) demonstrated that the kinesthetic method of teaching reading was effective.

Multisensorimotor Academic Training (Stuart, 1963)

Stuart, in her excellent book, recommends a multisensorimotor approach to specific language disabilities (dyslexia), centered on Fernald's program. She adds to it phonics, speech training, orientation practice and extensive memory training. Stuart also suggests mnemonic aids to recall and extends the training into artwork and music. Throughout the program, the emphasis is on activity and she quotes liberally from Montessori to make her points. The teaching of conceptualizing and reasoning is advocated. But it is Stuart's wide view of what education really is, even for the dyslexic child, which is a refreshing antidote to some of the passive, uninteresting, vocationally oriented programs put forward today. The latter are sometimes necessary but they must be supplemented and infused with the broader view of the purposes of education.

REGULAR SCHOOL READING PROGRAMS

Several reading courses are particularly useful with dyslexic children even though they were originally designed for use as regular reading programs in elementary schools. The three sets of books selected have several exclusive advantages and they complement each other as they approach reading from different angles.

Lift-Off to Reading (Woolman, 1966)

This series "provides a systematic pattern of growth in developing reading skills by controlling response conditions, sequence of letter presentation, and letter sound-letter shape relationships." Initially, the child is given only a small number of possible responses from which to choose but as he progresses, the number of response choices increases. He proceeds only after showing mastery of the material he has covered. The letters taught at any one time are as dissimilar in appearance as possible and only one response is learned for any letter or group of letters. Woolman claims that the continual built-in success a child experiences is a major factor in motivating him. There are three cycles to the program. In cycle 1, all the letters of the alphabet except Q are presented in upper-case form.

The child learns to recognize print and sound each letter through five controlled steps: the audial meaning level, the discrimination level, the identification level, the compounding level and the visual meaning level. The first associates the oral words the child will use with their meanings; in the second, the child discriminates between letter shapes and prints them; in the third, he can print the shapes of the letters when he hears their sounds; on the fourth level he learns to print the correct letter sequence when he hears meaningless blended sounds, and on the last level he reads and writes meaningfully the words he knows. In cycle 2, the child learns the lower-case alphabet and studies twenty-six phonetically consistent compounds, along with several other items. In cycle 3, variant sounds for letter shapes are introduced and he learns to master irregular orthography. At the end of cycle 3, the child must demonstrate his comprehension of several simple stories.

Lift-Off to Reading is an excellent series for teaching dyslexic children who are almost complete nonreaders or those who are in a complete muddle, up to the end of the second-grade achievement level. It is a very thorough, phonically oriented writing and reading program which requires full child participation. It is interesting to some children and thorough, but it progresses very slowly and takes children only to the end of the first-grade level. In practice, it has been found that dyslexic children, even though they know the content well, cannot really read simple sentences fluently after completing the program. However, as the title implies, it is an excellent lift-off for those children who learn slowly; those who learn quickly get bored at times, partly because of age, the program being for young children.

A second series by the same author and publisher, *Reading in High Gear*, is also available but has not been assessed.

Programmed Reading (Sullivan, 1966)

The Sullivan Programmed Readers and the Programmed Pre-reading Series (Buchanan, 1963) are together a comprehensive reading course designed to take children step by step from learning the letters of the alphabet and sound-symbol relationships through to the level of competent reading. The great advantage of the program is that once the student is under way in the main program, he can continue with only minimal attention from the teacher—that is, compared with most reading series. The child is very routinely active in this program, which has a phonic basis.

The main problem for dyslexic children who use this series is the absence of the auditory-sound component. Children who have major problems with sound-symbol relationships are very tempted to fill in the missing letters without really knowing or remembering the phoneme equivalents. Therefore, when working with dyslexic children, the teacher must hide the answers and get the child to read the words and sentences out loud. The series moves along at a reasonable rate, each student being able to determine his own pace. One favorable characteristic is that students can be screened on supplied tests to determine exactly where they should enter the program. Some children seem able to learn the cues to the answer system in the series by recognizing that the word or letter required is a particular one mentioned in the previous item. Thus, they complete the workbooks mechanically and do not learn to read; this is because they operate on a problem-solving short-term memory basis.

Basic Reading Series (McCracken and Walcutt, 1963)

In this program, the teacher participates fully; the program is suited to both class and individual tuition. It uses a phonic approach, is well illustrated and teaches both upper-case and lower-case letters at the same time. Letter discrimination is taught quickly and efficiently and some vocalization is provided for by associating sounds with the initial letters of the names of the objects pictured. The range of vocabulary develops quickly but irregular orthography is avoided in the initial stages. Blends are introduced in the pre-primer workbook. Taken overall, this series is well suited to those dyslexic children who do not have severe difficulties but who require a general "sorting-out" in terms of phoneme/grapheme matchings and sequencings. The workbooks, which have a linguistic-phonic basis, require the active participation of the student.

Palo Alto Reading Program (1969)

This program, also known as "Sequential Steps In Reading," is a basic reading program for the primary grades. The emphasis is on the sequential development of linguistic skills including decoding. The method is eclectic and develops the child's word power in a carefully sequenced progression. The materials comprise twenty readers, twenty workbooks, six teachers' guides, flannel board, wallcharts, pocket charts, spelling pockets, letter cards and various card boxes. This is one of the better programs for general classroom use.

Miami Linguistic Readers (Robinett, 1964)

This phonics-based experimental series has worked well for children with problems of expressive language as it was specifically designed to teach foreign-language-speaking immigrant children how to read English. One child who has been helped tended to miss phonemes in his speech, particularly center vowels and final consonants. The program is carefully organized, the workbooks are comprehensive and the wall charts are clear and easily used. The manuals are exceptionally instructive, and there is no possibility of the teacher being unaware of what she is doing; the lesson content is laid out in analyzed items and the principles involved. Considerable writing is required of the children and the variety of content, including the real-life stories, motivates the children well. I do not know how successful the series would be with various types of dyslexic children but it is very promising.

Phonics with Write and See (Bishop, 1968)

This is a three-book series of self-correcting, supplementary exercise materials to be used alongside the reading program the teacher is using in class. The books can be used in several ways— as a complete supplementary program, for practicing extra skills in isolation or for the remediation of individual pupils under the guidance of a tutor. The Write and See process lets the child know immediately whether he is right or wrong in his answer because he marks it with a pen which causes a yellow color to appear on the paper if he is correct. Concise teacher instructions are given in the teacher's edition. The exercises are mainly an initial-letter, multiple-choice answer system associated with a picture of an object. The child looks at the picture and marks under the letter he considers to be the initial sound of the object. If he is correct, the line turns yellow. This series should be very useful for the purpose for which it was designed, but by itself, it might become a little monotonous for the child. I have not yet used it sufficiently to evaluate it more fully.

The Royal Road Readers (Daniels and Dyack, 1960)

This reading scheme does not have workbooks, so the teacher has to participate fully all the time. The Royal Road Readers was one of the first "modern" phonics series to be published for regular classroom use and it quickly became an essential part of every remedial teacher's library. The whole program is based on words with relatively regular orthography. At the outset, only three-letter words are used (as is now the case with most recent programs), but the children are not directly taught the sounds of the letters; they work them out for themselves by abstraction much as they do in Stott's Reading Kit. The series moves very rapidly into longer words, blends and special words, the latter being those which do not follow the rule of phonic simplicity. The Royal Road Readers program moves very quickly, in fact, too fast on its own for many dyslexic children. However, if it is well supplemented by other activities, it can provide a sound basis for a remedial reading program, mainly because of the regular phonics on which it is founded. An "apparatus set" can also be purchased which supplements the readers with word and picture games. The apparatus sets are closely correlated with Book I of the series, amplifying the simple phonics learned there. In her critical survey of basal readers, Chall (1967) found the Royal Road Readers to be one of the best available for regular class teaching. When the Royal Road Readers are used with dyslexic children, I would recommend that a direct teaching of phoneme/grapheme matching, blending, etc., be used with them.

The Psycholinguistic Color System: A Reading, Writing, Spelling and Language Program (Bannatyne, 1968b)

This program has been described earlier in the chapter.

READING BOOKS FOR DYSLEXIC CHILDREN

A constant problem faced by remedial teachers is finding suitable reading books of a nonprogrammed kind which can be used to supplement the mainstream course work. In the past, the books which are at the first-, second- or third-grade level of reading have usually been babyish in content, while books for older boys and girls are, of course, far too difficult.

In previous chapters, I examined the differences between individuals with good verbal ability and those with superior spatial ability, and it is probably true that different types of people prefer quite different styles of writing. The spatial person might find the flowery verbal prose of Lawrence Durrell tedious, whereas the verbally talented person might find him fascinating. Of course, verbal people should be inclined to enjoy all types of authors, whereas those with spatial ability might prefer crisp reality-based styles such as Hemingway's. If this speculation has any substance, reading books for dyslexic children should be written by authors who themselves have been dyslexic. Critchley (1964) suggests that Hans Christian Andersen may have been a dyslexic as a boy and therefore his stories might yield a basic style to be emulated.

Schiffman (1967) has suggested rewriting textbooks in simple prose for disabled readers so that they can keep up with their classmates in subjects such as science, geography and English.

A useful reference book from which to select readers for dyslexic children is Spache's (1966) *Good Reading for Poor Readers*. One essential book all dyslexic children should have is a good children's dictionary, and the Thorndike series is excellent for this purpose. Gillingham and Stillman (1960) include in their method training in using dictionaries.

SPELLING REMEDIATION

There are many useful books and papers available on the teaching of spelling, including Hildreth (1955), Dolch (1960), Rudd (1962), Plunkett and Peck (1960), Plunkett (1963), Baron (1963), Arvidson (1961), Freyberg (1960), Shipley (1962), Fowler (1962) and Patton and Johnson (1960). No attempt will be made to summarize these works, each of which adequately deals with some aspect of the theory or practice of spelling. Nor shall I examine the techniques of teaching spelling in ordinary classes. The spelling of the dyslexic child should partially be taken care of by the remedial reading technique itself, particularly if writing and sequencing are emphasized within an overall phonics method. When dyslexic children have learned to read reasonably well, there is often a residual problem of poor spelling. Many boys who have learned to read at a comparatively late age have, through sheer reasoning ability, obtained a place in an academically inclined school, and while from the conceptualizing point of view they can hold their own, their work is marred by extremely irregular spelling. Such boys, who are often genetic dyslexics, require a program of intensive training in spelling, which may only require two separate half-hours of individual tuition per week. The reason is that they are usually intelligent enough to put into practice in their own ordinary schoolwork and homework the instructions and information they obtain during tuition lessions. The following techniques may be of help to these and other dyslexic children.

Spelling can only be learned by establishing the habit of looking at the individual letters or graphemes of words for their own sake as *unit* designs, at the same time momentarily disregarding the meaning of the word. This is a rather difficult trick for dyslexic children, although for those who are more verbally gifted it is a commonplace feat. Words of similar spelling and vowel phonemes should be grouped and learned at the same time, en bloc, because they then support each other and enable the conventions of Enlish spelling to be learned. In this respect, Fowler's Scientific Spelling: Books 1-4 (Fowler, 1962) should prove useful.

The above books or any others which list a graded basic vocabulary may also be used to screen out those everyday words which the child cannot spell, and these faulty words together with the child's own spontaneous errors should then be "overlearned" at the rate of only twelve per week. The twelve words should be used repeatedly in every way possible during that week, even after they are easily spelled. One recommended practice is to use as many of the words as possible in composite sentences, whether they are humorous or serious. Every effort should be made to prevent the child from writing the words incorrectly.

It will be remembered from the research in Chapter VIII that sound blending or sequential phonetic articulation is very important and that this sequencing should be linked with the individual grapheme configurations composing the word. *Therefore, spelling lessons should always involve first, a nonvisual training in a slow and careful articulation of the word and its blends, second, a study of the configuration of the individual grapheme units of which the word is visually composed and third, a careful matching and meshing of the two processes, preferably while writing the word.*

The basic spelling rules should be learned not only by rote but by frequently putting them into practice, so that the child can instantly recognize a particular rule in a given word or produce a word when presented with a specific rule (Bannatyne and Cotterell, 1966). Dyslexic children are unfortunate in that they have to learn mechanically those letter-sequencing processes which come naturally to most children. As Fernald suggests, the child should also attempt to write the words correctly without looking at the original. The spelling rules have been programmed for teaching machine use (Homme, 1962), but the efficacy of the program is not known.

Nevertheless, the lessons must not be allowed to become dull, routine or humorless. Competitions against oneself, rewards for success, humorous games and above all praise will lighten the work routine.

If difficult words are *broken into syllables,* the child will be able to see that a long word is really only a series of quite manageable short "bits" which can themselves be strung together in much the same way as letters are. Moreover, the child will come to understand that the "bits" or syllables have their own conventional spellings and can be arranged and rearranged in various sequences to form many other words. This can be the basis of several word games, especially if little cards with syllables, prefixes, roots and suffiixes are printed with a fiber pen, e.g., How many words can you make by adding prefixes and suffixes to the root *tract?* (*contract, extract, tractor, tractable, retractability, intractable,* etc.). The spelling of blends should be thoroughly taught at this time. Dictionaries are always allowed.

Speaking of dictionaries, as mentioned above, the child should be given one suitable to his or her age level. In addition, the child should be given a looseleaf, indexed pocket notebook in which he writes very clearly those words frequently misspelled. This notebook (which need not contain meanings) is to be used at all times in school, at home and in any circumstances calling for correct spelling.

In a spelling context, *sequencing* is the term used when each letter is individually selected from a "pile" of letters and placed *in the correct order from left to right*. Sequencing can be a visual, vocal, auditory or manual process and lessons for dyslexic children should incorporate all four. When sequencing, the child must manually place or write the letters. The motor-kinesthetic activity involved reinforces the eyes and ears. In very severe cases, finger tracing in large cursive letters on the table will also build up the correct sequencing of very hard-to-learn words (Fernald, 1943). If small grapheme cards are used for spelling and for breaking words into syllables, the correct sequences will be learned better. All the words must always be *spoken,* written, printed, traced and sequenced from left to right in the correct order. Children are never allowed to begin a word in the middle. *Words must be phonetically sounded out but not spelled orally* (Bannatyne and Wichiarajote, 1969a). The individual grapheme chips can also be used for breaking words into syllables or for building several words around a root. The teacher should always demonstrate a word with grapheme cards before having the child build it.

Rhythm (see Chapter VIII) is important in learning to spell, and teaching the child simple rhythmic poems with stresses and syllables marked can give him insight into the basic "pulsing" of speech.

A typewriter, even if it is very old, will assist the child to sequence correctly. It is yet another way of forcing the mind to sort out words letter by letter, and the novelty of tapping keys adds to the interest. The use of a typewriter should not be made into a reward. It should be used every day if need be, but, except in the case of responsible older children who may like to learn typewriting for its own sake, its use should be limited so that the novelty does not entirely wear off.

Serialized story writing by the child is a valuable aid to spelling, especially if the "difficult word list" for the week is incorporated into the text of the story. About one short paragraph a day, of perhaps ten minutes, is sufficient. The topic must be chosen by the child (e.g., ghosts, spaceships, photography, etc.), and considerable adult assistance should be given with the grammar, spelling and conceptual content. The child should be allowed to illustrate the story outside the lesson time if he wishes. Any incorrect spelling should be anticipated if possible, replacing it with the right one. Words which may be misspelled should be written out separately or perhaps independently sequenced with grapheme cards before using them in the story. Erasers may be used at any time and no recriminations should be given for any mistakes. The teacher must have as much patience as the child's difficulties demand.

Word games are of great value. Lexicon, Junior Scrabble, spelling bees, etc., all help, particularly if the teacher is tolerant. The child's particular problem must be brought into the open with brothers, sisters, friends and classmates, and these should all be encouraged to help sympathetically rather than to scoff. Nobody should pretend that the spelling difficulty does not exist and genuine allowances should be made for it in all games, even to the extent of giving the dyslexic child a "running start."

There is no substitute for motivation and serious work. The above techniques should bring a slow but steady progress; remember that sound blending and sequential articulation are very important, especially if they are linked to unit graphemes. Break up any lesson into several different activities of five to ten minutes each. Ring the changes frequently, but tend to keep to the basic list of twelve difficult words in any one week. Of course, many more words will be learned in the process, so that within two years, a healthy known vocabulary of some 3,000 words should have been achieved.

AUDITORY TRAINING AND LISTENING

As has been indicated in previous chapters, the auditory area and its deficits are at the heart of true language problems including most reading disabilities. Research findings have not supported blindfold while listening. If a child has a problem differentiating a stimulus phoneme from background noise, he should be given training which requires him to do just that. Games can be played in which children have to identify all kinds of noises and musical chords—animal noises, city and household noises, musical instrument notes and chords can all be taped and used for discrimination training, and there is no reason why this training should not proceed alongside work on the discrimination of phonemes. If the principles of various types of auditory discrimination tests are taken and applied in training procedures, preferably as games the children can play by keeping score, phoneme discrimination will be rapidly improved. High-fidelity tape recorders can be of great benefit in this work, and just as the speech correctionist can help a great deal in training the child's vocalization (see below), so in this area she can contribute much. However, she must realize that a much more subtle approach to listening and phoneme registration must be used with learning disability children who superficially may appear to be normal. These children have to be taught to hear the differences between sounds, and the criterion of correctness is not necessarily the child's ability to reproduce the sounds explicitly in speech. In one exercise, the teacher can say a series of five very similar sounding words more and more quickly at random, the child having to guess which one was spoken by pointing to a picture of the object. Of course, the teacher's pronunciation must be absolutely correct, and only one sound should be varied from word to word, e.g. *ball, bell, bull, bowl, bill.*

There is no reason why auditory discrimination should not be taught using phoneme/grapheme matching flash cards which can be color-coded as in the PGS (Bannatyne, 1968b), but this should be only one of a variety of auditory discrimination activities.

Memory

If the discrimination of phonemes is fundamental to the processing of auditory language, the sequencing of those phonemes and the retention of the order in which they occur in any given spoken word is equally fundamental. A deficit in auditory sequencing memory can lead to a variety of order-errors in blending, closure, letter reversals, spelling, malapropisms and melody discrimination. Many of these are discussed below or in later sections. One form in which an inadequate auditory sequencing memory is manifested in genetic dyslexic boys is the inability to remember the sounds, or series of phonemes, which make up a word they were trained to read a few lines previously. Auditory sequencing is a problem for all kinds of dyslexic children and, in particular, for genetic dyslexic boys (see Chapter IX).

The child with a serious deficit in this area will require a training program which will start with simple sequences of everyday sounds that he must try to reproduce in the correct order. Preferably, the sounds should not be meaningfully related and thus nonsense syllables can be used to advantage. The training should move from gross conglomerates of sound clearly sequenced with distinct gaps between groupings, and move gradually through words and syllables until finally phonemes can be sequenced rapidly, as in a word. Most genetic dyslexic boys can move very quickly onto phoneme sequencing once any discrimination problems have been cleared up. As dyslexic children are of average or higher intelligence, the purpose of each exercise and the objectives it is intended to achieve should always be explained in detail. Individual grapheme chips as found in the Norrie (1960) Letter-Case will be helpful (see the section on spelling above).

There is little doubt that auditory sequencing memory is A-reinforced by using other intact senses, e.g., tracing, the visual sequencing of grapheme chips and typewriting. However, even when these techniques are used, it must be remembered that the fundamental problem is that of an *auditory* sequencing memory and that the remediation should not get too far away from memorizing sequences of "heard" phonemes.

Auditory Closure

Closure in this context is the ability to "fill in" the missing phonemes or distorted phonemes within a word which the child hears. The word may be heard by the child during his own reading process as he translates a series of visual graphemes into a sequence of phonemes. If the latter sequence is slightly mispronounced by the child, he may have trouble closing on the true sound of the words; he may stress the wrong syllable or mispronounce a phoneme or two.

Training in auditory closure takes the form of having the child guess the correct pronunication of mispronounced words. If speakers with unusual or foreign accents tape record simple passages of prose at a slow pace, dyslexic children can "translate" the passages clause by clause. A tape recorder with a foot switch is useful for this purpose. As with most of the exercises in this chapter, two or more children can participate in mildly competitive games in which phonemes or syllables are distorted or left out of words which are prepared in lists for them by the teacher. It can be fun to have children pronounce short lists of one- and two-syllable words backwards to each other, the listener having to identify the word as it would be pronounced in a forward direction. By tape recording words in a voice which keeps a constant volume against a background of increasing "white" noise, the problem of closing on the stimulus words increases in difficulty; children can compete to see how many words they can get in spite of the increasing noise. If headphones with earmuffs are used, children with specific problems can be be trained in auditory sequencing and closure without interfering with the rest of the group or class who may be doing other kinds of work. The training should not last for more than ten minutes at the most in any one lesson.

Phoneme/Grapheme Matching

Some children may not even realize that visual pictures or designs can be associated in a regular way with sounds. Such children can acquire the idea by having them match pictures with recorded animal noises and other everyday sounds.

When introducing the child to phoneme/grapheme matching, *the teacher should make sure that both he and the child pronounce the phonemes correctly.* Therefore, /b/ will not be /bi/, and /t/ will not be /tuh/. *Before* introducing graphemes, the teacher should have the child identify the initial, middle and final sounds (phonemes) of words by multiple-choice picture matching such as is used in almost all prereading workbooks. It should be explained to the child that phonemes can be arranged and re-arranged in different sequences, e.g., *pin, nip, at, tab,* etc. This should be done before any visual or written letters, graphemes or words are presented. Graphemes are the visual *labels* for phonemes. Thus the phonemes must be clearly identified as sounds for the graphemes to be meaningful. All this is programmed into the PCS.

Single-Unit Phoneme/Grapheme Memory Training

Once the discrimination and sequencing of individual phonemes is accomplished, work can proceed on matching individual graphemes to each phoneme. The traditional way of doing this is to use flash cards (Gillingham and Stillman, 1960), and it is still one of the best ways, particularly if it is supplemented by the use of specific memory aids and equipment. The major objective is to train the child to recite each of the phonemes associated with a specific grapheme. Some authorities recommend that the sounds should always be associated with words (Stott, 1962; Daniels and Dyack, 1960), and it is an excellent practice to do so. However, Chall (1967), after reviewing the research, could find no evidence that children who are taught code breaking "name call" or "bark at print." Therefore, there would seem to be no harm in teaching phoneme/grapheme matchings directly as well as in key words—the two methods are not incompatible. Laubach (1955) has suggested using mnemonic drawings in the shape of the letter or grapheme which will aid the child's memory; e.g., an S is a picture of a snake. The problem here is to find enough suitable objects which adequately picture sound symbols. If the flash cards are color-coded as in the PCS, the child will receive an instant prompt which will facilitate memorization. The children should have regular practice and testing in black-and-white versions of the graphemes, both individually and in work, to insure that retention is taking place. If colored pencils (PCS) are available, Language Master blank cards (made by the Bell & Howell Co.) can be used with the individual child, the grapheme being printed in color on the card while the sound is recorded on the strip of tape.

All phoneme/grapheme matching should be overlearned to the point of instant recognition.

Phoneme/Grapheme Sequencing Memory Training

As phoneme/grapheme individual matchings are learned, they may be incorporated in sequences which, for a considerable time, should be regular in orthography. Most of the reading programs outlined above introduce phoneme/grapheme matching in a simple regular way, beginning with three-letter words and establishing simple regular sequences before moving on to more complex and irregular words.

Most remedial techniques in phoneme/grapheme sequencing training involve the child actively in spelling and writing because this is a matter of recall rather than simple recognition (see Chapter VIII). Here again, such aids as color-coding can be used to advantage. In the PCS, the child reads words and stories, at the same time color-coding the vowels by tracing over them with colored pencils, the vowels and words being introduced very gradually on a progressive system. Color-coded chips or Norrie Letter-Box pieces can be used for sequencing spelling words in a variety of ways. The advantage of placing separate letters or graphemes on little cards is that a word composed of them can be split into syllables and sounds can be isolated visually. Irregular words should be learned by rote so that the whole word is able to be pronounced in response to a flash card. Frostig (1950) has produced a list of the one hundred most often misspelled words, all of which should be overlearned.

Most dyslexic children will make very limited progress sitting down passively with the teacher and attempting to struggle through reader after reader without the benefit of specialized techniques. The automatization of the language at the reading level depends on overlearning (in both recognition and recall) sequences of phoneme/grapheme equivalents. Smooth reading cannot be attained until the basic units have been learned. As has been said, once a few phoneme/grapheme units have been learned, they can be successfully sequenced after suitable training; not all the matchings have to be learned before reading commences. I have found it useful in a large class, as *one* track of a remediation program, to select a child who can read well, sit him alongside a dyslexic child and get him to say any word the dyslexic child cannot read five seconds after the previous word in the sentence has been read. Thus, the good reader becomes an automatic human teaching machine who supplies the words the dyslexic child cannot read. If the good reader "teacher" counts to ten quickly before supplying the unknown word in the text, the right amount of time will have elapsed. The dyslexic child should receive many other types of training as well.

Whatever work they are doing, dyslexic children should always be allowed to *whisper* both sounds and words to themselves unless this seriously interferes with the activities of other children.

Aids, Prosthetic and Prophylactic Devices and Other Equipment

Tape recorders and the Language Master have already been mentioned as valuable adjuncts to auditory training. Stuart (1963) has used a tape recorder effectively in her classroom work by having the children sit in a circle with earphones on their heads, listening to a tape-recorded book, the text being at about the level of difficulty consistent with their needs. As they listen to the carefully pronounced text of the story, their eyes follow the actual words being spoken in their individual copy of the recorded book. It is a help if the children follow the text with their index finger, so that the teacher can check that they are reading the words corresponding to the voice. In a similar way, children can record their own stories, later listening to them as they read silently in phase. These techniques help establish sequential phoneme/grapheme associations and at the same time give the child a great deal of motivational enjoyment. If the group listening to a tape recorder wears headphones, this need not interfere with the other children in the class. Frostig will tape a whole lesson, with appropriate answering pauses, from a child's programmed workbook so that the child can carry on independently of the teacher. A foot switch for the child is an advantage here, too.

Atkinson and Hart (1963) have constructed some simple mechanical and electrical devices to assist the child in learning discrimination and phoneme/grapheme matching and sequencing. The actual exercises are similar to those in many reading readiness workbooks but the gadgets are novel and would motivate boys particularly. Moxon (1962) has invented a whole system of aids, devices and gadgets for teaching reading to mildly mentally retarded children. They are equally suitable for dyslexic children if the teacher has a constructional talent. I think that not enough use is made of prophylactic devices which children can carry with them permanently as memory aids. It should not be too difficult, for example, to make a small phoneme identification color-coded "wheel" of pocket size to which the child can refer when faced with an unknown grapheme; some effort would still be required on his part to choose between the alternative phonemes offered.

There is an excellent book called *Listening Aids Through the Grades* (Russell and Russell, 1959), which has many ideas helpful to dyslexic children. Learning to *listen* with precision is difficult for them and this book contains many ideas which are applicable to either individual children or the whole class.

Teaching machines and language laboratories have not yet been developed either technically or financially to the point where they can be used on a day-to-day basis in the classroom or reading center. Most of the training machines available to reading students are for competent readers who wish to speed up their rate of reading. A project at Stanford University reported by Atkinson and Hansen (1966), which uses a light-sensitive television screen, a taped voiceover program and a multilooped computerized feedback system, is very promising but also extremely expensive. So also is the Edison Responsive Environment System or "talking typewriter"; these elaborate machines are, as yet, only possibilities for the distant future. Here again I feel that the growing field of remedial education is ready for a variety of *simple* electronic devices which will facilitate auditory-visual associational learning. Certainly, some of the instruments available for teaching partially hearing and deaf children can be used to advantage with dyslexic children.

SPEECH TRAINING: LISTENING AND CLARITY OF ARTICULATION

The speech correctionist, or in her absence the remedial teacher, can contribute to the wider reading program in several ways. She can train the child in *listening* carefully because many dyslexics do not listen to sounds accurately. At the Word Blind Institute in Copenhagen, the child will listen to the speech therapist through an amplifier, using headphones, as she enunciates sounds, words and phrases which the child must repeat carefully. A corollary of careful listening is the retention of longer and longer series of instructions. At the Frostig School, children are trained to remember series of instructions, and they participate in mildly competitive games to see who can remember and act out the longest series of continuous order: e.g., stand up; go to the door; open it; close it; go to the chalkboard; pick up the red chalk; write your last name; take the chalk to the teacher; walk around the table twice; sit down.

Training in *articulation* will help children to learn reading (Sommers *et al.*, 1961b), but the content is more sophisticated than that used with deaf or aphasic children. The objective is to "clean up" and polish children's speech until they can pronounce clearly each and every phoneme in the language; therefore, in a sense, the exercise becomes a form of simple elocution. McNeil and Keisler (1963), in a research using programmed instruction with an oral response from beginning readers, found that the oral response is valuable in learning to read.

Oral training is a little different, the objective being rather to develop the child's ability to marshal his conversational content in an organized way. This is a kind of structured "show and tell," with the children being trained as "radio and television commentators." Once again, tape recorders are useful in this kind of work. A valuable practice in both auditory and speech training and, for that matter, reading, is to sound the phonemes or syllables which are usually slurred over in popular speech, e.g., *bus-i-ness, in*-ter-*est, sec-*re-tar-*y*. When every syllable is pronounced in this way, children will find the spelling of these words much simpler.

Sound blending can be taught by the speech correctionist both as an oral response and as a response to flash cards with blends printed on them or to whole words containing suitable blends. Several techniques are available in addition to the traditional one of saying the isolated phonemes more and more quickly until they run together as a word. Engelmann (Bereiter and Engelmann, 1966) always teaches one-syllable words by splitting off either the initial consonants or the final consonants, e.g., *c-at* or *ca-t*, *b-oat* or *boa-t*. In this way, the children come to understand blending without the difficult process of running several sounds together.

One good way to teach sound blending is to get the child to form the mouth in the position required for the pronunciation of the intial consonant but to actually voice the vowel sound immediatedly following that consonant. For example, in the word bat, the child would purse the lips ready to say the phoneme /b/, but would then quickly say the vowel /a/, equally quickly following it with the /t/. It is important that all unvoiced phonemes (e.g., /t/, /p/, /f/) be taught and spoken as unvoiced, otherwise the child is faced with the impossible task of blending vowels and consonants which frequently do not fit together. At the Frostig School, a few of the children (who I thought might be genetic dyslexic cases) were taught blending by whole-word recognition after phonics training in individual phoneme/grapheme matching. In other words, the two techniques are used until they meet in the center, so to speak, and so before long, a child who can both sound a word and sight-recognize it has acquired the idea of blending and can apply it to strange words. Hegge *et al.* (1955) recommend that blending be taught by demonstrating to the child how sounds are broken down. They start with a simple double sound and stretch it until it is two individual sounds. Thus, the child comes to understand the nature of the blending process and can reverse it as a synthesis of sounds.

In terms of *memory processes*, *blends* and common *syllables* are really "chunks" and certainly segments such as *sh, ph, ing, sub,* etc., should be taught as a gestalt of sound, each of which has its written equivalent in the form of several letters. Flash cards, and key words as used in the PCS, will facilitate this learning process. The PCS uses all the above techniques.

One approach I have found valuable with dyslexic children is to supply them with a one hundred-page drawing book (letter size), in which they divide each page into four sections. In the top left-hand corner, they write all the letters and letter combinations associated with a particular grapheme/phoneme association. In the upper right-hand section, they draw a stylized picture of the mouth, tongue, teeth, lips, etc., both in side-view cross-section and from the front. These drawings, which are not as difficult as they sound, show the position of the vocal organs while the sound is being produced. In the lower left-hand section, they draw two or three objects whose names contain the phoneme/grapheme combination written above. The words for these objects are written in the lower right-hand section. Usually, the whole book has a theme such as cowboys or pirates, and color-coding is used liberally. The drawings are also colored by the children. As each page takes some time, the drawings of the objects and the word-labels can be done as homework, using models written by the teacher. Besides all the phoneme/grapheme combinations of the language, blends and constant syllables can also be drawn and laid out in the way indicated. The children use the book continually for overlearning, having to recite the phonemes and words on every page rapidly each time before the next entry is made.

VISUO-SPATIAL AND VISUO-MOTOR TRAINING

Visuo-spatial deficits occur when the child has difficulty in visually manipulating the relationships between objects in two- or three-dimensional space. Visuo-motor activity occurs when objects are manipulated or drawn, thus involving eye-hand coordination. The motor aspects of this problem in certain dyslexic children will be discussed below in the appropriate section, and only the visuo-spatial aspects will be discussed here.

Piaget and Inhelder (1956, 1960) and Vereecken (1961) have observed the development of visuo-spatial activity through childhood to be a relatively systematic progression. Many MND children suffer from mild visuo-spatial deficits, the symptoms being many and varied. Experience and research (Hagin *et al.*, 1965) have shown that certain dyslexic children can profit from training designed to remediate defects in visual perception.

Frostig (1964, 1966) has pioneered training programs for the development of visual perception which follow naturally from her Test of Visual Perception (Frostig, 1964). The first five subsections below are aspects of her training and remedial programs (Frostig and Horne, 1964):

1. *Visuo-Motor Coordination:* This is the first part of the remediation program and involves the child in drawing lines precisely within confined limits, point to point or between guidelines.

2. *Perceptual Constancy:* These exercises develop the child's perception and identification of forms regardless of differences in size, color, texture, position, background or angle of viewing; in other words, they develop the child's ability to generalize visually from object to object or design to design. A typical exercise requires the child to pick out all the equilateral triangles from a page of assorted triangles.

3. *Figure-Ground Perception:* In these, the child has to isolate and recognize a figure of a given shape against overlapping, intersecting or very distracting backgrounds. The exercises are very like the popular hidden-figure puzzles children like to do.

4. *Spatial Relationships:* The objective of these exercises is to develop the child's ability to perceive positional relationships between various objects or points of reference; this is helpful to children when they have to understand the arrangement of material on a work page.

5. *Position in Space:* The work here develops the child's recognition of the formation and directionality of figures and characters. The exercises are mostly multiple-choice items in which the child is required to select the shape or design from a multiple-choice series which is exactly like the model provided.

Visual Discrimination

All the above exercises involve visual discrimination, but in the case of words, some MND children will have further problems. In order to teach discrimination of letters and words, one covers the page (using a typewriter) with spaced random letters or groups of letters and the child is required to circle or cancel specific letters or groups of letters. In another exercise, nonsense words are paired, some pairs being the same and some having a one-letter difference; the child is required to circle the pairs which contain dissimilar words. Many variations are possible on this theme. For reading purposes, children with serious discrimination problems should use the large-print reading books available for the partially sighted. The PCS includes visual discrimination exercises.

Memory for Designs and Letters

The Memory-for-Designs Test (Graham and Kendall, 1960) or the Banntayne Visuo-Spatial Memory Test (Bannatyne, 1968c) can be adapted for training exercises in which the child is shown a particular shape which is removed after a few seconds, at which point the subject has to draw or point to the correct shape. In both these types of exercises, it is preferable to use letter-like shapes, since the ultimate objective is to enable the MND child concerned to remember visually individual letters. Genetic dyslexic children do not tend to have problems remembering letter shapes.

Visual Sequencing Memory

The appropriate subtest from the ITPA can be converted to remedial ends by having the child practice remembering the sequences in which the design chips were originally laid out by the teacher. Of course, any set of designs on small cards will do as well. The letter chips from the Edith Norrie Letter-Case or other letter cards can be similarly used for visual sequencing memory training. To start with, one or two letters can be used in any sequence and slowly built up until the child can replace accurately six or seven letter chips. *It is most important in the teaching of spelling that any visual sequencing of letters and graphemes be tied to articulatory sequencing and sound blending, since it is these which determine the order of the letters* (Bannatyne and Wichiarajote, 1969a).

Parts-to-Whole Gestalt Assembling

The Block Design and Object Assembly subtests of the WISC present MND children with visuo-spatial deficits with a relational assembly problem. Although some design-matching materials are available (Fairbanks and Robinson, 1967), to my knowledge, nobody has thoroughly programmed constructional assembly tasks. Fortunately, many toys are available which accomplish this and children with difficulties in this area should have ample opportunity to copy Leggo designs, pattern mosaics, use Lincoln Logs, assemble jigsaw puzzles, etc.

Design Assembly, Spatial Relationships, Dimension and Perspective

Older MND boys who are quite intelligent may appreciate an understanding of the simple mechanics and physical relationships involved in levers, cogs and braces on an elementary engineering level. They will also appreciate training in perspective and vanishing points, as in architectural drawings. Of course, not too much remedial time should be devoted to these aspects of the work but it is surprising how an understanding of the logic behind the relationships of objects in space can help a boy understand not only letters and word shapes, but also the spatial content of his mathematics and science programs.

There is a need for someone to program a constructional abilities curriculum for all children in elementary and secondary schools. At the moment, Montessori stops before first grade and the subject begins again in architecture and engineering courses at the university, a serious education gap which must be filled.

Mirror Imaging and Reversals

These problems should gradually mature even in learning disability children. Eye movement lateralization (see below) may help. The letters *b* and *d* are best dealt with by printing the word *bed* on a card and by drawing a bed over the word, thus, b̄ed. Note, the letters can only face inward and the first one must be *b*.

MOTOR TRAINING

In this section, only direct motor and kinesthetic training will be considered; in other words, the emphasis will be on muscle training, kinesthetic feedback and haptic sensing.

General Physical Training

The theories and programs of Kephart (1966), Barsch (1965), Delacato (1954, 1964) and Ayres (1965, 1967) have been outlined in Chapter X, where it was concluded that muscle training which involves the whole body has little effect on reading processes except inasmuch as the training happens to involve those specific muscles which are directly concerned with reading processes. Creeping, crawling, posturing and balance are all valuable to a child's physical development, but the evidence (see Chapter X) is that *academically* they are of little value, and certainly of less value than a direct training of the muscles involved in reading and writing. Motor performance skills are highly specific from every point of view.

One type of training which might help with reading is the development in the child of a full appreciation of his own body image (M.L.J. Abercrombie, 1964). Spastic MND children and possibly others can be helped to develop an adequate body image by direct tuition, by working with the child in front of a large full-length mirror and by developing drawing skills involving the body in a deliberate way. It should be noted that throughout, the objective of this operation is psychological, not physiological.

A new type of psychophysical development program based on body image training and the internalization of instructions has been developed by M. Bannatyne and A. D. Bannatyne (1970). This successful technique enables a child to attain an extensive thought control mastery over his voluntary motor system. It is based on research by Luria (1961a). The technique thoroughly teaches (a) an excellent body image, (b) auditory sequencing memory for words, (c) vocal codes, (d) voluntary motor control, (e) sensorimotor coordination and (f) physical development.

Finger and Hand Control Training

On rare occasions, the MND child will be found to have slightly uncontrollable choreiform movements (twitching) of the hands and fingers or he may suffer from finger agnosia which is, in essence, a lack of kinesthetic and haptic sensory feedback and registration in the brain. It is possible that finger agnosia may be helped by presenting the child with a large number of familiar *textured* objects, etc., to feel and identify, preferably when he is blindfolded, but to my knowledge, nobody has yet tried this. Children with choreiform movements or any serious visuo-motor deficit (with the emphasis on the motor aspect) may be helped by any manual activity involving hands and eyes in precise movement. The Frostig hand-eye coordination exercises will prove useful and the teacher can invent many similar tasks such as joining dots, tracing between lines, tracing pictures through paper, outlining line drawings in color, copying line pictures, cutting out patterns with scissors, using stencils or creating ruled designs.

Handwriting Programs

MND dyslexic children, and for that matter untidy genetic dyslexic boys, may profit from a very thorough handwriting program. Younger children may first learn to print, using any of the traditional pre-primer programs. Satisfactory handwriting programs are the Zaner-Bloser Company's (1970) and Peterson's (1964). This course soon changes from manuscript writing to cursive writing. I would recommend that any dyslexic child at the third-grade level or over be taught cursive handwriting (as well as manuscript, if necessary) so that he quickly learns the various shapes which can represent a given sound. He will also tend to mirror-image less in his own writing, since cursive letters are irreversible. W.H. Gardner has published a text-manual for remedial handwriting to which the teacher can refer when preparing lessons. *Lift-Off to Reading,* by Woolman (1966), might be useful for dyslexic children with severe difficulties in motor functioning who are also beginners at reading, since it includes a script-writing program.

Other programs which teach writing within the reading program are Fernald (1943) and Spalding and Spalding (1962). The Fernald technique is particularly appropriate for children with writing disabilities as it contains much kinesthetic tracing activity. Chldren can also be taught cursive writing as they progress through the PCS.

Eye Movements and Eye Muscle Training

Lesevre (1966) and Calvert and Cromes (1966) have found that many (presumably) MND children suffer from choreiform-type eye movements. Lesevre also found that left-to-right lateralization of the gaze showed a lag in development in some poor readers. The key to reading is to be found in saccadic movements; that is, the eyes flick from point to point along a line of print, pausing between flicks long enough to register the content of the designs seen. The eyes do *not* track in one smooth motion and exercises of that nature in isolation will not necessarily improve reading performance.

Finger pointing helps establish saccadic movements in dyslexic children and is recommended by Frostig. Another technique I would suggest is the drawing of small crosses on ruled paper at random distances apart (say between half an inch and two inches), the child being required to look at and possibly point to each cross in succession as rapidly as possible, moving from left to right along each line in turn and going down the page as in reading. A page of print can be similarly organized by the teacher by circling a letter in each word about one-third of the way along the word from its beginning. The child then looks at and points to each circled letter in succession, moving along quickly. Geake and Smith (1965) have developed a workbook for training visual tracking in a routine way.

A technique I use is to cut a long slot, one line in width, from the center right-hand edge of a 6 × 4-inch file card, which is then slid along the line of print. The child reads the words which are moving along in the slot. This device not only concentrates the child's vision on the words being read, but also allows the child's right visual field to feed in the incoming stimuli farther along the line, a most important aspect of fluent reading. This device helps genetic dyslexic boys lateralize their gaze in one dimension. It is important to tell children that in order to read smoothly their eyes should run ahead of their voice when reading out loud. This will improve the fluency of both their oral reading and silent reading.

If a child has a serious problem following a line of print, it is possible to alternate the colors of the lines by typing the text using red and black typewriter ribbon. With one line in red, the next in black and the next in red, etc., the child's eye will be fixated to a color as an A-reinforcer.

Articulation Training

Training the articulatory apparatus to function correctly is the work of the speech clinician and should not be confused with the training for clarity of phoneme enunciation mentioned in the previous section on speech. Children who stutter, who are aphasic or who have any of the many speech apparatus defects which are possible should be sent to a speech and hearing clinic for treatment. Better still, the reading center or large school should employ a speech clinician as a permanent member of the staff. However, simple training in slow and careful articulation should be undertaken by the reading teacher when her purpose is to improve the child's performance in reading and spelling.

SENSORY AND MOTOR INTEGRATION TRAINING

All the lessons and activities described in this chapter involve intersensory and sensorimotor training, and there is no need to artificially invent sensorimotor integration exercises for dyslexic children. Although we strive to make diagnostic testing procedures and remediation methods as sensorially singular and pure as possible, it is fundamentally impossible to activate only one sense or motor activity to the exclusion of all others. All output of the human body is, in the final analysis, motor in nature. Therefore, motor functions must be involved and will be coordinated and trained whatever exercises the child does.

There is one single exception to the above statement. Some MND dyslexic children have constructional apraxic difficulties, probably because a particular area of the brain handles such activity and may be impaired (see Chapter X). Children with apraxic deficits should embark on a training program which involves manipulating objects in three-dimensional space. Once again, Leggo, Lincoln Logs and Erector Sets will be valuable for this purpose, but only if the child is actively trained by the teacher. Unfortunately, as has been mentioned above, no one has yet programmed such materials either for regular class use or for learning disability children.

In all multisensorimotor training, one should insure that the child works primarily in the deficit area and does not "slide off" into preferred intact areas during training lessons. Sometimes, when necessary, blindfolds and earmuffs should be used to prevent this from happening.

CONCEPTUALIZING, REASONING AND LATERALITY TRAINING

Without an appreciation of logical organization, a child cannot cope with the relationships between objects or concepts. This is a problem with mildly autistic children as well.

Once again, the deficit area has to be trained, in this case by developing the child's ability to appreciate comparisons and other conceptual relationships. He should be trained to manipulate concepts in the following areas: color, time, shape, weight, direction, family relationships, texture, length, volume, light, sound and density. Naturally, the teaching of these topics will involve the use of a considerable amount of equipment, some of which is available commercially.

Directionality Training

Some children seem to benefit from training in the concepts of direction, particularly left and right. Note that direction in this context is being considered as a conceptualizing problem, whose difficulties arise from mirror-image (body) confusion and a poor memory for associating verbal-labels to objects. Children who are truly spatially disoriented for reasons of serious neurological dysfunction may require elaborate expert training. Sceats (1965) has given dyslexic children successful training in simple directionality. He has reported how he marched a boy around the playground like a soldier, giving him directions to turn left or right. The reading aspects of directionality *skills* training can best be taught using techniques like those mentioned earlier in connection with eye movements.

Training Reasoning Abilities

Very often, primary emotional communicative dyslexic and socially disadvantaged children (as well as other dyslexics) may not appreciate the conventional formats in which intelligence test items and similar tasks are presented. A series of workbooks which will train children in this aspect of reasoning is the Learning To Think Series by Thurstone (1967).

Bereiter and Engelmann (1966) emphasize that socially disadvantaged (and other) children will profit from thorough training in formulating the sentences, syntax, questions and answers which are necessary to communicate logical discussion. The question-and-answer lessons, while supplying and training the children in linguistic conventions, also insure that the children learn to think.

The Cuisenaire rods (Cuisenaire, 1953) successfully help children understand the logic of mathematics.

MEMORY TRAINING

The background and theory of memory training was presented in detail in Chapters VII and VIII and there is no need to recapitulate it here. Specific techniques for training memory in various sensorimotor modalities have been suggested in the appropriate sections in this chapter.

It should be remembered that the major objective in teaching reading, writing and spelling at the elementary stages is skill automatization. Once a child can encode or decode automatically, he is freed from conscious communication skills to get on with the business of understanding, thinking and creating. Rote memorization is at the best of times rather an uninteresting task, and therefore it is wise to artificially motivate the child with tokens, stars, etc., for a job well done. Songs, poems, rhythms and so on may also help.

Mnemonic aids and prosthetic or prophylactic memory devices should be used to facilitate memorizing in difficult cases.

It will be remembered that the repetitive-part method (Postman, 1965) is the best method of learning by rote. Before adding each new item to any series, the child must re-repeat all the items that have gone before. This is particularly true for phoneme/grapheme matching training. Children should learn by both sight and sound the days of the week and the months of the year using the Postman method. Overlearning is automatic with this procedure.

Chunking, or the clustering of parts into subwholes, increases the memory span and is to be encouraged. If the chunks can be further organized into logical relationships, a vast array of material can be recalled at will. However, similarities (but not identity) will cause confusion and should be avoided, particularly when the material is auditory/vocal in nature. Thus, putting the words *blue* and *blew* together will cause trouble, but the grouping together of all the words spelled and pronounced in a similar way is beneficial, e.g., *sun, bun, run,* etc. The number of "bits" which can be remembered by most children is limited to seven, whether they are units, chunks or organizational wholes. All dyslexic children usually do poorly on sequencing memory tasks. Color-coding organizes hundreds of bits into a few color-clusters which, once they are overlearned, facilitate the automatization of phoneme/grapheme matching in reading, spelling and writing.

LANGUAGE TRAINING, LINGUISTICS AND SYNTAX

Many dyslexic children of all kinds may be perplexed by the order of words in different kinds of sentences (e.g., active and passive verbs, questions, etc.), by meaning-carrying prefixes and suffixes (e.g., -*ly* usually indicates an adverb) and by the usefulness of stress, intonation and pauses to convey meaning.

Fries (1963) has written at length on linguistics and reading. The Palo Alto Reading Program (1969) is sound. This series and the Miami Linguistic Readers have already been discussed; Bloomfield and Barnhart (1961) have also written a reading series based on a linguistic approach. Lefevre (1964) has written a text for teachers on linguistics and the teaching of reading which is a very useful handbook when instructing children directly. Personally, I have found that most dyslexic children are of an age when syntax, grammar and sentence patterns can be understood directly and that as long as the books they read are not too syntactically complex, they can get by quite well. Of course, very difficult sentence constructions should be avoided.

The PCS teaches syntax and linguistic structure as a natural element of language right from the beginning of the program.

A major theme of Chapters II through VIII was that syntax is fundamentally (but not entirely) determined by the *sequence* of nonverbal thought content (imagery, percepts, concepts and their relationships). This then devolves on the logicality of thought—it must make sense. The converse of "commonsense" syntax is to be found in the disorganized language of some aphasic and psychotic individuals who confabulate and have confused speech or writing. Some learning disability children exhibit similar if less acute symptoms. Therefore, remediation should always include training in reasoning and simple logic, mainly through matching *series* of pictures or objects with a complete sentence. The *sequence* of events which matches the *sequence* of words in the sentence is all-important. Of course, training in standard conventional syntax (in terms of syntactic structure) should parallel this instruction in coding sequences of meanings in a logical word system called a sentence.

Verbal Fluency Skills in Writing

The essence of fluency in writing is to be able to recall rapidly, "out of the blue," those specific words necessary to our flow of thought. Some of us "hum and hah" overmuch as we leaf through our internal thesaurus matching words with ideas. Dyslexic children who have difficulties of this nature require extensive vocabulary-building exercises and games, the emphasis being on the verbal labels and their production, not on meanings. Most dyslexic children know what they want to express—their difficulty lies in vocal encoding fluency. They should learn specific conventional sequences of words quite deliberately.

Developing fluency in *reading* was considered earlier in this chapter.

Context Clues in Word Recognition and Comprehension

Dulin (1970) has emphasized how children can use contextual aids such as layout, typographical, syntactical and structural aids to improve the word attack skills of children learning to read. Root words, prefixes and suffixes also help readers to decode difficult new words.

The Origins of Language and Words

Interest and understanding can be promoted in older dyslexic children if they are told briefly how the English language came to exist as it does today and where specific words originated. Gillingham and Stillman (1960) has a section in her handbook devoted to these topics.

Writing Poems

It may seem strange to recommend that dyslexic children write poetry, that most verbal of all activities, but I have found this to be an excellent motivator, one which is founded in the language itself. Dyslexics come to appreciate the linguistic structure of English when they have to organize words in metrically correct rhyming poems. The almost mathematical puzzle quality of the manipulation of words in structured poems seem to intrigue highly intelligent genetic dyslexic boys. Sometimes the poems can incorporate words from the spelling list, particularly the ones they repeatedly misspell. A rhyming dictionary may be consulted at all times.

REMEDIATING THE VARIOUS GROUPS OF DYSLEXIC CHILDREN

It would be redundant to rearrange the content of this chapter in such a way that the remediation for each type of dyslexic child would be precisely specified. Besides, many of the remedial techniques "work" equally well for more than one kind of reading disability case. Throughout the text, frequent references have been made to genetic dyslexics or MND children, and these can be used as pointers to appropriate methods. In the separate chapters on each type of dyslexic child, sufficient information is given to indicate in a general way which types of remediation would be most suitable. Another complicating factor is the incidence of reading disability cases with multiple dyslexia. It is not uncommon to find socially disadvantaged genetic dyslexic children or emotionally disturbed MND dyslexic children. In such cases, the teacher must use her discretion in selecting the precise techniques and motivators which will be most effective. A thorough diagnosis will take most of the trial-and-error element out of remediation, but one should not keep rigidly to a multiple prescription which is not working well. Furthermore, a policy of diagnostic remediation is recommended so that through task analysis, remedial techniques can develop to meet the immediate academic needs of the child. Endeavor to remediate children to a whole grade level above their chronological age grade level so that they are much more able to continue the progress they have made.

Primary emotional communicative dyslexics will require a considerable amount of language and linguistics training, and if they have been made afraid of words, they will have to be desensitized and strongly motivated in several ways. The reading program itself should be one of the linguistic series mentioned above.

Genetic dyslexic children will have to be remediated in most of the areas indicated in Table II, which is also reiterated in expanded form in Chapter IX. This should not be done blindly, but on a continuing assessment of the child's academic and sensorimotor needs. Most genetic dyslexic children will require a multitrack program, at least in the initial stages, one which effects auditory/vocal training on all four levels. The visual training of genetic dyslexic children is of a very different quality from that of MND children, being directed primarily against mirror imaging and lateralizing the gaze. The PCS is very useful with genetic dyslexic boys, and the whole program should be oriented toward spelling and writing activities. Lavish praise will help counteract a poor self-concept.

MND children, as a heterogeneous group, will involve the teacher in every type of training described thus far and probably many more, the specific techniques most suitable for a particular child being determined by a thorough diagnostic examination. It will be found that MND children frequently require training in visuo-spatial and visuo-motor skills on all four major levels simultaneously. MND children with emotional problems will require motivational reinforcement using tokens and high-interest topics in the program. They will also be more sensitive to distraction and therefore extraneous auditory stimuli should be kept to a minimum. Carpets on the floor are very useful and soundproof headphones can be helpful.

Socially disadvantaged children much as communicative dyslexics require a strong teacher-child relationship to motivate them to work. If possible, the whole family should be involved in a reorientation program, although this may be wishful thinking for the present. The teacher's attitudes to the children, in particular her expectancies and beliefs about their capabilities, are very important elements in the progress the children will make. All teachers should believe that the children in their class are bright and eager to learn and should plan their lessons accordingly. For one dyslexic boy in a rural school, I recommended to the class teacher that she start a farm project, with the entire language and reading program for the child being centered on farm activities. Three months later, the boy had improved only minimally, because the teacher and the class as a whole were enthusiastically building and equipping a model farm in the classroom, which was a hive of industry.

MOTIVATION

It cannot be stressed too often that motivation and a mutually rewarding (M-reinforcing) attachment relationship between teacher and child, and parent and child, are 75 percent of successful remediation. Motivation is the driving force without which the best techniques are impotent.

SCHOOL DISTRICT ORGANIZATION FOR LEARNING DISABILITY CHILDREN

The following brief descriptions may prove useful to administrators and professional people who have the responsibility of organizing the education of learning disability children.

Regular Class Placement

There are two ways of coping with learning disability children in the regular class. In the first, the teacher remediates each child individually. This will mean that she will be able to spend only a few minutes a day with any one child and will only rarely be able to give him specific deficit training. Usually, the child is given a little more practice in some basal reading series.

Some capable teachers group together the worst four readers in the class and devote twenty minutes or so to them while the remainder of the class is engaged in some quite different lesson, independently of the teacher. This arrangement is a viable proposition, provided that the teacher has excellent backup services such as diagnosis and a variety of workbooks and equipment. Sometimes she can enlist as aides the most intelligent readers in the class. Reading games (Stott, 1962) which can be played by two to four children facilitate group tuition.

School Tutorial Services

In sparsely populated districts, an itinerant teacher with a trailer can move from school to school or old buses can be equipped as mobile reading centers. In large schools, one or two teachers can be employed as reading tutors.

Ideally, the reading tutor will spend half an hour to forty-five minutes each day with one child, five days a week, with the child coming out of the regular classroom for these special sessions. This is probably the most effective and least costly way of handling learning disability cases from the long-term point of view. The tutor may group children in threes or fours (never just two), but then lessons must be at least an hour in duration. The members of the small group should be at approximately the same level of achievement and should be taught as a group; otherwise, the teacher might just as well see them individually.

In some schools, the tutorial teacher takes large groups of children for remedial work, usually for a two-hour period. This may benefit some of the children, but motivationally speaking, the operation becomes depersonalized and the variety of treatment is restricted. However, given extensive equipment and a large full resource cupboard, the enthusiastic inventive teacher may be successful with up to twelve children, but it is not recommended.

The Full-Time Remedial Class

The full-time remedial class usually contains somewhere between ten and twenty children and may last half a day or all day. The teacher is responsible for educating the group in all areas of the curriculum including the skill subjects. Unless there is a full-time qualified aide working with the teacher and unless the classroom is lavishly equipped, I am doubtful about the efficacy of such a program.

Reading or Learning Disability Centers

One of the most effective ways of handling learning disability cases in cities and towns is to establish a center to which the children come for tuition either singly or in small groups. The staff of the center may also advise on classroom remediation. Of course, several centers may be necessary—one for each district. The learning disability centers are staffed by a team of experts including psychologists, speech correctionists and fully qualified learning disability teachers. The person in day-to-day charge should be an experienced learning disability educator. The children are thoroughly diagnosed and prescriptions are written, very little being left to chance. Such centers can be fully equipped and should have an excellent resource room so that each child's needs can be precisely met. It is essential that a full liaison be kept with the child's class teacher and the school principal; when remediation has finished, the class teacher should be advised on how to carry on with a classroom program. Also, someone should be responsible for following up the child's progress year by year, if only because the continued interest will motivate him throughout his school life. The follow-up should be on a personal basis— not by letter. A social worker trained in teaching can handle such work along with parent counseling, etc.

Organizing a School in Sets

If part-time teachers can be hired who are specialists in reading, language and mathematics, and if space is available, groups of both high achievers and low achievers can be drawn from several classrooms in "sets" for specialized teaching. I have seen this system work very successfully in a large city school but it requires remarkably good scheduling and an enthusiastic team of teachers. In such an organization, the classroom teacher herself takes only the "middle group" for reading, arithmetic (mathematics) and the English language, but she takes the whole class for all other subjects. The groups in the "sets" contain no more than fifteen children at one time.

Special Schools for Learning Disability Children

Children with severe deficits who obviously cannot cope with any regular classroom instruction may be screened out and placed in a special school for learning disability children which would have specially trained teachers, smaller classes, special equipment and a less competitive atmosphere. I have visited several such schools that would seem to be working very successfully. Once again, such a school can have the advantage of a team of experts who can work with the children (not simply advise) both diagnostically and remedially. Only severe cases should be sent to special schools of this type and they may have to receive all of their education in such schools throughout much or all of their school lives, although in exceptional cases, a return to the regular school would not be precluded.

Involving the Classroom Teacher

Whether the child is removed from the classroom daily for half an hour or spends a half-day in a remedial class, it is imperative that the classroom teacher be kept continuously informed about the child's progress. She should also actively involve herself in the remediation program by providing the child with supplementary work in other school subjects. For example, she should be aware of the spelling list for each week so that it can be "worked into" the child's social studies lessons, for example, or his English language exercises. Some reading programs have a supplementary set of workbooks which the child can work through in regular class time if the remedial and class teachers get together and coordinate the program. Every effort should be made by the two teachers to work closely and harmoniously together in an integrated program under the general direction of the remedial teacher. As remediation comes to an end, the cooperative effort will have laid the groundwork for gradually phasing the program over to the classroom teacher without a break in continuity or approach. If this is done, it is less likely that there will be a remission of the academic improvement made by the child (Schiffman, 1964).

Organizing a Diagnostic Team

Many school districts or sets of districts already have the nucleus of a diagnostic team. By selecting an experienced remedial teacher or two, an educational psychologist, a speech therapist, a school pediatrician and a social worker, some of whom can work part-time, and by giving them shared office space (in addition to their other offices), a Learning Disabilities Center can be formed. The remedial teacher or psychologist should be the executive director of the group, and a competent secretary will be required to organize the children. Referrals should be able to be made from any source: schools, the family, doctors or other agencies. The reading center should work closely with the speech and hearing clinic and the child guidance clinic, but care should be taken to not accept children who are seriously emotionally disturbed. Children accepted for the clinic should have an IQ of 85 or over on at least one scale of the WISC. In order to avoid overloading the center with socially disadvantaged children of low intelligence (on tests) who should be catered to in other programs, referrals to the center should be on a quota basis. Quotas should be made on the basis of IQ groupings, subject-matter groupings and types of schools. Thus, a highly intelligent boy of thirteen in high school whose only handicap is very poor spelling would be able to find a remedial place in the center. Finally, the whole staff, including the diagnostic team, should have funds to take summer courses, attend conventions and purchase textbooks, while the learning disabilities center itself should be lavishly equipped in every imaginable way. A few centers approximating the type described already exist in various countries around the world and there are quite a few in the United States. However, many more are urgently required.

Often emotionally disturbed children also have learning disabilities, and it is my experience that in many cases, if they can be taught to read and can be given pride in academic achievement through an improved self-concept, their emotional disturbance will be somewhat ameliorated. The traditional child guidance clinic has had only limited success with emotionally disturbed children using traditional psychotherapy and play therapy. More emphasis on remediating the learning disabilities of severely emotionally disturbed children should be given consideration as an alternative treatment, not forgetting that it is the adult-child relationship which is fundamental to motivation (see Chapter XIII). Perhaps many child guidance clinics could be turned into learning disability centers catering primarily to maladjusted children.

SOURCES OF FURTHER INFORMATION ON REMEDIATION

It is impossible in one chapter to indicate in detail each specific remedial technique, and therefore the following sources are recommended for that purpose: Money (1962), Money and Schiffman (1966), Hellmuth (1965), Valett (1967), Johnson and Myklebust (1967), Cruickshank (1966), Morley (1965), Karnes *et al.* (1966b), Bereiter and Engelmann (1966), Stuart (1963) and four journals, *The Journal of Learning Disabilities, Academic Therapy, The Reading Teacher* (International Reading Association) and the *Orton Society Bulletin.* A directory of learning disability centers and schools entitled "Annual Directory of Facilities for the Learning Disabled" (1970), is already available from the Academic Therapy Press, San Rafael, California.

Chapter XVI

THE FUTURE

Sometimes one hears people say that the authorities in the area of reading, dyslexia and hearing disabilities disagree about the nature of these disorders, their etiology, their remediation and of course their definitions and labels. But this is an exaggeration of the true situation. Those who have personally worked extensively in diagnosing and remediating learning disability children are in much more agreement than disagreement about etiology, dysfunctions and remediation. As the research evidence builds up, it is becoming more and more apparent that almost everyone is correct in his viewpoint simply because, as I have tried to show in this book, the field is heterogeneous and very complex. Thus, each person, seeing it from a different perspective, stresses some aspects more than others. As future research increases in scope and more precisely delineates the groups, most of the remaining differences will disappear even though, in a way, this is not entirely a constructive trend. In almost every area of every profession, there is and should be some disagreement, which catalyzes both interest and progress in terms of knowledge.

THE CHILDREN

I have transferred several children from classes for the educationally mentally handicapped back to the regular school simply because other psychologists, using the Stanford-Binet Intelligence Scale (which is highly verbal), had originally classified them as having IQ's under 75. Two of these children had Spatial Ability equivalent IQ's of over 135. Recently, I tested a girl with a Stanford-Binet IQ of 45 who had a Spatial Ability equivalent IQ (Picture Completion plus Block Design plus Object Assembly, prorated) of 114. Her Block Design score was 15/20 (10/20 is average). Psychologists, administrators and educators must come to realize that the WISC, WAIS or WPPSI should be used as an intelligence scale for screening educationally mentally handicapped and learning disability children; furthermore, the subtests should be thoroughly scrutinized before a decision is made which is going to affect the child's whole future. Any subtest scaled score over 10 in an otherwise low record should be examined carefully. To say that verbal intelligence tests are the best predictors of scholastic achievement is a very tight and erroneous circular argument, longitudinally speaking. If verbal tests are used as the best predictors of achievement in the sciences of engineering, architecture, mathematics and medicine, and in many other occupations which involve spatial ability, then many potentially successful professionals in these areas will be needlessly screened out. How many bright genetic dyslexic boys are now mechanics who could have been professional engineers?

Without doubt, not a few genetic dyslexic and MND children (though for different reasons) suffer from a maturational lag in development which may render them less able to learn elementary reading and arithmetic skills in the first and second grades. Provision must be made in the educational system for these children to be taught continuously at their own rate of progression and with books and materials suited to their age levels and interests, so that they do not become dropouts as a result of getting farther and farther behind their peers. Most dyslexic children can read—they just read significantly less well than their intelligence would suggest.

Very occasionally, one comes across gifted dyslexic children who may be in one of two categories. The first group tends to be spatially gifted, whether they are artistic, excellent scientists or mechanical wizards, while the other group is verbally gifted and should have been taught to read at the age of two or three. It is worth mentioning again that Einstein, whose IQ was estimated at over 200, did not learn to speak properly until he was three, and did not learn to read until he was seven. The eminent physicist Niels Bohr (so I am told) and Leonardo da Vinci were mirror writers. One dyslexic child I taught invented, at the age of thirteen, a record player which did not require the records to be turned over to play the second side. Another boy, who could not read at the age of seven, was a genius who achieved six out of ten maximum scaled scores of 20 each on the subtests of the WISC. The other four subtests were 15, 16, 18 and 19, all at the age of seven in a child *not able to read.* It should not be assumed that dyslexic children are all dull or of only average intelligence.

PEOPLE AND TEAMWORK

Educational and mental health administrators on all levels must be made aware of the problems of learning disability children and the need to provide for them. In particular, directors of special education should come to realize that many children have been misclassified and placed in inappropriate classes who should be receiving attention as learning disability cases. They should also know that it is more economical to find them and teach them correctly in the first grade (Schiffman, 1964).

School principals and regular class teachers also need to be made aware of learning disability children who all too often are labeled as "lazy." It is especially important for regular class teachers to be briefed on the common signs and symptoms exhibited by learning disability children in general and the various types of dyslexic children in particular. They should feel no loss of self-esteem about not being able to teach these children in the regular classroom—they are often very difficult to teach even in a high specialized learning disability center. Rather, the regular class teacher should come to feel slightly guilty if she does *not* refer suspected learning disability cases for a specialized examination.

Many more learning disability teachers will have to be trained to cope with the increasing numbers of children who are detected as being in need of help. Training center and university courses should be short and intensive and the programs themselves should be eclectic in approach. Teachers of dyslexic children require a considerable amount of patience; the teacher often feels that dyslexic children, being intelligent by all the usual standards, should make rapid progress, and she is inclined to become irritable when her expectations are not met. The educational psychologist on the learning disabilities team will need to have had very broad experience in both education and child psychology. In England, all educational psychologists have to be qualified experienced teachers as well as possessing a degree in psychology and appropriate postgraduate training, an admirable set of requirements. If they work in a learning disabilities center, psychologists should also take occasional cases personally for remediation. Each member of the team should learn to listen carefully to what the remedial teachers have to say about the children; usually, teachers know "what is what" but their opinion is not sought. Everyone must have adequate and pleasant surroundings in which to work and very often the most satisfactory and readily available type of building is a solid old house with many rooms. If a new building is being erected, the walls and doors should be soundproof, the windows double-glazed and hung with drapes and all the floors carpeted.

A NEW TYPE OF TEACHER SPECIALIST

I would strongly suggest that a new type of special educator be trained, one who is qualified to work equally competently with children who have *speech and hearing difficulties, emotional disturbance* or *learning disabilities.* Such a person might have some such name as Specialist in the Education and Rehabilitation of Dysfunctioning Children. In many towns and suburbs, there is only one center or clinic of one type (reading, speech and hearing, guidance, etc.) and this specialist would expand its activities in several needed directions.

TESTS

There is a need to develop more precise, pure and predictively accurate diagnostic tests. Most of those that exist at the moment have been haphazardly developed, borrowed or adapted because of the urgency of the situation and the lack of financial support. There is a tremendous need for a *federally sponsored Children's Test Agency,* which would be extremely well funded to devise, create, construct and standardize all kinds of psychoneurological, psychological and educational tests for children. The director of the agency should have full *professional* responsibility for its operation without reference to a professional board or superior.

It is worth emphasizing, again, the need for screening tests in the first grade which will isolate potential learning disability cases and enable them to be taught correctly in the first place. It seems incredible that so much time, money and effort is being spent on "patching up" children, when a really good first-grade screening and tuition program would eliminate the need for almost 90 percent of remediation within five years. The money saved would pay many times over for a crash research program.

There is a lack of pre- and post-achievement tests which would assess children's academic abilities much more thoroughly at the first-, second- and third-grade levels. Most achievement tests at the moment are not truly *diagnostic* in "task analysis" terms. Many more academic tests should be expressly designed for learning disability children.

EDUCATIONAL PROGRAMS

Although many remedial techniques have been thoroughly developed and a wide variety are already available, there is still a great deal of room for improvement. In particular, there is need for more precision in the application of remedial methods, a topic which will be further elaborated below.

The continuing shortage of learning disability teachers means that children are going to have to work more on their own so that the teachers can handle larger groups. Therefore, fully programmed self-correcting remedial courses for children will have to be constructed, some of them highly specific in nature. Publishers and manufacturers will have to become more aware of the expanding learning disability market and stop regarding specialized educational materials as unprofitable.

Programmed course work, if it is to involve children in multisensorimotor activities, will require quite elaborate electronic audiovisual equipment, and education authorities will have to get used to the idea of furnishing learning disability centers elec-

tronically. First-class equipment in an affluent technological society can go a long way to make up for a shortage of teachers.
Besides, dyslexic children in general prefer an activity-workshop
approach to learning and provided the curriculum content is
intrinsically interesting and they are personally well rewarded
for their efforts, they will work away happily and independently.
This will occur only when the teacher-child relationship is particularly sound.

PREVENTION PROGRAMS

If all children are screened for potential learning disabilities
within six weeks of their entry in the first grade, there will be a
need for carefully thought-out reading, writing, spelling and
arithmetic programs and motivational reinforcers which will train
the children correctly in these subjects, thus preventing most
disabilities from ever occurring. The Psycholinguistic Color System (Bannatyne, 1968b) is one such program. Obviously, the
reading and other first-grade work programs as they are presently
constituted are not doing this and will need to be supplemented
by the proposed prevention courses. These are best administered
by the classroom teacher, who would be able to consult with
expert personnel on the regular assessment and prescription writing for serious cases.

Part of the dyslexia problem lies in such matters as early language training, and ideally, screening devices and predictors of
learning (and other) disabilities should be available to families
from birth onward. Eventually, there is no reason why such high-
risk groups as premature babies, asphyxiated children and genetic
dyslexic families should not have access to training programs
which would compensate for or ameliorate deficits almost before
they arise. Most parents would welcome such a plan. For example,
musical records could be made which might stimulate infants
into listening intently. One set of "baby" records has been made
by the Gesell Institute of Child Development and is sold commercially.

RESEARCH

Too much of the research in the area in learning disabilities and, in particular, dyslexia, has been small-scale and piecemeal in nature. Biased clinical samples and unrepresentative school-based samples abound. Ideally, a very large school district or group of districts comprising both city, suburban and rural communities should invite an expert research team (federally funded) to carry through large-scale ten-year research in screening, identification, diagnosis and remediation, not to mention follow-up studies.

Statistically, such a research project would be facilitated by the invention of computerized clustering techniques (not factor analysis) which would group characteristics and attributes for accurate syndrome-sorting data analysis. The objectives of such research are purely practical, because if homogeneous groups of learning disability children can be delineated, whole-group teaching with all its economies in time, money and effort becomes a viable proposition. However, a gross, oversimplified, once-only clustering research would probably not be enough because experience has shown that the tuition of dyslexic children calls for extreme precision of content and technique. Therefore, any continuing research would need to become more and more detailed.

Time is one of our most important elements, economically speaking, and the more precisely remedial methods can be matched to specific deficits, the more rapid remediation will be, with a consequent increase in turnover. Therefore, any research which investigates "track advancement effectors" should be encouraged. Remedial teachers can assist in this respect by keeping a detailed log of those aspects of their lessons which cause children to move ahead rapidly; in doing so, they should not forget the influence of motivators. Any really helpful techniques or constructed aids should be written up and published in appropriate journals. See Bannatyne *et al.* (1970) for a detailed research on the process analysis of tutoring.

Genetic factors in dyslexia urgently require investigation on the lines indicated above. If genetic dyslexic children can be identified at a very early age, much might be done in preschool years to improve their language functioning, thus preventing the problem of dyslexia from arising in the elementary school. Some people have the opinion that because something is "genetic" or caused by "neurological dysfunction" it cannot be prevented. On the contrary, once the causal factors have been discovered, a training program can commence which is all the more intensive in order to remediate the deficits.

As part of a major research project, a comprehensive longitudinal study of learning disabilities should be initiated on a representative sample of children, who preferably have been selected at birth on the basis of being in one of the various high-risk categories. Longitudinal research such as this would investigate etiological factors in detail and set up predictive hypotheses concerning the outcome for these children educationally and socially.

FINANCIAL SUPPORT

All the facilities and projects mentioned above will require considerable financial support. The investment, however, will be more than compensated for in the money saved with respect to what might have been the future lives of these children. The payoff in terms of human values would be immeasurable. Many illiterate boys are delinquent, and in a technological society, poorly educated citizens are far less productive than the well educated. A genetic dyslexic boy who is prevented from becoming a professional person simply because nobody has taught him how to spell is contributing far less to the community than he should be. The sociopathic boy who has to be kept in a corrective or penal institution by the state will account for a much larger sum of money than would have been spent remediating his reading problem. Investment in the prevention and early remediation of learning disabilities in intelligent children will save the community money even in the short run.

THE WIDER IMPLICATIONS OF DYSLEXIA

Some countries and states have passed laws which state that every child must be educated according to his or her individual needs, talents and disabilities. Every child has the birthright that the society in which he lives should give him the opportunity to develop to his *maximum potential in terms of both health and education*, and in an affluent democratic society anything less is sheer negligence. It is incumbent upon every country, state and school district to insure that the children in its charge, especially those with handicaps, receive an education and health care which will develop their capacities to their fullest potential.

As has been previously mentioned, some dyslexic children are well above average in intelligence and provided they are given successful remediation in childhood, there is no reason why they should not eventually attend the university. However, too often the prerequisites required for many courses by universities prevent bright dyslexics from entering their preferred profession. Foreign language requirements can be a bother and even core subjects such as English may be a barrier to success. Any examiner who is intolerant of poor spelling may fail a dyslexic child because educators traditionally equate poor spelling with a lack of intelligence. In England, a precedent was set by the Oxford and Cambridge Universities entrance examining board when it kindly agreed to disregard the spelling of a bright genetic dyslexic boy; he passed in every subject except English—which he passed on the second attempt. Some dyslexic children find it difficult to retain isolated facts and recall them at will, and they will find it difficult to cope with those time-limited machine-marked examinations which consist of a list of dozens of short questions requiring single "recall" answers. Older genetic dyslexics seem to do much better at essay-type examinations in which they can present short logical discussions.

Most elementary and even secondary schools are staffed by women teachers, with the result that the curriculum offered is invariably highly verbal and oriented to a female viewpoint. There is little opportunity for boys to identify with a male teacher or to get a masculine slant on engineering, transportation, manufacturing, farming, forestry, fishing and so on. In most normal families, the boys can get this identification and communication through a relationship with their father, but all too often, the handicapped child has no father with whom to identify. As it seems unlikely that male teachers will begin to move back into the elementary schools, it is incumbent on the women teachers to insure that the boys in their care have the opportunity to learn about electronics, engines, etc., even at a young age. Not only should the teachers make an effort to study these topics themselves, but they should invite men from the community into the school to describe their work and enthuse the boys.

Although there are many exceptions, most classrooms are still far too passive and verbal in their approach to instruction. There is a need for teachers to be more adventurous by introducing more activity methods, by grouping the children for particular lessons or projects, by using aids and equipment more imaginatively and by allowing much more experimentation in every subject right in the classroom.

Only if all these steps are taken will the number of children who drop out of education, or who are dropped out, significantly decrease. Money to buy better classrooms and a wide variety of equipment and materials will help. These things are very necessary, but they will have no effect on the class unless the teacher herself is strongly motivated to give the children many more enriching experiences for their future lives than they get from traditional coursework. Most schools now systematically set about training children to inhibit their curiosity, stifle their personal self-expression, dislike textbooks and look on school as a place of drudgery, so that ever afterward they regard reading as a boring dry-as-dust duty. Our schools and colleges are mostly mechanical, anxiety-producing, vocational assembly lines turning out automatons who will fit into a million job-slots as neatly and narrowly as keyed programs.

Education is life, and life is experience, evolution and service. Language, reading and communication are skills and tools whose purpose is to enrich that experience, evolution and service for the benefit of both the individual person and society as a whole.

REFERENCES

Abercrombie, M.L.J. (1964): *Perceptual Visuomotor Disorders in Cerebral Palsy*. London, Heinemann.

Academic Therapy, 1543 Fifth St., San Rafael, Calif. 94901.

Adams, J.A. (1967a): Engineering psychology. In Helson, H., and Bevan, W. (Eds.): *Contemporary Approaches to Psychology.** Princeton, N.J., Van Nostrand, pp. 345-383.

Adams, J.A. (1967b): *Human Memory.** New York, McGraw-Hill.

Adams, J.A., and Dijkstra, S. (1966): Short-term memory for motor responses. *J. Exp. Psychol.*, 71:314-318.

Adams, J.A., and Montague, W.E. (1967): Retroactive inhibition and natural language mediation. *J. Verbal Learning, Verbal Behavior*, 6:528-535.

Adams, P.A. (1967): Patterns of intellectual functioning in learning disability children. Paper read to Society for Research in Child Development, New York, N.Y. Mimeographed report from Palo Alto Unified School District, Calif.

Agranowitz, A., and McKeown, M.R. (1963): *Aphasia Handbook: For Adults and Children.** Springfield, Thomas.

Alexander, W.P. (1935): Intelligence, concrete and abstract. *Brit. J. Psychol., Mono. Suppl. 19*, p. 177.

Alwitt, L.F., and Bryant, N.D. (1963): Decay of immediate memory for visually presented digits among non-readers and readers. *J. Educ. Psychol.*, 54:144-148.

Ambrose, J.A. (1960): *The Smiling Response*. Ph.D. dissertation, University of London, England.

Ambrose, J.A. (1961): The development of the smiling response in early infancy. In Foss (1961, 1963), p. 179.

Ames, L.B., and Ilg, F.O. (1964): Sex differences in test performance of matched girl-boy pairs in the five-to-nine-year-old age range. *J. Gen. Psychol.*, 104:25-34.

Amster, H., *et al.* (1970): Learning and retention of letter pairs as a function of association strength. *Amer. J. Psychol.*, Vol. 83, No. 1.

Anderson, J.O. (1944): Aphasia from the viewpoint of a speech pathologist. *J. Speech Dis.*, Vol. 9, No. 3, Sept.

Annett, M., *et al.* (1961): Intellectual disabilities in relation to lateralized features in the EEG. In Abercrombie, M.L.J. (Ed.): *Hemiplegic Cere-*

*Key textbook on a specific topic.
†Test.

bral Palsy in Children and Adults. Report of an International Study Group, No. 4, Clinics in Developmental Medicine. London, Heinemann.

Annual Directory of Facilities for the Learning Disabled (1970): San Rafael, Calif., Academic Therapy Press.

Argyle, M., and Robinson, J. (1962): Two origins of achievement motivation. *Brit. J. Soc. Clin. Psychol.,* Vol. 1, Pt. 2.

Arnold, G.E. (1961): The genetic background of developmental language disorders. *Folia Phoniat. (Basel), 13:*246-254.

Arvidson, G.L. (1961): *Learning to Spell.* Wellington, N.Z., New Zealand Council for Educational Research.

Ashton-Warner, S. (1966): *Teacher.*° Harmondsworth, England, Penguin Books.

Association for Children with Learning Disabilities (1966): *Selected Conference Papers.* San Rafael, Calif., Academic Therapy Press.

Atkinson, J.K., and Hart, J.A. (1963): Establishing sound symbol association with severely retarded readers. *The Slow Learning Child, 10* (No. 2):85-93. Brisbane, Australia, University of Queensland.

Atkinson, R.C., and Hansen, D.N. (1966): Computer assisted instruction in initial reading: The Stanford Project. *Reading Res. Quart.,* Vol. 2, No. 1, Fall.

Ausubel, D.P. (1963): *The Psychology of Meaningful Verbal Learning.*° New York, Grune & Stratton.

Ayres, A.J. (1965): Patterns of perceptual-motor dysfunction in children: A factor analytic study. *Percept. Motor Skills, Mono. Suppl. 1,* Vol. 20.

Ayres, A.J. (1967): Reading—A product of sensory integrative processes. Paper presented at International Reading Association's Twelfth Annual Convention, Seattle, Wash.

Bachrach, D.L. (1964): Sex differences in reaction to delayed auditory feedback. *Percept. Motor Skills, 19:*81-82.

Baddeley, A.D. (1966): Short-term memory for word sequences as a function of acoustic, semantic and formal similarity. *Quart. J. Exp. Psychol., 18:*362-365.

Ballard, P.B. (1920): *Mental and Group Tests†.* London, University of London Press.

Bannatyne, A.D. (1966a): Personal communication with Dr. White Franklin.

Bannatyne, A.D. (1966b): A research evaluating teaching machines for junior school use. *Programmed Learning,* Vol. 3, No. 1.

Bannatyne, A.D. (1966c): Verbal and spatial abilities and reading. Paper presented at First International Reading Association Congress, Paris, France. Newark, Del., International Reading Association.

Bannatyne, A.D. (1966d): *Color Phonics System.* (See Bannatyne, 1968b.)

Bannatyne, A.D. (1966e): The Color Phonics System. In Money and Schiffman (1966), Chap. 12.

Bannatyne, A.D. (1966f): The etiology of dyslexia: *The Slow Learning Child*. (Aust. J. on Ed. of Backward Children.) Vol. 13, No. 1, July. Brisbane, University of Queensland.

Bannatyne, A.D. (1966g): A suggested classification of the causes of dyslexia. *Word Blind Bull.*, Vol. 1, Spring.

Bannatyne, A.D. (1967a): *Matching Remedial Methods with Specific Deficits*. Published Proceedings of 1967 International Convocation on Children and Young Adults with Learning Disabilities. Pittsburgh, Feb.

Bannatyne, A.D. (1967b): The etiology of dyslexia and the Color Phonics System. *Proceedings of the Third Annual Conference of Association for Children with Learning Disabilities, Tulsa, Okla.* San Rafael, Calif., Academic Therapy Press.

Bannatyne, A.D. (1967c): The transfer from the modality perceptual to the modality conceptual. In *Percept. and Reading*, Vol. 12, Pt. 4. Newark, Del., International Reading Association.

Bannatyne, A.D. (1968a): Diagnosing learning disabilities and prescribing remediation. *J. Learning Dis.*, Vol. 1, No. 4, Apr.

Bannatyne, A.D. (1968b): *Psycholinguistic Color System: A Reading, Writing, Spelling and Language Program*. Urbana, Ill., Learning Systems Press. (P.O. Box 64)

Bannatyne, A.D. (1968c): *Visuo-Spatial Memory Test*. Available for research purposes from the author.

Bannatyne, A.D. (1969): *A Comparison of Visuo-Spatial and Visuo-Motor Memory for Designs and their Relationship to other Sensori-motor and Psycholinguistic Variables*. *J. Learning Dis.*, Sept.

Bannatyne, A.D., and Cotterell, G. (1966): Spelling for the dyslexic child. *Word Blind Bull.*, Winter.

Bannatyne, A.D., and Wichiarajote, P. (1969a): Relationships between written spelling, motor functioning and sequencing skills. *J. Learning Dis.*, Jan.

Bannatyne, A.D., and Wichiarajote, P. (1969b): Hemispheric "dominance," learned and unlearned handedness, mirror imaging, and auditory sequencing: A research report. *Exceptional Child.*, Sept.

Bannatyne, A.D., and Bannatyne, M. (1970): *Motivation Management Materials (Elementary Level)*. South Miami, Fla., Kismet Publishing Company. P.O. Box 90

Bannatyne, M., and Bannatyne, A.D. (1970): *Body Image/Communication: A Psycho-Physical Development Program*. South Miami, Fla., Kismet Publishing Company. (P.O. Box 90)

Bannatyne, A.D., et al. (1970): One-to-one process analysis of learning disability tutorial sessions. *J. Learning Dis.*, Sept., Oct., and Nov.

Baron, K.D. (1963): *Teach Yourself To Spell*. London, English Universities Press.

Barsch, R.H. (1965): *A Movigenic Curriculum.* Bull. No. 25, State Department of Public Instruction, Madison, Wisc.

Bartlctt, F.C. (1932): *Remembering.* London, University of London Press.

Bateman, B. (1967a): *Reading: A Controversial View—Research and Rationale.* Curriculum Bull. No. 278, Vol. 23, School of Education, University of Oregon, Eugene.

Bateman, B. (1967b): Three eras in the education of children with learning disabilities. International Convocation on Children and Young Adults with Learning Disabilities. Pittsburgh, Pa., Feb.

Bayley, N., and Jones, M. (1955): Physical maturing among boys as related to behavior. In Martin, W.E., and Stendler, C.C. (Eds.): *Readings in Child Development.* New York, Harcourt.

Bayley, N., and Schaeffer, E.S. (1964): Correlations of maternal and child behaviors with development of mental abilities. Berkeley Growth Study. Monograph of Society for Research in Child Development, Ser. No. 97, Vol. 29, No. 6, p. 80.

Beard, R.M. (1965): The structure of perception: A factorial study. *Brit. J. Educ. Psychol., 35* (Pt. 2):210.

Beery, K.E., and Buktenica, N. (1967): *Beery-Buktenica Developmental Test of Visual-Motor Integration.*† Chicago, Follett.

Bellugi, U., and Brown, R. (1964): *Acquisition of Language.* Monograph of Society for Research in Child Development, Ser. No. 92, Vol. 29, No. 1.

Belmont, L., and Birch, H.G. (1965): Lateral dominance, lateral awareness and reading disability. *Child Develop.,* Vol. 36, No. 1.

Bender, L. (1938): *A Visual-Motor Gestalt Test and Its Clinical Use.*† Res. Mono. No. 3, American Orthopedics Association, New York, N.Y.

Bender, L. (1963): Specific reading disability as a maturational lag. *Bull. Orton Soc.,* Vol. 13.

Bene, E., and Anthony, E.J. (1957): *Family Relations Test.*† The Mere, Slough, England, National Foundation for Educational Research in England and Wales.

Benson, D.F. (1970): Graphic orientation disorders of left-handed children. *J. Learning Dis.,* Vol. 3, No. 3.

Bentley, A. (1966): *Measures of Musical Abilities.* New York, October House.

Benton, A.L. (1958): Significance of systematic reversal in right-left discrimination. *Acta Psychiat. Neurol. Scand.,* 33:129-137.

Benton, A.L. (1959): Benton protocol for right-left discrimination. In Benton, A.L. *Right-Left Discrimination and Finger Localization: Development and Pathology.* New York, Hoeber-Harper.

Benton, A.L. (1962): Discussion of session on Clinical symptomatology in right and left hemispheric lesions, by H. Hecaen. In Mountcastle (1962).

Benton, A.L. (1963): *The Revised Visual Retention Test.*† New York, Psychological Corporation.

Benton, A.L. (1966): The problem of cerebral dominance. *Bull. Orton Soc.,* Vol. 16.

Benton, A.L., and Kemble, J.D. (1960): Right-left orientation and reading disability. *Psychiat. Neurol. (Basel),* 139:49-60.

Bentzen, F. (1963): Sex ratios in learning and behavior disorders. *Amer. J. Orthopsychiat.,* Jan.

‡Bentzen, F. (1966): Sex ratios in learning and behavior disorders. *The National Elementary Principal,* Vol. XLVI, No. 2, Nov.

Bereiter, C., and Engelmann, S. (1966): *Teaching Disadvantaged Children in the Preschool.*° Englewood Cliffs, N.J., Prentice-Hall.

Berkowitz, L. (1962): *Aggression: A Social Psychological Analysis.*° New York, McGraw-Hill.

Berkowitz, L. (1967): The frustration-aggression hypothesis revisited. Notes from speech given at University of Illinois, Urbana, Sept.

Bernstein, B. (1961a): Aspects of language and learning in the genesis of the social process. *J. Child Psychol. Psychiat.,* 1:313-324.

Bernstein, B. (1961b): Social structure, language and learning. *Educ. Res. (NFER),* 3:3.

Biggs, J.H. (1962): *Anxiety, Motivation and Primary School Mathematics.* The Mere, Slough, England, National Foundation for Educational Research in England and Wales.

Bijou, S.W., and Baer, D.M. (1961, 1965): *Child Development I: A Systematic and Empirical Theory.*° New York, Appleton-Century-Crofts.

Biller, H.B. (1970): Father absence and the personality development of the male child. *Develop. Psychol.,* Vol. 2, No. 2.

Birch, H.G. (1964): *Brain Damage in Children: The Biological and Social Aspects.*° Baltimore, Williams & Wilkins.

Birch, H.G., and Belmont, L. (1964a): Perceptual analysis and sensory integration in brain-damaged persons. *J Genet. Psychol.,* 105:173-179.

Birch, H.G., and Belmont, L. (1964b): Auditory-visual integration in normal and retarded readers. *Amer. J. Orthopsychiat.,* 34:5.

Birch, H.G., and Belmont, L. (1965a): Social differences in auditory perception, *Percept. Motor Skills,* 20:861-870.

Birch, H.G., and Belmont, L. (1965b); Auditory-visual integration, intelligence and reading ability in school children. *Percept. Motor Skills,* 20:295-305.

Birch, H.G., and Belmont, L. (1965c): Auditory-visual integration in brain-damaged and normal children. *Develop. Med. Child Neurol.,* 7:135.

Birch, H.G., and Lefford, A. (1963): Intersensory development in children. *Child Develop.,* Mono. 89, Vol. 28, No. 5.

Birch, H.G., *et al.* (1964a): Excitation-inhibition balance in brain-damaged patients. *J. Nerv. Ment. Dis.*, Vol. 39, No. 6.

Birch, H.G., *et al.* (1964b): Behavioral development in brain-damaged children. *Arch. Gen. Psychiat. (Chicago)*, 2:596-603.

Bishop, W.E. (1968): Successful teachers of the gifted. *Exceptional Child.*, Jan.

Blau, T.H., and Schaffer, R.E. (1960): The Spiral After-Effect Test (SAET) as a predictor of normal and abnormal EEG records in children. *J. Consult. Psychol.*, 24:35-42.

Bleismer, E.P., and Yarborough, B.H. (1965): An evaluation of ten different reading programmes. Talk given at A.E.R.A., Chicago, Ill. Published by *Phi Delta Kappan*, June.

Blewett, D.B. (1954): An experimental study of the inheritance of intelligence. *J. Ment. Sci.*, 106:922-933.

Bloomfield, L., and Barnhart, C.L. (1961): *Let's Read: A Linguistic Approach*. Detroit, Wayne State University Press.

Bocca, E., *et al.* (1954): A new method for testing hearing in temporal lobe tumors. *Acta Otolaryng. (Stockholm)*, 44:219-221.

Bonin, C. von, *et al.* (1942): The functional organization of the occipital lobe. *Biol. Symp.*, 7.

Boshes, B., and Myklebust, H.R. (1964): A neurological and behavioral study of children with learning disorders. *Neurology*, 14:7-12.

Bower, E.M., and Lambert, N.M. (1965): In-school screening of children with emotional handicaps. In *Conflict in the Classroom*. Belmont, Calif., Wadsworth.

Bower, T.G.R. (1966): The visual world of infants. *Sci. Amer.*, Dec.

Bowlby, J. (1957): An ethological approach to research in child development. *Brit. J. Med. Psychol.*, 30 (Pt. 4): 230-240.

Bowlby, J. (1958): The nature of the child's tie to his mother. *Int. J. Psychoanal.*, Vol. 34, Pt. 5.

Bowlby, J. (1961): Processes of mourning. *Int. J. Psychoanal.*, 42 (Pts. 4-5): 317-340.

Boxall, J. (1962): Anxiety retardation in reading. Paper presented at Annual Conference, Educational Section, British Psychological Society, Sept.

Bradley, C. (1958): Tranquilizing drugs in pediatrics. *Pediatrics*, Vol. 21, No. 2, Feb.

Breland, K., and Breland, M. (1961): The misbehavior of organisms. *Amer. Psychol.*, 16 (No. 11):681-684.

Bremer, *et al.* (1956): Physiologie et pathologie du corps calleux. *Arch. Suisses Neurol. Psychiat.*, 78:31-87.

Brendtro, L.K. (1965): Verbal and conceptual factors in pre-adolescent boys with impaired relationship capacity. Ph.D. dissertation, University of Michigan, Ann Arbor.

Brewer, W.F. (1963): Specific language disability: Review of the literature and a family study. Honors thesis, Harvard University, Cambridge, Mass.

Broadbent, D.E. (1958): *Perception and Communication.*° New York, Pergamon Press.

Broadbent, D.E. (1962): Attention and the perception of speech. *Sci. Amer.,* Apr.

Broverman, D.M. (1960): Dimensions of cognitive style. *J. Personality, 28:* 167-185.

Broverman, D.M. (1964): Generality and behavioral correlates of cognitive styles. *J. Consult. Psychol., 28:*487-500.

Broverman, D.M., *et al.* (1964): The automatization, cognitive style and physical development. *Child Develop.,* 35:1343.

Brown, J.R., and Simonson, J. (1957): A clinical study of 100 aphasic patients. *Neurology,* 7:777-783.

Brown, R., and Fraser, C. (1964): The acquisition of syntax. In Bellugi and Brown (1964).

Bruun, K., *et al.* (1966): *Inheritance of Drinking Behavior, a Study of Adult Twins.* Helsinki, The Finnish Foundation for Alcohol Research.

Bryant, N.D. (1964): Some conclusions concerning impaired motor development among reading disability cases. *Bull. Orton Soc.,* 14:16-17.

Bryden, M.P. (1964): Tachistoscopic recognition and cerebral dominance. *Percept. Motor Skills,* 19:686.

Bryden, M.P., and Rainey, C.A. (1963): Left-right differences in tachistoscopic recognition. *J. Exp. Psychol.,* 66:568-571.

Buchanan, C.D. (1963): *A Programmed Introduction to Linguistics: Phonetics and Phonemics.* Boston, Heath.

Buckley, M.S., and Lamb, E.B. (1960): *The Phonovisual Game Book.* Washington, D.C., Phonovisual Products.

Buddeke, R. (1960): *Differential Factorial Patterns of Boys and Girls in Algebraic Computations.* Washington, D.C., Catholic University of America Press.

Burke, F. (1898): Growth of children in height and weight. *Amer. J. Psychol.,* 9:253-329.

Buros, O.K. (1965): *The Sixth Mental Measurements Yearbook.* Highland Park, N.J., Gryphon Press.

Burt, C. (1937, 1950): *The Backward Child.* London, University of London Press.

Butterfield, E.C. (1968): Serial learning and the stimulus trace theory of mental retardation. *Amer. J. Ment. Defic.,* 72 (No. 5):778-787.

Calvert, J.J., and Cromes, G.F. (1966): Oculomotor spasms in handicapped readers. *Reading Teacher,* Dec.

Carrow, M.A. (1968): The development of auditory comprehension of language structure in children. *J. Speech Hearing Dis.,* Vol. 33, No. 2, May.

Carter, C.O. (1962): *Human Heredity*. Harmondsworth, England, Penguin Books.

Cattell, R.B. (1960): The multiple abstract variance analysis equations and solutions: For nature-nurture research on continuous variables. *Psychol. Rev.*, 67:353-372.

Cattell, R.B., and Warburton, F.W. (1967): *Objective Personality and Motivation Tests.*† Urbana, University of Illinois Press.

Chall, J.S. (1967): *Learning To Read: The Great Debate.*° New York, McGraw-Hill.

Childs, S.B., and Childs, R.S. (1962): *Sound Phonics*. Cambridge, Mass., Educators Publishing Service.

Childs, S.B., and Childs, R.S. (1965): *Magic Squares*. Cambridge, Mass., Educators Publishing Service.

Chomsky, N. (1957): *Syntactic Structures*. The Hague, Mouton.

Chomsky, N. (1959): A review of B.F. Skinner's verbal behavior. *Language*, Vol. 35, Jan.-Mar.

Chomsky, N. (1964): Discussion of Miller and Ervin (1964). In Bellugi and Brown (1964).

Churchill, J.A. (1966): Pregnant woman's diet may affect baby's I.Q. *Med. News*, Mar. 4.

Clark, M.M. (1957): *Left-Handedness.*° London, London University Press.

Clements, S.D. (1966): *Minimal Brain Dysfunction in Children: Phase One.*° Washington, D.C., U.S. Department of Health, Education and Welfare, NINDB Monogr. No. 3, Public Health Service Publ. No. 1415.

†Clements, S.D. (1967): Some aspects of the characteristics, management and education of the child with minimal brain dysfunction. Glen Ellyn, Ill., West Suburban Assoc. for the Other Child.

†Cohen, A., and Glass, G.G. (1968): Lateral dominance and reading ability. *Reading Teacher*, Vol. 21, No. 4, 343-348, Jan.

Connolly, K. (1966): The genetics of behavior. In Foss, B.M. (Ed.): *New Horizons in Psychology*. Harmondsworth, England, Penguin Books, Chap. 9.

Conrad, K. (1949): Ueber aphasiche sprach-stoerungen bei hirnverletzten linkshaender. *Nervenarzt*, 20:148-154.

Conrad, R. (1962): An association between memory errors and errors due to acoustic masking of speech. *Nature*, 193:1314-1315.

Conrad, R. (1964): Acoustic confusions in immediate memory. *Brit. J. Psychol.*, 55:75-84.

Conrad, R., and Hull, A.J. (1964): Information, acoustic confusion and memory span. *Brit. J. Psychol.*, 55:429-432.

Cooke, B. (1968): The relationship between balance, performance and cognitive abilities. Ph.D. dissertation, University of Illinois, Urbana.

Coopersmith, S. (1968): Studies in self-esteem. *Sci. Amer.*, Feb.

Cowen, E.L., *et al.* (1965): The relation of anxiety in school children to school record, achievement and behavioral measures. *Child Develop.,* 36:685-695.

Critchley, M. (1953): *The Parietal Lobes.* London, Arnold.

Critchley, M. (1962): Speech and speech-loss in relation to the duality of the brain. In Mountcastle (1962).

Critchley, M. (1964): *Developmental Dyslexia.** London, Heinemann.

Cruickshank, W.M. (Ed.) (1966): *The Teacher of Brain-Injured Children.** Syracuse, N.Y., Syracuse University Special Education and Rehabilitation Monogr., Ser. 7.

Cuisenaire (1953): Cuisenaire Kits and Books, Cuisenaire Company of America, Inc. New Rochelle, N.Y.

Daniels, J.C., and Dyack, H. (1960): *Royal Road Readers.* Cambridge, Mass., Educators Publishing Service.

Davids, A., *et al.* (1957): The relation of the Archimedes spiral after-effect and the trail making test to brain damage in children. *J. Consult. Psychol.,* 21:429-433.

Davis, R., *et al.* (1961): Information content in recognition and recall. *J. Exp. Psychol.,* 61:422-429.

Day, E.J. (1932): The development of language in twins: I. A comparison of twins and single children. *Child Develop.,* 3:179.

Delacato, C.H. (1954): *The Treatment and Prevention of Reading Problems.* Springfield, Thomas.

Delacato, C.H. (1964): *The Diagnosis and Treatment of Speech and Reading Problems.* Springfield, Thomas.

Della-Piana, G., and Martin, G. (1966): Reading achievement and maternal behavior. *Reading Teacher,* Dec.

Denny-Brown, D. (1958): The nature of apraxia. *J. Nerv. Ment. Dis., 126:* 9-32.

Denny-Brown, D. (1962): Discussion of session on Clinical symptomatology in right and left hemispheric lesions. In Mountcastle (1962).

Deutsch, M. (1967): Problems of compensatory education programs. Paper read to Claremont Reading Conference, Claremont, Calif., Feb.

Dicarlo, L.M. (1960): Differential diagnosis of congenital aphasia. Reprint No. 743. Washington, D.C., Volta Bureau.

Dinnan, J.A., *et al.* (1970): Auditory feedback—stutterers versus nonstutterers. *J. Learning Dis.,* Vol. 3, No. 4.

Dolan, G.K. (1964): Counseling as an aid for delayed readers. *J. Reading,* 8:129-135.

Dolch, E.W. (1960): *Better Spelling.* Champaign, Ill., Garrard Press.

Doll, E.A. (1946): *The Oseretsky Tests of Motor Proficiency: A Translation from the Portugese Adaptation.†* Minneapolis, Minn., American Guidance Service.

Doll, E.A. (1959): *Vineland Social Maturity Scale.*† Minneapolis, Minn., American Guidance Service.

Doman, G. (1964): *How To Teach Your Baby To Read.* New York, Random House.

Domrath, R.P. (1968): Constructional praxis and visual perception in school children. *J. Consult. Clin. Psychol.*, Vol. 32, No. 2, Apr.

Douglas, J.W.B. (1964): *The Home and the School.** London, MacGibbon and Kee.

Downer, J.L. (1962): Interhemispheric integration in the visual system. In Mountcastle (1962).

Downing, J. (1967): *Evaluating the Initial Teaching Alphabet.** London, Cassell.

Downing, J. (1968): The implications of research on children's thinking for the early stages of learning to read. Paper read at Claremont Reading Conference, Claremont, Calif.

Drake, C. (1965): The diagnosis and treatment of dyslexia in children. Paper presented at Massachusetts General Hospital, May.

Drake, C. (1966a): *P.E.R.C. Auditory Discrimination Test.*† Wellesley, Mass., Perceptual and Educational Research Center.

Drake, C. (1966b): Time for a new look at the "Minimal Brain Damage" hypothesis. In *International Approach to Learning Disabilities of Children and Youth.* Association for Children with Learning Disabilities. Convention Selected Papers, Tulsa, Okla. San Rafael, Calif., Academic Therapy Press.

Drake, C., and Schnall, M. (1966): Decoding problems in reading. *Pathways in Child Guidance,* Vol. 8, No. 2, Apr.

Drever, J. (1963): *A Dictionary of Psychology.* Harmondsworth, England, Penguin Books.

Dulin, K.L. (1970): Using context clues in word recognition and comprehension. *Reading Teacher,* Vol. 23, No. 5.

Duncan, R. (1964): What's the best way to teach reading? *School Management,* pp. 46-47, Dec.

Durkin, D., and Meshover, L. (1964): *Phonics Knowledge Survey.*† New York, Teachers College Press, Columbia University.

Dykstra, R. (1966): Auditory discrimination abilities and beginning reading achievement. *Reading Res. Quart.,* 1:5-34.

Dykstra, R. (1968): The effectiveness of code- and meaning-emphasis beginning reading programs. *Reading Teacher,* Vol. 22, No. 1, Oct.

Eames, T.H. (1960): Some neural and glandular bases of learning. *J. Educ.,* Vol. 42, No. 4.

Ebner, F.F., and Myers, R.E. (1960): Inter- and intra-hemispheric transmission of tactile agnosis in normal and corpus callosum-sectioned monkeys. *Fed. Proc., 19:*292.

Eccles, J.C. (1965): The synapse. *Sci. Amer.*, Jan.

Eccles, J.C. (1966): Conscious experience and memory. In Eccles, J.C. (Ed.): *Brain and Conscious Experience.*° New York, Springer-Verlag, pp. 314-338.

Eisenson, J. (1963): Aphasia and dyslexia in children. *Bull. Orton Soc.*

Ellis, N.R. (1963): The stimulus trace and behavioral inadequacy. In Ellis, N.R. (Ed.): *Handbook of Mental Deficiency.* New York, McGraw-Hill.

Elze, C. (1924): Rechtslinksempfinden und Rechtslinksblindheit. *Z. Psychol.*, 24:129-135; Rechts und Links im Korperschema. *Med. Klin.*, 20: 525-526.

Ernhart, C.B., *et al.* (1963): Brain injury in the preschool child: Some developmental considerations; II. Comparison of brain injured and normal children. *Psychol. Monogr.*, 77 (Nos. 10-11):573-574.

Espschage, A. (1940): Motor performance in adolescence. Society for Research in Child Development, Monograph 5. New York, Harcourt.

Ettlinger, G. (1961): Lateral preferences in monkeys. *Behaviour.* (Details of reference not known.)

Ettinger, G. (1962): Lateral preferences in monkeys. In Mountcastle (1962).

Fairbanks and Robinson (1967): *Perceptual-Motor Development.* Teaching Resources. Boston, New York Times.

Falek, H. (1959): Handedness: A family study. *J. Hum. Genet.*, 11:52-62.

Fant, G. (1967): Auditory patterns of speech. In Wathen-Dunn, W. (Ed.): *Models for the Perception of Speech and Visual Form.* Cambridge, Mass., MIT Press.

Fender, D.H. (1964): Control mechanisms of the eye. *Sci. Amer.*, July.

Fernald, G.M. (1943): *Remedial Techniques in Basic School Subjects.*° New York, McGraw-Hill.

Ferster, C.B. (1967): Arbitrary and natural reinforcement procedures applied to the treatment of institutionalized autistic children. Speech (published) presented at International Convocation on Children and Young Adults with Learning Disabilities. Pittsburgh, Feb. Home for Crippled Children.

Fink, M.B. (1962): Self-concept as it relates to academic under-achievement. *Calif. J. Educ. Res.*, 13:2.

Fisher, G.H. (1963): Objects, models and two-dimensional shapes for use in visual and tactile kinaesthetic shape perception experiments. Thesis, Institute of Education, University of Durham, Newcastle, England.

Fisher, S. (1967): Two tests of perceptual motor function: The draw-a-person and the Bender-Gestalt. Paper read to Society for Research in Child Development, New York, N.Y., Mar. Mimeographed report from Palo Alto Unified School District, Calif.

Forness, S.R., and Weil, M.C. (1970): Laterality in retarded readers with brain dysfunction. *Exceptional Child.*, May.

Forrest, T. (1967): Neurological and medical factors discriminating between normal children and those with learning disability. Paper read to Society for Research in Child Development, New York, N.Y., Mar. Mimeographed report from Palo Alto Unified School District, Calif.

Foss, B.M. (1961): The functions of laughter. *New Scientist*, No. 242, July.

Foss, B.M. (1961, 1963): *Determinants of Infant Behaviour,*° Vols. I and II. New York, Wiley.

Fowler, W.S. (1962): *Fowler's Scientific Spelling: Books 1-4*. Edinburgh, McDougall's Educational Co.

Freeman, R.D. (1967): Special education and the electroencephalogram: Marriage of convenience. *J. Special Educ.*, Vol. 2, No. 1, Fall.

Freyburg, P.S. (1960): *Teaching Spelling to Juniors*. London, Macmillan.

Frierson, E.G., and Barke, W.B. (Eds.) (1967): *Educating Children with Learning Disabilities: Selected Readings*. New York, Appleton-Century-Crofts.

Fries, C.C. (1963): *Linguistics and Reading.*° New York, Holt.

Frost, B.P. (1965): Intelligence, manifest anxiety and scholastic achievement. *Alberta J. Educ. Res.*, 11:167-175.

Frostig, M. (1950): One hundred words most often misspelled by children. *J. Educ. Res.*, Oct.

Frostig, M. (1964): *Developmental Test of Visual Perception*. Palo Alto, Calif., Consulting Psychologists Press.

Frostig, M. (1966): The needs of teachers for specialized information on reading. In Cruickshank (1966). Syracuse, N.Y., Syracuse University Press.

Frostig, M., and Hart, W. (1965): Developmental evaluation and the institution of remedial programs for children with learning disabilities. Mimeographed paper from Frostig School, Los Angeles, Calif.

Frostig, M., and Horne, D. (1964): The Frostig Program for the Development of Visual Perception. Chicago, Follett.

Fry, D.B. (1966): The development of the phonological system in the normal and the deaf child. In Smith and Miller (1966).

Furth, H.G. (1964): Research with the deaf: Implications for language and cognition. *Psychol. Bull.*, Vol. 62, No. 3, Sept.

Furth, H.G. (1966): *Thinking Without Language: Psychological Implications of Deafness.*° New York, Free Press.

Gallagher, J.J. (1963): Sex differences in expressive thought of gifted children in the classroom. Unpublished paper, Institute for Research on Exceptional Children, University of Illinois, Urbana.

Gardner, R.W. (1966a): The development of cognitive structures. In Scheerer, C. (Ed.): *Cognition: Theory, Research and Promise*. New York, Harper.

Gardner, R.W. (1966b): The need of teachers for specialized information on the development of cognitive structures. In Cruickshank (1966).

Gardner, W.H. (1966): *Text-Manual for Remedial Handwriting.* Danville, Ill., The Interstate Printers and Publishers.

Gates, A.I., and McKillop, A.S. (1968): *Gates-McKillop Reading Diagnostic Tests.*† New York, Teachers College Press, Columbia University.

Gattegno, C. (1963): *Words in Colour—A New Method of Teaching the Reading and Writing of English.* New York, Xerox Corporation.

Geake, R.R., and Smith, D.E.P. (1965): *Visual Tracking.* Ann Arbor, Mich., Ann Arbor Publishers.

Georgiades, N.J. (1964): *Report on the Use of i.t.a. in Remedial Reading Classes.* London, Reading Research Unit.

Gerstmann, J. (1940): Syndrome of finger agnosia disorientation for right and left, agraphia and acalculia. *Arch. Neurol. Psychiat., 44:*398-408.

Gibson, E.J., *et al.* (1963): A study of the development of grapheme-phoneme correspondences. *J. Verbal Learning, Verbal Behavior, 2:* 142-146.

Gillingham, A. (1952): Pedagogical implications of specific language disability. *Independent School Bull.,* Jan.

Gillingham, A., and Stillman, B.W. (1960): *Remedial Training for Children with Specific Disability in Reading, Spelling and Penmanship.** Cambridge, Mass., Educators Publishing Service.

Glezer, I.I. (1955): New data on the development of the cortical nucleus of the motor analyzer in man. Proceedings of the Second Conference on Age Morphology and Physiology. *Izv. Akad. Ped. Nauk. RSFSR,* Moscow.

Goldberg, H.K. (1964): Dyslexia and ophthalmology. *Bull. Orton Soc.,* Vol. 14.

Goldberg, H.K. (1970): Ocular motility in learning disabilities. *J. Learning Dis.,* Vol. 3, No. 3.

Goldman-Eisler, F. (1958a): Speech analysis and mental processes. *Lang. Speech, 1:*59-75.

Goldman-Eisler, F. (1958b): The predictability of words in context and the length of pauses in speech. *Lang. Speech, 1:*226-231.

Goldman-Eisler, F. (1958c): Speech production and the predictability of words in context. *Quart. J. Exp. Psychol., 10:*96-106.

Goldman-Eisler, F. (1964): Discussion and further comments. In Lenneberg, E.H. (Ed.): *Directions in the Study of Language.* Cambridge, Mass., MIT Press.

Good, J. (1968): Color coded sound symbols in the teaching of speech and language. *Illinois Speech Hearing J.,* Vol. 1, No. 3, May.

Gorman, A.M. (1961): Recognition memory for nouns as a function of abstractness and frequency. *J. Exp. Psychol., 61:*23-29.

Gorton, A. (1964): The incidence of specific dyslexia. *Word Blind Bull.,* Vol. 1, No. 3, June.

Graham, F.K., and Ernhart, C.B. (1964): *Brain Damage Tests for Preschool Children.†* Mimeographed paper from Department of Psychology, University of Wisconsin, Madison.

Graham, F.K., and Kendall, B.S. (1960): Memory-for-Designs Test— Revised General Manual.† Missoula, Mont., Psychological Test Specialists; also, *Percept. Motor Skills*, 2:147-188.

Graham, F.K., *et al.* (1963): Brain injury in the preschool child: Some developmental considerations: I. Performance of normal children. *Psychol. Monogr.*, Vol. 77, Nos. 10, 11.

Graubard, P.S., *et al.* (1970): The introduction and use of token reinforcement in classes for disruptive children. *Amer. J. Orthopsychiat.*, Vol. 40, No. 2.

Gray, B.B. (1970): Language acquisition through programmed conditioning. In Bradfield, R.H. (Ed.): *Behavior Modification: The Human Effort.* San Rafael, Calif., Dimensions Publishing Co.

Gray, E.C. (1967): The synapse. *Sci. J.*, May.

Gray, S.W. (1967): Before first grade: The imprint of the low income home. Claremont Reading Conference Thirty First Yearbook. Claremont, Calif., Claremont University.

Gregory, R.E. (1965): Unsettledness, maladjustment and reading failure: A village study. *Brit. J. Educ. Psychol.*, Vol. 35.

Gregory, R.L. (1966): *Eye and Brain—The Psychology of Seeing.** London, World University Library.

Greulich, W.W. (1955): The rationale of assessing the developmental status of children from roentgenograms of the hand and wrist. In Martin, W.E., and Stendler, C.B. (Eds.): *Readings in Child Development.* New York, Harcourt, pp. 42-48.

Grissom, R.J., *et al.* (1962): Memory for verbal material: Effects of sensory deprivation. *Science*, 138:429-430.

Groninger, L.D. (1966): Natural language mediation and covert rehersal in short-term memory. *Psychon. Sci.*, 5, 135-136.

Hagin, R.A., *et al.* (1965): The basis of reading and task analysis. Paper read at Georgia Association for Children with Learning Disabilities Seminar, Atlanta, Ga.

Hagin, R.A., *et al.* (1965): Specific reading disability: Teaching by stimulation of deficit perceptual areas. *Proceedings of the International Reading Association Convention*, Vol. 10.

Hake, J.M. (1969): Covert motivations of good and poor readers. *Reading Teacher*, 22 (No. 8):731-738.

Hallgren, B. (1950): Specific dyslexia. *Acta Psychiat. Neurol., Suppl.*, 65: 1-287.

Halstead, W.C., and Wepman, J.M. (1949): The Halstead-Wepman aphasia screening test. *J. Speech Hearing Dis.*, 14:9-15.

Hamachek, D.C. (1965): *The Self in Growth, Teaching and Learning.* Englewood Cliffs, N.J., Prentice-Hall.

Hardy, W.G. (1956): Problems of audition, perception and understanding *The Volta Review*, Vol. 58, pp. 389-300, Sept.

Hardy, W.G. (1960): The causes of childhood aphasia. In West *et al.* (1960).

Hargis, C.H. (1970): The relationship of available instructional reading materials to deficiency in reading achievement. *Amer. Ann. Deaf*, Vol. 115, No. 1.

Haring, N., and Phillips, E. (1962): *Educating Emotionally Disturbed Children.* New York, McGraw-Hill.

Haring, N.G., and Schiefelbusch, R.L. (1967): *Methods in Special Education*. New York, McGraw-Hill.

Harlow, H.F. (1959): Love in infant monkeys. *Sci. Amer.*, June.

Harlow, H.F. (1961): The development of affectional patterns in infant monkeys. In Foss, B.M. (Ed.): *Determinants of Infant Behavior*, Vol. I. New York, Wiley.

Harlow, H.F. (1963): The maternal affectional system. In Foss (1961, 1963).

Harlow, H.F., and Kuenne, M. (1962): Social deprivation in monkeys. *Sci. Amer.*, Nov.

Harlow, H.F., and Suomi, S.J. (1970): Nature of love—simplified. *Amer. Psychol.*, Vol. 25, No. 2.

Harris, A.J. (1947): *Harris Test of Lateral Dominance.*† New York, Psychological Corporation.

Harris, A.J. (1957): Lateral dominance, directional confusion, and reading disability. *J. Psychol.*, 44:283-294.

Hebb, D.O. (1949): *The Organization of Behavior: A Neuropsychological Theory.* New York, Wiley.

Hebb, D.O., and Foord, E.N. (1945): Errors of visual recognition and the texture of the trace. *J. Exp. Psychol.*, 35:335-348.

Hecaen, H. (1962): Clinical symptomatology in right and left hemispheric lesions. In Mountcastle (1962).

Hecaen, H., and Ajuriaguerra, J. de (1964): *Left-Handedness.* New York, Grune & Stratton.

Hecaen, H., *et al.* (1952): Les déficits fonctionnels après lobectomie occipitale. *Mschr. Psychiatrie Neurologie*, 123:289-291.

Hegge, T.G., *et al.* (1955): *Remedial Reading Drills*. Ann Arbor, Mich., George Wahr, Bookstalls.

Hellmuth, J. (Ed.) (1965): *Learning Disorders*, Vol. 1. Seattle, Wash., Special Child Publications.

Hellyer, S. (1962): Supplementary report: Frequency of stimulus presentation and short-term decrement in recall. *J. Exp. Psychol.*, 64:650.

Hennebert, P.E. (1964): Troubles de l'audition et dyslexie. *Bull. Orton Soc.*, 45:104 (in English).

Herbert, M. (1964): The concept of testing of brain-damage in children: A review. *J. Child Psychol. Psychiat.*, 5:197-206.

Hermann, K. (1959): *Reading Disability.** Springfield, Thomas.

Hermann, K. (1964): Specific reading disability with special reference to complicated word blindness. *Danish Med. Bull.*, 2 (No. 1):34-40.

Hess, R.D., and Shipman, V. (1965): Early blocks to children's learning. *Children*, 12:189-194.

Hewett, F. (1964): A hierarchy of educational tasks for children with learning disorders. *Exceptional Child.*, 31:207-214.

Hewett, F.M. (1967a): Educational engineering with emotionally disturbed children. *Exceptional Child.*, Vol. 33, No. 7, Mar.

Hewett, F.M. (1967b): Institutional and public school application of behavior modification theory in programs for children with learning disorders. Paper (published) presented at International Convocation on Children and Young Adults with Learning Disabilities, Pittsburgh, Feb., Home for Crippled Children.

Hildreth, G. (1955): *Teaching Spelling.* New York, Holt.

Hinde, R.A. (1966): *Animal Behavior: A Synthesis of Ethology and Comparative Psychology.** New York, McGraw-Hill.

Hirsch, E. (1963): Training of visualizing ability by the kinesthetic method of teaching reading. Unpublished Master's thesis, University of Illinois, Urbana.

Hirsch, K. de (1964): The oral language performance of premature children and controls. *J. Speech Hearing Dis.*, 29 (No. 1):60-69.

Hirsch, K. de (1965): Plasticity and language disorders. In Hellmuth (1965).

Hirsch, K. de (1967): Differential diagnosis between aphasic and schizophrenic language in children. *J. Speech Hearing Dis.*, Vol. 32, No. 1, February.

Hirsch, K. de, et al. (1966a): Comparisons between prematurely and maturely born children at three age levels. *Amer. J. Ortho.*, 36:4, July.

Hirsch, K. de, et al. (1966b): *Predicting Reading Failure.* New York, Harper.

Hirshoren, A. (1968): Relaxation exercises for learning disability children. Personal communication, Champaign, Ill.

Hirst, W.E. (1970): Entrance age—a predictor variable for academic success? *Reading Teacher*, Vol. 23, No. 6.

Hockett, C.F. (1960): The origin of speech. *Sci. Amer.*, Vol. 203, No. 3, Sept.

Holroyd, J. (1965): Neurological implications of WISC verbal-performance discrepancies in a psychiatric setting. *J. Consult. Psychol.*, 29:206-212.

Holroyd, R.G., and Riess, R.L. (1968): Central auditory disturbances in dyslexic school children. *J. Special Educ.*, 2:2.

Homme, L.E. (1962): *TMI-Grolier Spelling Rules.* Programmed Course TM-101. New York, Teaching Materials Corporation.

Houghton, V.P., and Daniels, J.C. (1966): The phenomenon of eulexia. *U.K.R.A. Reading Bull. No. 6,* July.

Hubel, D.H. (1963): The visual cortex of the brain. *Sci. Amer.,* Nov.

Hughes, J.R. (1968): Electroencephalography and learning. In Myklebust, H.R. (Ed.): *Progress in Learning Disabilities,* Vol. 1. New York, Grune & Stratton.

Hunt, J.McV. (1961): *Intelligence and Experience.* New York, Ronald Press.

Hyden, H. (1961): Satellite cells in the nervous system. *Sci. Amer.,* Dec.

I.D.E.A. (1969): The role of the ophthalmologist in dyslexia: Report of an international seminar. An I.D.E.A. occasional paper, Melbourne, Fla. (Commented on by Rice, 1970.)

Ilg, F.L., and Ames, L.B. (1950): Developmental trends in reading behaviour. *J. Genet. Psychol.,* 76:291-312.

Ingram, T.T.S., and Reid, J.F. (1956): Developmental aphasia observed in a department of child psychiatry. *Arch. Dis. Child,* 31:161-172.

Inhelder, B., and Piaget, J. (1958): *The Growth of Logical Thinking from Childhood to Adolescence.* New York, Basic Books.

Jakobson, R., and Halle, M. (1956): *Fundamentals of Language.* s'Gravenhage, Netherlands, Mouton.

Jakobson, R., et al. (1952): *Preliminaries to Speech Analysis.* Tech. Rept. No. 13, Acoustics Laboratory, MIT Press, Cambridge, Mass.

James, J., et al. (1967): Pregnancy and teratogens. *JAMA (New York Times* Report).

Jansky, J. (1965): The phenomenon of plasticity in relation to manipulating numbers and early learning in arithmetic. In Hellmuth (1965).

Jastak, J.F., et al. (1965): *Wide Range Achievement Test.*† Wilmington, Del., Guidance Associates.

Jenkins, J.G., and Dallenbach, K.M. (1924): Obliviscence during sleep and waking. *Amer. J. Psychol.,* 35:605-612.

Jenkins, J.J., and Palermo, D.S. (1964): Mediation processes and the acquisition of linguistic structure. In Bellugi and Brown (1964).

Jerger, J. (1960): Observations on auditory behavior in lesions of the central auditory pathways. *Arch. Otolaryng. (Chicago),* 71:797-806.

Jinks, J.L. (1964): Behavior is a phenotype—the biometrical approach. Paper presented at the Annual Conference of British Psych. Society.

John, E.R. (1967): *Mechanisms of Memory.* New York, Academic Press.

Johnson, D.J., and Myklebust, H.R. (1967): *Learning Disabilities.* New York, Grune & Stratton.

Johnson, R.C. (1963): Similarity in I.Q. of separated identical twins as related to length of time spent in same environment. *Child Develop.,* 34:745-749.

Jones, J.K. (1965): Research report on phonetic color. *New Educ.,* 1:4, Feb.

Journal of Learning Disabilities, 5 N. Wabash Ave., Chicago, Ill.

Kagan, J. (1964): Formal discussion of paper on mediation processes and the acquisition of linguistic structure by Jenkins and Palermo. In Bellugi and Brown (1964).

Karnes, M.B., *et al.* (1966a): *An Approach for Working with Parents of Disadvantaged Children—A Pilot Project.* Urbana, Institute for Research on Exceptional Children, University of Illinois.

Karnes, M.B., *et al.* (1966b): *Activities for Developing Psycholinguistic Skills with Preschool Culturally Disadvantaged Children.* Urbana, Institute for Research on Exceptional Children, University of Illinois.

Karnes, M.B., *et al.* (1966c): *A Comparative Study of Two Preschool Programs for Culturally Disadvantaged Children—A Highly Structured and Traditional Program.* Urbana, Institute for Research on Exceptional Children, University of Illinois.

Karnes, M.B., *et al.* (1970): The effects of four programs of classroom intervention on the intellectual and language development of four-year-old disadvantaged children. *Amer. J. Orthopsychiat.,* Vol. 40, No. 1.

Kass, C.E. (1962): Some psychological correlates of severe reading disability. Unpublished Ph.D. dissertation. University of Illinois, Urbana.

Keller, F.S., and Schoenfeld, W.N. (1950): *Principles of Psychology.*° New York, Appleton-Century-Crofts.

Kellmer Pringle, M.L. (1965): *Deprivation and Education.* London, Longmans, Green.

Kellmer Pringle, M.L., *et al.* (1967): *11,000 Seven-Year-Olds.* London, Longmans, Green.

Kephart, M.C. (1960): *The Slow Learner in the Classroom.*° Columbus, Ohio, Charles E. Merrill.

Kephart, M.C. (1966): The needs of teachers for specialized information on perception. In Cruickshank (1966).

Keppel, G., and Underwood, B.J. (1962): Proactive inhibition in short-term retention of single items. *J. Verbal Learning, Verbal Behavior, 1*: 153-161.

Kettlewell, B. (1964): A theory of the origin of dyslexia. *Word Blind Bull.,* Vol. 1, Winter.

Keystone Telebinocular (1968), Keystone View Company, Meadville, Pa.

Kimura, D. (1964): Left-right differences in the perception of melodies. *Quart. J. Exper. Psychol.,* Vol. 16, Pt. 4, Nov.

Kinsbourne, M., and Warrington, E. (1962): A study of finger agnosia. *Brain,* 85:47.

Kinsbourne, M., and Warrington, E.K. (1963a): Developmental factor in reading and writing backwardness. *Brit. J. Psychol.*, 54 (No. 2):145.

Kinsbourne, M., and Warrington, E.K. (1963b): The development of finger differentiation.† *Quart. J. Exp. Psychol.*, Vol. 15, Pt. 2, May.

Kinsbourne, M., and Warrington, E.K. (1963c): The developmental Gerstmann syndrome. *Arch. Neurol.*, 8:490-501, May.

Kinsbourne, M., and Warrington, E.K. (1964): Disorders of spelling. *J. Neurol. Neurosurg. Psychiat.*, 27:224.

Kirk, S.A. (1966): The diagnosis and remediation of psycholinguistic disabilities. Urbana, Institute for Research on Exceptional Children, University of Illinois.

Kirk, S.A., et al. (1968): *The Illinois Test of Psycholinguistic Abilities,†* rev. ed. Urbana, Illinois University Press.

Kirk, S.A., and McCarthy, J.J. (1961): The ITPA—An approach to differential diagnosis. *Amer. J. Ment. Defic.*, Vol. 66, No. 3, November.

Kleist, L. (1934): Gehirnpathologie. Quoted in Critchley (1953).

Kline, C.L., and Lee, N. (1970): A transcultural study of dyslexia: Analysis of reading disabilities in 425 Chinese children simultaneously learning to read and write in English and Chinese. *Amer. J. Orthopsychiat.*, Vol. 40, No. 2.

Klopfer, P.H., and Hailman, J.P. (1967): *An Introduction to Animal Behavior: Ethology's First Century.*° Englewood Cliffs, N.J., Prentice-Hall.

Knoblock, P. (Ed.) (1964): *Educational Programming for Emotionally Disturbed Children: The Decade Ahead.*° New York, Syracuse University Press.

Knoblock, P. (Ed.) (1966): *Intervention Approaches in Educating Emotionally Disturbed Children.*° New York, Syracuse University Press.

Koffka, K. (1935): *Principles of Gestalt Psychology.* New York, Harcourt.

Kohlberg, L., et al. (1968): Private speech: Four studies and a review of theories. *Child Develop.*, 39 (No. 3):691-736.

Kolers, P.A. (1968): Bilingualism and information processing. *Sci. Amer.*, Mar.

Kolers, P.A., and Boyer, A.C. (1965): Interlingual transfer of reading skill. *MIT Q.P.R.*, 77:323-325.

Koos, E.M. (1964): Manifestations of cerebral dominance and reading retardation in primary grade children. *J. Genet. Psychol.*, 104:155-166.

Koppitz, E.M. (1964): *The Bender-Gestalt Test for Young Children.†* New York, Grune & Stratton.

Koussy, A.A.H. el (1955): *The Directions of Research in the Domain of Spatial Abilities.* Paris, Centre National de la Recherche Scientifique.

Krasner, L., and Ullmann, L.P. (Eds.) (1966): *Research in Behavior Modification.*° New York, Holt.

Krippner, S. (1963): Sociopathic tendencies and reading retardation in children. *Council for Exceptional Child. J., 29*:258.

Lansdell, H. (1962): A sex difference in effect of temporal-lobe neurosurgery on design preference. *Nature, 194* (No. 4831):852-854.

Lansdell, H., and Urbach, N. (1965): Sex differences in personality measures related to size and side of temporal lobe ablations. From *Proceedings of Annual Meeting of American Psychological Association.*

Lansdell, J.P. (1964): The carotid amytal test. *Maryland J. Speech Hearing*, Vol. 3, No. 1, Sept.

Lashley, K.S. (1929): *Brain Mechanisms and Intelligence*. Chicago, University of Chicago Press.

Lashley, K.S. (1950): In search of the engram. *Sympos. Soc. Exp. Biol., 4*:454-482.

Laubach, F.C. (1955): *Reading Readiness Charts and Stories.* Baltimore, Koinonia Foundation Press.

Lefevre, C.A. (1964): *Linguistics and the Teaching of Reading.*° New York, McGraw-Hill.

Lenneberg, E.H. (1964): Speech as a motor skill with special reference to nonaphasic disorders. In Bellugi and Brown (1964).

Lenneberg, E.H. (1967): *Biological Foundations of Language.*° New York, Wiley.

Lesevre, N. (1966): Les mouvements oculaires d'exploration. *Word Blind Bull.*, Vol. 1, Spring.

Levenstein, P. (1970): Cognitive growth in preschoolers through verbal interaction with mothers. *Amer. J. Orthopsychiat.*, Vol. 40, No. 3.

Lewis, M.M. (1963): *Language, Thought and Personality in Infancy and Childhood.*° London, George G. Harrap.

Liberman, A.M., *et al.* (1962): A motor theory of speech perception. Speech Communication Seminar, Royal Institute of Technology, Stockholm, Sweden. Published *Proceedings*, September.

Lilly, J.C. (1964): Animals in aquatic environments: Adaption of mammals to the ocean. In *Handbook of Physiology Environment*, Chap. 46.

Lilly, J.C. (1965): Vocal mimicry in tursiops. *Science, 147* (No. 3655):300-301.

Lilly, J.C. (1967): Dolphin vocalization. In *Brain Mechanisms Underlying Speech and Language.* New York, Grune & Stratton.

Lilly, J.C. (1968): *The Mind of the Dolphin: A Non-Human Intelligence.*° New York, Doubleday.

Lindgren, N. (1965): Machine recognition of human language. Part II— Theoretical models of speech perception and language. *IEEE Spectrum*, Vol. 2, No. 4, Apr.

Linn, S.H. (1968): Achievement report of first-grade students after visual-perceptual training in kindergarten. *Academic Therapy Quart.*, Spring.

Lombroso, C. (1891): *The Man of Genius*. London, Walter Scott Co.

Long, N.J., *et al.* (1965): *Conflict in the Classroom.*° Belmont, Calif., Wadsworth.

Lorber, J. (1965): Hydroencephaly with normal development. *Develop. Med. Child Neurol.*, 7:628-633.

Lorenz, K. (1951): The role of gestalt perception in animal and human behavior. In Whyte, L.L. (Ed.): *Symposium on Aspects of Form*. London, Lund Humphries.

Lorenz, K. (1952): *King Solomon's Ring*. London, University Paperbacks; New York, Thomas Y. Crowell Company.

Lorenz, K. (1963): *On Aggression.*° New York, Harcourt.

Lorenz, K. (1965): *Evolution and Modification of Behaviour*. London, Methuen.

Luchsinger, R., and Arnold (1959): *Lehrbuch der Stimm und Sprachheilkunde*, 2nd ed. Wien, Springer.

Luh, C.W. (1922): The conditions of retention. *Psychol. Monogr.*, Vol. 31, No. 142.

Luria, A.R. (1961a): The genesis of voluntary movements. *Voprosy Psikhologii*, No. 6, pp. 3-19.

Luria, A.R. (1961b): *The Role of Speech in the Regulation of Normal and Abnormal Behaviour*. London, Pergamon Press.

Luria, A.R. (1966): *Higher Cortical Functions in Man.*° New York, Basic Books.

Luria, A.R., and Yudovich, F.I. (1959): *Speech and the Development of Mental Processes*. London, Pergamon Press.

Lynn, R. (1955): Personality factors in reading achievement. *Proc. Roy. Soc. Med.*, 48:996-997.

Maccoby, E. (1966): *The Development of Sex Differences.*° Stanford, Calif., Stanford University Press.

MacNeilage, P.F., *et al.* (1967): Speech production and perception in a patient with severe impairment of somesthetic perception and motor control. *J. Speech Hearing Res.*, 10 (No. 3):449-467, Sept.

Madsen, C.H., Jr., and Madsen, C.K. (1970): *Teaching and Discipline*. Boston, Allyn & Bacon.

Maes, W.K. (1966): The identification of emotionally disturbed elementary school children. *Exceptional Child.*, 32:607-609, May.

Makita, K. (1968): The rarity of reading disability in Japanese children. *Amer. J. Orthopsychiat.*, July.

Mann, L., *et al.* (1963): The Spiral After-Effect Test (SAET) as a predictor of school adjustment and achievement in first grade children. *J. Clin. Psychol.*, 19:206-208.

Mather, K. (1949): *Biometrical Genetics: The Study of Continuous Variation*. London, Methuen.

Matzker, J. (1959): Two new methods for the assessment of central auditory functions in cases of brain disease.† *Ann. Otol.*, 68:1185-1197.

Maxwell, A.E. (1959): A factor analysis of the Wechsler Intelligence Scale for children. *Brit. J. Educ. Psychol.*, Vol. 29, Pt. 3.

Mayer-Gross, W. (1936): The question of visual impairment in constructional apraxia. *Proc. Roy. Soc. Med.*, 29:1396-1405.

McCarthy, D. (1954): Language development in children. In *Manual of Child Psychology*. New York, Wiley.

McCracken, G., and Walcutt, C.C. (1963): *Basic Reading Series*. Philadelphia, Lippincott.

McCulloch, W.S. (1943): Inter-areal interactions of the cerebral cortex. In Bucy, P.C. (Ed.): *The Precentral Motor Cortex*. Urbana, University of Illinois Press.

McFarlane, M. (1925): A study of practical ability. *Brit. J. Psychol.*, Mono., Suppl. 8, p. 75.

McFie, J. (1961a): The effects of hemispherectomy on intellectual functioning in cases of infantile hemiplegia. *J. Neurol. Neurosurg. Psychiat.*, 24:240-249.

McFie, J. (1961b): Intellectual impairment in children with localized post infantile cerebral lesions. *J. Neurol. Neurosurg. Phychiat.*, 24:361.

McFie, J. et al. (1950): Visual spatial agnosia associated with lesions of the right cerebral hemisphere. *Brain*, 73:167-190.

McGinnis, M.A., et al. (1956): *Teaching Aphasic Children* (reprint). Washington, D.C., Volta Bureau.

McGlannon, R. (1970): Comments on bio-chemical factors in dyslexia. Paper given at Florida Association of School Psychologists Convention, Miami Beach, Fla., May.

McLeod, J. (1965): A comparison of WISC sub-test scores of pre-adolescent successful and unsuccessful readers. *Aust. J. Psychol.*, 17 (No. 3): 220-228.

McNeil, J.D., and Keislar, E.R. (1963): Value of the oral response in beginning reading: An experimental study using programmed instruction. *Brit. J. Educ. Psychol.*, Vol. 33, Pt. 2, June.

McNeill, D. (1965): The capacity for language acquisition of syntax. In Stuckless, E.R. (Ed.): *Research on Behavioral Aspects of Deafness*. Proceedings of a National Research Conference, New Orleans, May.

Mead, M. (1950): *Male and Female*. Harmondsworth, England, Penguin Books.

Melton, A.W. (1963): Implications of short-term memory for a general theory of memory. *J. Verbal Learning, Verbal Behavior*, 2:1-21.

Menyuk, P. (1964): Comparison of grammar of children with functionally deviant and normal speech. *J. Speech Hearing Res.*, 7:199-221.

Michal-Smith, H., et al. (1970): Dyslexia in four siblings. *J. Learning Dis.*, Vol. 3, No. 4.

Miller, G.A. (1956): The magical number seven, plus or minus two: Some limits on our capacity for processing information. *Psychol. Rev.,* 63: 81-97.

Miller, G.A., *et al.* (1960): *Plans and the Structure of Behavior.* New York, Holt.

Miller, W., and Ervin, S. (1964): The development of grammar in child language. In Bellugi and Brown (1964).

Mills, R.E. (1964): *Learning Methods Test.*† Ft. Lauderdale, Fla., Mills Center.

Milner, B. (1958): Psychological defects produced by temporal lobe excision. *Res. Publ. Ass. Res. Nerv. Ment. Dis.,* 36:244-257.

Milner, B. (1960): Impairment of visual recognition and recall after right temporal lobectomy in man. Psychonomic Society Paper, Chicago.

Milner, B. (1962): Laterality effects in audition. In Mountcastle (1962).

Milner, B. (1965): Memory disturbance after bilateral hippocampal lesions. In Milner, P., and Glickman, S. (Eds.): *Cognitive Processes and the Brain.* New York, Insight Book, Van Nostrand.

Mishkin, M. (1962): A possible link between interhemispheric integration in monkeys and cerebral dominance in man. In Mountcastle (1962).

Mishkin, M., and Forgays, D. (1949): Experiments in the recognition of words in right and left visual fields. Reported in Hebb (1949).

Mittler, P. (1968): Heredity and language. Personal communication, Birkbeck College, University of London.

Money, J. (Ed.) (1962): *Reading Disability: Progress and Research Needs in Dyslexia.*† Baltimore, Johns Hopkins Press.

Money, J. (1966a): *Road Map Test of Direction Sense.*† Baltimore, Johns Hopkins Press.

Money, J. (1966b): The laws of constancy and learning to read. In *International Approach to Learning Disabilities of Children and Youth.* Tulsa, Okla., A.C.L.D. San Rafael, Calif., Academic Therapy Press.

Money, J., and Schiffman, G. (Eds.) (1966): *The Disabled Reader, Education of the Dyslexic Child.* Baltimore, Johns Hopkins Press.

Monsees, E.K. (1957): *Aphasia in Children: Diagnosis and Education,* Reprint No. 693. Washington, D.C., Volta Bureau.

Montague, W.E., *et al.* (1966): Forgetting and natural language mediation. *J. Exp. Psychol.,* 72:829-833.

Morley, M.E. (1965): *The Development and Disorders of Speech in Childhood.*° London, E & S Livingstone.

Morton, J. (1964): The effects of context upon speed of reading, eye movements and eye-voice span. *Quart. J Exp. Psychol.,* Vol. 16.

Mountcastle, V.B. (Ed.) (1962): *Interhemispheric Relations and Cerebral Dominance.*° Baltimore, Johns Hopkins Press.

Mowrer, O.H. (1960): *Learning Theory and the Symbolic Processes.* New York, Wiley.

Moxon, C.A.V. (1962): *A Remedial Reading Method.* London, Methuen.

Muller, S.D., and Madsen, C.H. (1970): Group desensitization for anxious children with reading problems. *Psychol. in the Schools,* Vol. 7, No. 2.

Mundy-Castle, A.C. (1958): Electrophysical correlates of intelligence. *J. Personality,* 26:184-199.

Murphy, P. (1933): The role of the concept in reading ability. *Psychol. Monogr.,* 44 (No. 3):21-73.

Myers, R.E. (1960): Interhemispheric interconnections between occipital poles of the monkey brain. *Anat. Rec.,* 136:249.

Myers, R.E. (1962): Discussion of session on Interhemispheric integration in the visual system. In Mountcastle (1962).

Myklebust, H.R. (1957): Aphasia in children, diagnosis and training. In *Handbook of Speech Pathology.* New York, Appleton-Century-Crofts.

Myklebust, H.R. (1964): *The Psychology of Deafness.* ° New York, Grune & Stratton.

Naidoo, S. (1961): An investigation into some aspects of ambiguous handedness. Master's thesis, University of London.

Nauta, W.J.H. (1962): Discussion of session on: Why do we have two brains? by Young, J.Z. In Mountcastle (1962).

Nazordva, L.K. (1952): The role of speech kinesthesias in writing. *Sovet. Pedag.,* No. 6.

Neale, M.D. (1964): *Neale Analysis of Reading Ability.*† London, Macmillan.

Nelson, W. (1959): Onset of skeletal ossification. In *Textbook of Pediatrics.* Philadelphia, Saunders.

Netter, F.H. (1962): *Nervous System,* Vol. 1. The CIBA Collection of Medical Illustrations. New Jersey, N.J. CIBA.

Newcomb, D.L. (Ed.) (1967): *Proceedings of the International Convocation on Children and Young Adults with Learning Disabilities.* Pittsburgh, Home for Crippled Children.

Newman, H.H., *et al.* (1937): *Twins, A Study of Heredity and Environment.* Chicago, University of Chicago Press.

Newson, E. (1955): The development of line figure discrimination in preschool children. Ph.D. dissertation, University of Nottingham, England.

Nielsen, J.M. (1938): Gerstmann syndrome: Finger agnosia, agraphia, confusion of right and left, and acalculia. *Arch. Neurol. Psychiat.,* 39:536-560.

Noble, C.E. (1953): The meaning-familiarity relationship. *Psychol. Rev.,* 60:89-98.

Noble, C.E. (1954): The familiarity-frequency relationship. *J. Exp. Psychol.,* 47:13-16.

Nolen, P.A., *et al.* (1967): Behavioral modification in a junior high learning disabilities classroom. *Exceptional Child.,* Nov.

Norrie, E. (1954): *Laesepaedagogen*, 2:61.

Norrie, E. (1960): Word-blindness in Denmark: Its neurological and educational aspects. *Independent School Bull.*, April.

O'Leary, J.L. (1962): Discussion of session on: Why do we have two brains? In Mountcastle (1962).

Olson, J.L. (1960): A comparison of receptive aphasic, expressive aphasic and deaf children on the Illinois Test of Psycholinguistic Abilities. Unpublished doctoral dissertation, Urbana, Univ. of Illinois, 1960.

Orme, J.E. (1970): Left-handedness, ability and emotional instability. *Brit. J. Soc. Clin. Psychol.*, 9:87-88.

Orton, S.T. (1937): *Reading, Writing and Speech Problems in Children.* London, Chapman and Hall; New York, Norton.

Orton Society, Bulletin of, Box 153, Pomfret, Conn.

Osgood, C.E. (1949): The similarity paradox in human learning. *Psychol. Rev.*, 56:132-143.

Osgood, C.E. (1953): *Method and Theory in Experimental Psychology.* New York, Oxford.

Osgood, C.E. (1957): Motivational dynamics of language behavior. In Jones, M. (Ed.): *Nebraska Symposium on Motivation.* Lincoln, University of Nebraska Press.

Osgood, C.E. (1963): On understanding and creating sentences. *Amer. Psychologist,* Vol. 18, No. 12, Dec.

Osgood, C.E. (1964a): Semantic differential technique in the comparative study of cultures. *Amer. Anthropol.,* Vol. 66, No. 3, Pt. 2, June.

Osgood, C.E. (1964b): A behavioristic analysis of perception and language as cognitive phenomena. In *Contemporary Approaches to Cognition.* Cambridge, Mass., Harvard University Press.

Osgood, C. E., and Miron, M.S. (1963): *Approaches to the Study of Aphasia.* Urbana, University of Illinois Press.

Osgood, C.E., and Sebeck, T.A. (1965): *Psycholinguistics.* Bloomington, Indiana University Press.

Owen, F.W. (1967): *Learning Disability—A Familial Study.* New York, Society for Research in Child Development, Mar. Mimeographed report from Palo Alto Unified School District, Calif.

Paine, R.S. (1965): Organic neurological factors related to learning disorders. In Hellmuth (1965).

Paine, R.S., *et al.* (1968): A study of minimal cerebral dysfunction. *Develop. Med. Child Neurol.,* Vol. 10, No. 4, Aug.

Painter, G.B. (1964): The effect of a rhythmic and sensory motor activity program on perceptual motor spatial abilities of kindergarten children. Master's thesis, University of Illinois, Urbana.

Palo Alto Reading Program (1969): New York, Harcourt Brace & World.

Parson, B.S. (1924): *Left-Handedness.* New York, Macmillan.

Patton, D.H., and Johnson, E.M. (1960): *Spelling for Word Mastery.* Columbus, Ohio, Charles E. Merrill.

Penfield, W. (1938): The cerebral cortex in man: I. The cerebral cortex and consciousness. *Arch. Neurol. Psychiat.*, 40:417-442.

Penfield, W. (1952): Epileptic automatism and the centrencephalic system. *Res. Publ. Ass. Res. Nerv. Ment. Dis.*, 30:513-528.

Penfield, W. (1954): Mechanisms of voluntary movements. *Brain*, 77:1-17.

Penfield, W., and Rasmussen, T. (1950): *The Cerebral Cortex of Man.* New York, Macmillan.

Penfield, W., and Roberts, L. (1959): *Speech and Brain-Mechanisms.*° Princeton, N.J., Princeton University Press.

Penrose, L.S. (1949): *The Biology of Mental Defect.* London, Sidgwick and Jackson.

Peters, M.L. (1965): The influence of certain reading methods on the spelling ability of junior school children. Paper read to the British Psychological Society.

Peters, M.L. (1967): *Brit. J. Educ. Psychol.*, Vol. 37, Pt. 1, Feb.

Peterson (1964): *Adventures in Handwriting.* New York, Macmillan.

Peterson, L.R., and Peterson, M.J. (1959): Short-term retention of individual verbal items. *J. Exp. Psychol.*, 58:193-198.

Piaget, J. (1950): *The Psychology of Intelligence.* London, Routledge & Paul.

Piaget, J. (1962): *Comments on Vygotsky.* Cambridge, Mass., MIT Press.

Piaget, J. (1965): *The Language and Thought of the Child.*° New York, Humanities Press.

Piaget, J., and Inhelder, B. (1956): *The Child's Conception of Space.* New York, Basic Books.

Piaget, J., and Inhelder, B. (1960): *The Child's Conception of Geometry.* New York, Basic Books.

Pidgeon, D.A., and Yates, A. (1956): Use of tests in the classroom (6); the relationship between ability and attainment—An examination of current theory. *NFER Bull.*, No. 8, pp. 24-29, Nov., London.

Pidgeon, D.A., and Yates, A. (1957): Ability and attainment, a further note. *NFER Bull.*, No. 10, pp. 22-25, Nov., London.

Pierson, G.R. (1964): Current research in juvenile delinquency with IPAT factored instruments. *IPAT Information Bull.*, No. 11.

Pines, M. (1967): *The Crucial Years: From Birth to Six.* New York, Harper.

Plunkett, M.B. (1963): *A Spelling Workbook for Corrective Drill.* Cambridge, Mass., Educators Publishing Service.

Plunkett, M.B., and Peck, C.Z. (1960): *A Spelling Workbook.* Cambridge, Mass., Educators Publishing Service.

Posner, M.I., and Konick, A.F. (1966): Short-term retention of visual and kinesthetic information. *Organiz. Behavior and Hum. Perf.*, 1:71-86.

Postman, L. (1950): Choice behavior and the process of recognition. *Amer. J. Psychol.*, 63:576-583.

Postman, L. (1962): Retention as a function of degree of overlearning. *Science*, 135:666-667.

Postman, L. (1963): Perception and learning. In *Psychology: A Study of a Science*, Vol. 5. New York, McGraw-Hill.

Postman, L. (1965): Invariance in learning and retention. In Stuckless, E.R. (Ed.): *Research on Behavioral Aspects of Deafness*. Proceedings of a National Research Conference on Behavioral Aspects of Deafness, New Orleans.

Postman, L., and Goggin, J. (1964): Whole vs. part learning of serial lists as a function of meaningfulness and intralist similarity. *J. Exp. Psychol.*, 68:140-150.

Postman, L., and Goggin, J. (1966): Whole vs. part learning of paired-associate lists. *J. Exp. Psychol.*

Postman, L., and Rau, L. (1957): Retention as a function of the method of measurement. *Psychology*, 8:217-270. Berkeley, University of California.

Postman, L., *et al.* (1948): An experimental comparison of active recall and recognition. *Amer. J. Psychol.*, 61:511-519.

Prechtl, H.F.R. (1962): Reading difficulties as a neurological problem in childhood. In Money (1962).

Pribram, K.H. (1962): Discussion of session on Interhemispheric integration in the visual system, by Downer, J. In Mountcastle (1962).

Price, B. (1950): Primary biases in twin studies. *Amer. J. Hum. Genet.*, 2:293-352.

Price, H.H. (1953): *Thinking and Experience*. London (Publisher not known).

Quay, H.C. (1968): The facets of educational exceptionality—A conceptual framework for assessment grouping and instruction. Mimeographed paper, Children's Research Center, University of Illinois, Urbana.

Quay, H.C., and Peterson, D.R. (1965): Behavior problem checklist. Mimeographed paper, Children's Research Center, University of Illinois, Urbana.

Quay, H.C., *et al.* (1966): Personality patterns of pupils in special classes for the emotionally disturbed. *Exceptional Child.*, 32:297-301.

Rabinovitch, R.D. (1962): *Hawthorn Concepts Scale for Children.*† Northville, Mich., Hawthorn Center.

The Reading Teacher. Journal of the International Reading Association, Newark, Del.

Redl, F., and Wineman, D. (1957): *The Aggressive Child.*° New York, Free Press.

Reed, H.B.C. (1966): The use of psychological tests in diagnosing brain damage in school age children. Mimeographed paper, Neuropsychology Laboratory, Indiana University Medical Center, Bloomington, Indiana.

Reed, S. (1967): A genetic basis for intelligence. Colloquium speech, Psychology Department, University of Illinois, Urbana.

Reitan, R.M. (1966): A research program on the psychological effects of brain lesions in human beings. In *International Review of Research in Mental Retardation,* Vol. I. New York, Academic Press.

Reitan, R.M., and Heineman, C.E. (1966): Interactions of neurological deficits and emotional disturbances in children with learning disorders— Methods for differential assessment. Unpublished mimeographed paper, Indiana University Medical Center.

Reitan, R.M., and Tarshes, E.L. (1959): Differential effects of left and right cerebral lesions on the trail-making test. *J. Nerv. Ment. Dis.,* *129*:257-262.

Renfrew, S. (1962): *An Introduction to Diagnostic Neurology,* Vol. II. London, E & S Livingstone.

Rice, D. B. (1970): Learning disabilities: An investigation in two parts. *J. Learning Dis.,* Vol. 3, No. 3.

Richardson, S. (1966): Learning disabilities: An introduction. In *International Approach to Learning Disabilities of Children and Youth.* Tulsa, Okla., A.C.L.D. Convention Papers. San Rafael, Calif., Academic Therapy Press.

Rimland, B. (1964): *Infantile Autism.* London, Methuen.

Risley, T., *et al.* (1970): Behavior modification with disadvantaged preschool children. In Bradfield, R.H. (Ed.): *Behavior Modification: The Human Effort.* San Rafael, Calif., Dimensions Publishing Co.

Roach, E.G., and Kephart, N.C. (1966): *The Purdue Perceptual-Motor Survey.†* Columbus, Ohio, Charles E. Merrill.

Robbins, M.P. (1966): The Delacato interpretation of neurological organization. *Reading Res. Quart.,* Vol. 1, No. 3, Spring.

Robinett, R.F. (1964): *Miami Linguistic Readers.* D. C. Heath.

Rock, I., and Harris, C.S. (1967): Vision and touch. *Sci. Amer.,* May.

Rodin, E., *et al.* (1964): A study of behavior disorders in children by means of general purpose computers. *Proceedings of the Conference on Data Acquisition and Processing in Biology and Medicine.* New York, Pergamon Press.

Rogers, C.A. (1952): A factorial study of verbal fluency and related dimensions of personality. Ph.D. dissertation, University of London.

Rose, S. (1967): The molecules of memory. *Sci. J.,* Vol. 3, No. 5, May Special Issue, London.

Rosenthal, R., and Jacobson, L.F. (1968): Teacher expectations for the disadvantaged. *Sci. Amer.,* Vol. 218, No. 4, Apr.

Roswell, F.G., and Chall, J.S. (1963): *Roswell-Chall Auditory Blending Test.*† New York, Essay Press.

Rubin, E.B., *et al.* (1967): *Emotionally Handicapped Children and the Elementary School.* Detroit, Wayne University Press.

Rudd, J. (1962): *Word Attack Manual.* Cambridge, Mass., Educators Publishing Service.

Russell, D.H., and Russell, E.F. (1959): *Listening Aids Through the Grades.** New York, Teachers College, Columbia University.

Rutter, M., *et al.* (1966): Interrelations between the choreiform syndrome, reading disability and psychiatric disorder in children 8-11 years. *Dev. Med. Child. Neurol.,* Vol. 8, 149-159.

Sarason, S., *et al.* (1960): *Anxiety in Elementary School Children.*† New York, Wiley.

Sceats, G. (1965): A technique of developing conscious awareness of laterality and general orientation in space. *Word Blind Bull.,* Vol. 1, Sept., London.

Schiffman, G. (1964): Early identification of reading disabilities: The responsibility of the public schools. *Bull. Orton Soc. 14:*42-44.

Schiffman, G. (1965): Particulars of 240 clinically retarded readers. Speech delivered at IRA Convention, Detroit.

Schiffman, G. (1967): Rewriting textbooks for disabled readers. Preconvention Institute, IRA Convention, Seattle, May.

Schonell, F.J., and Schonell, F.E. (1960): *Diagnostic and Attainment Testing.*† London, Oliver & Boyd.

Schoolfield, L.D., *et al.* (1960): *The Phonovisual Method—A Phonics Program.* Washington, D.C., Phonovisual Products.

Schrock, R.E., and Grossman, M. (1961): Pilot study: Motivation in reading. *Reading Teacher,* Vol. 15, No. 2, Nov.

Schroeder, L.B. (1966): A study of the relationships between five descriptive categories of emotional disturbance and reading and arithmetic achievement. *Exceptional Child.,* 32:111-112, Oct.

Schwachman, H., and Kopito, L. (1968): Tale of a hair. *Newsweek,* Aug. 5.

Sears, P.S., and Feldman, D.H. (1966): Teacher's interactions with boys and with girls. *Nat. Elementary Principal, 46* (No. 2):30-38, Nov.

Sears, R.R., *et al.* (1957): *Patterns of Child Rearing.* Evanston, Ill., Row Peterson.

Seashore, C.E., and Lewis, D. (1960): *Seashore Measures of Musical Talents.*† New York, Psychological Corporation.

Seuss, Dr. (1963): Beginner Books. New York, Random House.

Shackel, B. (1967): Eye movement recording by electro-oculography. In Venables, P.H., and Martin, I. (Eds.): *A Manual of Psychophysiological Methods.* New York, Wiley.

Shapiro, M.B., *et al.* (1962): Experimental studies of a perceptual anomaly. VII. A new explanation. *J. Ment. Sci., 108*:655-668.

Shaw, M.C. (1960): The self conception of bright under-achieving high school students as revealed by an adjective check list. *Personnel Guidance J.*, Vol. 39.

Shepard, R.N. (1967): Recognition memory for words, sentences, and pictures. *J. Verbal Learning, Verbal Behavior, 6*:156-163.

Sheridan, M.D. (1964): Disorders of communication in young children. *Monthly Bull. Minist. Health (London)* 23:20.

Shields, J. (1962): *Monozygotic Twins.* New York, Oxford.

Shipley, J.T. (1962): *Word Games for Word Power.* Englewood Cliffs, N.J., Prentice-Hall.

Shriner, T.H. (1968): Morphological structures in the language of disadvantaged and advantaged children. *J. Speech Hearing Res.,* 2:3, Sept.

Silver, A.A., and Hagin, R. (1960): Specific reading disability: Delineation of the syndrome and relationship to cerebral dominance. *Compr. Psychiat., 1* (No. 2.):126-134, Apr.

Silver, A.A., and Hagin, R. (1966): Maturation of perceptual functions in children with specific reading disability. *Reading Teacher,* pp. 253-259, Jan.

Skinner, B.F. (1938): *The Behavior of Organisms,* New York, Appleton-Century-Crofts.

Skinner, B.F. (1953): *Science and Human Behavior.* New York, Free Press.

Skinner, B.F. (1957): *Verbal Behavior.* New York, Appleton-Century-Crofts.

Slingerland, B.H. (1964): *Screening Tests for Identifying Children with Specific Language Disability.†* Cambridge, Mass., Educators Publishing Service.

Slingerland, B.H. (1966): Public school programs for the prevention of specific language disability in children. *Educ. Therapy,* Vol. 1. Seattle, Wash., Special Child Publications.

Slingerland, B.H., and Gillingham (1965): *The Slingerland Kit.* Cambridge, Mass., Educators Publishing Service.

Sloan, W. (1955): *Lincoln-Oseretsky Motor Development Scale.†* Chicago, Stoelting.

Smith, D.E.P., and Carrigan (1959): *The Nature of Reading Disability.* New York, Harcourt.

Smith, F., and Miller, G.A. (Eds.) (1966): *The Genesis of Language.* Cambridge, Mass., MIT Press.

Smith, I.M. (1964): *Spatial Ability: Its Educational and Social Significance.°* London, University of London Press.

Sokal, R.R. (1966): Numerical taxonomy. *Sci. Amer.,* Dec.

Sommers, R.K., *et al.* (1961a): Pitch discrimination and articulation. *J. Speech Hearing Res.,* 4:56-60.

Sommers, R.K., *et al.* (1961b): Effects of speech therapy and speech improvement upon articulation and reading. *J. Speech Hearing, 26*:27-37.

Spache. G. (1957): Personality patterns of retarded readers. *J. Educ. Res., 50*:461-469.

Spache, G.D. (1966): *Good Reading for Poor Readers*. Champaign, Ill., Garrard Press.

Spalding, R.B. (1970): *The Writing Road to Reading.*° New York, William Morrow.

Spearman, C. (1946): Theory of general factor. *Brit. J. Psychol., 36* (No. 3):117-131.

Spearman, C., and Jones, L.W. (1950): *Human Ability*. London, Macmillan.

Sperry, R.W. (1962): Some general aspects of interhemispheric integration. In Mountcastle (1962).

Sperry, R.W. (1964): The great cerebral commissure. *Sci. Amer.*, Jan.

Spitz, H.H. (1963): Field theory in mental deficiency. In Ellis, N.R. (Ed.): *Handbook of Mental Deficiency*. New York, McGraw-Hill.

Spitz, H.H. (1966): The role of input organization in the learning and memory of mental retardates. In Ellis, N.R. (Ed.): *International Review of Research in Mental Retardation*. New York, Academic Press.

Spreen, O., *et al.* (1965): Auditory agnosia without aphasia. *Arch. Neurol., 13*:84-92.

Stafford, R.E. (1962): Analyzing parent-child test scores for evidence of hereditary components. Report No. 62-7, Pennsylvania State College.

Stark, J., *et al.* (1968): Teaching the aphasic child. *Except. Child.*, Oct.

Steiner, S.R. (1967): Comparison of high and low achieving readers on certain basic visual functions. Unpublished Master's thesis, University of Illinois, Urbana.

Stemmer, C.J. (1964): Some psychological aspects of the choreatiforme syndrome. Ph.D. dissertation, University of Groningen, Netherlands.

Stephens, W.E., *et al.* (1967): Reading readiness and eye hand preference patterns in first grade children. *Except. Child.*, March.

Stettner, L.J., and Matyniak, K.A. (1968): The brain of birds. *Sci. Amer.*, June.

Stevens, K.N., and Halle, M. (1967): Remarks on analysis by synthesis and distinctive features. In Wathen-Dunn, W. (Ed.): *Models for the Perception of Speech and Visual Form*. Cambridge, Mass., MIT Press.

Stott, D.H. (1962): *Programmed Reading Kit*. Glasgow, W & R Holmes.

Stott, D.H. (1965): How to learn to read. *New Society, 127*:14-16, Mar.

Stott, D.H., and Sykes, E.G. (1958): *Bristol Social-Adjustment Guides.†* London, University of London Press.

Strauss, A.A., and Lehtinen, L.E. (1947): *Psychopathology and Education of the Brain-Injured Child*. New York, Grune & Stratton.

Stroud, J.B. (1956): *Psychology in Education*. London, Longmans, Green.

Stuart, M.F. (1963): *Neurophysiological Insights into Teaching.** Palo Alto, Calif., Pacific Books.

Subirama, A. (1958). The prognosis in aphasia in relation to the factor of cerebral dominance and handedness. *Brain, 81*:415-425.

Sullivan, M.W. (1966): *Remedial Reading Program*. Palo Alto, Calif., Behavioral Research Laboratories.

Swift, D.F. (1966): Social class and achievement motivation. *Educ. Res.*, Vol. 8, No. 2, Feb.

Taylor, E.M. (1961): *Psychological Appraisal of Children with Cerebral Defects.** Cambridge, Mass., Harvard University Press.

Templin, M.C. (1957): *Certain Language Skills in Children.** Minneapolis, University of Minnesota Press.

Templin, M.C., and Darley, F.L. (1960): *The Templin-Darley Tests of Articulation.*† Iowa City, Bureau of Educational Research and Service, University of Iowa.

Templin, M.C., *et al.* (1960): What we must still learn about childhood aphasia. In West *et al.* (1960).

Terrace, H.S. (1959): The effects of retinal locus and attention on the perception of words. *J. Exp. Psychol., 58*:382-385.

Teuber, H-L. (1962): Discussion of paper on Laterality effects in audition, by Milner, B. In Mountcastle (1962).

Teuber, H-L. (1964): Discussion of paper on Speech as a motor skill with special reference to nonaphasic disorders, by Lenneberg, E. In Bellugi and Brown (1964).

Thackray, D.V. (1965): The relationship between reading readiness and reading progress. *Brit. J. Educ. Psychol., 35*:252-254.

Thoday, J.M. (1965): Geneticism and environmentalism. In Meade, J.D., and Parkes, A.S. (Eds.): *Biological Aspects of Social Problems*. Edinburgh, Oliver and Boyd.

Thorpe, W.H. (1963): *Learning and Instinct in Animals*. London, Methuen.

Thurstone, T.G. (1967): *Learning To Think Series*. Chicago, Science Research Associates.

Thurstone, T.G., *et al.* (1955): A psychological study of twins. Rep. 4, Psychometric Laboratory, Chapel Hill, N.C.

Tinbergen, N. (1951): *The Study of Instinct*. New York, Oxford.

Tinker, K.J. (1964): The role of laterality in reading disability. In *Reading and Inquiry*. Proceedings of International Reading Association Annual Convention, Detroit.

Tschirgi, R. (1958): Spatial perception and central nervous system symmetry. *Arq. Neuropsiquiat., 16*:364-366.

Ucko, L.E. (1965): A comparative study of asphyxiated and non-asphyxiated boys from birth to five years. *Develop. Med. Child Neurol., 7* (No. 6):643.

Underwood, B.J. (1964): Degree of learning and measurement of forgetting. *J. Verbal Learning, Verbal Behavior*, pp. 112-129.

Valenstein, E.S., *et al.* (1970): Re-examination of the role of the hypothalamus in motivation. *Psychol. Rev.*, 27 (No. 1):16-31.

Valett, R.E. (1967): *The Remediation of Learning Disabilities.*° Palo Alto, Calif., Fearon Publishers.

Vandemark, A.A., and Mann, M.B. (1965): Oral language skills of children with defective articulation. *J. Speech Hearing Res.*, 8:409-414.

Vandenberg, S.G. (1966): Methods in human behavior genetics. Paper presented at a colloquium on Human Behavior Genetics, Illinois State University, Nov.; also in Human behavior genetics: Present status and suggestions for future research, *Merrill-Palmer Quarterly of Behavior and Development* (1969), 15:121-154.

Vereecken, P. (1961): *Spatial Development—Constructive Apraxia from Birth to the Age of Seven.* Groningen, Netherlands, G.B. Wolters.

Vernon, M.D. (1957): *Backwardness in Reading.* New York, Cambridge University Press.

Vernon, P.E. (1953): *Personality Tests and Assessments.* London, Methuen.

Vernon, P.E. (1960): *Intelligence and Attainment Tests.* London, University of London Press.

Vernon, P.E. (1961): *The Structure of Human Abilities.*° London, Methuen; New York, Wiley.

Vorhaus, P.G. (1952): Rorschach configurations associated with reading disability. *J. Project. Techn.*, Vol. 16.

Vygotsky, L.S. (1962): *Thought and Language.* Cambridge, Mass, MIT Press.

Waddington, M. (1965): Color blindness in young children. *Educ. Res.*, Vol. 7, No. 3, June.

Waja, J. (1949): A new method for the determination of the side of cerebral speech dominance: A preliminary report on the intracaroted injection of sodium amytal in man. *Med. Biol.*, 14:221-222.

Walker, L., and Cole, E.M. (1965): Familial patterns of expression of specific reading disability in a population sample. Part 1: Prevalence, distribution and persistence. *Bull. Orton Soc.*, 15:12-24.

Walker, M (1965): Perceptual coding visuomotor and spatial difficulties and their neurological correlates: A progress note. *Develop. Med. Child Neurol.*, 7:543-548.

Walsh, E.G. (1964): *Physiology of the Nervous System*, 2nd ed. London, Longmans, Green.

Walter, W.G. (1953): *The Living Brain.* New York, Norton.

Warburton, B. (1966): Games useful in the teaching of reading and spelling. *Word Blind Bull.*, Winter.

Wartenberg, A. (1970): A parent-teacher speaks. *Reading Teacher*, Vol. 23, No. 8.

Watson, J.B. (1924): *Behaviourism.* New York, Norton.

Weaver, S.J. (1963): Psycholinguistic abilities of culturally deprived children. In *Early Training Project,* Murfreesboro, Tenn.

Webster, R.L., *et al.* (1970): Changes in stuttering frequency as a function of various intervals of delayed auditory feeback. *J. Abnormal Psychol.,* Vol. 75, No. 1.

Webster's New World Dictionary (1966): Cleveland, World Publishing Company.

Wechsler, D. (1967): *Wechsler Preschool and Primary Scale of Intelligence (WPPSI).*† New York, Psychological Corporation (also publishes the Wechsler Intelligence Scale for Children).

Wechsler, D., and Hagin, R.A. (1964): The problem of aerial rotation in reading disability. *Percept. Motor Skills, 19*:319-326.

Wedell, K. (1960): The visual perception of cerebral palsied children. *Child Psychol. Psychiat., 1*:215-227.

Weiner, P.S. (1967): Auditory discrimination and articulation. *J. Speech Hearing Dis.,* Vol. 32, No. 1, Feb.

Weinstein, S. (1962): Differences in effects of brain wounds implicating right or left hemispheres. In Mountcastle (1962).

Weinstein, S. (1964): Deficits concomitant with aphasia and lesions of either cerebral hemisphere. *Cortex, 1*:154-169.

Wells, M.E. (1970): Preschool play activities and reading achievement. *J. Learning Dis.,* Vol. 3, No. 4.

Wepman, J. (1958): *Wepman Auditory Discrimination Test.*† Chicago, Chicago Language Research Associates.

Wepman, J. (1960): Auditory discrimination, speech and reading. *Elementary School J., 60*:325-333.

Wepman, J.M., *et al.* (1960): Studies in aphasia. *J. Speech Hearing Dis., 25*:323-332.

Werry, J.S., and Sprague, R.L. (1967): Hyperactivity. Mimeographed paper, Children's Research Center, University of Illinois, Urbana.

West, R., *et al.* (1960): *Childhood Aphasia: Summing Up of Institute Proceedings.*° San Francisco, California Society for Crippled Children and Adults.

White, L. (1966): Mumps may cause birth defects. *Med. News,* Apr. 29.

Whiting, D., *et al.* (1966): Automatization in dyslexia and normal children. Mimeographed paper, Reading Research Institute, Fryeberg, Me.

Wickelgren, W.A. (1965): Acoustic similarity and intrusion errors in short-term memory. *J. Exp. Psychol., 70*:102-108.

Wiseman, D.E. (1964): Program planning for retarded children with psycholinguistic abilities. *Selected Convention Papers, 42nd Annual CEC Convention,* Washington, D.C., Council for Exceptional Children.

Wiseman, D.E. (1965): Remedial suggestions for learning disabilities as diagnosed by the ITPA. Unpublished mimeographed paper, IREC, University of Illinois, Urbana.

Wolf, C.W. (1966): Memory and dyslexia. Personal communication, Dallas, Tex.

Wolf, C.W. (1967): An experimental investigation of specific language disability (dyslexia). *Bull. Orton Soc.*, Vol. 17.

Wolff, S. (1967): The contribution of obstetric complications to the etiology of behaviour disorders in childhood. *J. Child Psychol. Psychiat.*, 8:57-66.

Wollman, E.L., and Jacob, F. (1956): Sexuality in bacteria. *Sci. Amer.*, July.

Wood, N.E., *et al.* (1960): The semantics of childhood aphasia. In West *et al.* (1960).

Woodburne, L.S. (1967): *The Neural Basis of Behavior.** Columbus, Ohio, Charles E. Merrill.

Woolman, M. (1965): Cultural asynchrony and contingency in learning disorders. In Hellmuth (1965).

Woolman, M. (1966): *Lift-Off to Reading*. Chicago, Institute of Educational Research, Science Research Associates.

Word Blind Bulletin, Word Blind Center for Dyslexic Children, London, England.

Worster-Drought, C. (1957): Central deafness and aphasia. *Postgrad. Med. J., 33*:486.

Wortis, J. (1957): A note on the concept of the brain-injured child. *Amer. J. Ment. Defic., 61*:204-206.

Yates, A.J. (1963): Delayed auditory feedback. *Psychol. Bull., 60*:213-232.

Yule, W., and Rutter, M. (1968): Educational aspects of childhood maladjustment. *Brit. J. Educ. Psychol.*, Vol. 38, Feb.

Zaner-Bloser Co. (1970): *Expressional Growth Through Handwriting*. Columbus, Ohio, Zaner-Bloser Co.

Zangwill, O.L. (1960): *Cerebral Dominance and its Relation to Psychological Function*. Edinburgh, Oliver and Boyd.

Zangwill, O.L. (1962): Dyslexia in relation to cerebral dominance. In Money (1962).

Zelder, E. (1966): A screening scale for children with high risk of neurological impairment. Tulsa, Okla., Association for Children with Learning Disabilities. Published Proceedings of Third Annual International Conference, Tulsa, Okla. San Rafael, Calif., Academic Therapy Press.

NAME INDEX

SUBJECT INDEX

288, 299, 312, 317, 327, 405, 470,
542, 547, 557, 571, 575, 639, 640,
648, 673, 688, 696, 707
A-reinforce, 258, 261, 265, 299, 312,
317, 327, 470, 575, 648, 673, 688
M-Reinforcement, 299, 405, 542, 557,
648, 696
motivational, 707
operant, 558
operant with points at home, 571
programs, 640
reinforcer, 557
reinforcing memory, 244, 251
social reinforcement, 547
T-Reinforcement, 255–256, 286, 288,
299, 648
token, 639, 640
see also Behavior modification
Relational operations, 95, 131
Relationships, 96, 154
negative, 154
Remediation, 29, 58, 171, 334, 383, 385,
394, 398, 399, 405, 417, 434, 441,
453, 462, 469, 470, 471, 475, 508,
510, 515, 525, 526, 541, 549, 552,
561, 569, 574, 579, 580, 632, 640,
641, 645–670, 688, 689, 697–701
articulation, 405, 688
diagnostic, 640
of deficit areas, 574
drawing book, 681
educational   therapy—remediation,
561
environment, 632
emotional factors, 541
eye movement, 453
Fernald Kinesthetic Technique, 659
flexible and adaptable materials, 645
fluency, 688
fluency of one skill at a time, 644
ideal reading technique, 644
integrative dysfunction, 453
laterality, 689
matching to specific deficit, 640
memory training, 660
mirror images, 393
multitrack, 580, 641

of one skill at a time, 644
positive training, 549, 552
prescription writing, 579, 641
primary emotional communicative
dyslexia, 171
programming tasks, 640
published techniques, 645–670
reasoning, 689
remedial class, 697
remedial reading drills, 654
sensory and motor integration, 688
spelling, 666
syntax, 569, 574
task analysis, 640
techniques, 383, 405
technology, 640
training against nature, 549
Reminiscence, 316
Repetition
repetitive part method, 316, 691
trial repetition, 244
Representational level, 53
Research, 3, 6, 7, 8, 13, 28, 116, 216,
220, 224, 239, 260, 272, 311, 318,
339–342, 346, 348, 351, 354, 362,
367, 373, 376, 387, 422, 464, 594
706
(This category only covers some
special research references.)
billboard study, 335
biochemical, 272
cluster-analysis, 17, 239, 426
comparative study of preschool programs, 521
cut-off area, 387
experimental design, 34
extensive programs, 346
heterogeneous samples, 373
lateralized hemispheric function research, 594, 707–709
Learning Disabilities Research Project Report, 362
Longitudinal, 709
Louisville Twin Study, 351
natural language mediators (NLMs),
260
reading, 357
spelling, 318, 357